I0047037

Unreal Development Kit Game Design Cookbook

Over 100 recipes to accelerate the process of learning
game design with UDK

Thomas Mooney

[PACKT]
PUBLISHING

BIRMINGHAM - MUMBAI

Unreal Development Kit Game Design Cookbook

Copyright © 2012 Packt Publishing

All rights reserved. No part of this book may be reproduced, stored in a retrieval system, or transmitted in any form or by any means, without the prior written permission of the publisher, except in the case of brief quotations embedded in critical articles or reviews.

Every effort has been made in the preparation of this book to ensure the accuracy of the information presented. However, the information contained in this book is sold without warranty, either express or implied. Neither the author, nor Packt Publishing, and its dealers and distributors will be held liable for any damages caused or alleged to be caused directly or indirectly by this book.

Packt Publishing has endeavored to provide trademark information about all of the companies and products mentioned in this book by the appropriate use of capitals. However, Packt Publishing cannot guarantee the accuracy of this information.

First published: February 2012

Production Reference: 1150212

Published by Packt Publishing Ltd.
Livery Place
35 Livery Street
Birmingham B3 2PB, UK.

ISBN 978-1-84969-180-2

www.packtpub.com

Cover Image by Thomas Mooney (tomofnz@gmail.com)

Credits

Authors

Thomas Mooney

Michael S. Prinke (Chapter 10)

Reviewers

Pralie Dutzel

Daniel G. Haddad

Matt Lefevere

Michael S. Prinke

Kyle R Umbenhower

Acquisition Editor

Wilson D'souza

Lead Technical Editor

Wilson D'souza

Technical Editor

Aaron Rosario

Project Coordinator

Leena Purkait

Proofreader

Aaron Nash

Indexer

Monica Ajmera Mehta

Production Coordinator

Shantanu Zagade

Cover Work

Shantanu Zagade

About the Authors

Tom grew up in New Zealand. He is a lecturer in design and also works as an artist. He has picked up UDK over the last few years, having worked previously as a 3D artist on games using 3ds Max and Maya. You can learn more about his work at www.tomofnz.com.

I'd like to thank Mike Prinke for his contribution to the last chapter on Scaleform, for the programming, and for the reviews. For getting this book done, I owe a lot to the kindness and patience of Cindy Devina for keeping me going during my first book commission. I'd also like to tip my hat to the members of the UDK forum, particularly those who helped me with particular problems, including slowJusko, Adam Jaggers, EFF, Xendance, Blade[UG], silsin, John J and Matt Doyle. Thanks also to Hywel Thomas (http://www.3dality.co.uk/) and Ryan Pelcz: (http://pelcz.squarespace.com/ for their very helpful UnrealScript snippets. I'd also like to thank Wilson D'souza and Aaron Rosario for smart and cogent development guidance and support.

Mike Prinke is an MFA graduate student in SCAD's interactive design and game development program. During his studies, he has assisted many projects and works with a wide variety of tools, with special emphasis on Unreal, Kismet, UnrealScript, and Scaleform/ Flash, and he is also conducting his MFA thesis on choice-driven narrative in games.

I want to give great thanks to Aram Cookson, without whom I would not have been equipped to work on this book. I also want to thank Timothy Valuato, who showed me how cool it can be to teach.

About the Reviewers

Pralie is currently a game and level design student and independent game developer. She has been studying both game and level design extensively for the past two years, and more recently became an indie developer at her own studio, Katastrophe Games. Although she has only been working in the Unreal Development Kit for almost two years, she has quickly become proficient and now offers guidance to fellow UDK users. On her blog and in her UDK workshop videos, she explains her level design process and offers advice to other students, indies, and anyone working in UDK.

After graduating with a Bachelor in Computer Science, **Daniel** decided to work on games independently. He started his career by working on several mods for The Elder Scrolls 4: Oblivion game. Shortly after that, he became part of the Ultima Return team and contributed to writing Ultima systems into the Neverwinter Nights 2 engine. At around the same time he decided to get cracking with the newly released UDK and he has been using it ever since. With the release of UDK-Mobile, Daniel has a couple of projects in the works that are sure to be a treat. He also recently won the local Microsoft Imagine Cup competition and third place in the world final People's Choice awards with a game he developed called Tale of a Tree Wisp.

I would like to thank Mr. Wilson D'souza and Ms. Leena Purkait for allowing me to do this, and especially so for their patience while I was too busy with the Imagine Cup World Finals.

Matt Lefevere is a level designer with experience working with each generation of the Unreal Engine. He is active in the Unreal community working as a level designer and scripter on UDK games such as Angels Fall First: Planetstorm and Tactical Assault. His portfolio is located at `http://mattlefevere.daportfolio.com/`. Matt is a graduate of George Mason University where he earned a Bachelor of Science in Management. He is a lifelong musician, with experience performing percussion, piano, and guitar.

Kyle Umbenhower is a level designer at the Guildhall at SMU, graduating in December of 2011. He worked as a designer and scripter for Barking Lizard Technologies, on an unannounced iPhone game. You can see Kyle's work at `www.umbygames.com`.

I would like to thank my family and my girlfriend Lynea for their support during this project.

www.PacktPub.com

Support files, eBooks, discount offers and more

You might want to visit www.PacktPub.com for support files and downloads related to your book.

Did you know that Packt offers eBook versions of every book published, with PDF and ePub files available? You can upgrade to the eBook version at www.PacktPub.com and as a print book customer, you are entitled to a discount on the eBook copy. Get in touch with us at service@packtpub.com for more details.

At www.PacktPub.com, you can also read a collection of free technical articles, sign up for a range of free newsletters and receive exclusive discounts and offers on Packt books and eBooks.

http://PacktLib.PacktPub.com

Do you need instant solutions to your IT questions? PacktLib is Packt's online digital book library. Here, you can access, read and search across Packt's entire library of books.

Why Subscribe?

- ▶ Fully searchable across every book published by Packt
- ▶ Copy and paste, print and bookmark content
- ▶ On demand and accessible via web browser

Free Access for Packt account holders

If you have an account with Packt at www.PacktPub.com, you can use this to access PacktLib today and view nine entirely free books. Simply use your login credentials for immediate access.

Table of Contents

   These recipes are not in the book, but are available as a free download from `http://www.packtpub.com/sites/default/files/downloads/1802EXP_Unreal_Development_Kit_Game_Design_Cookbook_Bonus_Recipes.pdf`

Preface

Unreal Development Kit Game Design Cookbook explores how real-time environments are built. Key features of UDK are examined—assets, animation, light, materials, game controls, user interface, special effects, and interactivity—with the objective to make UDK more technically accessible so that users can transcend technique and focus on their creative design process. The book has well prepared recipes for level designers and artists of all levels. It covers core design tools and processes in the editor, particularly setting up characters, UI approaches, configuration, and scripting gameplay. It is a technical guide that allows game artists to go beyond just creating assets, based upon creative, extensive demonstrations.

What this book covers

Chapter 1, Heads Up—UDK Interface Essentials will get you started with UDK, discussing some very easy to follow procedures, glancing over the interface, UI conventions, level building, and even testing the level in PC or iOS, and packaging it to send it out into the world.

Chapter 2, Notes From an Unreal World—Constructing Game World Elements will discuss some of UDK's more important content generation principles.

Chapter 3, It Lives!—Character Setup and Animation shows you how to make your character's movements more life-like using ActorX and FBX, allowing you to create fully customized, animated character performances.

Chapter 4, Got Your Wires Crossed?—Visual Scripting of Gameplay in Kismet deals with Kismet, its UI, and all the wild scenarios that level designers can use to allow actors and objects to act and react in their scene with functionality driven by events and actions.

Chapter 5, It Is Your Destiny!—Scripting Complex Gameplay Flow in Kismet is more about Kismet, showing you how to do more with gameplay such as casting spells, interacting with Bots, and creating level checkpoints.

Chapter 6, Under The Hood—Configuration and Handy Tweaks for UDK contains lessons in adjusting configuration, scripts, and even supplying additional actors and Kismet actions.

Chapter 7, Hi, I'm Eye Candy!—Ways to Create and Use Particle Effects will teach you about the VFX editor Cascade and its myriad of features. You will learn how to use Emitters and Particles to enhance the artwork in your level.

Chapter 8, Then There Was Light!—Manipulating Level Light and Shadows will cover Post Process and everything to do with lighting, shadows, and how they can bring your environments to life.

Chapter 9, The Devil Is In the Details!—Making the Most of Materials unravels some of the Material Editor's deepest, darkest secrets, showing you how to create slick surfaces which radiate attention to detail.

Chapter 10, The Way Of The Flash UI—Scaleform, CLIK, and Flash Interfaces discusses ways to use Flash animation and more to make your UI more vibrant.

More on CLIK, ActionScript, dialog boxes, and menu functionality, as well as creating an animated day-to-night transition is available as a free download at: `http://www.packtpub. com/sites/default/files/downloads/1802EXP_Unreal_Development_Kit_ Game_Design_Cookbook_Bonus_Recipes.pdf`.

A PDF file containing colored screenshots used in this book is available for download at `http://www.packtpub.com/sites/default/files/downloads/1802EXP_Unreal_ Development_Kit_Game_Design_Cookbook_ColoredImages.pdf`.

What you need for this book

- ▶ Windows (XP, Vista, or Windows 7)

- ▶ UDK (`http://www.udk.com/download`)

- ▶ Autodesk 3ds Max 2012 or a similar 3D editing application

- ▶ Adobe Photoshop CS5 or a similar image processing application

- ▶ ConText (`http://contexteditor.org/`)—a free text editor with UnrealScript template, or a similar coding oriented text editing application

- ▶ Vue 9.5 PLE (`http://www.e-onsoftware.com/try/vue_9_ple/`)—Personal Learning Edition of a popular terrain generation tool

- ▶ Heightmap Conversion Software 2 (`http://www.lilchips.com/hmcs2.asp`)—a free utility that processes heightmap data

- ▶ Caustics Generator (`http://www.dualheights.se/caustics/`)—a free utility which creates animation of caustic light patterns

- ▶ Contact Sheet X (`http://csx.riaforge.org/`)—a free add on for Photoshop to process frames into a single tiling image

▸ Camstudio 2 (`http://camstudio.org/`)—a free utility for PC screen video capture, or a similar screen recording application

Who this book is for

This book is meant for game artists who are getting used to UDK but may feel the need for guidance on matters of implementation. It also targets brave beginners who are struggling to find an all in one package for getting started with UDK, and want a reference ready at hand. Level designers can use this book to gauge their understanding of the editor, check for specific problems, and discover gems they may not have come across before.

Conventions

In this book, in an effort to provide a pleasant user experience, we've established a layout style that distinguishes between different kinds of information in UDK. This section provides examples of these styles and explains their meaning.

There is not a lot of code in this book, only a bare minimum of short excerpts required to set up some assets. Where lines of code occur in the text body, they are shown as follows: "The `DefaultProperties` entry `HUDType=class'MyGame.MyHud'` sets the class from which the game calls its HUD instructions."

A block of code is set as follows:

```
class MyGame extends UDKGame
       config(MyGame);

DefaultProperties
{
    HUDType=class'MyGame.MyHUD'
//     bUseClassicHUD=true
// This code sample cannot use the line above as it does not extend
from UTGame but from UDKGame...

}
```

Lines that bear upon the current discussion are shown in bold within the block of code. In this book you will not need to make up any code, and the samples can be typed as they appear in the text, without having to worry about line breaks.

Any command-line input or output is written as follows:

```
C:\UDK\~\UDKGame\Binaries\Win64>UDKGame.exe gfximport Yourfolder\Mouse.
SWF Yourfolder\Button.SWF
```

If you want to learn more about writing UnrealScript, I highly recommend the new Packt book by Rachel Cordone, *Unreal Development Kit Game Programming with UnrealScript: Beginner's Guide*. available at `http://www.packtpub.com/unreal-development-kit-game-programming-with-unrealscript-beginners-guide/book/`.

Besides the fact that you can check it out, the above website link demonstrates how this book presents URLs that you can follow for more information. Paths to your computer's folders are shown as: `C:\UDK\~\UDKGame\Content\Maps\`. File names mentioned in isolation are shown in italics, like this: *UTGame.UC*.

Likewise, where you are required to enter text in a text field, or assign a name to a file or an asset this will be shown as follows: "For the current value, type *Ending*. Here you would type *Ending*. Frequently you are asked to search out an asset already given a unique name; its name is also shown in italics, like this: *Packt.Texture.SkyDome_Night*.

New terms and important words are shown in bold, as are words that help you navigate menus, dialog boxes, and editor-defined properties of objects. Here's an example: "Go to **View | World Properties** and expand the **Game Type** section and click on *MyGame* in the roll-out." Here you can distinguish the **menu commands** from the user entry *MyGame*.

UDK features many special nodes or modules which we've chosen to highlight amongst the many menu entries, properties and text fields that go along with them. These include event, action and variable types in Kismet, module types in Cascade, node types in the Material Editor, and node types in the AnimTree Editor. Except where they occur in menu navigation instructions, which are always in bold, nodes are shown as follows:" **Level Loaded** event". Connectors belonging to a node are shown in bold: "**Loaded and Visible**".

Compare the text formatting against the next image, where it is marked with floating arrows (as is typical with many images in the book). The action is at the top, and its property is in the dialog underneath:

"The **Play Sound** action in Kismet has a property called **Play Sound**, which is set to *None* by default."

The next image, similarly, shows Material Editor nodes. The nodes are at the top and the properties are below.

"In the *Panner* node's Properties, set the **Speed X** value to 2.0 to make the texture that it feeds slide sideways."

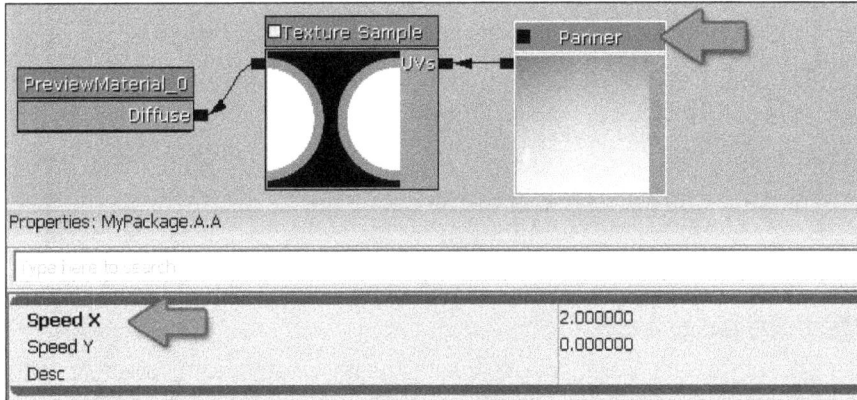

The next example deals with the Cascade Editor, used for creating particle effects:

"Highlight the *Color Over Life* module to expose its properties. Currently this module is disabled."

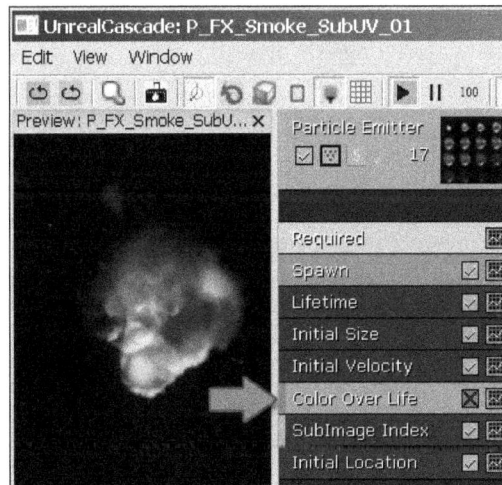

Key strokes and mouse clicks are shown as follows: "Hold *Ctrl* + *LMB* and drag". Sometimes a contraction like *Alt-drag* is used to shorten some instructions, such as "hold *Alt* + *LMB* and drag". In some cases we say to press *LMB* (for **Left Mouse Button**) and *RMB* (for **Right Mouse Button**), but quite often we simply say click or right-click.

Wherever possible, we've included icons within the text to help direct you to tools in the UI. These are formatted as in the example: "The icon [⊲] is for **Use Selected Object in the Content Browser**". Quite often I've referred to this particular icon as the Assign icon, to save space. Also to save space I have often called a **Connector** a 'nub', as others do.

> Warnings or important notes appear in a box like this.

> Tips and tricks appear like this.

Reader feedback

Feedback from our readers is always welcome. Let us know what you think about this book— what you liked or may have disliked. Reader feedback is important for us to develop titles that you really get the most out of.

To send us general feedback, simply send an e-mail to feedback@packtpub.com, and mention the book title through the subject of your message.

If there is a topic that you have expertise in and you are interested in either writing or contributing to a book, see our author guide on www.packtpub.com/authors.

Customer support

Now that you are the proud owner of a Packt book, we have a number of things to help you to get the most from your purchase.

Downloading the example code

You can download the example code files for all Packt books you have purchased from your account at http://www.packtpub.com. If you purchased this book elsewhere, you can visit http://www.packtpub.com/support and register to have the files e-mailed directly to you.

A PDF file containing colored screenshots used in this book is available for download at http://www.packtpub.com/sites/default/files/downloads/1802EXP_Unreal_ Development_Kit_Game_Design_Cookbook_ColoredImages.pdf.

Errata

Although we have taken every care to ensure the accuracy of our content, mistakes do happen. If you find a mistake in one of our books—maybe a mistake in the text or the code—we would be grateful if you would report this to us. By doing so, you can save other readers from frustration and help us improve subsequent versions of this book. If you find any errata, please report them by visiting http://www.packtpub.com/support, selecting your book, clicking on the **errata submission form** link, and entering the details of your errata. Once your errata are verified, your submission will be accepted and the errata will be uploaded to our website, or added to any list of existing errata, under the Errata section of that title.

Piracy

Piracy of copyright material on the Internet is an ongoing problem across all media. At Packt, we take the protection of our copyright and licenses very seriously. If you come across any illegal copies of our works, in any form, on the Internet, please provide us with the location address or website name immediately so that we can pursue a remedy.

Please contact us at copyright@packtpub.com with a link to the suspected pirated material.

We appreciate your help in protecting our authors, and our ability to bring you valuable content.

Questions

You can contact us at questions@packtpub.com if you are having a problem with any aspect of the book, and we will do our best to address it.

1
Heads Up
UDK Interface Essentials

This chapter is for people who are starting out with the **Unreal Development Kit** (**UDK**). It walks you through some very easy procedures such as obtaining and installing UDK, glancing over the interface, UI conventions, level building, and even sending the level off to iOS emulation to play.

In this chapter, we'll cover the following topics:

- ▶ Installing UDK and folder structure
- ▶ What content comes with UDK
- ▶ Beginning, building, and testing a new level
- ▶ Deciding on your preferences
- ▶ UI survival steps
- ▶ Navigating the Content Browser
- ▶ Accessing assets in the Content Browser
- ▶ Creating and managing packages
- ▶ Importing your own content
- ▶ Cooking a map with Unreal Frontend
- ▶ Mobile device emulation
- ▶ Kismet debugging

Introduction

UDK is a robust game editor that welds several different tools together; it offers many areas of specialization. New users should try to gain a broad understanding of the complete scope of what UDK includes, then start building individual prowess in areas that they care about. Whether you like to build things up or knock things down, you'll confront a base set of asset handling processes which deal with **actors** and **game objects** placed in the world, and the properties and interactions which we can assign to influence them. You'll also have to handle **packages**, which store content used to construct levels. The following lessons may seem at first difficult for those unfamiliar with UDK, but after a short while they'll become second nature. The examples here are intended to furnish anyone picking up UDK from scratch with some interface and asset handling awareness so they can then follow upcoming chapters.

Installing UDK and folder structure

Since 2009 **Epic Games** has updated UDK every month. The software is distributed as a download from their front page at www.udk.com. The website foregrounds the current version, along with its new features, and provides a list of previous versions that users can still access for legacy reasons. If you are following tutorials based on a previous version it is useful to run an older version of UDK to ensure the content referred to is available, as shipped content does change somewhat from time to time.

Getting ready

Install **GetRight** from http://getright.com/get.html to ensure that the large installer file for UDK is easy to obtain. It supports resumed downloads. Then visit www.udk.com.

How to do it...

1. UDK has a **Download UDK** button on the upper tab of their front page. Click this. Also take a look at the **UDK News** for the current version.

2. Under **Download Latest Release** there should be a direct link to the installer file. With GetRight running (or any downloader that supports resumable, large file downloads), right-click on it and choose **Copy Link Address**. Through the Windows tray choose GetRight's **Enter New URL to Download** command and paste in the copied link. You should also be prompted for a folder destination for the file, such as your desktop.

3. Once the installer has downloaded, locate it and run it. During the installation you'll be prompted to agree to **Epic Games**' license terms, which you should read at least once to answer questions about what you are permitted to do with UDK, and then set a directory to install to. Usually, it makes sense to install to the offered directory. This includes the **version number**, customarily in the format of the date of release, like UDK-2011-08, which in this book we refer to as **~**.

4. UDK installs its own required utilities including **DirectX**. If there is a problem with that step (which is rare) you can go to `C:\UDK\~\Binaries\Redist\UE3Redist.EXE` and run it as administrator. Supposing the dependencies install okay, UDK should then install correctly. Users using Windows XP may face this.

5. UDK offers to launch itself at the end of the installation, and after that you can find it in the **Start | Programs | Unreal Development Kit | Editor** shortcut. UDK also adds a desktop shortcut, and you can pin this to the start menu. It is a good idea to edit the UDK shortcut to include a running **Log**, by right-clicking on it and choosing **Properties**, then adding `-log` to the end of the text in the **Target:** field.

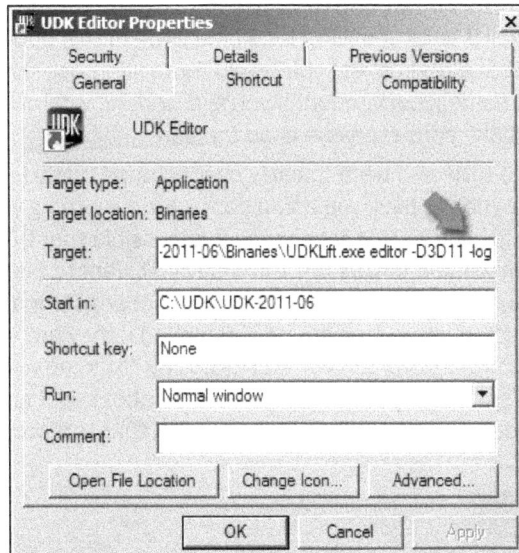

There's more...

Folder structure and updating UDK

UDK so far has had regular updates, and it is possible to concurrently run several installations of UDK as well as several different versions all on the same machine. Each installation has its own folder. Remember to track whether the shortcut to the editor is opening the version you want to use if you have several UDK copies installed. The files used need to be maintained by the user. In this recipe we'll discuss ways to make this easy.

How to do it...

1. When you uninstall UDK all the user files created can be deleted too, or maintained if you so choose. When you update, this can provide you with a way to access exactly what needs to be transferred over to a new installation.

2. It is best to keep your content in a few packages all within a single folder (which can then be easily backed up and transferred to other machines too).

3. Create a subfolder called *Yourname* in the `C:\UDK\~\UDKGame\Content\` folder. In here drop all the model, texture, sound, and animation files you create as you go. To start with you may well have nothing to add, but create the folder anyway for easy access when the time comes.

4. Flash content is handled differently. This should go in another *YournameUI* subfolder created in `C:\UDK\~\UDKGame\Flash\`. This will include any SWF files you import and further subfolders containing content that each SWF uses.

5. Code is handled separately too. You will need to create a folder called `C:\UDK\~\Development\Src\MyGame\Classes\`, where *MyGame* is your folder. You can call it what you like, but all the code in this book assumes you are using *MyGame*. For a real project you would more likely use the title of the game and create your own naming convention. If you are working with others, consult with the team leader to make sure everyone is on the same page.

6. When you update UDK and want to carry over settings that you changed in the previous version's config files, you could copy over everything wholesale, but it wouldn't be a safe choice. This is because it is possible that UDK's initial settings may change from version to version. You really just want to take the lines which your game depends on across (the ones that you changed or added yourself). For example, your custom class files are only compiled if they are assigned a path in `C:\UDK\~\UDKGame\Config\DefaultEngine.INI`, as we'll see later. When you update UDK, you have to tell the new version about your custom classes all over again, and set other default settings for UDK that you want changed too.

See also

The configuration of UDK depends on how you intend to use it. More information on this is covered in *Got Your Wires Crossed?*

What content comes with UDK?

From version to version the content bundled with the editor changes. Usually this is incremental, like the face of a moving glacier, while sometimes it is abrupt, like a melted one. Also, the package structure in the Content Browser changes from time to time. This matters if you transfer levels made in one version to another.

How to do it...

1. Some tutorials refer to maps, the scenes built using UDK, that no longer come with the current installer. For example, the very good **Introduction to the Unreal Development Kit** DVD by *Waylon Brinck*, published by **The Gnomon Workshop**, is based on a map called *DM_Sanctuary* which is found in the March 2010 release. Later releases don't include it. You would have to download the entire March 2010 release from www.udk.com to obtain the relevant content to follow that DVD (which is well worth it).

2. Some old releases included a set of material network demonstrations which, after May 2011, seem to have been dropped from the *TestPackages* folder.

3. The folder structure for versions after June 2011 has been simplified so that there are now Maps, *Mobile*, *Shared*, *Showcases*, *TestPackages*, and *UT3* folders in the Content Browser. Not all of the original UT3 content is still included.

4. Older tutorials, those by **3DBuzz** for example, sometimes include deprecated tools. One case in particular is the **UIScenes** editor used to build HUD graphics, whose functionality has been superseded by the incorporation of **Autodesk Scaleform** tools (through *GFxUI* nodes in Kismet). Some users didn't like this switch, preferring the old UI building editor, shown below, and their objections still echo through the forums; but on the whole it is generally accepted that the change to GFxUI represents a step forward, though one that takes an effort.

5. The UIScene editor actually still functions, but is turned off in newer versions in the configuration. Very little is actually preventing it from working. All you have to do is designate in your **GameType** script (such as *MyGame.uc*) in the **DefaultProperties** the line: useclassicHUD=true and it will be enabled after recompiling.

There's more...

Binaries

UDK includes some external software to interface with other programs. These are found in `C:\UDK\~\Binaries\`.

How to do it...

1. **Actorx** enables users to export models and animation as assets from 3D applications such as Autodesk 3ds Max, Autodesk XSI and Autodesk Maya. Each supported software has its own plugin folder within the `C:\UDK\~\Binaries\actorx\` folder. The plugin or plugins can be copied and pasted to the relevant application.

2. Additionally, **FaceFX**, the facial animation tool in UDK, has plugins that work the same way, also including an interface to Autodesk MotionBuilder. To use FaceFX, which is a third party technology, refer to `www.facefx.com`.

3. Next, the `C:\UDK\~\Binaries\GFx\` folder includes requirements for using SWF [assets] from Adobe Flash in UDK through Scaleform. Information for installing those and using them is covered in *Chapter 10, The Way of the Flash UI*.

4. **Speed Tree Modeler**, a third party foliage generation software is bundled with UDK in a format that only permits assets from it to be compiled for UDK levels. Refer to `http://www.speedtree.com/games/` for technical information. It is possible to pick up the functionality of SpeedTree within a few hours. Since it installs with UDK, you can access it from Windows **Start | All Programs | Unreal Development Kit | ~ | Tools | Speed Tree Modeller**.

5. In the binaries folder, you will also find *Unrealfrontend.EXE* [🗐], which is an interface for compiling and publishing completed levels (or sets of levels) into a single installer for distribution. It also allows script compilation. This can be run from **Start | Programs | Unreal Development Kit | ~ | Tools | Unreal Frontend**. Its usage will be discussed briefly in an upcoming recipe.

See also

Some of the topics mentioned are discussed in depth later on:

▶ **Unreal Frontend** is discussed in this chapter's recipe *Cooking a map in Unreal Frontend*.

▶ **ActorX** is detailed in *Chapter 3, It Lives!* The recipe covers how to install ActorX, export skeletal animation, and import content into UDK.

▶ **Scaleform GfxUI** is discussed in *Chapter 10, The Way of the Flash UI*.

Beginning, building, and testing a new level

In versions prior to June 2011 the user was confronted with a blank scene on loading the editor. This is still possible, if one likes that, but there is now also a set of templates to get started quickly. The templates each emulate a certain time of the day (Night, Day, Morning, Afternoon). These are not extensive maps, just a staging point to help move around the space easily and to help make visual prototyping faster. They come with already established lighting (**Dominant Directional Light**), a **sky dome** StaticMesh, a **LightmassImportanceVolume**, and a **KillZ** height, all of which the user would have to fuss with previously.

How to do it...

1. Install UDK post June 2011 and start UDK. Go to the **File menu** and choose **New**. Choose the *Afternoon Lighting* template.

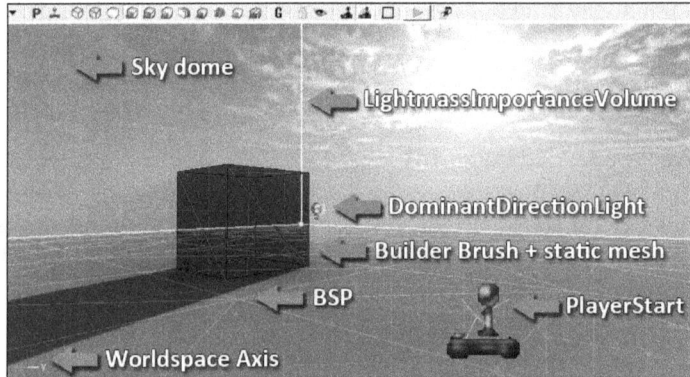

2. The map that opens has a large **StaticMesh** box for the ground, and a small **StaticMesh** cube where the **Builder Brush** is. This StaticMesh is not useful except for scale reference, so select and delete it by pressing *Delete*. You can't delete the red **Builder Brush**.

3. After deleting the box, notice the current lighting (shadows most obviously) doesn't change. Therefore we need to build the scene. Click on the menu **Build** and choose **Build All** or press [🔧]. **Swarm Agent** will start and you can watch it process the scene (in the first instance you may be asked for administrator approval to run this utility). For more information on **Swarm**, and distributed rendering, consult: http://udn.epicgames.com/Three/Swarm.html.

4. When the **Build** is finished, which should be fast given the scene simplicity, hit *F8* (to **Play in Editor** (**PIE**)) or *Alt + F8* to play in the active viewport.

5. Notice you have no gun and there's no **HUD** (**Heads-up display**). Press *Escape* to close the play session and return to the editor. This time go to the menu **View | World Properties**. Under **Default Game Type**, change *None* to *UTGame* and do the same for **Game Type for PIE**. Press *F8* or press [▷] and this time when you PIE you'll be able to shoot and see a crosshair for aiming and so on.

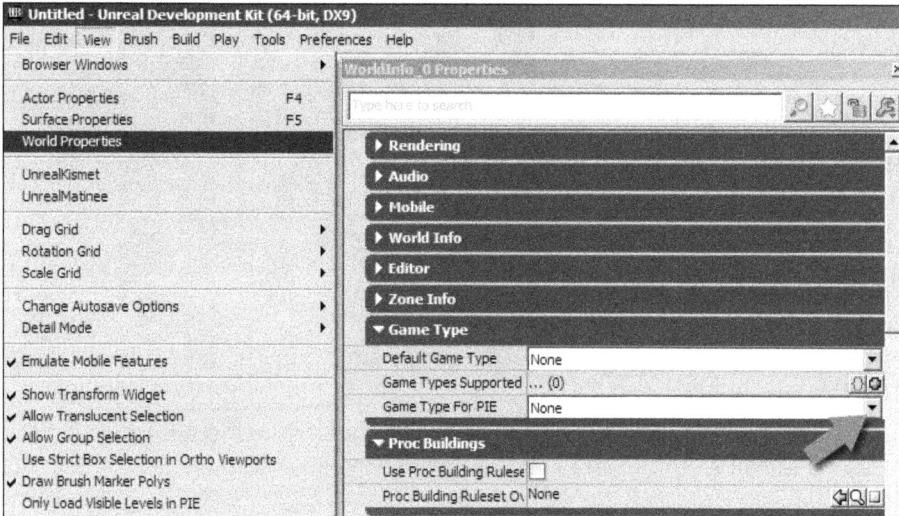

6. Save the map to
   C:\UDK\~\UDKGame\Content\Yourfolder\Yourfirstmap.UDK.

7. If you want to you can set any of your maps as one of the map templates that show when UDK loads. To do this we need to save the map to the folder C:\UDK\~\UDKGame\Content\Maps\Templates which is a location specifically for templates. In this case use the extension **.UMAP**, for instance: *YourFirstMap.UMAP*.

8. In the Content Browser, locate the folder or **package** called *Engine.Content. MapTemplateIndex*. Add your map here by right-clicking in the Content Browser and choosing **New TemplateMapMetadata**. When the dialog for this opens, give the **Info | Name** as *YourFirstMap* (or whatever you saved your .UMAP file as, without including the ending). Click **Okay**.

9. You can add a picture to your newly created **TemplateMapMetadata** asset. You could take a screen grab and save it as .PNG from Photoshop, and then in the UDK Content Browser right-click and choose **Import**, and browse to your .PNG. Import the texture to the same package as your **TemplateMapMetadata** asset.

10. To complete adding the picture to the template, right-click on the imported texture and choose **Copy full name to clipboard**. Then find the **TemplateMapMetadata** asset and double-click it to show its **Properties**, and in the **Thumbnail** field of the **Template Map Metadata** paste the texture name. Save your package and next time you start UDK and choose **New Map**, yours should appear in the offered templates.

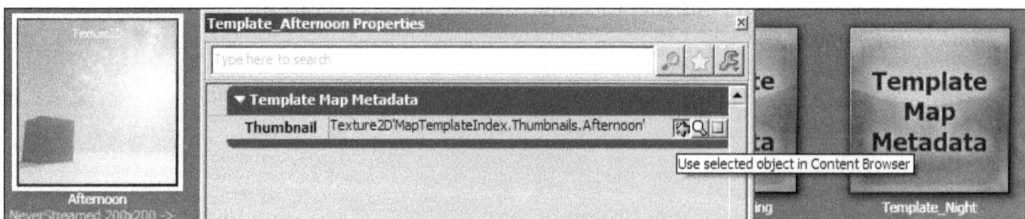

Deciding on your preferences

UDK offers some tweaks to customize the user experience. We'll explore some of the ways to alter the default settings. There are two ways to set preferences. One is the **Preferences menu**, and the other is the **View menu**. If you choose to use a version of UDK prior to June 2011, all preferences appear in the **View menu**. This recipe details some of the more immediately useful available settings.

Getting ready

Load one of the default map presets. Also, have a read through the UDN interface information at `http://udn.epicgames.com/Three/MainEditorMenuBar.html`.

How to do it...

1. Click on the **Preferences** menu, and turn on **Load Simple Map on Startup**. This toggle will prevent or allow skipping through the startup menu to immediately load a set map.

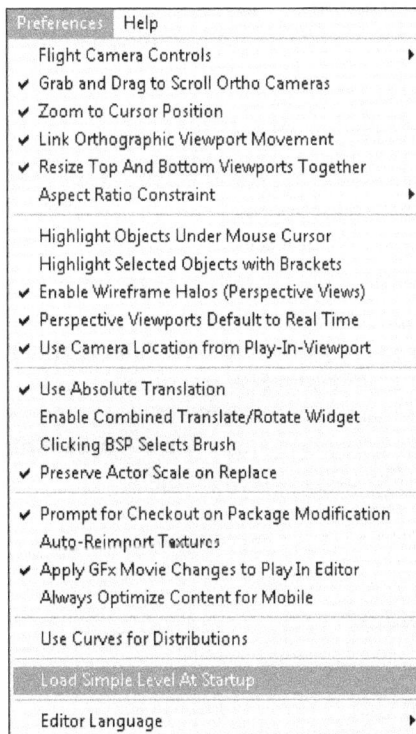

Preferences	Help
	Flight Camera Controls ▶
✔	Grab and Drag to Scroll Ortho Cameras
✔	Zoom to Cursor Position
✔	Link Orthographic Viewport Movement
✔	Resize Top And Bottom Viewports Together
	Aspect Ratio Constraint ▶
	Highlight Objects Under Mouse Cursor
	Highlight Selected Objects with Brackets
✔	Enable Wireframe Halos (Perspective Views)
✔	Perspective Viewports Default to Real Time
✔	Use Camera Location from Play-In-Viewport
✔	Use Absolute Translation
	Enable Combined Translate/Rotate Widget
	Clicking BSP Selects Brush
✔	Preserve Actor Scale on Replace
✔	Prompt for Checkout on Package Modification
	Auto-Reimport Textures
✔	Apply GFx Movie Changes to Play In Editor
	Always Optimize Content for Mobile
	Use Curves for Distributions
	Load Simple Level At Startup
	Editor Language ▶

2. The map which is already loaded (which ought to be a .UMAP as was discussed in the previous recipe) is defined in the configuration file `C:\UDK\~\UDKGame\Config\DefaultEditorUDK.ini` in the lines at the end:

```
[UnrealEd.SimpleMap]
SimpleMapName=..\..\Engine\Content\Maps\Templates\Template_MidDay.
umap
```

3. If you are certain you're developing for mobile you can set **Preferences | Always Optimize Content for Mobile** which helps to ensure compiled materials and meshes are maintained within platform limitations. View more information at: `http://udn.epicgames.com/Three/MigratingMobileJune2011.html`. The setting enables ImgTec's PowerVR **PVRTC compression** when building lighting, which is a lossy, fixed rate texture compression used because mobile devices don't support **DXT** (**DirectX textures**). What UDK actually does is cache both **DXT** and **PVRTC** compression of the texture and dumps one or the other when cooking the game depending on the destination format (PC or iOS).

4. Textures for iOS should be larger than `16 x 16` pixels. iOS doesn't support textures that do not have their width-height resolution in powers of two, so what UDK does under the hood is automatically stretch any you use so they'll work. Lightmaps, the scene lighting baked into textures during a build, are often not square so these may need special attention. This command is already set in UDK's configuration in `C:\UDK\~\UDKGame\Config\UDKLightmass.INI`:

```
[DevOptions.StaticLighting]
bRepackLightAndShadowMapTextures=True
```

5. If you want to alter this state, just add the suffix `nopvrtclightmaps` to the line in the **Target:** field of your editor shortcut before launching UDK. If you're just starting out then you won't need to, but it's good to understand how it works.

6. Moving on, a useful preference to set comes from the fact that clicking on **BSP geometry** in the perspective view selects the surface under the cursor, not the entire BSP model. In **Preferences | Clicking BSP Selects Brush**, you can reverse this. Remember, click *Ctrl + Shift* on a BSP by default selects the entire brush or you can just select it in an orthographic view instead. You can make the BSP brush show shaded faces when selected by going to **View | Draw Brush Marker Polys**. Try this out, and check the effect of it being on and off.

7. **Preferences | Perspective viewports default to real-time** means that when you launch the editor, your perspective view will display running particle systems and animated content in materials and so on. This can use considerable memory in large scenes. To toggle Real Time display, press *Ctrl + R* or click the joystick icon [🕹] in the icons row above the desired viewport. You can test this in the June 2011 version or later straight away if you've loaded one of the templates that include a sky. With real-time playback enabled you'll see clouds moving. With it off, you won't.

8. Some designers like to see a visual guide to what is selected. You can go to **Preferences | Highlight Selected with Borders** to enable white bounding boxes which face the camera and surround each object in a selection. For better depth perception you can tick **Preferences | Enable Wireframe halos** so that objects further away get fuzzy edges. Also, you can tick **Preferences | Highlight objects under the mouse cursor** so as you mouse over objects it identifies one over another in a busy scene. The effect is more obvious in some shading modes (like wireframe or unlit) than others (lit or detail lighting).

9. If you like to split up your views, you can disable the default **Preferences | Resize Top and Bottom Viewports Together**. This means that when you drag a view, it is free from the others. By default when you zoom and pan an orthographic view the others follow it. This can also be disabled, through **Preferences | Link Orthographic Viewport Movement** and will make your viewport response a little more like 3ds Max. A related feature which you may find disconcerting if you use another 3D application is that UDK's default view panning is to move the camera in the direction of the drag (which sends the scene apparently panning away from the drag direction). This can be inverted to a generic style of map panning where the scene stays fixed relative to the cursor during the drag. **Preferences | Grab and Drag to Scroll Ortho Cameras** sets this.

10. If you want to work full screen, press *F11* or go to **View | Fullscreen**. This fits the editor to the maximum available space. If you want to switch from the default view 2 x 2 split to a single view, each view has an icon [▢] for this on the extreme upper right -hand corner of the view. When maximized, it restores down. If you have multiple monitors it can be useful to **Tear Off** additional views by going to **View | New Floating Viewport** and choosing between **Perspective** or an **Orthographic** view. Each view (and the Content Browser) has icons for this [⧉].

11. In versions of UDK from June 2011 on, you can **Group** actors to make handling them in the view easier. Go to **View | Allow Group Selection** and tick it. Refer to `http://udn.epicgames.com/Three/ActorGrouping.html` for further information on grouping. All grouping is controlled by having a selection of objects then right-clicking on them and choosing **Group Actors**, or **Groups** if the objects are already grouped.

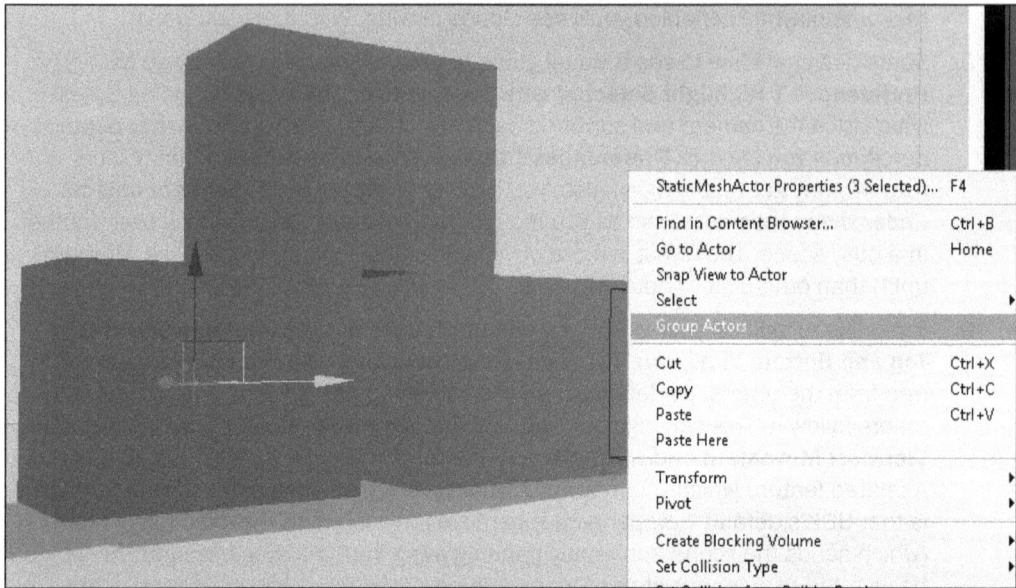

UI survival steps

UDK's interface has changed from time to time; it is an outgrowth from the UT3 Editor of several years ago. There's no reason to think it will remain the same as the software improves. Still, its essential layout has remained intact since day one.

How to do it...

1. Look down the side of the editor and you'll see a range of square buttons that are grouped together. The top set is **Editing modes**. The second is **Brushes** (the base geometry creating tool in UDK). The third is **Volumes**, which opens a list of volume types you can generate from the active brush in the scene. Then there are some **Show/Hide** tools and **Selection** aid tools at the bottom. Click on the **Go To Builder Brush** icon [🔲]. You can also press the *Home* key to frame whatever is selected in the view. Notice it frames the red Builder Brush in all views, and also selects it. Click on the sky dome actor in the scene, then press **Go to Actor** [🔲] and it will likewise frame the entire scene as that actor is really big. Below, the icons, for the tool set have been set into a smaller area to fit the page.

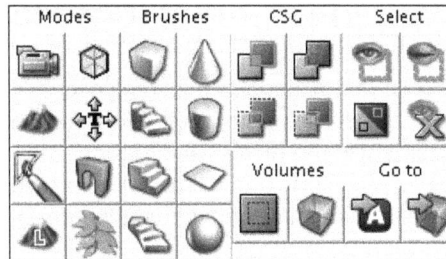

2. The four views can be sized by dragging their frames. At the end of the icon row each viewport has, shown below, there is a **Tear Off** command that creates a floating copy of the view. You can change the layout of the views using the options under the menu **View | Viewport Configuration**. The default 2 x 2 split is probably easiest to get used to. As with most 3D software, you can shade the views in various modes, using the icons running along the top of each view. Just hold the mouse over the button to get its **tooltip**, and test each one out to see how it behaves. Each viewport's icon row starts with a letter (**P** for perspective, **T** for top, **F** for front, and **S** for Side) that you can click to cycle between views.

3. To navigate the perspective view there are two systems. One way is to use the left mouse to move forward and back, right mouse to look around, and both together to move up and down. This way can be extended by right-clicking and using W A S D for movement, Q and E for up and down, and Z and C for camera zoom. There is an option to use W A S D without holding the right-click under the **Preferences** menu in the **Flight Camera Controls**. If you use this you'll have to switch from using W to hide StaticMesh models to using Alt + W.

4. In the orthographic views you can pan the view using left or right click, zoom using both together or by mouse scrolling. Middle mouse dragging creates a handy ruler that measures units as you draw a red line.

5. Many of the icons down the side of the editor and along the top of each viewport are just graphics for the same tools or commands in the menu at the top of the editor.

6. The **File menu** lets you save and open maps, as well as packages, and import and export terrain content. There is also a list of **Recent files** which becomes very handy.

7. The **Edit** menu allows you to **Select**, **Copy**, and **Paste** actors and also **Find Actors** through search filters. The icon for that is a pair of binoculars [🔍].

8. The **View** menu has a lot of functionality including access to the Browsers (**Content**, **Actor Classes**, **Levels**, and so on), actor properties, surface properties and world properties windows, and also the Kismet and Matinee editors. You can enable and adjust the **grid scale** for viewports and the editor **autosave period** here, or at the lower right-hand side of the screen through the roll-outs shown here:

9. In the **View** menu there are some toggles, including **Allow Translucent Selection** (which is also on the top row of icons) [🔲], which makes actors that have a translucent material (like water) selectable. At the bottom of the **View menu** you'll find some handy **Lighting Info** tools too. These help you monitor your scene and adjust lighting variables.

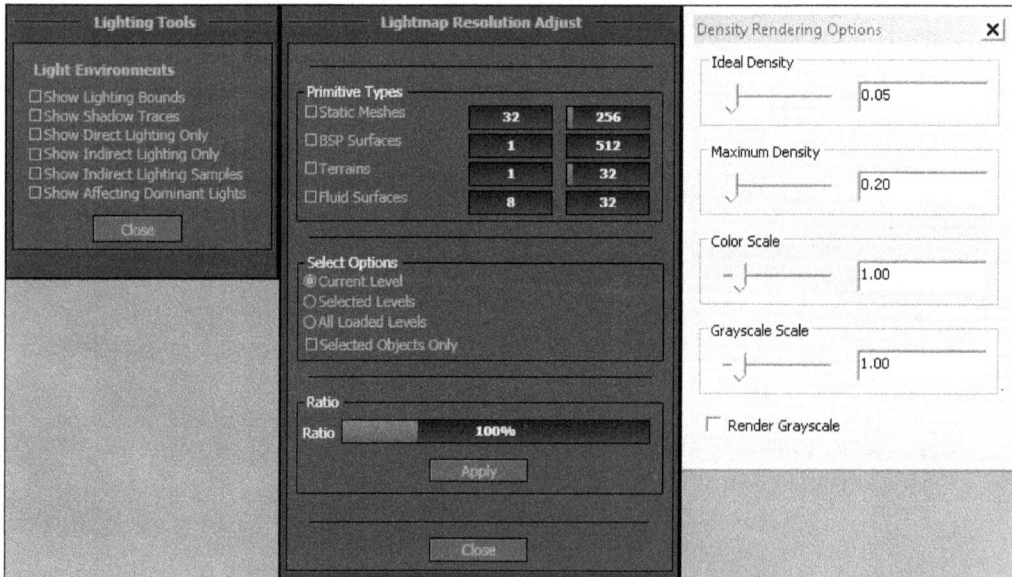

10. The **Brush menu**, **Build menu**, and **Play menu** each provides access to the tools we already mentioned as well as lists their hot keys. The **Tools menu** offers a few extra utilities, in particular the **New Terrain** generation window.

11. With actors in the scene, you can transform them using the **Move**, **Rotate, Scale**, and Local **Non-Uniform Scaling** tools, which can be accessed through icons in the top row or through the **Edit** menu or by repeatedly pressing *Space* to cycle them. **Non-uniform scale** is always in Local space. The hotkey to switch between the World and Local transform modes is the grave key ` or tilde key ~

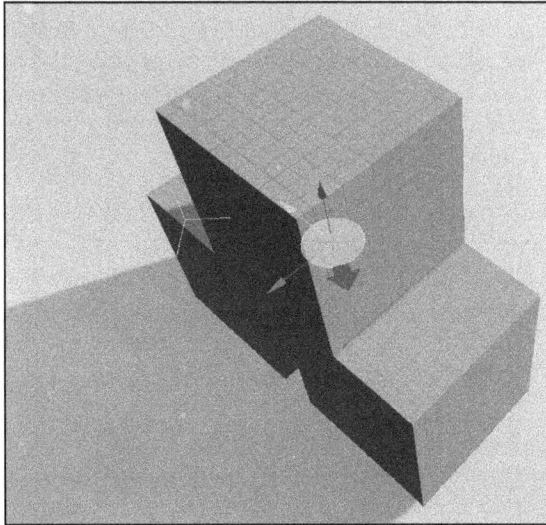

12. In one of the UDK updates, a combined transform tool was introduced which can be enabled through the **Preferences | Enable Combined Translate/RotateWidget** and then cycling the *Space* bar till it appears. Shown above, this features regular RGB=XYZ axis arrows for movement, a yellow XY movement circle, and a blue arrow to orient an object through a world Z rotation.

13. Once you have fleshed out a scene, press *G* to view it in **Game mode** [**G**], where all symbolic object icons, boundaries like collision or volumes, and labels will be hidden. Press *Ctrl + R* to toggle **Real Time** mode to see all the effects playing out. Finally, **Camera Movement Speed** can be adjusted using the icon in each view as shown next. If you right-click on it, you can access it through a roll-out or just tap it until you get the camera speed you like.

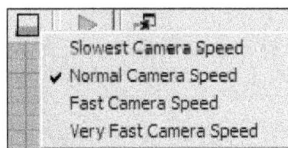

Navigating the Content Browser

How it works...

The **Content Browser** opens with each session of UDK. It can be a good idea to use two monitors with UDK and push it off onto a second screen. In older versions, the editor would first display the **Start Page**, which is essentially a web page within the editor that shows news and tips. Looking at the top of this window, you'll see tabs that include **Content Browser**, **Actor Classes**, **Levels**, **Scene**, **Groups**, and **Start Page**. We are going to be dealing with just the Content Browser and Actor Classes here.

The Content Browser is quite large, so make sure you know how to resize windows and move them around to make screen space. If you accidentally close the Content Browser, press **Ctrl** + *Shift* + *F* to open it back up. In the top of the main editor you will see a graphic icon which also opens it [🎮] (dating back to Unreal, the game from which UDK springs, the icon is meant to be a **U** for Unreal, but it's scaled down to illegibility). Its location in the editor is shown here:

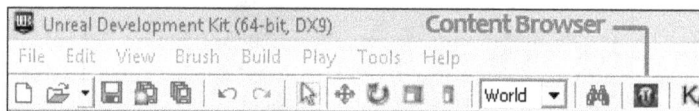

On either side of the Content Browser you'll find black vertical strips with gray triangle arrows. These expose or hide panels for viewing your current UDK folder structure (**Packages List** on the left-hand side), and sorting objects through user tags (**Tags List** on the right-hand side, as shown here).

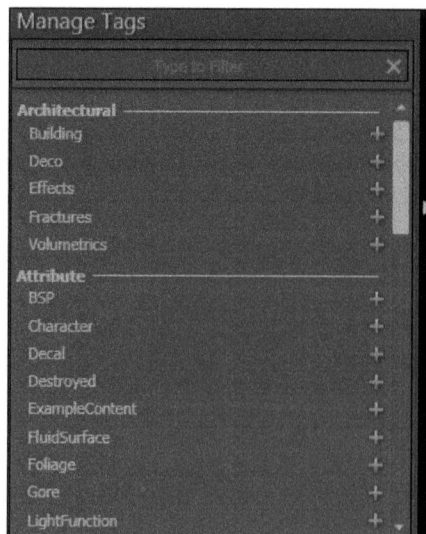

The tags won't be that useful to start with, since this is a tool for arranging large sets of content, but since the arrow icon is near the often used asset list slider you may hit it by mistake and be momentarily disoriented by the tags emerging into view. To use tags, notice how the tag categories have a **+** icon on the right-hand side which highlights green on mouse-over:

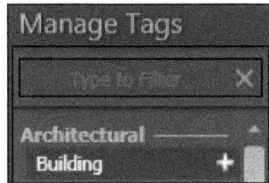

These are used to apply a tag to objects you have already highlighted in the Browser. Highlighted objects are framed in yellow and their tags, if any, are shown in the **Applied Tags** panel at the very top of the tags area when that is exposed. You can search tags using the field called **Type to Filter**. If you right-click on a tag, you will see a pop-up menu for further adjusting tags. If you create a tag of your own this way it will appear in whichever **Group** was current at the time (or one you then assign, as shown here).

You can also use the [Create Tag] **Create Tag** icon at the bottom of the tags panel, which defaults to a group called *None*. Next to **Create Tag** is an icon named **Destroy**. If you press it, the **–** icon appears next to each tag, as shown next. They highlight red on mouse over, allowing you to destroy by clicking:

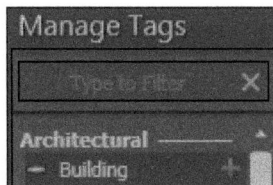

Once you are used to tagging, you can search the Browser with a 'tagged' or 'untagged' or 'both' filter, shown in the **Status** panel of the main search tool:

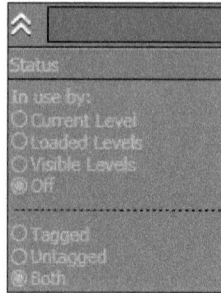

The status of a search is quite important as it defines the scope of the search either narrow or wide. If you have ticked the radio button to limit your search to the current level (**In Use By: Current Level**) [⊙ Current Level] and you are starting a scene, you won't see many *UDKGame* assets at all, just some assets used by the *Engine*.

Above the **Status** section of the search tool, there is the icon [⊼]. This simply minimizes the search filters so you can see more of the content. Next to this is a **Type here to search** (*Ctrl + Shift + F*) field. At the right of this type field (and also the tags type field) is the [✕] icon which will clear text. Beside it, a spanner icon [🔧 ▾] provides access to the kind of 'match any' and 'match all' that **Find** tools usually have. Next to the spanner icon is a text button called **Clear**. This not only removes text in the search field but also any ticked entries in the search by **Object Type** and **Tags** areas seen in the next screenshot:

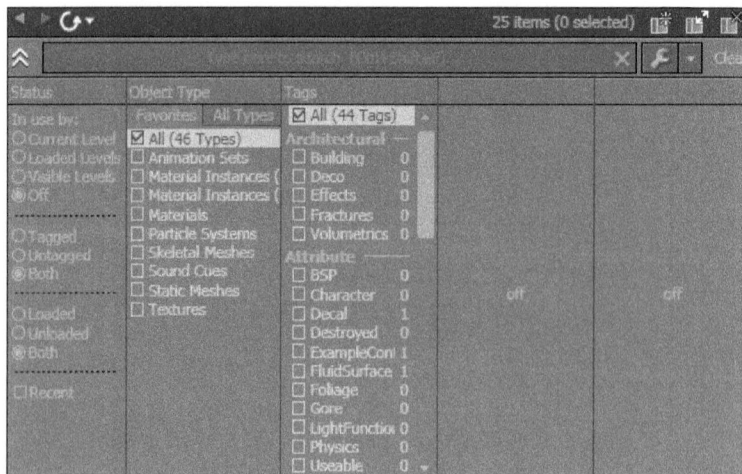

Above the search filter panel there are some small icons that are really useful for those often using the Content Browser (which is everyone really). Two left and right triangle arrows [◄ ►] allow us to browse using a kind of history of filter and search settings. There is also a **Refresh** button (*Ctrl* + *F5*) [⟳] alongside these which can ensure your search shows everything current. On the right-hand side of these buttons are three square icon [▦ ▦ ▦] that allow control of the Browser window itself. You can duplicate a new tabbed Browser window, you can **float** the Browser (and re-dock it into tabs), and you can kill off duplicated Browsers (the original one ignores this command).

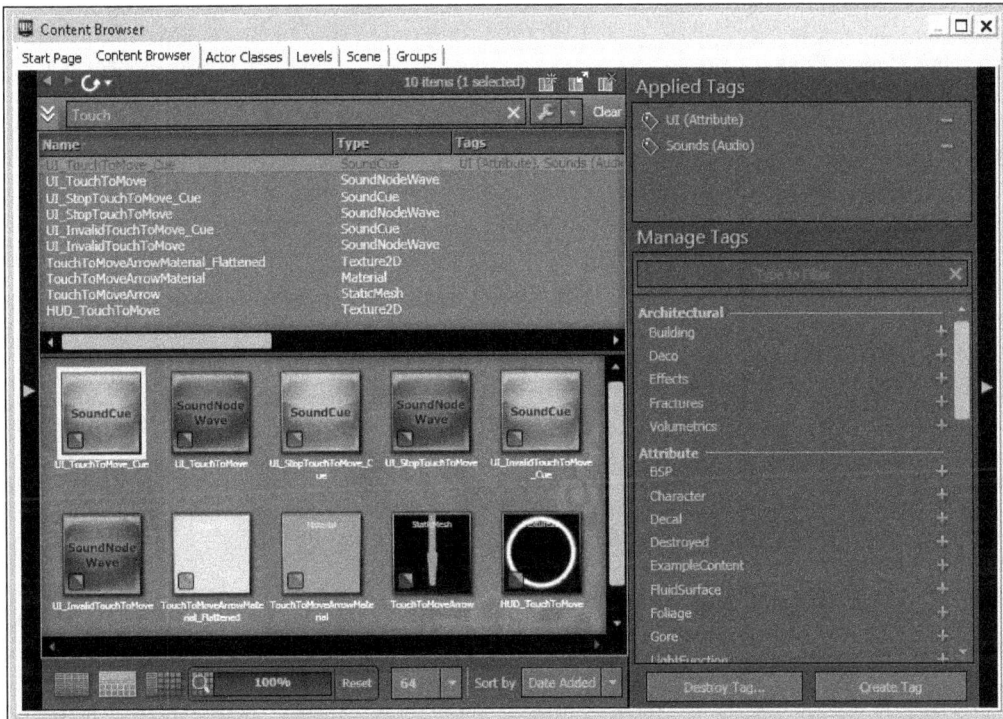

Shown here is a slightly atypical arrangement of the **Content Browser**. The folder structure usually exposed on the left-hand side is toggled to hidden. Using the layout buttons at the bottom of the image, the panel showing asset icons has been switched to **horizontal split view** to also show the names of assets as well. The search filters below the text field have been minimized. Tags have been applied to the highlighted **SoundCue**. Double-clicking an asset will open it in an editor for inspection, or in the case of a **SoundCue**, preview how it sounds. You can also press *Space* to preview highlighted sounds. Previously created assets which have not been used or loaded yet in the current editing session are marked in one corner with a small orange box icon [▇] in one corner. Click this to **Fully Load** the asset. It saves memory to load only the assets you need. The assets are sorted here by **Date Added** rather than by **Name** (bottom of the image). The icon size has been reduced to 64 x 64 (also at the bottom of the image). Finally, the frame dimensions of the views have been altered by dragging on their edges.

This example is shown to indicate how the UI of the Browser is flexible and packed full of search and layout tools designed to enable ready access to game content.

There's more...

Right-clicking is the way to go!

Editing assets shown in the Browser is usually done by right-clicking on them and choosing the appropriate task. You will have noticed that right-clicking everywhere in UDK typically provides access to tools related to what is selected in the scene or highlighted in the Content Browser. Using the **Find in Content Browser...** command through right-clicking over a scene actor is very useful, and likewise so is right-clicking over an asset in the browser to access the **Find Package** command. Both allow us to find any assets related to the current one. Because a lot of UDK assets are intended to be modular, this is particularly important. Also, right-clicking an object in the **Content Browser** lets you access any examples of the asset already in the scene through the command **Select Level Actors Using This Object**. Right-clicking in empty space in the assets panel of the Content Browser lets you create new items, which leads us to the next topic.

See also

▶   The next recipe, *Accessing assets in the Content Browser*, looks closer at handling assets

▶   The recipe following that, *Creating and managing packages*, covers the process for introducing or modifying the actual assets in the Content Browser

Accessing assets in the Content Browser

The Content Browser is the key staging area of assets used to furnish levels. Before you make a level, this is the window UDK opens up onto. If your job is making assets then you may do a lot of work here without even doing any level layout. In this recipe, we look at how to find something that we need to find, how to move content around, how to create or import new content, and shortcuts to using the Browser effectively.

How to do it...

Examining the assets belonging to a plant model

1.   After starting UDK, the Content Browser should be open. If not, press *Ctrl + Shift + F* or the icon: [🖼]

2.   Locate the **Type here to search** field, which is near the top. Click in there if your cursor isn't already flashing there and type *PLANT*.

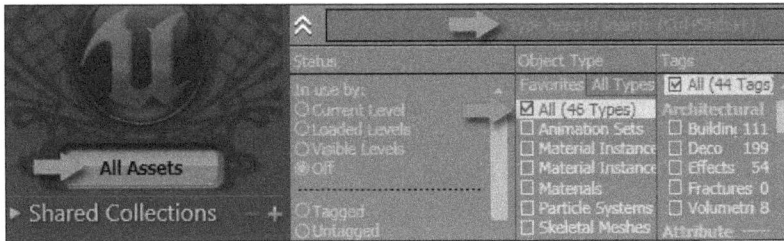

3. You will probably see a lot of textures of leaves display in the assets panel under the filters. If not, make sure **ALL** [☑ All] is ticked in the **Object Type** filter, just below the search field. Click on **All Assets**. This ensures that we're searching the entire body of provided content.

4. Now filter only **Static Meshes** in the **Object Type** list.

5. Look for *S_BananaPlant_01* in the resulting display of assets. If necessary use the sliders on the edges of the red-edged asset panel to scroll and locate it. You can also scroll the middle mouse scroll wheel.

6. When you mouse over *S_BananaPlant_01* it turns orange. When you click on it, it turns yellow. Assets the scene is not using aren't loaded with the editor, which saves memory for the scene. When an asset is **fully loaded**, its dependencies are also loaded, for instance the material and textures used by a model like the *Banana Plant*. Click on the small orange square [■] in the corner of the banana plant asset's icon, which will **fully load** the mesh. The asset will state there is **NO COLLISION MODEL**! This means that if the model is placed in the level then a player will be able to run right through it. For now, ignore that. We discuss collision later.

7. Drag the icon over the perspective view to drop an instance of the asset into the editor. You should see a purple tinted banana plant in the editor. This tint indicates it is selected. You should also see a movement cursor.

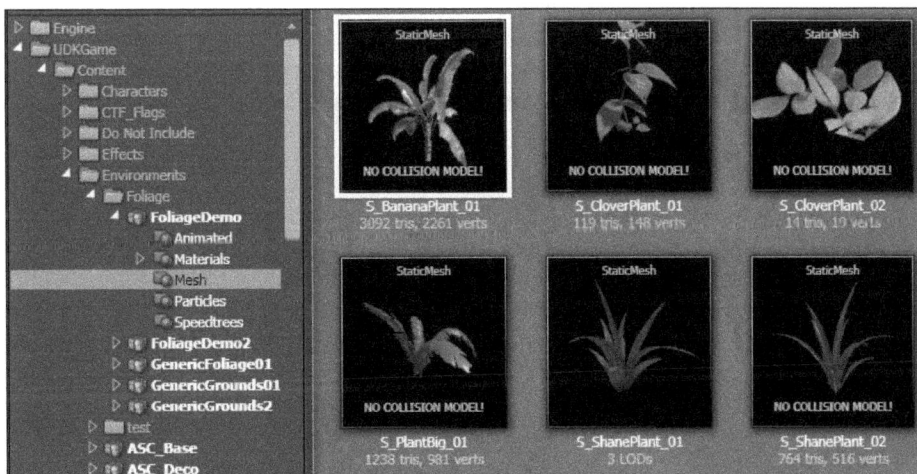

8. This screenshot shows the highlighted *BananaPlant* asset in its specific package. Right-click on the model in the editor window (not in the Browser) and choose **Show in Browser**. Notice how the Browser will jump from showing just *PLANT* in the search field to showing other objects too. These are all the objects in the same package as the banana plant asset. You don't actually need to pull the object into the editor for this step. Instead, you can right-click on the asset in the Browser and choose **Find Package**.

9. For convenience, you can also right-click on the asset and choose **Copy Full Name to Clipboard**. This allows you to paste its name into search strings or assign it to property channels where needed.

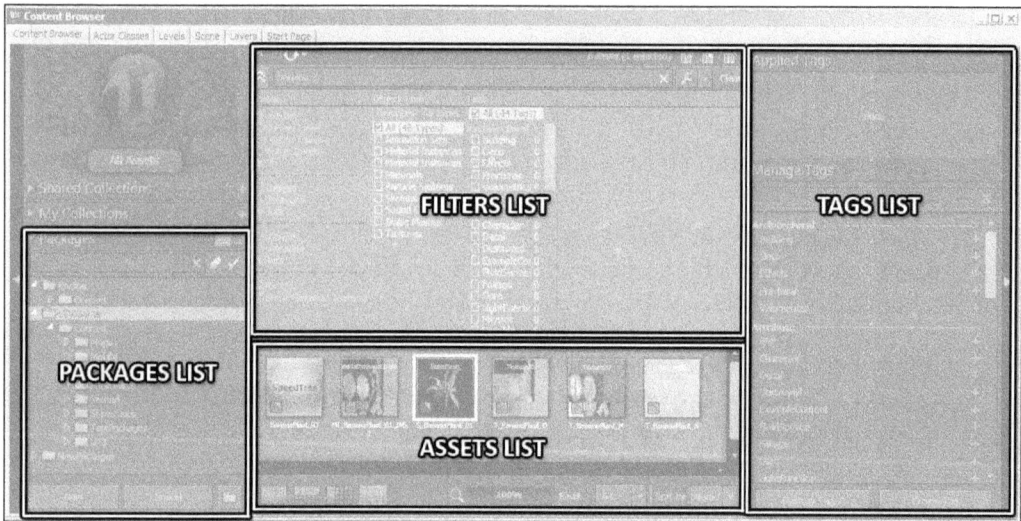

10. Look to the left, in the **Packages** list, and see how the package displaying is `UDKGame/Content/Environments/Foliage/FoliageDemo/Mesh`. This indicates the folder structure for the package *FoliageDemo*. The current model is properly indicated as *FoliageDemo.Mesh.S_BananaPlant_01* because the naming convention is **Package.Group.Asset** for all assets in UDK.

Accessing materials used by a model

1. Double-click the *Banana Plant* model to open it in the **Static Mesh Editor**, which provides us with a closer look at the asset and allows key properties to be set for the asset, including collision, mesh simplification, and materials. On the right of the mesh viewer you will see a list of **Properties** (as with most panels in UDK this can be dragged by its heading to be floated and docked on either side of the view). Here, expand **LODInfo**, to reveal the **Material** the object uses.

2. Next to the Material name there are three small icons [⬅🔍⬜]. If you click the green arrow you can load a new Material, if one is highlighted in the Browser. The magnifying glass takes you to the current Material asset in the Browser. The square clears the Material channel. For now, click on the magnifying glass.

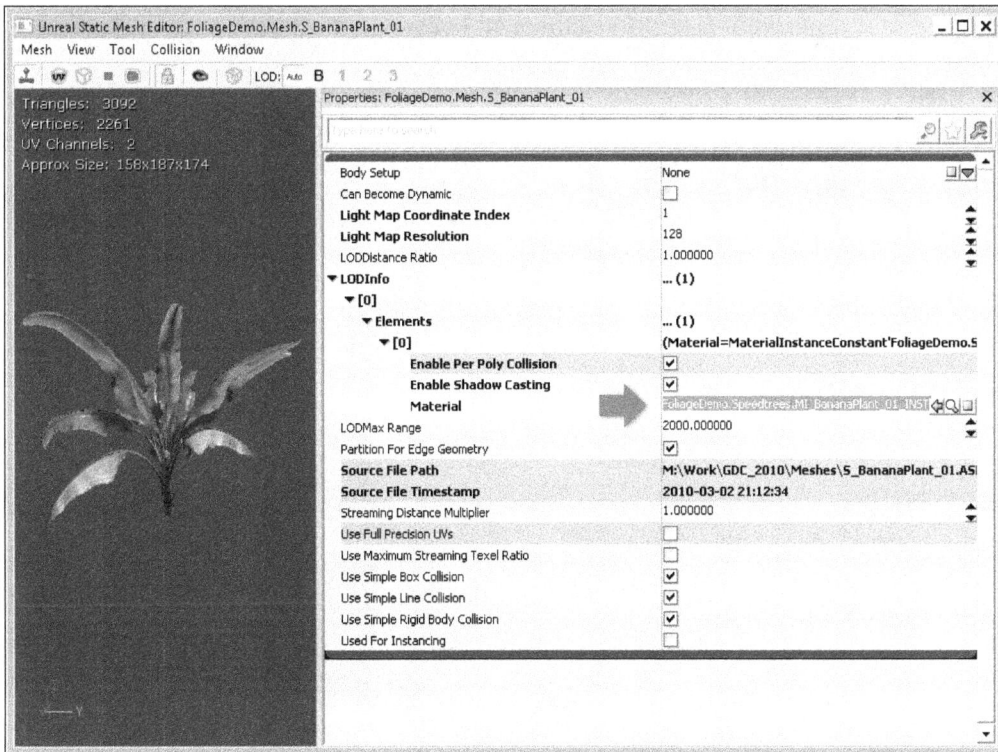

3. Notice that in the Content Browser the Material for the plant is highlighted. It just so happens this mesh uses a **Material Instance Constant**, a special type of material which depends on a **parent Material** for certain variable parameters (which can be animated or allow you to create many variations from one parent). The **Material Instance Constant**, discussed in depth later, has its own editor. Double-click *MI_BananaPlant_01_INST* to open the **Material Instance Editor**, and notice the **Parent** channel in the left-hand side **Properties** panel also has a green arrow, magnifying glass, and a **Clear text** icon. Click the Parent's magnifying glass [🔍] to highlight the **Parent** Material in the Content Browser.

4. That's quite a long thread to follow if you're new to these ideas, but it does expose how elements in UDK may connect together. You'll find that from editor to editor the icons for navigating between the assets remain the same, and hopefully you'll quickly get used to the assign icon [⬀], the find in browser icon [⬁] and the add entry icon [⬂], which appear everywhere.

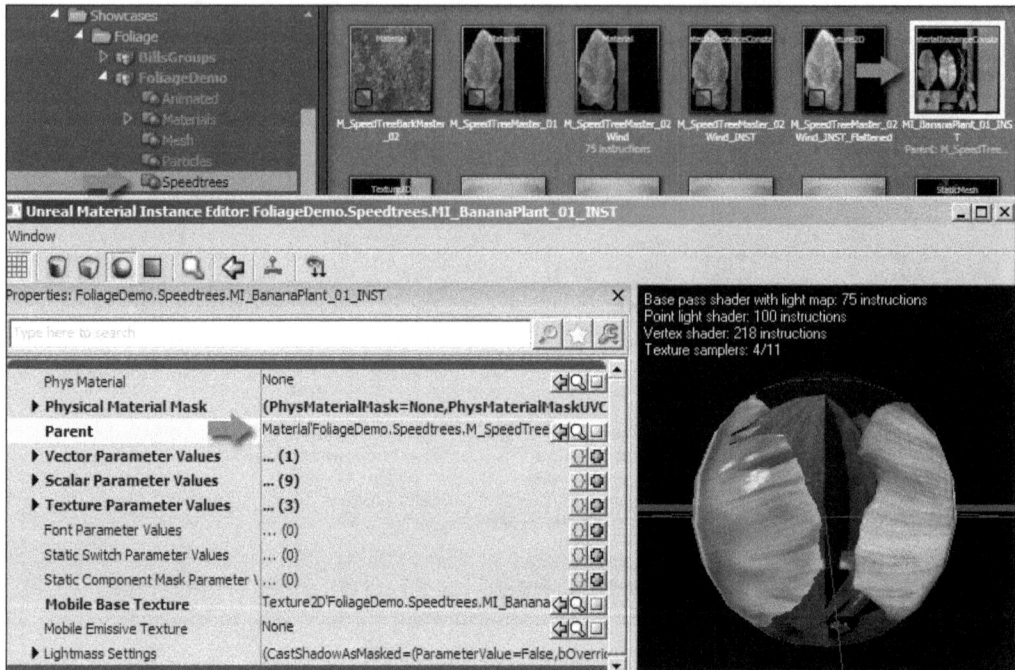

5. To see what textures a Material uses (and there may be many) you can right-click on a Material in the assets panel of the Content Browser and choose **List Referenced Objects**. This will display a lot of information. Amongst this, the texture nodes are the ones named **Texture2D** in the list, for example: *Texture2D FoliageDemo. Speedtrees.T_ShaneTobacco_D*.

6. You can also simply double-click on a Material to edit it and follow the Material channels back to their Texture2D or Param2D nodes in the Material Editor. Doing so is a good way to become familiar with Material shader instructions. Without going into the Material Editor, you can see how many **Texture Samplers** nodes are in use by the Material by holding your mouse over the Material and reading the floating display info. A **Texture Sampler** is a node that holds a **Texture** asset.

7. Double-click the highlighted **Parent** Material which the **MIC** of the banana plant is based on. The Material Editor is discussed later, but you should be able to spot in the network the texture assigned to the Material by following the nodes from the **Diffuse** channel. You'll also see a huge network of nodes controlling the orientation of the leaves of the tree (which are mostly math operations).

Creating and managing packages

Let's consider how packages work and how to manage them both inside UDK and through Windows. All the assets you use are saved in packages. They have the suffix .UPK and are distinct from .UDK files, which are maps or levels. Both of these are external files stored in folders within the UDK installation, typically in C:/UDK/~/UDKGame/Content/ where ~ is the version number you have installed, such as *UDK-2011-08*. When using package files keep in mind that they can be transferred between users sharing a project or between computers independently of maps or scenes you may have been working on. However, maps that depend on certain packages will not load completely if those packages have been removed or renamed. An important thing to watch for is pasting packages to a different computer which have the same name as existing packages but have different content.

We'll be creating a particle asset in this recipe, in a very basic way, not at all to focus on the particle procedure, but the way to deal with the asset itself and the package the asset is created in. The intention is to get used to package naming, renaming, saving, and moving assets around.

Getting ready

This book assumes you have installed UDK using its default folder option. If you already have UDK open, close it down.

How to do it...

1. In Windows Explorer, within the folder C:/UDK/~/UDKGame/Content/ create a *Yourname* sub-folder named after yourself or your project. It is highly advisable to put everything you personally create in here, rather than in default folders, because then you can readily transport content from computer to computer or even from one version of UDK to another (assuming you are rolling forward). Since UDK is updated frequently, this can save a lot of noodling around with files. If you work in a team, a folder naming convention may be imposed which you should follow.

2. Restart UDK. If you then look in the **Packages list** in the Content Browser you should now see your folder showing there. If you didn't reset, and create a package, you will still be able to save the package into the newly named subfolder but it won't display in the **Packages list** until you restart. Instead it will display at the bottom of the list, under **New Packages** in a temporary package called *Untitled_1* (and the number will increment if you start a new scene).

3. A package typically includes some content, and there are two ways to get started. The first is to press the **New** button at the bottom of the **Packages List**. This floats a menu for creating content. The other way is to right-click in the gray space of the Content Browser's assets panel and choose **New...** according to the type of object you want to create.

4. If you highlight an existing folder in the packages list, such as the one with your name that you created just before, the new object will follow suit and save to that folder. Anyway, you can choose from the floating menu whatever folder you like. You should also give the object a **Group** and a name. Setting a **Group** is optional, but really helps a lot. It allows you to organize content that is similar together inside a package. You could put all your meshes in a group called *Mesh* and all your textures in a group called *Texture* for example.

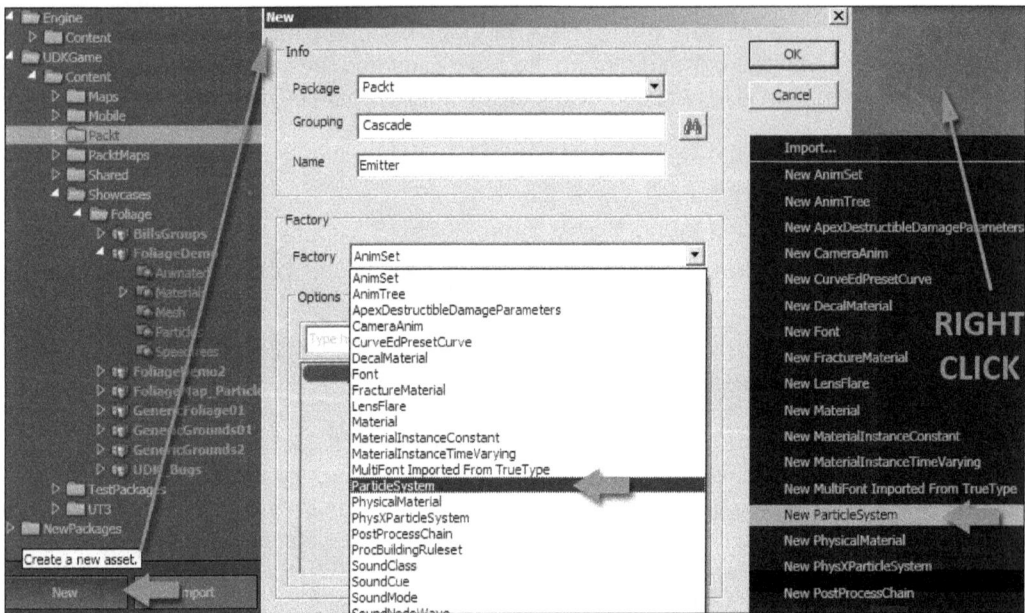

5. Based on the information above, create a **New Particle System** in your folder, something like this: *Yourname.Cascade.DemoPS1* where *Yourname* is the folder name, *Cascade* is the group name, and *DemoPS1* is the unique asset name. Notice when you create a particle system by using the right-click approach it automatically assigns a **Factory** preset called **Particle System** in the creation menu, and after you hit **Okay** then Cascade opens. **Cascade** is UDK's particle asset editor. If you use the **New** icon, you have to set the **Factory** type yourself from a roll down list, shown above. You should then see a thumbnail in the Content Browser, as shown in the next illustration. Notice the asterisk ***** next to both the package name and the asset name. This indicates the need to save changes, and is visible in the following screenshot:

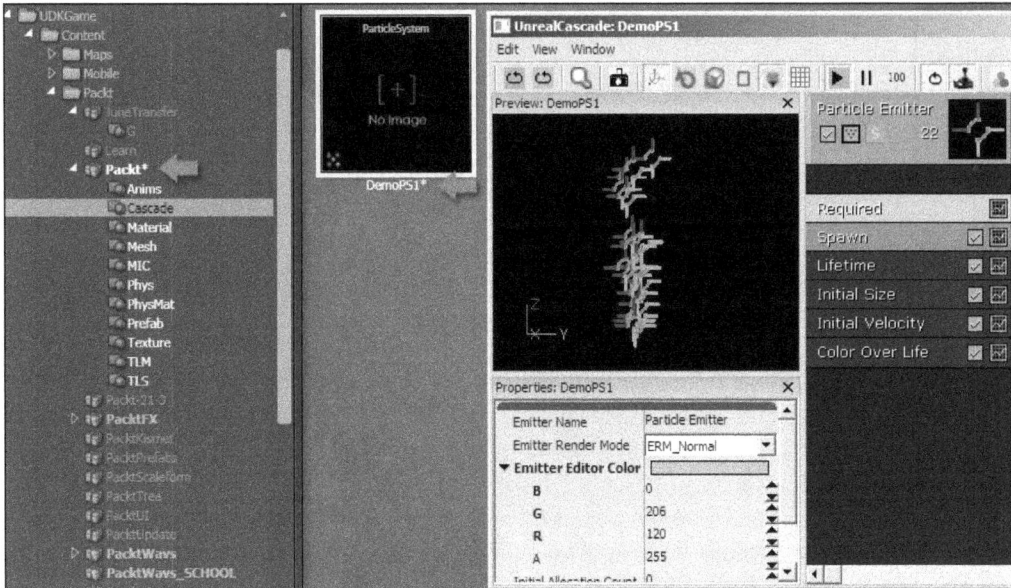

6. This new particle system is nothing special. We'll edit particles later. The goal here is just to have a new asset to play with. For now, set an icon thumbnail for it in the Cascade editor menu by going to **View | Save Cam Position**. This ensures that the thumbnail of the asset displayed in the browser doesn't remain empty and instead looks more like the particles in the Cascade editor, which is important if you want to browse through a large number of asset thumbnails. To set a thumbnail you can also use the icon which looks like a black and white camera [🖭]. When ready, close the Cascade editor then right-click on your package folder and press **Save**, which will save all of its content.

7. If you get a warning saying **Cannot Save via the Browser** then your new particle system must be in the *Untitled_0* package. You should redefine it by pointing it to your own package *Yourname* in the folder `C:\UDK\~\UDKGame\Content\Yourname`. To do so, right-click on the asset and choose **Move or Rename...** and then just enter a specific folder; it would be good to use the folder name you created at the start for your custom assets. If you are starting out with UDK, and have never saved a package of your own already you'll be prompted for a .UPK file save location in Explorer, and should use the folder we've pointed to: `C:\UDK\~\UDKGame\Content\Yourname`.

8. You can set as many packages in your folder as you want, or put all your assets in one package. If a single package grows over 300 MB or so, you may hit a performance ceiling for it and get a warning when you save.

> A good way to keep package size down is to use simpler **Lightmaps**. To do so, avoid raising the StaticMesh and BSP sampling resolution too high. StaticMesh resolution is higher when its value raised, BSP resolution is higher when its value is lowered. This is further discussed in *Chapter 8, Then There Was Light!*

9. If you now delete your folder in Explorer or a .UPK inside of your folder, the Content Browser will no longer include what you deleted next time you run UDK. So, if you save your scene or map, and reload it after deleting content, you will get missing content errors. This is something to be very careful of. Deleting a folder containing a package with an unused, empty particle system won't matter, but deleting a folder with packages full of textures used by model assets in different packages could keep you up fretting long into the night. It is a good idea to periodically copy out and rename backups of your key packages.

10. If, in the Browser, you want to modify the content which ships with UDK, you shouldn't directly edit it but instead right-click on it and choose **Create a Copy...** then set the new package name to one of your own, located in your `C:\UDK\~\UDKGame\Content\Yourname` subfolder, and probably rename the asset too. You can then modify the copy as you wish.

11. Finally, if you have content from another graphics software you want to import, like a texture or a model, click on the **Import** button at the bottom of the packages list or right-click in the assets Browser panel and choose **Import** there. It is the top entry and you may have to scroll up the list to see it.

Importing your own content

If you don't have any resource files, you can download sample content from `http://www.packtpub.com/support` (select **Unreal Development Kit Game Design Cookbook** from the drop-down list) including textures, models, sounds, and animation. Note that UDK likes textures which have squared dimensions (or powers of 2) such as `256 x 256`.

How to do it...

1. Download the book's content from the above mentioned URL and extract it into a folder such as `C:\Packt\`. In the main extracted folder `...\Files\` select the `\Development` and `\UDKGame` subfolders and copy or merge them into your UDK installation `C:\UDK\~\` where ~ is the version number. These files do not replace any default UDK files, but add additional content referred to in the book. The extra folder `...\Files\Provided Content` contains a few additional files such as 3ds Max source scenes. Look for the included archive *ImportTest.rar* and extract that to a subfolder `\ImportTest`.

2. In UDK, in the Content Browser, select *YOURFOLDER* and choose **Import** as discussed above. You can import multiple assets at one go. Select the files extracted to `C:\UDK\~\UDKGame\Content\Packt\ImportTest` and press **Open**.

3. When UDK notices the SWF file it will give the following warning:

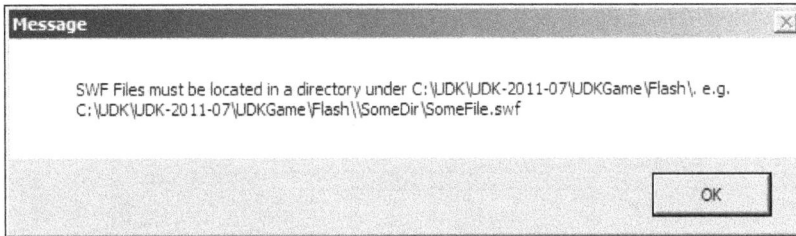

4. All the other assets will still come in. As mentioned earlier, SWF file import should be from assets in the `C:\UDK\~\UDKGame\Flash\UI\` folder, not from the `\UDKGame\Content` folder. Don't import the SWF now; instead, move it where it should be, then import it separately. When they are used later in the lessons, each important file's requirements are talked about more.

5. The rest of the content will go into a package we'll call *Packt UDK* (just treat it as a throw-away package). While it's possible to do so, it isn't a good idea to press **Okay to all** if the content is not all of the same type, and here it isn't. There are textures, meshes, and .WAV files. So check that each item you import has the appropriate **Group** (Mesh, Texture, Mesh, Wav) and press **OK** for each one. The next few steps detail this.

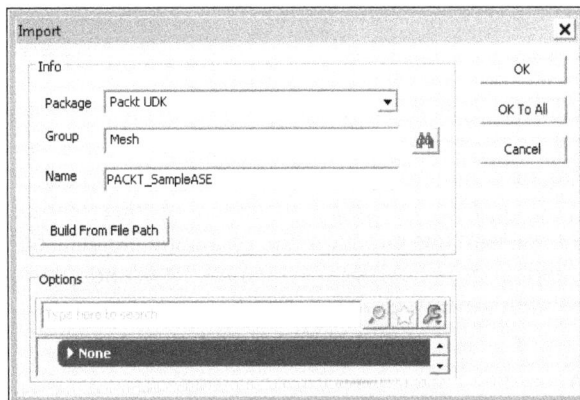

6. The included mesh file is an .ASE and was sent out from **Autodesk 3DS Max** using **File | Export Selected** with .ASE as the file type. Now you can also use .FBX to transfer between Autodesk modelers and UDK. To import it, it just needs its group name set to *Mesh* or something to distinguish it from a texture. This goes for the included WAV file, which are sounds, and should have a group named *Wavs* or *Sounds*.

7. The textures mainly import with default settings. Give them the group name *Texture*. The exception is *256x256_SampleIII_NRM.TGA*. The filename ending _NRM is so named to indicate that it contains a normal map. If you are importing **Normal map** assets which help describe bumpy surfaces in a material in the **Import** dialog, they require the **Compressing Settings:** *TC_Default* setting to be changed to *TC_Normalmap*. A properly imported normal map will show up pale pink in the Browser. If it shows up dark blue in the Browser, then it has probably been imported without the correct compression settings.

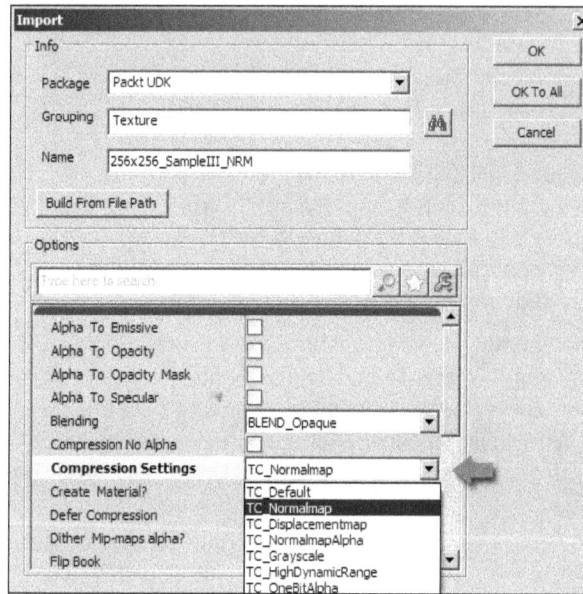

8. Having imported all the files, your package needs to be saved. Right-click on it and choose **Save**. The next screenshot shows the imported content, and the **Save Package** dialog for committing your .UPK file. When prompted for the folder location to save *Packt UDK.UPK* choose your own folder that you created earlier. Actually this package is not one we'll use directly in the upcoming projects; so deleting it later on and using content from \Yourname\Yourname.UPK and \Packt\Packt.UPK instead will be what's mostly likely to happen.

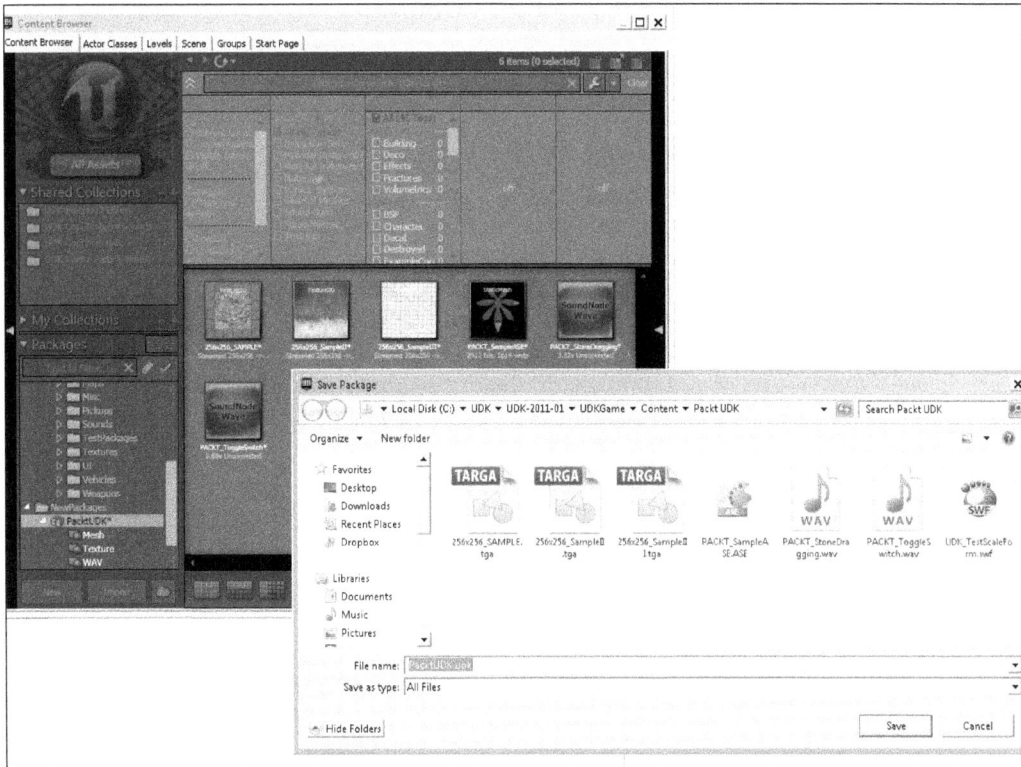

There's more...

How to open an external package

From time to time you will come across a useful package that someone else has made, such as those that come with many of the video tutorials that exist for UDK. The usage here is for when you want to extract content from an existing package without putting it into your *UDKGame* folder structure (and then put the extracted content to your own package).

1. To load the .UPK file click in the Content Browser on the folder icon next to **New** and **Import** which has the tool tip (mouse-over): **Open an External Package**, shown next. This method is okay if all you want to do is select assets from the external package and move them into other packages.

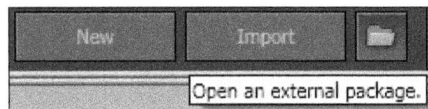

2. If you simply paste a .UPK into your folder structure `C:\UDK\~\UDKGAME\Content` and restart UDK, the pasted content will show up in the **Packages** list when you restart. Normally this is considered a safer way to bring in new content.

Copying and pasting content between scenes

UDK allows you to open one scene, select any number of objects in the world, and copy them to be pasted into a second scene. Copying and pasting is fairly easy between scenes; just use **Copy** and **Paste** from the editor's main **Edit** menu. You can also right click in the scene and choose **Paste Here**. Pasting generally works unless you are pasting an object that references another, such as terrain, which also includes **Terrain Layer Setup** and **Terrain Material** assets, where those assets may be tied into a particular scene. This example may be unusual, which is why it provides a good illustration for how important package handling can become. Changing UDK default library assets causes all kinds of headaches like this one and should be avoided:

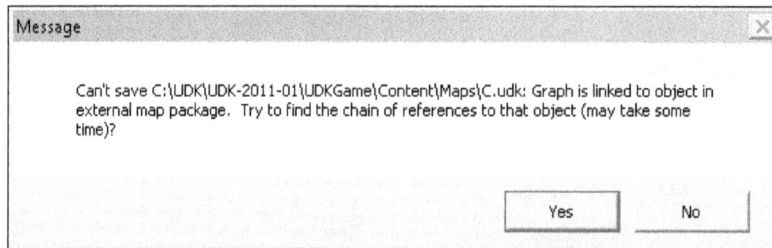

The image above is what shows if you have tried to copy content from one scene to another and some dependencies are not included, and the validity of the pasted content is therefore called into question. The solution is to list the required assets and copy those over too, then reassign them where they ought to go.

Over the last few topics, while learning about package handling and assets, we opened up several editors within UDK: the **Properties Editor** (*F4*), the **Static Mesh editor**, **Cascade**, and the **Material Instance editor**. Most actors have their own editor type. You can examine the types of assets that UDK provides by going to the **Actor Classes** list, which is in the tab alongside the Content Browser. Once you highlight any given actor type you can add it into the scene by right-clicking in the viewport and assign it from the context options.

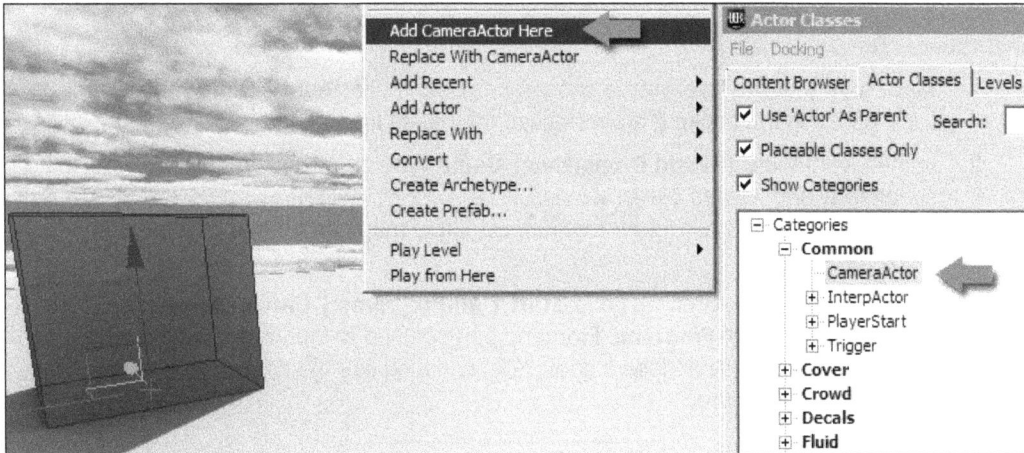

Let's tie this in better with the copying and pasting topic.

1. Use the **Actor Classes** list to locate the *CameraActor* type, and add one to the scene from the right-click menu in the Perspective view, as seen in the previous screenshot.

2. To match this camera exactly into another scene so that its position and location are the same, go to the **Edit** menu and choose **Copy**. If you want, save the scene.

3. Open a new scene template and from the **Edit** menu, choose **Paste**. Another instance of the first camera will appear with exactly the same settings.

> This works even when the camera is animated, but you'd also have to copy and paste the relevant Kismet. You can't copy both at once, unless the animated camera is converted to a **Prefab**. Prefabs are discussed under the first recipe in *Chapter 5, It Is Your Destiny!*

Cooking a map in Unreal Frontend

Once you've made a level, or a set of them, you can cook the content (to distil out from the editor only what is used) and then package that to a game installer that can run on any capable PC without having to have UDK itself there too. In this recipe the cooking process is outlined for a simple test case.

Getting ready

Load any map, or the `C:\UDK\~\UDKGame\Content\Yourfolder\Yourfirstmap.UDK` you made in the recent recipe *Beginning, building and testing a level*.

How to do it...

1. Make sure that the level you've chosen has been built (**Build | Build All**) or press [🔩], because the cooking process uses the baked lighting information.

2. In the level's **View | World Properties | Game Type** property set *UTGame*, if it isn't set already and save to `C:\UDK\~\UDKGame\Content\Maps\CookMe.UDK`. It is good to have a different folder for final, cookable maps and maps that are still being developed.

3. Close UDK, then in Windows go to **Start | All Programs | Unreal Development Kit | ~ | Tools | Unreal Frontend**. Frontend can be used to launch the editor, to launch a game to play, or to package a game. You can also use the search field to pop it up quickly, as shown here:

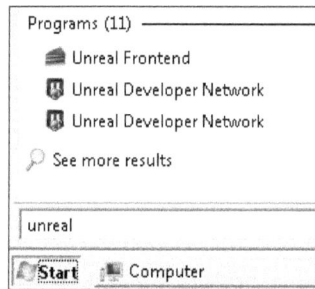

4. Once Frontend launches, choose the type of game you are cooking using the preset. Two types are for mobile, and one is for PC. In this case, choose the PC version which is called **DM-Deck**.

5. In the **Maps to Cook** window, highlight the entry **DM-Deck** and choose **Remove**. Then click the **Add...** text button, and choose it from the list (which shows all the valid maps UDK can find in *UDKGame\Content*). If you haven't got a map to use, the name of any map in the list will do. After all, this is just a test run.

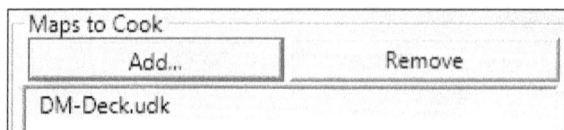

6. If you intend to bundle together several maps for cooking, you can specify the initial launch map in the field called **Launch Map**, by turning on **Override Default** and choosing one from the list, which is based on the maps to cook. Remember, if an included level depends on another (for a menu or go to map upon completion), to avoid errors you will have to include that to cook too.

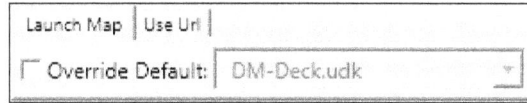

7. You can set the **Target Directory** for the output file (although to be safe, you may as well leave the default setting for this alone).

8. Along the top of the Frontend interface there are big glossy icons. Click **Launch** to show the options for it (on mouse release), and click the checkbox to disable this feature. Then, since for now you don't need to compile any scripts, just click on **Cook** and choose **Clean and Full Recook**. Then wait till you see the report in the feedback panel showing success.

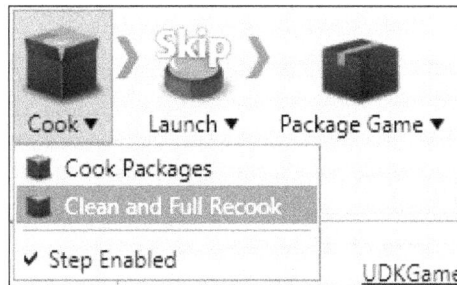

9. Now click the icon for **Package Game** and enable its **Step Enabled** checkbox, and then click the embedded **Package Game** command. A dialog will appear asking for a **GameLongName** and a **GameName**. **GameLongName** determines the way your game will appear in Windows in the **Start | All Programs** menu. The **GameName** is what's given to the installer filename. Appended to this will be the prefix **UDKInstall**, so if you typed in *MyGame* as your **GameName**, you'd get *UDKInstall-MyGame.EXE*.

10. Press **Package Game** after entering these names, and wait till you get the success notice returned in the messages in Frontend. Once finished you'll have an .EXE installer which installs the same way UDK installs in the folder you specified in the **Target Directory** field.

Mobile device emulation

If you are using a UDK version from June 2011 onwards, once you've made a level, you can test how it may appear on an iPad or similar mobile device. This recipe covers the feature and also briefly explains how to deploy a game to a device.

How to do it...

1. With your map loaded press the **Emulate Mobile Features** icon, the first in the row of icons pictured below. This shows how the game may appear visually.

2. Save your level, then click the icon **Edit Mobile Previewer Settings** [ ]. Choose **Resolution | iPad** and also choose **Orientation | Landscape**. Of course, you can set these according to your target output. In **Features**, ensure that **iPad** is set. Press **Save Settings**. You could alternatively choose all the iPhone 4 settings.

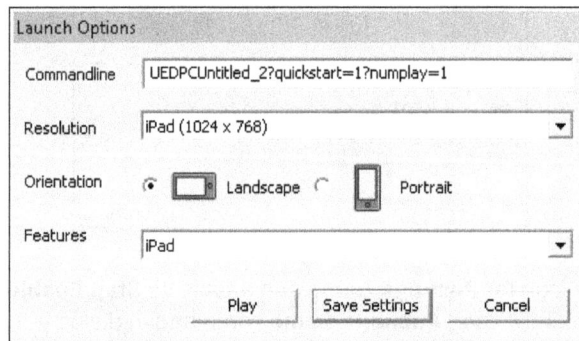

Launch Options	
Commandline	UEDPCUntitled_2?quickstart=1?numplay=1
Resolution	iPad (1024 x 768)
Orientation	⦿ Landscape ○ Portrait
Features	iPad
	Play Save Settings Cancel

3. At the bottom of the **Settings** window there is a **Play** button.

4. Alternatively, you can also click the icon in the editor next to the settings icon, called **Start this level on Mobile Previewer** [ ]. That's really all there is to it. Your PIE session should include a UI with on screen joysticks that emulate iPad controls. Mouse dragging stands in for input from fingers on a touch screen.

5. When you are happy with your level performance running in device emulation mode, you can actually install to an iOS game directly from the editor using the **Install on iOS device** icon [ ]. Right-click on this to use a command line in order to enter game-specific settings such as the number of players.

6. The game will cook through a background instance of Frontend then provide a dialog for deployment.

7. Bear in mind that to actually send an iOS game to hardware you need to be an **iOS registered developer**. You can register as one from the dialog after pressing **Install on iOS device**, or do so through Apple's website: `http://developer.apple.com/programs/ios/`; though because Apple does levy an annual fee for the right to develop on their platforms you want to be ready to do so before you start paying out. Once you are registered you can proceed through the **Unreal iOS Configuration dialog** to provision and deploy your game. More information on this is available through a link to UDN inside the dialog itself. If you run this by mistake, it is quite okay just to cancel it.

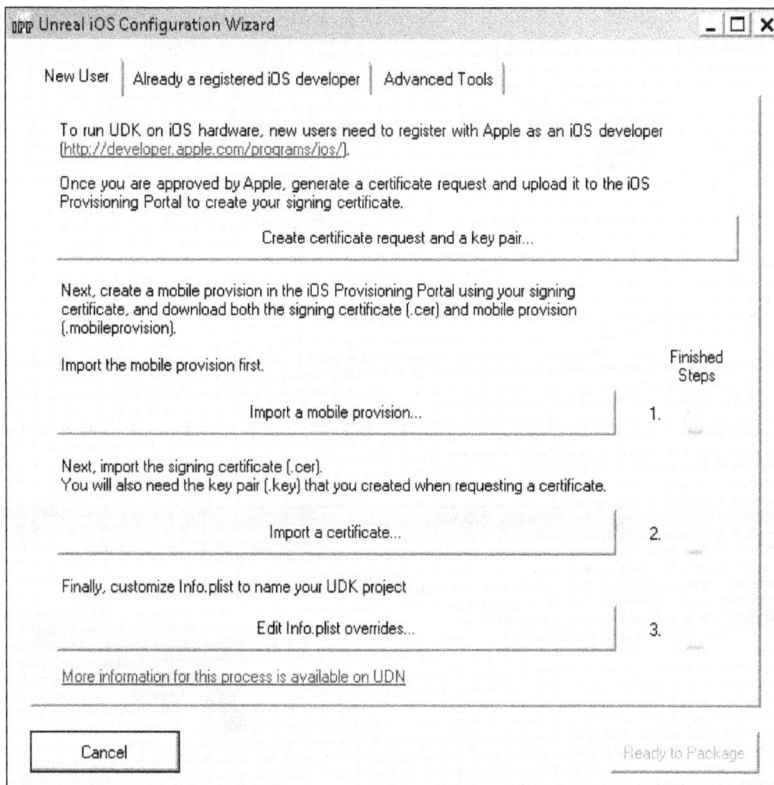

8. For provisioning, should you be taking things that far, it is recommended on PC to use Safari, given it is Apple's main web platform, as iOS provisioning is generally aimed at Mac computers. Once through the provisioning stage you'll wind up with **certification files** to import back into the **Unreal iOS Configuration wizard**, and once those are imported, the last step is to set the bundled content names and display names that will be used by the device for your game's icon.

9. Once those steps are complete, and you press **Ready to Package**, your game is sent to the device. This assumes you have gone through the steps starting from the editor, as currently Unreal Frontend itself doesn't complete this stage.

10. Existing developers of iOS applications who wish to develop iOS games using UDK must export their certificate and private key from the **Keychain Access** application in order to import it on a PC running UDK.

Kismet debugging

If you are using a UDK version from June 2011 onwards, when you are using Kismet to create events and actions to enliven the actors in the scene, you can track the nodes that are being used (or not used) and also check some statistics for how frequently nodes are firing. There is a lengthy chapter on Kismet operations in *Chapter 4, Got Your Wires Crossed?* This recipe is not a Kismet lesson, just a procedure for enabling the Kismet debugging tool using an existing scene.

Getting ready

Load the scene from the provided content: *Packt_01_BreakPoints_START.UDK*.

How to do it...

1. This map is set to *UTGame* for its **Game Type**, so when you **Play in Editor** (**PIE**) [▣] you will have a **HUD** and you can use weapons. The level has a rocket launcher weapon pickup placed near the **PlayerStart**, and you can shoot it at a platform to allow you to create a set of stairs.

2. The Kismet for the scene is contained in a sub-sequence *BlockAB*. Its functionality is covered in *Chapter 4, Got Your Wires Crossed?* in the recipe *Allowing the player to pick up, carry, and place an object*. For now, we just want to get the **Breakpoints** used to check the Kismet is working.

3. First off, press the **Enable Kismet Debugging** icon [K], which is located in the top icon row of the main editor next to the **PIE** icon as shown here:

4. Open Kismet [K], and expand the list in the **Sequences window**, then click on the **Sub-Sequence** labeled *BlockAB*.

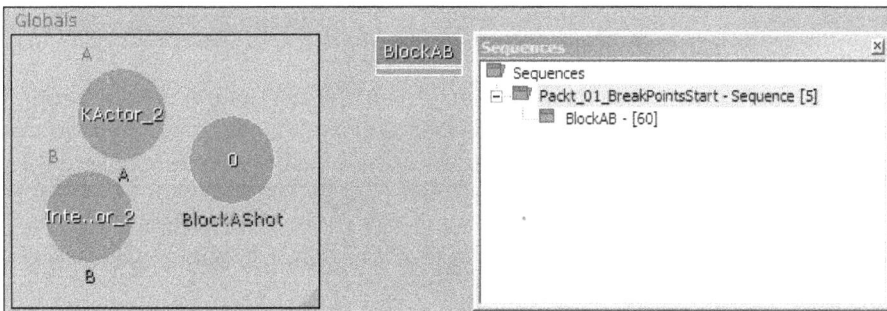

5. Right-click on the first event in the sequence and choose **Set Breakpoint**. Repeat this with all the other events in the sequence. Events are easy to spot, since they have a hexagon shape, and red outlines (that turn yellow when selected).

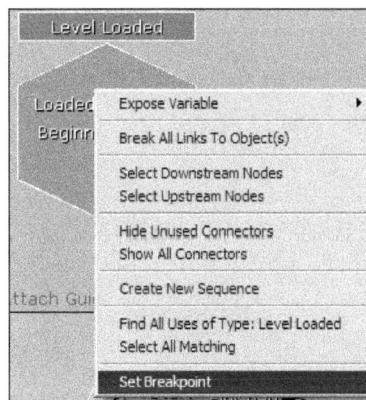

6. Use the **Search** tool, which is the Magnifying glass icon [🔍] in the top row of Kismet icons, and set the **Search Type** to **Object**. In the **Search For** list you'll be able to access a roll-down list and choose *Destroy*. Click **Search**, and click on the item that is found in the **Results** panel. Right-click on the action that is focused, and choose **Set Breakpoint** for this too. You should now have six breakpoints.

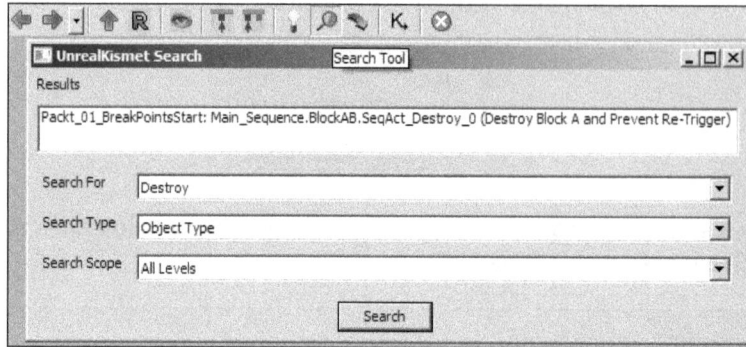

7. In the editor, press *F8*. Immediately after the **PIE** window shows, you'll be paused and shown Kismet again. This is because the first breakpoint is on the **Level Loaded** event, which fires when the session begins. The icon for breakpoints that have been tripped shows with an arrow over their red dot [🔴]. At the top of the Kismet debugging window there is a **Play** icon (*Alt + F8*). Press this, and you'll resume playing. And you'll get a pause again to show the **Player Spawned** event has fired. Again, press **Play**.

8. The next **Breakpoint** will likely occur after you pick up the rocket launcher and fire a rocket at the platform on the ground. Looking at the Kismet debugger you can see some statistics showing above each involved node, the time it was last activated and the number of times it has activated.

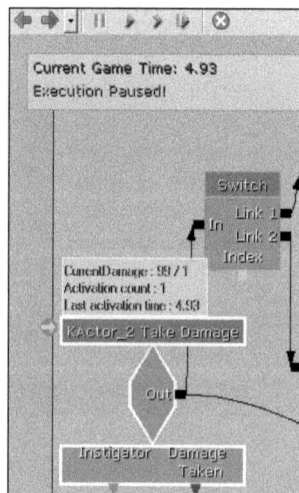

9. Rather than pressing **Play** this time, select the event labeled ***KActor_2 Take Damage***, right-click on the icon on its right-hand side called **Run to Next Action**. Choose **Selected** and the game will let you play up till the point when the Trigger involved takes damage from the rocket. The statistics above the node will show for the ***Take Damage*** event the current level of damage to the involved Trigger. You may see many nodes stepping through as they fire one after the other. This is where you can track the order or correctness of your Kismet sequence.

10. If you are playing and you want to check the Kismet debugger without waiting for a **Breakpoint** to occur, press *Shift + F1*. It prevents the cursor being locked to the **PIE** session. This is useful if you have the debugger open and accidentally set focus on the game again, while it's still paused. That will happen if you jump from one application in Windows to another then back to **PIE**. You still have to resume playback by pressing the **Play** icon [▶] in the debugger.

11. After this point, pressing **Play** again from Kismet, you may notice that there is a kind of strange, continual pausing every time you hit **Play**. This is because one of the events involves a Trigger attached directly to the player, which is triggered by the player continually. So, while the Kismet is showing, look for and select the event ***Trigger_0 Touch*** and right-click on it and choose **Clear Breakpoint**.

12. Unless you shoot the platform continually, the next **Breakpoint** to fire will be when you place the carried platform in the space for it against the wall. The event is called ***Trigger_3 Touch***. It's inside the *Check Block Int* comment box. Directly after that event, the game should pause and show the debugging window again because the platform is removed immediately from the scene by the ***Destroy*** action on which we set a **Breakpoint** earlier.

Hotkeys for the Kismet debugger window

> ▸ *Alt + F7* = Pause
> ▸ *Alt + F8* = Continue
> ▸ *Alt + F9* = Step through
> ▸ *Alt + F10* = Run to next action

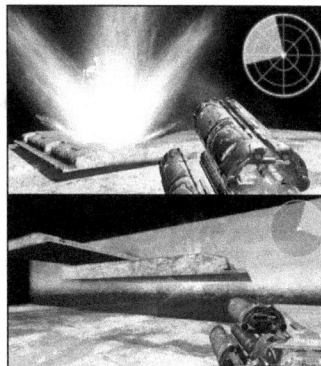

2
Notes From an Unreal World
Constructing Game World Elements

In this chapter, you'll find essential lessons covering principle features of UDK:

- How to handle BSP geometry
- Building a hollow room
- Adjusting surface properties of BSP
- Generating a Volume from the BSP brush
- Handling StaticMesh actors in the scene
- Setting collision in the Static Mesh Editor
- Creating Terrain, Deco Layers, and Material Layers
- Creating a Landscape
- Scattering meshes on Landscape using Foliage
- Creating a steamy plume in Cascade

Introduction

In *Chapter 1*, *Heads Up*, we ripped through getting started with UDK, establishing a scene, using the Content Browser to build and package a level or map, albeit in a bare bones fashion. Now let's look at actual environment features. To begin developing a scene, we need a geometry modeling tool (BSP), a method of terrain editing (for which UDK now has two). Also, while covering these basics, it's a good point to introduce other content generation tools that UDK provides, such as the scattering tool **Foliage**, and the particle creation tool **Cascade**.

How to handle BSP geometry

BSP stands for **Binary Space Partition**. BSP allows you to quickly create and lay out surfaces such as floors, walls, and ceilings which are lined up with each other without having to worry about using any other software. BSP helps you in the design stage, and generally geometry made with BSP can later be replaced by more efficient, more detailed StaticMesh assets. But besides being a modeling tool, BSP can be used to do a lot more, like serve as triggers, lighting volumes, and collision. We'll look at how to generate BSP and how to convert it to a StaticMesh and to a Volume.

Getting ready

Open a **Blank Map** from the UDK templates. Make sure you follow these steps:

1. Go to **Viewport Options** [▼] (which appears in the upper corner of each viewport) and choose **Show | Use Defaults**. If you ever hide scene elements accidentally and get lost, restore them by using **Show | Use Defaults**.

2. In the main menu choose **View | Viewport Configuration | 2x2 split**.

3. In the perspective viewport, choose **Unlit** mode [⃝] or press *Alt + 3*. This is so when we add the BSP geometry it won't be so much in shadow we can't see it.

How to do it...

Getting to know the BSP geometry tools

1. Along the side of the editor are light blue buttons representing some preset geometry. Almost always, a box is the best starting point for BSP. Pick the **BSP cube brush** [⃝] from the brushes.

2. Nothing much will change, because UDK levels always have a BSP cube at the world center when they open. However, if you right-click on that same icon you get options for changing the brush size. Set the brush size to something that will suffice for a floor, say 1024 x 1024 x 16. The XYZ values we set conform to powers of two, so it will mean the brush is easy to align on the grid.

3. Now press the **Close** button. There's no need to press **Build** (in this dialog) as what this is for is moving the Builder Brush over to whatever object is selected in the scene, like an align.

4. Before we start modeling, let's examine what the Builder Brush is. Edit the brush by pressing the **Geometry Mode** icon [⊚] at the top of the buttons, above the brushes. It looks like a box wireframe, and this is because that's what it gives us access to. You can alternatively press *Shift + 2*.

5. Having done so, click on the **BSP** brush in the Perspective view and notice how a surface is picked (it's shaded red) and the points at the corners are larger, so they are easy to pick. In the Perspective viewport, you will almost always just select a surface, not the entire brush.

6. To circumvent this you can *Ctrl + Shift + click* on the BSP to grab the whole thing or click on it in the orthographic view.

7. Now that the BSP is already selected, in one of the orthographic viewports, click directly over an edge. Doing so will actually select two edges, through the model, that align with each other in depth. It is rather hard to select edges directly in the perspective viewport by comparison, which is why we've set the view to **2x2 split**. Try it if you want. If you must do it, zooming in a bit helps.

8. Selecting a point is a matter of clicking on it. Then you can *Ctrl + click* on another to add to the selection. If you *Ctrl + click* on an already selected point it will deselect. Finally, you can *Ctrl + Alt + drag* to marquee select points falling inside the selection box in any view. If you marquee select one group of points then try adding to it using the same method it will only select the new points. To extend the current point selection using a marquee, use *Ctrl + Shift + Alt + drag*.

9. In the perspective viewport, select one corner of the box, a single point, and use the Move tool (which should be active but if it isn't try pressing *Space* to cycle transforms), and nudge the point some distance along an axis, creating a spike. Your moved point will snap to the grid and appear to stagger a little. It's good to keep snapping on so model components align well. This is particularly important for placing architectural features but less so for elements like rocks, plants, or scattered objects that don't need to line up to anything. You can adjust and turn off snapping at the bottom right of the screen or through the **View | Drag Grid** options.

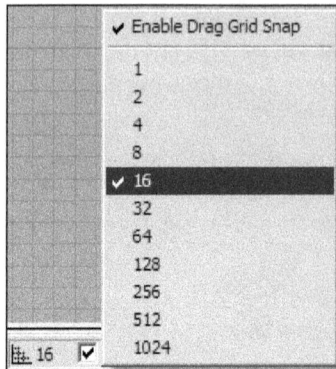

10. When moving models and model components in the viewports there is a **Drag Grid** spacing or snap by default set to 16 units. This can be toggled and adjusted using the setting at the bottom of the editor, and you will also see the **Rotation Grid** snap toggle, **Scale Grid** snap toggle, and auto-save toggle and frequency setting there too. Click the little triangles to set the actual amounts for each.

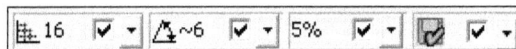

11. Try pressing **Undo** [⤺] or *Ctrl + Z* to undo the spike you made earlier. Notice nothing happens except the pivot of the BSP jumps to the middle of the brush. Press undo once more and notice this time the spike is returned to its box shape. Create a spike again, but this time we'll commit the change.

12. At the top of the editor are a row of buttons that are short cuts for menu items, highlighted below. The first button is **Build | Geometry for Visible Levels**. Press this. Alternatively, if you go to the menu and choose **Build** you will see the list of build methods.

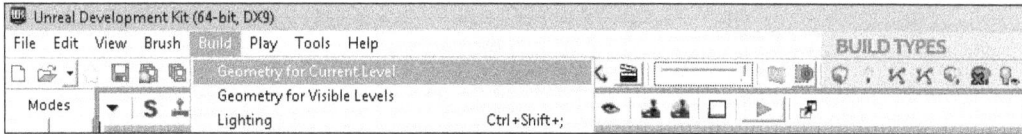

13. Now press undo twice, as before. This time there's no going back and indeed the **Undo** icon is greyed out, because after a build any geometry edits from beforehand are committed. However, you can always restore a basic BSP cube by pressing the BSP cube brush button again.

14. Notice that your spiked BSP brush is now split from one corner to another by an added edge. This is to ensure the geometry remains convex. If you don't like the direction this edge has been added you can turn it by clicking on the edge in question then pressing **Turn** in the **Geometry Tools** floating window.

15. We can extend this simple cube and give it more complexity. In **Geometry Tools**, change from **Edit** to **Extrude** mode. Now when you drag a selected surface of the brush along an axis it will extend new geometry in that direction. To stop extruding, just switch back to **Edit** mode. The following screenshot shows two extrude operations, before and after, in two directions:

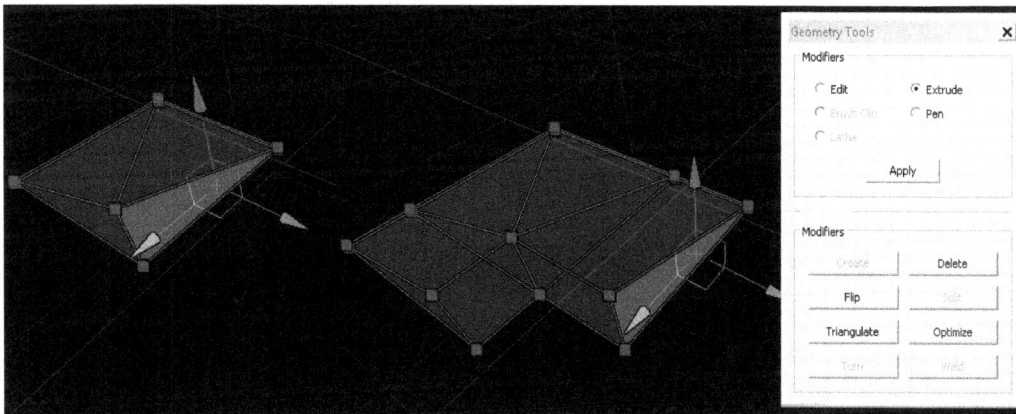

16. Besides the **Extrude** tool there is a method of creating new geometry in a brush called the **Pen** tool. This lets you use *Space* successively to define points on the viewport grid (orthographic) and create a closed shape, which is then extruded according to a preset depth. Press *Space* to add pen tool points. Pressing *Space* will create a point where the mouse is located. Dashed lines between points mark the edges of the geometry. You can hit *Enter* to stop adding points, which will connect the first and last points and form a new BSP brush.

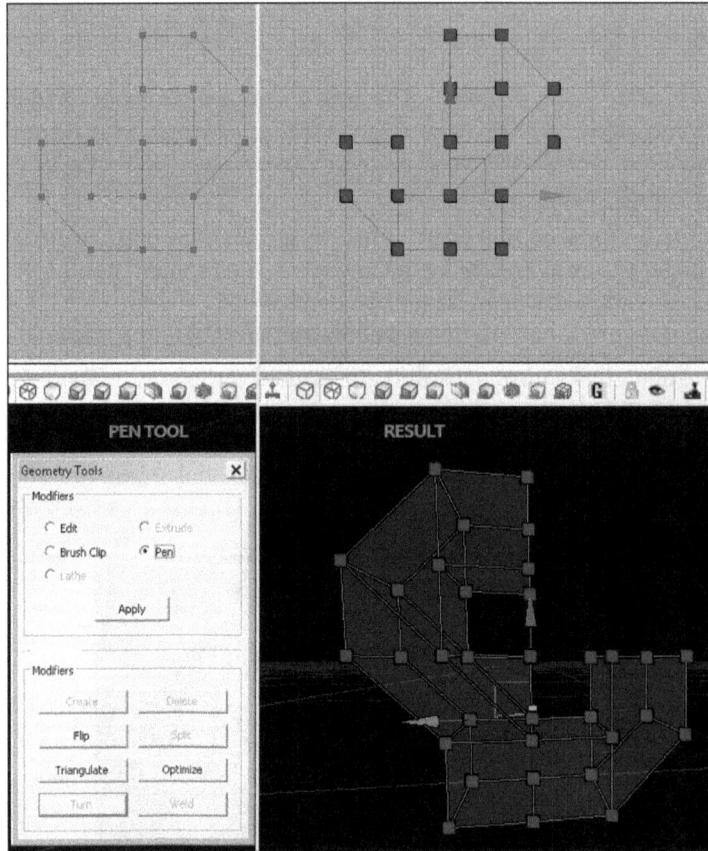

17. When you close the shape you've made with the **Pen** brush, its depth is auto extruded from the floating window **Geometry Tools | Properties | Extrude Depth**. This property, shown in the next screenshot, appears only when the **Pen** tool is active:

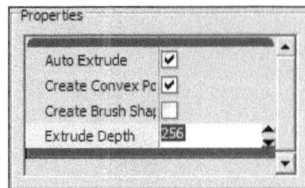

Starting construction of objects with BSP

1. Now we have covered how to alter a BSP brush, we want to see what we can do with it. BSP is most often converted into geometry and then textured. It can also be used as a collision blocking volume, a spatially based moving trigger, and much more. First let's create some geometry from a basic BSP by recreating the 1024 x 1024 x 16 floor block we made earlier (remember to right click on the BSP cube brush [🔍] to set this up), and this time go to the icon set called **CSG**).

2. Click on **CSG Add** [▣], the first of those four icons, and your BSP brush will leave its footprint in the form of a blue/white checkered surface. This coloring is from a default UDK Material: *EngineMaterials.DefaultMaterial*, and can be replaced later.

3. Click on the top surface of the additive BSP then hold *L* and click to create a light shining on the surface. Move the light up in the Z axis and enlarge it a bit using scale. It helps us see what we are doing. Press *Alt + 4* to see the effect of this light. *Alt + 4* is the hot key for **Lit mode** [▣], and it is more appealing than **Unlit mode**. Press *F4* if you want to edit the light's intensity and color, under **Light | Light Component | Light Component | Brightness** and so on. Lighting is covered in *Chapter 8, Then There Was Light!* Here, adding the one light will be fine since we're just starting.

4. When you press **CSG Add** [▣] (*Ctrl + A*), the Builder Brush isn't replaced. It is still there and the geometry is stamped into place at its location. Move the brush out of the way, and maybe press *Ctrl + A* again to create a second mesh.

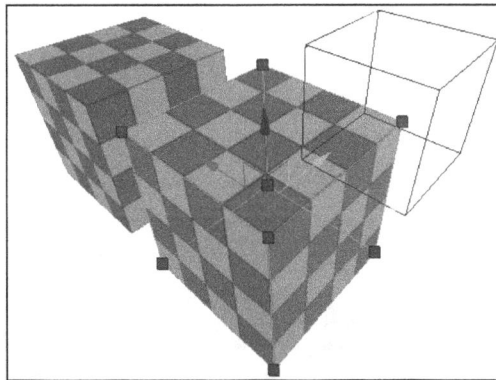

5. You may notice the **Builder Brush** is singular and is red. CSG **additive geometry** is blue. If you click on it in the orthographic viewports, it can be selected directly and moved around. If you click on it in the perspective viewport you will more likely select the surface under the cursor. To circumvent that, hold down *Ctrl + Shift* when clicking on BSP. When you move the BSP geometry however, unlike the brush, you just move its frame, and the surface itself remains behind. This is because any geometry edit needs a rebuild. As well as moving the BSP geometry, you can readily clone it by holding down *Alt* when moving it.

6. Suppose you want to cut a corner from a wall or dig a trap in the floor, based on an existing BSP geometry. This is fairly easy. First size the BSP brush to fit the area you want to remove, and then press **CSG Subtract** [🔳], which is next to **CSG Add**. You may also notice there's **CSG Intersect** and **CSG De-Intersect** too, which handle combining brushes, a lot like Boolean operations. The next image is an arbitrary example of a subtraction; notice subtractive geometry is orange:

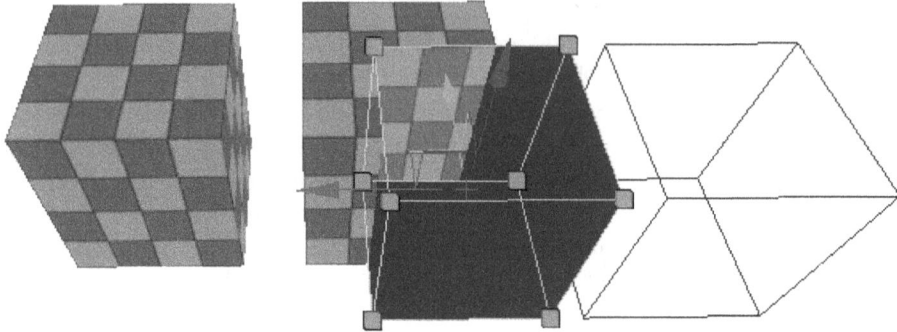

7. To control the subtraction you may consider using Scale to adjust the area of the BSP brush. It is usually better to move the edges or points of the brush in **Edit Geometry mode**, because then you can be sure the sides align to the grid. Scaling is faster though. You will get an idea of when it is okay to scale and when you'll need the precision that manual point control offers. If you only ever use the precise method, and follow the grid all the time, it will take you a long time to get things done.

8. With your large, flat additive BSP framed in the view, press *Shift + 2* and select and move corners of the Builder Brush so it sits within the floor space with a bit of space around it, then press **CSG Subtract**.

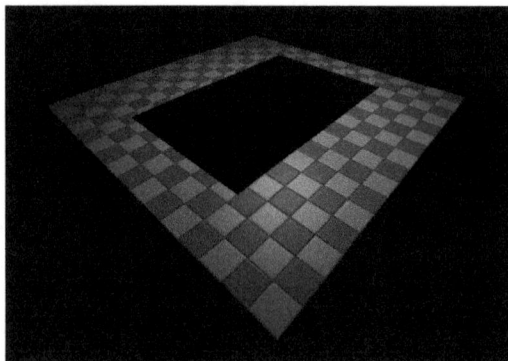

9. The order in which you make BSP geometry matters. If you build another additive mesh inside the hole created by the subtractive operation, then it will happily sit there. However, if you choose the subtractive BSP and right click and choose **Order | To First** or **Order | To Last** you can move its order upwards and downwards, reversing the overlap of each, or the build order. This is something to keep in mind at all times when using subtractive geometry. Always rebuild after sorting the BSP order. From now on, choose **Build All** so lights build too.

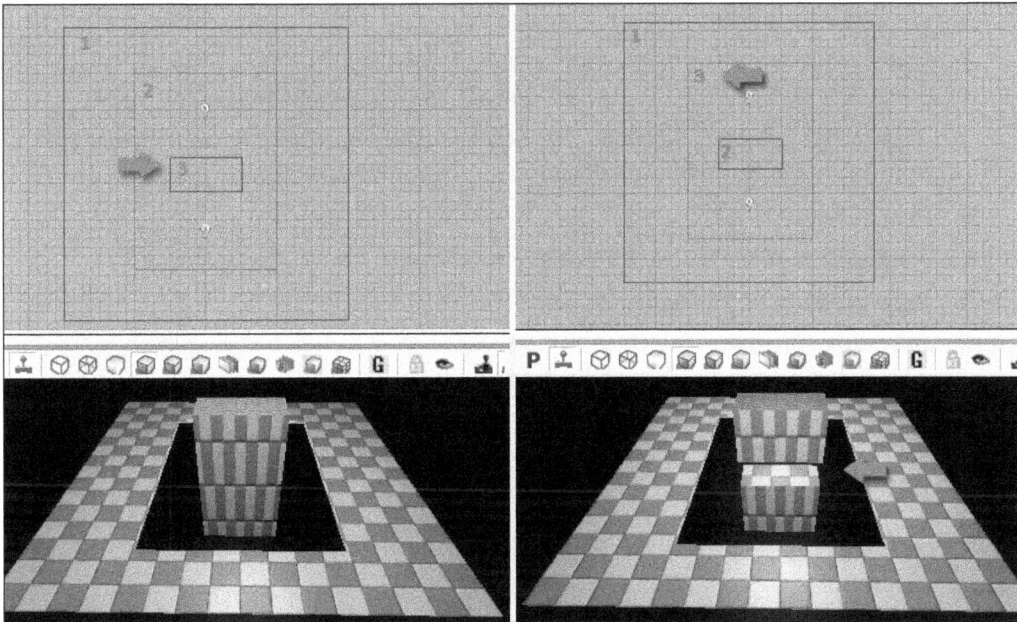

10. Subtracted geometry will have a yellow outline in the orthographic views. If you delete the subtractive mesh the hole will remain until you rebuild. Delete the subtractive BSP and choose **Build All** [🔍] to leave you with two boxes.

If you want to export BSP out of UDK as a mesh to use in another 3D editor, you can click on the BSP in the orthographic view then right-click and choose **Convert | Convert to Static Mesh**. This will create an asset you can store in a package. To export the asset, just right-click it in the Content Browser and choose **Export to File.** Once you alter the .OBJ in another software, remember to export the result back as .ASE or .FBX. This process is particularly useful if you want to match a model to specific BSP proportions in a scene.

Building a hollow room

You may have noticed there are more BSP brush creation options than we've discussed. A useful one is to create a hollow BSP with a preset thickness. This allows us to quickly create interiors.

How to do it...

1. Start a new scene and right click the BSP cube brush icon [●] and set it to something like `512 x 512 x 512` and set the **Wall Thickness** setting to 64.

2. Click on the tick box for **Hollow**. If for some reason you can't find your brush in the scene click the **Go To Builder Brush** icon on the left-hand side of the editor.

3. Press **CSG Add** [●] or *Ctrl + A*.

4. Turn on **Unlit mode** (so you can see inside the hollow box) by pressing *Alt + 3*.

5. Drive the camera inside the geometry.

6. Hold down *L* and click on a surface inside the box. Drag the resulting light up a bit, so it lights the scene well. Turn on **Lit mode** by pressing *Alt + 4*.

Placing imagery on BSP geometry

1. Let's assign a Material to the geometry. Select a surface of one of the wall surfaces visible in the perspective viewport and right click and choose **Select Surfaces | Adjacent Walls**.

2. Now go to the Content Browser (*Ctrl + Shift + F*) and filter **Materials**. Highlight one that would look nice for a wall and right-click in the perspective viewport and choose **Apply Material**. You will see the name of the Material in question there. When you choose this the geometry should acquire that Material.

3. For the as yet untextured geometry, right-click over it and choose **Select Surfaces | Matching Texture**. Highlight another Material in the Browser then right-click in the viewport and choose **Apply Material** as before. The next screenshot is an example of surface selection using a hollow cube.

4. Besides selecting matching textures, you can also select adjacent surfaces such as walls, floors, and ceilings. In particular, notice that at the bottom of the list is a **Memorize Set** command (*Shift + M*) and related recall and combining commands that allow custom surface control.

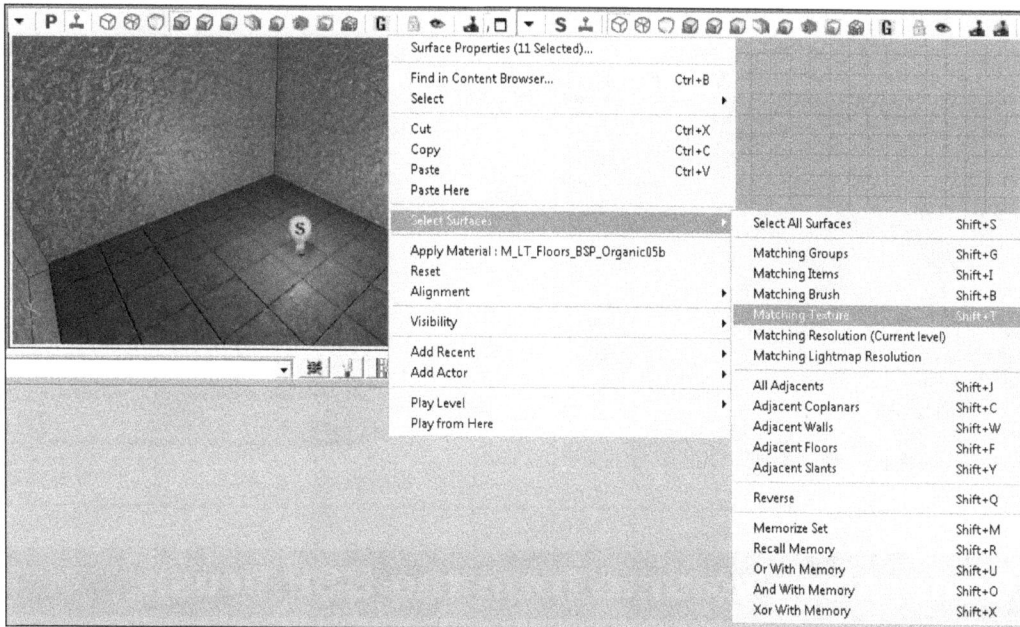

Adjusting surface properties of BSP

Once you have applied a Material to a BSP surface, you may want to resize or shift it on the selected surface. This can be done directly in **Texture Alignment Mode** (*Shift + F4*) which is slightly clumsy, or through the menu **View/Surface Properties** Editor (*F5*).

How to do it...

1. Create a **Hollow BSP** room, as in the last recipe, and assign a Material to the entire brush from the browser. Select the interior floor, which should tint purple. Give it a unique Material.

2. Press *F5* and notice the window which pops up. This includes **Pan UV**, **Rotation**, **Scaling**, and **UV Tiling** parameters, shown below. Try panning the texture 4 units horizontally (which is the U value) and 16 vertically (which is the V value). Use *Shift* when clicking **Pan UV** buttons to reverse the direction. You can also press **Custom** and enter a negative number to do this. Experiment with **Scaling** too. To scale in the Surface Properties Editor use the UV tiling **Options**. Note the requirement to press **Apply** to see the changes.

3. The **Flip U** and **Flip V** commands under **Rotation** can be used to mirror a texture on a surface, which is great when creating elements that face each other.

4. Close this window, then enter **Texture Alignment** mode [✲] (*Shift + 4*). Try using the Move tool to repeat the last panning action. For finer control hold *Ctrl* when moving or scaling the texture.

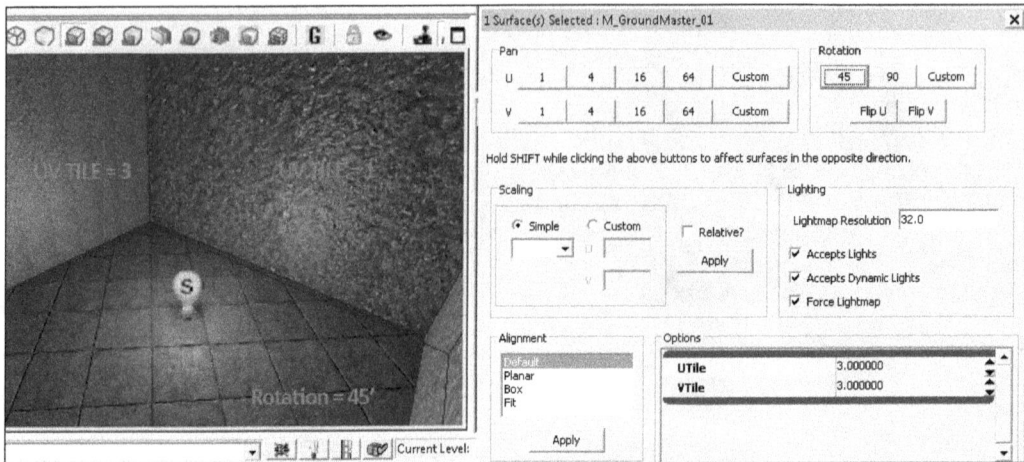

Generating volume from the BSP brush

The BSP brush can be used to generate volumes that cover functionality like defining a spatial zone for something to happen (or not happen) inside. In later chapters we'll be using all kinds of volumes. For now let's choose a simple one, a **PostProcess Volume**. This volume type effects the coloration and focus of the image seen by the camera. The use of a volume provides a boundary for the effect.

How to do it...

1. Create a new scene and create a hollow cube, as above, with a pointlight inside it (hold *L* and click on an interior surface). The repetitive start for the last few recipes will help you get faster at this common process.

2. Highlight and apply any likely wall Materials from the Content Browser using **Apply Material** as we did before. You can copy Materials from one surface to another using right-click and choosing **Copy** then **Paste**.

3. Duplicate this room alongside itself by selecting it in the Top viewport and then hold down *ALT* and move it until the outer walls of the rooms just touch. You can even copy over the PointLight at the same time.

4. Adjust one of the lights to red, and the other to blue, through its properties (*F4*). Place each in its own room which was created by the hollow cubes. Scale each PointLight so its decay area (the pale blue circle bounding the light) just covers the room it is inside, so we can see distinct colors bounded to each room.

5. Subtract a doorway by shaping a new, non-hollow BSP brush in the touching walls then pressing **CSG Subtract** [🔳].

6. Now reset the BSP cube and move it and shape it to fill the red room's space.

7. On the left-hand side of the editor, right-click on the **Volumes** icon [◉] (below the CSG icons) and choose **PostProcessVolume**. This adds a volume where the Builder Brush is. It may not be easy to see, because of the Builder Brush, but it will be selected after its creation. Press *F4* to see its properties.

8. Change the following in **Post Process Volume | Settings**: first tick on **Enable DOF** so we can blur the scene, then tick off **Max Near**, and then tick on **Min**. Set **Min** to 20, and set **Max** to 100. Above, set the **DOF_Falloff Exponent** to 16. These values blur the volume in a simple way. Don't worry for now about what all the available properties are for. That is discussed in *Chapter 8, Then There Was Light!* For now, we just want to see a noticeable difference to the normal focus.

9. Select the floor in the blue room and right click and choose **Add Actor | Player Start** here. Now you can build [🔦] and play this little scene (*F8*). The blue room should be in focus and the red room out of focus. At this stage, if you return to the blue room it will probably also be out of focus now. Once a PostProcessVolume is turned on, leaving the volume won't change the look of the scene back, unless you enter another volume.

10. To fix that, in the top viewport select the PostProcessVolume you made earlier, and move it while pressing *Alt* to create a copy of it. Place the copied volume over the blue room. Press *F4*, then set these properties for it: Tick on **Max Near** and ensure it is 0. Change **Max Far** to 16 and **DOF_Falloff Exponent** to 4. So we have now a 'no blur' volume to enter.

11. **Build All** [🗔] and press *F8*. You should observe how both rooms now toggle in and out of focus as you go back and forth. This scene is provided in the book's downloadable content: *Packt_01_Volumes_DEMO.UDK*.

See also

▸ For more on **PostProcess** features see *Chapter 8, Then There Was Light!*

▸ For more on **Materials**, see *Chapter 9, The Devil is in the Details!*

Handling StaticMesh actors in the scene

StaticMesh actors are the meshed geometry in the scene used by designers to represent fixed environment components. A large library of these comes with the content provided by **Epic Games** in UDK. In this recipe we'll look at ways to bring that content into the scene, shift it around and adjust it, and make sure that lining it up with other content is no problem. We'll also look at converting a StaticMesh for other uses. In the previous recipe we set up a small scene just using BSP elements. This time we'll only use meshes from the Browser.

How to do it...

1. Open the Content Browser (*Ctrl + Shift + F*). In the **Packages List**, make sure *UDKGame* is the selected folder. You can click on it to expand the sub-folders it contains.

2. Click on the **Object Type** filter for *Static Meshes* and, under **Tags**, click on *Building*.

3. Scroll down the assets (or type in the search field) to find *S_NEC_Roofs_SM_Tiled_Solid*.

4. Drag this into the perspective viewport. While it is selected, press *F4* and expand the properties section **Movement | Location**. Adjust the XYZ values to 0,0,0. This ensures the StaticMesh is situated at the world center or origin.

5. *Alt-drag* a copy of this up to about 300 in **Z** (you can fine-tune this, as before, in the **Movement | Location** section of the mesh's properties). This will be a ceiling. Having the floor at Z = 0 and the ceiling at Z = 300 will ensure the default character can easily walk in between.

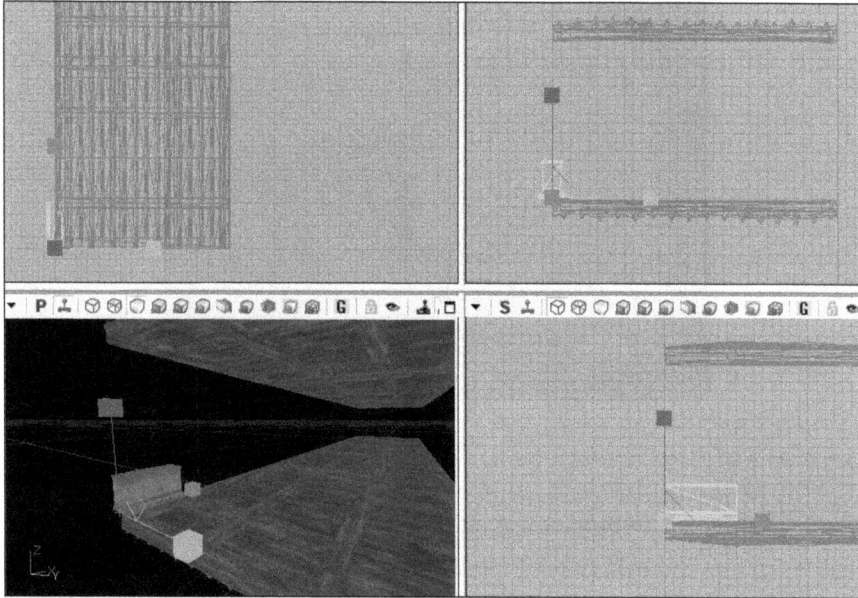

6. Select and rotate the lower mesh 180 degrees. We'll use it as a floor. Press *Space* to cycle the transform mode, and make sure the wood boards face up. In Move mode, *Alt-drag* both meshes sideways to create a string of them. Repeat this to form a passageway about five blocks deep, as in the previous screenshot.

7. Following the same image, where it is shown highlighted, drag into the view from the Browser the mesh called *S_NEC_Trims_SM_Plain_STRb*. Place it along the edge of the floor, and then **Non-uniform Scale** [ ] it to match the dimensions of the first floor piece, effectively creating a wall. This is shown in the next screenshot. It can help to set the **Scale Grid Snap** [ ] to 1% so it is easier to fit the two pieces to the same dimensions. The values I used for scaling were X=4, Y=1, Z=4.2 but yours may differ. The values can be set in the fields at the bottom of the screen.

8. Note that the scale along the X axis that I used was 4, an even number. Because the asset is modular, that is a safe amount to scale it up by and still have the ends touching without crossing into each other. It is okay to have meshes penetrate each other at an angle, but not at the same angle (co-planar) because then you'll see Z fighting (flickering) in the overlap. Also you want to avoid gaps.

9. When you are happy with the scaling, move copies along to match the entire floor, and reproduce this on the other side too using *Alt-drag* on the set again.

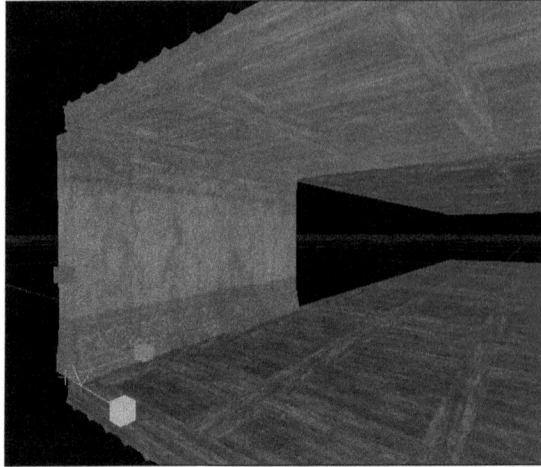

10. At either end of the passage we've made, add the StaticMesh called S_NEC_Walls_SM_Archwalls_01 and then fit a pillar called S_NEC_Walls_SM_CASup1 on either side, into the corners.

11. In the Content Browser, turn off the *Building* tag filter which was set before. Then search for *LAMP* to expose the asset *S_NEC_Lights_SM_TurkLamp01*. With the asset highlighted, select a right-hand side wall in the viewport, right-click, and choose **Add Static Mesh: S_NEC_Lights_SM_TurkLamp01**. Note that if you added the light based on the left-hand side wall, the object might be facing through the wall, so in that case choose **Rotate** and turn it 180 degrees to face the correct direction, into the passage.

12. Press *F4* with the light selected and expand the setting **Static Mesh Actor | Static Mesh Component | Lightmass | Lightmass Settings | Use Emissive For Static Lighting**. Turn this on. What this does, since the mesh has a Material with an active Emissive channel, is cast light into the scene based on its Material.

13. Distribute copies of this lamp at regular intervals. To select all the lamps, right-click one and choose **Select | Select all with matching Material**. Now right-click on this set and choose **Create Prefab**. This encapsulates all those assets into a single one for easier handling. When creating the **Prefab**, you'll have to name it. Set the **Package** to *YourPackage*, the **Group** to *Prefab,* and the **Name** to *TurkLamps*. You'll be asked if you want to replace the source meshes with an instance of the prefab, which you can, but you can't edit the lights' properties after having done so. A way around the problem of editing prefab constituent parts is to right-click on the prefab in the scene and choose **Convert Prefab to Normal Actors**. Then you can edit the component lamps' properties. Prefabs are discussed in greater detail in the first recipe of *Chapter 5, It Is Your Destiny!*

14. Right-click one of the lamps and **Select | Select all with matching Material**. Changing the **Emissive Light Falloff Exponent** to 1, the **Emissive Light Explicit Influence Radius** to 0, and the **Emissive Boost**, at 3 should illuminate the passage adequately. Those values accumulate together to control the brightness and range of the light cast by the lamp's texture. You can hold your mouse over each property to get a tool-tip explaining what it does. The effect of the emissive lighting from the lamps is shown in the next screenshot, where there is a yellow glow constrained around the walls around each lamp:

Moving on, let's delete the middle piece of the passage floor to create a hole. Place a point light in the scene and move it into this hole. Fill the black void by extending the walls down with a stone foundation made from *S_NEC_walls_SM_CAWall_STRc* and at the base of those, add the mesh *SM_GEN_Ruins_512Block04* and scale it so it fits two by two into the lowered floor space.

> Note that if you have an actor selected in the scene, you can press *Home* or the new **Go To Actor** icon [🔘] on the left-hand side of the editor, to jump all viewports to it. You can press *End* to align a mesh to the surface directly below it, though this works best if both surfaces are flat, and aligned. On a slope, it has limitations.

The intended result is shown in the next screenshot.

There's more...

Rigid Bodies in action!

1. Select *UDKGame* as the folder level in the **Packages List** in the Content Browser, then type *crate* into the search field. Highlight and fully load the mesh asset *S_LT_Mech_SM_Cratebox02a*.

2. At one end of the passage, right-click on the ground and choose **Add RigidBody: LT_Mech_SM_Cratebox02a**. A **RigidBody** is a mesh that is enabled for physics calculation, and consequently it will collide with objects in the scene when under a kinematic impulse such as a hit impact, a throw, or gravity. A **RigidBody** will be listed in the current level as a **KActor**.

3. You could also drag the asset from the browser into the scene as a StaticMesh and then right-click on it and choose **Convert | Convert StaticMeshActor to KActor**.

4. Be sure to also right-click on it and choose **Set Collision Type: Block All**. This prevents objects like the player or bullets from traveling through it.

5. If you have trouble placing the crate accurately on the ground, try raising it into the air and pressing the *End* key to drop it to the nearest surface.

6. Select the floor at the bottom of the hole, press *F4*, and take note of the **Movement | Location** value of **Z** for the floor mesh.

7. Go to the menu **View | World Properties**, and open up **ZoneInfo**. Set the **KillZ** value to the height you took note of, then adjust it so the value is a little higher. You'll see a red line in the orthographic view that indicates the **KillZ** height. The point of doing this is so if the player falls in the shaft they will die upon hitting that line. Otherwise, you'd have to build in some way to let them climb out.

8. Also in the **View | World Properties** menu, adjust the **Game Type For PIE** to *UTGame*. This ensures that when you play you'll have a preset body and gun. Formerly, *UTGame* was a default setting in UDK, but it has been deprecated for a setting that allows designers to more easily insert their own player controller.

9. Add a **PlayerStart** just by the RigidBody, then **Build All** [🔧] and **PIE** [▶].

10. Try to knock the RigidBody into the hole and use it as a bridge to get across. While playing, use the mouse scroll wheel to cycle guns until the PhysicsGun is showing. It has just a white X cross-hair, shown in the next screenshot. You can left-click with it to poke an object, and right-click drag to take hold of an object then right-click release to throw it. Note that the PhysicsGun will more easily knock rigid bodies than the impulse from the default LinkGun, and using the PhysicsGun with the right mouse button will let you hoist RigidBody actors into the air.

11. If you made your hole too deep, try raising the **KillZ** value accordingly. You may also need to adjust the the crate's **DrawScale3D** property so it enables you to bridge the hole. An example scene is included in the available content: *PACKT_01_StaticMesh_DEMO.UDK*.

Setting collision in the Static Mesh Editor

When you convert BSP to a StaticMesh, and when you import a new model from an external source, the mesh will have no collision calculated. UDK provides an easy way to automatically generate collision geometry for imported StaticMesh assets. Collision geometry can be calculated from the actual mesh, but that is seldom efficient. It is better to use a proxy mesh with far fewer polygons, encasing the visible model. Instead of bumping into the visible model while playing, you'd instead be bumping into the low res collision model linked to it. Without collision you'd run right through the model, though that may be desirable for some models, such as grass, flowers, the canopies of trees, and things that would otherwise be troublesome to snag against when moving.

How to do it...

1. For the base meshes that come with UDK, it isn't a good idea to try changing them. However, you can **Create a Copy** and edit that instead.

2. In a new scene, open the Content Browser, click **All Assets**, then filter **Static Meshes**. Type *Mesa* in the search field. This model is a rock without collision.

3. Right-click on the mesh and choose **Create a Copy**... to duplicate it into a package of your own.

4. Double-click on the resulting copy and the **Static Mesh Editor** will open.

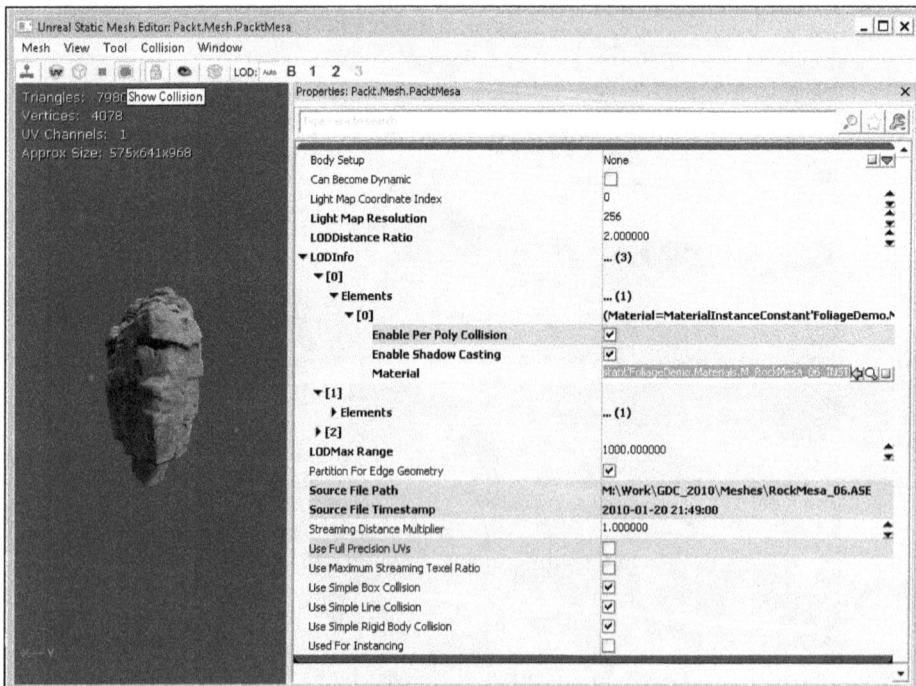

5. The fifth icon along [▣] toggles the collision preview. At present, there is no collision so toggling it won't make any difference yet.

6. Above, in the menu, under **Collision**, choose **6DOP simplified collision**. This will create a box collision only. It should show up as a wireframe around the object and you will see that there is a lot of negative space within the collision box.

7. In the same menu, try using **Auto Convex collision** using the settings shown in the next screenshot, which accumulate together to give a collision proxy, then hit **Apply**:

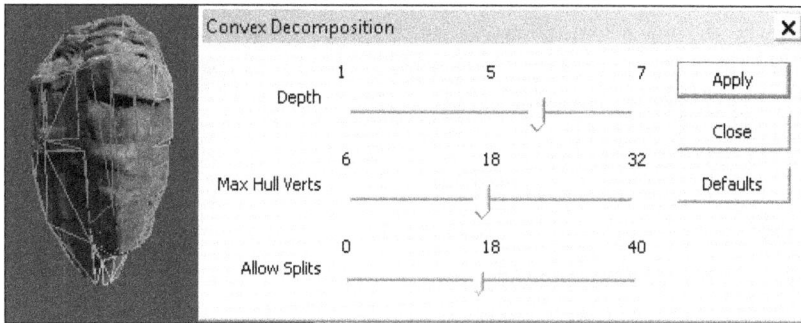

8. The convex collision sliders allow for splitting the collision component into chunks to better fit concave shapes. Splitting it up too much can cause a slow calculation. Take the time to experiment with values to get the optimal result.

9. Once you press **Close**, don't forget to save your asset.

10. Place the mesh in the scene and press *Alt + C* to view the collision in the scene.

There's more...

Changing the Material on a StaticMesh

Meshes that ship with UDK don't respond well to direct changes in the Static Mesh Editor. If you want though, you can place in the scene a mesh you've already copied to a new package, then highlight a new Material in the Content Browser, and right-click on the mesh in the scene and choose **Materials | Assign from Content Browser**. Changes in the scene like this aren't stored on the original asset, but on an instance saved with the map.

Visibility in the scene of StaticMesh actors

1. Select the *Mesa* StaticMesh actor and right-click in the viewport, then choose **Visibility | Hide Selected**.

2. To restore hidden objects, choose instead **Visibility | Show All**.

3. There are icons for these commands on the editor's side toolbar under **Select**.

Creating Terrain, Deco Layers, and Material Layers

This recipe covers the basics of adding a **Terrain** to your scene, and shows how StaticMesh actors can be distributed over its surface. We also look at brushes that can touch up the **HeightMap** to support meshes on the deco layer, and then improve the look of the terrain's surface by adding decals. We don't cover everything involved in terrain editing, since you can probably make your own inroads after doing this example. Also, the **Terrain** tool is somewhat overshadowed by the newer **Landscape** tool, and its accompanying addition **Foliage** which takes over the role of **Deco Layers**. Still, both tools are powerful. A terrain can even be converted into a landscape later on.

How to do it...

1. Create a new **Blank Map** and go to the main menu and choose **Tools | New Terrain**. Give it dimensions of 32 x 32.

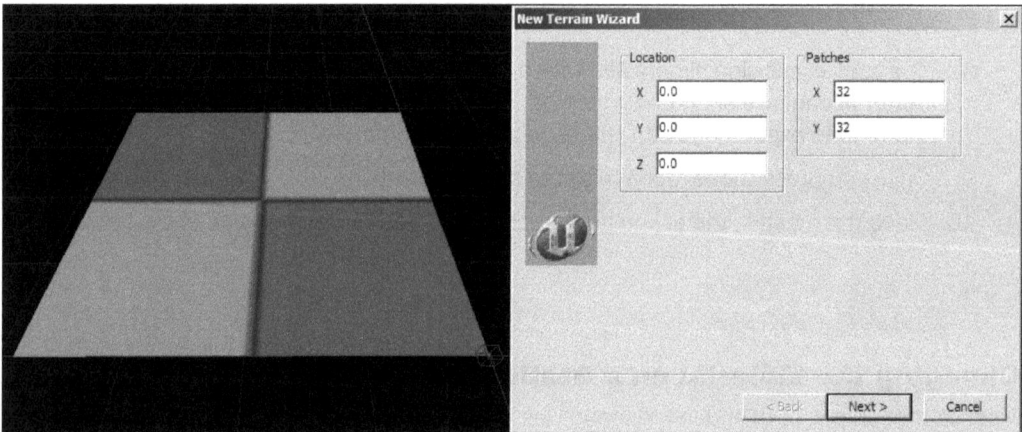

2. In the Content Browser, highlight the Material *M_ASC_Floor_BSP_Tile01*.
3. Enter **Terrain Editing Mode** (*Shift + 3*). Right-click in the space below the **HeightMap** layer then choose **New Terrain Setup Layer from Material (select package)**.

4. Assign the package to one of your own, and the **Group** to *TLM*.

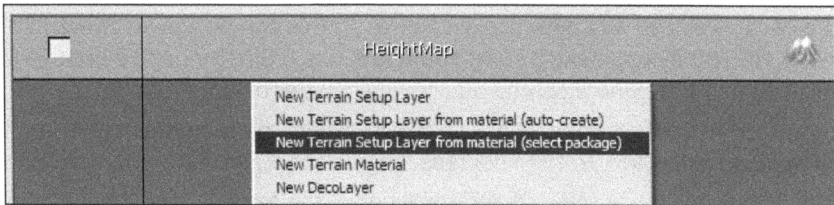

5. Assets will be created in the chosen package and group, as shown in the next screenshot. This differs from the approach of the Landscape tool, which is discussed in the next recipe.

6. Next highlight the Material in the Content Browser called *Packt.Material.M_Wet*. Create another terrain Material layer as before.

7. With the **Paint** brush, mask out the top Material (hold down *Ctrl + LMB* when brushing on the terrain). Also, don't forget to set strength and radius for the brush first. To invert the paint direction, hold *Ctrl + RMB* while brushing.

8. The brush settings for the Terrain Editor are distributed across the **Tool, Settings**, and **Brush** sections of the **Terrain Editor**. Since the **Paint** tool is highlighted by default, all that's required to get ready to paint is to adjust the brush **Strength** slider and also adjust the **Radius** and **Falloff** sliders. **Falloff** creates a decay from the brush radius outward. If you like, you can turn on symmetry for the brush using the **Mirror** option there too. Below the **Mirror** tool there are some brush shape presets that automatically set **Radius** and **Falloff** values. You can adjust **Falloff** by holding *Ctrl* and scrolling the mouse wheel. You can adjust **Radius** by holding *Alt* and scrolling the mouse wheel. The brushes in the tools set can be explored easily by holding the cursor over their icon and reading the tooltip.

9. You can only add so many Material layers to a terrain before it overloads. Instead, you can try using **decals** to add complexity. Set your Content Browser filter to include **Material Instance Constant** and search for *BloodSplatter*. Then right-click above the ground in the viewport and choose **Add Decal: CH_Gibs.Decals.BloodSplatter**.

10. You can scale up the decal by opening its properties (*F4*) and adjusting **Decal Actor Base | Decal | Decal | Width and Height**. Make it `2048 x 2048`.

11. The decal is placed off a gray circle icon [   ]. This can be scaled directly. In Move mode, *Alt + drag* it to make a copy, and rotate it to a different angle relative to the first, just to make a more spread out looking splatter on the ground.

12. Enter **Terrain Editing** mode again (*Shift + 3*). Select the HeightMap layer and use the **Paint** brush with *Ctrl + RMB* to depress the surface a little.

13. Enter wireframe mode (*Alt + 2*) and you'll notice the terrain doesn't have a lot of geometry detail. You can add more detail by editing the properties of the terrain (*F4*) and raising the **MIN** and **MAX Tessellation Level** to 16 and the **Editor Tessellation Level** to 16. The same result can be achieved in the **Terrain Editor** during **Terrain Editing** mode by clicking on the icons in the **Tessellation** section to **Increase** or **Decrease** the geometry detail.

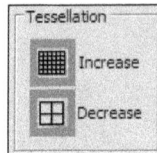

14. Create a light, raise it up in the space above the ground, and right-click on it and choose **Convert Light | Directional Lights | Dominant Directional Light**. This effectively adds a sun to the scene. Rotate this sun to an angle facing three quarters downward to the ground (it has a little blue directional arrow). If you want, tint it slightly yellow in its properties. Also, open its **Light | Light Component | Light Component | Shadow Filter Quality** and set this to **SFQ_High**.

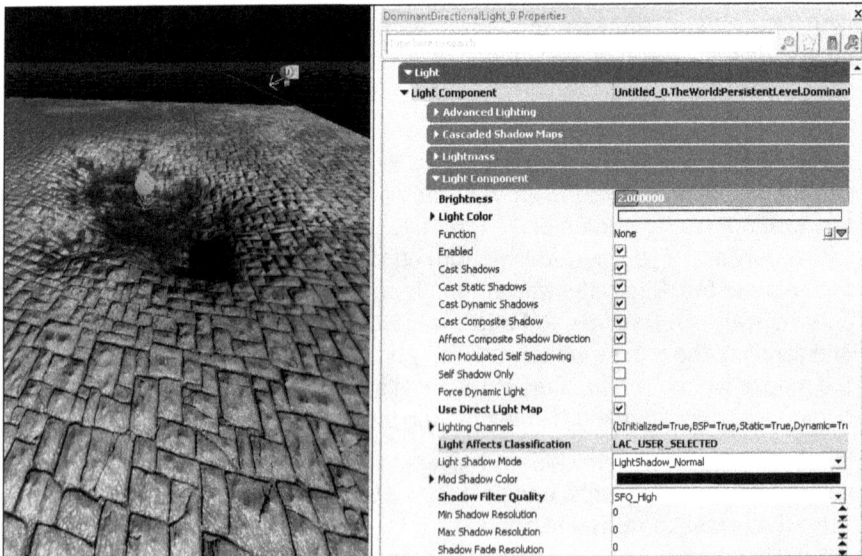

15. Now let's add a **Deco Layer** to sprinkle some plants on the terrain. For the depression in the ground, choose the StaticMesh in the Content Browser called *S_CloverPlant_01* and in the **Terrain Editor** right-click under the layers already added and choose **New Deco Layer**.

16. With the terrain object selected in the viewport, press *F4* and go to the **Terrain | Layers | Deco Layers** roll out. Expand it and click on the add entry icon [🖼] on the **Decorations** channel. This will add an empty factory, with two options. Use the blue downward triangle [🔽] to choose *StaticMeshComponentFactory*.

17. Expand the **Factory** settings to reveal the **Static Mesh** entry, and click on its assign icon [🖼]. This will add the mesh that was selected in the Content Browser.

18. Change the **Density** property (below the factory settings) to 1. Otherwise, the default value may be too low to actually see any meshes added on the terrain.

19. **Lock** this set of properties using the little padlock icon [🖼] at the top of the properties window. This keeps them present in the view no matter what other object you may choose. Ordinarily, changing from object to object updates the properties panel to show the current selection's properties.

20. Make sure the *Plant* Deco Layer is highlighted in the **Terrain Editor** and use the **Paint** brush (with *Ctrl held down* and a fairly large brush radius), to brush plants into the hole in the ground. When you paint , if you don't see plant meshes, increase the **Density** property until you do.

21. Set a **Slope Rotation Blend** of about 1 so plants on angled polygons will tilt instead of standing vertically, as shown in the following screenshot:

22. Notice the decals we applied to the terrain also effect the plants, which are StaticMesh actors. This looks strange, so select the decals, press *F4*, then turn off their property: **Decal Actor Base | Decal | Decal | Project on Static Meshes**. Individual actors also have a property **Static Mesh Actor | Static Mesh Component | Rendering | Accepts Static Decals**, which you can turn off if you don't want them to receive a decal.

23. You can continue adding Deco Layer entries to add pebbles, trees, grass, or other repeatable objects. You can see in the next screenshot that the properties for the plants spread across the ground are supplied by Deco Layer [0] | Decorations | [0] | Factory, which is expanded out to show the StaticMesh asset used, the **Density** value of 100, the **Min Scale** and **Max Scale** factor, and the **Slope** value which helps the plants orient on the surface of the terrain. **Build All** to see the lit result.

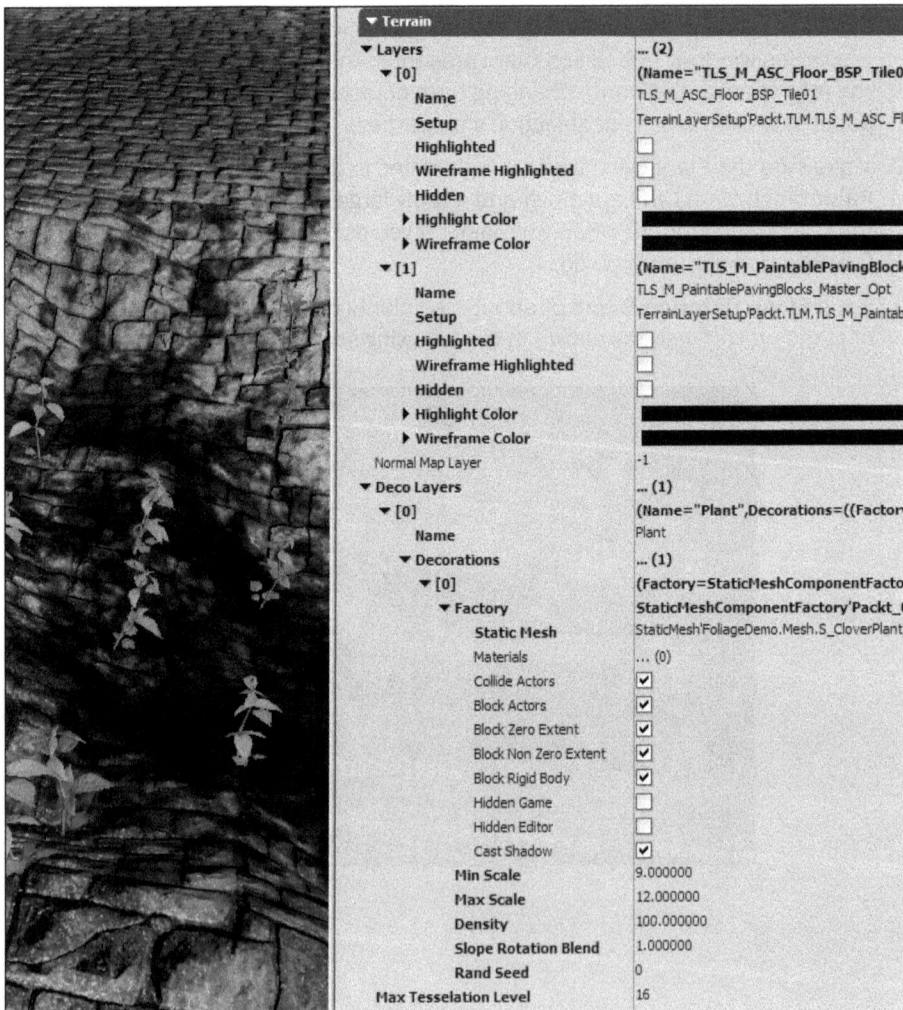

There's more...

Can I export a Terrain Heightmap to use in a Landscape?

A **Heightmap** is a texture that uses variance in black and white tones to depict altitude, where white is more and black is less.

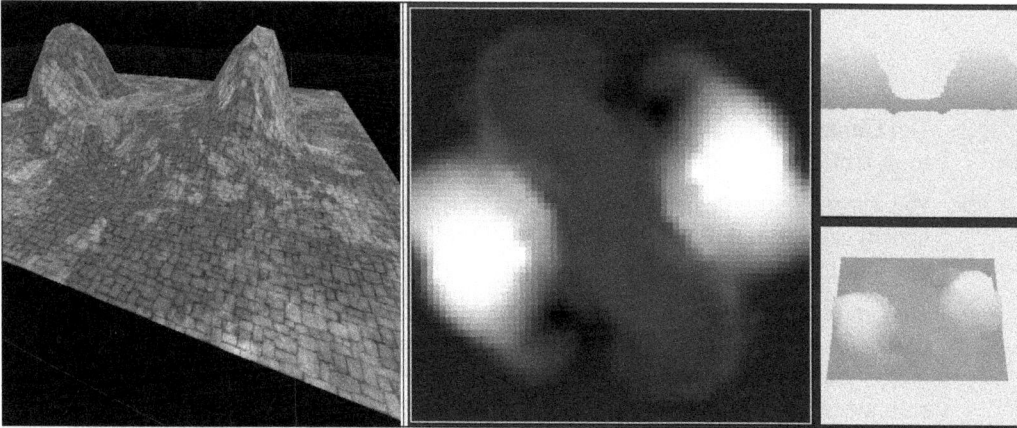

The newer **Landscape** tool covered in the next recipe can handle `.raw` and `.r16` heightmaps. The **Terrain Editing Mode** dialog includes an **Export Heightmap** section, shown below, which sends out a `G16MPT3D` file, a .BMP essentially, which you can open and convert using an external utility like **HMCS (Heightmap Conversion Software)**; this is discussed in the next recipe too. In this utility you can resample the size of the image and also adjust the altitude value for the black and white intensity.

Creating a Landscape

This recipe covers the basics of making a Landscape, which is a newer alternative to using the Terrain tool. It features a more painterly tool set, and can also import Heightmaps from software such as Vue or Terragen. Heightmaps are black and white textures where light tones influence a surface to push it upwards, and darker tones effect it less. Our goals will be to model a simple Landscape asset, and paint texture layers on it. Afterward, we'll scatter trees and rocks across it using the **Foliage** tool (which isn't limited to foliage).

Getting ready

Open UDK fresh, and from the **File | New** menu load the map template *Midday Lighting*. You may want to read about the technological basis for the Landscape tool at
`http://udn.epicgames.com/Three/Landscape.html`.

How to do it...

Generating a Landscape asset:

1. To open **Landscape Mode**, click the icon which resembles a mountain with an **L** on it, shown here. Above it, the other icon with a mountain is for Terrain.

2. The **Landscape Edit** dialog will display. Drag its top or bottom to show the range of tools it offers. Click the icon [▲] next to **Editing** to hide that section.

3. You will see in the **Create New** section a **Heightmap Import** field in which you can specify an external .RAW or .R16 file of the type generated in **Vue** for instance. That's one way to get started, based on existing topological data.

4. The other way is to start from scratch. Adjust the **Heightmap Size | Size (vertices) 0x0** field to 255 x 255. Underneath, set the **Component Size** to 257. You will notice the **Create Landscape** button below become available. Click that, and your settings will be transferred onto a new actor in the scene, situated at 0,0,0 in the world. You can read about valid heightmap sizes (and other creation notes) at `http://udn.epicgames.com/Three/LandscapeCreating.html`. They even provide a **Recommended Landscape Sizes** table.

5. Press *Shift + 1* then select the actor *Landscape_0*, and move it down a little in the side view to avoid running through the default box geometry in the scene, as in the next screenshot. Notice the orthographic wireframe reveals the density of the Landscape. Compared to the Terrain tool, it can retain a lot more detail and still function well. The values we've entered have also yielded a fairly large surface.

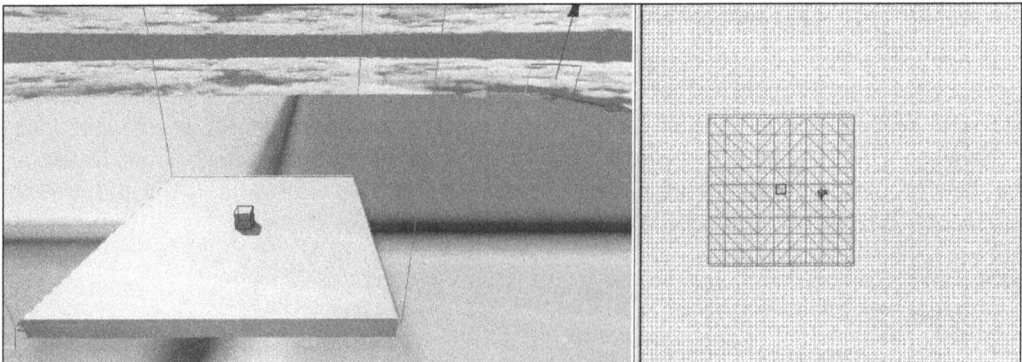

6. Activate **Landscape Mode** again, to restore the **Landscape Edit** dialog. The **Editing** section will now be exposed again, and now it will show the asset name. Under this notice the active **Paint Tools** tool is **Paint**. Further down you'll see a **Tool Strength** slider, which effects intensity of strokes applied to the surface. Below that there is a **Brushes** section, which includes a highlighted **Falloff** type that is set to **Smooth**. Below that, there are sliders for **Brush Size** (which is the radius of the brush cursor), and **Brush Falloff**, which provides a control for softness/hardness for the stamp. For the most part these tools are similar to the Terrain editing tools.

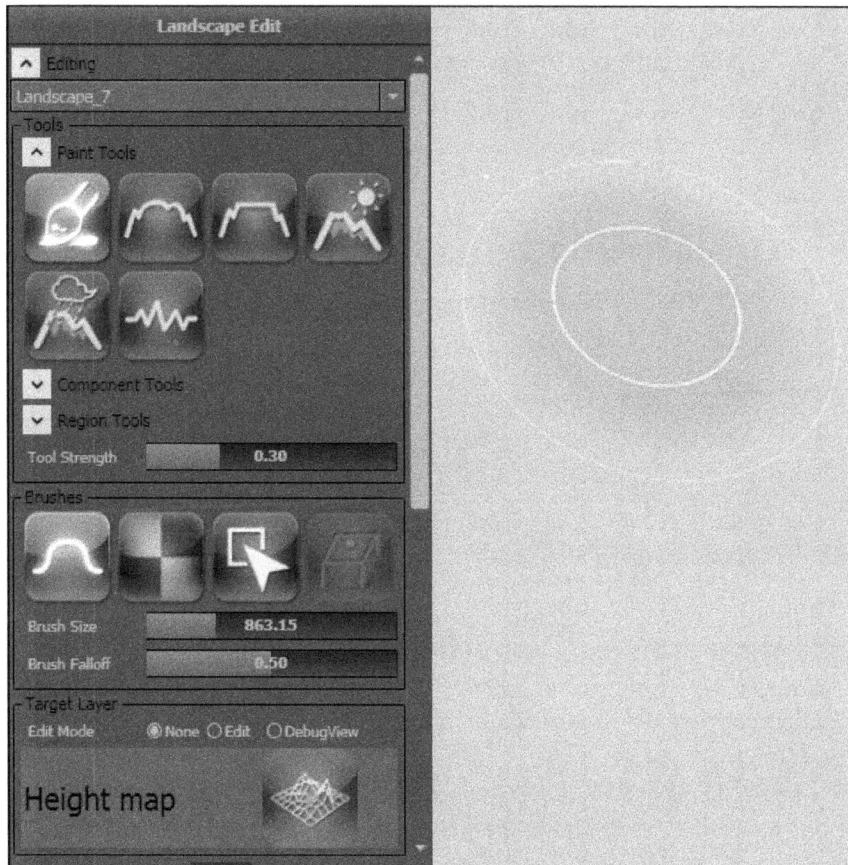

7. As you adjust the **Brush Size** you will notice in the view there is a radius/falloff circle which pulses and will interactively scale.

8. Stroke on the surface and you'll notice nothing much happens. This is because the brush will only work with *Ctrl* held down. Hold *Ctrl* and brush around the base of the default block in the scene. Don't worry if it isn't very elegant.

9. The default brush raises the landscape by 0.3. Raise this if it helps you get the height you want quicker. Or you can increment your strokes to let it build up.

10. To paint downwards, or to depress the surface, hold *Ctrl + Shift* while making a brush stroke. Again, work around the boundary you just built up, as below. After this, in terms of where to brush, it becomes an artistic endeavor, and it would be a good idea to play a bit before continuing. Pay particular attention to the horizon of the scene, or the straight edge of the Landscape component, to hide the flat edge from players. The next example can be found in *Packt_01_LandscapeBasics_DEMO.UDK*.

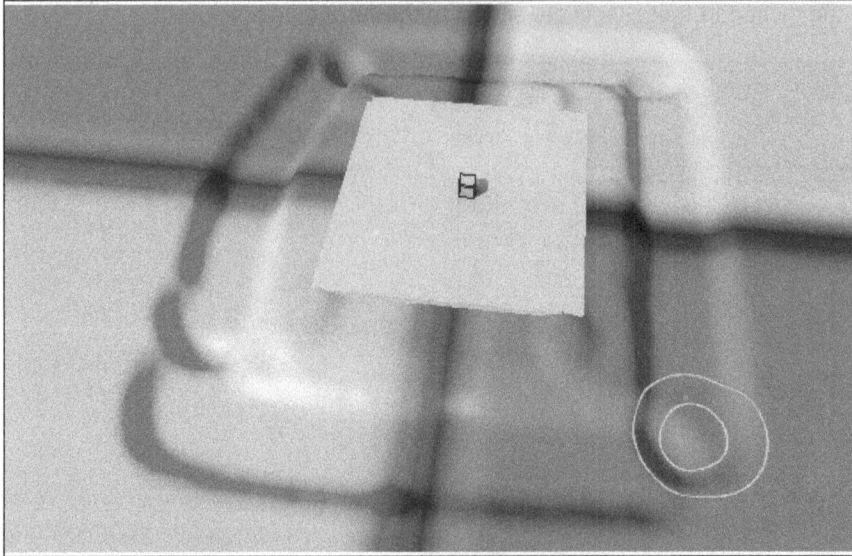

There's more...

What about creating and importing heightmaps?

1. The measures to generate a valid heightmap will vary depending on where you get your source data. To keep things simple, I am going to just use Photoshop for this example. On www.udk.com/forums you will find some information on heightmap generation in software such as Vue, Terragen, and so on.

2. Open Photoshop, and choose **File | New document**. Set it at 509 x 509 (this is one of the recommended landscape sizes). **Fill** it with black.

3. Apply the **Filter | Difference Clouds**. This generates a noisy base. Then select the **Burn** tool, size it quite big, and darken around the picture edges. This will mean the edge of the terrain is a bit lower than the center in the final output, which is good for dealing with the eventual visible horizon. You can **Dodge** white or **Burn** black features as you wish everywhere else.

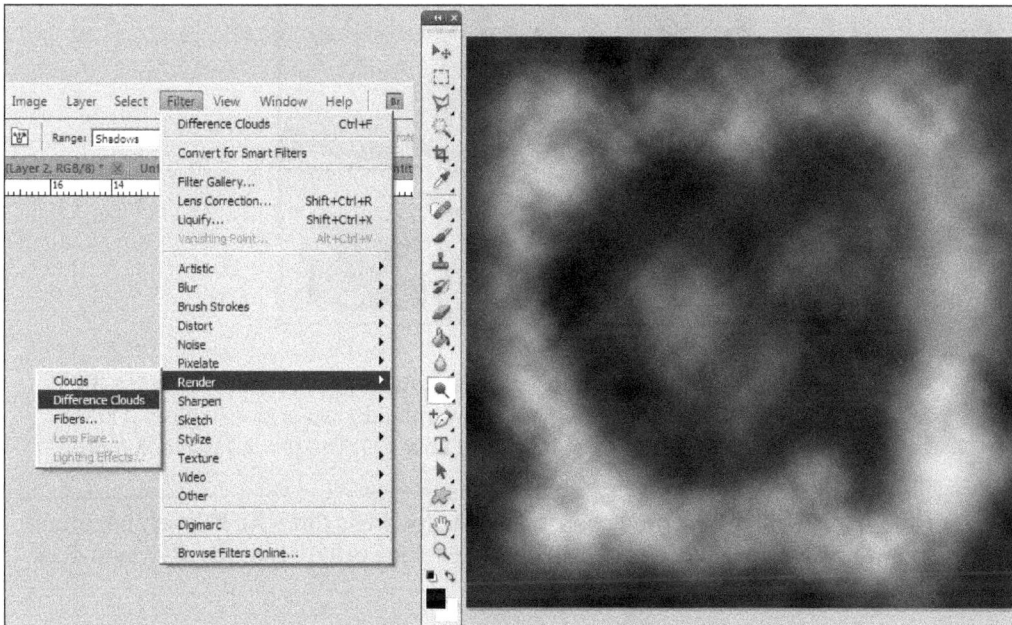

4. This next part is the most important step for getting a valid heightmap. Go to **Image | Mode** and set it to **Greyscale** and 8 bit. Save the image in .BMP format as *HeightmapTest.BMP* to your desktop.

   Why that step matters is because the UDN documentation says to save out a grayscale .RAW file in 16 bit mode. You can try it, but it may not work, and if it does you may get extreme results for the landscape altitude.

5. Instead, saving a .BMP allows us to use a handy free tool **HMCS (Height Map Conversion Software)** from `http://www.lilchips.com/hmcs2.asp`. Download and install this, open it, and choose **File | Open** and grab *HeightmapTest.BMP* from your desktop. You should get immediate feedback in the viewer as to the altitude interpolation of your image, which looks rather steep.

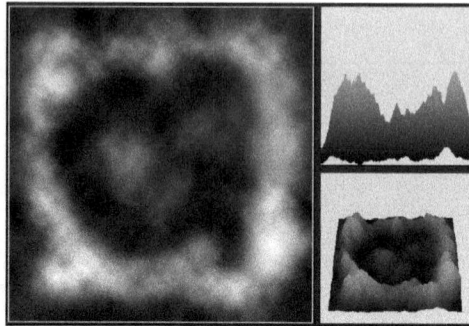

6. At the top of the **HMCS** menu, choose **Adjust | Altitude**. You can also press the icon [🖼] or press *Ctrl + L*. A dialog will show that lets you specify high and low settings for altitude. Enter **High** = 4096 and **Low** = 0. The results will look more modest in HMCS, but look nicer in UDK.

7. Now go to the **File** menu and choose **Save As** (or press *Ctrl + A*). It is very important in **Save as type** to choose not .BMP but .R16 (since UDK only reads .RAW and .R16 files for heightmaps). An example is shown:

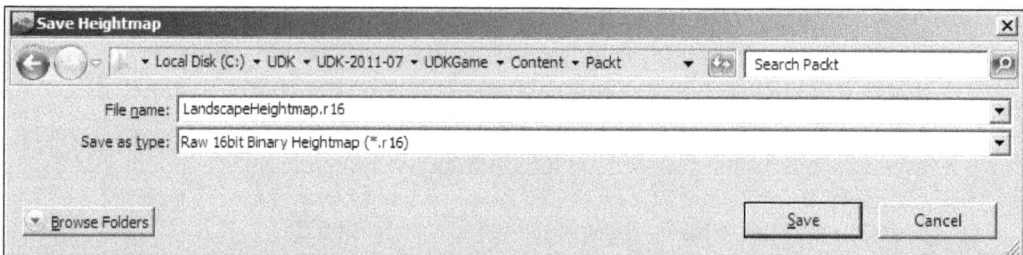

8. Now in UDK, delete any Landscape you may have already, and click on **Landscape Mode** [🏔]. By the **Heightmap Import | Heightmap** field, click the browse icon [⬛] and choose your saved .R16 file. It will show up there and auto-assign **Heightmap Size | Size (vertices)** and **Component Size** settings.

9. Click on the **Format | Unsigned** and **Format | PC** radio buttons, then click the **Create Landscape** icon below, which should now be available. If you cannot see a landscape suddenly jump into view don't be scared. The pivot will be at Z=0 but the geometry may import much lower in the scene, well below Z=0. Switch to **Wireframe** view (*Alt + 1*) to find the actor. Press *Shift + 1* to enter **Camera Mode** and move the landscape up to a position where it lines up with the map template's central block. Watch out for the red **KillZ** line in the side view, as shown next. The terrain should be completely above that if you intend the player to walk on it, and you should place the **PlayerStart** above the land too.

Applying Materials to your Landscape

1. The Terrain tool applies several Materials to a Terrain patch using layers driven by unique assets, shown here, that are generated through the **Terrain Editing Mode** dialog:

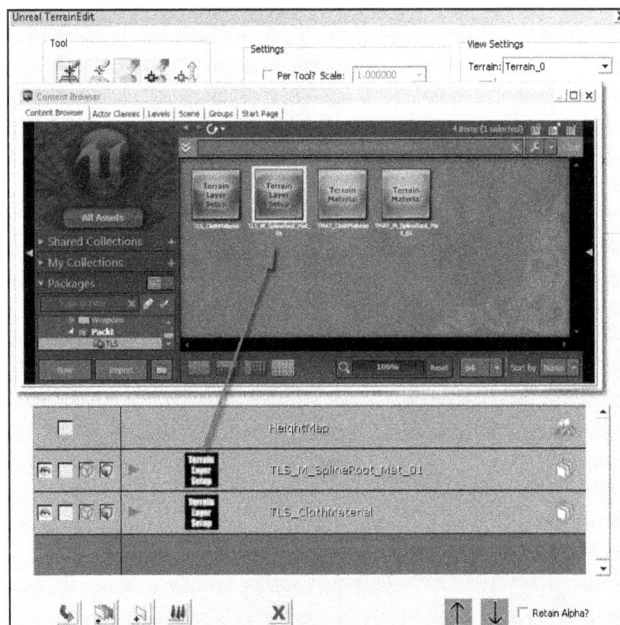

2. Landscape takes a different approach, using just one Material, which has its layers of textures built up in the Material Editor. The content of the layers is set there and given **Parameter Names**. These are matched with named **Layers** added in the **Landscape Editor**. The designer then uses the **Paint** tool to brush on masks for each layer. The layers don't require any additional asset to be saved out. The same layers that hold the Material mask can be locally sculpted too. The contribution of each layer can be set through a **Blend** value.

3. Load the file *Packt_01_LandscapePaint_Start.UDK*. You'll see an untextured landscape waiting for a Material to be assigned to it.

4. Select the Landscape actor and press *F4*. Its properties will appear. The first section, **Landscape**, contains a **Landscape Material** field. This is where you'll assign a Material from the Content Browser. You can at a pinch choose a regular Material, but it will simply cover the entire surface and won't be editable.

5. To allow layer painting, create a new Material in the Content Browser called *YourPackage.Material.Landscape_LayersTest_mat*. Double-click the Material.

6. Set up the nodes as shown in the next screenshot. To load a texture, highlight the desired texture in the browser then in the Material Editor *hold T and click* in the canvas area. If you haven't chosen a texture, the keyboard shortcut will work, but give you an empty **Texture Sample**, and you can fill it in the node's properties using the **Use selected object in Content Browser** icon [◙]. The nodes have had unused inputs and outputs hidden using the icon [▓].

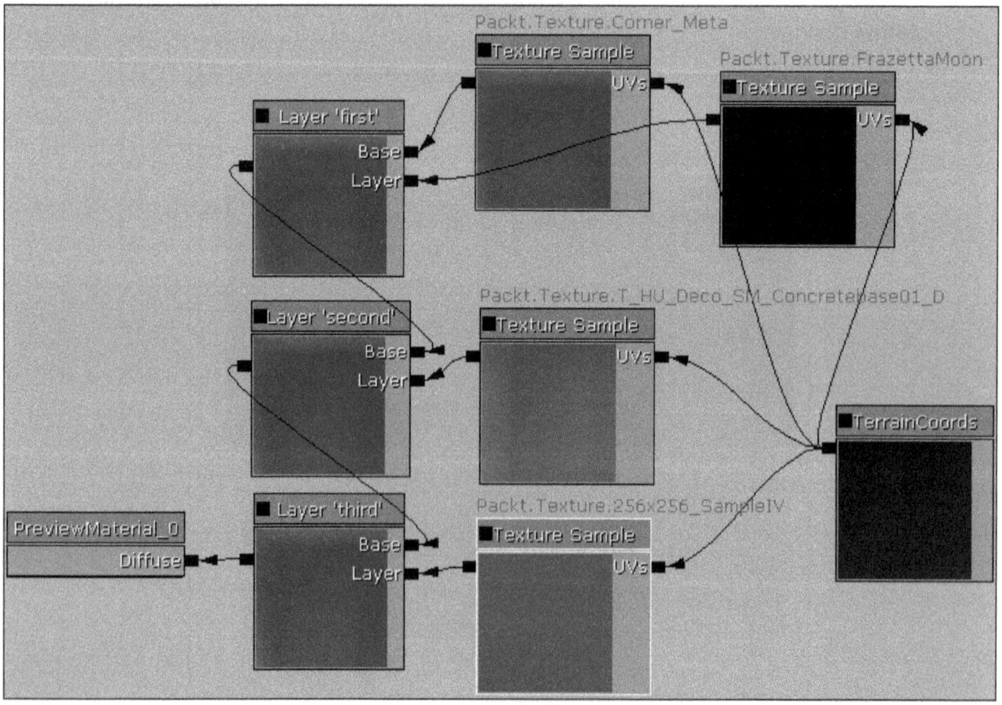

7. To add the node ***TerrainCoords***, which tells the texture how to distribute on the Landscape surface, right-click in the canvas, and choose **Terrain | New Terrain Layer Coords**. In its properties set the **Mapping Scale** to 256 which matches the landscape component size. If you have good tiling textures to source, then this value can be smaller and you'll get nicer texture resolution.

8. To add the node ***Layer***, right-click and choose **Terrain | New Terrain Layer Weight**. What this does is set which texture will appear on which layer of the Landscape. In its properties, give each ***Layer*** node a **Parameter Name**. It is normal to name the layers after the texture they represent such as grass, snow, dirt, and so on. In this case, enter *first* and *second* and *third*. Then compile the Material by pressing [▓].

9. In the scene, select the Landscape actor and press *F4*. In its **Landscape | Landscape Material** and assign your **Material** from the Content Browser: *YourPackage.Material.Landscape_LayersTest_mat*. On the object only one layer of the Material will be apparent.

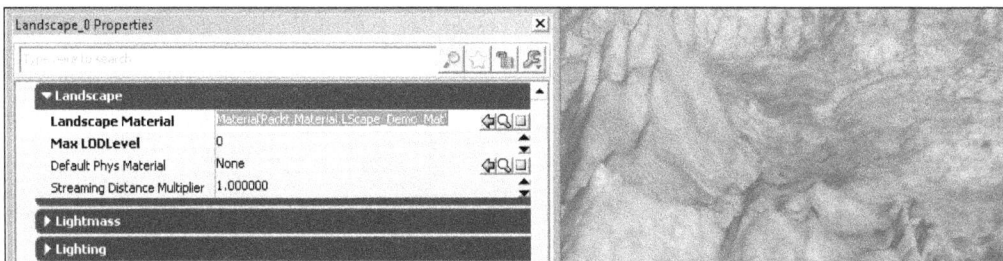

10. Click on **Landscape Mode** and go to the editor section, under **Target Layer | Edit Mode** click the **Edit** radio button, as show below. This allows you to add a new layer. In the **Add Layer Name** field type *first*, then click the icon next to it [▓].

11. Again, in the **Add Layer Name** field type *second*, then click the [▓] icon again. Add another called *third* to complete matching the layers against the textures.

12. Now with either of these layers highlighted you can hold *Ctrl* and brush with the **Paint** tool to apply a hand-drawn weight mask for the texture. Hold *Ctrl + Alt* to decrease the weight mask (although actually what this does is increase the weight of all the other layers as they combine to a value of 1.0). For this reason it seems best to have more than two layers contributing.

13. This covers the basics of getting up and running with the Landscape creation and Material tools. There is a lot more about improving the land forms using Normal maps and the **Landscape Gizmo** in the UDN documentation, in particular: http://udn.epicgames.com/Three/LandscapeEditing.html.

14. A simple example of the Landscape layering process using a Material set up with a ***Terrain Layer Weight*** network, shown below, can be found in the provided content *Packt_01_LandscapePaint_DEMO.UDK*.

A **Landscape Gizmo** is a tool similar to a volume which is used to copy and paste, and export, selections of the Landscape through a heightmap for duplication purposes, modularization, and external refinement. They can be automatically fitted to a region selection and their properties allow the height value of data contained in the gizmo to be relatively scaled. Gizmos are created as a function of the **Region Tools | Region Selection** tool in the **Editing** brushes of the **Landscape Editor**.

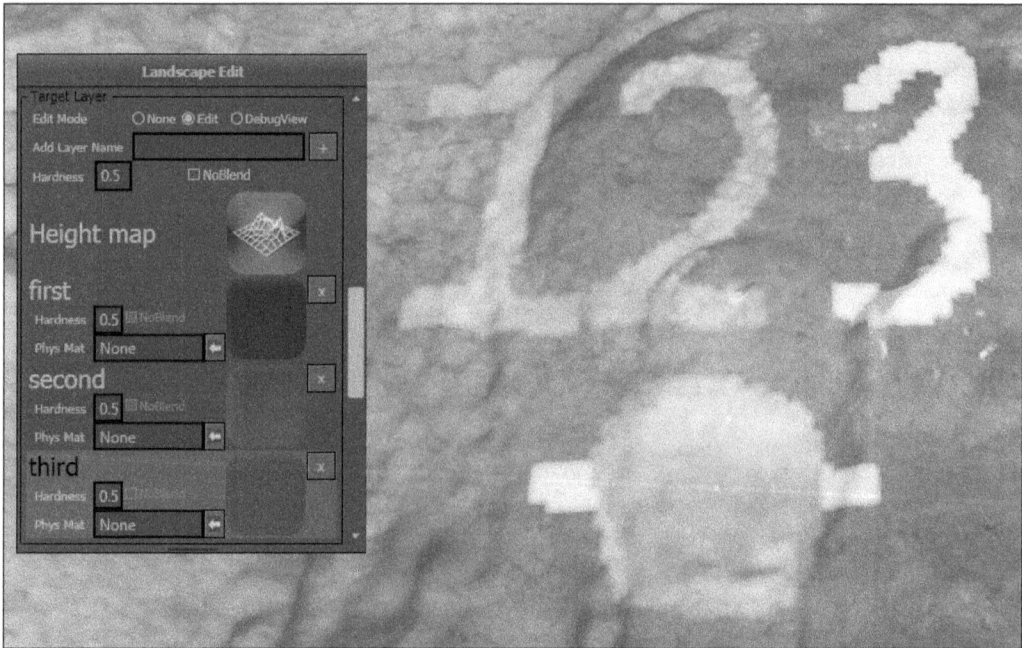

Scattering meshes on a Landscape using the Foliage tool

Foliage Mode extends the **Landscape** tools, and sits alongside **Landscape Mode** in the editor. In this recipe we'll scatter rock meshes on a Landscape surface, since the **Foliage** tool, while great for making forests and grass, is not limited to just that.

Getting ready

Open the file *Packt_01_Foliage_Start.UDK*. This extends from the previous example.

How to do it...

1. Press **Foliage Mode**, shown on the right-hand side in the previous image. Then press *Ctrl + Shift + F* and in the Browser search for *rock* to expose StaticMesh assets of that type (although you can use whatever meshes you like).

2. In the **Foliage** dialog there is an area, **Meshes**, to drop assets to be used. You can drag in several.

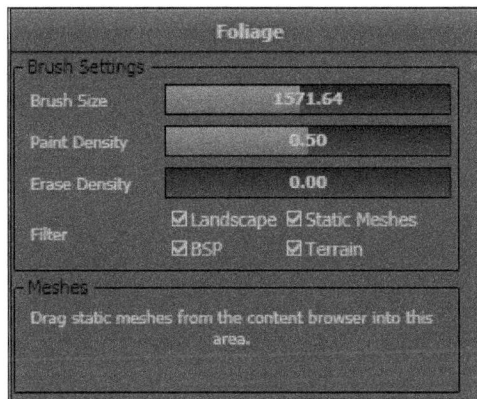

3. The meshes will appear there and each will have parameters for setting scale, count, and angle when brushed. They can also be assigned to separate layers in the Landscape using existing **Parameter Names** (such as *first*, *second*, *third*).

4. There are three icons that allow you to control the StaticMesh assets used. The first icon is **Hide Details** [🔲], which deselects and effectively disables the mesh from being brushed to the Landscape. The next screenshot shows one of the layers grayed out. The second icon is **Show Paint Settings** [🖊], which exposes values for controlling scale and density. Highlight an available mesh and set a **Scale Min** value of 1 and a **Max** value of 5 (though a good value depends on the actual size of the mesh used). The third icon is **Show Settings for Placed Instances** [ℹ️], which returns info for the meshes where they are used, such as the total count in the scene.

5. To paint, at the top of the Foliage Editor, you can adjust a slider for **Brush Size** and **Paint Density**, which you should see update in the scene as a pulsing white circle cursor. Then in the view, move the cursor over the Landscape, hold *Ctrl*, and click or stroke.

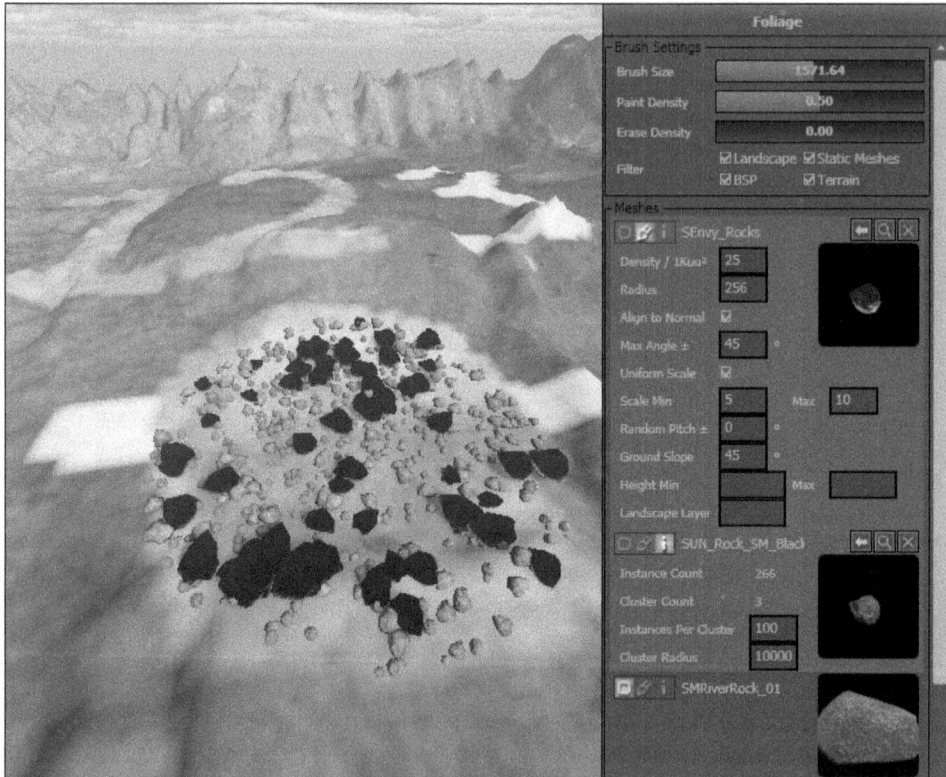

6. The last thing to point out is that you can remove meshes from the list using the icon [✕] and you can swap out meshes from the browser using the assign icon for the Foliage Editor [⬅], and locate the current mesh in the browser using the magnifying glass [🔍].

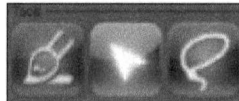

In versions from September 2011, two new tools shown here (individual instance selection and paint selection) have been added to the foliage edit mode. Selected instances can be moved, rotated, and scaled with the widget, and also snapped to the floor, deleted, and cloned with *Alt-drag*.

Creating a steamy plume in Cascade

The goal of this chapter has been to overview a broad spectrum of the UDK content generation tools, so now we jump to a new area, particle effects. In the first chapter we created an asset which was an empty particle system, aiming to show how its package would be created and saved, but having left it at that it would be good to flesh it out. So we'll look a little deeper into Cascade and create a steamy plume which can be applied in a scene as a set dressing. This recipe is a quick guide to the essentials. We will deal with advanced Cascade challenges in *Chapter 7, Hi, I'm Eye Candy!*

How to do it...

1. Create a **Blank Map** and, in the Content Browser, select your package folder. If you haven't created one, just click on **New Packages**. You'll be prompted for a package save location later. Right-click in the assets panel and choose **New Particle System**. Make the **Group** name of the Particle System *Cascade* and the asset name *SmokePlume*. The **Unreal Cascade Editor** will open after the asset is created. Later, when you need to re-open Cascade, just double-click on the asset.

2. The Cascade Editor has three windows (**Preview**, where we see what's happening, **Properties**, for defining the look and behavior of the particles, and **Curve Editor**, for adjusting animated values). The main part of the editor is a set of emitters and their modules. This section defaults to one emitter, which should be currently playing. Commands to adjust modules are accessed by right-clicking.

3. In the **Preview** window, hold the *RMB* and drag to zoom in and frame the playing particles. If you wish to stop them playing you can either toggle **Real Time** [🔦] or press the **Pause** button in the **Play/Pause** icon pair [▶❙❙]. Notice they use a default Material designed to be memory light and provide a clear illustration of the individual particles. Let's change this to something more smoky. In the Content Browser, search for a Material called *M_EFX_Smokeball* and highlight it. Now go to the list of operators currently active in **Particle Emitter**. Choose **Required** and look in its properties (at the bottom of the Cascade Editor) for **Emitter | Material**. Click the assign icon [◁] to assign the Material that's highlighted in the Content Browser.

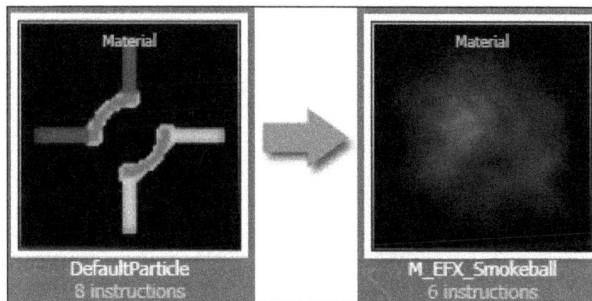

[
For navigation, Cascade's preview panel works a lot like any preview panel in UDK, where *LMB+drag* orbits in Z around the object, *RMB+drag* up and down zooms in and out. *MMB+drag* pans. *LMB+RMB+drag* orbits in Y around the object. There is also an axis free orbit mode, accessed by clicking on the icon [🔍].
]

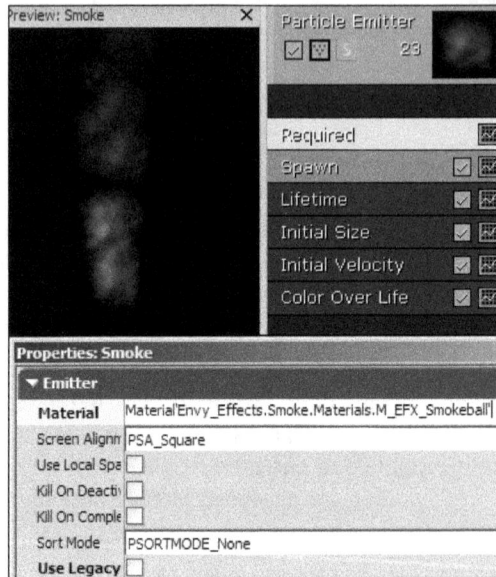

4. The Material we're using is slightly regular as it plumes up. Change this by finding it in the Content Browser (use the magnifying glass in the Material channel [🔍] or just search by name for *M_EFX_Smokeball*. Right-click on the asset and **Create a Copy** to your own package. Now double-click the displayed asset to open the **Material Editor**.

5. We're going to make the texture rotate and include a link into the **Distortion** channel too, so whatever is behind the smoke in the scene will ripple a little. To create the rotation, type *Rotator* in the **Material Expressions** search field on the right at the top. Drag a ***Rotator*** operator from the list to the canvas and hook up its output to the texture sample UV's input. When you have an expression (or node) selected, its properties are exposed in the **Properties** window. For the ***Rotator***, in its properties set the rotation **Speed** to 0.4 and in its **Desc** field type **Positive** (just to recall its purpose). Create a copy of the ***Rotator*** and set its **Speed** to -0.4 and name its **Desc** *Negative*. Now reorganize the nodes so that they're arranged like what you see in the next screenshot. Click-and-drag to pan the canvas. *Ctrl-drag* on a node to move it. *Ctrl+Alt+drag* around some nodes to select several. Press *Alt* over a wire's **In** or **Out** connector (or nub) to break a connection. Reducing the nodes used where possible gives the asset fewer instructions, making it process faster. Check the little square in the corner of the ***Multiply*** node to preview the resulting rotation effect.

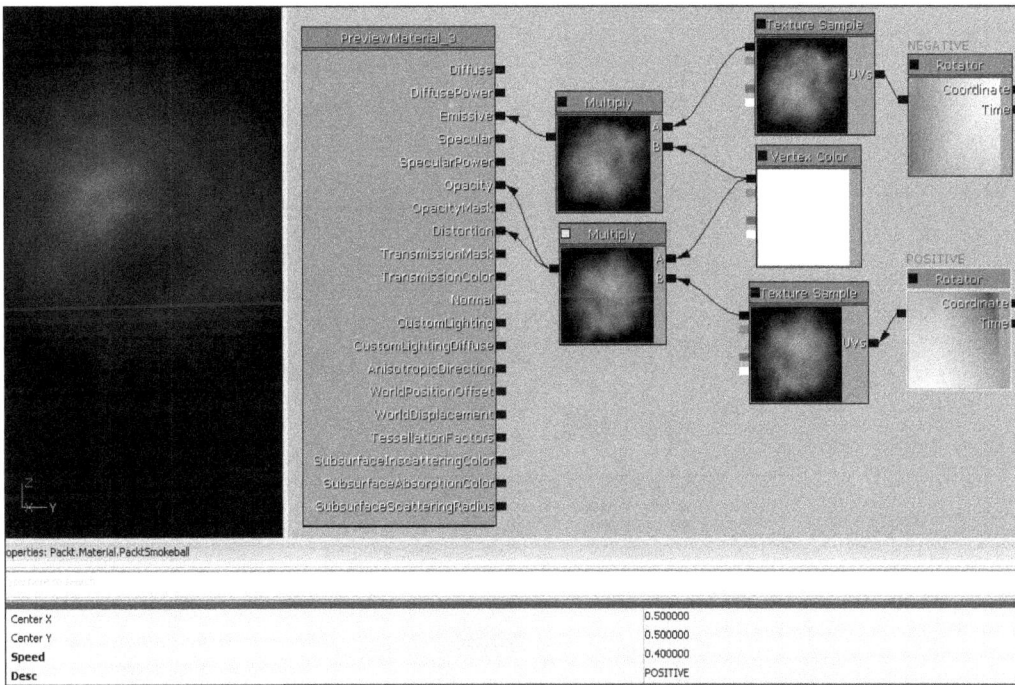

6. This screenshot shows the *Negative* and *Positive* nodes for the ***Rotator*** we made. In the image, besides the **Emissive** channel giving the steam its whiteness, the same spinning texture drives the **Distortion** channel of the Material. What this does is slightly squiggle the background behind the steam.

7. Now tick the **compile** icon [🗹] in the top corner of the Material Editor. This commits your changes to the original Material and its use in the world, and you can close the editor and go back to the particle system to assign it, given we now have an adjusted copy of the Material initially set there. Also, right-click and choose **Save** on the Material in the Browser.

8. You can also rotate the particles themselves in Cascade. Right-click in the *Particle Emitter* module list and add an item called **Rotation | Initial Rotation**. With this highlighted, in its properties set **Rotation | Start Rotation | Distribution** so the **Max** value is 90.

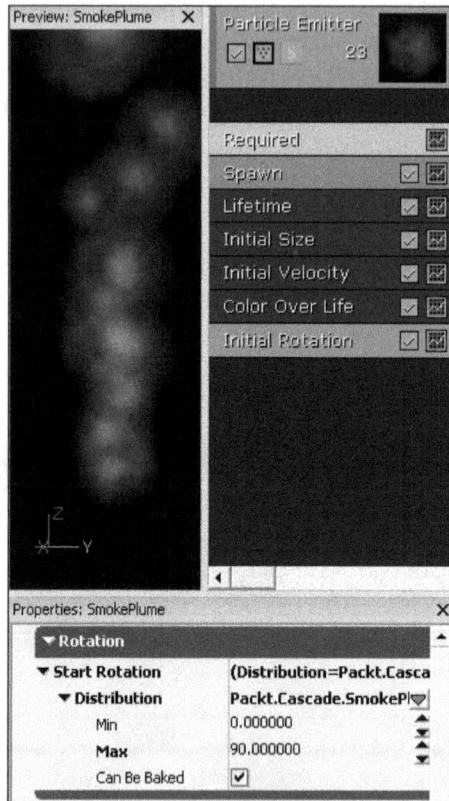

9. To change the speed of the puffs of smoke in the plume, click on the *Spawn* module in the Particle Emitter modules. Go to the module's properties and expand **Spawn**. Change **Rate | Distribution | Constant** to 75 and, below it, the **Rate Scale | Distribution | Constant** to 5. It would be a good idea to experiment with different values to see how they alter the look of the plume.

10. At the moment our steam is straight white, and it might be nice to tint it. Click the **Color Over Life** module in the Particle Emitter list, then adjust its property **Color | Color Over Life | Distribution | Constant Curve | Points | [0] | Out Val | Y** to 2 and notice how the base turns slightly blue.

11. Now change the **Color | Color Over Life | Distribution | Constant Curve | Points | [0] | Out Val | X**, **Y** and **Z** to 0.1, 2 and 3 respectively. This should effect the color of the top of the plume. The next screenshot shows this coloration.

12. Let's change the character of the smoke by adjusting the **Initial Velocity** module in the Particle Emitter list. In its properties change **Velocity | Start Velocity | Distribution | Max** to Z=222 and **Min** to Z=2, and the stream of particles should become tall and thin.

13. If you want to make the plume less regular, change the **Lifetime** module in the **Particle Emitter** list. In its properties change **Lifetime | Distribution | Max** to 5. You should see little breakaway puffs come off the main plume.

14. Our plume is now pretty tall, so to moderate its maximum height, we can add a **Kill** module to the Particle Emitter list as shown above. In its properties, set the **Kill | Height | Distribution** type using the blue downward triangle [▽] to **Distribution Float Uniform**. This gives you a **Min** and **Max** value to edit. Set those to Min=200 and Max=300.

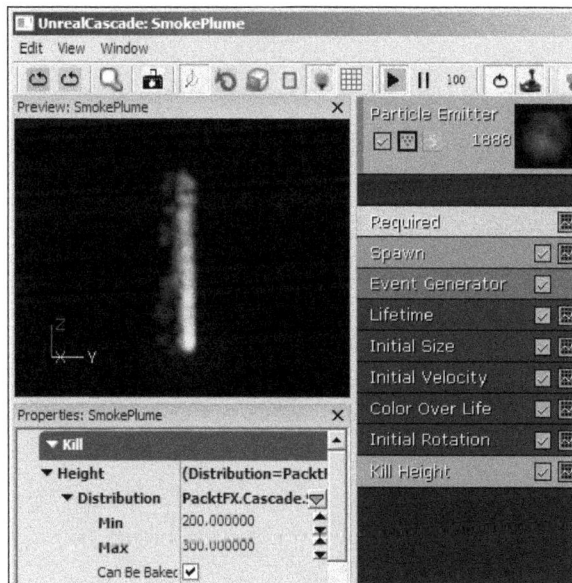

15. In the **Kill** module properties, don't turn on **Absolute** unless you want to use world space for the calculation of the height the particles can reach. What that would do is constrain the particle within that range of the scene's height.

16. That's probably enough to get things started. To explore Cascade more you can examine similarly each of the items available by right-clicking the Particle Emitter list, such as **Collision**, **Attraction**, and **Event** modules. When you finish experimenting, save your asset in its package. You can also save a thumbnail of the particle system using the menu command **View | Save Cam Position** [🔒].

17. To add your asset to the scene, just drag it from the Browser into the viewport or right-click in the scene and choose **Add Emitter: SmokePlume**.

See also

▸ For adding a particle system to a skeletal mesh socket see *Chapter 7, Hi, I'm Eye Candy!*

3
It Lives!
Character Setup and Animation

In this chapter we examine key processes for handling animated characters:

- ▶ Installing ActorX and exporting skeletal animation
- ▶ Importing SkeletalMesh content into UDK
- ▶ Morph targets and .FBX importing
- ▶ Setting up sockets
- ▶ Attachments to SkeletalMeshes without using sockets
- ▶ Setting up a custom AnimTree
- ▶ Defining animations in your AnimTree
- ▶ Configuring your character to use your AnimTree
- ▶ How to use a single bone control chain to correct an offset crouch animation
- ▶ Setting up a physics asset using PhAT
- ▶ Adding limits to physics asset joint rotations
- ▶ Adding a physics-driven tail to a key framed SkeletalMesh
- ▶ Enabling the head to face in a given direction for tracking purposes
- ▶ Setting a LookAt target for head rotation in code
- ▶ Setting morph weights in code
- ▶ Calling up SkeletalMesh animations using Matinee
- ▶ Associating sounds with character moves in Matinee
- ▶ Sounds for non-Matinee controlled animation

Introduction

When you consider game character animation, it's normal to ask how to import external animation content into the Game Editor, and how to make it work during gameplay. This is going to be our starting point. It's assumed if you are dealing with this chapter that you already know how to animate a character. The questions that follow implementation of a character tend to revolve around issues of internal control. For example, one might ask: how to access and offset bones directly in UDK, how to let UDK control the animation procedurally, how a weapon's aim direction can be accessed on the fly, or how to switch between animations according to events dynamically occurring in the scene.

The path to enlightenment in UDK can be a rocky one, and it is helpful to think of it like gaining levels of experience.

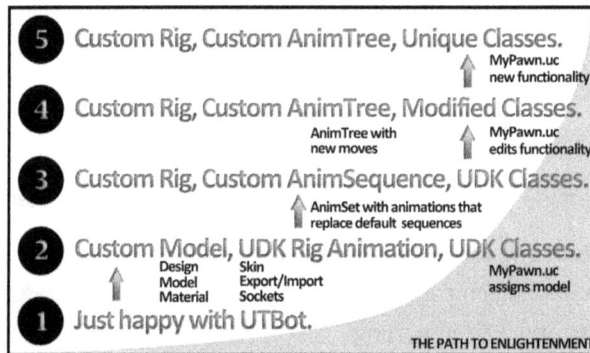

Be sure to distinguish the difference between simply replacing the mesh or adjusting the behavior of an existing character class, and creating a new custom character from scratch. For the examples that we will be dealing with, given this is not a rigging or an animating tutorial, we will be using a character based on the rig *UT3_Female.MAX* that **Epic Games** provides online through their documentation for 3ds Max users: `http://udn.epicgames.com/Three/UDKCustomCharacters.html`.

Installing ActorX and exporting skeletal animation

Getting ready

ActorX is provided with UDK. It can be found in the folder `C:\UDK\~\Binaries\ActorX` (where ~ is your version number). You will notice there are many variants, supporting popular 3D software. For 3ds Max users like myself, all that is required to get ActorX working is to choose the version of the supplied *ActorX.dlu* files which matches the 3ds Max version, and copy it to `C:\Program files\Autodesk\3ds Max ~\plugins`. At the time of writing, users of 3ds Max 2012 have to use the .FBX format instead of ActorX, which is discussed later. Maya and XSI tutorials can be found at `http://udn.epicgames.com/Three/ActorX.html`.

If you don't use 3ds Max but still want to read the UDK importing information, skip to the next recipe.

There is a pipeline for handling characters in UDK:

1. Create and skin a model that matches the rigs supplied by **Epic Games**, or create a model and rig it yourself using a rig naming convention that matches the convention established for UDK. Create any LODs and morph targets too.

2. Export the mesh from 3ds Max to .PSK or .FBX into the UDK content folder along with the textures needed by the character.

3. Export any animations you want to use on the character to .PSA, or use .FBX.

   If you are using ActorX, export morph targets and any LODs you have made.

4. Import the textures to UDK, and create a Material that uses them.

5. Import the Skeletal Mesh to UDK.

6. Create an AnimSet and add the mesh and animations.

7. Apply the Material, and import the morphs and LODs if needed. Generating a physics asset may also be required.

8. Create an AnimTree to drive the character animations in game.

9. Define a custom pawn class *MyPawn.UC* for your character by extending the game character class or maybe try writing one of your own. Here, you essentially tell the player what assets to use, and what drives the player's behavior.

10. Set the *MyGame.UC* class to use your new character class. Finally, in its engine configuration, instruct UDK to compile the code for *MyGame*.

How to do it...

Accessing ActorX after installation and accessing the UDK export rig:

1. Upon reloading 3ds Max go to the **Utilities** panel (the little hammer icon) [⚒] and press **More**. ActorX should now appear in the list. It is a good idea to add ActorX to the shortcut for **Utilities** using the **Configure Button Sets** [🔧] icon.

2. Once you have opened ActorX, you will see that it provides two export options. You can export **SkeletalMesh files** (.PSK) and export **animation sequences** (.PSA), sets of keyed bone transforms and rotations. We'll provide these.

3. Load the file *PACKT_FemaleMesh_Idle.MAX*. This scene provides a 14K polygon mesh that has a **Skin** modifier and a **Morpher** modifier. 14K polygons is an acceptable target for a UDK character model. The model design follows the joint locations of the rig *UT3_Female*. The biped skeleton overlays and directly drives the **b_** boned based skeleton which itself matches the preset UDK rig used for the default player character animation set that UDK ships with: *K_AnimHuman_BaseMale*. The *K_AnimHuman_BaseMale* set of animations works well with *UT3_Female* bones (despite the engendered names). In the scene, these two rigs can be accessed through the **Layers Manager** [📑].

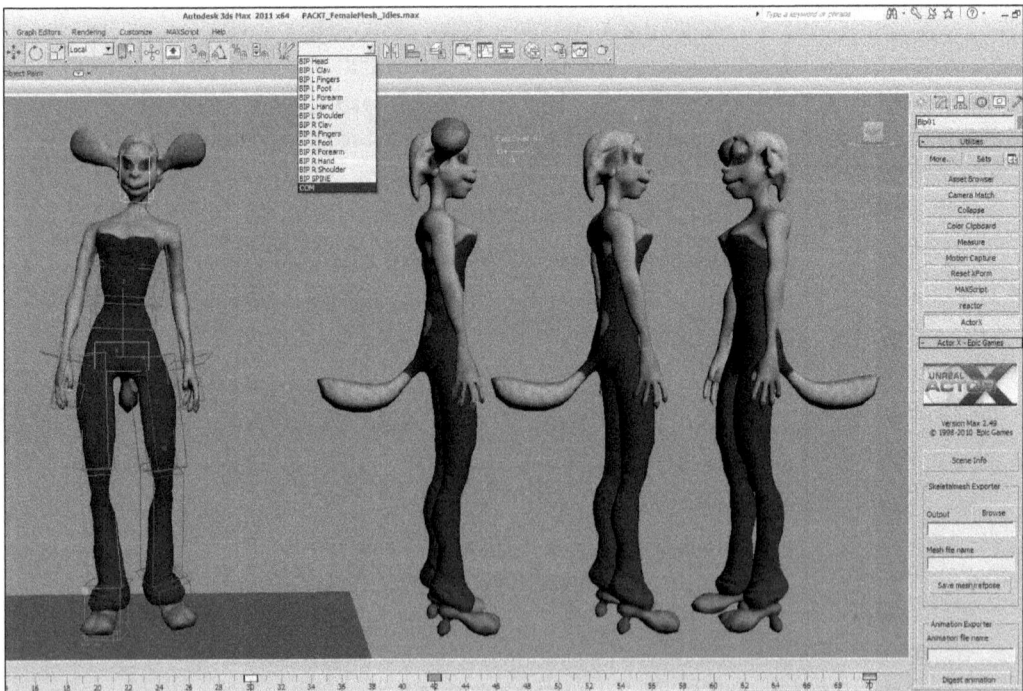

4. The next screenshot shows, on the left, the **Motion** panel of the **Biped**. This is where animation is driven from, and on the right, the **ActorX** utility allows you to export animation.

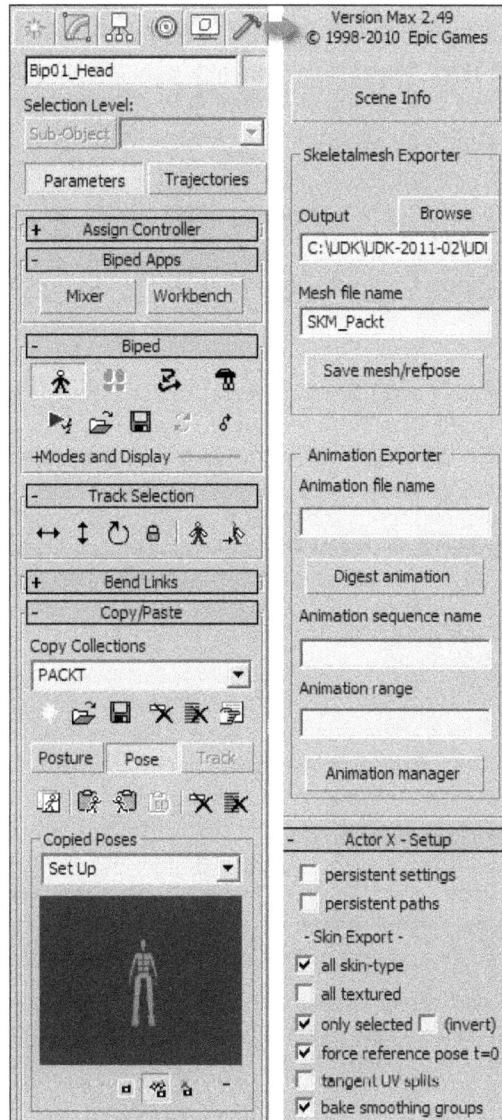

5. Press *H*, or **Select by Name** [🔲], and from the listed objects choose *Bip_01*.

6. Go to the **Motion** panel [⊙] in the **Biped** control section, and choose **Figure** mode [🚶]. It turns blue when active. With it active, expand the roll out called **Copy/Paste** and use the **Collection** called *Packt*, that's already been added to this biped. These steps are indicated with arrows in the previous screenshot.

7. In the collections panel, make sure **Pose** mode (not Posture mode) is active, and press the **Copy Pose** button. You can rename the pose snapshot to *Set Up*.

8. Now leave **Figure** mode by pressing its icon again, and turn on **Animation** mode by pressing the *N* key.

9. In the **Motion** panel [⊙], press the **Paste Pose** icon to set at frame 0 a reference pose for our character.

10. Your model should now be keyed standing with its arms out. This is all we'll export for now to UDK.

> This model uses only one Material. In UDK, this will lead the imported SkeletalMesh to have one available Material channel (or **chunk** in UDK parlance). If you want to include several different Materials in UDK for different body parts it is a good idea to add a multi-sub object Material to your model (by applying Materials to relevant polygon selections). It doesn't actually matter what maps you assign to the Materials in 3ds Max. You'll still have to assign textures to a Material asset in UDK

Exporting the asset

1. Select the *Packt_Character* model, then press **Utilities | ActorX** and scroll down to find **Output**, and press **Browse** to define a folder in `C:\UDK\~\UDKGame\Content\YOURFOLDER\Characters`. When you have done so, press **Use Path** which lets you set the output for the exported content. YOURFOLDER is just a name for a folder. You may have established it already at an earlier stage. Many designers prefer to use a dedicated character asset folder and package. That is so they only need to load relevant assets when testing the character.

2. We also need to give the exported content a name. Let's use *Test_Character*. The supplied content already includes a completed *Packt_Character* for later use. The first step is to export the mesh with its skin data (that matches to bones in UDK's provided skeleton). It is possible that you will see vertex skin data warnings when you export.

3. To prevent errors, a good first step is to turn on the following filters in the **Actor X—Setup roll out: All Skin Type** (because we only want to export skinned models); **Only Selected** (because we only want to export the mesh we selected already); **Force Reference Pose = 0** (because we want the pose to accurately represent the skinning solution on the model); and **Cull Unused Dummies** (so that bones that aren't relevant to the skinning solution will not be included).

Exporting Animations

1. Now we need to export the animation too, which is something ActorX does separately from model export. We'll look at how to export our idle sequence, create a copy of the *K_AnimHuman_BaseMale* set, and add our idle into it.

2. We have an idle animation that can be exported. So we can use the **Animation Exporter** part of ActorX to deal with that. The components in ActorX we'll define are a file name and path to save everything into, each **animation sequence** in the file (the unique moves to include one by one), and the **animation range** in frames for the sequence.

3. Click **ActorX** in the utilities. In the dialog for **ActorX**, enter the **Animation File Name**: *Packt_TestCharAnim*, **Animation Sequence** name: *PacktIdle*, and *Animation Range*: `0-219` (a frame count of 220 matches the range of the default UDK idle). As with the mesh export, the path to set would be `C:\UDK\~\UDKGame\Content\YOURFOLDER\Characters`.

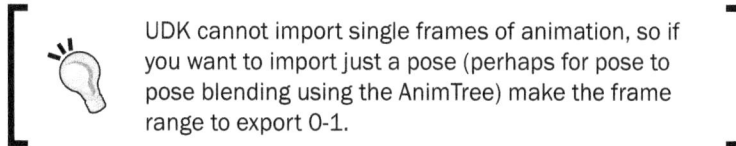

> UDK cannot import single frames of animation, so if you want to import just a pose (perhaps for pose to pose blending using the AnimTree) make the frame range to export 0-1.

4. Press **Digest Animation** to send the *PacktIdle* motion to the **Animation Manager**.

5. Press **Animation Manager** to open it, then highlight *PacktIdle* in the dialog (where it will be the only entry), and press the right facing arrow to move the digested sequence into the output list.

6. Optionally, in the **Group** field, type *Anims*. Note that here you can also set the target frame rate and a key reduction value. In most cases there is no need.

7. Press **Save As**, and make sure the output folder is in the UDK content folder structure, and set the file name to *Test_CharAnims.PSA* and press **Save**. Now we've exported the model and animations, we can move on to the next recipe on importing them into UDK.

Suppose you plan to animate all the moves a character might need; it is worthwhile to consider the speed with which your character will move and the dimensions of the space in which they will move, and the obstacles in that space. The height in units of the standard character in UDK is 96 unreal units = 192 cm = 75.59 inches = a bit over 6 feet. Another influencing factor is weight. Most **Epic Games** characters are heavily armored and don't jump very high or far, and also don't move all that fast.

While the values for these can be changed in configuration settings and by creating character classes, the nature of game animation is that it tends to suffice if a cycle loops well for a given distance moved. A sequence's playback speed can be adjusted in its properties in the UDK animation tree. If you want to replace the UDK animations with those of your own, it is worth considering that there are 124 key framed animation clips and poses in the *K_AnimHuman_BaseMale* set.

Importing SkeletalMesh content into UDK

This recipe continues the previous one, although from this point you can begin using the provided content where noted in the steps. Where before we exported content, now we're going to import it into UDK and set up the character content there.

How to do it...

Importing SkeletalMesh content and animations in UDK:

1. Open UDK. If you used ActorX for exporting the model and animation, and don't need morphs, you can import the `.PSK` and `.PSA` files you exported already. If you didn't use ActorX, you can use the provided asset `Packt_Character.PSK` in `\UDKGame\Content\Packt`.

2. The textures for the character are also available in the same location. You'll need to import them to your package too, though they are already in the *Packt* package: *PACKT_Female_Diffuse.PNG* and *PACKT_Female_Normal.PNG*.

3. Select your folder in the UDK Content Browser's **Packages List**, and choose **Import** and load either the .PSK exported in the previous recipe to an asset called *Yourfolder.Mesh.Test_Character*. A fully finished example is also included, shown next:

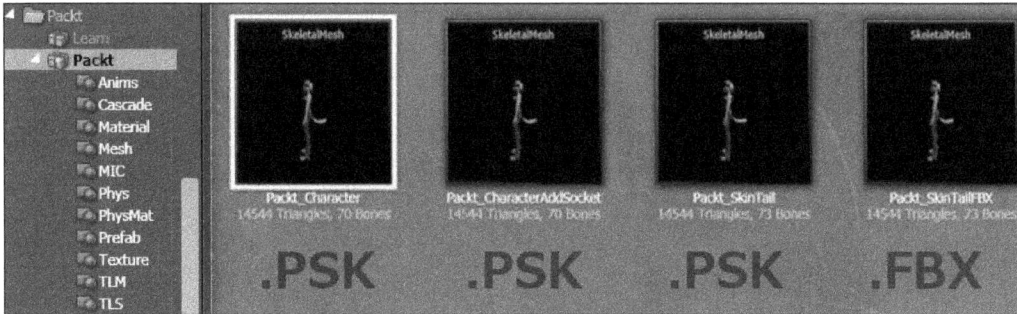

> To avoid confusion, the *Packt_Character* asset doesn't have additional tail bones; it just uses the original *UT3_Female b_* bones. The *Packt_SkinTail* asset has three additional bones and therefore uses different skin data.

4. In the Browser, double-click on the asset then, in the AnimSet Editor **Properties** panel, expand the **Mesh** tab's **Skeletal Mesh | Materials** component. In **Materials [0]** , with *Packt.Material.Packt_CharMat* highlighted in the Content Browser, press the assign icon [🔄].

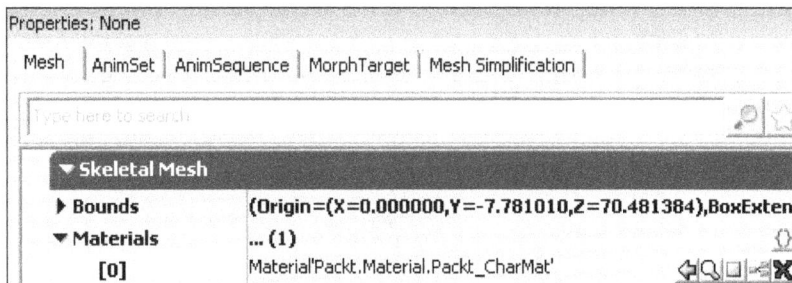

5. Right-click, select **New Material**, and call it *YourFolder.Material.DemoMat*. The Material Editor will open blank.

6. Go into the browser and select a texture asset called *Packt.Texture.PACKT_Female_ Diffuse*. In the **Material Editor**, hold *T* and click to add a new **Texture Sample**. This defines the texture. There's also a corresponding normal map, which you'll also want to add as a **Texture Sample**.

7. Allocate the **Texture Sample** node's black **RGB** output to the ***PreviewMaterial***'s **Diffuse** channel. The normal map is furnished the same way, as shown below. Press the **Compile** icon [▨] and close the Material Editor. Save the package.

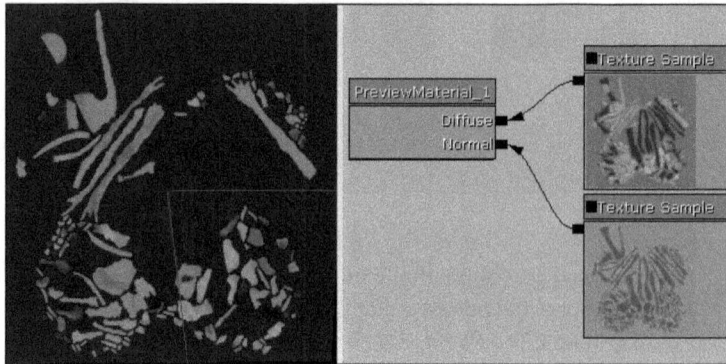

8. A feature of the provided character's Material is the inclusion of a Physical Material, which plays different sounds and particle effects depending on where on the body the character receives hit impacts. The construction of Physical Materials can be learned in the recipe *Getting varied hit impacts off models using a PhysicalMaterial* in *Chapter 9, The Devil is in the Details!*

9. Some imported models need to be adjusted to face along the viewer's **X axis**. The appropriate adjustment can be made in the properties section of the **AnimSet** editor: **Mesh | Skeletal Mesh | Rot Origin**. You'll probably need **Yaw: -90'** or whichever transform gives you the model facing along the X axis in the viewer. When you have set the correct rotation, close the AnimSet Editor window and save the asset.

▶ Origin	(X=0.000000,Y=0.000000,Z=0.000000)
▼ **Rot Origin**	**(Pitch=0.00°,Yaw=-90.00°,Roll=0.00°)**
Roll	0.00°
Pitch	0.00°
Yaw	-90.00°

10. Now we have the model asset dealt with, let's handle the animations. Remember that if you import FBX you can import the animations at the same time you imported the model, but with ActorX this is done separately.

11. Right-click in the content browser and choose **New AnimSet** and call it *Yourfolder. Anims.Test_CharAnims*. When the **AnimSet** asset appears, right-click on it and choose **Edit Using AnimSet Viewer**.

12. Click on the **Browser** panel's **Anim** tab, and from the **AnimSet** roll-down list choose the entry *Packt_TestCharAnims*. This is there just to represent the name of the asset. At the moment it should be empty. Choose **File | Import PSA**.

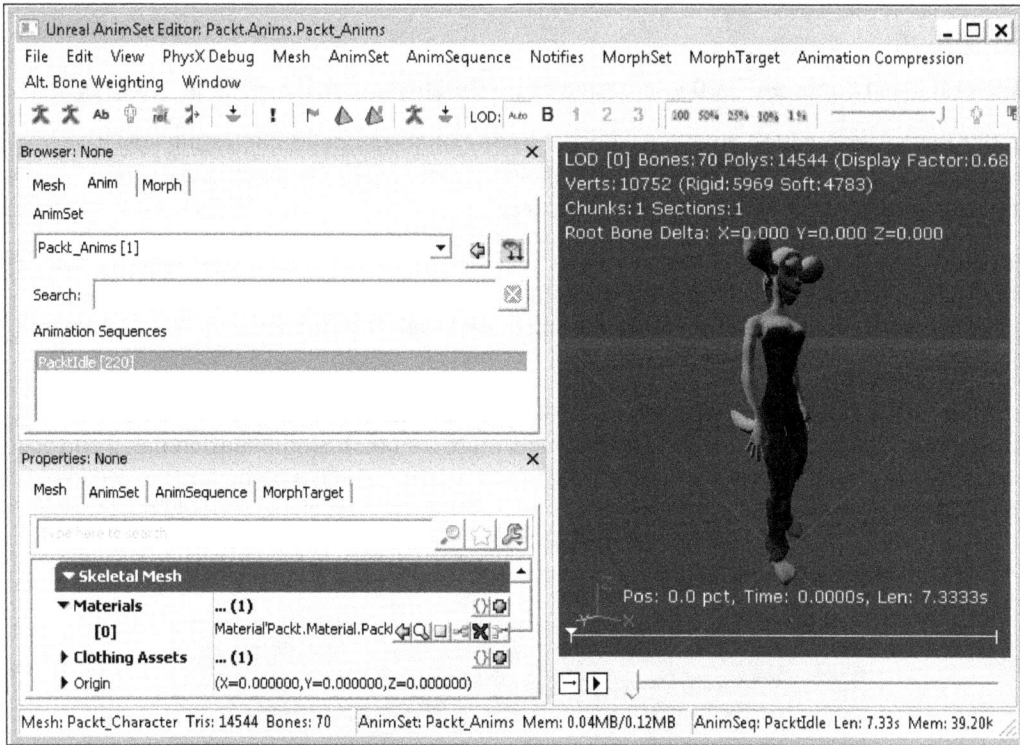

13. You need to import the .PSA you exported earlier from 3ds Max, (or use *Packt_TestCharAnims.PSA*) and then check that what has loaded is indeed what we expected to see, the *PacktIdle* clip with 220 frames. This is shown loaded in the above screenshot. There is a play button with a loop option at the bottom of the preview display.

> If you don't plan to build a comprehensive set of animated moves, you can **Create A Copy** of the *CH_AnimHuman.Anims.K_AnimHuman_ BaseMale* set and put it to *YOURFOLDER.Anims.YOURSET*, and then simply open it and choose **File | Import PSA** to load any additional or replacement animations into it. Likewise, if you don't want to make an AnimTree, you can edit the default human AnimTree so your animations are swapped in place of the existing ones.

There's more...

Skeletal Mesh Simplygon LOD generation vs ProOptimiser and SkinWrap in 3ds Max

In this recipe we imported our model. Part of setting up the model is controlling how it performs in game, including creating LODs (**Level of Detail** variants which show lighter models further away and the detailed model only close up).

For automatic SkeletalMesh polygon reduction an option added to UDK betas starting from July 2011, is **Simplygon**, a third-party utility that efficiently decimates the mesh into lower polygon counts. Doing this is useful for getting quick **Level Of Detail** variants. It works with both StaticMesh and SkeletalMesh assets.

Starting with a StaticMesh, highlight an asset in the browser and double-click it to open the **Static Mesh Editor**. Below the **Properties** panel there's a **Mesh Simplification** panel and you can generate an LOD with a distance setting from the camera and a percentage to reduce the model by. The changes you make remain open for further tweaking. It would make sense to assign new LODs before starting to actually reduce the polygons using the slider. Do so through the **Mesh | Generate LOD** menu command at the top of the Mesh Editor.

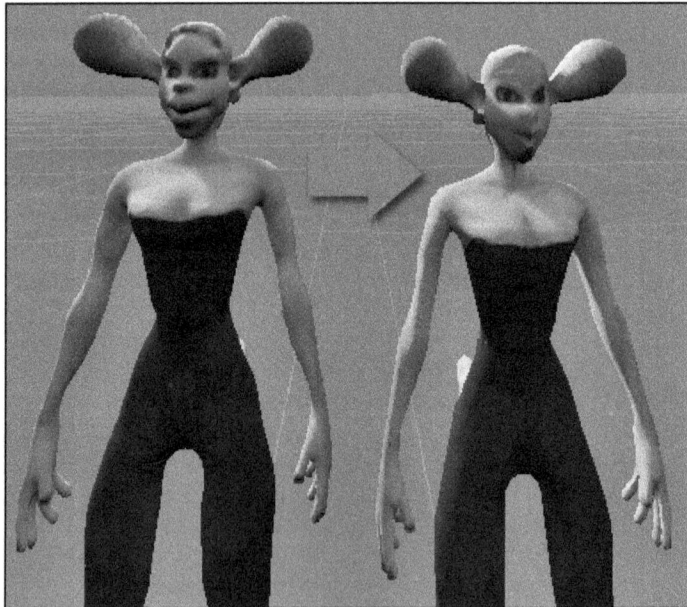

For a SkeletalMesh, generating new LODs is the same, through the **Mesh | Generate** menu command at the top of the AnimSet Editor. For polygon reduction the control process is found in the **Properties** panel, under the tab **Mesh Simplification** shown next.

Properties: None ✕

Mesh | AnimSet | AnimSequence | MorphTarget | Mesh Simplification

Original Mesh

Triangles: 14544

Vertices: 10744

Desired Quality

0   100   100

Silhouette	Normal ▼
Texture	Highest ▼
Shading	High ▼
Animation	High ▼
Normals	Recompute Normals ▼

Simplify LOD0

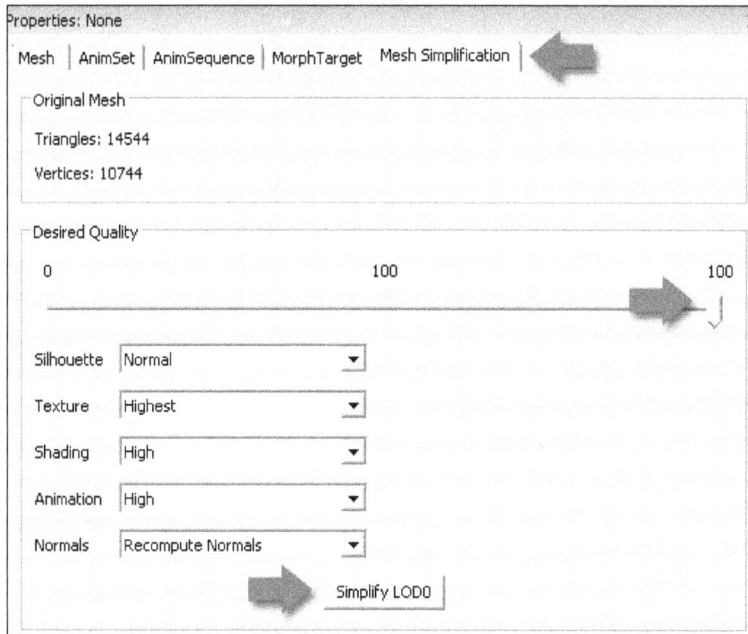

Simplygon works similarly to **ProOptimiser**, a 3ds Max modifier. For a **SkeletalMesh**, it may prove best to use **ProOptimiser** (with **Keep Textures** and **Keep UV Boundaries** turned on) and then use the **Skin Wrap** modifier to carry the original model's skin weights across, because you can then further tweak the skinning if needed. Once done, export it as FBX and then in UDK use the AnimSet Editor's tool **File | Import LOD**.

Morph targets and .FBX importing

In recent versions of UDK, importing of characters via the FBX format has been increasingly supported. The best way to try out this approach is to first jump to the official documentation from **Epic Games** on the Unreal Developer's Network: `http://udn.epicgames.com/Three/FBXImporterUserGuide.html`.

In the export dialog from 3ds Max there is the option to include **Animation and Skinning** and **Morph Targets**. When importing an .FBX asset to UDK, the import dialog offers the same options, including StaticMesh only import from a rigged mesh.

Like other software, the FBX file format is updated from time to time. Prior to December 2011, UDK did not support FBX 2012, so it is advisable to use a current version of both 3ds Max and UDK. With older versions it is possible to switch the FBX export to an older variant when exporting the model. which can be done in the **Advanced Options | FBX File Format | Version** roll-out.

How to do it...

1. In 3ds Max open *PACKT_FemaleMesh_Idle.MAX*. Select the model *Packt_Character*, which has the required **Morpher** modifier already there. To export **Morph targets** you need to send them out from the main character model, not export the target meshes. FBX handles this automatically. Within the **Morpher modifier**, press **Load Multiple Targets** and add *EarShrinkR* and *EarShrinkL* as targets. Keep their channel weights on zero.

2. You may need to place the bones for the character on a **Layer** of their own in the **Layer Manager** and hide the layer. The *b_* layer has already been populated, so hide the contents of the layer in the layer manager.

3. Use the **Select Highlighted Objects and Layers** icon [▣], then select all the *b_* bones and right-click in the scene and choose **Object Properties** from the quad menu. Ensure **By Layer** is active rather than **By Object**, as shown in the next screenshot.

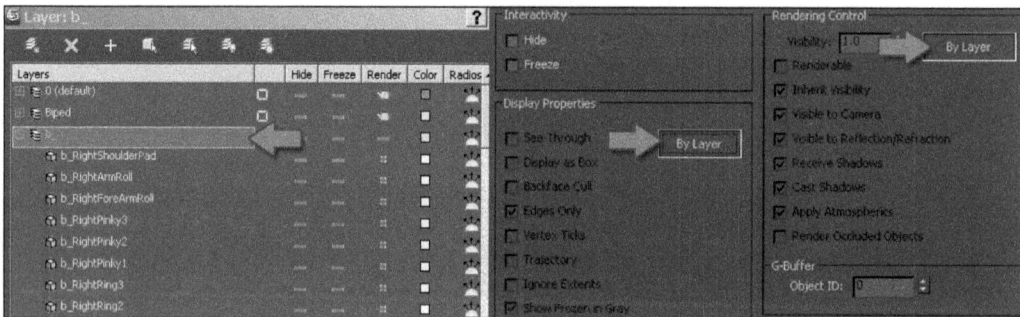

4. Select the mesh and choose **File | Export | Export Selected**. Then, set **Morphs** to be enabled under **Deformations** in the **Animation** export options, along with **Skin**. That should be on by default however, but it's good to check it.

5. Press **OK** at the bottom of the export dialog.

6. Now in UDK we need to import the morph targets we exported from 3ds Max through FBX's automatic functionality. A holder for loaded content is created for the morphs when you import the FBX. In the AnimSet you can also manually load morph targets from the AnimSet Editor's **File | Load Morph targets** menu. For that you have to first make a **MorphTargetSet** by right-clicking in the content browser and choosing the **MorphTargetSet** asset type. The FBX import creates its own asset automatically, and you should be able to locate it in the package along with the SkeletalMesh.

7. Just in case you are exploring the **Advanced** section of the FBX import dialog, as you might if you are troubleshooting, don't be tempted to click on **Import Meshes in Bone Hierarchy**. If you do, you'll get visible bones along with your character model, as shown here:

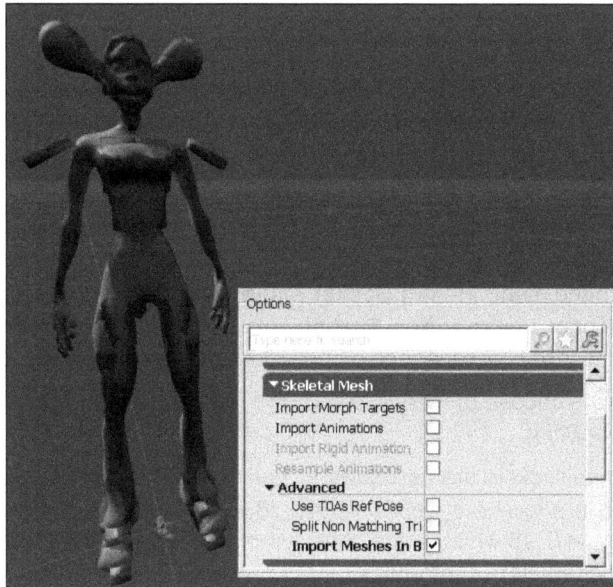

8.   Meanwhile, in the AnimSet Editor, click on the **Morphs** tab, and there you should see *Packt_SkinTailFBX_Morphs*.

> Even if you loaded your SkeletalMesh through ActorX as a .PSK, if the mesh is the same, the morphs from the FBX export can still be assigned to it in the **AnimSet Editor | Morphs Section**.

9.   If you are loading morphs from a .PSK file instead of FBX, choose **File | Import MorphTarget** in the AnimSet Editor and select the morph target .PSK files exported from 3ds Max earlier. The morph targets should now appear in the AnimSet Editor's **Morph** section with 0-1 sliders. If you try out the sliders, the model should show their influence. Adjusting the sliders in the AnimSet editor is just for previewing purposes; for in-game adjustment of the morphs we can use a coded method, or a *Matinee* driven **Morph** track through Kismet.

Setting up sockets

Sockets are points on the model where elements that are not part of the character can be fixed on it, such as weapon points, particle emitter points, or any other kind of contact point that you can think of. Typically a character in UDK needs to have two weapon sockets to work as a player character and also two jump boot sockets and a neck gore socket because they are defined in the default player class, at least for *UTGame*. They should be defined, but they don't need to actually have anything assigned to them.

Getting ready

Make sure the *Packt* package is fully loaded, and open *Packt_Character_AddSocket* in the AnimSet Editor. This mesh is different to *Packt_Character*, which already has the sockets added.

How to do it...

1. Choose from the menu **Mesh | Socket Manager** or click its icon [☀]. In the dialog window that pops up press **New Socket**. You will be prompted to select a bone name from the bones that comprise the active skeleton to add a socket to.

2. In this example choose *b_RightWeapon*. You will be prompted to label the socket. Enter *WeaponPoint*.

3. Other common sockets are as follows: *b_LeftWeapon = DualWeaponPoint*, *b_Neck = HeadShotGoreSocket*, *b_LeftAnkle = L_JB* which is a jump boot designation, and *b_RightAnkle = R_JB* which is the other jump boot designation. These designations are used by characters conforming to UT3 presets. Of course, you can create sockets where you like as well.

4. Let's create a socket on the head bone *b_head* called *Hat*. Notice that it takes the pivot of the bone itself, which isn't really a suitable place for a hat.

5. In this case, we'll move the socket to the model's crown simply by dragging on its widget in the view port. If you prefer you can set a **Relative Location** for the socket in the properties section of the **Socket Manager**. The location is relative to the chosen bone's pivot.

6. In the Content Browser highlight *Packt.Mesh.Packt_TopHat* and then in the **Socket Manager** properties section, find **Preview Static Mesh** and assign *Packt_TopHat* to it using the assign icon [☀] as in the next screenshot.

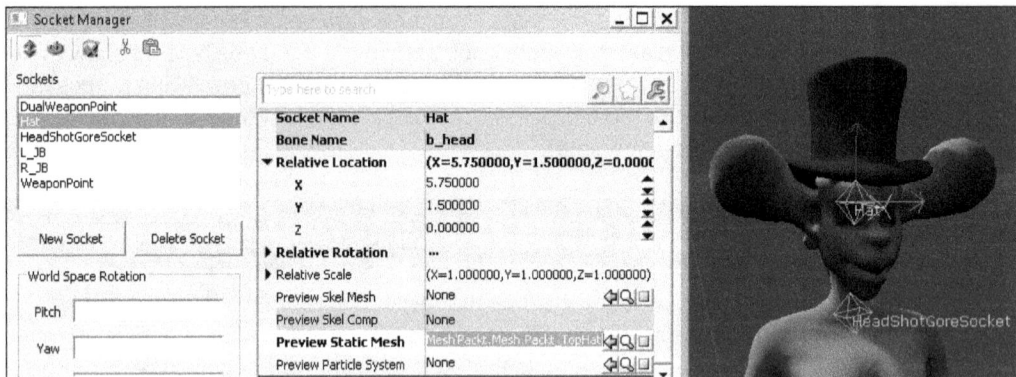

7. If the added mesh does not show up where expected you may need to adjust the **Relative Rotation** (something like **Roll=0**, **Pitch=-90**, **Yaw=11**), and you can also adjust it directly by pressing *Space* in the preview and rotating it there.

8. Tweak the placement of the *Hat* socket until the mesh is sitting agreeably on the model and follows the AnimSet animations accurately.

> If you build your own prop to add to a socket, note that when exporting from 3ds Max the mesh must be placed at 0,0,0 rather than where it sits relative to the model, or the offset from 0,0,0 will be added in UDK.

9. At the start we mentioned that there are already sockets for *Packt_Character*. The problem is, the mesh lacks an animated tail and isn't as complete as the model we'll use later. Putting sockets on again would be tedious. Luckily there are **Copy Sockets** and **Paste Sockets** tools in the socket manager. Open *Packt_Character* in the AnimSet Editor, then press the **Socket Manager** icon [⬆]. Along the socket manager dialog's icons you will see a scissors icon [✂] and a clipboard icon [📋]. These are **Copy Sockets** and **Paste Sockets** tools, so press **Copy Sockets**, then open *Packt_SkinTail_LODtest* and its socket manager (which should be empty) and press **Paste Sockets** to complete the transfer.

Attachments to SkeletalMeshes without using sockets

Sockets are handy to use because they can be called on in code no matter the actual object is that is active in the socket. Sometimes though, it's sufficient to just directly attach an object to another already in the scene. By default, objects attach to the target object's main pivot. You can also define an attachment to the pivot of a bone in a SkeletalMesh object's hierarchy. In the **Attachment** section of the **Properties** panel (*F4*) of the object you want attached, you can point to a **Base Bone Name** in the target's skeleton if you want the selected object to stick to it. To get a bone's name just open the SkeletalMesh in the AnimSet Editor and click on the icon **Show Skeleton** [✻].

How to do it...

1. Start the map template *Midday Lighting*. In the Content Browser, find *Packt_Character* and drag the asset into the Perspective view.

2. Find the particle **Emitter** *SmokePlume* in the browser. Drag *SmokePlume* into the scene also.

3. Press *F4* with *SmokePlume* selected to access its properties, then **Lock** the properties using the padlock icon [🔒] at the top of the properties window. This lets you keep *SmokePlume*'s properties displayed while selecting other objects.

4. Expand the **Attachment** roll-out of *SmokePlume*'s properties.

5. Now click on *Packt_Character* in the scene, and press the green arrow [🔄] of *SmokePlume*'s **Attachment | Base** channel.

6. In the **Base Bone Name** channel, type in *b_head*. In the scene, line up the two assets so the particles look like they are emitting just above the character's head. You may want to turn off **Grid Snapping** to do so, and also you may want to scale down the emitter slightly.

7. The properties for SmokePlume should still be exposed. Turn off **Emitter | Particle System Component | Particle System Component | Auto activate**. This will make the particle system stop emitting (assuming you had on the real-time playback icon [🔳]). Instead, we'll toggle the particles through Kismet. We'll also add some animation to the character.

8. In the scene add a Trigger actor, from which we'll fire the action in Kismet. So you can see the Trigger when you play, press *F4* and uncheck **Display | Hidden**.

9. With the Trigger selected, in Kismet [K] right-click and choose **New Event** using the *Trigger_0 | Touch* event and add a regular *Toggle* action (hold *T* and click).

10. Connect the **Touched** nub of the *Trigger_0 | Touch* event to the **Turn On** nub of the *Toggle* action. Also, connect the **Untouched** nub of the *Trigger_0 | Touch* to a 3 second *Delay* action then run the *Delay* action's **Out** nub into the **Turn Off** nub of the *Toggle*.

11. In the properties of the *Trigger_0 | Touch*, make sure the **Max Trigger Count = 0**.

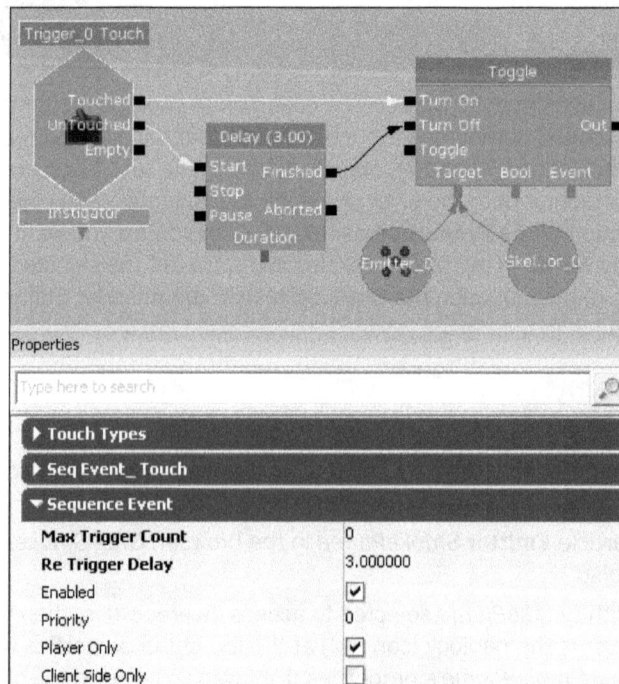

12. Select the SkeletalMesh in the scene, and press *F4* to open its properties. Expand **Skeletal Mesh Actor | Skeletal Mesh Component | Skeletal Mesh Component | Animations**.

13. Here there are two channels we need to set. The first is the name of the clip we want to play, which is **Anim Node Sequence | Anim Seq Name**. Enter *Kick*, as shown in the next screenshot. The second is **AnimSet**. This needs to have its add entry icon [🔲] pressed.

14. Then you can highlight *Packt_CharAnims* in the Content Browser and assign it here using the green arrow [🔲] into **[0]**. This is shown at the bottom of the next screenshot. If everything is good, you should see the character shift its pose in the viewport. It won't play just yet though.

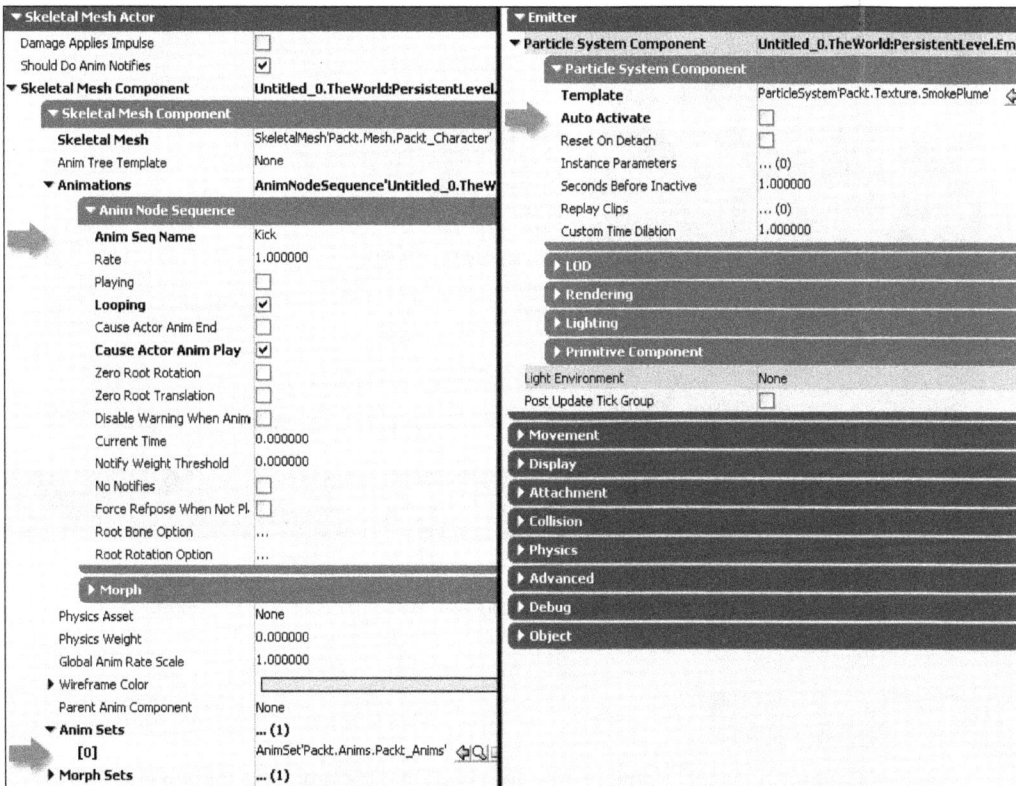

15. This screenshot also shows (on the right) the tick box to set **Auto Activate** off for the Emitter.

16. Set the properties, then select both the emitter *SmokePlume* and the **SkeletalMesh** in the scene. In Kismet [🔲] assign them as targets of the *Toggle*.

17. In the next screenshot, you can see **Kismet** with the ***Trigger Touch*** event toggling both an ***Object Variable*** to which the Emitter is assigned and an ***Object Variable*** to which the SkeletalMesh is assigned, prepped to play the chosen animation. On the right, we see the result. Build and PIE, and you should be able to start and stop both the animation and the emitter by bumping into the Trigger.

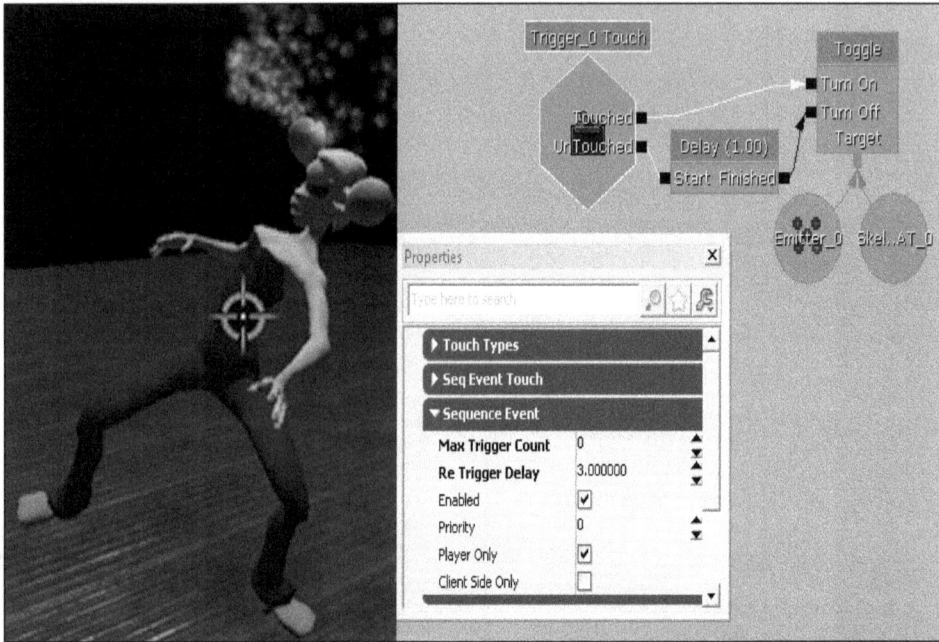

Setting up a custom AnimTree

This recipe shows how to furnish a custom AnimTree with asset link ups that allow our character to preview what will occur in a game and to play animations that reflect its assigned moves.

How to do it...

1. In the Content Browser, highlight your folder, right-click amongst the assets, and choose **New AnimTree**.

2. Name it *YourFolder.Anims.TestTree*. Double-click the newly created **AnimTree** and it will open in the **AnimTree Editor**, showing only a base ***AnimTree*** node.

3. Before adding more nodes, we must set the **Properties** of the ***AnimTree*** node so it understands the assets we'll be using, much as we did with the SkeletalMesh in the previous recipe after we placed the asset in the scene. Let's work down the list, using the next screenshot as a reference:

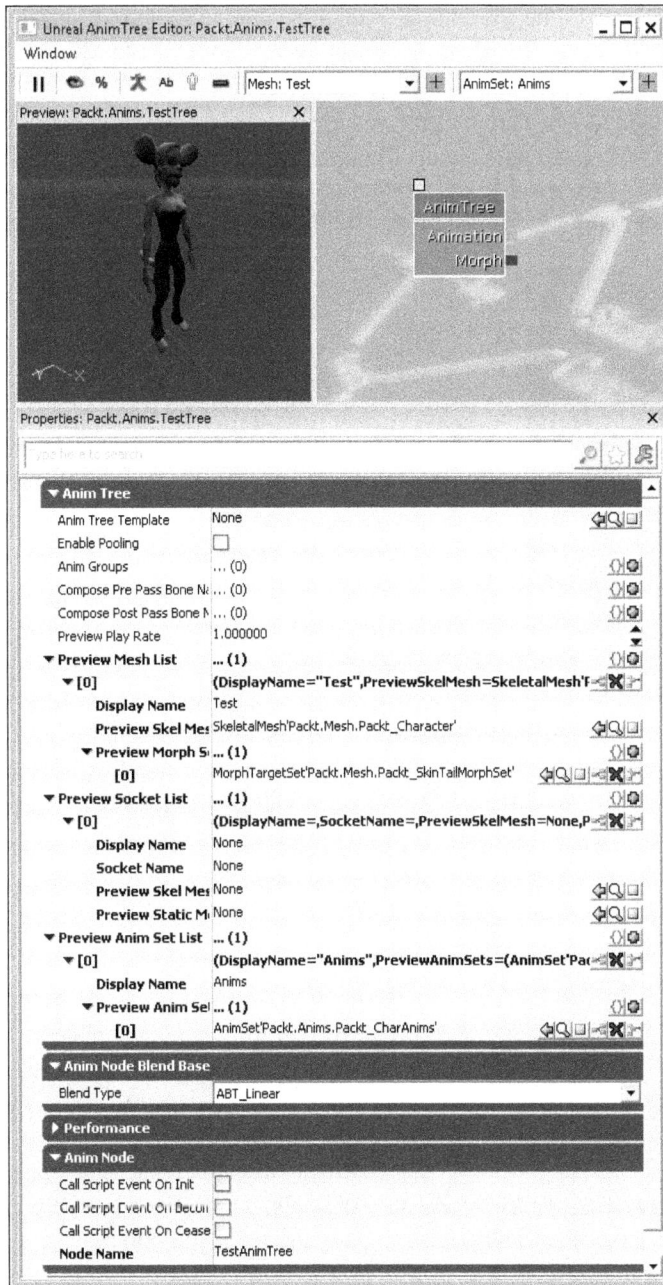

4. Expand the **Anim Tree** section in the properties of the ***AnimTree*** node and look at the channel **Preview Mesh List**. This requires *Packt_Character* (or another SkeletalMesh) to be added here, which will then show in the preview window.

5. If you plan to animate **Morphs**, you will also need to add at least one asset directly below the **Preview Morph Sets** channel, such as: *Packt.Mesh.Packt_SkinTailMorphSet.*

6. The **Preview Socket List** is included for if you want to preview the inclusion of some extra asset attached to a socket. This will be unnecessary here, but you just have to add the SkeletalMesh to use, the StaticMesh to preview, and the socket name the StaticMesh should fix to. You could add the mesh *Packt_TopHat* to the socket *Hat*.

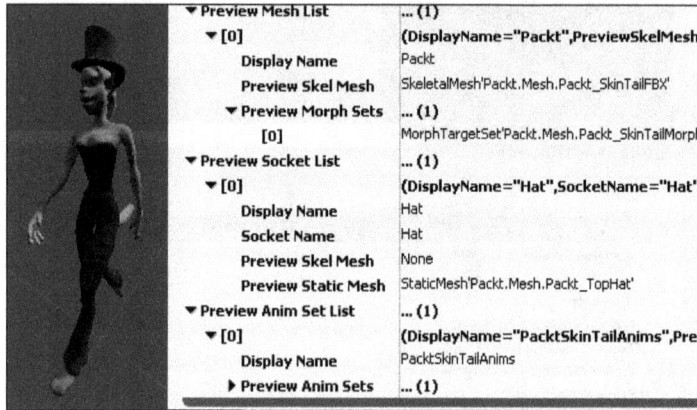

7. In the next channel, the **Preview AnimSet List** should be set to *Packt.Anims.Packt_SkinTailAnims*. Setting this lets us see the moves that belong to the character when active nodes in the AnimTree show their sequences.

8. Finally, if your ***AnimTree*** will be called by UnrealScript it needs a **Node Name**, which can be entered further down in **Anim Node section | Node Name**. You can give this any name, but it is good to choose something sensible and clear.

How it works...

The **AnimTree Editor** is rather like Kismet in terms of view navigation in that left mouse will pan, and *Ctrl-drag* will select and move nodes, while the middle mouse will zoom. It is also similar in structure, involving nodes linked in a visual, branch-like set of connections. Here they serve as switches. The nodes won't show very much without first having assets assigned to the AnimTree for preview purposes. The AnimTree needs to know what your mesh is, what your AnimSet is, what your morphs are, and even what sockets you want to show. The channels for adding these actually allow multiple entries. If you add more than one character mesh for instance, at the top of the AnimTree editor you can choose from the **Mesh roll-down list** which one will be current.

Still, this set up process does not actually tell the AnimTree how to work in game. For that we'll follow this up with another recipe. Meanwhile, you can compare your results with the next screenshot, which shows the channels filled with the assets mentioned so far.

Defining animations in your AnimTree

This recipe shows how to furnish the AnimTree we have been working on with actual animation controls and sequences. It extends the previous recipe, which set up the properties of the AnimTree to include our character assets. We won't be creating an entire animation tree, only the bare bones needed for walking around, including an Idle.

How to do it...

1. With your *TestTree* AnimTree asset open, right-click in the editor and choose **New Animation Node | UDKAnimBlendByPhysics**, shown next, which you can hook up to the **Animation** output of the *AnimTree* node. This node is usually the end node for all the animation to parse through. It covers situations such as walking, falling, and swimming. Additional inputs can be added by right-clicking and choosing **Add Input**.

2. From the **PHYS_Walking** output extend to a **New Animation Node | BlendBy | UDKAnimBlendByIdle**, shown in the next screenshot. This gives us a control to switch between **Idle** animations and **Moving** animations. There is a previewing slider at the base of this node which ranges from 0 (Idle) to 1 (Moving).

3. We could add some additional blends to the idle, such as between sitting and standing, or even lying down, but for now a basic idle will be fine. Right-click and choose **New Animation Sequence | AnimNodeSequence**. This will produce a node which says *None*. Connect the **Idle** output of the *UDKAnimBlendByIdle* to this. Highlight the *AnimNodeSequence None*, and look in its **Properties**. For the **Anim Seq Name** enter *PacktIdle*, which renames *None*. You can get the list of available animations for the preview AnimSet in the rightmost roll-down list at the top of the editor.

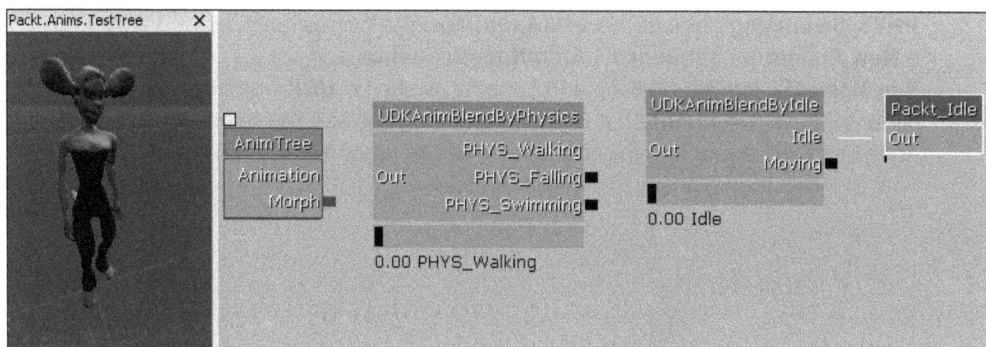

4. For *PacktIdle*, in the properties panel, click on **Playing** and **Looping**. Further down, in the **Anim Node** section, for **Node Name**, enter *Idle*. Hooking the nodes up will let you see the *Idle* animation playing in the preview window.

5. From ***UDKAnimBlendByIdle*** extend from its **Moving** output a **New Animation Node | Directional | AnimNodeBlendDirectional**. This provides a mixer for user directed movement typically assigned to *W A S D* keys in a game.

6. For each output of the new node, assign a **New Animation Sequence | AnimNodeSequence**, and respectively set their **Anim Seq Name** channels to *FWD*, *BWD*, *LeftStep*, and *RightStep*, as defined in the AnimSet *Packt_CharAnims*.

7. Your four nodes should all be set to **Playing** and **Looping** in their properties. Slide the ***UDKAnimBlendByIdle*** slider to 1.0 **Moving** to see the results. Then slide the ***AnimNodeBlendDirectional*** slider (which ranges around 360') to cycle through the movement directions.

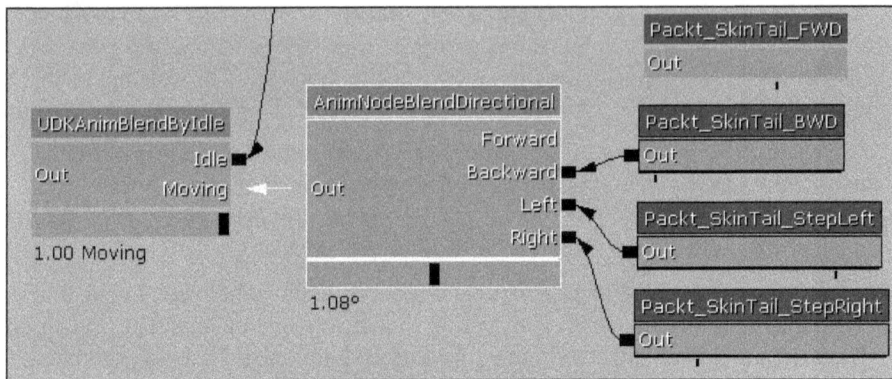

8. Activate the ***AnimNodeSequence*** *SkinTail_BWD* and in its properties set the **Rate** to 0.75, since usually a character doesn't move as fast backwards as forwards. The overall speed a character will move is defined in its pawn class.

9. Just for an extra step, since we have one swimming animation, from the **PHYS_Swimming** node of the ***UDKAnimBlendByPhysics*** node, extend a wire to a **New Animation Sequence | AnimNodeSequence** and set its properties to **Anim Seq Name**: *SwimFWD*, Playing and Looping. Slide the ***UDKAnimBlendByPhysics*** slider till **Phys_Swimming** highlights and is active to see the result. To fill out an AnimTree tree requires many sequences. Get to know the available nodes and how they mix then plan your own sequences.

10. You will notice that there is an available output off the main ***AnimTree*** node called
Morph. Using this you can add the morph targets your character uses. The quickest
way to examine how this works is to open the *Packt_CharTree* asset, which already
has the *EarShrinkL* and *EarShrinkR* morphs added. To add a Morph Target just
right-click and choose **New Morph Node | MorphNodeWeight**. This creates a slider
you can name. From that, extend to a **New Morph Node | MorphNodePose**, which
references the actual morph target by its name in the AnimSet **Morph** section.

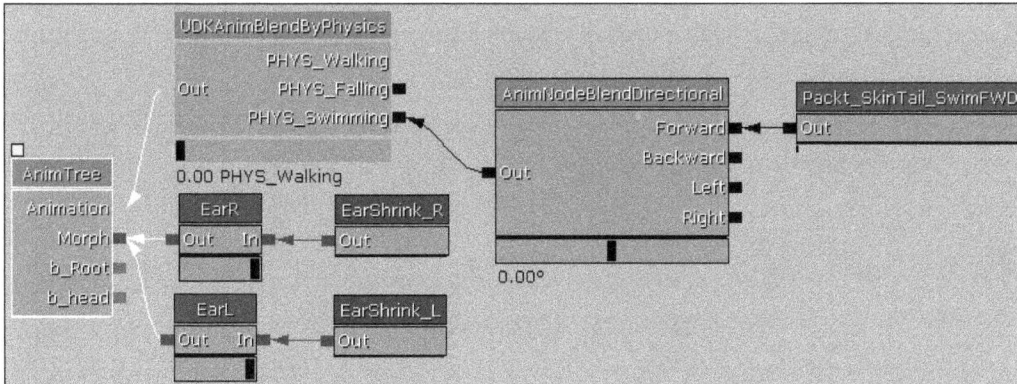

11. To familiarize yourself with the workings of AnimTrees a good start is to search the
content browser using **AnimTree** as a filter and open up those that ship with UDK.
A good next step is to look for the great set of free video tutorials by **Wraiyth** at:
`http://udkc.info/index.php?title=Tutorials:Wraiyth's_AnimTree_`
`crash_course`.

Configuring your character to use your AnimTree

This recipe shows how to set up the environment of UDK to allow our character to use
an AnimTree we have been working on. While in the editor we can preview the AnimTree
performance, that isn't the same as seeing it in action during gameplay. To deploy our
AnimTree requires us to create a custom pawn class derived from the default pawn UDK
includes. To do so, we first need to adjust some of UDK's configuration so it will accept the
adjustments we're going to make.

Getting ready

The configuration steps are not very difficult, it is just that all the changes are made outside of the editor, an approach which may feel unfamiliar to designers used to working totally *inside* a software environment to produce content. In short, we just edit a few UnrealScript files to alert UDK to use our AnimTree when it loads. I am going to use a tool called **ConTEXT** for this example. This is a text editor which sits in the middle ground between Notepad and Microsoft Visual Studio. It is freely available from `www.contexteditor.org` and the **Desktop Version** is what I'll be using, along with its *UnrealEd* **Highlighter** template that can be found in the list at `http://www.contexteditor.org/highlighters/`.

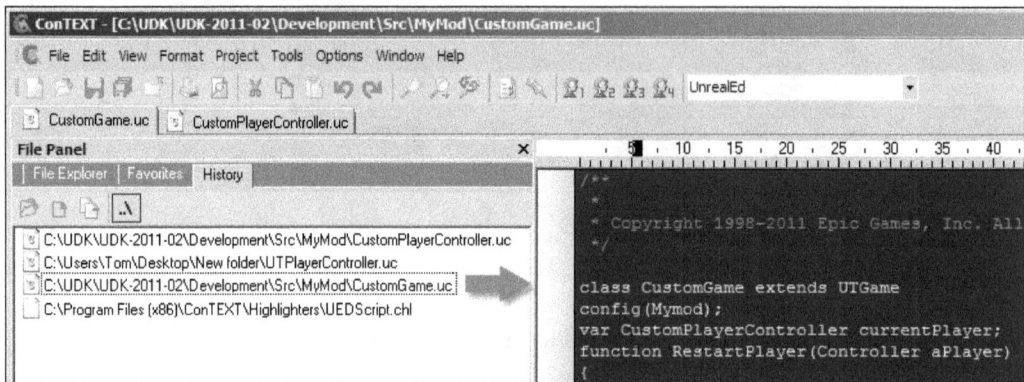

This screenshot shows the simple, tabbed interface of ConTEXT, its convenient **History** list, and an open UnrealScript. Note that the UnrealScript Highlighter displays as *UnrealEd* in the icon row. Highlighters can be added by following the instructions from the ConTEXT website: **To add a new highlighter to ConTEXT, download the highlighter and copy it to the Highlighters folder of your ConTEXT installation's folder. If ConTEXT is running, restart it to update the list of external highlighters**. For full information on how ConTEXT works, look to their documentation. For us, it is only necessary to set the *UnrealEd* Highlighter to be active in an open document from the **Select Active Highlighter** list on the right-hand side end of the icon row.

Note that a dark blue background will be applied, which is a visual aid as it is easier on the eyes than a bright white color. If you are fond of changing colors, just edit the color entries in *UEDScript.chl* using HTML color codes (for instance `CommentCol: clLime` could be replaced with `CommentCol: $00FF00`) and you can find a list of color codes at `http://www.w3schools.com/html/html_colors.asp`. Bear in mind there is a foreground and background color pair that needs to be defined.

How to do it...

1. **ConTEXT** is a text editor with nice highlighting and code template tools, but it doesn't help to set up the UDK folders or settings that are the entry point for creating a custom game. Assuming you have a fresh install of UDK, and haven't already set up your own game folders besides those created to store assets in the `\UDKGame\Content\` folder, you will need to create a folder called *MyGame* in the location: `C:\UDK\~\Development\Src\` (where ~ is your version). The folder name *MyGame* can be any name but the upcoming code refers to it repeatedly, so you may find it helps to stick with this if you aren't sure you can track it all the way.

2. In `C:\UDK\~\Development\Src\MyGame`, add a new sub-folder called *Classes*.

3. In the folder `C:\UDK\~\Development\Src\MyGame\Classes`, create three new text files, *MyGame.UC*, *MyPlayerController.UC*, and *MyPawn.UC*, then right-click on each and choose **Properties** and ensure their **Read Only** checkbox is not ticked.

> What is *MyGame* anyway? When a designer creates a level, UDK requires a game type to be set, especially in later versions which no longer default to *UTGame*. The game type defines what kind of allocations hold out for the game, such as camera type, HUD used, details about the player, and everything that needs to be set at the entry point of the game.

4. In ConTEXT open `C:\UDK\~\Development\Src\MyGame\Classes\MyGame.UC`. This will be empty currently. Paste in the following code to define how *MyGame.UC* configures the player:

```
class MyGame extends UTGame
config(MyGame);

DefaultProperties

{
DefaultControllerClass = class'MyGame.MyPlayerController'
DefaultPawnClass = class'MyGame.MyPawn'
}
```

5. Above we set a variable referring to *MyPawn*, which is there to set all the information for how a player can behave and appear in game. Next, we'll provision that. After it, we'll provision *MyPlayController*.

6. Open the file we made before which should be empty: `C:\UDK\~\Development\Src\MyGame\Classes\MyPawn.UC`. Treat lines in the code which are darkened as particularly important. Author comments are demarcated using `//` and explain what follows. Type in the following code:

```
class MyPawn extends UTPawn
config(MyGame);
```
//The Object class defined below provisions the player model.
```
DefaultProperties

{
Begin Object class=SkeletalMeshComponent
Name=SkeletalMeshComponent0
SkeletalMesh=SkeletalMesh'Package.Group.Asset'
AnimSets(0)=AnimSet'Package.Group.Asset'
AnimTreeTemplate=AnimTree'Package.Group.Asset'
PhysicsAsset=PhysicsAsset'Package.Group.Asset'
bEnableSoftBodySimulation=True
bSoftBodyAwakeOnStartup=True
bAcceptsLights=True
End Object
Mesh=SkeletalMeshComponent0
Components.Add(SkeletalMeshComponent0)
```
//The setting below sets the apparent camera distance from its pivot, which is where the player model is located. The DrawScale of the pawn can be increased or decreased to suit, with testing.
```
DrawScale=1
CameraScale=30
}
```

> This code doesn't refer to specific character assets; they are listed only as *Package.Group.Asset*. It is important to realize code will vary according to different needs. Our examples will include only what's needed to produce a result for the problem of this chapter, using the *Packt_SkinTailFBX* character. The following section deals with referencing the existing SkeletalMesh assets to work with our own animation.

7. You will need to replace the asset names according to the package files of interest. In our case, we are using the provided content from the Packt folder.

8. In the code entered so far, find the line `SkeletalMesh=SkeletalMesh`. Here's how the entries below that need to be adjusted for the character we've worked with so far in the chapter:

   // The top part of the code entered in the previous steps doesn't change, just the following lines:

   ```
   SkeletalMesh=SkeletalMesh'Packt.Mesh.Packt_SkinTailFBX'
   AnimSets(0)=AnimSet'Packt.Anims.Packt_SkinTailAnims'
   AnimTreeTemplate=AnimTree'Packt.Anims.Packt_CharTree'
   PhysicsAsset=PhysicsAsset'Packt.Mesh.Packt_CharPhysics'
   ```

9. The assets shown here are those for the most complete version of our character that's provided with the book. The **AnimTree** we have been referring to all along has now been set. Of course, eventually you'll want to use your own.

10. Now we need to furnish the *MyPlayerController.UC* class we referred to earlier in the *MyGame.UC* file we wrote. Open this file, which should be empty:
    `C:\UDK\~\Development\Src\MyGame\Classes\MyPlayerController.UC`

11. UDK defaults to a first person view. We can't test the character works if we can't see it, so what we need is an entry to set the camera view behind the player. Type in the following:

    ```
    class MyPlayerController extends UTPlayerController;

    DefaultProperties
    {
    bBehindView=True
    }
    ```

12. Save all the open .UC files. As things are, the classes are ready. Now we have to tell UDK to use the folder `MyGame` and its classes, and then test them out.

13. Make sure UDK is not running and go to `C:\UDK\~\UDKGame\Config\` and open the file *DefaultEngine.INI* in ConTEXT.

14. That change at the moment is simply to type in: `+ModEditPackages=MyGame` under the last entry in the section headed: `[UnrealEd.EditorEngine]` (which you can search for using the menu command **Edit | Find**). The added line should come last because the list order determines the order that classes get loaded and compiled. Save the *DefaultEngine.INI* file.

15. In Windows choose **Start | All Programs | Unreal Development Kit | ~ | Tools | Unreal Frontend** where ~ is your install version for UDK. Frontend will load, and you can recompile the scripts for UDK using either the **Script | Full Recompile** command or **Script | Compile Scripts** command. If you have changed scripts and start up UDK, it will also prompt you to recompile scripts automatically. If you choose not to, changes will be ignored.

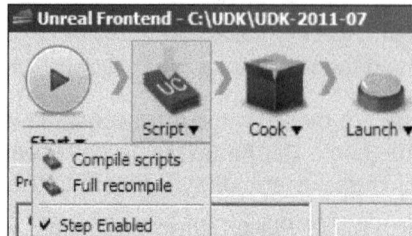

16. If you have made any typos or other errors in your classes, the compiler should feedback errors in red and warnings in yellow in the analysis at the bottom of Frontend after compiling. You can open the .UC file with a problem in ConTEXT and use *Ctrl + G* to go to the line mentioned in the error. Here is a hypothetical example of an error report:

    ```
    C:\UDK\UDK-2011-02\Development\Src\MyGame\Classes\MyGame.UC(16) :
    Error, Illegal character in name. Compile aborted due to errors.
    ```

    In this case *MyGame.UC* contained a typo fault on line 16; the line is found in brackets after the file name.

17. If your *MyPawn.UC* has incorrect package references, warnings will be listed in yellow at the end of compiling. Here is another hypothetical example:

    ```
    ...\MyPawn.UC(47) : Warning, ObjectProperty MyGame.
    MyPawn:DefaultMesh: unresolved reference to 'SkeletalMesh'Package.
    Group.Asset''.
    ```

    The problem is that the asset is still in the abstract, not specifically one that exists such as *SkeletalMesh'Packt.Mesh.Packt_SkinTailFBX*. Again in ConTEXT, loading *MyPawn.UC* and using *Ctrl + G* to find line 47 would allow us to locate and fix this. Since you may periodically update the assets you want to use, this kind of oversight can easily occur.

18. To recover from a non-compiling custom game, you can temporarily comment out the line in C:\UDK\~\UDKGame\Config\DefaultEngine.INI that points to your classes by adding ; in front of the line +ModEditPackages=MyGame.

19. In UDK, there are a couple of requirements to complete the process we've been through. Although it's been set already for the final character asset *Packt_SkinTail*, a **Z** offset from the **Origin** is required in the AnimSet Editor to avoid the character walking in the air. For *Packt_SkinTailFBX* a value of Z = -40 works well. The next screenshot shows this setting. Note in the small image that the character's feet are no longer on the ground line and she has dropped below. While this looks disconcerting in the viewer, in gameplay it looks okay.

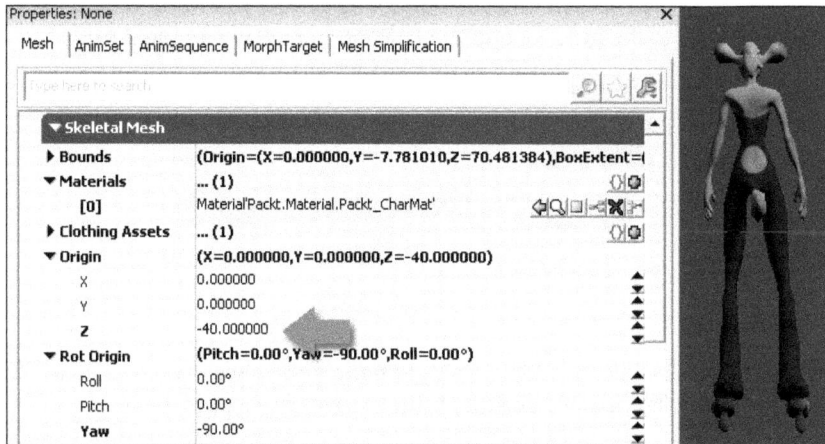

20. After setting the **Origin | Z** offset, close the AnimSet Editor and save the package. Finally, go to the **View** menu and click on **World Properties**. Expand the section **Game Type** and in the entries **GameType** and **GameType for PIE** choose from the list *MyGame*.

How it works...

To provision the player model is a matter of telling *MyGame.UC* to use your *MyPawn.UC* and configuring UDK to use the *MyGame* folder. You should extend *UTPawn.UC* and set the default properties in the new *MyPawn.UC* class to those of your assets. There are plenty of examples of this on the **UDK** forum www.udk.com/forums. An example using the asset *Packt_SkinTailFBX* is included in this book's provided content: /files/Development/MyGame/Classes/.

After recompiling scripts, to place her in the scene as an NPC, place a Trigger actor and a PathNode actor. Create a ***Trigger*** event which connects to an ***Actor Factory*** action in Kismet. In its properties choose the **Factory** setting for an NPC by clicking [▼] and choosing **UTActorFactoryAI** then under it set the **Controller Class** to *None* and the **Pawn Class** to *MyPawn*, which should now show up in the list within the factory.

An example is in the provided map *Packt_03_CheckMyPawnworks.UDK*.

How to use a single bone control chain to correct an offset crouch animation

In a crouch, the *b_Root* bone has to move down towards the ground. In UDK all the character animations are stored in the **AnimSet** and in this is a property called **AnimSet | Anim Rotation Only** that forces UDK to read off only rotations from the *b_Root* bone; this is helpful where you will create cyclic character moves but not so good if you want to create a crouch, where the feet are local to the ground, and the *b_Root* drops down in the Z axis.

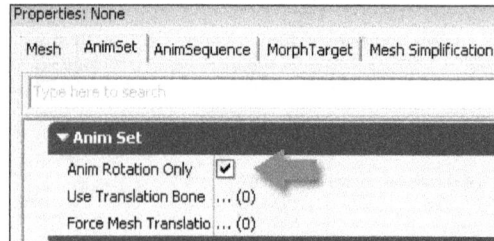

In the **AnimTree** we can fix this by adding a **single bone controller** to *b_Root* called from the character rig. The controller also has a **Node Name** so we can access it in code.

Getting ready

In this example we'll create an empty AnimTree asset, and start from there. For ease of use later, in the Content Browser filters click **All Types** and right-click on the **Animation Trees** filter and choose **Add to Favorites**. This will allow you to easily locate your AnimTree asset as we go. Remember that if you want UDK to use this new AnimTree in-game, you'll have to tell *MyPawn.UC* to use it in the `DefaultProperties`, just as we did in the previous recipe.

How to do it...

1. Make sure the *Packt* package is fully loaded. Right-click in the Content Browser and choose **New AnimTree** and call it *Yourfolder.Test.BRootOffset*.

2. Add the *Packt_SkinTailFBX* SkeletalMesh to the **Preview Mesh List** channel of the **AnimTree** properties. Likewise, add the *Packt_SkinTailAnims* AnimSet to the **Preview AnimSet List**, just like in the last recipe on starting an AnimTree.

3. As in the last recipe, add a **UDKAnimBlendByIdle** (we'll forego doing the movement clips) and hook up to its **Idle** input an **AnimNodeBlendByPosture**.

4. Add two **AnimNodeSequence** nodes. Make the first refer to *Packt_SkinTail* (an idle) and the second refer to *Packt_SkinTail_CrouchIdle*. Make sure both are **Playing** and **Looping** in their properties. These sequences hook up to the **AnimNodeBlendByPosture**. *PacktIdle* goes to **Standing**. *PacktIdleCrouched* goes to **Crouched**.

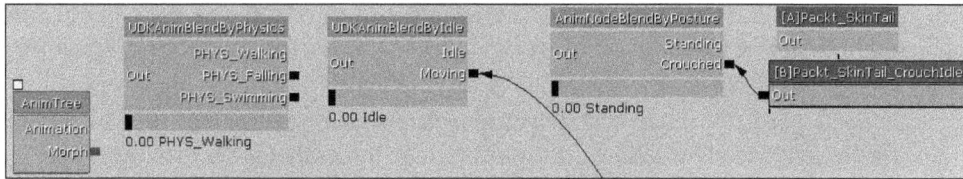

5. Slide the **AnimNodeBlendByPosture**'s weight value and notice the crouched animation appears to make the character look like she's levitating. This is what we'll fix by adding a control for *b_Root*.

6. Right-click on the **AnimTree** node and choose **Add NewSkelControl Chain**. From the prompt, choose *b_Root*. Note that this can't occur if the **Preview** content including the **AnimSet** hasn't been defined in the earlier steps.

7. Right-click on the canvas and choose **New Skeletal Control | Single Bone | SkelControlSingleBone**. Copy this and add another one chained to it, as shown next:

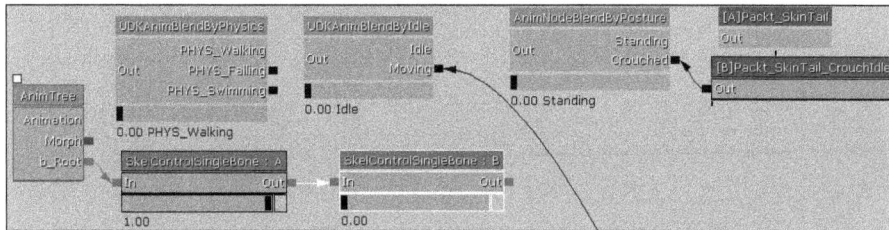

8. As shown in the next screenshot, select the **AnimNodeSequence** *Packt_SkinTail* and in its **AnimNode | Node Name** field type *A*. Then select the **AnimNodeSequence** *Packt_SkinTail_CrouchIdle* and in its **AnimNode | Node Name** field type *B*. These names can really be anything unique. Something short is usually better. They will be referenced by the node chain we made.

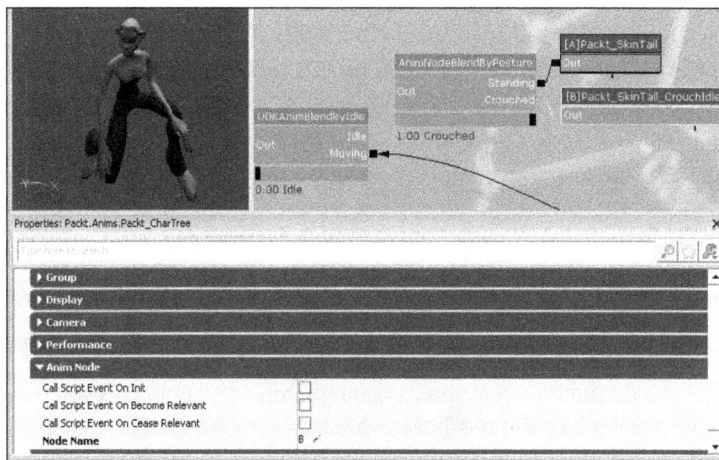

9. In the first of the two **SkelControlSingleBone** nodes, find the property **Adjustments | Apply Translation** and turn it on. Further down, also turn on the property **Translation | Add Translation**. Here, leave the XYZ values at 0,0,0.

10. In the property **Controller | Strength Anim Node Name List** add an item by clicking the new entry icon [🔾]. Name it *A*. Also, turn on the property **Set Strength from Anim Node**. Repeat this for the second **SkelControlSingleBone**, but this time name the added item *B*. Set the **Translation | Bone Translation | Z** offset to -40. This corresponds with the **Origin Z** offset we gave the model.

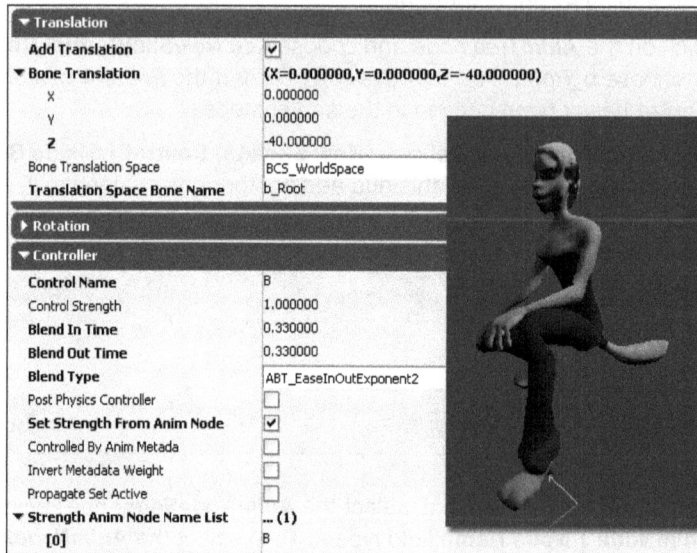

11. Slide the **AnimNodeBlendByPosture** node's weight value and notice the crouched animation appears to drop down onto its feet, rather than raise its feet up. You could also add further offsets for the *b_Root* using new nodes in the chain for situations such as *Flying*, *Lying Down*, or *Sitting*. The next image shows the **SkelControlSingleBone** pair which controls the crouch offset from *b_Root*, and the properties that make this work.

12. Note that when you adjust the offset value for *A* or *B* and test it in the editor, the one currently set active by the slider completely takes over the pivot. This is something of an update problem, but you can work around it if you adjust a value, save the package, and then restart **UDK**; the change will be as expected.

Setting up a physics asset using PhAT

Physics assets let you animate your character using forces and impulses such as gravity or hit impacts, using collision calculations between simple geometry objects assigned to your character's bones.

It is relatively easy to provision a SkeletalMesh with a physics asset. It takes some tinkering around to make the initial results more pleasing. The main editor to get used to is the **Physics Actor Tool** (**PhAT**).

Getting ready

Previously we created an AnimTree for the SkeletalMesh *Packt_Character*. To keep the focus of the exercise on the AnimTree, a physics asset was already prepared and included in the script that drives the character. It was just a placeholder. In this exercise we'll make the real physics asset for this model.

We'll start with just the *Packt_Character* SkeletalMesh, and we'll create and test out some physics attributes in the PhAT Editor. In the Content Browser, make sure the *Packt* package is fully loaded in the **Packages list**.

How to do it...

1. Right-click on *Packt_Character* in the browser and choose **New Physics Asset**. Name it *Packt.Mesh.Test_Character_Physics*.

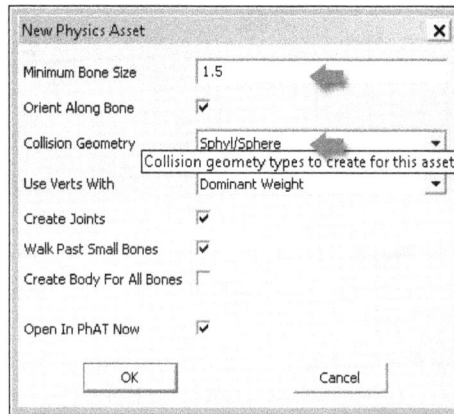

2. You'll be prompted for some initial conditions, as shown here. The **Minimum Bone Size** value you set in the dialog will determine how many bones get collision geometry. In this case, entering 1.5 will give us a result on many bones.

This approach means we'll have to adjust the collision geometry UDK generates. Another approach is to start with no collision geometry by setting a really large **Minimum Bone Size** so the threshold becomes too high for UDK to generate geometry, then add custom geometry bit by bit to suit your needs. In the end, both ways take about the same amount of work.

3. In the dialog, for **Collision Geometry** choose **Sphyl/Sphere**, not **Box**. The **Box** type is offered by default, but a **Sphyl** is cheaper in terms of memory and suits an organic character's collision requirements. Having said that, a character's feet would do best with **Box** geometry, because they have flat soles. Since the geometry assigned can be changed later on, we'll just assign the whole body to **Sphyl** now.

4. After your press **OK** the **UnrealPhAT** Editor will open, showing the *Packt_Character* SkeletalMesh covered in wireframe circles.

5. Straight away, if you press S to toggle **Simulation** mode, the character should collapse in an odd, but at least operational kind of way. Press S again to turn this off. You can't select part of the bone hierarchy or geometry when simulations are playing.

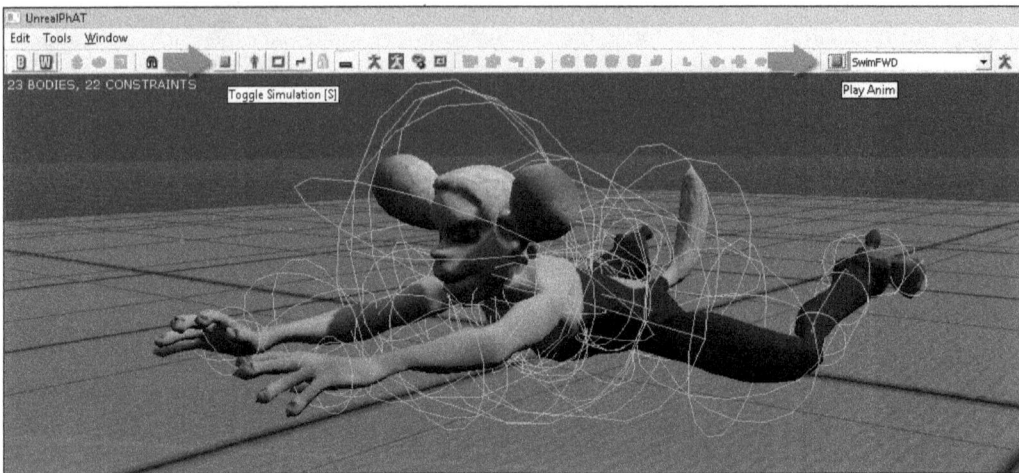

6. In the right-hand side **Properties** panel, notice there is a **Preview AnimSet** channel. To fill it, highlight *Packt.Anims.Packt_CharAnims* in the content browser, then click the channel's assign icon [◀].

7. Underneath **Preview AnimSet** find the checkbox **Blend On Poke** and turn it on. Now when you press S nothing will happen until you **Poke** the character by pressing *Ctrl + LMB* in the view. Then it will blend from animation mode to physics simulation mode. These are the settings that effect the **Poke**:

   ❑ **Poke Strength**—how hard you Poke the character

   ❑ **Poke Pause Time**—the time the Poked character will stay lying down

   ❑ **Poke Blend Time**—the time to blend from physics back to animation mode

   ❑ **Sim Speed**—allows you to slow things down

   ❑ **Floor Gap**—an arbitrary offset of the character from the floor

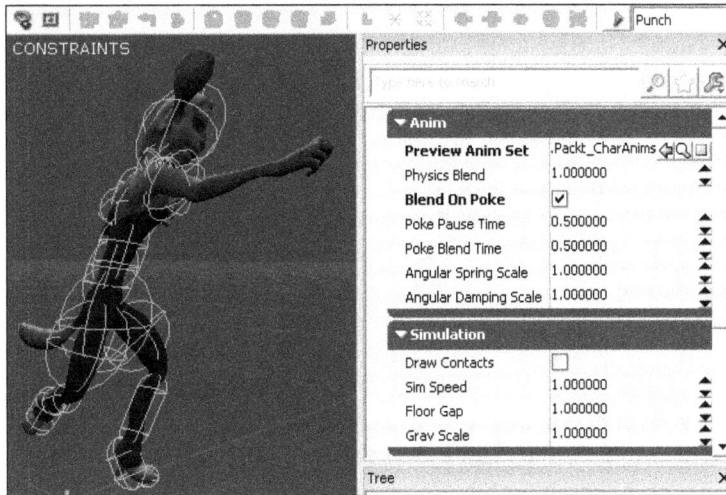

8. To play an animation from the AnimSet, first press S to turn on **Simulation** mode, or tap its **Play** icon [🔊]. This will enable the selection of a sequence on the far right side of the icon row through a drop-down list. Here there is another **Play** button which tells the sequence whether to be playing or just showing its first pose. Make sure **Blend on Poke** is on.

9. Turn off **Simulation** mode (S). Click on one of the wire frames enclosing the head and notice how the properties panel now refers to the highlighted object. To access the main asset properties at any time just click in the editor view's blank space if a particular object is selected and showing its own properties.

10. You can also select geometry objects by clicking on the corresponding bone in the **Tree** panel under **Properties** on the right-hand side of the editor. The **Tree** panel shows a hierarchy of bones in the character, fully expanded. Given our initial value of 1.5 for the **Minimum Bone Size** that we set in the **Physics Asset** creation dialog, you should have a hierarchy that extends down to the hands but doesn't include the fingers, as shown here:

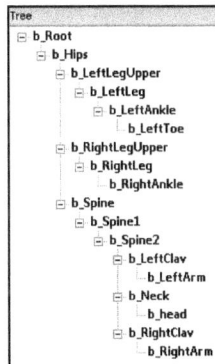

11. In the **Tree**, first click on *b_Root* then *b_Hips* and see the corresponding geometry in the view switches too. Highlight *b_Root* and press *W*, then *E*, then *R* and notice the transform widget changes. You can also use *Space* to cycle it. The PhAT editor follows the transform hot keys of most 3D applications. Try moving, rotating, and scaling the root.

12. It doesn't matter how much, because then we'll delete it by pressing the *DEL* key (there is also a **Delete Current Primitive** icon for this in the icon row [🔳]). It would be strange for the root to collide. You will see a warning dialog about removing the bone and its constraints, but it won't remove the bone, just the collision geometry on it. The *b_Root* bone in the tree will now be grayed out.

13. You will need to select each bone in turn and move, rotate, and scale so it has a snug fit to the geometry. Notice the *b_Hips* collision geometry includes the tail. For this recipe, let's ignore the mesh area of the tail completely, and make the pelvis a smaller sphere containing only the hips.

14. The thighs have large spheres where stretched Sphyls will probably be better. Select *b_LeftLegUpper*, then use the **Add Sphyl** icon [🔳] to add a replacement. Select and delete the original sphere. You will have to rotate and scale the new Sphyl to fit the leg well. Press *Space* to cycle transforms. Don't worry about overlap with surrounding collision geometry.

15. Rather than adjusting the upper-right leg the same way, select the *b_LeftLegUpper* bone's Sphyl and press *C* to copy its transforms, then just click on the existing geometry for *b_RightLegUpper*. The transforms will be immediately pasted across.

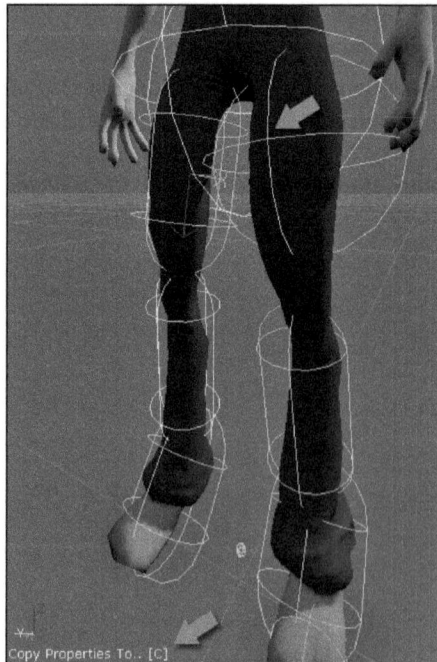

16. The lower legs are probably okay, but the feet may be better suited to have **Box** collision. First delete the collision geometry on the two toe bones. Then add a **Box** [🔲] to the foot (*b_RightAnkle*) and rotate it so it is aligned to the floor and scale it so it fits the shoe of the character. Delete the previous primitive the foot had. You can then simply press *C* then click on *b_LeftAnkle* to swap out the left foot's sphere for a box automatically. This copy-and-paste approach can also allow you to swap a thin Sphyl onto the forearms too, off of the leg. The spine and neck can be dealt with by scaling them down to hug the figure better.

17. The head, given its odd shape, needs three sphere objects rather than one, so you can add and position two more to each side. Note you can't copy and paste transforms across different primitives belonging to the same bone, but you can use the **Duplicate Current Primitive** icon [🔲].

18. For our character, the *b_LeftClav* and *b_RightClav* bones don't appear to need collision geometry because they are absorbed in the larger spine bone. However, removing their collision causes the arms to disconnect and stretch when simulation occurs. Delete the collision geometry on the Clav bones and press S. Poke the character and notice her arms appear to be free in the physics simulation. Once you take away collision from a bone in the **Tree** you can use the **Add New Body** icon [🔲] to re-include it. Clicking the icon will expose the entire tree, and you can click on the bone you want to add. Available choices will display in bold type. Then you'll be prompted, as at the start, to define the geometry type, and for the Clavs that were deleted, choose **Sphyl | Sphere**.

19. In the case of *Packt_Character* it would probably be advantageous to **weld** the Clav collision geometry to the *b_Spine2* bone to simplify its physics calculations. Select *b_Spine2* and use the **Weld To This Body...** icon [🔲] to include *b_RightClav*'s collision in its own set. You can also press D, so use D to join in *b_LeftClav*'s collision to the spine also. Remember to start from the bone to be welded to, then click on the bones to weld to it.

20. If you **Poke** (*Ctrl + RMB*) the character now it will behave differently than the first time, but it still isn't ready yet. This is because none of the joints have limits which set how much they can rotate, so the limbs flop all over the place. But we've reached the end of this stage, so now would be a good time to save the asset. Now you can either continue the next recipe from where you are or switch over to the example *Packt. Mesh.Packt_CharPhysicsLimitsStart*.

See also

Epic Games' technical animator **Jeremy Ernst** provides a great video on these stages in the official documentation at `http://udn.epicgames.com/Three/VideoTutorials.html` and there is also technical reference in the **Physics Actor User Guide** online at `http://udn.epicgames.com/Three/PhATUserGuide.html`.

Adding limits to physics asset joint rotations

Try turning your forearm as far as you can. You'll immediately see it rotates more in some angles than others. This is true of many joints in your body. To allow a character's physics asset to work correctly we create such joint rotation limits in the PhAT Editor.

How to do it...

1. Either continue from where you were in the previous recipe, *Setting up a Physics Asset using PhAT*, or, if you haven't completed the asset so far, double-click instead the provided asset *Packt.Mesh.Packt_CharPhysicsLimitsStart*.

2. In the PhAT Editor, press *J* a couple of times to cycle collision to shaded, and press the **Draw Ground Box** icon [▬] to turn off the ground.

3. Setting up rotation limits will help the joints behave more naturally. UDK uses a one dimensional arc limit and a two dimensional cone limit. Exit simulation mode (S) and press the **B** icon [▣] under the edit menu. This will turn to a **C**, and the view should change, showing that we're now in **Constraints** mode. The hotkey *B* toggles back and forth between the **Editing** and **Constraints** modes.

4. Select the character's right knee pivot. The lower leg should turn red and the upper leg blue. Press the icon **Convert to Hinge** [✦], to more faithfully realize the possible motion of that joint. Repeat this with the character's left knee joint.

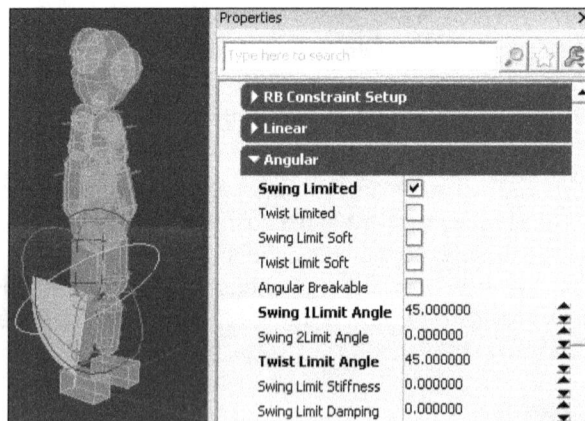

5. Look to the properties of either joint and expand the **Angular** parameters. Adjust **Swing 1Limit Angle** to 45. This is shown in the above screenshot. Click in the preview window then press *E* to let you rotate the resulting green pie shape in the view to about where the leg could realistically bend. Remember your leg can't bend forwards and you don't normally want a 3D character to be able to kick their own butt because the foot geometry might overlap the body. Repeat this same step for the other knee.

6. Press *K* to cycle **Constraints Rendering Mode** (so you can see the angle limit for both legs at the same time).

7. It is a little tedious to plot the constraints for every joint. It just requires some thinking about how much a given bone can freely rotate in each axis.

8. The forearm can't rotate backwards or upwards for example, but it can twist and rotate forwards. Select either **ForeArm** bone and set the **Swing 1Limit Angle** to 55, then rotate the pie shape so the forearm can't swing backwards. Turn on **Twist Limited**, and set the **Twist Limit Angle** to 110. These aren't quite realistic values, but they should be adequate. Under physics, it is better to allow slightly less rotation than can be achieved by a real person so the body doesn't appear too elastic. Repeat the same step with the other forearm.

9. Some joints permit XYZ rotation, but can only rotate a certain amount around each axis. The neck for instance can rotate in XYZ but not all the way round. In our case, it is probably a good idea to **weld** b_Neck to b_Spine2 in order to avoid the head flipping round erratically to face the wrong way. Do this in **Editing** Mode (*B*) by selecting b_Spine2, pressing *D*, then clicking on b_Neck. Then press *B* again to return to **Constraints** Mode. Also, using a **Twist Limit Angle** value, give b_Head just a little freedom of movement, so it isn't too floppy.

10. The spine needs a **Twist Limit** and can only rotate a certain amount for each bone (there are three spine bones plus the hips and the bendiness of the back is the accumulation of a few fairly limited possible rotations). Each bone's constraint may require rotation of the widget to suit the bone alignments.

11. At this stage, you may find it handy to know *Q* cycles the alignment of the cone to an axis. *Ctrl + Q* lets you transform the pivot based on the *W-E-R* current transform.

12. Given next is a table of **Swing** and **Twist** limit values used for *Packt_Character*. Note that the clav and neck bones have been welded to b_Spine, so they aren't listed below. It would be good practice to set up the rotations, observe the rig performance as it collapses under physics (*S*), then start from there to make adjustments. To simulate the character, switch back to **Editing** mode (*B*).

Joint	Swing1	Swing2	Twist
b_LeftLegUpper, b_RightLegUpper	40	40	40
b_LeftLeg, b_RightLeg	45	5	45
b_LeftAnkle, b_RightAnkle	22	6	66
b_Spine	6	6	15
b_Spine1	15	15	33
b_Spine2	22	22	33
b_Left Arm, b_RightArm	33	33	66
b_LeftForeArm, b_RightForeArm	55	0	110
b_LeftHand, b_RightHand	22	22	22
b_Head	5	5	5

13. Adjust the values to suit by testing and varying what changes occur by pressing *S* to simulate and then watching the figure collapse; on the ground she should lie with limbs facing in agreeable angles, not crazily broken—particularly the head, feet and arms. It is normal for the thighs to make the splits. One way to address this peculiarity is to enter **Editing** mode (*B* toggles editing and constraint mode), go to the upper leg's properties and adjust the **Mass Scale** higher than that of the upper body. Again, perfect values are a matter of trial and error. If the chest is 2, the upper legs could be 5.

14. The next screenshot shows green cones visualizing the rotation limits for the skeletal joints. On the right-hand side of the image, we see how disabling collision of the chest with the nearby bones is displayed, and this is discussed in the following steps.

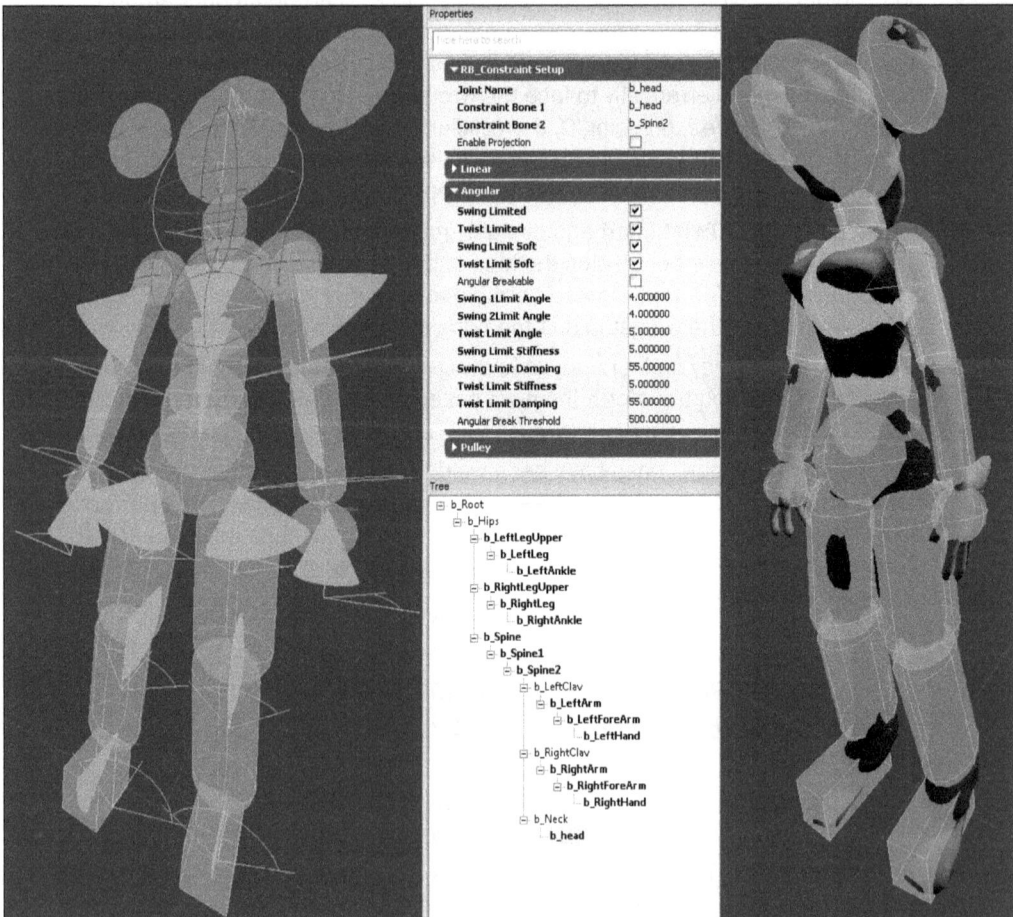

15. A fun way to test out the performance of the rag doll is to hold *Ctrl + Right-click*, drag part of the body, and see how the body follows the cursor. If you let go during this, the body will free wheel as though thrown.

16. While by now the rag doll should be less floppy than at the beginning, we can improve things by adjusting collision pairs to compensate for where geometry overlaps the geometry of neighboring joints. Turn off **Constraints** mode [▦], and select *b_Spine2*. Notice how that some previously grayed out icons are now exposed by the selection. Click the **Disable Collision With...** icon [▥], then choose *b_Spine1*, which will turn gray. You can press *J* to cycle shading to see this better.

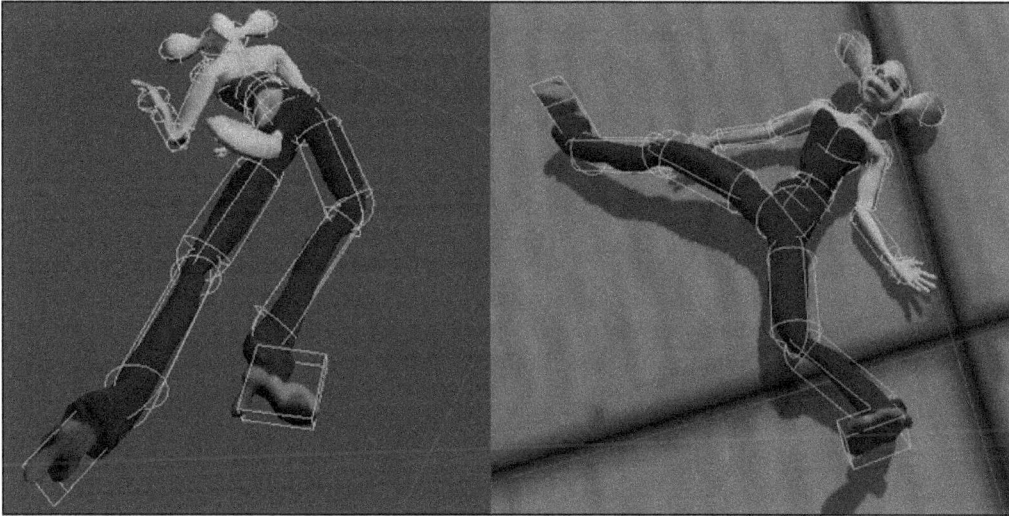

17. In our skeleton, by default, most of the neighboring pieces should acquire their collision pairs automatically. After fixing the spine link, a good test to see if things are performing okay would be to **Poke** the model and see whether the tail and chest stay facing in opposite directions when it falls to the floor (*Ctrl + RMB*). They shouldn't flip to the same direction ideally.

18. The final result of adding the rotation limits is shown in the provided asset *Packt_Character_Physics*, which is used with the feature complete asset *Packt_SkinTailFBX* in later recipes.

Adding a physics-driven tail to a key framed SkeletalMesh

Our model has a prominent tail, and it would be good to be able to use physics on this to control its behavior. The process also works with capes and long hair.

How to do it...

1. So the tail can work, back in 3ds Max we would need to add tail bones to our original model, which ideally would occur right at the original rigging and skinning stage. To speed things up, we will use an alternative model *Packt_SkinTail.PSK* with a tail already weighted to additional bones, and a corresponding AnimSet *Packt_SkinTailAnims*. In this replacement character, three tail bones have been skinned to the mesh after being linked to *b_Hips*.

2. To avoid wasting the work we did on your **physics asset** so far, find it in the Content Browser, right-click on it, and choose **Create a Copy**. Name the copy *CharPhysics_TailAdd* and open it. This asset uses the *Packt_Character* SkeletalMesh, which has no tail bones. Luckily there is a tool, in the PhAT Editor **Edit** menu called **Change Default Skeletal Mesh**. Highlight *Packt_SkinTail* in the Content Browser and then choose **Change Default Skeletal Mesh**.

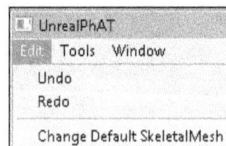

3. Click the **Add New Body** icon [🔵] and browse down the **Tree** to find *Bone1*, *Bone2*, and *Bone3*, which should be newly exposed at the bottom. Add them one by one (it is necessary to double-click them to add them), setting up for each an appropriately sized **Sphyl | Sphere**.

4. For these bones you could now turn on **Enable Continuous Collision Detection** and **Always Full Anim Weight** in their **Properties**. Hover the mouse over these commands to check their purpose, displayed in a tool tip. In essence, they ensure the tail is always controlled by physics, overriding any other animation and calculated continually, to reduce the risk of penetration with other bodies.

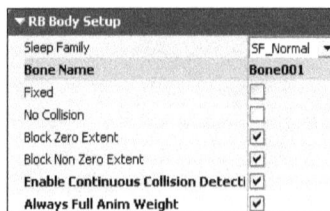

5. After adding the tail, it could be a good idea to go to the Properties of each tail bone and turn off the **Block Zero Extent** and **Block Non Zero Extent**. This will make UDK stop calculating weapon impacts or similar traces on the tail (given it is furry).

> Another case where this might be useful is if the character was wearing some kind of trailing scarf or had long hair controlled by similar bones. You wouldn't want a headshot if someone hit a trailing scarf. In this case, possibly a hit on the tail might hurt the character, but you wouldn't want to fire off into a full simulation if just the tip of the tail got hit. Instead it would perhaps be better to make a Morph target for a tail flick triggered in Kismet by Take Damage events, using an animation track for the Morph in a Matinee to fire off the effect.

6. For the tail bones, adjust the **Swing** angles and **Twist** to 30, and set the **Mass Scale** of the end of the tail to 2 to give it a little extra pull downwards. In the illustration below the tail bones are visible and hopefully in your own scene you can get the rag doll to be swung around by her tail in the preview window.

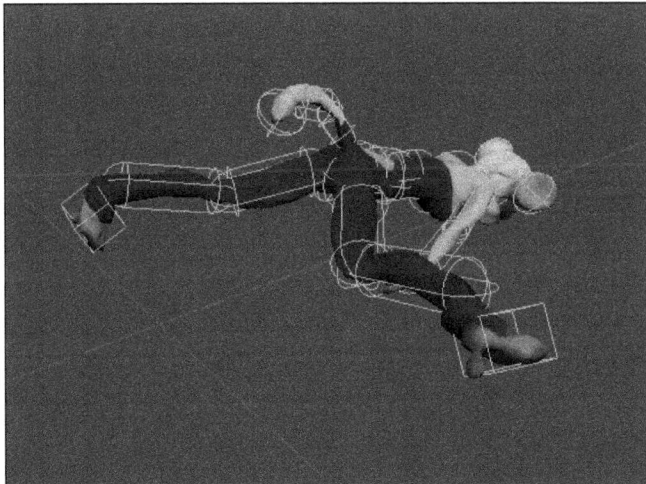

7. To see the result of all this in gameplay is our final step. Select the *b_Hips* bone and right-click on it in the view, and choose **Fix All Bodies Below**. This makes the entire body not respond to physics. In the scene, it will only play the specified sequence from the AnimSet. Select each tail bone and unfix them all by turning off their **Fix** check box in each bone's properties.

8. From the Content Browser, place an instance of the *Packt_SkinTail* SkeletalMesh in the scene and open its properties (*F4*). Look for, and turn on, these two tick boxes: **Skeletal Mesh Actor | Skeletal Mesh Component | Skeletal Mesh Component | Has Physics Asset Instance** and **Update Kinematic Bones from Animation**.

9. In the SkeletalMesh properties also assign the following: Anim Tree Template = *Packt_CharTree*; **PhysicsAsset** = *Packt_Character_Physics*; **AnimSet** = *Packt_ SkinTailAnims*. Refer to the illustration showing the **Properties** panel settings to · clarify all the elements you'll need to add.

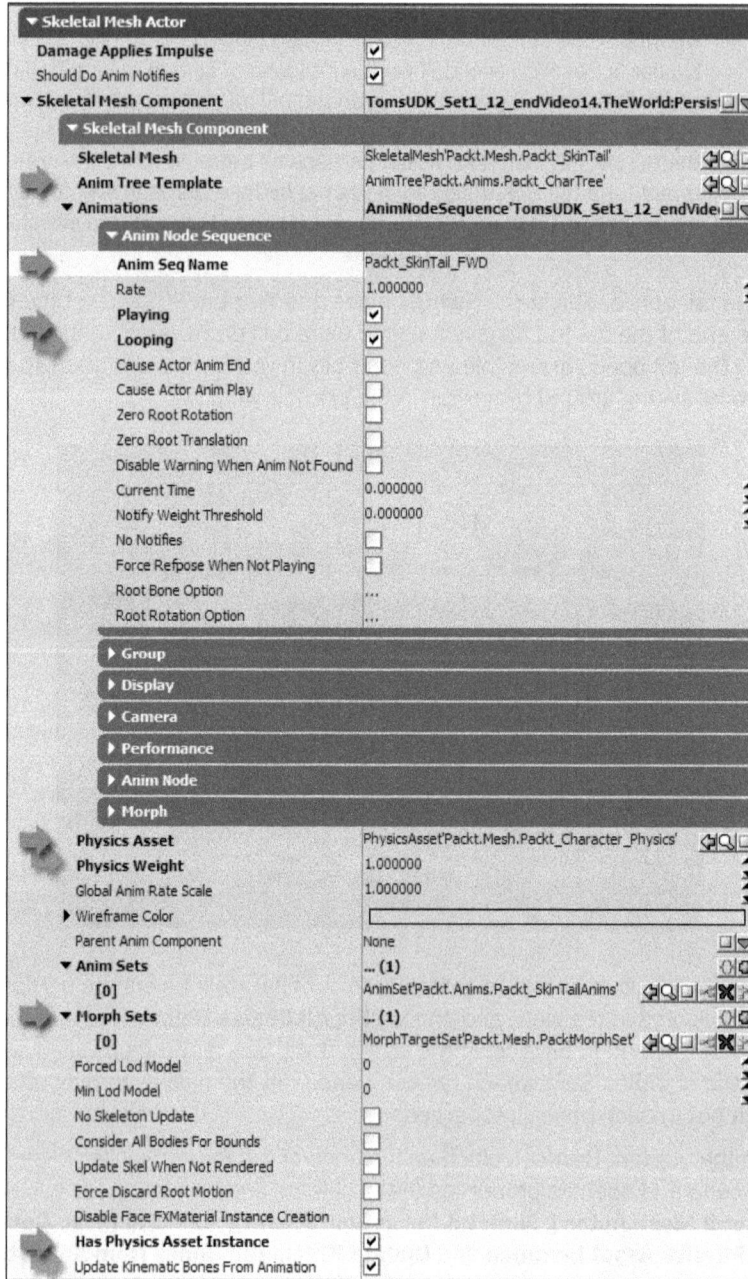

10. This screenshot shows the necessary inputs to furnish the NPC placed in the scene with assets to drive its animation. In **Skeletal Mesh Actor | Skeletal Mesh Component | Skeletal Mesh Component | Animations | Anim Node Sequence | Anim Seq Name** enter *Packt_SkinTail_FWD* (which is just the walking animation). Underneath, tick on **Playing** and **Looping**.

11. When you **PIE**, you should see the tail hanging down under physics rather than playing the key frames of the FWD sequence.

12. We're done, but to be fair, this is a testing situation. In an actual game, you would only want your character's tail to be controlled by physics when walking or the like, and possibly have the body switch to full physics if you happen to shoot at the character. Enabling these kinds of transitions is done in the character's class, and every case would be different. **Epic Games** admits that physical animation presents difficult challenges, and provides examples at `http://udn.epicgames.com/Three/PhysicalAnimation.html`.

Enabling the head to face in a given direction for tracking purposes

Animators can import any key frame animation as a sequence, but it is very hard to cover all the conditions whereby a part of a character will face or follow or track another moving object during gameplay. In the next lesson, we'll show how to use the AnimTree nodes to let you rotate a bone after assigning it a controller.

Getting ready

Fully load the *Packt* package by right-clicking on it in the **Content Browser Packages List**, then highlight the group **Anims**. Open the **AnimTree** *Packt_CharTree_AimStart*.

You can also find an example of **Aim** functionality in the *AT_CH_Human* AnimTree for upper body movement. For the case of the upper body on our character, we'll apply an offset control to the swimming physics blending. In the next screenshot, you can see our starting point where the *PHYS_Swimming* channel feeds a ***Forward*** directional sequence:

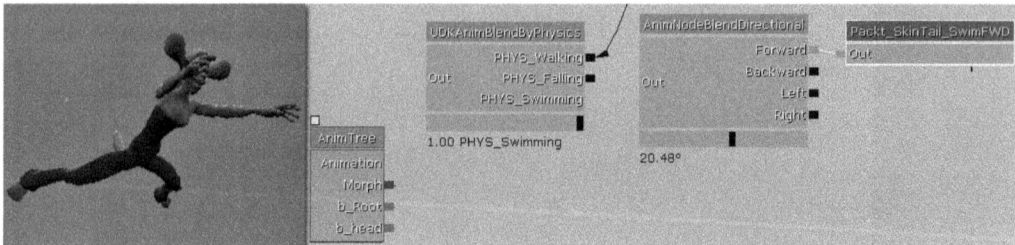

How to do it...

1. Right-click and add the node called **New Animation Node | AnimNodeAimOffset**. This creates an XY field that has nine directions which can be used to tell the character where to aim. You can also think of these as compass directions.

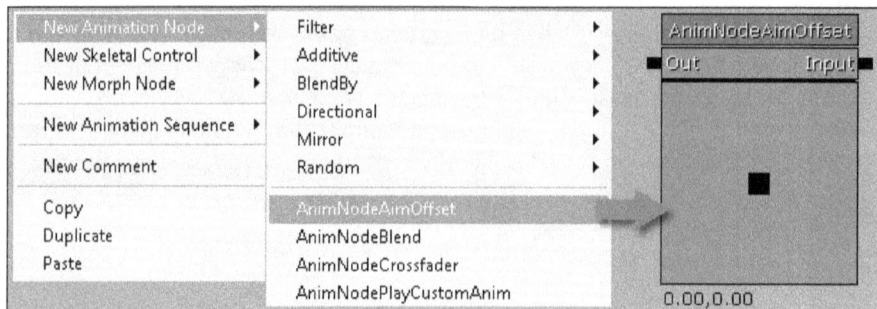

LU—LeftUp	CU—CenterUp	RU—RightUp
LC—LeftCenter	CC—CenterCenter	RC—RightCenter
LD—LeftDown	CD—CenterDown	RD—RightDown

2. Hook up the node to the *PHYS_Swimming* input of the **UDKAnimBlendByPhsyics** node, in between the existing **AnimNodeBlendDirectional** node which calls up *Packt_SkinTail_SwimFWD*.

3. In the properties of the new aim node, set the **Anim Node | Node Name** to *SwimLook*. This name can be called in code.

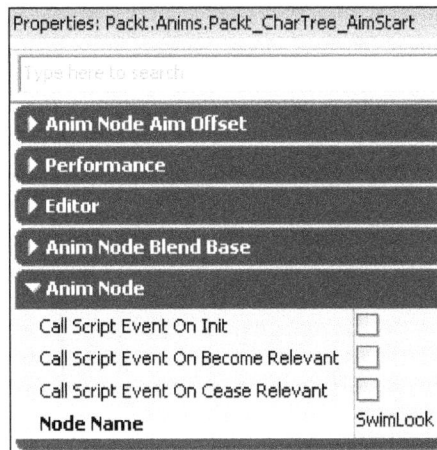

4. Double-click on the label of the node. A special editor will open, the **AimOffset Editor**. Here, we need to create a **Profile**. In the **Profile** section, click **New** and call your profile *SwimLookProfile*. An example *SwimLookProfile* is in the provided content *SwimLook_SwimLookProfile.AOP*.

5. For each **Aim Direction** you need to add bones that will have a set rotation offset, which can be defined in the **AimOffset Editor's** view using a rotate widget. It may help to turn off **World Space Widget** under the **Bone Rotation XYZ** fields while rotating the bone. Note that you can **Save** the settings in the profile to file and load this on any **AnimTree** with a similar skeleton and an **AimOffset** node.

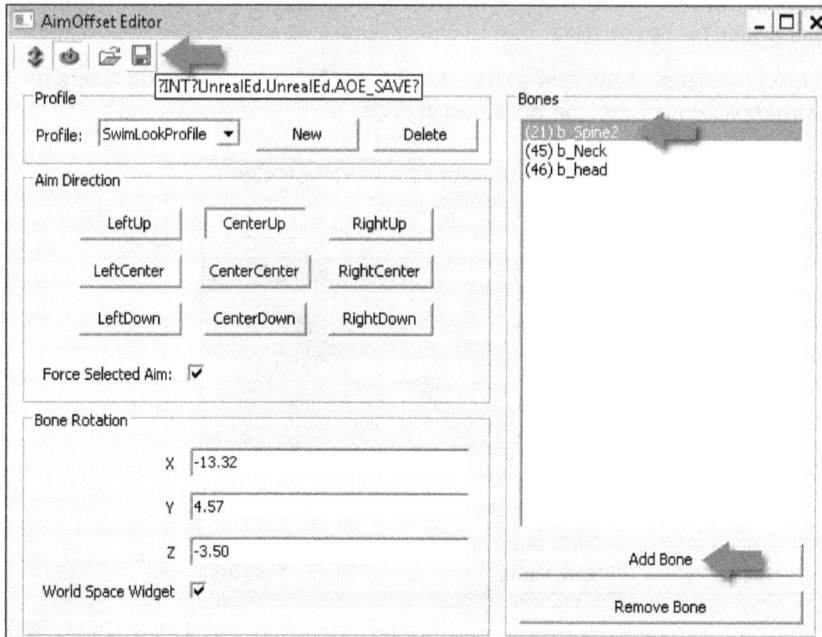

6. Since we're just going to animate bones directly, select **CenterUp**, then press **Add Bone**, and from the list, choose *b_head*. Don't worry about the numerical values, just rotate the figure using the widget in the preview window. You may need to move the floating editor away from the preview window.

7. Using the rotation widget, tilt the head back, looking up. You may also want to similarly add *b_Neck* to increase the tilt back effect.

8. Now set an appropriate rotation for each bone for each of the remaining eight directions by highlighting *LeftUp*, *RightUp*, and so on. Each time you switch from direction to direction the character rotations will update.

> Note that for our purposes it isn't necessary, but it is great to know also that there is not only a rotation widget but a translation widget, accessed by the first icons in the **AimOffset Editor**. This could be useful for adding shimmy moves for example in a dance, or dodges. Normally an aim is controlled by the player input (the mouse direction you drag as you are running about in the game). It is also possible to associate the aim direction to an object in the scene, again through coding.

9. Once you have your directions set, you can waggle the **AimOffset** *SwimLook* node's XY slider to check things look alright. You can always go back and adjust things later on. Generally speaking, the direction the character will look is dictated by activity in the game, not the node's little field, so instead tick on the **AnimNodeAimOffset | Force Aim Dir** to make the direction come from the **ForcedAimDir** enumerator, which is driven by code. For the next recipe, the artist enabling *HeadLook* to be accessed by the programmer is as far as we'll go. An example AnimTree including the completed **AimOffset** is in *Packt.Anims.Packt_CharTree_Aim*.

Setting a LookAt target for head rotation in code

Our model can look in an XY cone of rotation while swimming, but so far we haven't associated this looking behavior with any controller in gameplay. Normally, either the player controls the look, or the look is controlled by an object in the scene dynamically, using a **LookAt** control.

How to do it...

1. Fully load the *Packt* package by right-clicking on it in the Content Browser **Packages List**, then highlight the group **Anims**. Create a copy of the AnimTree *Packt_CharTree*. Call the copy *MyTreeLookat*.

2. Select the main ***AnimTree*** node and right-click on it and choose **Add SkelControl Chain** using *b_head*. Right-click on the canvas and choose **New Skeletal Control | SkelControlLookAt**.

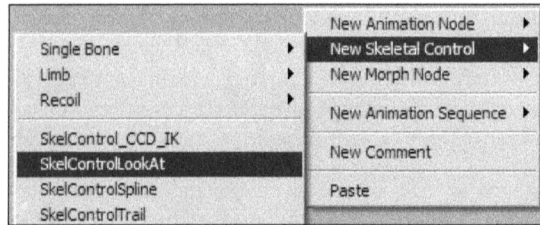

3. In the Properties of the new ***SkelControlLookAt*** expand the **Controller** section and in **Control Name** type *HeadControl*. This is a name we'll reference in code. Underneath the **Control Name**, set the **Control Strength** to 1.0 so that there will be a visible effect.

4. In the **AnimTree** Editor, set the slider weight of the ***HeadControl*** node to 1.0 and hook the **In** nub of this to the *b_Head* nub you added to the ***AnimTree*** node.

5. In the ***SkelControlLookAt*** Properties expand the **LookAt** section and set **Target Location X**=20, **Y**=0, and **Z**=45. Set the **Target Location Space** to *BCS_WorldSpace*. Set the **Look At Axis** to *AXIS_Y*. Set the **Up Axis** to *AXIS_None*. Set the **Target Space Bone Name** to *b_Head*. Tick on the checkbox for **Invert Look At Axis**. All of this is shown in the next screenshot.

What we are doing here is telling the character's head where it's able to focus its attention. In the preview window your character should now be looking at a little blue diamond widget just ahead of itself. You can move the widget directly in the viewport.

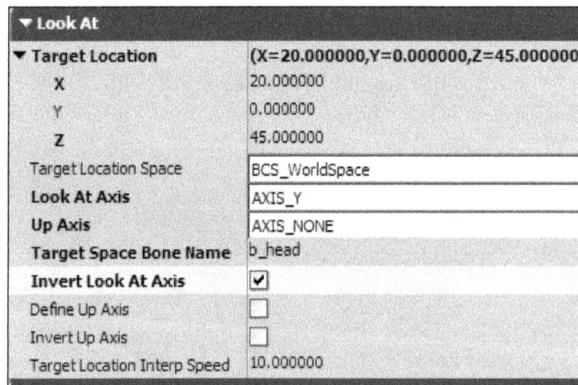

6. To avoid the head flopping too much, we'll now add **Limits** to the possible head rotation. Expand the Properties section **Limit**. Tick the checkbox **Enable Limit**. Tick the checkbox **Show Limit**, and you should see a green cone which represents the space the head can look within (which is a bit like the aim space we covered in the prior part of this recipe). **Show Limit** just displays in the Preview window so you know what you're doing. Turn off **Allow Rotation Z** (this prevents the character looking up and down). This is shown here:

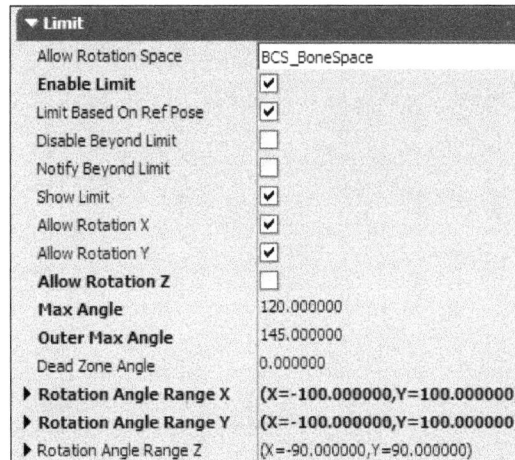

7. In the property **Limit | Max Angle**, and also set the **Outer Max Angle** to 145. Set the **Rotation Angle Range X** between -100 and 100. Do the same for **Rotation Angle Range Y**. This allows the head to turn a little more than the defaults. Don't set **Rotation Angle Range Z**, since you'll want to make sure that the head turning works around side to side axis first. It can always be set later on.

8. Save your package and close UDK.

9. Now you need to code a custom class that extends *UTPawn.UC*. You should already know how to make UDK use your custom class by setting configuration and recompiling. If not, see the earlier recipe in this chapter called *Configuring your character to use your AnimTree*.

10. Create a new file in `C:\UDK\~\Development\Src\MyGame\Classes` called *MyPawnLookAt.UC*. Using ConTEXT, enter the following code in the file:

```
class MyPawnLookAt extends UTPawn;

var SkelControlLookAt SkelControlLookAt;

simulated event PostInitAnimTree(SkeletalMeshComponent
SkeletalMeshLookAt)
{
  Super.PostInitAnimTree(SkeletalMeshLookAt);
  if (SkeletalMeshLookAt == Mesh)
```

```
    {
      SkelControlLookAt =
        SkelControlLookAt(mesh.FindSkelControl('HeadControl'));
    }
}

simulated event Destroyed()
{
 Super.Destroyed();

 SkelControlLookAt = None;
}

simulated event Tick(float DeltaTime)
{
 local PlayerController PlayerController;

 Super.Tick(DeltaTime);

 if (SkelControlLookAt != None)
 {
  PlayerController = GetALocalPlayerController();

  if (PlayerController != None && PlayerController.Pawn != None)
  {
   SkelControlLookAt.TargetLocation =
     PlayerController.Pawn.Location
       + (Vect(0.f, 0.f, 45.f)); //+45 in Z
  }
 }
}

DefaultProperties
{
Begin Object class=SkeletalMeshComponent
 Name=SkeletalMeshLookAt
 SkeletalMesh=SkeletalMesh'Packt.Mesh.Packt_SkinTailFBX'
 AnimSets(0)=AnimSet'Packt.Anims.Packt_SkinTailAnims'
 //This assigns the AnimTree you've just been working on.
  AnimTreeTemplate=AnimTree'Yourfolder.Group.MyTreeLookAt'
 PhysicsAsset=PhysicsAsset'Packt.Mesh.Packt_Character_Physics'
 bEnableSoftBodySimulation=True
 bSoftBodyAwakeonStartup=True
 bAcceptsLights=True
End Object
Mesh=SkeletalMeshLookAt
Components.Add(SkeletalMeshLookAt)
Physics=PHYS_Walking

DrawScale=1
CameraScale=30
}
```

11. Reloading UDK will force you to recompile scripts. Once that's working, load _Packt_03_SkelControlLookAt_Start.UDK_, where we'll cause a Bot to be spawned at a PathNode by touching a visible Trigger.

> **Bots** are variously described as pawns, AI, enemies, NPCs. They are really just another actor or game object spawned in the level. Thinking this way, it would be easy, using the LookAt skelcontrol script, to create a turret which turns to face the player by assigning a different SkeletalMesh with a weapon socket. Then all you'd have to do in Kismet would be to give it a weapon inventory and set a **Start Firing At** action with a suitable target.

12. Select the Trigger actor in the scene then open Kismet [K].

13. Right-click in Kismet and choose **New Event Using Trigger | Touch**.

14. Right-click near it and choose **New Action | Actor | Actor Factory**.

15. In the scene, select the PathNode actor, which is there to show pawns the paths they can traverse. Back in Kismet, right-click on the pink **Spawn Point** connector of the **Actor Factory** and choose **New Object Var Using PathNode_0**.

16. Right-click on the pink **Spawned** connector of the **Actor Factory** and choose **Create New Object Variable**.

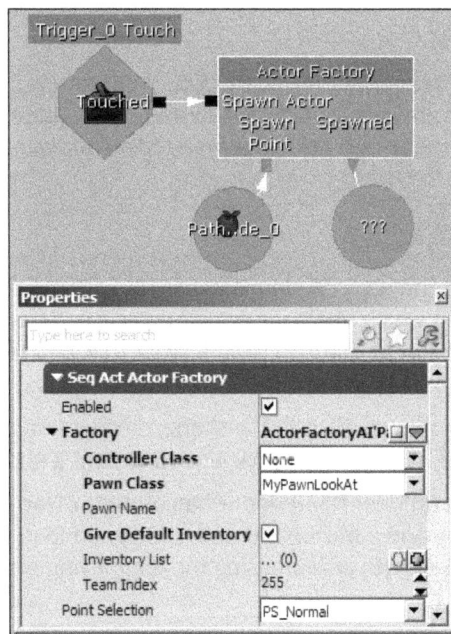

17. In the **Actor Factory** properties, click the blue triangle icon [▼] in the **Factory** channel, and from the list choose *UTActorFactoryAI*. Then expand **Factory** and set the **Controller Class** to *None* and the **Pawn Class** to *MyPawnLookAt*.

18. In the editor go to the **View** menu, choose **World Properties**, and expand **Game Type**. There, ensure that **Game Type for PIE** is specified as *MyGame*. Now when you **PIE** and spawn the Bot from the Trigger its head should face you as you walk around it (within the **Rotation Angle Limit** we set in the AnimTree so that it won't break its neck).

19. An example scene is in provided: *Packt_03_SkelControlLookAt_DEMO.UDK*. Observe that in this case, if you jump up and down in front of the Bot then the Bot will look up and down with you. This is because in the AnimTree used, which is *Packt.Mesh. Packt_CharTreeLookAt*, the **Limit** properties of the **SkelControlLookAt**, include **Allow Rotation Z**.

Setting morph weights in code

In this recipe we'll compare setting Morph target values on a pawn through UnrealScript with doing so on a **SkeletalMeshMAT** using Matinee. This will bridge us between the previous lesson and the next one, which is also about character handling in Matinee. Both the examples in this lesson use the MorphTargets included in the FBX SkeletalMesh asset, which in the case of *Packt_SkinTailFBX*, our character, shrink each of her rather large ears.

Getting ready

Load the scene *Packt_03_MatineeMorph_Start.UDK*. This already includes a placed SkeletalMesh asset, and its preview assets have already been added to save time, since we already did similar steps in the recipe *Attachments to SkeletalMeshes without using sockets*.

How to do it...

1. In the scene, select the actor *SkeletalMeshMAT_0*. This is a special instance of a **SkeletalMesh** asset which has been added using the right-click command: **Add SkeletalMeshMAT: Packt_SkinTailFBX**. Press *Ctrl + B* to highlight the asset in the browser and try assigning another one the same way.

2. We'll keep with the actor already in the scene, since it has been scaled up 1.25 times bigger, and also has its properties provisioned. Select it and press *F4*.

3. Note that the **SkeletalMeshComponent** has an **Anim Tree Template**, a **Physics Asset**, an **Anim Set**, and a **Morph Set** asset assigned to it. Find the **Morph Set** by expanding **Morph Sets>[0]** and pressing the magnifying glass icon [🔍].

4. Now double-click the highlighted asset *Packt_SkinTailMorphSet* and double-click it. The **AnimSet** Editor will open, showing the SkeletalMesh *Packt_SkinTailFBX*. On the left panel you will see sliders for the **MorphTargets**. Make sure the ears on the model shrink when the sliders are set to 1. These are preview sliders only. The real control for the **Morphs** come from the **AnimTree**.

5. In the Browser, highlight *Packt_CharTreeLookAt*, right-click on it and choose **Create A Copy**. Call the copy *Yourfolder.Anims.MyCharTreeMorph*. This already has nodes that create controls for the ear morph targets. Adjust the sliders under the nodes *EarR* and *EarL* to ensure they work. Click on the node *EarShrink_R* (which references the morph target in the **Morph Target Set**). In its properties, in the **Morph Node Base | Node Name** type *EarRight*. Likewise, click on the node *EarShrink_L* and in its property **Morph Node Base | Node Name** type *EarLeft*. These are strings that will be used by both Matinee and UnrealScript to drive the target weights.

6. Save the AnimTree, and open Kismet [ᴷ]. Here you will see a **Level Loaded** event. Next to it hold *M* and click to add a new **Matinee**. Open the Matinee editor by double-clicking on the **Matinee**.

7. In the dark gray panel on the left-hand side, right-click and choose **Add New Empty Group**. With the track *NewGroup* highlighted, look at its properties panel, and notice a channel there for **Group Anim Sets**. Press **Add a New Item** [⊚] with the *AnimSet Packt.Anims.Packt_SkinTailAnims* highlighted in the Content Browser. This morph example doesn't require AnimSets, but it is good to add the AnimSet because later it's easy to forget if you start increasing the Matinee tracks. With the *NewGroup* track highlighted, right-click and choose **Add New Morph Weight**. This sets a track we can add keyframes to.

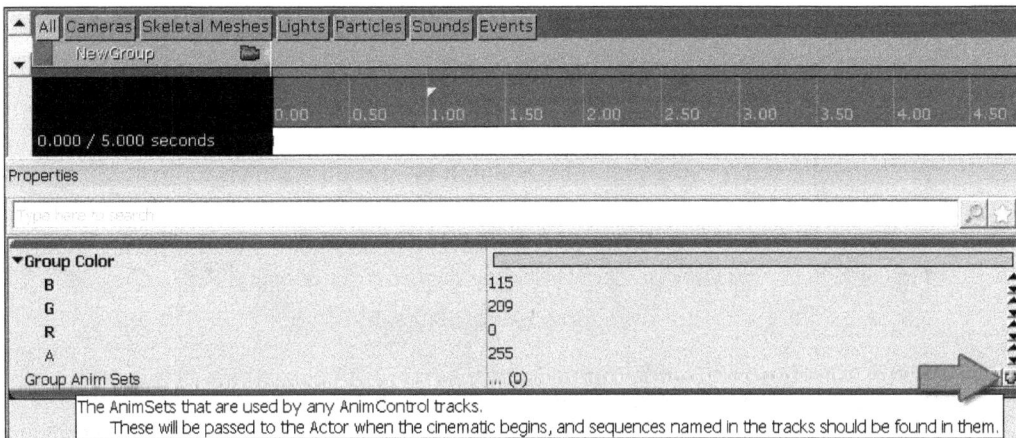

8. Highlight the new track, and in its **Properties**, in the **Morph Node Name** channel enter *EarRight*.

9. Add another **Morph Weight** track, and this time give it a **Morph Node Name** of *EarLeft*.

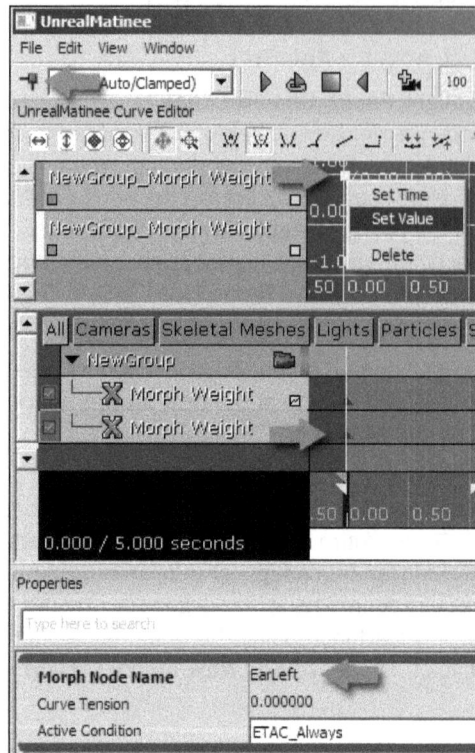

10. Key both the tracks at 0s by selecting each and pressing *Enter* or the icon [➕], then right-click on the keyframe and set a value of 1.0, as in the above screenshot.

11. At the moment, the **SkeletalMeshMAT** ears should always be small. If you like, you can key different values along the **Morph Weight** tracks to obtain animation of the ears.

12. Close the Matinee Editor and connect the *Level Loaded* event to the *Matinee* action's **Play** nub. In the *Matinee* properties tick the checkbox for **Looping. PIE** to check it.

13. Note this method will only work on a **SkeletalMeshMAT**, not a spawned pawn.

Driving morph targets on a pawn in UnrealScript

1. You've seen how the AnimTree **Node Name** is called on in the **Morph Weight** track in *Matinee* for the **SkeletalMeshMAT** assigned to it. This is really what we'll leverage in UnrealScript now for the pawn.

2. Close UDK and open ConTEXT. There, open `C:\UDK\~\Development\Src\MyGame\Classes\MyPawnLookAt.UC` (or use *MyPawnLookAt.UC* from the provided content if you have not yet done the previous recipe).

3. Rename a copy of it *MyPawnLookAtMorph.UC* in the same folder.

4. Within the existing code we need to enter three things. First, change the first line to the following, so the new class name matches the file name.

   ```
   class MyPawnLookAtMorph extends UTPawn;
   ```

5. Second, so we can make the code talk to the morph targets specifically, under the line below starting with `var SkelControlLookAt`... type the following:

   ```
   var MorphNodeWeight   EarRightMorphNode;
   var MorphNodeWeight   EarLeftMorphNode;
   ```

6. Third, above the code starting with `simulated event Destroyed()` type the following:

   ```
   simulated function FindMorphNode()
   {
   //Notice the reference below to EarRight, the node name we set in
   the AnimTree.
     EarRightMorphNode == MorphNodeWeight(Mesh.
   FindMorphNode('EarRight'));
     if(EarRightMorphNode == none)
     {
     }
     EarRightMorphNode.SetNodeWeight(1.0f);

   //Notice the reference below to EarLeft, the node name we set in
   the AnimTree.
     EarLeftMorphNode == MorphNodeWeight(Mesh.
   FindMorphNode('EarLeft'));
     if(EarLeftMorphNode == none)
     {
     }
     EarLeftMorphNode.SetNodeWeight(1.0f);
   }
   ```

7. Press *Ctrl + R*, the **Replace** tool. In the **Find** field type *SkeletalMeshLookAt* and in the **Replace** field type *SkeletalMeshLookAtMorph*. Press **Replace All**. This will avoid a class mismatch with the existing class *MyPawnLookAt*, which also uses *SkeletalMeshLookAt*.

8. There is one extra step. At the moment the class is using a Packt AnimTree, not the one you copied and adjusted to include **Morph Node Names** referenced in the code. So in the `DefaultProperties` part of the code replace the line `AnimTreeTemplate=AnimTree'Packt.Anims.Packt_CharTreeLookAt'` with `AnimTreeTemplate=AnimTree'Yourfolder.Anims.MyCharTreeMorph'`, being careful to match the asset name of the AnimTree you edited in UDK before.

9. Save the new class, and compile the changes by restarting UDK. Sparing typos, you should be able to reload the map *Packt_03_MatineeMorphDEMO.UDK*. Open Kismet and look in the properties of the **Actor Factory** already there. In its **Factory | Pawn Class** access the class list [▾] and replace the current entry *MyPawnLookAt* with *MyPawnLookAtMorph*. Then PIE to test it out.

10. In this lesson we handled Morphs through Matinee and through code. In the next lesson, we will direct AnimTree sequences from within Matinee.

Calling up SkeletalMesh animation using Matinee

In Kismet, a **Matinee** action can be used to fire off events in a time-based manner, and an **AnimNotify** is an AnimTree node that lets us associate AnimTree content with *Matinee* tracks. For example, you could have a looping animation for a SkeletalMesh walking or idling, then use a Trigger in the scene to fire off a **Matinee** which swaps in a falling animation to replace the idle. A **Matinee** can also be used to control Morph target keys.

Getting ready

Load the map template *Midday Lighting*.

How to do it...

1. Right-click in the scene and add a Trigger actor on the ground. In its properties turn off the check box for **Display | Hidden** so it shows during gameplay.

2. In the Content Browser, locate and right-click on the AnimTree *Packt_CharTreeSlotStart* and choose **Create a Copy** and call the copy *Yourname.Mesh.TestSlotTree*.

3. Double-click the result, then right-click in the canvas and choose **New Animation Node | AnimNodeSlot**.

4. Place this in between the **UDKAnimationBlendByPhysics** node and the **UDKAnimBlendByIdle** node, as shown in the next screenshot.

5. An extra input has to be added to the **AnimNodeSlot** by right-clicking and choosing **Add Input**. In the past, an **AnimSequenceNode** would need to go into the **Channel 0** and **Channel 1**, but now it is no longer necessary to set this. We are going to drive a sequence into these channels in a Matinee. **SlotName** is not a very inspiring name for a node, but keep it as such, since we need to reference it later. The name *SlotName* appears in the node's properties under **Anim Node | Node Name**.

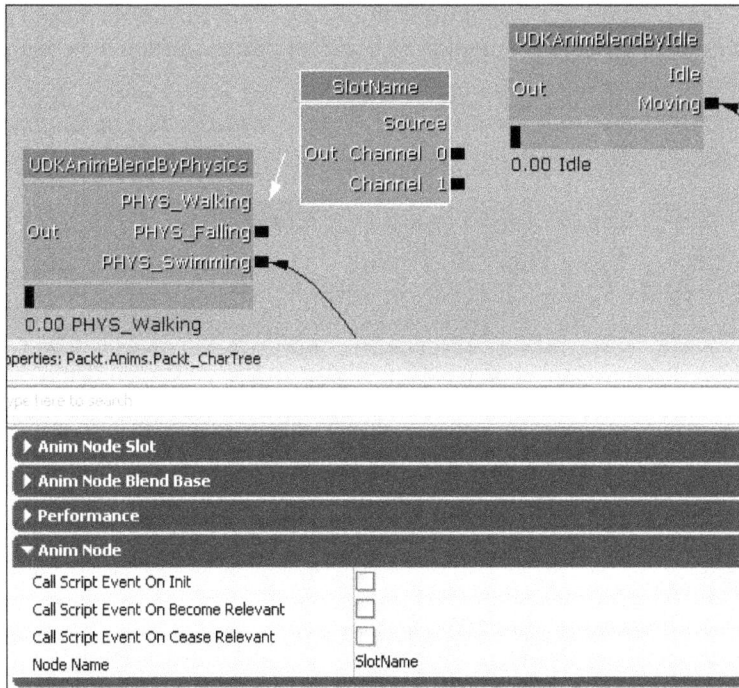

6. In the Content Browser, find *Packt_SkinTailFBX*. Highlight it and right-click in the scene and choose **Add SkeletalMeshMAT: Packt.Mesh.Packt_SkinTailFBX**. This differs from just dragging and dropping the asset, because there are actually three kinds of SkeletalMesh actors that you can place in the scene. The **MAT** suffix means this actor can have blending animation driven by Matinee. Set the scale of the actor to 1.25 and ensure it is standing on the ground.

7. With the *Packt_SkinTail* actor selected, press *F4* and add the necessary **Anim Tree Template** *MyCharTreeSlot* (that you just created), the **AnimSet** *Packt_SkinTailAnims*, and also the **Physics Asset** *Packt_Character_Physics* and **Morph target set** *PacktMorphSet* if you wish, as in earlier recipes covering the SkeletalMesh placed directly in the scene.

8. Note that in the **SkeletalMeshMAT** properties there is no channel for naming an animation sequence to play. Instead, this is done in the Kismet.

9. In the **SkeletalMeshMAT** properties, under the **Movement** section, set the **Physics** method to *PHYS_Interpolating*.

10. In the scene, select the Trigger actor. In Kismet [K], right-click and choose the **New Event Using Trigger_0 | Touch** event using the Trigger. Set its **Max Trigger Count** property to 0.

11. Next to the ***Trigger_0 Touch*** event hold *M* and click to add a new ***Matinee***, and tick its **Looping** property. Connect the **Touched** nub to the **Play** nub, highlighted below.

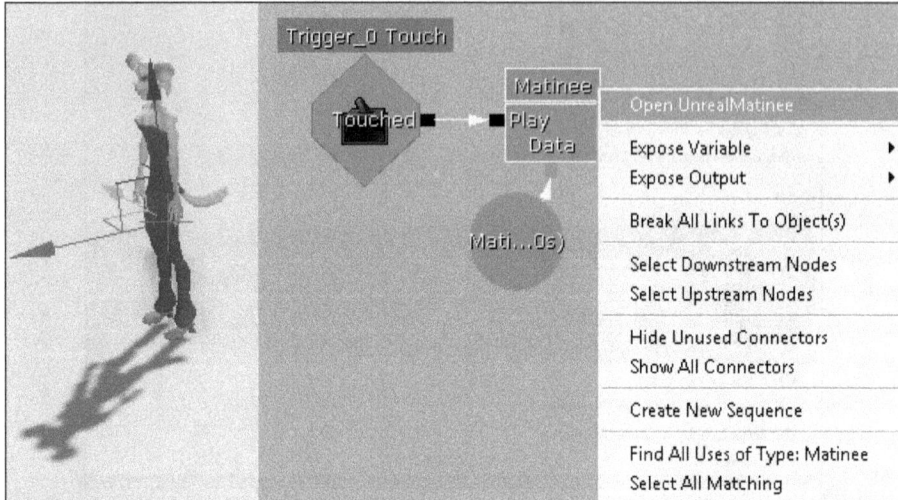

12. As shown here, with *Packt_SkinTail* selected in the scene, right-click the **Matinee** action and choose **Open UnrealMatinee**. In the Matinee Editor's tracks panel, right-click and choose **New Empty Group**. Call this *AnimTrack*.

13. In the Content Browser, highlight the *AnimSet Packt_SkinTailAnims*. Back inside the Matinee Editor, click on the *AnimTrack* we just added then look to its **Properties** panel; you'll notice there is a channel **Group AnimSets**. Press the add entry icon [⊕] to add *Packt_SkinTailAnims* here. If you don't, you won't be able to add animation sequences to the timeline later.

14. Right-click on *AnimTrack* and choose **Add New Movement Track**. Again, right-click on *AnimTrack* and choose **Add AnimControl Track**. You will be prompted to select amongst **AnimSlot** nodes in your **AnimTree**. Ours is *SlotName*. If it's not already there, type *SlotName* in the properties of the **Anim: SlotName** track.

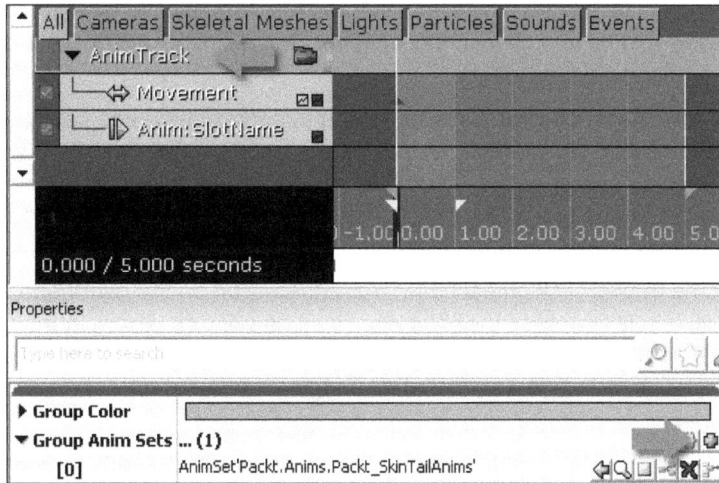

15. With the **Anim: SlotName** track highlighted, press *Enter* to place a key on the timeline or click the icon [✦].

16. You will be prompted to choose a sequence from a pop-up list based on your **Group AnimSet** *Packt_SkinTailAnims*. Choose *Packt_SkinTailPunch*, which is an attacking move.

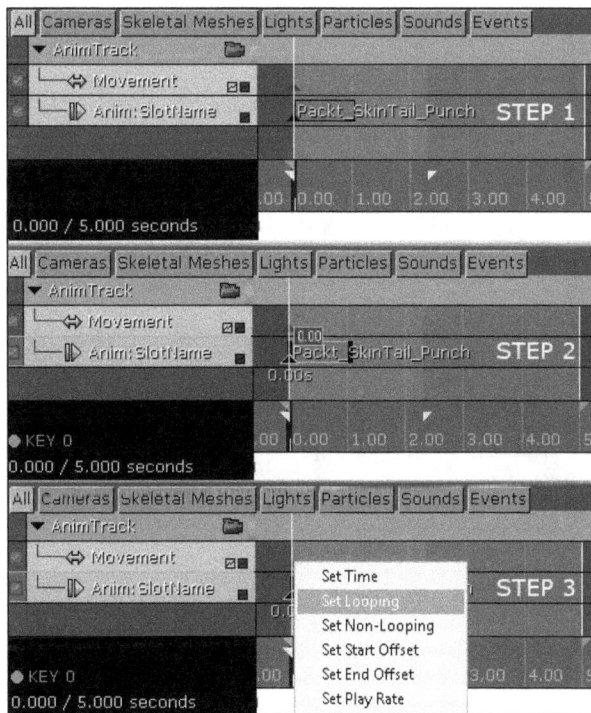

17. You'll notice it fill the timeline with a colored bar. As shown here, right-click on the key in timeline at 0.0s and choose **Set Looping**. The solid bar will fill the timeline with cycles of the current sequence.

18. Add another **Anim Control Track** and key it to add from the pop-up list of animation sequences *Packt_SkinTailKick*. You can't add more because the AnimTree node **SlotName** has only been given two **Channels**. Notice the kick animation is the same base length on the timeline as the punch animation. Right-click on the timeline key at 0.0s and choose **Set Looping**, as before.

19. To edit the tracks, click on each tiny gray square icon on the right-hand side of the track labels to access their **Curves**. The icon will turn yellow. In the previous screenshot, the Curve Editor, you'll see the track's curve. Each curve at the moment displays a line. Adding keys on it, and changing their values produces curves, hence the name.

20. At about 1.00 on the *Punch* curve/line press *Ctrl + LMB* to add a new key. After that hold *Ctrl* and *drag* the key to set a value of 1. You can also right-click on any key and choose **Set Value** to enter a value. Repeat this along the timeline to create an ease in-ease out bell curve for the punch. Create a similar curve by adding keys to the *Kick* track, but offset it so one turns off while the other turns off. Your result should resemble the next screenshot. For timing, check the beginning and ending frames of the looping sequences. PIE to verify the touched Trigger fires off the animation. *Packt_03_AnimTrackDEMO.UDK* shows the result.

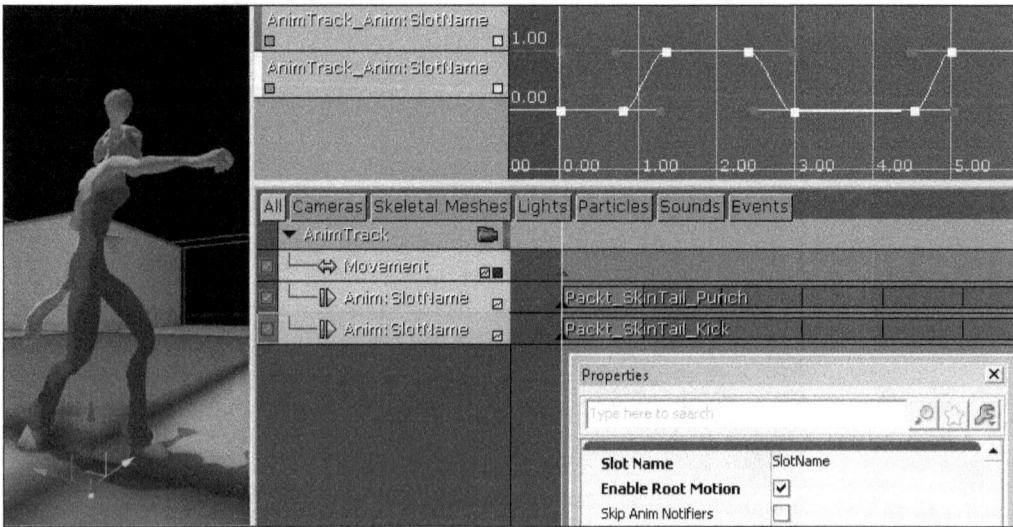

Associating sounds with character moves in Matinee

An action appears more lively if a sound goes with it. When you are playing a character animation from Matinee, there is no player input to cue the animated SkeletalMesh as to what sound to play, so whenever a sound is needed we'll have to provide a cue through a sound track or event track on the timeline.

Getting ready

Load the scene *Packt_03_SoundTrack_Start.UDK*. This map continues from the end of the last recipe. Note the added particle emitter attached in its **Attachment** property to the *b_LeftHand* of the *SkeletalMesh Packt_SkinTail*.

How to do it...

Associating sounds with animation using Matinee sound tracks and event tracks

1. Quite often, to open a *Matinee*, users will open Kismet and then open the *Matinee* that they want to edit from there. There's another way to get there. Click the **Open UnrealMatinee** icon [▤] next to the Kismet icon in the editor. What this does is expose any single *Matinee* in the scene (which is the case here) or offer a list of *Matinee* actions to choose from. It's good to add **Obj Comment** names to your *Matinee* actions because the names show up on the ends of the list entries.

2. Having pressed the icon [▤] you'll get the warning shown next. Avoid this by selecting the **SkeletalMeshMAT** actor in the scene, pressing *F4*, then changing the **Movement | Physics** property to **PHYS_Interpolating**.

   > UnrealMatinee detected the following warnings:
   >
   > WARNING: Tracks [Movement Track] in Group AnimTrack are associated with Actor SkeletalMeshActorMAT_2 whose Physics mode is not set to PHYS_Interpolating. This object may not animate correctly in game! Consider changing the physics type to PHYS_Interpolating.

3. The Matinee Editor will open whether or not you fix the issue. There, right-click under *AnimTrack* and choose **Add New Director Group**. Highlight the **DirGroup** track and right-click and choose **Add New Sound Track**.

4. Highlight the cue *PacktWavs.Cue.Impact_Cue* in the Content Browser.

5. Move the time slider along to where the graphs for the two moves cross, and add a key to the **Sound Track**. *Impact_Cue* should appear on the timeline. A colored bar represents its active duration. Adjust the onset time of the key by right-clicking at the start of the sound cue on the timeline and choosing **Set Time**. Alternatively you can also hold *Ctrl* and drag on the key to move the cue.

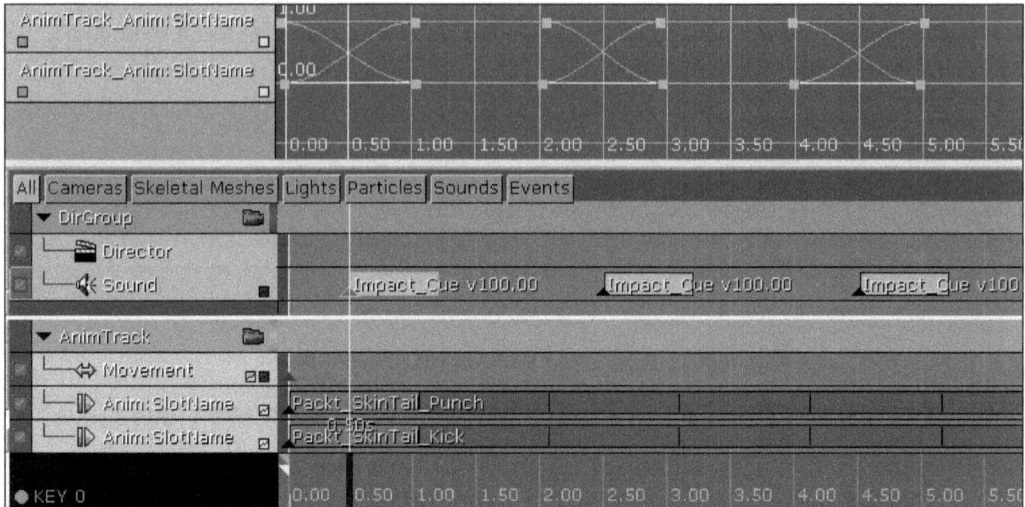

6. By right-clicking the key of the *Impact_Cue* you can set the **Sound Volume**, set the **Sound Pitch**, or locate the asset in the Content Browser, which is handy in a large scene.

7. PIE and check whether the sound plays at the right time.

8. That is one way to add sound. Another is to add an event track by right-clicking the **DirGroup** track and choosing **New Event Track**. When you key an **Event** track you can add a named key, as shown here:

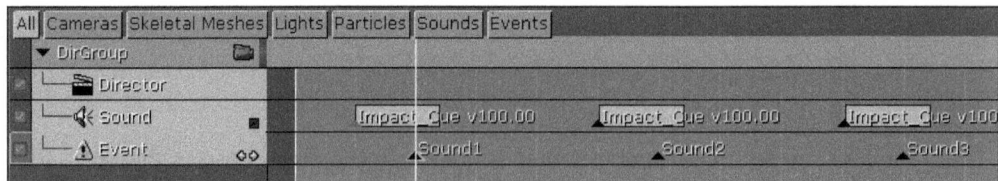

9. The keys will appear as connectors on the **_Matinee_** action in Kismet, and you can hold S and click to add a **_Play Sound_** to hook up to each one. For its **Play Sound** property, select a **SoundCue** in the content browser then click assign [⬧].

10. Using **Event** tracks instead of **Sound** tracks lets you add things other than sound such as particle effect toggles. Load the file _Packt_03_SoundTrackDEMO.UDK_ and PIE to see a result based on both approaches.

How it works...

The previous step states you can make an **Event** track control a sound. The **Event** track keys are set on the timeline in Matinee Editor and then feed out of the **_Matinee_** into Kismet actions. You don't have to fire off sounds from an event; it allows you to hook up any action which you want to occur based on the **_Matinee_** timeline playing. In the next screenshot, besides sounds, we also have a particle emitter attached to the girl's hand. It is good to give visual and audio cues to events so the player is alerted to them.

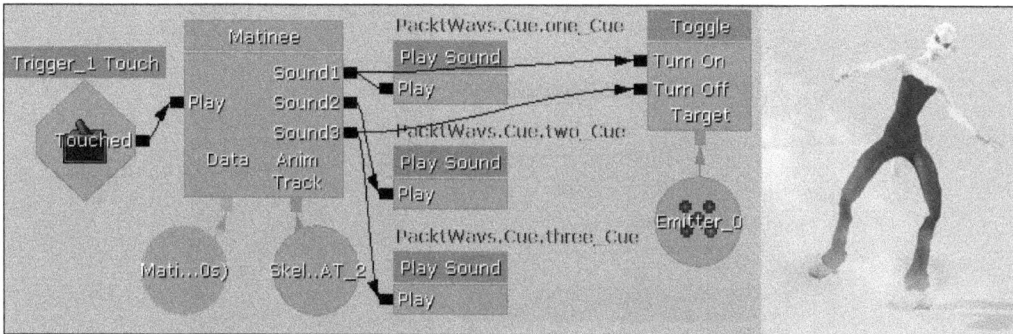

Sound for non-Matinee controlled animation

In the last example we fired off sounds from the **_Matinee_** timeline, but this doesn't allow us to influence the playing of sounds such as player or Bot footsteps that will occur every time an animation sequence plays. In this recipe we will assign sounds directly with animation sequences, allocating them so they are tracked by the AnimSet associated with the character.

How to do it...

1. In the Content Browser, find and open the AnimSet *Packt_SkinTailAnimsAudio*. This is just a test copy of the AnimSet that we've been using so far. Once it opens, highlight *Packt_SkinTailFWD* in the animation sequences list. Look down to the properties panel, and click on the **Anim Sequence** tab. Here you can expand **Anim Sequence** and see a channel called **Notifies**.

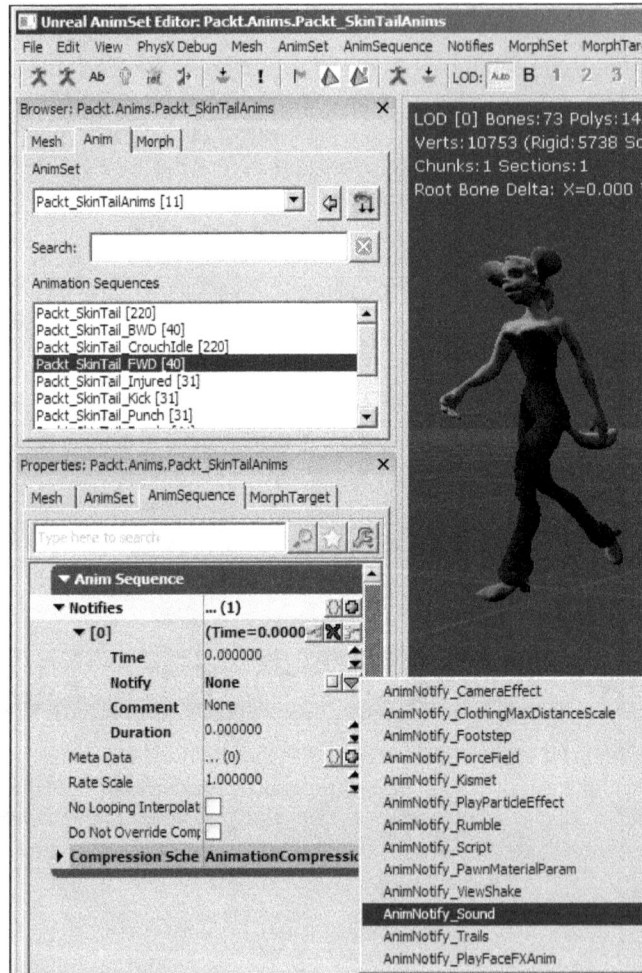

2. Click on the add entry icon [⚙] and a **[0]** will appear that you can expand. Click its blue triangle [▽] to select the kind of notify you want to add. For footsteps it might be an **AnimNotify_Sound** but you may equally require splash particles coming off the feet for watery levels through the use of **AnimNotify_PlayParticleEffect**. As shown here, in this case, go with **AnimNotify_Sound**.

3. You will now be able to assign an asset from the Content Browser. In this case, choosing a footstep cue would be helpful. I chose a default one: *A_Character_Footsteps.FootSteps.A_Character_Footstep_DefaultCue*.

4. You will also want to set the **Time** when the footstep will be fired during the sequence. Once this is set, you can drag the marker in the preview to change it.

5. Set the bone the Notify is related to (especially if you are sending off particle effects, as for sound it doesn't matter much). In this case I used *b_LeftToe* as that is the end of the leg chain, and at 0.0s that is the model's ground contacting joint.

6. You can add another item to the **Notifies** list by clicking the add entry icon [🔘] again, and repeating these steps to create a right foot step sound for *b_RightToe* at about 0.7s.

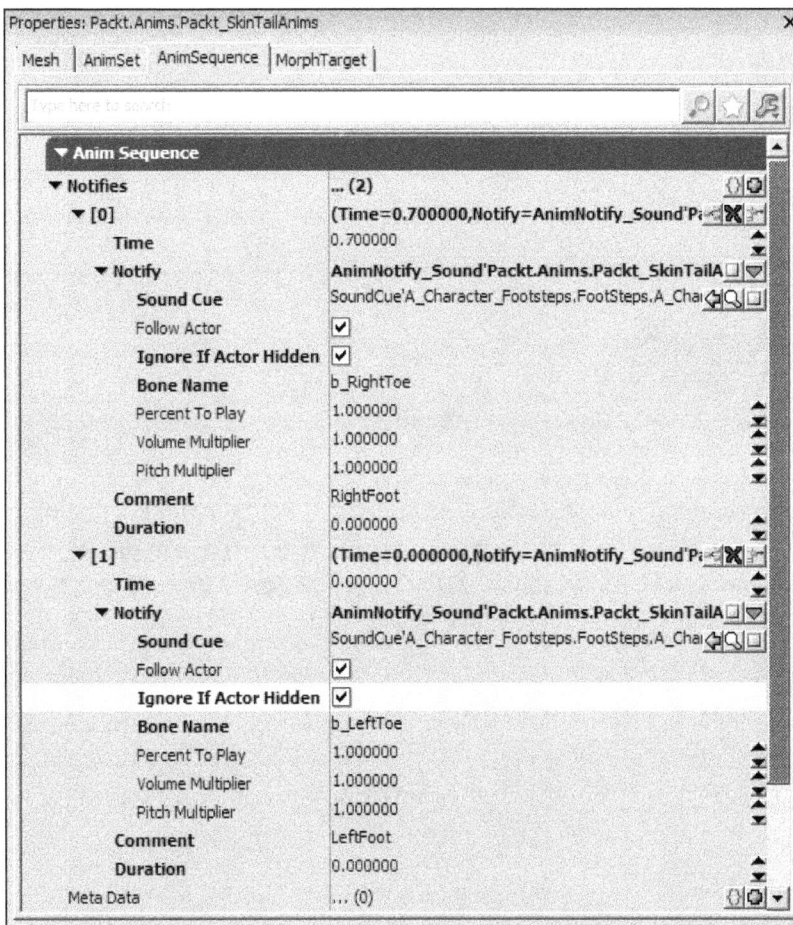

7. It helps to add a **Comment** like *Left foot* and *Right foot* to each item, as these show up on the **AnimSet** preview timeline.

8. When playing games, once in a while you may have noticed hidden characters walking in the scene with audible footsteps. In the properties, there is a check box to eliminate the chance of this called **Ignore if Actor Hidden**. Still, there might be some cases where you want this spooky effect.

9. When you assign each **AnimNotify_Sound** you might have noticed in the list that there are plenty of other kinds of Notify available. Assigning them and checking through their properties would be a good way to familiarize yourself with what they offer. One in particular that is relevant here is the **AnimNotify_FootStep**. This has a preset foot down channel with a value of 0 for Left and 1 for Right, so once you add one **AnimNotify_Footstep** entry you've covered the requirement for stepping sounds. However, you may notice that there is no SoundCue set here, which is because it must be set in the custom pawn class for a given character. The benefit of this is that you could add some kind of array for different sounds to play when walking on different surfaces or when wearing different shoes, or at different movement speeds and so on.

```
simulated event PlayFootStepSound (int FootDown)
{
local SoundCue FootSound;
FootSound = SoundCue'YOURPACKAGE.GROUP.YOURSOUNDCUE'
PlaySound(FootSound, false, true,,,true);
}
```

See also

This chapter has covered a wide range of Material, from 3ds Max asset handling, to Kismet, Matinee, and UnrealScript basics.

▶ For more information on Kismet, see *Chapter 4, Got Your Wires Crossed?*

▶ For more information on UnrealScript, see *Chapter 6, Under the Hood*. This chapter deals mostly with configuration. It is not a deep guide to UnrealScript, but some of the content there may help make entering code feel a bit more friendly.

4
Got Your Wires Crossed?
Visual Scripting of Gameplay in Kismet

This chapter deals with Kismet, which enables level designers to provision the actors in their scene with functionality driven by events and actions. Our goal is to hone in on a few of the many interesting challenges Kismet provides, and some basic understanding of the UDK editing environment is assumed.

- ▶ Kismet UI essentials
- ▶ Creating a simple enemy Bot
- ▶ Event based movement of scene objects in Matinee
- ▶ Trace actions in a shooting situation
- ▶ Revealing and hiding scene actors during gameplay
- ▶ Producing sounds through Kismet
- ▶ Using Take Damage events to produce explosions
- ▶ Understanding the usage of Named Variables
- ▶ Tidying up Kismet networks using Sub-Sequences
- ▶ Tidying up Kismet networks using Remote Events
- ▶ Toggling Materials through Kismet
- ▶ Toggling lights through Kismet

- ▸ Animating PointLights in Matinee to mimic texture animation
- ▸ Making a comparison following a countdown
- ▸ Using an Integer Counter to count enemy deaths
- ▸ Controlling node flow using a Gate action
- ▸ Making Bots follow a path

Introduction

The process of explaining Kismet in this chapter includes some formatting that you will want to get used to. Nodes in Kismet, that carry actions and events, are formatted as follows: **Event**. Properties of those nodes, and menu choices are formatted as follows: *Property*. Values that you type in property fields or unique names we've assigned things will be formatted as follows: *field name*.

Kismet lets us tell game actors how to behave in relation to each other and the player. The editor is a canvas on which to construct a network of connected nodes. It has a **Properties** window which exposes properties for the selected node, and a **Sequences** window for navigating layers of the canvas created using **Sub-Sequences**.

In this chapter we give essential explanations that will allow you to set up your own Kismet, and cover common cases of Kismet-driven functionality in UDK that many games leverage frequently. In the next chapter we cover more challenging examples.

Kismet UI essentials

In this recipe we'll construct a simple network and explain its anatomy. Since the word **Kismet** means destiny, we'll add a random hurt/heal loop to doom the player to a slow, unavoidable death (but you can always come back afterwards). We'll do this using actions entirely within Kismet to affect the player.

Getting ready

Open UDK and choose **File | New** and select the *Midday Lighting* map template. Click in the **View** menu and choose **World Properties** and there set the **Game Type for PIE** to *UTGame*. This gives us a head-up display in which we can see, amongst other things, the health changes this recipe involves.

Open the Kismet Editor by pressing the icon [K].

How to do it...

1. Hold *P* and click to add a *Player Variable*. The *Player Variable* currently says **All Players**, which for now is fine as that's just us. A list of hotkeys for adding Kismet nodes is at `http://udn.epicgames.com/Three/KismetUserGuide.html`.

2. To move a node, hold *Ctrl + LMB* and drag it. Hold *LMB* and drag to pan the view. *MMB* scrolling zooms the view in steps or *LMB + RMB* dragging zooms smoothly.

3. Right-click and choose **New Event | Player | Player Spawned**. This event fires when the player spawns in the game. Actions which stem from it will fire too.

4. Click the *Player Spawned* event and notice it displays its properties in the **Properties** window. This window can be dragged around. Close it by pressing the icon [✕] then restore from the **Window** menu (*Alt + W*).

5. In the *Player Spawned* properties, set the **Max Trigger Count** to 0. This means the sequence we're making will fire off every time you die and spawn again.

6. The right-click menu exposes sets of **Events**, **Actions**, **Variables**, and **Conditions**. Right-click on the canvas and choose **New Action | Actor | Modify Health**. The player is variously referred to as a pawn, controller, object, or actor. So we can bring about a change in the player using actions from the Actor category.

7. Select the event and the action by *Ctrl + Alt + LMB* dragging a red marquee around them, then right-click the empty canvas nearby and choose **New Comment**. Call this *Random Doom!* Enlarge the comment box by clicking its edge and dragging, and you can position it if you hold *Ctrl* and drag its label.

8. The *Modify Health* action has a black **In** and **Out** nub (or connector or link). Draw a wire from the **In** nub to the **Out** nub of the *Player Spawned* event. Right-click on the **In** nub and choose **Set Activate Delay** and set the value to 2.00. This will mean the action doesn't fire until two seconds have passed. Note that if you want to disconnect the wire, you can *Alt-click* on it or right-click on the nub and choose **Break All Links**. Now you know how to add and remove wires.

9. At the moment the *Modify Health* doesn't do anything. First, it needs a value to say how much health it should modify. In its properties, in the **Damage Type** field choose *DmgType_Crushed*. In the **Amount** field, type 25.0.

10. Under the *Modify Health* you'll see a pink **Target** nub. It is expecting an *Object Variable* (these variables are always pink). Connect the *Player Variable* which says **All Players** to it by dragging from the **Target** nub to the variable. Now go in the properties of the *Player Variable* and turn off the checkbox which says **All Players**. It will swap to an **Index** value of 0. If you had more players, you'd have to start assigning them distinct index values.

11. With the *Modify Health* selected, press *Ctrl + C* and then *Ctrl + V*. You'll get a copy of it, and notice the *Player Variable* links up to both. This is what we want.

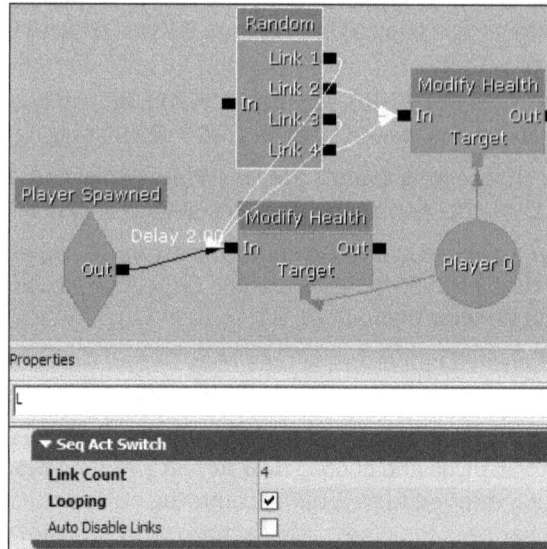

12. Right-click on the canvas and choose **New Action | Switch | Random**. This creates an action with a **Link 1** output.

13. Select it, and type *L* in the **Properties | Search** field as shown here. It will show all the properties for the *Random* action starting with *L*.

14. To add more links, go to its properties and type *4* in the **Link Count** field. Also, tick on **Looping**. This means when an input fires up the action, you'll get any of four random outputs and this will happen for as long as there's some input happening.

15. Now feed the **Link 1** to **Link 4** outputs into the *Modify Health* actions, as shown here. You could choose any order you like.

16. Hold *D* and click, or choose **New Action | Misc | Delay**. A *Delay* action prevents the flow for a set duration, which can be set in its property **Duration** or as a *Float Variable* through its blue **Duration** nub. Floats are always shown in a blue color.

17. Right-click and choose **New Variable | Float | Random Float**. This gives us a number which can range between a **Min** and **Max** value. In its properties set **Min** to 3 and **Max** to 9. Connect a wire from the **Duration** nub of the *Delay* action to the *Random Float Variable*. If a *Float Variable* is used for the **Duration** nub it will override any value typed in the **Duration** property.

18. Feed the **Out** nub of both *Modify Health* actions into the **Start** nub of the *Delay*.

19. Feed the **Finished** nub of the *Delay* to the **In** nub of the *Random* switch action, the one with four **Link** outputs, as shown in the next screenshot. This creates a sequence loop.

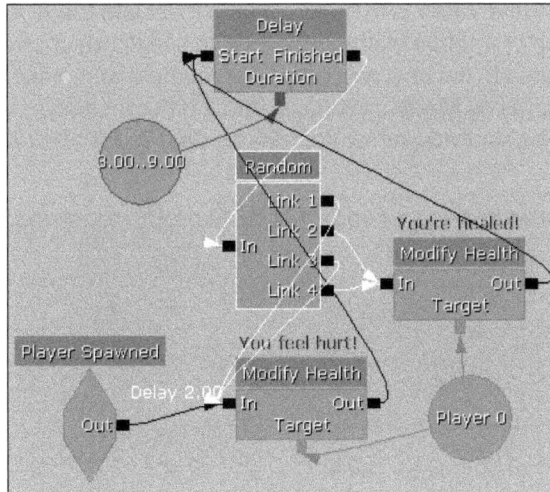

20. To give some simple feedback to the player select the **Modify Health** which damages the player and in its **Object Comment** field type *You feel hurt!* The text will display above the **Modify Health**. Then tick the **Output Obj Comment To Screen** checkbox below to ensure it displays on the screen during gameplay too.

21. For the **Modify Health** that heals the player, in its **Object Comment** field type *You're healed!* Also tick **Output Obj Comment to Screen**.

22. Right-click on the **Random** switch action's label to create a breakpoint. Close the Kismet Editor then enable **Kismet Debugging** by pressing [🔑] in the main icon row. **Kismet Debugging** was discussed in *Chapter 1, Heads Up*.

23. Finally press *F8* to PIE in order to see how quickly you die off in game. In particular look for whether or not you are healing at all.

How it works

Even though you didn't add any actors or traps or monsters in the scene, you can still create a process that acts upon the player. In this case you hurt them. Also, you've been exposed to the notion that the Kismet layout is highly flexible. In this book, we've directed the recipes at intermediate users who probably know a bit about handling the Kismet UI, but in case you're a brave beginner, here is a rapid run through of how Kismet works.

Most uses of Kismet are built around the idea of an event firing off a series of actions that call on scene actors through variables. Within each event, action, or variable there are property values that can be given as a **Float Value** (a number like 0.001), **String Value** (which is essentially a line of text), **Var Name** (which is usually an actor in the scene or that will be placed in the scene during gameplay), **Integer Value** (a whole number like 0, 1, 2) or **Boolean** (which is true or false). It can take quite a while to get used to using these, so in a way the recipes in this chapter have that kind of rehearsal in mind.

Very often the use of a **Float Value** is to measure time or isolate the X, Y, or Z component of the world space location or rotation of something in the scene (which is given within a **Vector Variable**) and is calculated to decimal accuracy from moment to moment for XYZ. A **Float Value** can be converted (using **Math** operations) into a different kind of variable value, such as an **Integer Value**, and vice versa. Kismet has **Cast to Int** and **Cast to Float** for this purpose.

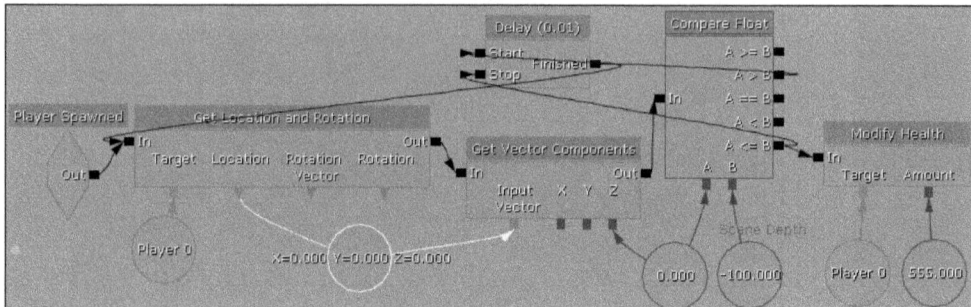

The sequence above is called *Alternative Kill Z*. **Kill Z** is a measure of how far the player can go downwards in the level before being considered 'fallen off the map'. It is set through the editor menu **View | World Properties | Zone Info**. The benefit of using Kismet for this, is that the *Scene Depth* value can be adjusted during the game through other Kismet nodes.

In the example, after the player is spawned the **Vector** (XYZ) representing their location has its **Z** component isolated and cast to a **Float Variable**. The value is derived from the player's present Z location. The value is compared against -100 straight away. If the Z value is above -100 this sequence loops through a 0.25 second **Delay**. If it gets to -100 or below the loop is stopped and the player is killed by a **Modify Health** which has a **Damage Amount** set higher than the **Player Health** amount.

Suppose you have a magic carpet game where if you step off it you always fall to your death. The higher you go, the longer it would take for the **Kill Z** to be reached. At high altitudes this would be boring if the player needs to fall for a really long span. Using the above method, you can add an adjustment to the *Scene Depth* target Float which always matches the Z depth of the magic carpet, with a slight offset. Another way to achieve this effect could be by using a **DynamicTriggerVolume** attached to the magic carpet. There's often more than one way to achieve a desired result when constructing game mechanics.

Setting up an iPad controller for an iOS game depends on the kind of **Vector Variable** conversions shown here. **Sjoerd Dejong** made a great tutorial on this available at http://eat3d.com/udk_mobile, called **iOS Mobile Game Production**. Be sure you have an iPad at hand if you want to get the most out of that tutorial.

For those really new to Kismet, navigation is the first thing you'll want to master. To add nodes, you can right-click and access events, actions, and conditions through the menu. Actions are what happen. Conditions are ways to evaluate whether something has happened or not, or to limit whether something can happen. Events are what is used to fire off actions.

Barring niche examples, there are just a few kinds of events employed often: touching, or running into something, using something, beginning the level, spawning actors in the level, dying, being damaged, damaging something else, actors having a line of sight with each other, AI reaching a path goal, physics impulses, UI events (such as user input and clicks), and events based on custom user commands or player input.

Visually, nodes for events are red and pointy shaped. Actions are pink boxes. Conditions are blue boxes. Variables are circular. Nodes can be commented as a group or individually with text to clarify their function.

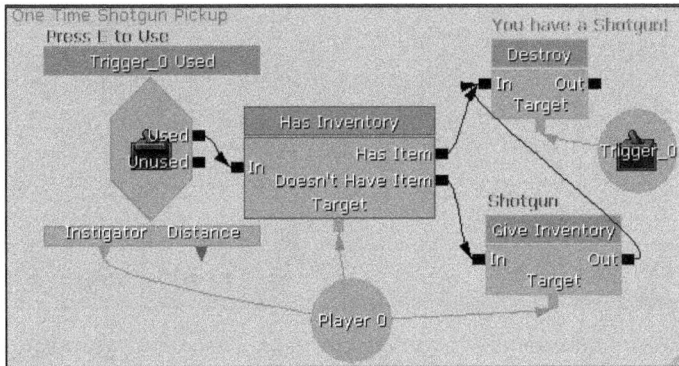

To move a node hold *Ctrl* and drag it. To select multiple nodes, Hold *Ctrl + Alt* and drag a marquee around them. To connect nodes, drag from connector to connector. I've called these nubs a lot because it saves space on the page. To remove a connection (or wire), hold *Alt* and click on it. *Del* will remove nodes. You can paste a selection using *Ctrl + C* and *Ctrl + V*. It's even possible to copy and paste a selection from a sequence between scenes or to Notepad as plain text.

It is possible to re-arrange the order of connectors or nubs on a node if you hold *Ctrl* and drag them. This is useful for reversing nubs that have crossed wires. In this book's images, nub order has been changed here and there from the defaults to help improve legibility in the connection wiring. It may make some of the nodes look unfamiliar if hiding unused nubs is a new concept for you, but try it out and hopefully you'll quickly see the benefit of this toggle.

Kismet offers you some convenient right-click commands for assigning scene actors to variables or selecting objects in the scene that the Kismet already references. These include **Assign From Scene**, **Select in Scene**, and **Select in Kismet**. For complex scenes you can also use the **Search Tool** icon [🔎] from the menu to find nodes and variables.

A very important feature of the Kismet UI is that networks can have their unused nubs (or connectors) hidden so the network can be compacted in space. An example is shown next. This is usually done on a finished piece, but has been used a lot in the book so the examples can fit on the page. If you want to toggle the unused nubs there is an icon which handles this globally [🔲]. Individual control of exposed nubs can also be accessed through right-clicking and choosing **Hide Unused Connectors**. Along with this goes **Show All Connectors**.

The toggle icons are shown in the following screenshot. They can be found in the Kismet Editor's top row of icons.

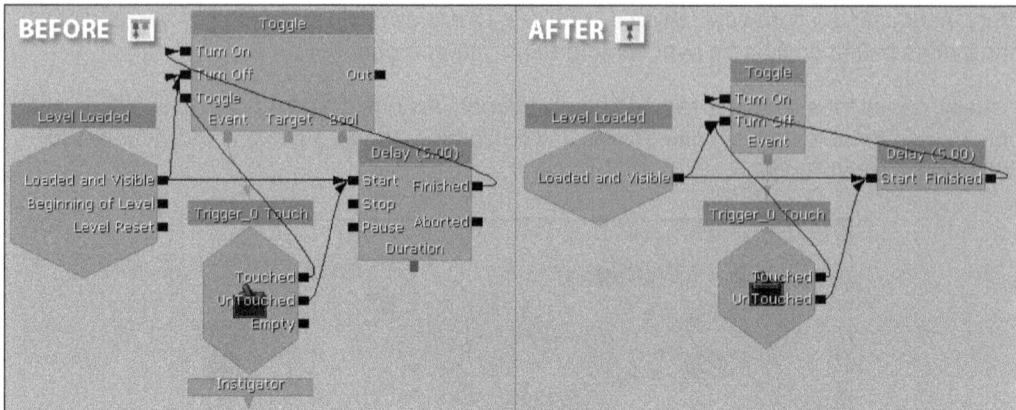

Creating a simple enemy Bot

In this recipe we'll introduce some AI handling concerns. We're setting up for future lessons where Bots will be used frequently. In this lesson, we'll just set up the Bot and make him fire at the player.

Getting ready

Open *Packt_04_BotHandling_Start.UDK*. Click in the **View** menu and choose **World Properties**; there set the **Game Type for PIE** to *UTGame*. This gives us a heads-up display in which we can see, amongst other things, the health changes this recipe involves.

How to do it...

1. Open the Kismet Editor by pressing the icon [K]. Hold *P* and click to add a *Player Variable*. Highlight this variable and in its properties turn off the tick box called **Seq Var Player | All Players**. This means the variable is specific to a single player. Every player can be given an **Index** to ID them. The default is 0.

2. Right-click and choose **New Event | Player | Player Spawned**. In the properties for this event look for **Max Trigger Count** and replace the default value of 1 with 0. This means that the event can fire off unlimited times.

3. Right-click and choose **New Action | Pawn | Give Inventory**. Connect the *Player Spawned* event's **Out** nub to the **In** nub of the *Give Inventory* action. Connect the **Target** nub to the *Player Variable*.

4. This action comes from a category which is specific to players and Bots. This **Give Inventory** action will put in the hands of the player whatever we specify in its properties. For the property **Inventory List** we need to add an entry. Hit the [🔂] icon to add an entry [0] will be added underneath. In this entry there's a roll-out list. From the list choose *UTWeap_RocketLauncher_Content*. Also tick on the properties below, **Clear Existing** and **Force Replace**, as shown here:

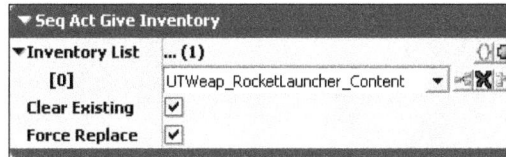

5. Now the player is packing a heavy weapon, let's account for the fact you still might get killed. Right-click and choose **New Action | Event | Attach to Event**. The **Attach to Event** action lets you associate a player (or Bot) with another event. Right-click and choose **New Event | Pawn | Death** to add the event we're going to attach it to.

6. Connect the nodes you've added as shown here:

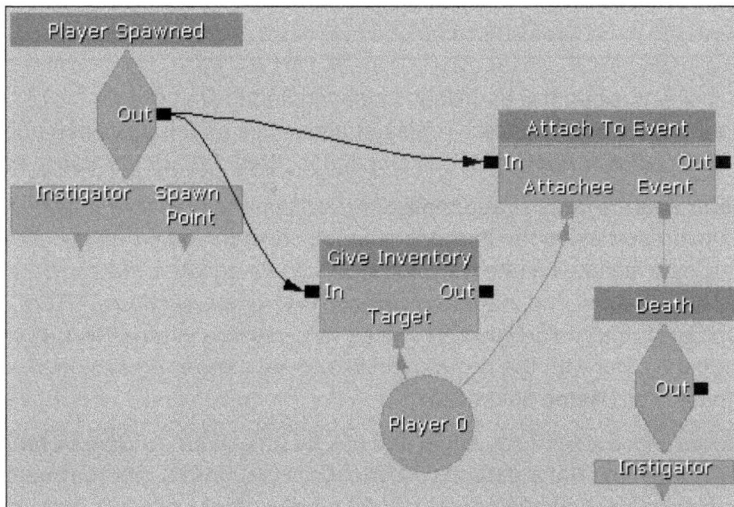

7. These steps have been a bit of preparation before adding the Bot, which is needed to just get things rolling. To create the Bot, we need an **Actor Factory**. Right-click and choose **New Action | Actor | Actor Factory**. This can be used to spawn all kinds of actors in the scene, not just Bots. But no matter what is spawned, it needs to start somewhere.

8. A **PathNode**, shown in the next screenshot, is provided to spawn a Bot. PathNodes include a cylindrical collision object, and when you press **Build Paths** [✕], UDK attempts to draw a direct line between each pair. Bots can then use these to navigate the scene. The (white) line in the screenshot shows the calculated path, displayed by pressing *P*. In this case we only need one, since the Bot will just stand in place and shoot at us. Add one as shown here:

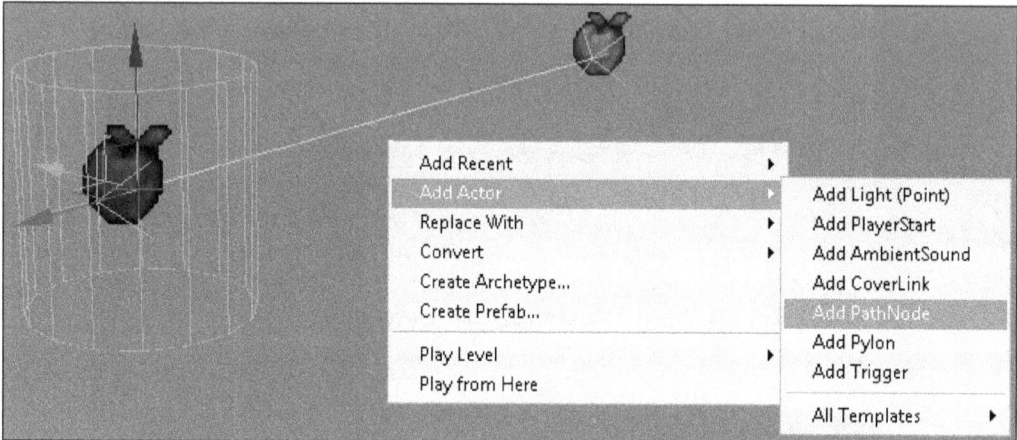

9. In the scene, position the PathNode actor you added so it sits on top of the cube in the map. With this highlighted, in Kismet, right-click on the **Spawned** nub along the bottom of the ***Actor Factory*** action and choose **New Object Var Using PathNode**.

10. The ***Actor Factory*** doesn't automatically provision the actor it will produce. We set that in its properties. In the **Factory** channel, press the blue triangle [▽] to expose a list of types of actor. The one we want is *UTActorFactoryAI*. Once this is added, expand the **Factory** channel and in the **Controller Class** property choose *UTBot*. In the **Pawn Class** property choose *UTPawn*. These point to classes in the UDK scripts folder that provision the actor with the desired mesh and animations and so on. If you want, type something in the **Name** field below.

11. How do we arm the Bot? You could just tick the checkbox for ***Give Default Inventory***. This will assign the Bot a default *LinkGun*. Or, if you want a different weapon leave that unchecked and instead press the **Add a new item** icon [◉]; then, in the added entry [0], choose from the available options by clicking where it says **None** then making a selection, such as *UTWeap_ShockRifle*, as shown in the next screenshot:

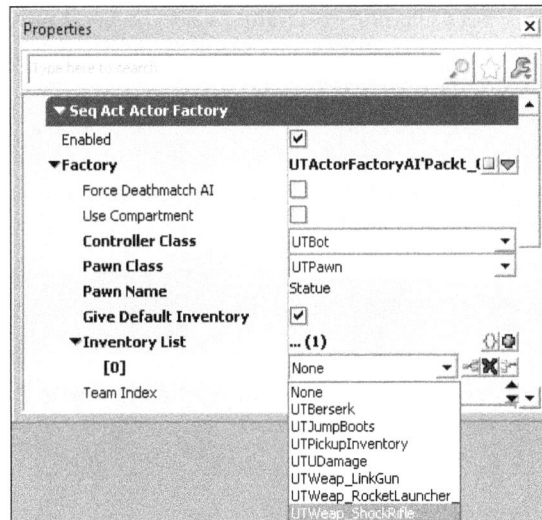

12. Our Bot needs to be referenced in Kismet once he's spawned, so right-click on the **Spawn** nub along the base of the *Actor Factory* action and choose **New Object Variable**. This displays a *???* node. The *???* doesn't mean it's an error, but just that it's not a specific scene actor, which is okay, since we're specifying what this *Object Variable* is from the *Actor Factory*.

13. Hook the **Out** nub of the *Attach to Event* action to the **In** nub of the *Actor Factory*. If you PIE now, you'll see the Bot just standing still on top of the StaticMesh cube. Press *Esc* and return to Kismet. Later on, some of the actions we're going to add will require us to slightly delay the spawning of the Bot. So right-click on the **In** nub of the *Actor Factory* and choose **Set Activate Delay** and set the value to 1. This means you'll see the Bot suddenly blink into existence after you start PIE again. Later we fix this.

14. The next screenshot shows what you'll have now. In the image the *Actor Factory* has had its unused nubs hidden. To do that right-click and choose **Hide Unused Connectors**, but be sure to right-click again and choose **Expose Output | Finished**, since next we'll be using this to tell the Bot what to do.

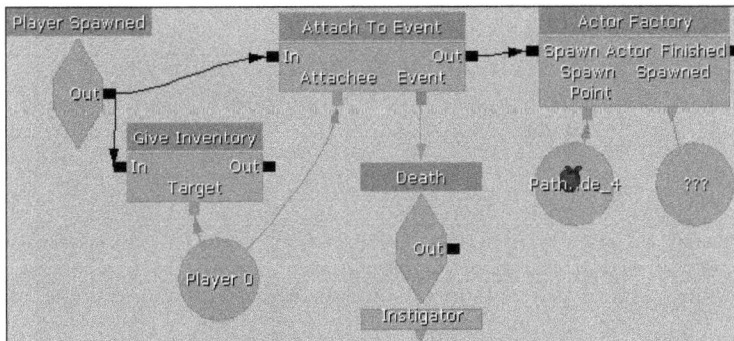

15. Since we want the Bot to be our enemy, he should be told to shoot at us. To do this, right-click and choose **New Action | AI | Start Firing At**. Also right-click again and choose **New Action | AI | Stop Firing**.

16. Hold *D* and click to add a **Delay** action. This we'll use to loop between the previous added actions. Highlight the existing **Player Variable** and press *Ctrl + C*, and under the **Start Firing At** action right-click and choose **Paste Here** (or press *Ctrl + V*). Connect the nodes as follows:

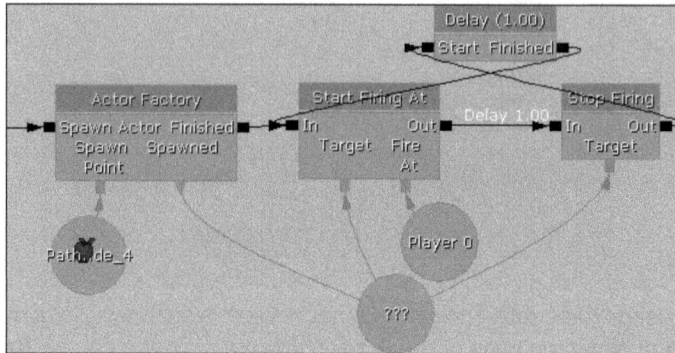

17. The **Delay** action's **Duration** property defaults to 1 second (as does the **Set Activate Delay** duration going into the **Stop Firing** action). The duration moderates how frequently the enemy fires at the player. You can vary it to suit yourself. Later, when we want to permanently stop the Bot's attack, we can just fire off the **Stop** nub of the **Delay** from another action.

18. If you PIE now and let the Bot win, when you respawn there will be an error, because our sequence is set up to spawn a new enemy just after the player spawns, however often. This is a problem because the previous Bot is still there. To remedy this, right-click and add a **New Action | Actor | Destroy**. Connect the **Out** nub of the **Death** event you added earlier to the **In** nub of the **Destroy** action. Set the **Target** of the **Destroy** action to the **Object Variable** *???*, belonging to the **Spawned** Bot.

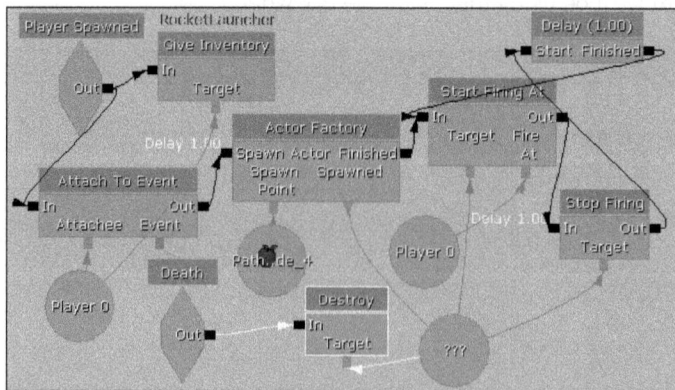

How it works

Adding the **Delay** for **Start Firing At** and **Stop Firing** isn't something that would be needed in every case for a Bot, it's just a simple way to set up a firing pattern where you can control the rapidity of the shots. In this sequence we introduced a **Player Spawned** event that recurs, and the need to Attach the player to the event of their **Death**. At the end of the sequence we added a consequence for that, which is to **Destroy** the enemy too, so we can respawn everything fresh. An important part of specifying the actor that is spawned was to set the **Pawn** class and **Controller** to use in the **Actor Factory** properties. For the Bot, we added a one second activation delay and because of this we see the Bot appearing out of nowhere after the level has begun. In the next recipe this will be disguised behind a wall that drops down to reveal the Bot.

This scene is demonstrated in the map _Packt_04_BotHandling_DEMO.UDK_.

Event-based movement of scene objects in Matinee

For the Bot in the previous recipe, we have an activation delay for his spawning, which means he seems to pop into existence out of nowhere. We can disguise this with a moving wall that surrounds him, then drops down to expose him to view after he's already spawned. To do so, we'll use the Matinee Editor to key the moving object's motion.

Getting ready

Open _Packt_04_SimpleMatinee_Start.UDK_ or continue from where you were in the last recipe if you wish.

How to do it...

1. Open the Content Browser (_Ctrl + Shift + F_) and set the filter type to **StaticMesh**. Type _Dropper_ in the search field. If nothing shows up, right-click on the _PacktKismet_ package and choose **Fully Load**.

2. You should see a StaticMesh that looks like a four-sided tube. Drag it into the scene and place it where the Bot spawns on top of the cube in the middle of the scene. Scale it up too, by about 5.5. You can do this using the numerical input at the bottom of the editor called **DrawScale** or in the actor's properties (_F4_) under **Static Mesh Actor | Static Mesh Component | Static Mesh Component | Primitive Component** in the XYZ fields of **Scale3D**.

3. A StaticMesh cannot be referenced in Kismet, so right-click on the actor and choose **Convert | Convert StaticMeshActor to Mover**. With it still selected, open Kismet.

4. Hold *Ctrl + S* and click to add a ***Level Loaded*** event. Next to it hold *M* and click to add a ***Matinee*** action. Connect the **Loaded and Visible** nub of the event to the **Play** nub of the ***Matinee*** action. To open the Matinee Editor you can either double-click on the action, or right-click on it and choose **Open UnrealMatinee**.

5. The Matinee Editor has a section on the left-hand side called **All** which is dark gray. Here, right-click and choose **Add New Empty Group**. You'll be prompted to name it. Type *Dropper*. A group track will appear called *Dropper*. Right-click on this and choose **Add New Movement Track**, and this track will likewise appear nested under the *Dropper* group track. Make sure the **Movement** Track is highlighted.

6. Use the middle mouse to scroll out the view of the time line to the right-hand side of the **Movement** Track. This should expose a red triangle key frame at 0.0 seconds on the time line. This doesn't need to be changed. Under it, down by the 0.0, is a black vertical slider. Slide this along to 2.0 seconds.

7. To add a keyframe, press *Enter* or the icon [🔲] at the top corner of the Matinee Editor. Highlight this newly added key. In the scene you will see the viewport displays a notice **Adjust Key Movement1**, which lets you know you're in the Matinee Editor's key adjustment mode. It means if you move the Mover its new location will be set for the 2.0s key. Move the Mover down so it sinks into the cube StaticMesh that it starts on top of. You should see dotted yellow line in the viewport, representing the trajectory of the animated actor. If you scrub the timeline slider, you'll see the playback.

8. In the Matinee Editor, click the little square on the right-hand side of the **Movement** Track label. This will show the curve for the motion you've animated above. Press the icon **Fit View to All** [🔘] to ensure the curve fits the view. We've only animated the Z value, so turn off the red and green boxes under the *Dropper_Movement* label in the curves panel, as shown in the following screenshot:

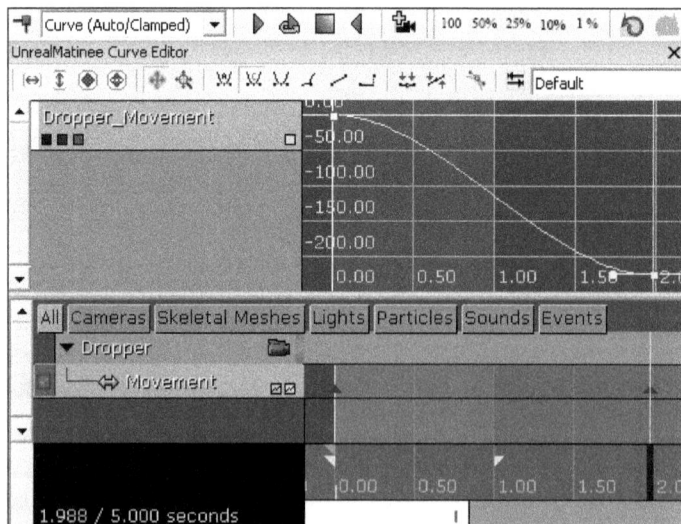

9. Let's adjust the key so it occurs later. Right-click on the key on the curve and choose **Set Time**. Enter 4.

10. You can also choose **Set Value**, which will give you fine control of the height by which the Mover drops. We've used -225.

11. If you want to adjust the rate of the animation, you can select then right-click on the triangular red keys on the time line and choose **Interp Mode**. At present they are on **Curve** (**Auto**). Try setting them to **Linear**. This would mean the animation happens at a uniform speed. In later recipes where Matinee is used we'll need that but for this example switch it back to **Curve** (**Auto**). The linear motion is particularly handy if you are doing rotations of objects that need to cycle or loop smoothly.

12. To add more keys in between the start and finish keys, hold *Ctrl* and click on the yellow curve in the upper panel. To move in a freehand way the key you added, hold *Ctrl* and drag the highlighted key.

13. To change the rate of the movement another way (useful if you don't want to adjust the existing keys), in the properties of the *Matinee* action adjust the **Play Rate** value. A value of 0.5 makes it half as fast.

14. An important feature of the time line to understand is that tracks have an end time, which defaults to 5.0s. Since we keyed our Mover to 4.0s we have an extra second of 'silence'. You can fix this if you right-click on the pink out point triangle on the time line and choose **Move to Longest Track Point**.

How it works

Adding this *Matinee* action does cause one problem. The Bot is set to start firing at the player before the Mover has dropped out of the way. To prevent this, we can either delay the onset of the firing, or add a *Trace* action for the shooting (which is a more dynamic method) so that Bot only fires if he sees us. We'll do this in the next recipe. An example of the current scene can be found in *Packt_04_SimpleMatinee_DEMO.UDK*.

The Matinee Editor and its tracks and key frames do take a while to become familiar with, but before long you will find it very easy to repeat the above steps. There's also a lot more you can do with *Matinee* actions besides move objects in the scene. They can be used to play sounds. They can be used to adjust parameter values in Materials, in animation trees, and in particle systems. We discuss all of this later.

An additional point to consider, particularly for rotation of moving objects, is whether to set the movement mode to be either **Relative to Initial** or **Relative to World** (which is set by right-clicking on a given **Movement** track and selecting one or the other from the menu). What this means is that you can either allow an object to move based on whatever its initial position is in space, or it can be based on a set of exact, absolute world coordinates. To clarify, if you took a door, and made it **Relative to World** instead of **Relative to Initial**, then copied it, the copy would end up snapping back to the original door's coordinates. Being set to **Relative to Initial**, though, allows you to copy it, and it will mimic the motion relative to whatever *new* position you move it to.

With rotating doors, when the wrong mode for a mirrored half of a door is set, you might not get the rotation you expect, even though the keys for the rotation were set correctly. To explore this, open the scene *Packt_04_RelativeMove_Start.UDK*. If you PIE and run into the visible Trigger, the gates in the scene rotate open, but one rotates 270' to reach its keyed angle. In Kismet, just open the ***Matinee*** action and highlight the *WrongWayDoor* group's **Movement** track and in its properties tick on **Show Rotation on Curve Ed**, which exposes individual curves for Rotation XYZ so you can see the blue Z rotation curve is keyed incorrectly from -180' at 0.0s to 90' at 5.0s. This isn't because of bad keyframing—it's because the keys were shifted automatically by an earlier swap from **World Frame** to **Relative to Initial**. Highlight the curve for the **Z** rotation of *WrongWayDoor_Movement*. Correct the key value to 180' at 0.0s and the door will work just fine. Then, to reproduce what caused the error in the first place, right-click on the **Movement** track under the group *WrongWayDoor*, and tick on the property **World Frame**. The initial key value will flip to -180' when you do so. This is because the model is a flipped copy of the first, correct door model. Highlight the key at 0.0s and set it back to 180' and the motion will be fixed for **Relative to Initial**. For the same **Movement** track, right-click on it and set it to use **Relative to Initial** and it will flip again to -180' and you'll have to rectify the shifted keyframe to 180' at 0.0s again.

See also

▸ More Matinee Editor procedures are covered in: *Chapter 5, It Is Your Destiny!*

▸ Particle effects are covered in: *Chapter 7, Hi, I'm Eye Candy!*

▸ Character assets are discussed in: *Chapter 3, It Lives!*

▸ Material Instance Constants, for animating parameters in Matinee, are discussed in: *Chapter 9, The Devil Is in the Details!*

Trace actions in a shooting situation

In this recipe we'll introduce the ***Trace*** action, which is very useful for testing whether the space between two actors is obstructed or unobstructed. The example we'll use continues from the last scene, where a wall drops down to reveal a Bot who wants to shoot at us. Being told to shoot at us, he does so regardless of the wall, which is not plausible, so adding the ***Trace*** will help with that.

Getting ready

Open *Packt_04_SimpleTrace_Start.UDK* or continue from where you were in the last recipe if you wish.

How to do it...

1. Open Kismet and, following the existing **Actor Factory** that provisions and spawns an enemy Bot, right-click and choose **New Action | Misc | Trace**. A **Trace** action draws a line between a **Start** object and an **End** object. You can also specify an exact **HitObject** it is looking for but in this case we don't need to. That would be more likely if you wanted to check against a NPC rather just a wall, which is what's getting in the robot's firing line on the player.

2. In the scene, select the Mover that is assigned to the **Matinee** action's *Dropper* nub (*InterpActor_5*) by right-clicking on the **Object Variable** and choosing **Select InterpActor_5 in Level**. Then right-click on the **HitObject** nub of the **Trace** action and choose **New Object Var using InterpActor_5**. Or you could just drag an additional wire to the existing variable. Also hook the **Object Variable** *???*, which is the spawned Bot, to the **Start** nub and the **Player Variable** to the **End** nub, as seen in the following screenshot:

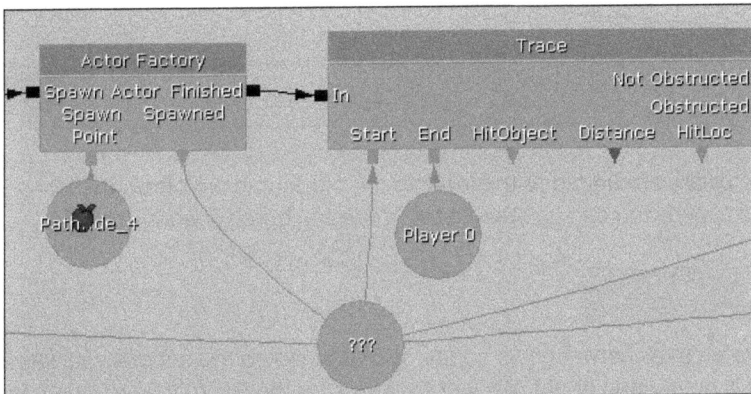

3. In the properties of the **Trace**, do not tick on the check box for **Trace Actors**. It will prevent the line of sight. Because the wall is a Mover, actually it is already part of the world and doesn't need to be set specifically set as an **Object Variable** under the **HitObject Object** nub of the **Trace**.

4. What we need now is to provision the outputs for the **Trace** action. **Not Obstructed** fires off actions if the player is seen by the Bot. If the wall is still in the way, then the **Obstructed** nub fires off and it can be left empty, since nothing happens in that case. For the **Not Obstructed** nub, hook it up to the existing **Start Firing At** action, which harks back to the earlier recipe *Creating a simple enemy Bot*.

5. At present the **Trace** will only fire off once. We need to make it loop, so the Bot is constantly checking whether it can see what it is supposed to shoot at. The sequence shown next is a suitable loop back, with two **Trace** actions occurring, one for the first case, and one for repeated tracing after that. You need this because the **Obstructed** nub, once firing has begun, should go to a **Stop Firing** action. But initially, it should just loop back on itself and check again for further obstruction, all this before any shooting has begun.

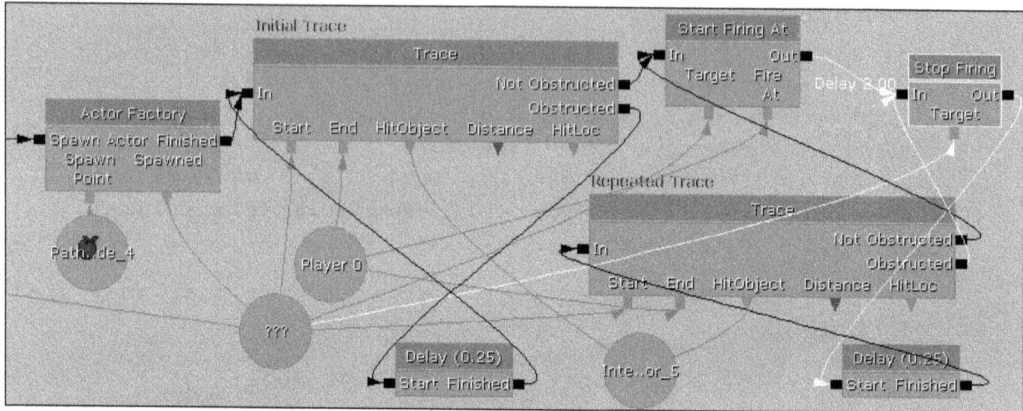

6. Some pillars are added to the level so the player can hide from the Bot once the wall has dropped. You can use this to test if the trace works when you PIE.

How it works

A **Trace** generates a ray between two points. You then set up the actions you want to occur when that ray is obstructed or not. We just set loops for the Bot to follow to decide whether to fire or not, then whether to continue firing or stop.

In the properties of the **Trace** there are **Offset** amounts you can set from the specified **Start** and **End** actors which can help control the ray that's cast. For example, part of the player model or Bot model (such as a swinging arm or gigantic weapon) might get in the way of the trace from the actor's pivot, so an offset slightly ahead of the character might work to prevent that.

You can also set a **Trace Extent**, which means that even if there's a direct line of sight between the two actors, if the distance or extent is too great then it will be discarded.

You might see a warning in the log when you kill the Bot about the **Stop Firing** action having no handler. This is because once the Bot is killed, there's no **Target** for the **Stop Firing** action to register to. This matters because of the 2 second **Set Activate Delay** on its **In** nub. It's like yelling stop shooting when there is no longer anyone around shooting. To fix this, instead feed the connections coming to the **In** of the **Stop Firing** action into a **Delay** action's **Start** nub. Feed the **Delay** action's **Finished** nub into the **In** of the **Stop Firing** action instead. From the **Death** event's **Out** nub, extend a connection to the **Delay** action's **Stop** nub. You should also do this with the **Stop** nubs of the two other **Delay** actions in this section. It cancels the loops around the **Trace** when the Bot **Death** event occurs.

You can view an example in *Packt_04_SimpleTrace_DEMO.UDK*. The **Delay** actions have been stopped there.

Revealing and hiding scene actors during gameplay

In this recipe we'll look at revealing and hiding actors in the scene using Trigger events and Kismet actions. One consideration is that even though we can hide an object, that won't prevent it from being there, and it's possible to collide with it even when it isn't visible. We'll use a **Change Collision** action to handle that, and a **Toggle Hidden** action to handle the visibility.

Getting ready

Open *Packt_04_RevealActors_Start.UDK* or continue from where you were in the last recipe if you completed it. In this map the Bot handling is already set up, from previous recipes.

How to do it...

1. In the map are four glowing white spheres. With these, we'll create a sequence where one is visible when the level loads, and touching it hides it and reveals another. In many games, this is a core process for collecting objects, though they might as easily be destroyed as hidden. Usually in such cases there is additional feedback to the player to strengthen the illusion of picking up the object.

2. The spheres are KActors contained in a collection called a **Prefab**. Its source in the Content Browser is *PacktKismet.Prefab.OrbsPlusTriggers*. It also contains Trigger actors that we'll use in the Kismet. Right-click on the Prefab and choose **Convert PrefabInstance to Normal Actors**. This breaks apart all the items in the Prefab.

3. Go to the **Edit** menu and choose **Find Actors**, and type *KActor* in the search field. Highlight all four in the list and press **Go To**, which selects them, then open Kismet.

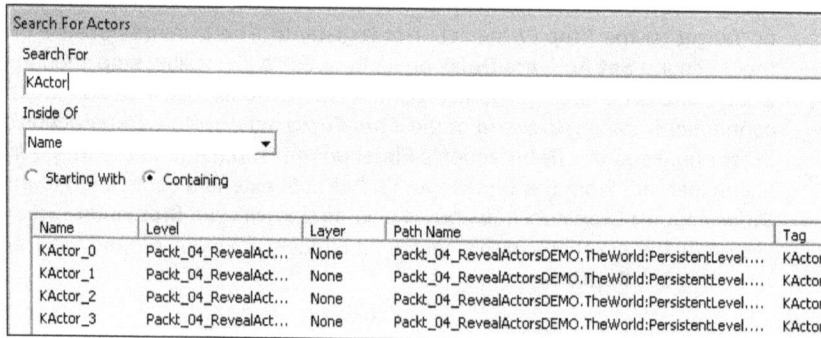

Name	Level	Layer	Path Name	Tag
KActor_0	Packt_04_RevealAct...	None	Packt_04_RevealActorsDEMO.TheWorld:PersistentLevel....	KActor
KActor_1	Packt_04_RevealAct...	None	Packt_04_RevealActorsDEMO.TheWorld:PersistentLevel....	KActor
KActor_2	Packt_04_RevealAct...	None	Packt_04_RevealActorsDEMO.TheWorld:PersistentLevel....	KActor
KActor_3	Packt_04_RevealAct...	None	Packt_04_RevealActorsDEMO.TheWorld:PersistentLevel....	KActor

Search For Actors — Search For: KActor — Inside Of: Name — ○ Starting With ◉ Containing

4. In Kismet, right-click and choose **New Object Vars Using KActor...** to bring them all into the sequence.

> Note that they are numbered KActor_0 to KActor_3, not 1 to 4. Kismet has a funny way of naming the newest additional item KActor_0 and existing items get renumbered each time you add another, but luckily all the references to them in UDK also get updated accordingly.

5. Right-click on the **Object Variable** in Kismet called *KActor_0*. This will be the first one to set up. Choose **Select KActor_0 in level**.

6. Overlapping the actor in the scene is a Trigger actor. Select that and in Kismet right-click and choose **New Event using Trigger_0 | Touch**. This event will fire when you touch the trigger.

7. Right-click and choose **New Action | Toggle | Toggle Hidden**. Connect the **Touched** nub of the ***Trigger_0 | Touched*** event to the **Hide** nub of the ***Toggle Hidden*** action. Assign the **Object Variable** *KActor_0* to the **Target** nub of the ***Toggle Hidden*** action.

8. PIE (*F8*) to verify that when you run up to the sphere it will hide, but you'll still bump into it after that even though it is hidden. Press *Esc*.

9. In Kismet, right-click and choose **New Action | Actor | Change Collision**. In the ***Change Collision*** action's properties, set the **Collision Type** to *COLLIDE_NoCollision*. Set the **Target** nub to the **Object Variable** *KActor_0*. Join the **Out** nub of the ***Toggle Hidden*** action to the **In** nub of the ***Change Collision*** action.

10. Next we want to deal with the remaining spheres. They are all visible, so we actually need to tell them to be hidden when the game begins. In Kismet, hold *Ctrl + S* and click to add a new **Level Loaded** event. Connect its **Loaded and Visible** nub to the **Hide** nub of a new **Toggle Hidden** action. Connect the **Object Variables** for *KActor_1*, *KActor_2*, and *KActor_3* to the **Target** nub of the added **Toggle Hidden** action. In the **Obj Comment** property for the **Toggle Hidden**, type *Extra Spheres Hidden at Start*.

11. While we're here, you will want to also inform the player what they should do in this level. In Kismet, hold *L* and click to add a **Log** action. In its **Obj Comment** property type *Collect four Orbs to Disarm the Enemy!* Hook this up as shown in the next screenshot to the **Level Loaded** event, and add a **Set Activate Delay** of 1.0. What this does is briefly display the text on the screen after the game begins in a simple way. It also shows above the **Log** in Kismet. Other ways to give feedback to players are discussed in later recipes.

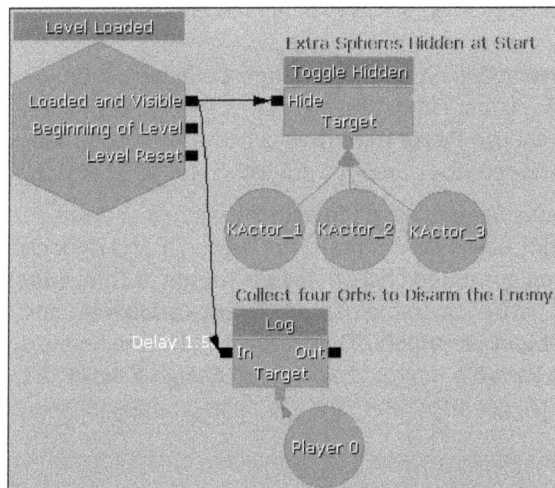

12. Highlight the three spheres together in the scene, then right-click and choose **Set Collision Type | No Collision**. This prevents us bumping into them before they are revealed.

13. So, the spheres are hidden, now we want to reveal them each time you touch a Trigger in the scene. You already dealt with the first sphere, *KActor_0*, as shown in the next screenshot. Extend from the **Out** nub of the **Change Collision** action to a new **Toggle Hidden** action, into its **UnHide** nub. Set the variable of this to the **Object Variable** *KActor_1*. So now we've revealed one of the three hidden spheres.

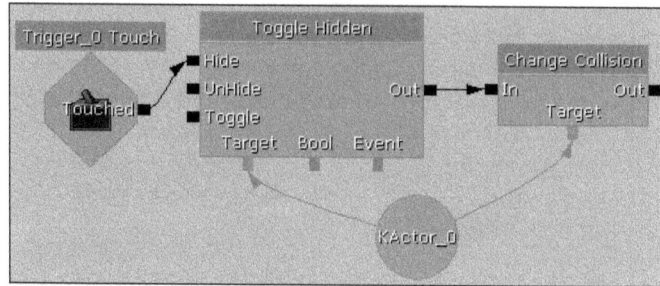

14. Select the above nodes except the **Change Collision** action. Also select the extra **Toggle Hidden** you just added, then press *Ctrl + C* to copy these. Somewhere below, right-click and choose **Paste Here** (this is better than just pressing *Ctrl + C* because it will paste them where the cursor is, not with some arbitrary offset).

15. The pasted nodes need to have the actors assigned to them changed. We can step through this fairly easily. Select the actor Trigger_1 and right-click on the pasted **Trigger_0 Touch** event and choose **Assign Trigger_1 to event(s)**. Select KActor_1 in the scene and right-click on the pasted **Object Variable** *KActor_0* and press **Assign KActor_1 to Object Variable(s)**. Select KActor_2 in the scene and right-click on the pasted **Object Variable** *KActor_1* and press **Assign KActor_2 to Object Variable(s)**. This is what you'll get after renaming the pasted nodes for this step:

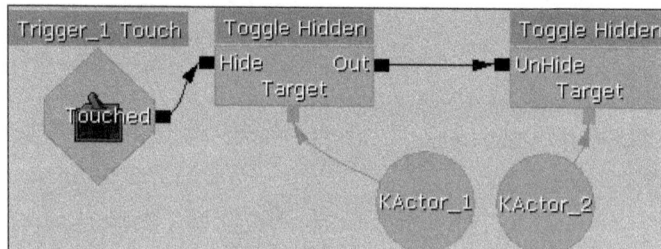

16. Seen next is what you'll get for the next repetition of this. Repeat this for the remaining **Trigger_3** and **Trigger_4** events, and the corresponding *KActor* variables.

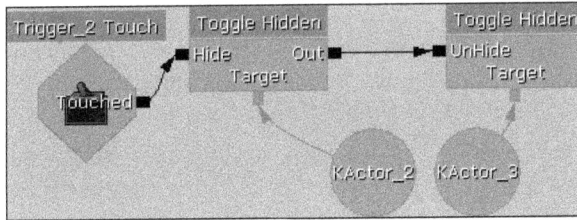

17. Having set those up, it's not much good to have all these **Trigger Touch** events available in gameplay straight away. Only the very first trigger should be available at the start. So we need to disable the other triggers until they're needed. To do so hold *T* and click to add a **Toggle** and in its **Obj Comment** property type *T1*. Repeat this till you have **Toggle** actions named *T1*, *T2*, and *T3*.

18. From the **Touched** nub of the **Trigger_0 Touch** event, connect to the **Turn On** nub of **Toggle** *T1*. From the red **Event** nub of **Toggle** *T1*, drag a wire down to the name label on top of the **Trigger_1 Touch** event. This is called a **Dynamic Binding Event**. Once you've done so, right-click on the **Toggle** *T1* and choose **Hide Unused Connectors**. In the properties of the **Trigger_1 Touch** event, look for the **Sequence Event | Enabled** checkbox and turn it off. This means that this **Trigger Touch** event will only be enabled by the first one.

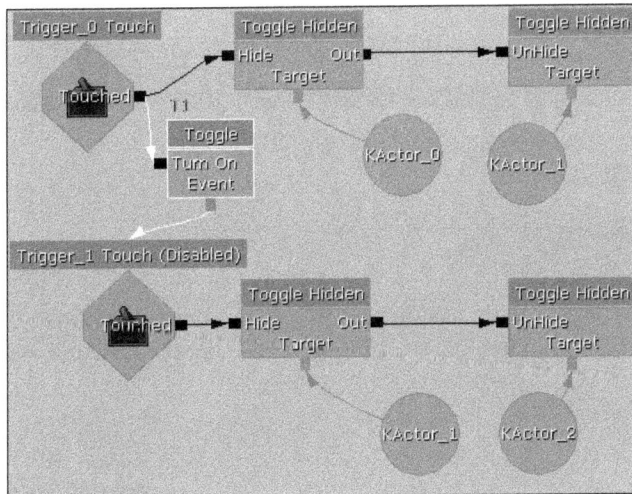

19. Repeat this pattern using both **Toggles** *T2* and *T3* until you can reveal the spheres one after the other.

20. The next few steps simply provide a result to go at the end of collecting the orbs. When the player collects them all, we want to disarm the enemy and make him vulnerable. We have already used the actions to do this, a **Change Collision** action and a **Give Inventory** action which removes his weapon.

21. After the ***Toggle Hidden*** action effecting **KActor_3**, add a new ***Change Collision*** and assign it to the ***Object Variable*** *???* assigned to the **Spawned** nub of the **Actor Factory** producing the Bot. Set the **Collision Type** property of this to *COLLIDE_CustomDefault*. This means we can hit him.

22. After he's spawned, the Bot needs his collision turned off. So copy and paste the same action, and hook the pasted action up to the **Finished** nub of the **Actor Factory** instead. This time set the **Collision Type** property to *COLLIDE_NoCollision*.

23. To disarm him, highlight the ***Give Inventory*** action already assigned to the player. It's labeled *RocketLauncher*. Press *Ctrl + C* then *Ctrl + V* and hook it up to the ***Toggle Hidden*** effecting the ***Object Variable*** KActor_3. It will still be assigned to the ***Player Variable***, so hold *Alt* and click on its **Target** nub, then assign the ***Object Variable*** *???* that's spawned by the **Actor Factory** instead. Instead of being given a *RocketLauncher*, we want to disarm the Bot, so set the **Inventory List | [0]** entry to *None* (and the **Obj Comment** too).

24. PIE to check that when you first fire at the Bot, you can't hit him at all. Then collect the four orbs and try again. You will get a Kismet warning. This is because giving the Bot *None* as a weapon replacement isn't really a viable option. Change this to *UTJumpBoots* (which aren't a weapon) instead. Test it again.

25. The last steps spread the Kismet out broadly, so it would probably be easiest to check the provided demonstration map *Packt_04_RevealActors_DEMO.UDK*.

Producing sounds through Kismet

In this recipe we'll introduce actions that allow you to accompany events with sounds when an actor picks up objects in the scene.

Getting ready

Open *Packt_04_PlaySound_Start.UDK* or continue from where you were in the last recipe if you completed it. In this map the Bot handling is already set up, from previous recipes.

How to do it...

1. In the map are four glowing white spheres. At present when you pick them up they just vanish. Let's provide some feedback to the player in the form of a sound too. Locate in the Kismet the event called ***Trigger_0 Touch***. In some clear space that's near, hold *D* and click to add a ***Delay***. Hook the **Touched** nub of the ***Trigger_0 Touch*** event to the **Start** nub of the ***Delay***. Set the ***Delay*** action's **Duration** to 0.25.

2. In the Content Browser, locate *PacktWavs.Cue.one_Cue*. This is a **SoundCue** asset that uses an imported .WAV file. Press *Space* to preview it. With this highlighted, in Kismet hold *S* and click to add a ***Play Sound*** node. In the node's properties, in the **Play Sound** field press the **Use selected object in browser** icon [🔄].

3. For the **Target** nub of the ***Play Sound*** action set a ***Player Variable*** (hold *P* and click). From the **Finished** nub of the ***Play Sound*** action, extend a wire to a ***Log*** (hold *L* and click). In the ***Log*** action's **Obj Comment** field, type *1 of 4*. This will display on screen after the sound plays.

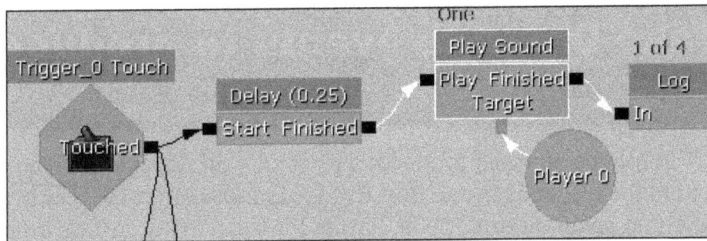

4. Repeat this set up for the ***Trigger_1 Touch*** event using the Sound Cue *PacktWavs. Cue.two_Cue* and entering the **Obj Comment** *2 of 4* in the ***Log*** following the ***Play Sound*** action. Since the name of the assets in the **Play Sound** property are much the same, you can just type the name change by replacing one with two in the field entry.

5. You can select and copy the ***Delay***, the ***Play Sound***, its ***Player Variable***, and the ***Log***, and paste them below, then re-assign *PacktWavs.Cue.three_Cue* to the **Play Sound** property, and *3 of 4* to the **Obj Comment** of the ***Log***. The same pattern would go for *4 of 4* and *PackWavs.Cue.four_Cue* in another pasted set. Make sure each set is assigned to the respective ***Trigger Touch*** event.

6. It would also be good to add a sound which is more of a special effect, to accompany the collection event. This can be a single ***Play Sound*** node that is fed by all the ***Trigger Touch*** events.

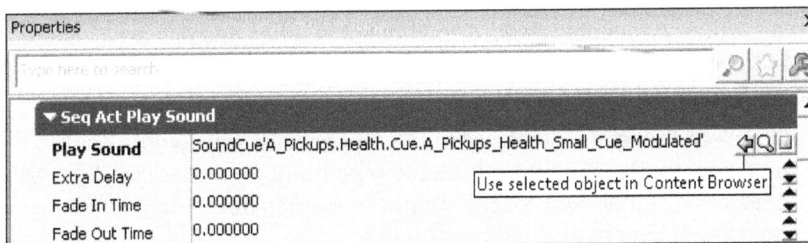

7. Hold S and click to add the **Play Sound** action and in its property **Play Sound**, and assign from the Content Browser *A_Pickups.Health.Cue.A_Pickups_Health_Small_Cue_Modulated*. Don't be misled by the name of the asset; it's the sound itself that counts. Feed its **Play** nub to the **Touched** nub of the *Trigger_0 Touch* event, the *Trigger_1 Touch* event, the *Trigger_2 Touch* event, and the *Trigger_3 Touch* event.

8. PIE to check that when you pick up the orbs you get a voice chiming in 1, 2, 3, 4. A demonstration is in the map *Packt_04_PlaySound_DEMO.UDK*. Look in the commented section **Collect Orb Sounds**.

Using Take Damage events to produce explosions

In this recipe we'll introduce an event that allows you to fire off actions when an actor happens to take damage from the player or from a Bot. This lesson will also cover how to add particle emitters to the event to generate explosions. Rather than use many particle emitters we'll teleport a single emitter from place to place whenever it is needed.

Getting ready

Open *Packt_04_Explosions_Start.UDK* or continue from where you were in the previous recipe if you completed it. In this map the Bot handling is already set up, from previous recipes.

How to do it...

1. In the map are four glowing white spheres. In gameplay, they are exposed in order by touching one after the other. Each of these is represented in Kismet by an *Object Variable*. These are indicated as *KActor_0* to *KActor_4*. Locate the *Object Variable KActor_0* in the commented section *Collect All Four Orbs*. Right-click on it and choose **Select KActor_0** in level.

2. In the section commented *Initial Conditions*, the other KActor's are clustered together. Hold *Ctrl* and click them in series to select all four variables, then right-click and choose **Select Actors in Level**.

3. In some clear space in Kismet, right-click and choose **New Events** using **KActor_0... | Take Damage**. This will add a *Take Damage* event for each actor. With all these selected, change their **Max Trigger Count** properties from 1 to 0. This means they can be damaged more any number of times.

4. Set the **Re Trigger Delay** property below it to 3.0 seconds, to slow down the event's availability.

5. Hold *D* and click to add a *Delay*. Give it a **Duration** of 0.3. Hook up the *KActor_0 Take Damage* event's **Out** nub to the **Start** nub of the *Delay*.

6. Right-click on the **Out** nub of the **KActor_0 Take Damage** event and choose **Copy Connections**. Go to each **Out** nub of the other **Take Damage** events and right-click and choose **Paste Connections**. This is a handy way of duplicating links to actions. In other situations you can transfer links by using **Cut Connections**. What you should have now is all the events feeding into the same **Delay** action's **Start**.

7. Next, hold *T* and click to add a **Toggle** action. Hook the **Finished** nub of the **Delay** into the **Turn On** nub of the **Toggle**.

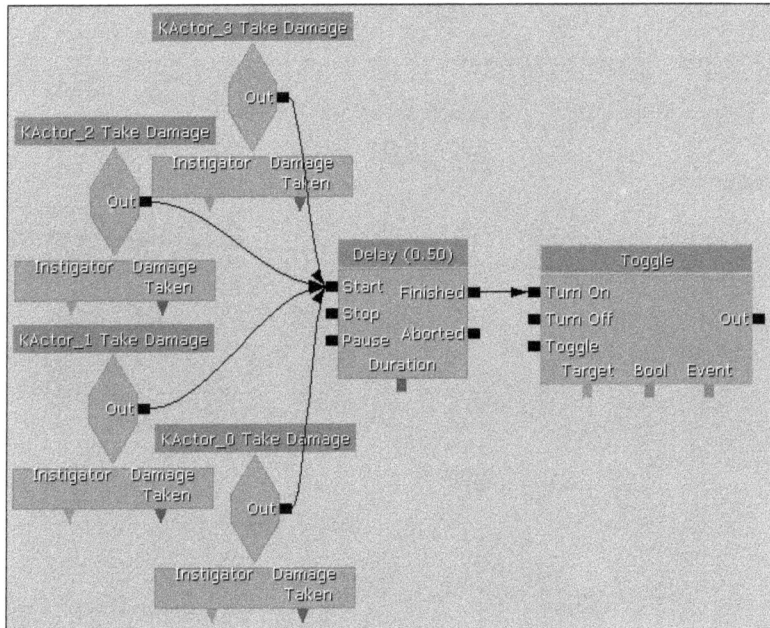

8. Now we'll add the particle effect to the scene. In the Content Browser, search for the *ParticleSystem WP_ShockRifle.Particles.P_WP_ShockRifle_Explo*. Drag it into the scene where the white sphere *KActor_0* sits. You'll have to scale it to suit the size of the sphere, down to about 0.6 **DrawScale 3D**.

9. With the Emitter selected, press *F4*, and expand the property **Emitter | Particle System Component | Particle System Component** to locate **Auto Activate**. Turn this off. We only want the particle to activate when we tell it to in Kismet, otherwise it would just fire off once when the game starts and that would be all.

10. In Kismet, right-click on the **Target** nub of the **Toggle** you added and choose **Assign Emitter_0 to Object Variable(s)**. What we now have is this: whenever one of the KActor spheres takes damage then the particle will activate, making a brief explosion. However, currently it will always occur at the same location. So, let's make sure it gets teleported where we need it at the appropriate time.

11. In the section called *Collect All Four Orbs* locate the ***Trigger_0 Touch*** event. Coming from its **Touched** nub is a ***Toggle*** *T1* which **Turns On** the next event. Send an additional wire from the red **Event** nub of the ***Toggle*** *T1* to make a **Dynamic Binding Event** to the top label of the ***KActor_1 Take Damage***. Likewise, send an additional wire from the red **Event** nub of the ***Toggle*** *T2* to the top label of the ***KActor_2 Take Damage***. Do the same from ***Toggle*** *T3* to ***KActor_3 Take Damage***. This means the events we've added can't fire in the wrong order. The following is what you should finally have for the *Take Damage* comment block shown below, including the enabling of the events by the ***Toggle*** *T1, T2,* and *T3*:

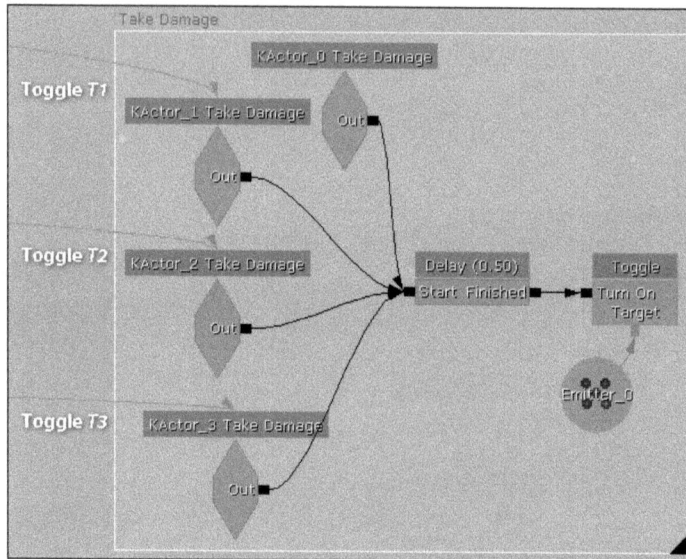

12. Near the ***Trigger_0 Touch*** event right-click and choose **New Action | Actor | Teleport**. Hook the **Touched** nub of the ***Trigger_0 Touch*** event to the **In** nub of the **Teleport** action. Set ***Object Variable*** *Emitter_0* as the **Target**. Select the ***Teleport*** action and the assigned ***Object Variable*** for the **Target** and press *Ctrl + C*. Set for the ***Object Variable*** *KActor_1* the **Destination** nub of the ***Teleport*** action. Press *Ctrl + V* to paste what you copied previously. For the pasted action, connect its **In** nub to the ***Trigger_1 Touch*** event's **Touched** nub. For the **Destination**, set the ***Object Variable*** *KActor_2*. Paste again, and for the second pasted action, connect its **In** nub to the ***Trigger_2 Touch*** event's **Touched** nub. For the **Destination**, set the ***Object Variable*** *KActor_3*.

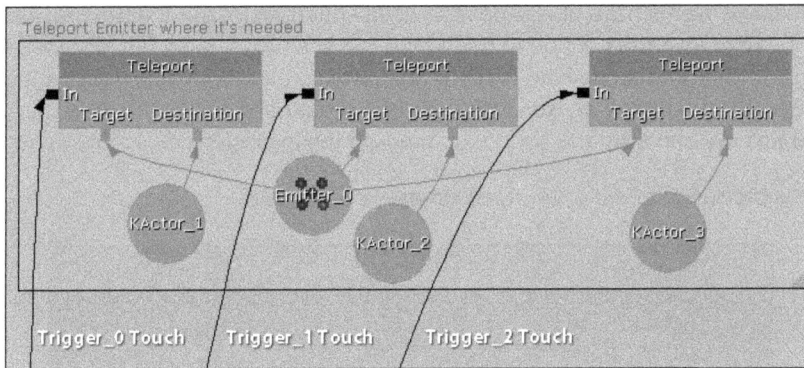

13. Select the four **Trigger Touch** events and in their properties expand the **Touch Types** category. Here, look for **Ignored Class Proximity Types** and add an entry [🔘] and in the [0] channel choose *UTWeap_RocketLauncher_Content* from the list. This prevents the rockets we fire causing a touch event on the Triggers that are supposed to be touched by the player.

14. What we have now is that each time the available **Trigger Touch** event is touched, the Emitter in the scene jumps to the location of the next exposed white sphere. PIE and shoot at the spheres to see if the Emitter fires off a purple flashy explosion at the right location. The Rocket Launcher will also produce a radius-based explosion, which is built into the weapon.

15. Last of all, to give some contextual meaning to shooting at the orbs, as opposed to just collecting them, let's reload the player's rocket launcher each time the player shoots at and hits an orb. Go to the section commented *Take Damage Events* and hook up all the **Take Damage** events into a **New Action | Pawn | Give Inventory** action. We've set up this before, so you'll find it easy to add the **Player 0 Variable** to the **Target** of the action, and then in the properties of the **Give Inventory** action add an entry to the **Inventory List** [🔘] and in the [0] channel select *UTWeap_RocketLauncher_Content*. PIE and shoot the orbs and you should notice that your ammo doesn't deplete unless you miss the orbs.

How it works

The particle system fires off when the level loads by default—this is to allow looping effects such as smoky chimneys, or leaves blowing in the wind, to run continually. For explosions, you want to turn off **Auto Activate** and instead use a **Toggle** action to fire them. In this example, it's it's better to use one Emitter instead of four. We can **Teleport** it to where it's needed through the **Trigger Touch** events that hide and expose the orbs. It's much cheaper to set up a Kismet network than to add four emitters. The calculation time for this is negligible at run-time.

The **Take Damage** events have been added to each sphere to let the Emitter fire. Also, we've added a **Give Inventory** action to reload the player's rocket launcher. It's good to match a visual effect with some kind of result that affects the player. It gives us a justification to shoot the orbs, and means we won't be likely to run out of ammo by the time we shoot at the exposed Bot. We can also add sound to round off the explosion.

An example is provided in *Packt_04_TakeDamage_DEMO.UDK*.

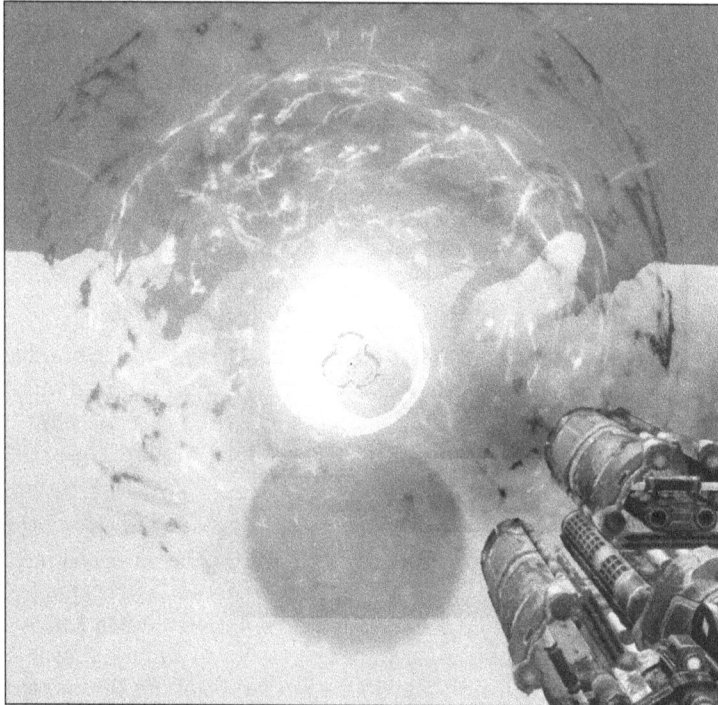

Understanding the usage of Named Variables

In this recipe we'll introduce a way to simplify the connections of **Object Variables**. The reason to do so is because in the next recipe we'll introduce **Sub-Sequences**, which are a way to layer out sections of Kismet, and using **Named Variables** are often necessary when doing so. A good case for introducing the benefit of **Named Variables** is in the case of Bots. When a spawned actor is referenced by actions many times, you wind up with connections to it from multiple locations, which can get messy. We'll take steps to clean up a section of Kismet we've made in previous recipes to show how **Named Variables** are set up.

Getting ready

Open *Packt_04_NamedVariable_Start.UDK* or continue from where you were in the last recipe if you completed it. In this map the Bot handling is already set up, from previous recipes. Look at the section *Bot Handling*.

How to do it...

1. In the top row of Kismet there is a *means* to set bookmarks of the Kismet canvas so you can jump around between areas you plan to work on a lot. Under the **Window** menu there is a little black downward triangle icon [⊿], which expands a roll-out menu for setting and jumping to bookmarks. Use this to jump to an existing bookmark. You can also set a bookmark with the hot keys *Ctrl + 0, Ctrl + 1*, and so on, and then jump between them using 0 and 1 and so on. Locate the section called *Bot Handling* and press *Ctrl + 0* to bookmark it for later recall with *0*.

2. The hotkey for adding an **Object Variable** is to hold *O* and click in Kismet. This creates an unnamed **Object Variable** *???*. Hold *O* and click, and in the new variable's properties, locate the **Var Name** field and type *Boss* (it can be any name you like so long as it is followed consistently). *Boss* will appear in red under the variable. Don't confuse this with an **Obj Comment**, which would appear above the variable in blue.

3. A **Var Name** is a distinct name that is declared so we can identify it anywhere. This is one of the key lessons to learn for UDK. Highlight the **Named Variables** *Boss*, right-click on the canvas nearby and choose **New Comment (Wrap)** and enter *Global Variables* in the **Obj Comment** property for the comment box, as shown in the next screenshot. Global variables are kept aside from everything else so they're easy to find, and must be in the main sequence of Kismet, not in a Sub-Sequence (of which we'll talk more about in the next topic).

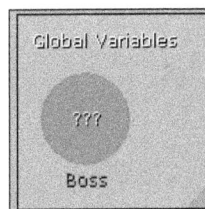

4. Notice that the other **Object Variable** *???* that comes from the **Spawned** nub of the **Actor Factory** in *Bot Handling* has many connections. This is where we can use a **Named Variable** to take up the strain on a single **Object Variable** node.

5. Hold *N* and click to produce a **Named Variable**. It will have a big red cross over it. In its **Find Var Name** field type *Boss*. This will tell the **Named Variable** who it represents. When any variable with the **Var Name** *Boss* is found, the **Named Variable** *Boss* gets a green tick. We already set one up, so that should happen immediately.

6. Copy and paste the **Named Variable** Boss and move it under an action that feeds the **Object Variable** ??? that has many wires. Press *Alt* on the action's nub and instead wire the nub to the **Named Variable** Boss. Paste the **Named Variable** Boss again and move it to the next action, and re-connect the wires. The next two images show a before and after comparison of the replaced nubs linked to the original variable. The first image shows the many connections to the **Object Variable** ???, which supplies us with an enemy Bot.

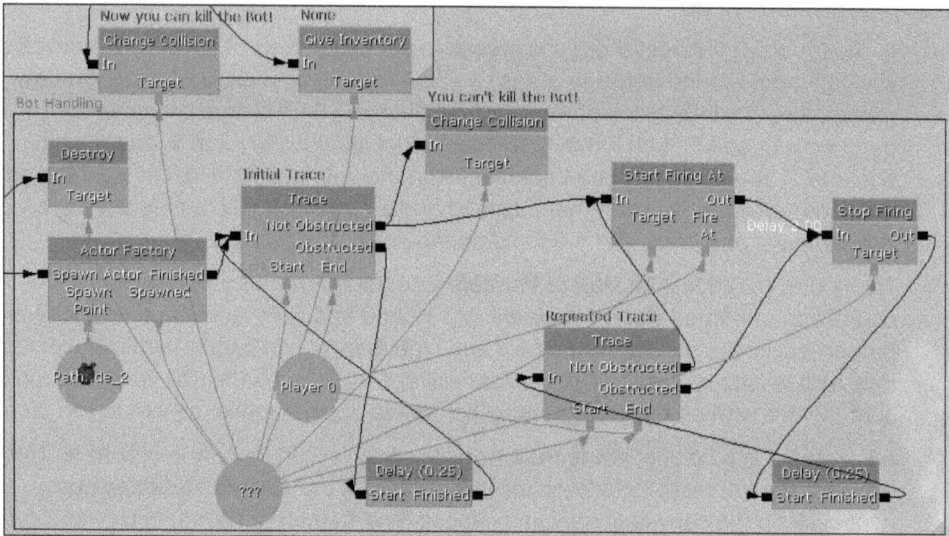

7. This is the result of replacing the connections to the **Named Variable** Boss. You'll notice that this frees up a lot of space to tidy and compact the Kismet layout too.

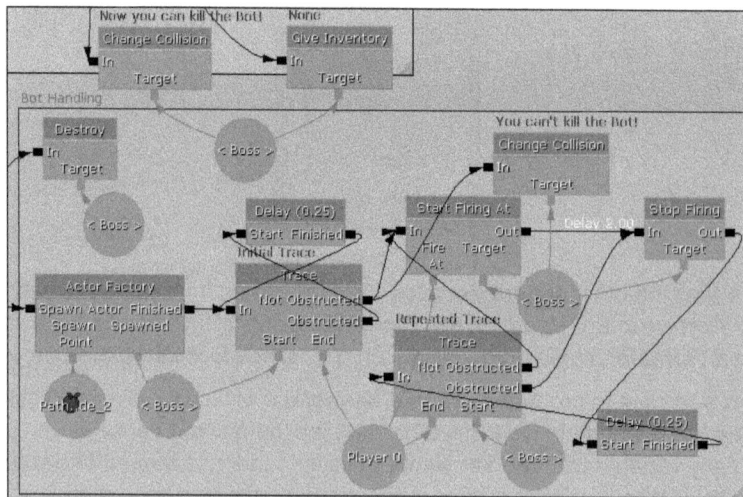

Tidying up Kismet networks using Sub-sequences

In this recipe we'll introduce the way to create **Sub-Sequences**. Sub-Sequences allow you to contextually split up parts of the Kismet network that can stand in isolation. You can still connect to them, and send out connections to other Sub-Sequences. Kismet has a **Sequences** Window usually docked at the lower right-hand side. When you create Sub-Sequences they show up here, nested under the main sequence. You can create Sub-Sequences inside of other Sub-Sequences. In the icons row at the top of the Kismet Editor, there is an up arrow [⬇] that lets you navigate from a Sub-Sequence to the main sequence.

Getting ready

Open *Packt_04_SubSequences_Start.UDK*. This continues from where you were in the previous map. In this map the Bot handling is already set up, from previous recipes. Look at the section *Bot Handling*.

How to do it...

1. Hold *Ctrl + Alt* and drag a selection marquee around the entire section of Kismet, as shown here:

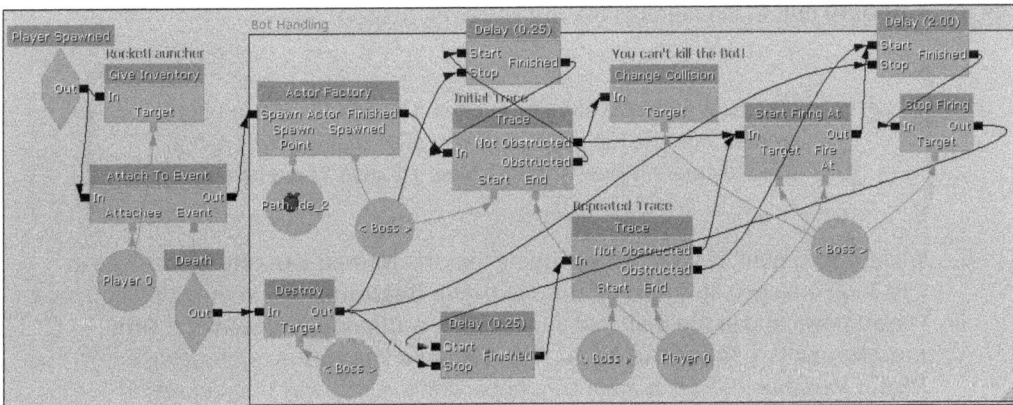

2. Right-click over the empty canvas and choose **Create New Sequence: 21 Objects**. You'll be prompted to name the sequence. Call it *PlayerPlusBoss*. Don't add space to the name as it isn't permitted. You'll get a little node with a blue background, and in the **Sequences** window you can also expand the list to show the nested *PlayerPlusBoss* Sub-Sequence. Clicking on that will open it, as will double clicking the node.

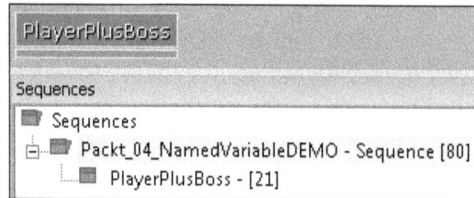

3. You can also jump to Sub-Sequences using the **Bookmarks** icon [⊒] and choosing them from the list.

4. Inside the Sub-Sequence *PlayerPlusBoss*, select the nodes outside of the *Bot Handling* comment box. Right-click and choose **Create New Sequence: 8 Objs**. Call it *PlayerSpawn*. Now we've added a nested Sub-Sequence.

5. Because this *PlayerSpawn* Sub-Sequence feeds out to the *PlayerPlusBoss* Sub-Sequence, a **Finish Sequence** action is automatically added. You can add one yourself by right-clicking and choosing **New Action | Misc | Finish Sequence**. Double-click the automatically added **Finish Sequence** node and it will jump you to its destination. Notice there, that there is a Sub-Sequence *PlayerSpawn* node with an **AutoOut0** nub which feeds to the *Bot Handling* network.

> Manually, a **New Event | Sequence Activated** event can be created with the hot key [, and similarly the hot key] can be used to create a **New Action | Misc | Finish Sequence** action.

6. While we are here, it's worth mentioning that the **Named Variable** Bot is used in this Sub-Sequence. It is also referred to by the **Destroy** action in the Sub-Sequence *PlayerSpawn* and in the main sequence under a **Change Collision** and **Give Inventory** action. This works because the **Named Variable** is referencing an **Object Variable** *???* in the main sequence. It is the only way that actions in various Sub-Sequences can refer to the same spawned actor (*Boss* in this case).

7. Hit the icon [↟] to go up to the main sequence. The section *Initial Conditions* could easily be selected and added to a new Sub-Sequence, as it stands in isolation from other parts of the network.

8. In the section commented *Collect All Four Orbs*, select the nodes highlighted below and create a Sub-Sequence from these called *Toggled0*.

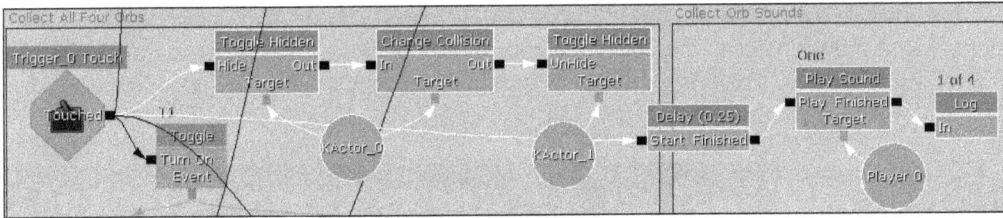

9. The result will show up as shown in the next screenshot. Notice it has two inputs. Actually it only needs one. We'll edit that next.

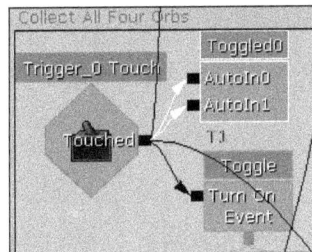

10. Double-click on the Sub-Sequence *Toggled0* and run a wire from the first **Sequence Activated Event** (*AutoIn0*) to the Delay that the other **Sequence Activated Event** (*AutoIn1*) is firing. Then delete the **Sequence Activated Event** (*AutoIn1*). Although you could leave it as it was, you only need one of the two, as shown in the next screenshot.

11. If you make a typo, to rename a Sub-Sequence, right-click on it and choose **Rename Sequence**.

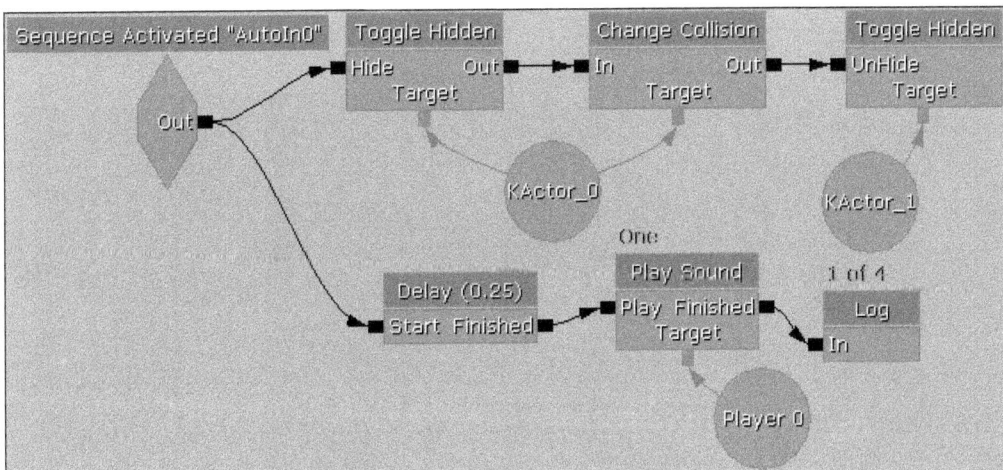

12. You can repeat the pattern for *Toggled1*, *Toggled2*, and *Toggled3* using the respective chains in the *Collect All Four Orbs* section of the main Kismet network. An example of this scene, tidied up using Sub-Sequences is in the provided map *Packt_04_SubSequence_DEMO.UDK*.

Tidying up Kismet networks using Remote Events

In this recipe we'll introduce **Remote Events**. These let you send a connection from one part of a Kismet network to another part far away, even in another Sub-Sequence. The purpose is to reduce the number of wires crossing over nodes, to make the network easier to read. In this example we'll do a very quick simplification of some nodes that are otherwise difficult to tidy up.

How to do it...

1. Open *Packt_04_RemoteEvent_Start.UDK*. Look at the section **Teleport Emitter Where It's Needed**. This would be a prime candidate for sending to a Sub-Sequence if it didn't have three separate links coming into it from events below.

2. Go to the **Trigger_0 Touch** event and hold *R* and click. You'll be prompted for an **Event Name**. Type `FirstTeleport`. This automatically creates a **Remote Event** event with the **Event Name** *FirstTeleport* but also an **Activate Remote Event** action with the **Event Name** *FirstTeleport* as well.

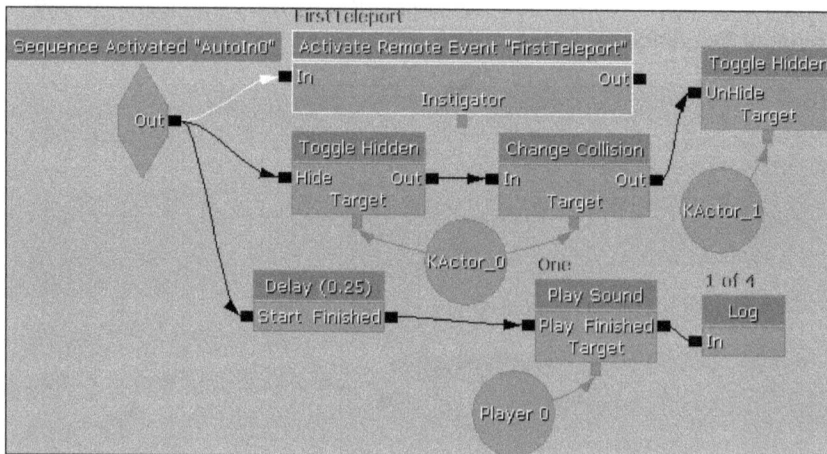

3. Select the newly added action and press *Ctrl + X* to cut it and then double-click on the Sub-Sequence *Toggled0*. As shown in the screenshot, press *Ctrl + V* with the Sub-Sequence to paste the action and hook its **In** nub to the **Sequence Activated AutoIn0** event's **Out** nub.

4. Double-click on the **Activate Remote Event** *FirstTeleport*. This will send you to the corresponding event, the **Remote Event** *FirstTeleport* up in the main sequence. Drag this to the **Teleport** action affecting *Emitter_0*, with the **Destination** being the **Object Variable** *KActor_0*, as shown in the next screenshot. Now, when the Sub-Sequence *Toggled0* fires off, the **Remote Event** will fire the **Teleport** action too. Press *Alt* on the wire feeding the same **Teleport** to the **Trigger_0 Touch** event. Instead hook the **Remote Event** up to the **Teleport** action, as shown below:

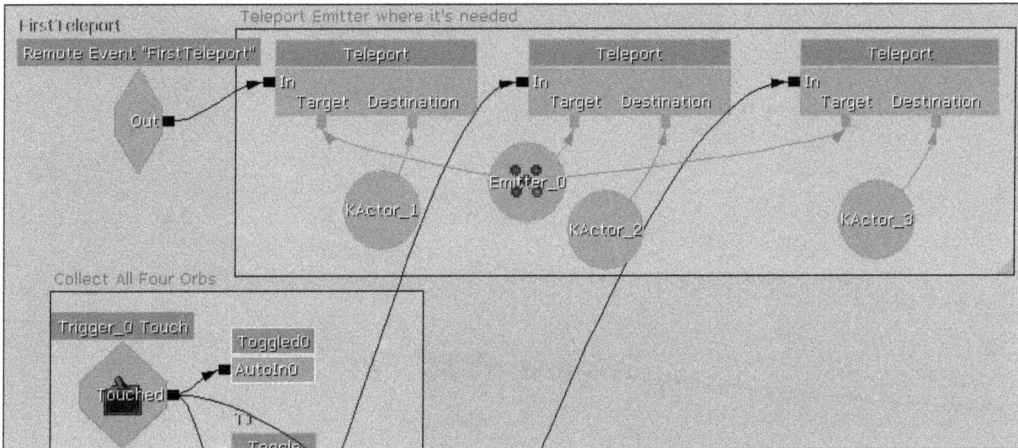

5. We'll have to repeat a similar step to provision a **Remote Event** for the second and third **Teleport** actions, as shown in the next screenshot. When that's done it can be turned into a stand-alone Sub-Sequences *Teleporters*.

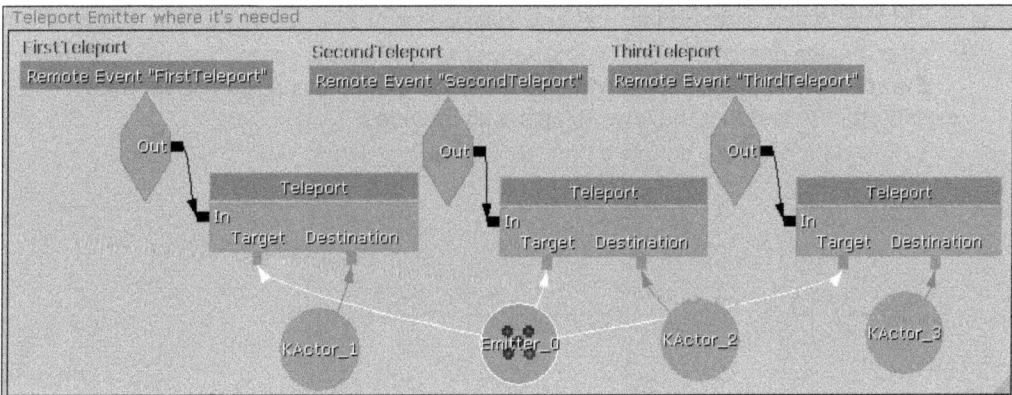

6. A similar staging using **Remote Events** could be done for the **Take Damage** event, as shown below:

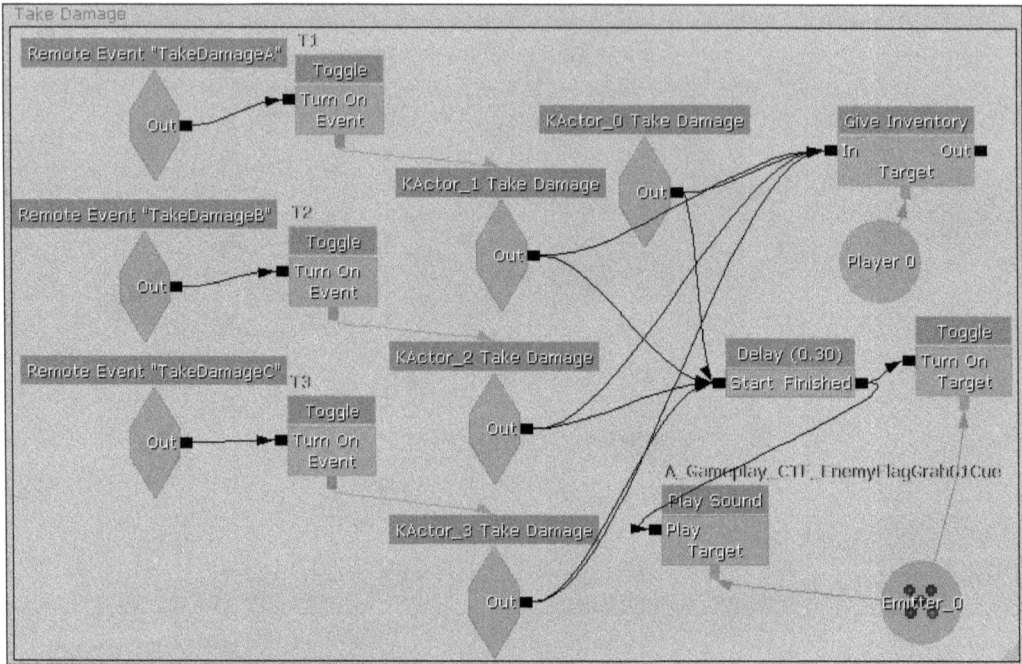

7. This would leave us with a final main sequence something like the next example, which can be viewed in the map *Packt_04_RemoteEvent_DEMO.UDK*, provided in this book's download bundle.

8. After making changes to an existing sequence so that it is compacted using **Remote Events**, Sub-Sequences, and when you are cleaning up using **Named Variables**; it is important to test that the level still plays as intended.

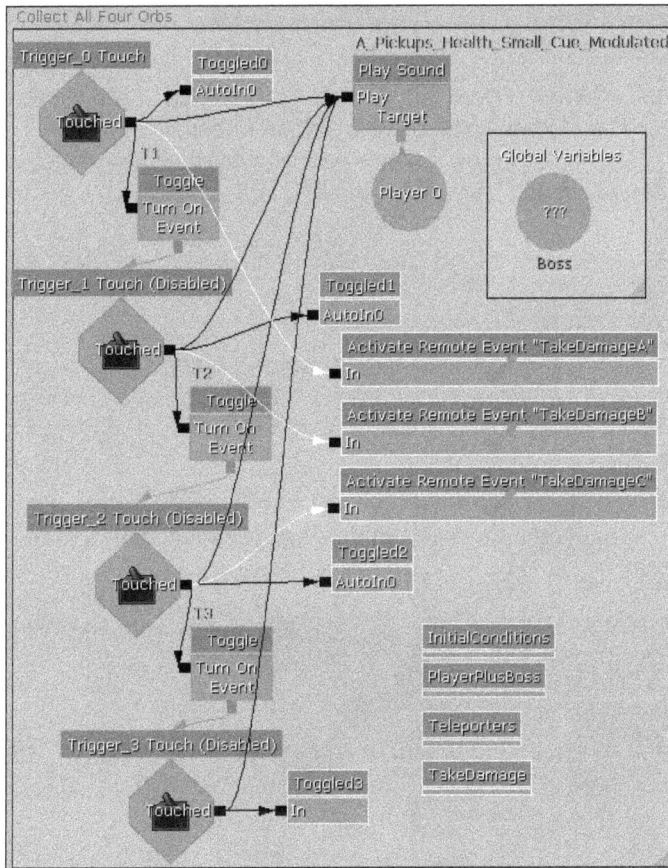

Toggling Materials through Kismet

Quite often you will want to adjust lights in the scene to turn them on and off according to events that happen during gameplay. Now we'll look at how to convert a lamp mesh so it has a Material with an Emissive feature and an alternative Material with no Emissive feature. This will help create the illusion of a lamp being turned on and off. This will be followed by a lesson on how to toggle a PointLight in the scene to continue to set up of that illusion. We're dealing with a lamp mesh as the source of illumination, and that requires a Material to be swapped for an on and off variant, so we'll look at the use of the **Set Material** action in Kismet.

Getting ready

The scene we'll work with would take a while to set up, so a starting point has been provided. From the provided content, load the map *Packt_04_SetMaterial_Start.UDK*. The scene includes at one end of a passage two switch elements and some lamp meshes. The lamps have a Material with a flickering Emissive channel. This is what needs to be turned off when the lamp is switched off.

How to do it...

1. There are two things to consider with the toggled lights: one is the light cast from it, and the other is the texture showing on it. The lamp mesh, which has a Material for "lights on" also needs a replacement Material for "lights out". We will create a **Set Material** action in Kismet.

2. If you can't spot it, select the lamp mesh *InterpActor_7* using the **Edit | Find Actor** menu. Press either the **Go To** text button in the floating window or the toolbar icon **Go to Actor** [▣], or *Home*.

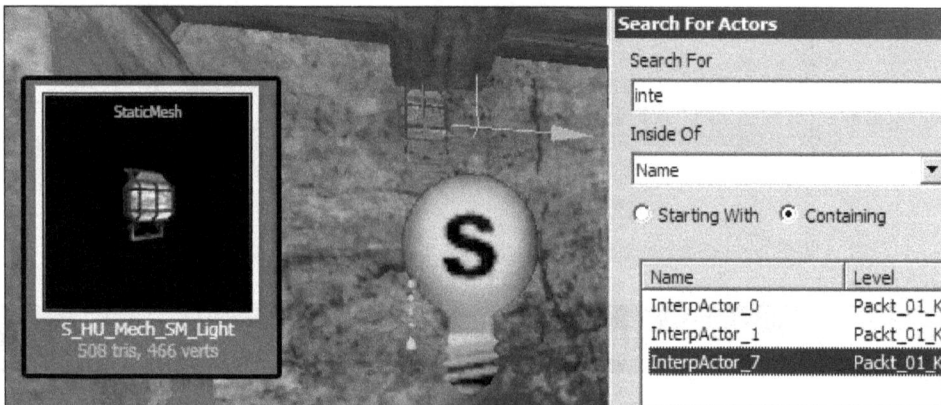

3. Right-click and choose **Materials | Find in Browser** or press *Ctrl + Shift + B*.

4. The Material *HU_Mech.Material.M_HU_Mech_SM_Light01* should now be highlighted in the Content Browser. Right-click on it and choose **Create a Copy**, and set a copy to your own package and rename it *Yourfolder.Material.LampOff*.

5. Double-click the result and the Material Editor will open. Here, simply *press ALT + LMB* on the wire feeding into the Material's Emissive channel to disconnect it. Then press the green tick [▢] in the top corner of the Material Editor to compile the change, and close. Right-click on the changed Material asset in the Content Browser and choose **Save**.

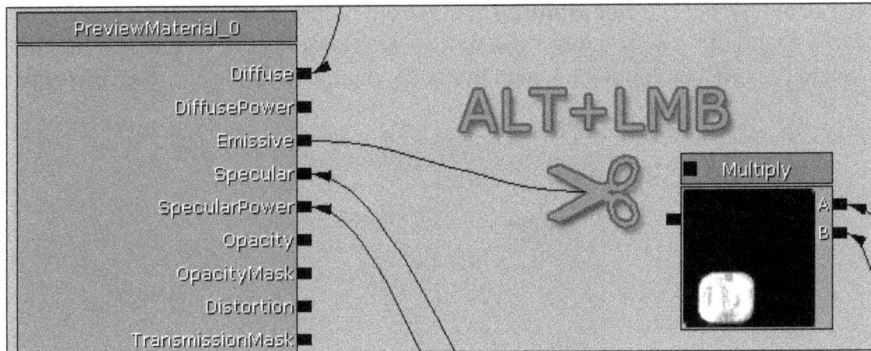

6. Make sure that your new *LampOff* Material is highlighted in the Content Browser and right-click on the lamp mesh and choose **Material | Assign from Content Browser**. Also, right-click on the lamp mesh in the scene, and choose **Convert | Convert StaticMeshActor to Mover**. This is so it can be accessed in Kismet.

7. Still in the Content Browser, filter Materials, then search for *LampOff*.

8. In Kismet, right-click and choose **New Action | Actor | Set Material**.

9. In this action's properties, expand **Seq Act_Set Material**. In the channel **New Material** we'll assign the Material *M_HU_Mech_SM_Light01* from the Content Browser. Tick the assign icon [🔄] to assign *M_HU_Mech_SM_Light01*.

10. With the lamp mesh selected in the scene, right-click on the **Target** nub of the *Set Material* action, and choose **New Object Var using InterpActor**.

11. Now *Alt-drag* the mesh across the wall so a copy sits opposite the first.

Notice the name of the copy is the same as the old version. The old version gets renamed, which is recursive and something that can take some getting used to. Any references to the old object will be updated automatically to reflect the name change.

12. In Kismet, select the **Set Material** action from before, and copy and paste it using *Ctrl + C* and *Ctrl + V*. You may have to *Alt + Left-click* on the **Target** nub to break the link to the original variable. Assign the second lamp mesh to this **Set Material** action.

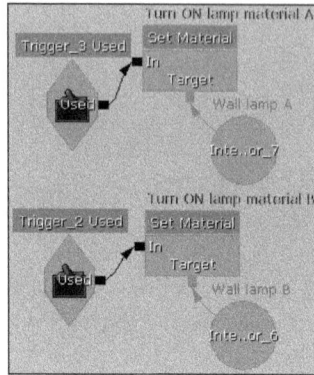

13. Connect each **Set Material** to the relevant **Trigger** event's **Used** nub, as in the previous screenshot. Remember that in your network other wires will be connected to the events too. If you want to duplicate the events to space things out and keep things clean that is fine, but usually it is best to make the most use of a single node where possible. Using duplicate nodes can make later editing harder.

14. Build again and PIE to see if the Material is being swapped from unlit to lit on the lamp when you trigger each switch. Make sure the left switch fires the left lamp, and the right switch fires the right lamp. An example is provided in the scene *Packt_04_SetMaterial_DEMO.UDK*.

Toggling lights through Kismet

In the previous recipe we set a Material toggle using two **Set Material** actions in Kismet. This only changes the Material on a mesh however, not the light cast in the scene. For that we are using PointLights. However, to make a PointLight so it can be turned on and off, it must be converted to a PointLightToggleable. This is what we'll cover in the recipe, along with setting up a control for this converted light using a simple **Toggle** action.

Getting ready

The scene we'll work with would take a while to set up, so a starting point has been provided. From the provided content, load the map *Packt_04_ToggleableLights_Start.UDK*. The scene includes at one end of a passage two switch elements and some lamp meshes. The lamps have a Material with a flickering Emissive channel, but the Material is insufficient to illuminate the surroundings. A standard PointLight sits in front of the smallest lamp, and we'll convert it to a light type that can be toggled in Kismet.

How to do it...

1. Select PointLight_4 by searching for it in the menu **Edit | Find Actors**. It is the light at the dark end of the passageway. Right-click on it and choose **Convert Light | PointLights | PointLightToggleable**. Notice its name and enumeration now change. Making the light toggleable is necessary to let the light operate in Kismet.

2. Open Kismet [K] and right-click in the Kismet canvas and choose **New Object Var Using PointLightToggleable_0**. Notice the light has been renamed and renumbered. Its icon [ ] has also changed to include a little dangling chain like old style lamps used to have. This reminds us we can switch this light on and off.

3. Minimize Kismet. Notice it pops down into the corner of the editor. You can actually place this minimized floater where you like and it will remember that position. Place it under the Kismet icon [K]. It will remain there till closed.

4. Now, we need to toggle the PointLight, which we already converted to be toggleable. This requires only a *Toggle* action (hold *T* and click) in Kismet. First, duplicate the PointLight so a copy of it covers the second wall lamp. Create the *Toggle* in Kismet, and assign the first PointLight as its **Target**.

5. Hook up the first *Trigger Used* event's output to the **Turn On** input on the *Toggle* action. Also, hook up the *Level Loaded* event's **Loaded and Visible** output to the **Turn Off** input of the *Toggle*. Repeat this for the second PointLight using the second trigger so you obtain a network functioning like the one shown in the next screenshot:

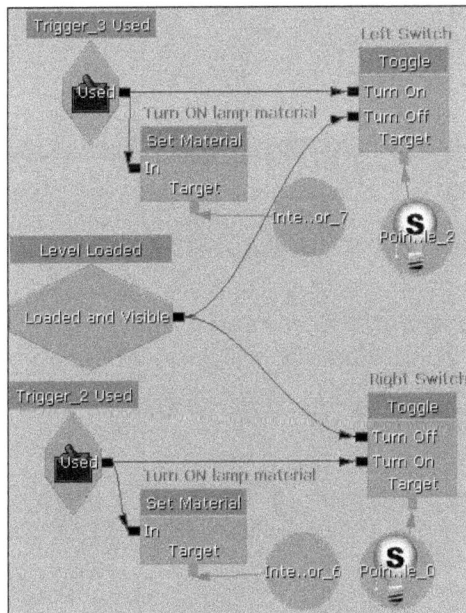

6. Press **Build All** [🔍]. You should now have a scene where the end of the passage is dark, and the two Triggers, when used with *E*, turn on the lights and depress the switches with a sound to enrich the event. The next image shows the toggling the triggers cause. Notice how the highlighted **Level Loaded** event sets the initial state for everything. Next we'll set up the **Matinee** action to control the lights flickering so it matches the flicker built into the lamp model's Material.

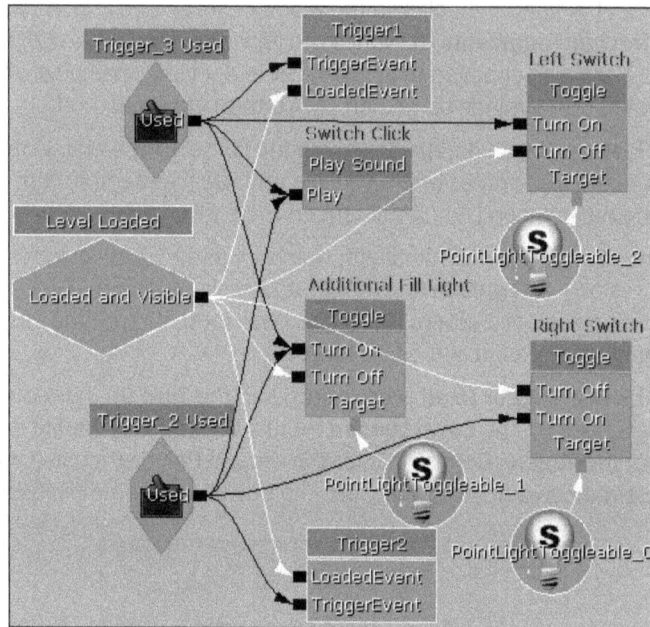

Animating PointLights in Matinee to mimic texture animation

In this recipe we'll animate PointLights associated with a lamp asset, a model with a flickering texture, so that the light emitted in the scene also appears to flicker. We'll do this using Matinee, and in particular the Constant interpolation mode of a set of noisily keyed values.

Getting ready

Open the map *Packt_04_MatineeFlicker_Start.UDK*. This progresses on from the previous recipes on toggling materials and toggling lights. Notice that that functionality has been compacted into a Sub-Sequence *ToggleableLighting*.

How to do it...

1. In the previous screenshot, you can see the Kismet for the entire sequence. Notice the importance of the highlighted **Level Loaded** event to set initial conditions. We can drive a **Matinee** for the light flicker straight from the **Level Loaded** event because the animation will just loop whether or not the lights involved are toggled on or off.

2. In Kismet hold *M* and click to add a **Matinee** next to the Sub-Sequence *ToggleableLighting* and type *Flicker* in its **Obj Comment** property. Also tick on the checkbox for **Looping**.

3. Hook up the **Matinee** action's **Play** input to the **Out** nub of the Sub-Sequence *ToggleableLighting*.

4. In the scene, select both PointLightToggleable actors and return to Kismet. Right-click and choose **New Matinee**.

5. Double-click on the **Matinee** to open it, and position the editor window to suit. Right-click in the dark gray space, and choose **Add New Empty Group**. At the prompt, name it *Flicker*.

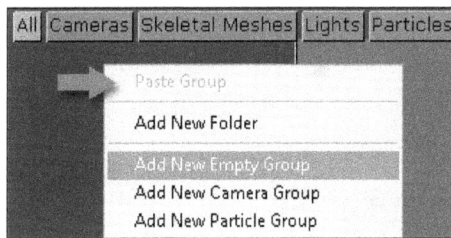

6. Make sure the PointLight actors are what is actually assigned to the **Flicker** track by checking in the Kismet Editor. If you don't see them attached to the **Flicker** nub of the **Matinee** action, select them in the scene and right-click on the new **Flicker** nub and add them both with the **New Object Vars using the PointLight...** command.

7. Right-click on the *Flicker* track in the Matinee Editor and choose **New Float Property Track** and at the prompt choose *PointLightComponent.Brightness*. This will not work unless the PointLights are already properly assigned to the **Matinee** action.

8. The **period** of the lamp's emissive flicker is driven by a panning noise map in the Material, so we have to more or less guess the key framing of the flicker. It will be a loop, over about two seconds. In the Matinee Editor, highlight the **Brightness** track and press *Enter*. This will create a key frame on frame 0, or at 0.00 seconds.

9. Drag the sequence time slider to 0.50 (it is a black bar with a white line above it, currently at 0.00s and a bit hard to spot). At 0.50 press *Enter* again to create a new key frame. This time, select the new key frame by right-clicking on it and choose **Set Value** and change the number to 2.

10. Use the mouse scroll wheel to zoom out the time range of the sequence until you see a red marker at 5.00s and move this to 2.00s instead. If you want to hit exactly 2.00s you may need to turn on the **Snap** tool (the magnet icon [🧲] in the Matinee Editor icon bar). It defaults to 0.50 increments

11. After setting the animation range, turn **Snap** off again. Between 0.00 and 2.00 add as many key frames as you want values varying between 0.3 and 2.33 or so. Don't go all the way to 0 for the brightness value and don't raise it too high, as a value of 1 is quite bright anyway.

12. Now select all the keys by using *Ctrl + Alt + LMB* and *drag* to define a marquee around them, and then right-click. Change their interpolation type to **Constant** by right-clicking on the time line keys as shown next. Drag the time slider, and in the viewport you should see the lights faithfully following their keyed animation. To see a better playback, extend the green arrows on the time line to fit from 0.00 to 2.00 and press **Loop Section** [🔁] in the Matinee Editor icon bar.

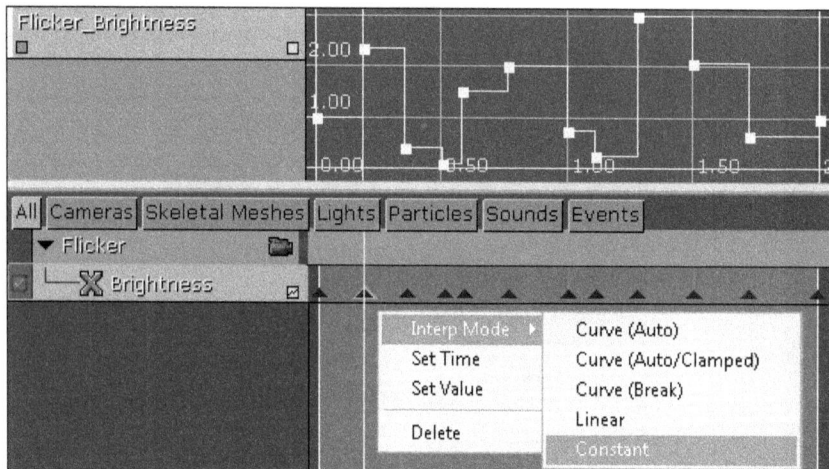

13. You may decide the flicker is too slow and stuttery. Rather than add more keys, in Kismet open the Matinee action's **Seq Act_Interp** properties, locate **Play Rate** and set it to 2, for example.

14. Your scene may still be quite dark around the locally lit lamps. Clone a new *PointLightToggleable* in the scene and place it over the gap in the floor after the two switches. Scale it up, but also change its **Brightness** property (*F4*) to 0.5 in order to make it seem like a fill light. In Kismet create a **New Action | Toggle | Toggle** and assign the fill light to its target. Then hook the **Used** outputs of both *Trigger | Used* Events to the *Toggle*'s **Turn On** input. Don't forget to ensure it is turned off when the level loads.

15. An example scene is included in the available content: *Packt_04_KismetLighting_Demo.UDK* and the following screenshot shows the before and after difference for the toggled lights:

Making a comparison following a countdown

In this recipe we'll shoot at a flying monster. What we'll check for is whether or not the player can shoot the dragon out of the sky in a set time. If they do, then they will get to load the next level. If they haven't the current level will reload. Given the reward of progression, we also discuss the difference between PIE, which is a quick emulation of the game in the editor, and **Play on PC** mode, which emulates all the features of a cooked, packaged game (see *Chapter 1, Heads Up*, under the recipe *Cooking a map with Unreal Frontend*).

Getting ready

Open the map *Packt_04_Comparison_Start.UDK*. This scene features an enclosure around which a monstrous creature is circling. PIE to see if you can shoot down the monster with provided rocket launcher. There is a need for deflection shooting, where you aim ahead of the trajectory of the target, to get a hit.

How to do it...

1. Once you are competent at shooting down the monster, you may want to inspect the Kismet set up for how this works. In the main sequence there are some results of hitting the monster with a rocket. Actually we don't hit the monster (or its SkeletalMesh), we just hit a Trigger actor attached to it.

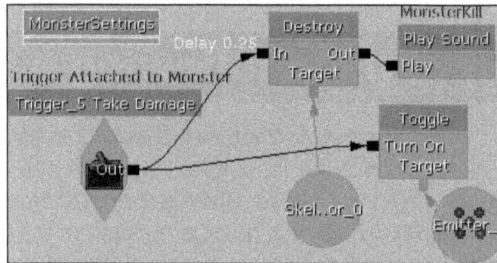

2. Unhook the **Play Sound** *MonsterKill* and move it off a bit into clear space. Select the **Destroy** action and its **Object Variable** and also the **Toggle** action firing the **Object Variable** *Emitter_0*. Create a New Sequence from these, to get them out of the way. Call this Sub-Sequence *DestroyMonster*.

3. The Sub-Sequence *MonsterSettings* is where the attachment of the Trigger to the SkeletalMesh *Monster* occurs. A particle Emitter actor in the scene is also attached to the Monster when the level loads, and the Monster is attached to a Cylinder that is being rotated 360 by a looping **Matinee**.

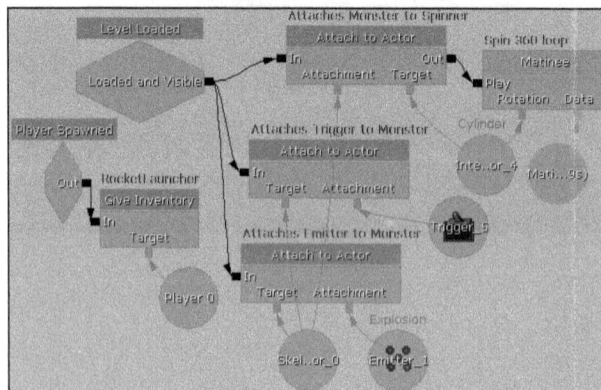

4. We'll want to add some results following the shooting besides those provided. We'll focus on setting up a *Timer* that we can compare against when the player finally shoots the monster out of the sky. To do this, in Kismet, in the main sequence, right-click and add a **New Action | Misc | Timer**. This simply acts like a stop from when its **Start** nub is fired to when its **Stop** nub is fired. Right-click its **Time** nub and choose **New Float Variable**.

5. Right-click and choose **New Event | Player | Spawned**, and connect its **Out** nub to the **Start** nub of the *Timer*. Connect the **Out** nub of the *Trigger_5 Take Damage* event to the **Stop** nub of the *Timer*. From when the player begins running around in the level to when the monster is shot down, the timer will be busy keeping time.

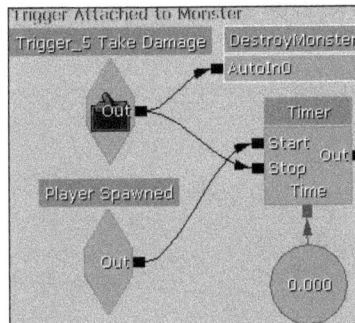

6. The timer will work but there's no way to either display the count on screen during PIE or to compare the time against something. To display the **Float value** on screen would be easy enough; a *Log* would do fine, but it would count upwards from 1 and would also have decimal places. It would be better to create a countdown from 30, and make sure the number displayed is a whole number (or Integer). To get started on this part, hold *L* and click to add a *Log* and hook it up so the **Player Spawned** event's **Out** nub feeds the *Log* node's **In** nub. Right-click on the *Log* and choose **Expose Variable | Float—Float**.

7. Set the **Float** nub to be the same *Float Variable* that's connected to the **Time** nub of the *Timer* action. Set a *Player 0 Variable* as the **Target** of the *Log*, as shown here:

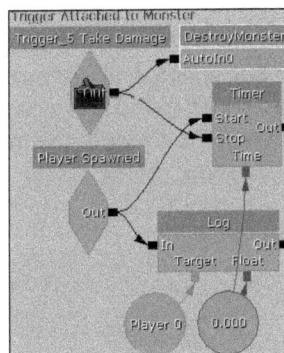

8. This **Log** requires a loop back to keep displaying the **Timer** action's count through the **Float Variable**, but we've still got a couple of things to do first. This **Log** would count up from 0 and we want to count down from 30. So right-click and choose **New Action | Math | Subtract Float**. The **Subtract Float** should be connected to the **Log**, and then the **B** nub should be connected to the existing **Float Variable** which is attached to the **Timer** (and the **Log**). Under the **A** nub hold F and click to add a **Float Variable**. Set its **Float Value** property to 30. If you want to, give the **Float Value** more or less than 30 depending on how hard you think it is to shoot the monster and how much time you want to count down. Hold F and click under the **Float Result** nub and connect the resulting **Float Variable** to it. Lastly, right-click on the **IntResult** nub and choose **Create New Int Variable**. This converts the **Float Result**, which goes to decimal point precision such as 29.013 or 28.004, to a round number like 30, 29, or 28.

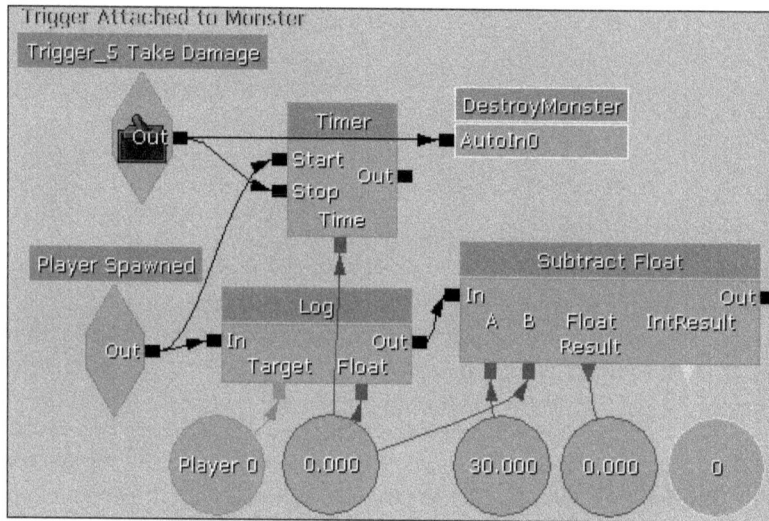

9. Hold L and click add another **Log**, and likewise set its **Target** as the **Player 0 Variable**. This time right-click on the Log and choose **Expose Variable | Int–Int**. Hook the exposed **Int** nub up to the same **Integer Variable** added in the previous step to the **IntResult** nub of the **Subtract Float**.

10. This sequence, from **Log** to **Log** should loop, so hold D and click to add a **Delay**. Hook the **Out** nub of the **Log** added in the previous step to the **Start** nub of the **Delay**. Hook the **Finished** nub of the **Delay** to the **In** nub of the **Log** connected to the **Player Spawned** event, as shown below:

Player Spawned

Time

Subtract Float

Log

Log

Out | In | Out | In | A B Float IntResult | In | Out

Target Float | Float Result | Int Target

Player 0 | 0.000 | 30.000 | 0.000 | 0 | Player 0

Delay (1.00)

Stop | Finished
Start

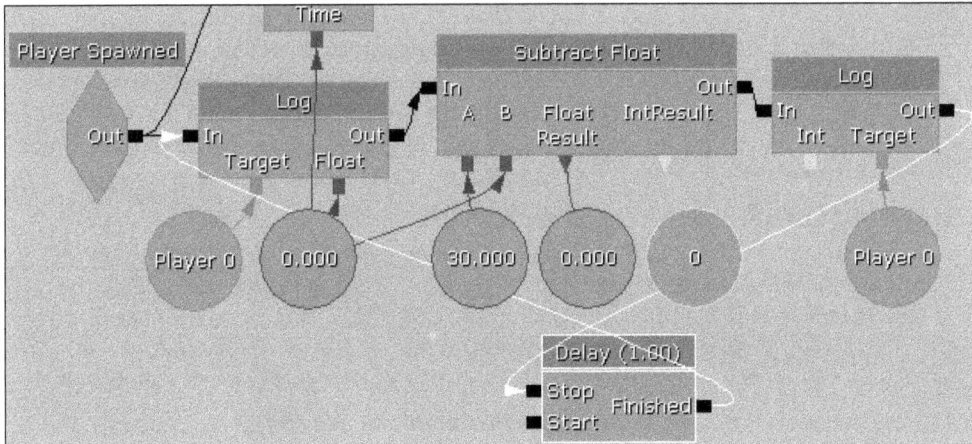

11. When the monster is destroyed, or more exactly, when the **Trigger_5 Take Damage** event occurs, we want to stop the loop which now should be counting down from 30 seconds, second by second. Hold *R* and click and when prompted enter the **Event Name** *EndLog* for a new **Remote Event** and **Activate Remote Event** action. Connect the **Trigger_5 Take Damage** event's **Out** nub to the **In** nub of the **Activate Remote Event** action. Move the **Remote Event** down by the **Delay** we added in the last step and hook its **Out** nub to the **Stop** nub of the **Delay**. This completes the looping timer and the time display.

12. Now we'll set up a condition for whether you killed or did not kill the monster within 30 seconds. Right-click in some clear space and choose **New Condition | Comparison | Compare Int** or hold *Ctrl + I* and click. This node takes its **A** value and compares it to its **B** value, and then sends out actions based on whether **A == B**, **A < B**, **A > B**, and so on. Hook the **In** nub of the **Compare Int** to the **Out** nub of the **Trigger_5 Take Damage** event. Connect the **Integer Variable** that's the **IntResult** of the **Subtract Float** and connect it to the **A** nub of the **Compare Int**. Right-click on the **B** nub and choose **Create New Int Variable**. The new **Integer Variable** can be left on 0 since we're counting down from 30 to 0, and so a target of **B = 0** works well.

13. Left hanging in the scene is a **Play Sound** action *MonsterKill*. Hook this up to the **A > B** nub of the **Compare Int**. If the time we take to shoot down the monster is not 30 seconds or longer we win.

14. In the Content Browser locate *PacktKismet.Cue.TooFast_CUE*. Back in Kismet, hold *S* and click next to the existing **Play Sound** *MonsterKill* and choose *PacktKismet. Cue.TooFast_CUE* for the **Play Sound** entry using the assign icon [ ]. Connect the **Finished** nub of **Play Sound** *MonsterKill* to the **Play** nub of **Play Sound** *TooFast*. This is an announcer congratulating us on our swift annihilation of the monster.

15. In the Content Browser locate *PacktKismet.Cue.TooLate_CUE*. Back in Kismet, hold S and click to add a **Play Sound** and use the assign icon [🔁] for the **Play Sound** property to assign *PacktKismet.Cue.TooLate_CUE*. Hook up the **Play Sound** action's **Play** nub to the A <= B nub of the **Compare Int**. The announcer in this case regrets that we took too long, even though we shot the monster. This will occur if the timer ran down all the way to zero (or more) before it was stopped.

16. Finally, let's create a concrete result to all this, besides sounds playing. Right-click and choose **New Action | Misc | Console Command**. Expand its property **Commands** to reveal the [0] channel, and in the text field type *open Packt_04_RemoteEventDEMO*. Don't add *.UDK* at the end. This lets the player progress on to a new level. Ideally it'd be one that leads on from this one, not an arbitrary one. You could choose any existing map you like as the target of this console command.

17. Right-click on the **In** nub of the **Console Command** and choose **Set Activate Delay**. Enter a value of 1.

18. Copy and paste the **Console Command** action. Type *open Yourfile_04_ComparisonDEMO* in the **Commands | [0]** property. Save the map you are working on with that name. The **Console Command** therefore will simply reload the current level, and the player will have a chance to try again. Here is the final sequence:

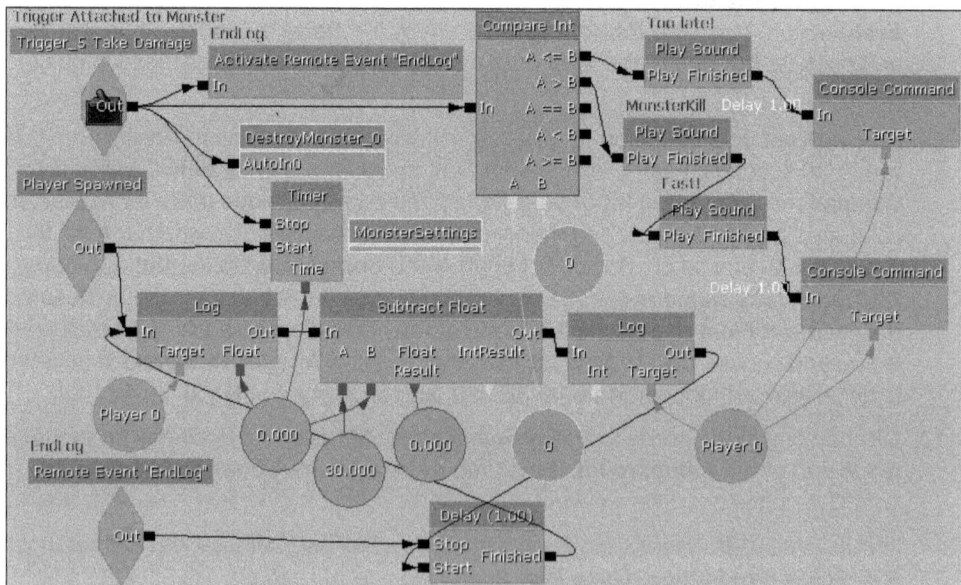

19. If you PIE (*F8*), everything will work except the final **Console Command** actions. They will only work in **Play on PC** mode [🖥], which emulates the final packaging of the game, complete with menus. An example scene is provided: *Packt_04_Comparison_DEMO.UDK*.

How it works

In this recipe we covered a lot of ground using the **Compare Int** action to see whether or not the player shot down the monster within 30 seconds. We rewarded and punished them accordingly with feedback and level loading and reloading. We set up a Timer, and a Math operation to count down 30 seconds, and we logged the result to the screen. We used a **Remote Event**, which we introduced in the previous recipe to jump from the **Take Damage** event down to the **Log** loop's **Delay** to stop it when required. To visualize the **Timer**, admittedly, it might be more elegant to create and display a proper 30 second clock animation through a graphic animated in Flash and imported as an .SWF rather than as a trail of numbers ticking off on the side of the screen.

Using Integer Counter to count enemy deaths

Death comes in many forms, and sometimes it's necessary to count them. In this recipe we'll keep track of how many times an enemy Bot that keeps re-spawning in the level is killed by the player. When the total is 10, we'll reward the player. The Bot spawning sequence is already set up and should be familiar from the recipe _Creating a simple enemy Bot_, back at the start of this chapter.

Getting ready

Open the map _Packt_04_IntegerCounter_Start.UDK_.

How to do it...

1. In Kismet, in the main sequence press _Ctrl + 1_. This sets 1 as a bookmark you can return to. The bookmarks only work in the current UDK session, which is a limitation but they are still handy.

2. Examine the Sub-Sequence _Enemies_ and in there press _Ctrl + 2_. This sets the hotkey 2 as a bookmark for the _Enemies_ sequence. The Sub-Sequence _Enemies_ spawns a Bot but this is respawned after the previous one dies. This is a loop.

3. In the **Sequences** window, click on the Sub-Sequence _EndSequence_. Press _Ctrl + 3_ to set 3 as a bookmark for this. Notice that there is a commented section that prevents bots spawning after 10 are killed. This is provisioned by an **Is Alive** condition. After 10 Bots are killed, the looping spawn fires the condition to be marked true and a **Destroy** action kills them in a loop behind the scenes. In a later recipe we'll handle this instead with a **Gate** action.

4. Press _2_ again, and notice the Bot searches for the player using the exact **Trace** action loop which comes directly from the recipe earlier in the chapter _Creating a simple enemy Bot_.

5. Also notice that upon the Bot's death an **Activate Remote Event** action is fired. This is there to send us to a **Remote Event** we'll add in a moment.

6. Press *1*, the bookmark you set for the main sequence, to return there.

7. Under the **Player Spawned** event, right-click and choose **New Event | Remote Event**. In its **Event Name** property type *KilledBot*. Connect the **Out** nub of the **Remote Event** to the **AutoIn0** nub of the Sub-Sequence *Enemies*. This ensures that when the Bot dies another is spawned again.

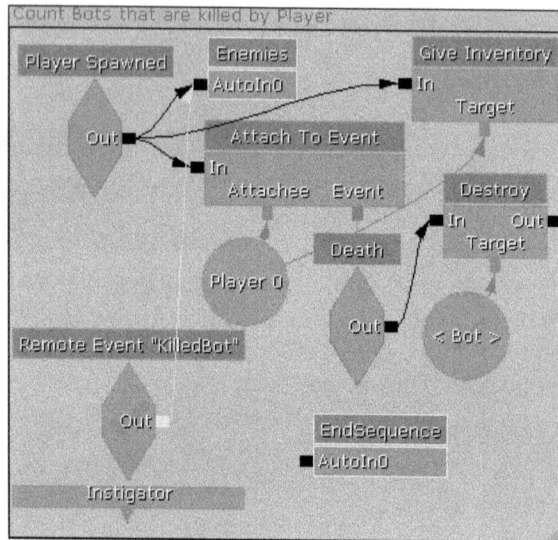

8. Next to the **Remote Event** *KilledBot*, right-click and choose **New Condition | Counter | Int Counter**.

9. Feed the **Out** nub of the **Remote Event** *KillBot* into the **In** nub of the **Int Counter**.

10. Right-click on the **A** nub of the **Int Counter** and choose **Create New Int Variable**.

11. Do the same for the **B** nub, but for the **B** nub in its **Int Value**, enter 10. What this provisions is a way to count up to 10 and then pull a result whenever the **Remote Event** fires the condition. Each time the condition is fired it takes the value from **A**, adds the number set in its **Increment Amount** property, which is 1, and then stores that back in **A** again. The **Remote Event** firing increments **A** from 0 to 1. Then next time it fires it increments **A** from 1 to 2, and so on.

12. There is a Sub-Sequence *EndSequence* in the main Kismet. Connect its **AutoIn0** nub to the **A == B** nub of the **Compare Int**.

13. Open the Sub-Sequence *EndSequence* and you'll see it plays a message *You Killed All the Enemies!* and also toggles a hidden *PowerCore* to show in the level and a looping Emitter to flash. Then you can go grab the *PowerCore* and be declared the winner.

14. We can display the sequence from 0 Bots killed to 10 Bots killed on screen using a **Log**. Next to the **Remote Event** *KilledBot* hold *L* and click to add a **Log**. Right-click on the **Log** and choose **Expose Variable | Int—Int**. Then hook up the **Log** as shown below:

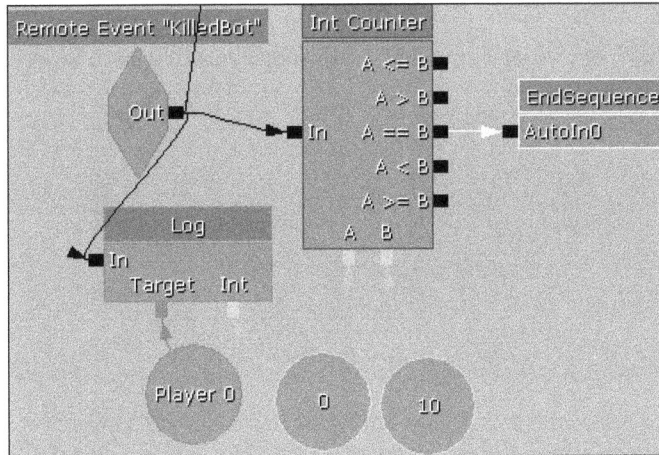

15. It is rather hard to kill all 10 enemies with them shooting at you in close quarters. Your 100 health doesn't last very long. For testing you could just select every **Actor Factory** action in the Sub-Sequence *Enemies* altogether and remove their Inventory entry with one click. Or you could, in the main sequence, add a **Modify Health** action effecting the **Player 0 Variable**, with its **Heal** property ticked and a **Damage** amount of 100.

> Actually, the **Damage** property is misnamed. It would make more sense if it was called **Amount**, as it's a **Modify Health** amount. If **Heal** is not ticked though, the player will take damage, which is more common perhaps. Hooking the healing **Modify Health** to the **Remote Event** means the player is restored to full health each time a Bot dies. Adjusting the value of the **Damage** amount (also known as **Healing** amount) would allow you to insert a measure of *Difficulty* level.

16. If the player does die, the entire sequence starts over, but the incremented *KilledBots* **Integer Variable** keeps its current value. To clear it if the player dies, right-click near the **Destroy** action and choose **New Action | Variable | Set Variable** action. Hook it up as shown next. Right-click on its **Value** nub and choose **Create New Integer Variable**. Connect its **Target** nub to the **Integer Variable** that is feeding the **A** nub of the **Int Counter** we made earlier. What happens here is the **Integer Variable** connected to the **A** nub is set by the **Set Variable** action back to 0 when the player is killed (through the **Death** event that clears out the current Bot too), which resets the total for the number of Bots killed.

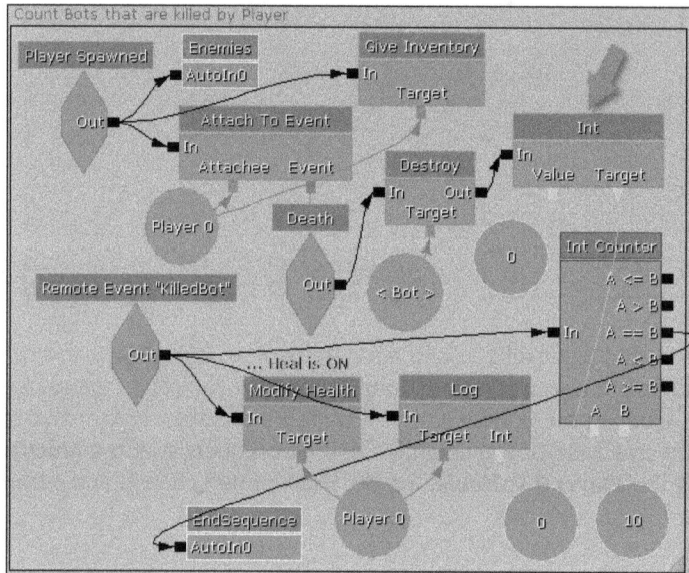

How it works

The **Int Counter** is used to count the Bots, incrementing the value **A** each time one dies. If the player is killed this should be reset. A **Log** with its **Int** nub exposed lets us display the current count of dead Bots. Much of the rest of the Kismet network is an elaboration from the recipe *Creating a Simple Bot*, except we spawn 10 in series. By the way, the platform in the center of the level that is raised by using the JumpPads is controlled by two **Matinee** actions that are moderated by **Int Counter** conditions too. Check the Sub-Sequence *Scenery* to inspect this. An example map is provided *Packt_04_IntegerCounts_DEMO.UDK*.

Controlling node flow using a Gate action

In this recipe we'll change the way that the spawning of Bots, which occurs in a loop, is culled when a target number of 10 Bots have been spawned. In the previous recipe you learned to keep track of how many enemy Bots in the level have been killed by the player, with winning conditions occurring upon a desired total of 10.

Getting ready

Open the map *Packt_04_GateAction_Start.UDK*. The lesson continues on from the previous one. Note that in Kismet, for the scene, *1* can be set as a bookmark for the main sequence, *2* as a bookmark for the Sub-Sequence *Enemies*, and *3* as a bookmark for the Sub-Sequence *EndSequence*.

How to do it...

1. The Sub-Sequence *EndSequence* is fired when an **Integer Counter** reaches a goal of ten Bot **Death** events. This is what we set up in the last recipe. Double-click on it to open it. Notice that it is set to fire off straight away a comparison called **Is Alive** which will **Destroy** any Bots from that point onward (if there are any). This loops, which works well, but it means there is a continual spawn of extra Bots and a culling loop behind the scenes.

2. To remedy this we'll instead use a *Gate* action to block the flow of Bots once 10 have been killed, instead of using the *Is Alive* condition. Select all the nodes in the *Comment* box *Prevents More Bots* after 10 die then press the *Del* key.

3. Press the [✦] icon to go the main sequence or press *1*. Here, find the *Int Counter* node and next to it hold *G* and click to add a new *Gate* action. You can also right-click and choose **New Action | Misc | Gate**.

4. The *Gate* action has and **In** nub and an **Out** nub. This lets you stream though it from one action or event to another. There are also **Open** and **Close** nubs. When one of these are set, the *Gate* opens and closes accordingly, based on whichever was set most recently. Hook the **A == B** nub of the *Int Counter* to the **Close** nub of the *Gate* action. Note that above the *Gate* there is text saying **bOpen=True**. This is the state of the *Gate* when the game begins. It can be set to false in the properties, but for this case, true is fine.

5. Press *Alt* on the wire leading from the *Remote Event* *KilledBot* to the **AutoIn0** nub of the Sub-Sequence *Enemies*.

6. Instead, connect the **Out** nub of the *Remote Event* *KilledBot* to the **In** nub of the *Gate* action. Then connect the **Out** nub of the *Gate* action to the **AutoIn0** nub of the Sub-Sequence *Enemies*. This change means a Bot can spawn through the loop through the *Remote Event* while the *Gate* is **Open**. Once 10 Bots have been killed the gate will **Close**, and no more will come forth. That means we no longer need to test the *Is Alive* condition for the Bot and cull extras. There won't be any.

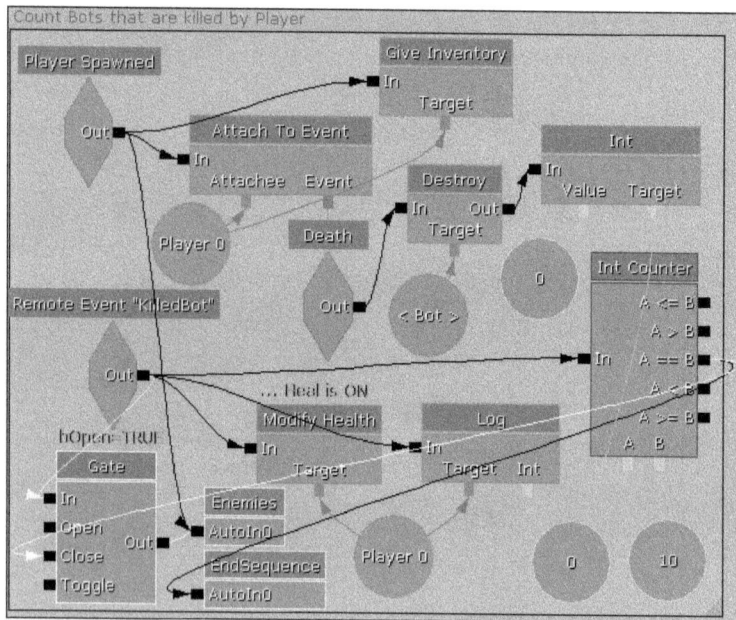

Making Bots follow a path

In this recipe we'll make Bots follow a patrol then, when they are shot, make them try and hide. This introduces some essential control for AI path following.

Getting ready

Open the map *Packt_04_PathFollowing_Start.UDK*. The lesson continues on from the previous one.

How to do it...

1. Open the Sub-Sequence *Enemies*. Here add a **New Action | AI | Move to Actor**. A **Move to Actor** action is for getting the **Target** object (which must be a pawn's **Object Variable**) to make its way to another game object, which is a path goal such as a PathNode, a JumpPad, a Trigger, or even the player. Add the **Named Variable** *Bot* as the *Target* of the **Move to Actor**.

2. In the scene, go to the **Edit** menu and choose **Find Actors**. From the list select *Pathnode_0*, *Pathnode_7*, *Pathnode_1*, and *Pathnode_6*. Press **Go To**.

3. In Kismet, right-click on the **Destination** nub of the **Move to Actor**, and choose **New Object Vars Using Pathnode...** to add all four selected actors at once.

4. For the **Look At** nub of the **Move to Actor**, assign the **Player 0 Variable**. This forces the Bot to look at the player while running around.

5. Add another **Move to Actor** action, and assign the **Named Variable** *Bot* to the **Target** nub, and the **Player 0 Variable** to the **Look At** nub. This time, in the scene use the **Edit | Find Actors** command to **Go To** the actors *Pathnode_2*, *Pathnode_3*, *Pathnode_4*, and *Pathnode_5*. Assign these to the **Destination** nub.

6. Now you need to add two **Delay** actions (hold *D* and click). Hook the **Delay** actions to the **Move to Actor** actions as shown next. Also, connect the **Death** event's **Out** nub to the **Stop** nub of the each **Delay**. This is necessary so that when the Bot dies, the looped patrol knows he's no longer running around.

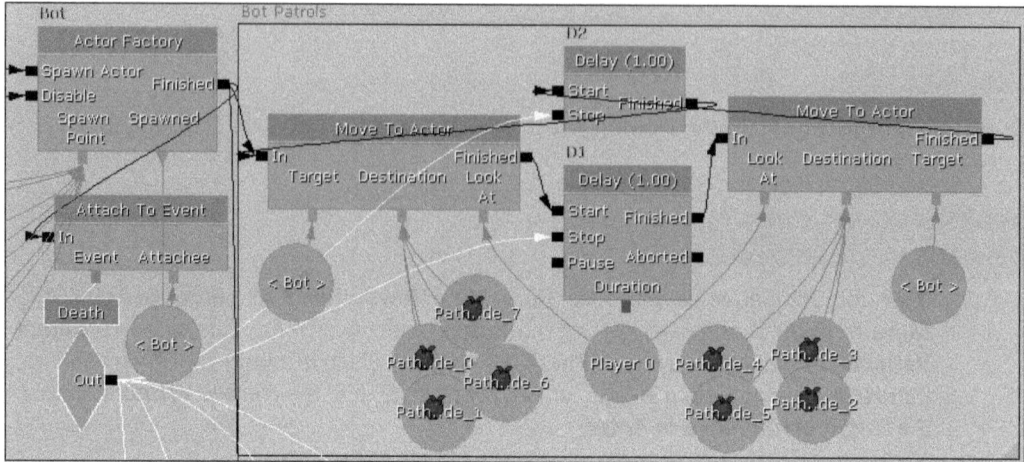

7. We can add a variation to the behavior of the Bot, which is that when he is hurt he runs and hides. He's going to run to the closest JumpPad actor in the scene. These are navigation points even though they aren't PathNodes. Since they will rapidly ping him elsewhere they may give him a moment of respite. Anyway, to balance the gameplay it'll be good to heal him if he manages to reach one.

8. To do this, right-click and choose **Create New Sequence** within the current Sub-Sequence *Enemies*. Call it *HideIfHurt*. Inside this, hold *]* and click to add a **Finish Sequence** action, and create nodes as follows:

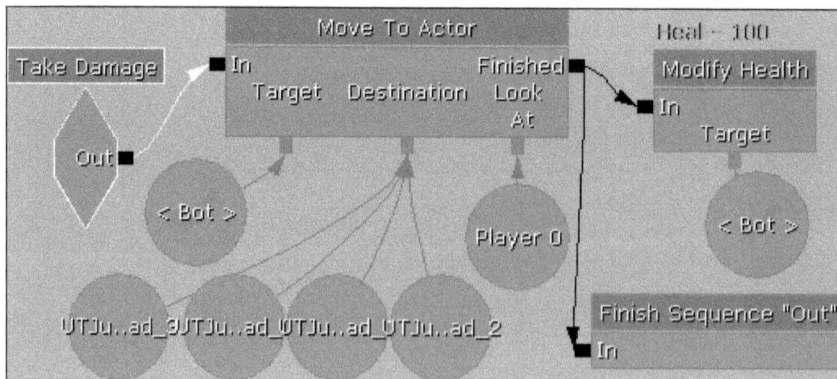

9. The *Take Damage* event needs its **Min Damage Amount** set to 1. Set its **Damage Threshold** to 1.

10. The *Move to Actor* action needs its property **Pick Closest** ticked on.

11. The *Modify Health* node must have its **Target** as the *Named Variable* Bot, so it heals him, and its **Damage** property set to 100, with the **Heal** checkbox ticked on.

12. In the Sub-Sequence *Enemies*, hook the **Out** nub of the Sub-Sequence *HideIfHurt* to the **Start** nub of either *Delay D1* or *D2* in the *Bot Patrols* section. The Bot resumes patrol after he's fled from being hurt.

13. A final step, but quite important now the enemies can move around, is that there's a chance that a Bot might pick up the discarded ShockRifle should the player die. This is a problem because the impact from this gun is sufficient to push the player out of the level. This could be fixed by putting an invisible collision ceiling over the level, but it can also be fixed by re-arming the Bot who picks it up straightaway with the LinkGun instead, since that gun doesn't have the same kick. The way to do this is to extend from the *Bot* **Actor Factory** a **New Condition | Is Using Weapon**, and from the **Using It** output of that, hook up a **New Action | Pawn | Give Inventory**. The *Is Using Weapon* should be set to look for the use of a *UTWeap_ShockRifle*, and the **Give Inventory** should be set to provide a *UTWeap_LinkGun*. **Clear Existing** and **Force Replace** should be ticked on.

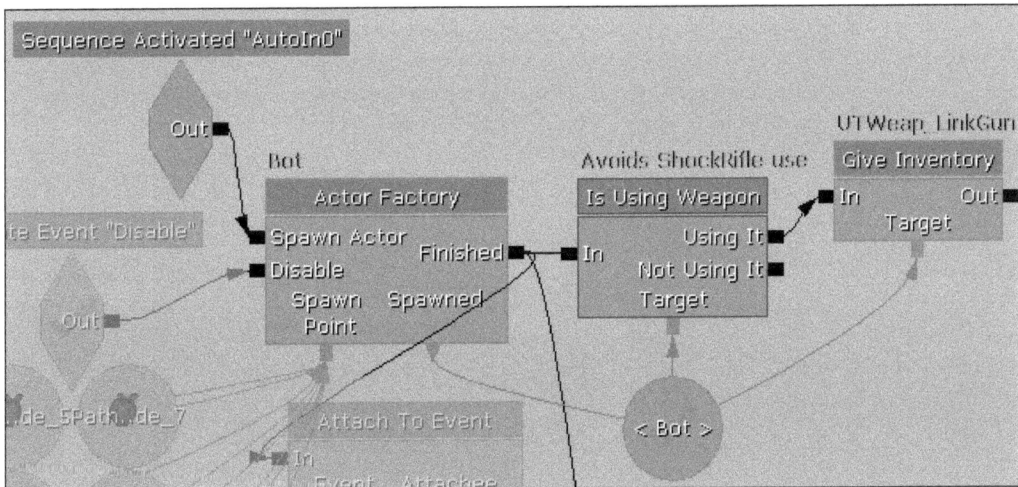

How it works

The recipe before this one set up the goal of shooting ten Bots. This was rather easy, but now the Bot can run around in the scene too, it is a lot more of a challenge. The simplest way to get the Bot running around is to use a **New Action | AI | Move to Actor** action. If the Bot moves between only two points, or follows a regular sequence, the action is quite easy to predict, so instead, in this example, we added four possible destination points for the Bot to try and reach. It would choose the closest based on its current location. We added to this the variation that if the Bot were to be shot he'd run off to a JumpPad to get some air and that would heal him. You may notice when you PIE that the Bot's patrol path also sends him running over the JumpPads anyway, but he's not healed if he steps on it 'accidentally'.

An example map is provided: *Packt_04_PathFollowing_DEMO.UDK.*

5
It Is Your Destiny!
Scripting Complex
Gameplay Flow in Kismet

This chapter further deals with Kismet, with a focus on constructing processes that allow you to do more with gameplay, such as creating cinematic effects, creating puzzles, spell-casting behavior, creating a regenerative health shield, or allowing the player to guide a Bot that follows you, and creating a per-session checkpoint.

In this chapter, we'll cover the following topics:

- Prefabs including Kismet references
- Swapping control of a Bot using Possess Pawn
- Ways to stop a recurring loop
- Setting up cinematic cameras
- Animating cinematic cameras
- Obtaining a trigger event off a RigidBody
- Creating a firing pattern based puzzle
- Allowing the player to pick up, carry, and place an object
- Exploring 'following' and 'attracting' behaviors
- Creating a regenerative health shield
- Creating a per-session checkpoint series

Prefabs including Kismet references

In this short recipe we'll furnish the scene with two Shrines using a pre-built asset that has been saved as a Prefab. A **Prefab** combines any number of actors into a single unit. The point of this recipe is to note that if the Prefab actors include references to Kismet, then the Kismet is saved with the Prefab asset as a Sub-Sequence.

Getting ready

Open the map *Packt_04_Prefabs_Start.UDK*. The scene consists of a cave mouth, looking out onto a landscape that the player cannot reach during gameplay.

How to do it...

1. First, let's look at how to create a Prefab which includes objects that participate in Kismet. Open Kismet [K] and look for the section commented *NightDayCycle*. This is an example that is set up in the bonus online recipe *Creating an animated day to night transition* (available at `http://www.packtpub.com/sites/default/files/downloads/1802EXPUnrealDevelopmentKitGameDesignCookbook_BonusRecipes.PDF`) introducing topics such as sky dome creation, a Night to Day transition, and using **MaterialInstanceActors**. What you want to look for in the networks is a *Log* called *Dusk*, coming from the bottom **Matinee** *ChangesMaterials*.

2. Next to the *Log Dusk*, add a **Toggle** (hold *T* and click). Select in the scene all the particle **Emitters**. These are flames for torches in the scene's cave. Press *F4* and turn off their **Auto-Activate** property so they don't simply play when the level loads.

3. In Kismet, right-click on the **Target** nub of the **Toggle** and choose **New Object Vars Using Emitters...** and hook up the **Out** node of the *Log* Dusk to the **Turn On** node of the **Toggle**.

4. Now hook up the **Out** node of the *Log* Dawn to the **Turn Off** node of the **Toggle**. This makes the particles only play at night.

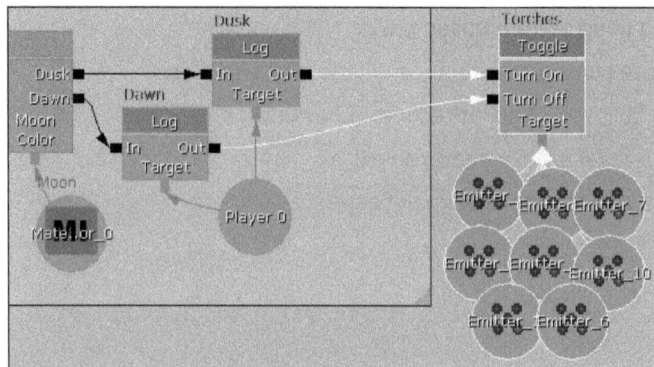

5. PIE, and you'll see that when *Dusk* arrives, the torches in the cave turn on at that time. However, if we were to make a Prefab out of the Emitters and Torches now, the problem is that the Emitter's use in Kismet comes out of the **Matinee** *ChangesMaterials*. That'd have to be included in the Prefab too. So we need to break it off, while still keeping it connected. Passing the **Toggle** through a **Remote Event** is the way to do this.

6. Hold *R* and click; you'll be prompted for an **Event Name**. Type in *TorchesON*. Hold *R* and click again, and this time when prompted for an **Event Name**, type *TorchesOFF*.

7. *Alt-click* on the **Turn On** and **Turn Off** links feeding the **Toggle**.

8. Hook up the **Activate Remote Event** action *TorchesON* to the **Log** *Dusk*. Hook up the **Activate Remote Event** *TorchesOFF* to the **Log** *Dawn*.

9. Hook up the **Remote Event** *TorchesOn* to the **Turn On** nub of the **Toggle**. Hook up the **Remote Event** *TorchesOff* to the **Turn Off** nub of the **Toggle**, as shown:

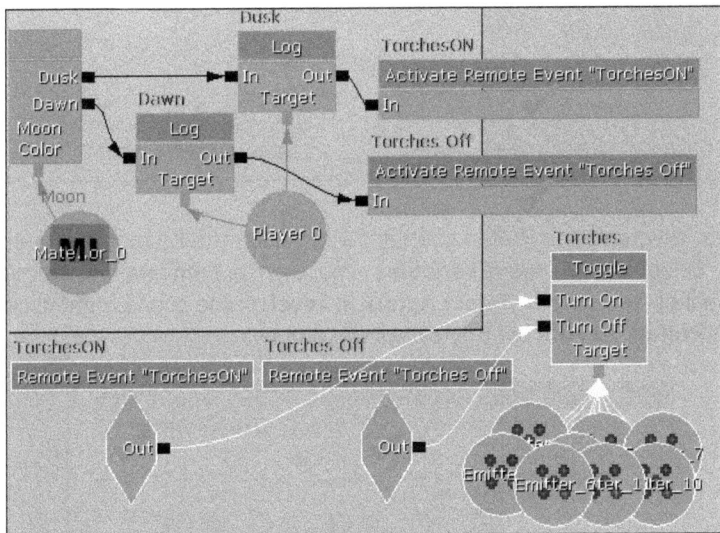

10. Select the nodes highlighted in the given screenshot, right-click, and choose **Create New Sequence**. Call the Sub-Sequence *TorchesToggle*.

11. In the Kismet there is a commented section *Torches*, which includes **Object Variables** for the torch mesh actors and *PointLightToggleable* actors. Select these, press *Ctrl + X* to cut them, and then open the Sub-Sequence *TorchesToggle* you just made and press *Ctrl + V* to paste them there.

12. Right-click and choose **New Action | Actor | Set Material**. Copy and paste this. Hook the added nodes up as shown in the following screenshot, including adding each *PointLightToggleable* **Object Variable** to the **Toggle** action's **Target**:

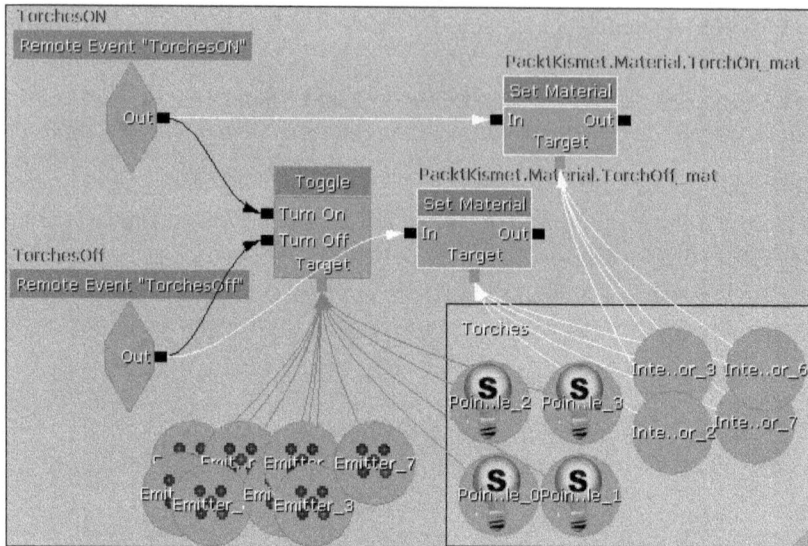

13. Now we can create the Prefab so that it will include the Kismet that goes with these actors. Select all the **Object Variables** including the **Emitters**, the four lights, and the four meshes and choose **Select Actors in Level**. In the scene, right-click and choose **Create Prefab**. You will get the following prompt:

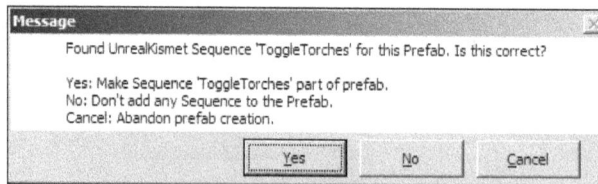

14. Press **Yes**, and then you'll be asked to name your new Prefab. Choose *Yourfolder. Prefab.WallTorches*. You'll then be asked **Would you like to replace these Actors with an instance of the new Prefab?** and here you can also press **Yes**. Don't forget to save your package.

15. To set up for the next recipe's level we can add a couple more Prefabs, for practice. Open the Content Browser and locate *PacktKismet.Prefabs.Shrine*. This is an asset including a plinth, a glowball, and a Kismet Sub-Sequence. If an actor in a Prefab is referenced within a Sub-Sequence in Kismet the script network involved also gets saved as part of the Prefab. In the case of our Shrine, this is just a **Matinee** for the *GlowBall* to bob up and down.

16. Place the *Shrine* prefab at *Trigger_0*, where the **PlayerStart** is. Place another right at the back of the cave, as shown in the next screenshot, at *Trigger_2*. These Shrines (or the Triggers they go with) will give us events to fire off the swapping of characters.

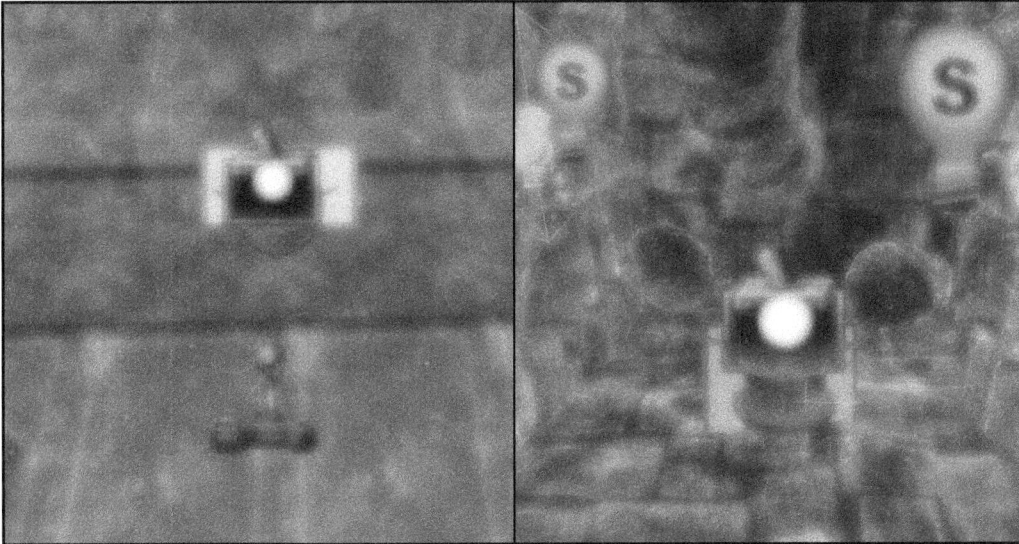

17. Open Kismet [K] and you'll see Kismet has automatically added a Sub-Sequence *Prefabs*, and you can't delete this since the Prefab actor in the scene depends on it; but if you delete the Prefab actor in the scene, it clears the Sub-Sequence *Prefabs*.

18. Optionally, in the Content Browser, locate the Prefab *PacktKismet.Prefab.SlidingGate* on top of the *StaticMeshActor_158* and *StaticMeshActor_164*. This is used in the next recipe. An example map is provided: *Packt_04_Prefabs_DEMO.UDK*.

How it works

A prefab pulls together selected assets so you can easily place many copies of them, or place them in various levels without having to arrange the parts again. You can actually update, reset, and collapse a Prefab.

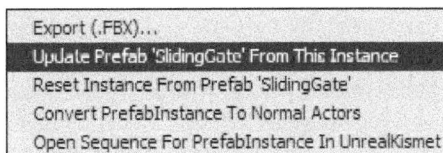

To collapse it back to individual actors, right-click in the scene with the Prefab selected and choose **Convert PrefabInstance To Normal Actors**. You can also open the Kismet nodes used by the Prefab from the scene by choosing **Open Sequence for PrefabInstance In UnrealKismet**.

There's more...

Editing a Prefab

One of the Prefabs we've added to the scene has an incorrect lighting setting. The *SlidingGate* has two halves, and one is an InterpActor that is animated by a **Matinee**. The other side is just a StaticMesh. An InterpActor and a StaticMesh have different shadows because one is static and one is dynamic. To fix this, we can open the Prefab and edit it by converting the StaticMesh half of the gate to an InterpActor too.

How to do it...

1. First, select the Prefab *PacktKismet.Prefabs.SlidingGates* that you added in the scene.

2. Now go to the **View** menu and turn off **Lock Prefab from Selection**. This is on by default, to stop us accidentally adjusting the Prefab contents.

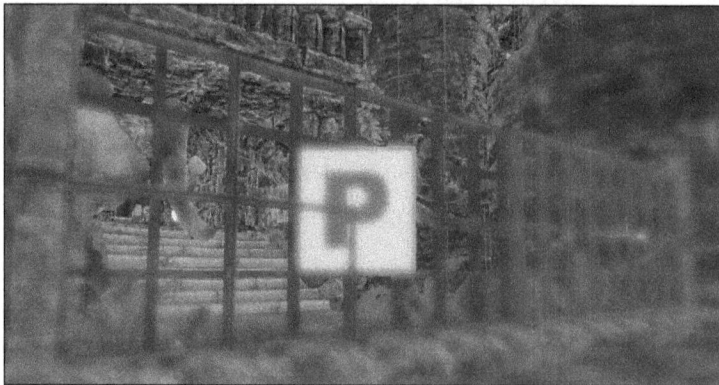

3. Once that is off we can select the gate mesh pieces individually. Select the piece shown in the screenshot, that is a Static Mesh actor, right-click on it and choose **Convert | Convert StaticMeshActor to Mover**. This turns it into an InterpActor that has a dynamic lighting channel. When you are done, *Ctrl + Left-click* on all the Prefab's elements (or click the icon for the Prefab actor then press *Ctrl + LMB* on the actor you adjusted too) then right-click and choose **Update Prefab from Selection**. You'll be prompted **Are you sure you want to update Prefab 'SlidingGate'**? Click on **Yes**. Later, where this asset is used in other maps, the first time the map is loaded you'll get an updating Prefab notice.

4. Now you should get shadows that match for both sides of the gate in every scene where it occurs.

See also

Prefabs are also covered in *Chapter 2*, *Notes From an Unreal World*, under the recipe *Handling StaticMesh actors in the scene*.

Swapping control of a Bot using Possess Pawn

In this recipe we'll allow the player to take control of an AI pawn, or Bot. This allows the player to jump to a different area of a level while their character remains where they left it. We'll then swap control back again. This is a fairly simple operation, but will lead in to the following recipe, on cinematic staging using camera director groups in Matinee.

Getting ready

Open the map *Packt_04_Possess_Start.UDK*. The scene consists of a cave mouth, looking out into a landscape the player cannot reach during gameplay. The player starts in a small compound outside the cave, and a Bot is spawned on the other side of a sliding gate. The scene is a continuation of the previous recipe's scene and we'll just be adding functionality in Kismet.

How to do it...

1. For this scene, let's view the action in third person. Open Kismet [K] and right-click and add a **New Action | Misc | Console Command** to the existing ***Player Spawned*** event. In the **Commands | [0]** property type *behindview*.

2. Hold *P* and click to add a ***Player Variable***. Set its property **All Players** off. Hook this up to the **Target** nub of the ***Console Command***.

3. In the scene, select the *Trigger_0* actor near the PlayerStart that the first Prefab is now sitting on. Right-click and choose **Select | All Triggers**.

4. In Kismet, right-click and choose **New Events Using Triggers | Used**. In the properties of both events turn off **Aim to Interact**. This makes it somewhat easier to use the Trigger during game play (*E*).

5. Right-click next to the event and choose **New Action | Pawn | PossessPawn**. Set the **Player 0 variable** as its **Target**. From the **Actor Factory** Gremlin copy the **Named Variable** Gremlin and assign a pasted copy to the **Possess Pawn** action's **Pawn Target** nub, as shown here:

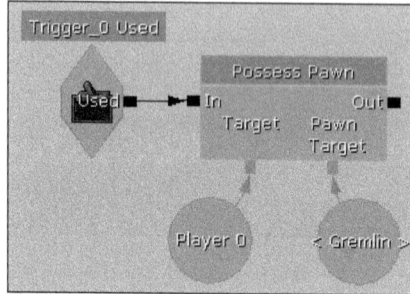

6. So far *Gremlin* only exists as an **Object Variable**. Let's spawn *Gremlin* in the game using an **Actor Factory** just like in the previous chapter's recipe *Creating a simple enemy Bot*. Put the **Named Variable** Gremlin to the **Spawned** nub of an **Actor Factory**, and set the **Spawn Point** as the scene *Pathnode_0* at the foot of the stairs to the cave.

7. Furnish the **Actor Factory** with the proper **Factory Type**: *UTActorFactoryAI*, **Controller**: *UTBot*, and **Pawn**: *UTPawn*. If you'd like to, set the name as *Gremlin* in Kismet using the **Named Variable** Gremlin. Connect the **Spawn Actor** nub of **Actor Factory** Gremlin to the **Player Spawned** event.

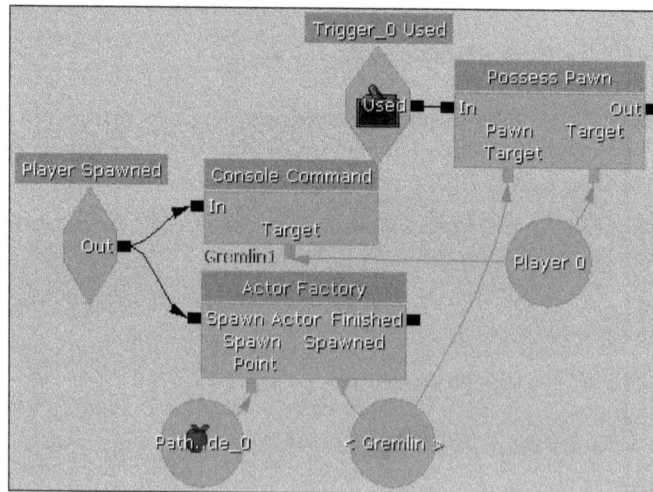

8. PIE to see that the swap works. If you look through the fence you'll see a Bot that used to be you, standing there by the Shrine. In the cave there's another Shrine. Now we have to make it possible to swap back to where we started from there.

9. In Kismet, copy-and-paste the **Possess Pawn** action, then reverse the variables connected to its **Target** and **Pawn Target** nubs. This would seem the intuitive approach, but if you PIE you'll see a problem.

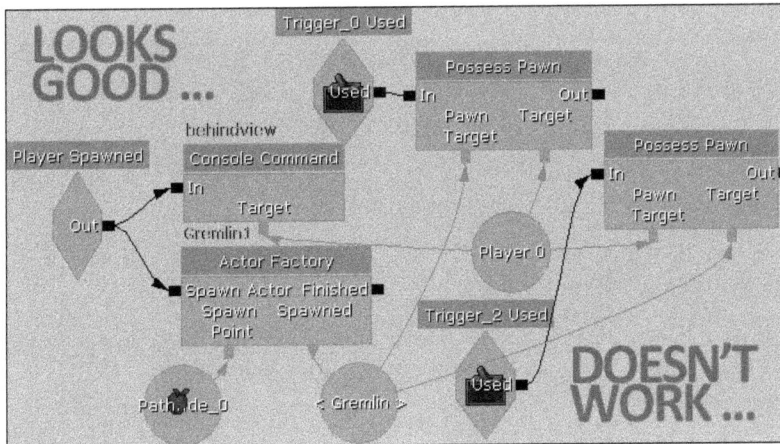

10. You'll notice that the possessed *Gremlin* still can't swap back to the player. That's because when the player possesses *Gremlin* to start with, *Gremlin* literally becomes the player so our Kismet is telling the player to possess themselves. The body that was left behind has no controller; it's just a husk in effect, and can't be possessed.

11. The method to solve this problem is simple; we'll destroy that husk and spawn a third Bot called *Zombie* at the location where the first **PossessPawn** occurs. In this case we'll use the Trigger actor to determine the location, but you could also try using a **Get Location and Rotation** of the player at the time of the triggered event. That's harder though, and we want to keep things straightforward.

12. Our real challenge lies in destroying and re-spawning suitable candidates to possess. One of the handy mechanisms we can use to moderate the re-spawning is a built-in **Kill Old Pawn** checkbox in the properties of the **Possess Pawn** action. Turn this on for all the **Possess Pawn** actions we'll make in this lesson. This wipes out the Bot husk you depart from each time. Think of it as good housekeeping. An alternative way is to use a **Destroy** action.

13. We can parse through the condition **Is Alive** when either *Gremlin* or *Zombie* needs to be checked. We'd be checking whether or not they are there in the scene, a check for possession readiness. If one or the other is not there, we spawn them in. It's like playing Tennis where after each stroke of the ball the players get zapped and replaced with fresh clones without anybody noticing.

14. The following sequence ensures on the first **Trigger_0 Used** event, the player possesses *Gremlin*, and the next time this same event occurs, *Zombie* possesses *Gremlin*. Note that after the first *Gremlin* is destroyed we re-spawn a new one at the Trigger_2, since that's what used by the player.

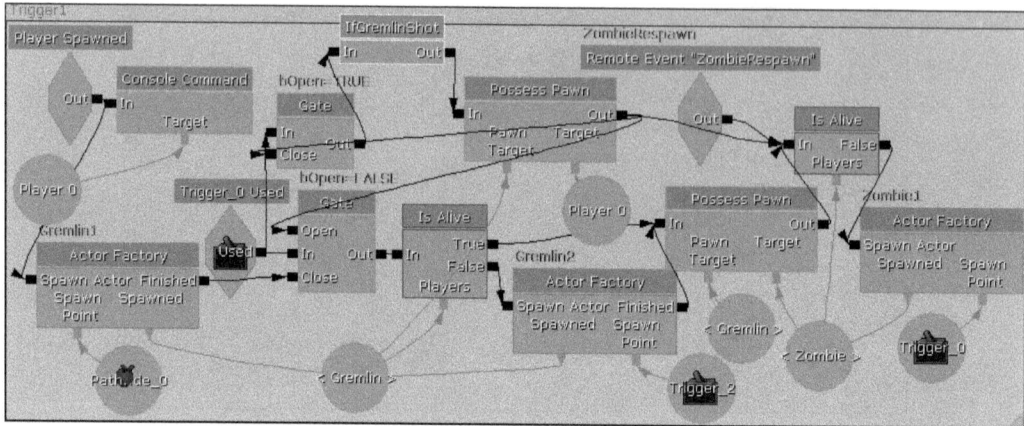

15. A mini Sub-sequence *IfGremlinShot* has been added, just to cover the chance the player may shoot at *Gremlin* before trying to use the **PossessPawn**. Its contents are simple enough, just an **Is Alive** condition which, if *Gremlin* is not around, gives us another before we can swap. In some cases you would want that kind of safety measure, and in others you would run some other action, like a losing condition or a possibly a winning condition. It seems contrived to have *Gremlin* re-appear after he's been shot dead, however that can be solved by storytelling. Suppose you were to add, when *Gremlin* takes full damage, a quick cinematic showing another Bot entering the level, then there'd be no continuity issue. Another way around this is to only implement such swapping in scenes where the player has no access to weapons. Another way would be to allow the killing and make it possible only to possess a corpse. A further way to approach the issue would be to make *Zombie* and *Gremlin* impervious to mutual 'friendly fire' while still vulnerable to enemy fire. If an enemy killed one of them, you'd prevent the swap, which is what we'll do in the next recipe.

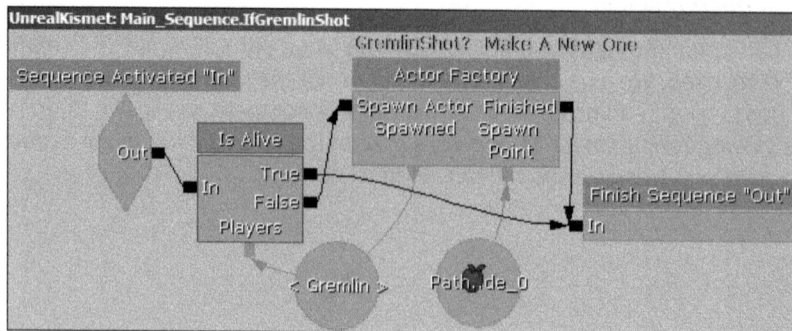

16. In the given screenshot, the contents of the small Sub-Sequence *IfGremlinShot* checks if he needs re-spawning and only re-spawns him if he does.

17. In the next screenshot we see how the ***Trigger_2 Used*** event is handled, which is rather similar except it includes some aggressive looping back so we can repeat the spawn process over and over. Also notice the **Activate Remote Event** action *ZombieRespawn* which effectively creates another loop back by taking us to the ***Remote Event*** in the ***Trigger_0 Used*** section.

18. An example scene is provided in *Packt_04_Possess_DEMO.UDK*.

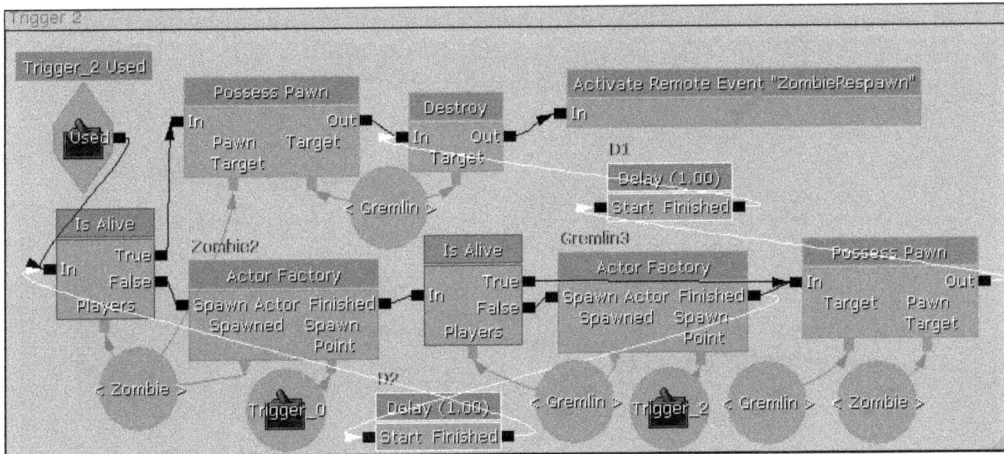

A similar topic based on firing at a Bot to possess it is handled by **Carl Newby**. He made the excellent 'Bill and Bob' series of videos from **The Underground Game Design Course**. The difference here is that there's no need to rely on UI Scenes, which are now somewhat deprecated, to flush input from the husked Bot, because it gets removed from the game. Also, the videos include a topic that discusses what to do if one of the Pawn Targets dies by misadventure.

Ways to stop a recurring loop

In the previous recipe we created a swap between two Bots called *Gremlin* and *Zombie*. We can perform this swap all day and all night. Being able to jump back and forth forever might be a good dynamic in some games, but you might want to build in a way to prevent the swapping at a certain point, perhaps when a quest goal is reached or a mission objective achieved. It would be good to show how to interrupt the possession sequence. In this recipe we'll try out two methods, a **New Action | Switch | Switch** action and a **New Action | Misc | AND Gate**.

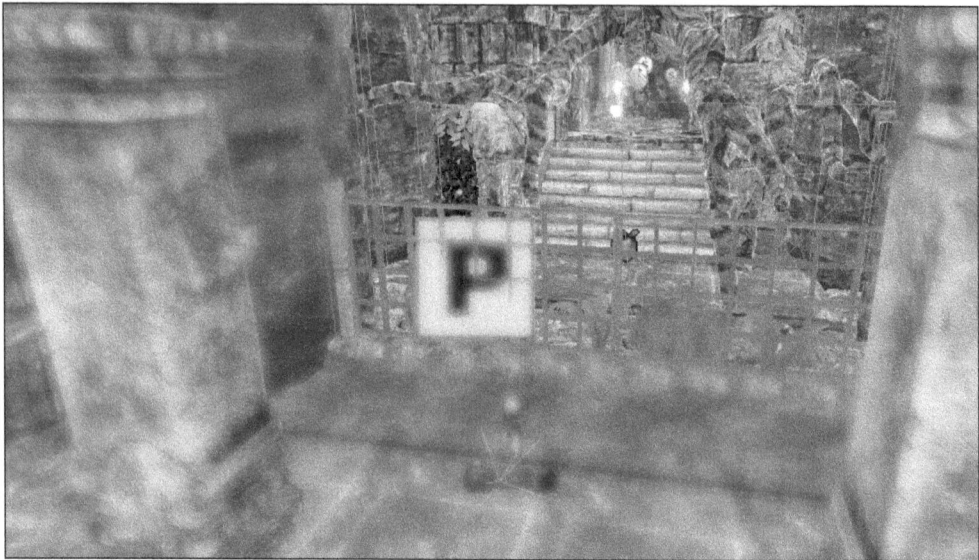

If *Zombie* shoots the gate shown here **and** dawn has arrived, the possession mechanism we set up in the previous recipe will stop. Instead a sliding gate (provisioned by a prefab) will open and *Gremlin* will start shooting at *Zombie*. There's our reason to use an **AND Gate** as both events must occur first. The problem is, as soon as the level begins it is dawn, we want to limit things so they player has to wait through the night (the day is much briefer than a real one). This is a good reason to use the **Switch** action.

Getting ready

Open the scene *Packt_04_GremlinZombieStart.UDK*. This continues from the previous recipe. In Kismet, two **Integer Variables** we'll call on have been added to the *Globals* section: *GateOpen* and *DawnSet*. Also, this game has been set to work best in **Play On PC** mode [🖳] as a **Console Command** has been added that sends the player back to start the level again if they get killed. This means that the **View | World Properties | Game Type | Default Game Type** (as well as the **GameType for PIE**) has been set to *UTGame*.

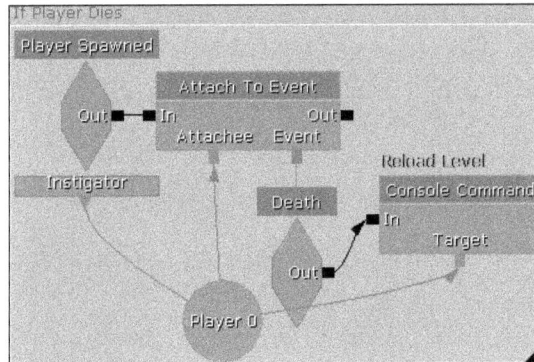

How to do it...

1. Our goal is that the actor *Packt.Prefabs.SlidingGate* will open under two conditions. One is that it has been damaged by the *Zombie* incarnation of the player (not *Gremlin*) and the other is that *Dawn* has come. Right-click in Kismet and choose **New Action | Misc | AND Gate**.

2. This simple action has no properties but lets us flow actions through it only when all the incoming connections have been met. We need to provision a check for whether it is Dawn and a limitation and check on the damage applied to the gate. If we run a check from the Dawn output of the **Matinee** *ChangeMaterials* (or its **Log** *Dawn*) into the **AND Gate** we're halfway there. The problem is, the Event Track *Dawn* in the Matinee fires almost immediately when the level loads. What we'll do is add a **New Action | Switch | Switch** action in between, as shown in the next screenshot. The **Switch** action has a property called **Link Count**. Set this to 2. The **Link 1** nub of the **Switch** now has a friend called **Link 2**. We're going to ignore **Link 1** completely, and instead connect to the **AND Gate** through **Link 2**.

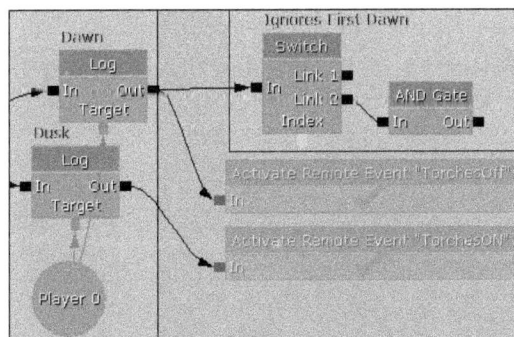

We can add to this the following set up. All the nodes here should be familiar from previous lessons. Try out the *Using Take Damage to produce explosions* recipe if not.

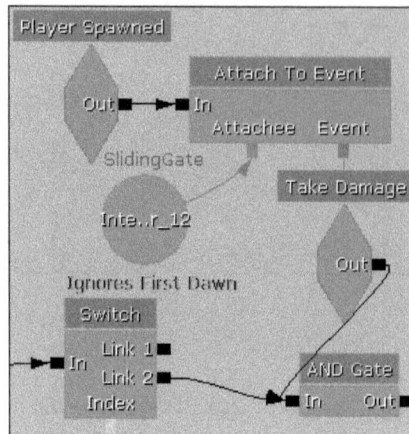

3. The **Take Damage** event should have its **Max Trigger Count** set to 0, so it can be used as much as we need, and the property **Min Damage Amount** set to 1 and its **Damage Threshold** set to 1 so it's easy to fire off this effect. Add an entry to the **Damage Types** channels so [0] is *UTDmgType_LinkBeam* and [1] is *UTDmgType_LinkGun*, since the LinkGun is the weapon the player has access to in this map.

4. The main thing in this sequence is the **Object Variable** *InterpActor_12* representing the *SlidingGate* prefab is attached to the **Take Damage** event when the player spawns, so whenever damage occurs it sends off the second input to the **AND Gate**. The damage may occur frequently, while *Dawn* only needs to come once, then both conditions will have been met. The order in which they occur isn't important.

5. At present nothing happens when the **AND Gate** is fired. Let's set up a result. Right-click and choose **New Action | Event | Activate Remote Event**. For this, enter the **Event Name**, type *GateShot*. Hook up the **Out** nub of the **AND Gate** to the **In** nub of the **Activate Remote Event** *GateShot*. There is already a **Remote Event** that matches this action. It is embedded in the Sub-Sequence **Prefabs | SlidingGate_Seq** that comes with the *Packt.Prefabs.SlidingGate* asset.

6. In the **Sequences** window, expand the Sub-Sequences to show *SlidingGate_Seq* and click on it.

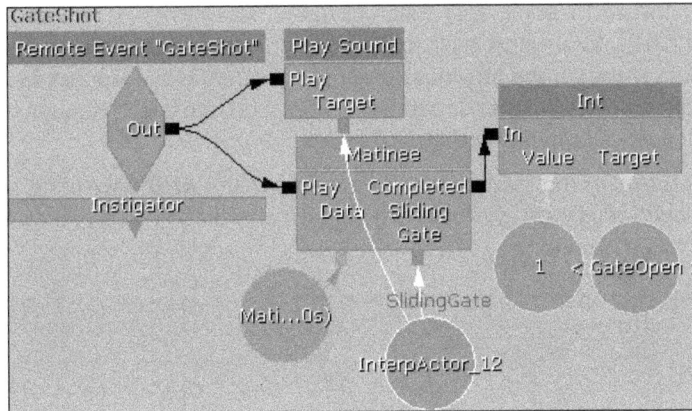

7. The **Matinee** is just a transform of one side of the gate, and there's a sound to go with it. After that, a **New Action | Set Variable | Int** sets a *Named Variable* *GateOpen* to 1.

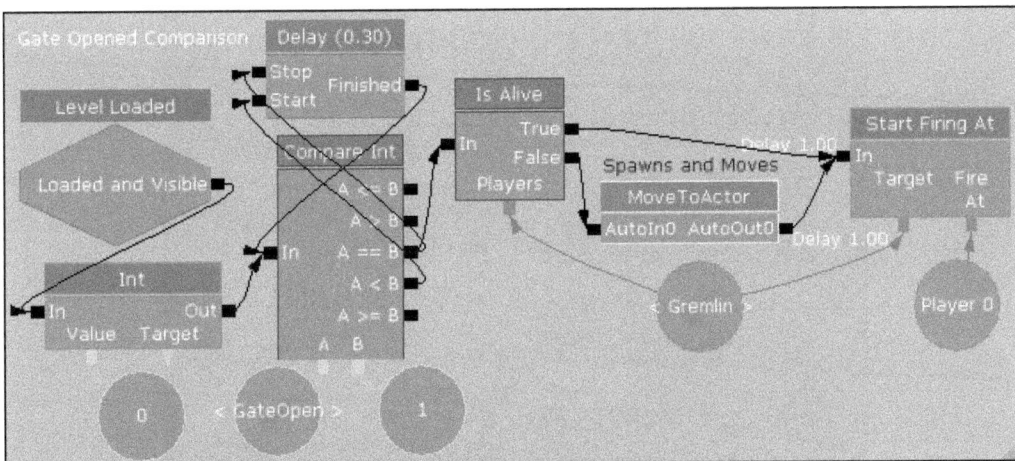

8. Here, after the **Level Loaded** event, the **Named Variable** *GateOpen* is set by another **Set Variable | Int** to 0. Then a **Compare Int** checks it, with a rapid loop, to see when the value it has actually does change to 1.

9. This will only happen when the **AND Gate** is opened and the **Matinee** plays for the Prefab *SlidingGate*.

10. What we can add is some aggression from the Bot *Gremlin*. If he's alive, he'll start to fire, and if he's not around, he'll spawn, then run towards the player and start to fire. This result, shown in the previous screenshot, is set up in a way we've covered several times before in this chapter. It can be compressed into a Sub-Sequence itself, called something like *GremlinAttack*.

11. Why is it *Gremlin* who starts firing? At the time of the **AND Gate** firing, as things are now, it could well be the player is *Gremlin*, which wouldn't work. So we need to add a method to get around this.

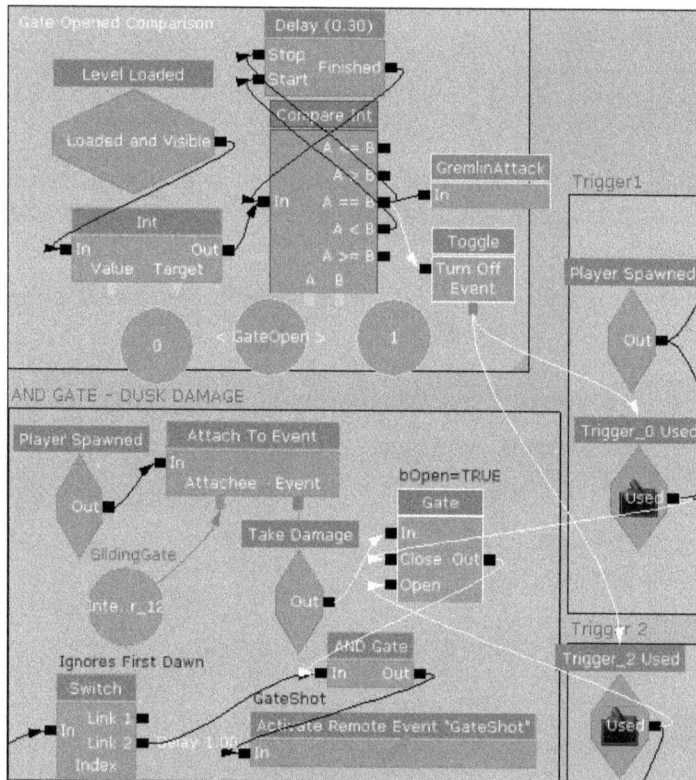

12. The highlighted **Gate** action (hold G and click) forces the **AND Gate** to only work if it is *Zombie* who damages the sliding gate. This is set up by the **Trigger_0 Used** event closing the **Gate**, and the **Trigger_2 Used** event opening the **Gate**.

13. The result is that, after Dawn has finally come and *Sliding Gate* has been damaged, and opens, a well placed **Toggle** lets us **Turn Off** the events **Trigger_0 Used** and **Trigger_2 Used**. These simply stop the **PossessPawn** actions from occurring, so the recurring loop for this can no longer occur.

14. An example scene is include *Packt_04_Zombie_DEMO.UDK*. Note that for this scene it is best to use **Play on PC** mode [▣] not PIE.

Setting up cinematic cameras

In this recipe we'll add a wider angle camera to the scene we constructed in the previous few lessons, and a cut away camera for when a sliding gate opens. A cinematic camera is one that isn't locked to the movement of the player. It can be used to show areas where the player should try to reach later on, or perhaps can see but cannot reach, or to show a wider view of the scene. It can also be used to show the player's activity from an alternative view, such as the front, or to show a close up view of what the player is looking at. In this lesson we'll place some cameras for use in the next recipe, where we animate cinematics. We'll show a view of the scene, then add two more cameras. We'll position them and add variables for them in Kismet.

Getting ready

Open the scene *Packt_04_Cameras_Start.UDK*.

How to do it...

1. Open the Content Browser (*Ctrl + Shift + F*) and choose the **Actor Classes** tab. Highlight *CameraActor* in the list of actors.

2. In the scene, select the ground that the **PlayerStart** actor sits on and choose **Add CameraActor Here**. The camera is represented by the non-colliding mesh shown in the next screenshot. Note that this model of a camera is pretty much just an icon and can penetrate walls or the floor without clipping the camera view so long as the actor's pivot has a clear view of what you want to look at through the camera. It is the pivot that really serves as the camera location, and the facing direction of the camera is along its local X axis.

3. We're going to need three cameras for this scene, so press *Ctrl + C* and *Ctrl + V* twice and move the pasted cameras slightly apart from each other. You'll have *Camera_0*, *Camera_1*, and *Camera_2*.

> A time-saving tip when creating a camera is to move the viewport to the vantage point where you want the new camera to be positioned, then press the **View Options** icon [▾] (found in the top-left corner of each view). At the bottom of the roll-out for **View Options** is a command **Add camera actor here**.

4. Select the *Camera_0* actor, zoom out, then move and rotate the camera so it is up above the scene, looking down on the **PlayerStart**. A nice way to do this is to press the **Lock Selected Actors to Camera** icon [👁] on the viewport icons toolbar which will align the selected Camera actor to the editor view camera. The actor will appear to vanish because it's jumped to the location of the viewport vantage point. It will stay locked there till the same icon is pressed again.

5. While choosing a viewing angle for the wide shot, make sure that the horizon (the lowest edge of the sky dome) and any unplayable area is not showing. When you're happy with the angle looking over the scene, release the camera actor with [👁] and select the *Camera_1* actor.

6. Move *Camera_1* so it is looking at the *SlidingGate* Prefab, something similar to the next screenshot:

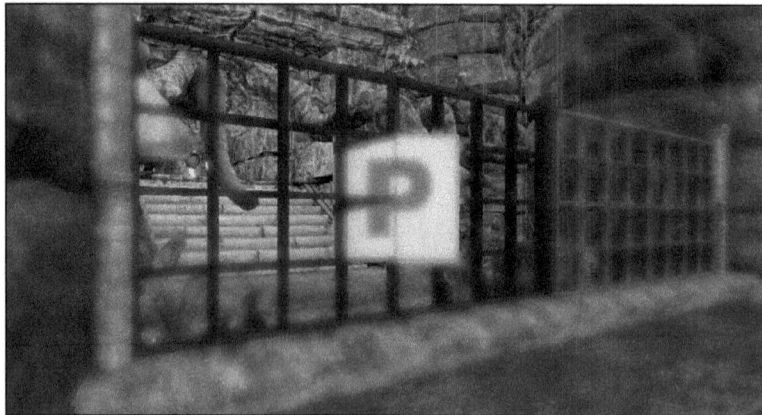

7. For the *Camera_2* actor, set it facing into the cave, with a view between the two pillar meshes. Make sure the **PlayerStart** is visible, as shown here:

8. With the camera actor still selected right-click and choose **Select | All CameraActor Actors**. Then open Kismet [⬈], right-click, and choose **New Object Vars Using Camera Actor_0...** and move the resulting ***Object Variables*** to the section commented **Globals**.

9. Select the ***Object Variable*** *Camera_0* and in its **Var Name** property type *WideCam*. Select the ***Object Variable*** *Camera_1* and its **Var Name** property type *CaveCam*. Select the ***Object Variable*** *Camera_2* and in its **Var Name** property type *GateCam*. The start scene in the next recipe continues from where we are now.

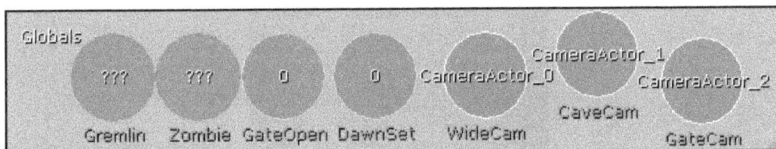

Animating cinematic cameras

In this recipe we continue from the previous lesson where we created and placed cameras in their initial positions and assigned variables for them in the Kismet. This time we'll animate those cameras to embellish the level with some cut scenes. One is an introduction and the other highlights a key event in the gameplay.

Getting ready

Open the scene *Packt_04_Cinematic_Start.UDK* or continue on from the previous recipe.

How to do it...

1. In Kismet, next to a **Player Spawned** event, hold *M* and click to add a **Matinee** action. Right-click on the **Object Variable** *WideCam* and choose **Select Actor in Level**. Then double-click the **Matinee** action. It's useful to have the actor you want to animate already selected when you open the Matinee Editor so that it is automatically assigned the Groups you create tracks for. Some tracks are only available to certain kinds of actors.

2. In the Matinee Editor, under **All** in the dark gray tracks panel, right-click and choose **New Camera Group**. Call this *WideCam*. Notice a **Movement** Track is added automatically. This lets us animate the position of the camera. The additional **FOVAngle Track** can also be animated, but we don't really need to do that now.

3. Back in the Kismet, right-click on the **Object Variable** *CaveCam* and choose **Select Actor in Level**. In the Matinee Editor, create a **New Camera Group** again, and call this one *CaveCam*. Make sure the **Matinee** action shows the new nub **CaveCam** and has the **Object Variable** *CaveCam* connected to it.

4. Right-click under the two group tracks you've added and choose **Add New Director Group**, as shown here:

5. A **DirGroup** is added above. The **Director Track** lets you set keys to switch to a given camera in the scene. Since we've added two **Camera Groups**, we can choose either of these when we keyframe the **Director Track**. Highlight the **Director Track**, and at frame 0.0s, press *Enter* or the key icon [ ].

6. You'll be prompted to choose which camera to use at frame 0.0s. Choose *WideCam*.

7. Move the time slider to 3.0s and, with the **Director Track** selected, press *Enter* or the key icon [➷] again. Extend the range of the time line to 8.0s by dragging the pink out point range handle shown in the next screenshot. You can scroll with the mouse wheel to zoom the time line in and out. Also move the green triangle icon, which sets the internal play loop range.

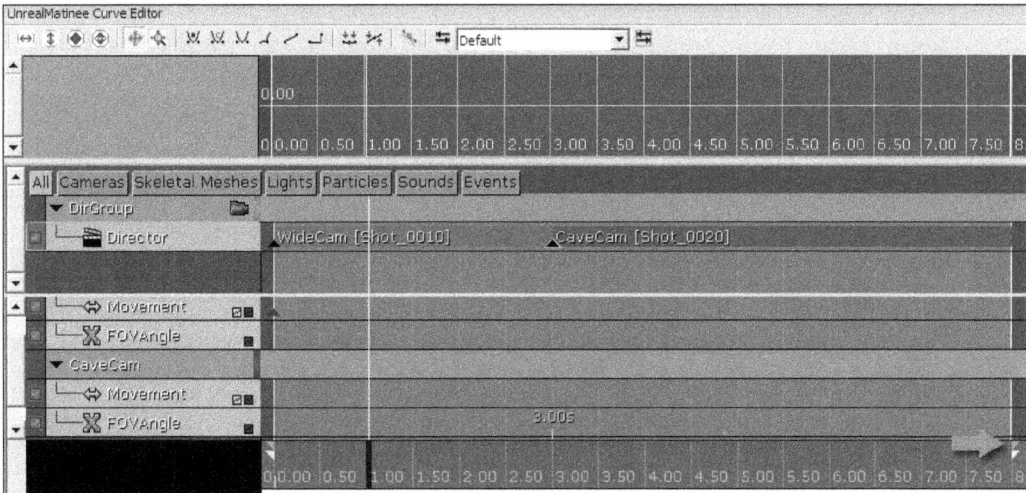

8. *WideCam* won't be animated, but it will have a **Fade Track** added to it. Right-click on the **Director Track** under **DirGroup** and choose **New Fade Track**. Highlight this and at frame 0.0s, press *Enter*. Right-click on the key that is created and choose **Set Value**. Enter 1. This means the view is fully faded, so don't be alarmed if the view goes black. There is a small checkbox to the left-hand side of tracks in the Matinee Editor that lets you disable them, which is handy for **Fade Tracks** at times, to temporarily prevent blacking the view.

9. Drag the time slider to frame 2.0s and press *Enter* again. This key has a value of 0 by default, which means we now have a fade in over 2 seconds. You can visualize this by pressing the show curves icon [■] at the end of the **Fade Track**. It will turn yellow, and in the Curve Editor a curve representing the fade will display. Make sure you can see the entire track by pressing the **Fit View to All** icon [◉].

10. Now we need to create some camera motion for the second camera in the **Director Track**. We'll drive the camera inside the cave to reveal one of the level goals. Highlight the **Movement Track** for the **Camera Group** *CaveCam*. At 4.0s on the time line, when the **Director Track** swaps from the first camera to this one, press *Enter*. Then drag the time line to 8.0s and press *Enter* again. With the new key at 8.0s highlighted, move *CameraActor_1* into the back of the cave. You can use toggle the **show view through camera** icon, shown here, which is at the end of the *CaveCam* Group, to show its current view.

11. The view should track forward if you scrub the timeline. Your last key should look similar to the next screenshot. In between the key at frame 3.0s and the key at 8.0s you may need to insert another key to help adjust the camera's in between motion. To add a key you can press *Ctrl + LMB* on its curve on the time line and to move it you can *Ctrl-drag* on keys that are highlighted. Close the Matinee Editor when finished.

12. If you want to, add further keys to the **Fade Track** to make the sequence fade out at the end.

13. Since the player has already been spawned into the level while this **Matinee** action is playing, we need the use of a **Toggle Cinematic Mode** action in Kismet to prevent the player running around until the introduction movie ends. In Kismet, right-click and choose **New Action | Toggle | Toggle Cinematic Mode**.

14. The **Toggle Cinematic Mode** action needs to be connected as shown here. Don't forget to add the **Player 0 Variable** as its **Target**.

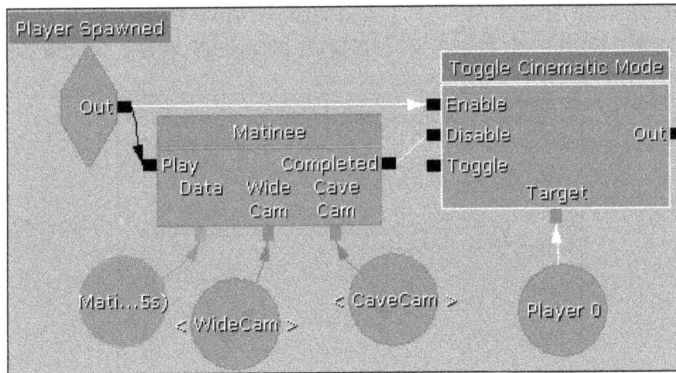

15. In the properties of the **_Toggle Cinematic Mode_** turn off **Hide Player** (since we want to see ourselves) and turn off **Disable Turning**. Turning and movement are disabled by default by this action, but let's allow the player to spin on the spot even though we don't want them to run around—this can be good to let the character feel they're still active in the game world while the cinematic plays. The HUD is also hidden by default, since removing all the gameplay feedback can help sell the film-like quality of a cinematic. Turn off **Disable Input**. This allows the player to skip the cinematic if that functionality has been enabled for this map. In the properties of the **_Matinee_** action, check on **Is Skippable**. When this is enabled it lets you skip the playing **_Matinee_** action if the command *CANCELMATINEE* is entered by the player. For the player to input this command, it has to map a **_Console Command_** to a keystroke. Adding such a keystroke is discussed in *Chapter 6, Under the Hood*.

> Kismet provides an easy to use key capture event. The event simply fires off any actions you connect to it if the player presses the defined key. Right-click and choose **Input | Key/Button Press** to add it. A specific key can be established as an entry in its **Add Input** property.

16. Now we'll create one more **_Matinee_** action for the *GateShot* camera, which simply cuts in to show the *SlidingGate* Prefab when it opens just in case the player were to be off somewhere else and miss this important event. In the section commented *Globals*, right-click on the **_Object Variable_** GateCam and choose **Select CameraActor_2 in Level**.

17. In Kismet, use the search tool [🔍] to locate the **AND Gate** action that, when its two conditions are both met, fires the *GateShot* sequence which opens the **Gate**.

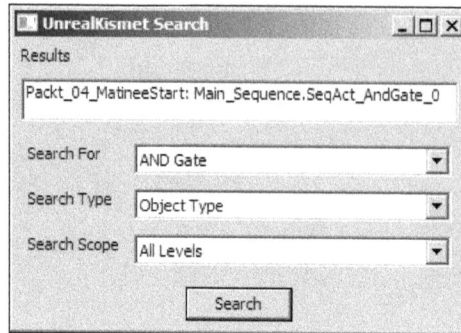

```
UnrealKismet Search                          _ □ ×
Results

Packt_04_MatineeStart: Main_Sequence.SeqAct_AndGate_0


Search For      AND Gate                         ▼

Search Type     Object Type                      ▼

Search Scope    All Levels                       ▼


                    Search
```

18. From the **Out** nub of the **AND Gate**, connect to the **Play** nub of a new **Matinee** action.

19. Double-click on it and add a **New Camera Group** called *GateCam*. Also add a new **Director Group** and at 0.0s set *GateCam* to play by keying the **Director Track** and assigning *GateCam* to the keyframe. The camera itself doesn't need to move but we can add a **Camera Shake** at 0.0s by adding an **Event Track**, and keying that at 0.0s too. You'll be prompted to enter a new **Event Name** for the key. Call it *Shake*. This adds a nub to this **Matinee** action. Note that the default Matinee Editor time line length is 5.0s, which is about how long we want this **Matinee** action to play.

> Music and sound make a big impact during a cinematic sequence. You can use an **Event Track** to set keys for outputs that let you fire **Play Sound** nodes. Or you can right click on the **Director Group** and choose **New Sound Track** so you can assign audio to play internally from the **Matinee** action. When designing for mobile devices an alternative option for having a **Sound Track** is to use the console command: `mobile PlaySong SONGNAME` along with `mobile StopSong`. An example is in `C:\UDK\~\UDKGame\Content\Maps\Mobile\EpicCitadel.UDK`. The file must be placed into your game's music directory, such as: `C:\UDK\~\UDKGame\Build\IPhone\Resources\Music\MySong.MP3`.

20. Given there is an action **New Action | Camera | Camera Shake**, you might think it is the choice to try out. Unfortunately, it's not working. Instead we can use a **New Action | Camera | Play Camera Animation**.

21. Close the Matinee Editor, right-click, and choose **New Action | Camera | Camera Shake**. Hook the **Matinee** action's new **Shake** nub to the **Start** nub of the **Play Camera Animation** action. Hook the **Completed** nub of the **Matinee** action to the **Finish** nub of the **Play Camera Animation** action.

22. In the properties of the ***Play Camera Animation*** action, to set its motion, we need to set a **Camera Animation** asset. For this, you can use *PacktKismet.Anims.Shake* which you can search for in the Content Browser using the filter **All Types | Camera Animations**.

23. Use the assign icon [⊕] in the **Play Anim** property of the ***Play Camera Animation*** with the asset *PacktKismet.Anims.Shake* selected in the Content Browser. If you prefer to make your own, you can right-click in the Content Browser and choose **New Camera Animation**, name it *Yourfolder.Anims.MyCameraAnim* and double-click on it to open it for editing. A special mode of the Matinee Editor will open with an **InterpGroup_Movement** curve already supplied that let's you animate a jiggle in XYZ. We want a three second shake. You can get a taste for this by opening existing UDK **Camera Animation** assets.

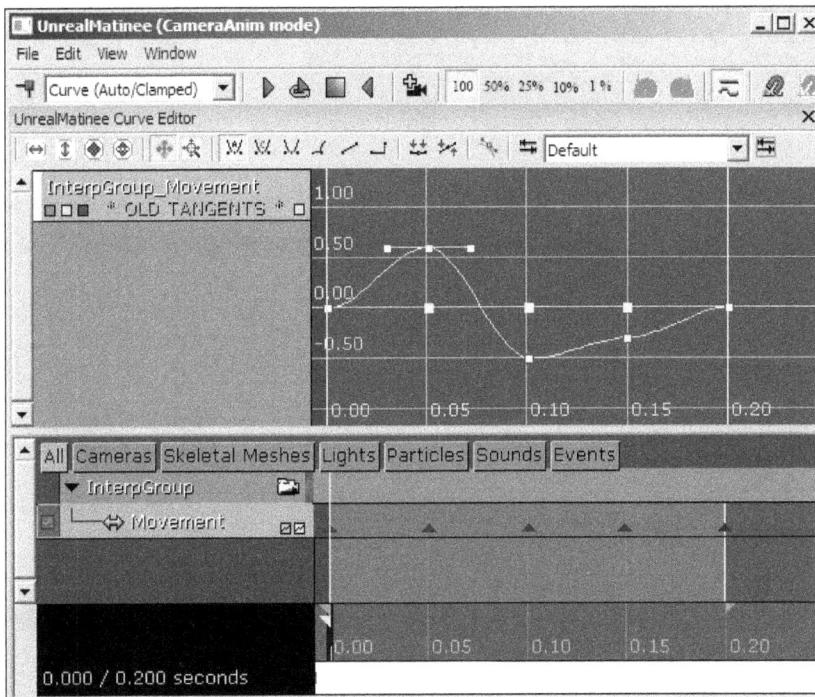

24. The next screenshot depicts the Kismet for placing the **Play Camera Animation** action. Note the properties include a value 1.5 for the **Intensity** of the shake, so you can adjust how it performs without having to edit the keys again.

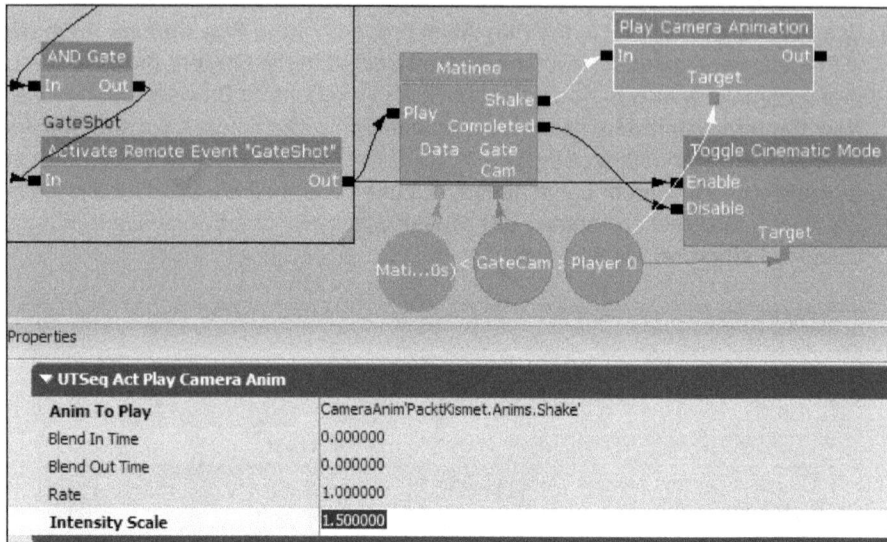

25. Copy the **Toggle Cinematic Mode** action you made earlier, right-click by the current Matinee action that we're working on and then press **Paste Here**. Hook it up as shown in the previous screenshot.

26. Play on PC to see how it goes. An example is in the provided content *Packt_04_Matinee_DEMO.UDK*.

How it works

The way **Matinee** actions work within the Kismet network makes them useful for animating any actor from models to particles to Bot skeletal controls. A cinematic camera briefly taking control from the player can be used in an enormous number of ways and this lesson is only a sampling of some essential features. From the September 2011 version of UDK, the documentation includes steps required to capture video and audio playback of a cinematic (for conversion to a highly compressed .BIK movie or perhaps just to let you take a fly through of a scene to a video editing application). The documentation for this is available at `http://udn.epicgames.com/Three/CapturingCinematicsAndGameplay.html`. For more information on using **Matinee** actions to create cinematics, and some Matinee Editor control hotkeys, check out `http://udn.epicgames.com/Three/CreatingCinematics.html`.

The use of SkeletalMeshMAT actors, characters you want to work within the Matinee Editor, is covered in *Chapter 3, It Lives!*

The use of special effects like particle systems within the Matinee Editor is covered in *Chapter 7, Hi, I'm Eye Candy!*

Obtaining a trigger event off a RigidBody

It is possible to cause a Trigger event to only fire off upon contact with a RigidBody thrown around in the scene under physics. This would be good in a case where a door at the bottom of some stairs is locked and you can't open it. Tipping over a fridge so it falls down some stairs under physics to break the locked door would offer a plausible solution and a good game play challenge.

How to do it...

1. Create a basic scene using the *Midday Lighting* map template. Set the **GameType for PIE** to *UTGame*. This is done through **View | World Properties** under **Game Type**.

2. Ensure the scene has a Trigger and a Mover at the same location animated by a **Matinee** action. The **Matinee** will be set to play when the Trigger is touched, so you'll need to add a **Trigger Touch** event in Kismet, but we want it so the player doesn't launch this event. So in the **Trigger Touch** event properties turn off **Player Only**.

3. In the **Trigger Touch** event's properties set the entry for **Class Proximity Types** to *KActor*, since we want the RigidBody to trigger the event. In the **Ignore** types, include an entry *Pawn*. Also tick on the checkbox for the property **Use Instigator**.

4. In the Content Browser locate a StaticMesh that would be good to bounce around the scene. A crate or box would suffice, something like *PacktKismet.Mesh.BlockMover*. Highlight the asset you chose, and in the **Perspective** viewport right-click and choose **Add Rigid Body: BlockMover**. A RigidBody actor is named in the scene as a *KActor* (or kinematics actor) and can perform under physics.

5. Select the added *KActor* in the scene, then in Kismet, under the **Instigator** nub of the **Trigger Touch** event right-click and choose **Create New Object Variable using KActor_0**.

6. Hook the **Object Variable** *Kactor_0* up to the **Instigator** nub of the **Trigger Touch** event.

7. In the editor, with the *KActor* still selected, press *F4* to edit its properties. Ensure that the **Collision Type** property is *COLLIDE_BlockAll*.

8. Also ensure that **No Encroach Check** is ticked off, since, as it says in the mouse roll-over note: **If you want touched events from triggers or volumes, you need to set this to FALSE**.

9. Now you can throw the object around in the scene and bang it on the Trigger to see if it will set off the Mover. You will have to use a physicsgun to do so. Remember to ensure that a player can't open the door directly.

How it works

The PhysicsGun is obtained in *UTGame* by scrolling the mouse, which is why we specified *UTGame* at the start of the recipe. The idea of this recipe is to edit the ***Trigger Touch*** event so there's a set type of actor assigned to flip it. For this case, we make the default **Player Only** setting to be ignored and set *KActor* as what it responds to. It can be both, so to only allow *KActor* we must set **Pawn** to be ignored, since the player is a pawn. When you convert a model to be a rigid body its collision type may be discarded and you will have to manually re-assign it to *COLLIDE_BlockAll*. Its easy to overlook that a touch occurs when the trigger and *KActor* encroach on each other, but by default the *KActor* doesn't have an encroach check enabled. **No Encroach Check** is on by default. So we must turn this off in its properties. The remaining part is to use an **Instigator** for the **Trigger Touch** event, defined by the ***Object Variable*** *KActor_0*.

There is a guide I made about this topic on YouTube (you4tom): `http://youtu.be/vNtenIWzEbQ?hd=1`. The next image is a screen grab from the video, where the ball under the PhysicsGun cross-hair is the RigidBody used to trigger the door:

Creating a firing pattern based puzzle

In this recipe we will make a puzzle that is based on shooting targets in a specific order cued by color coding in the level.

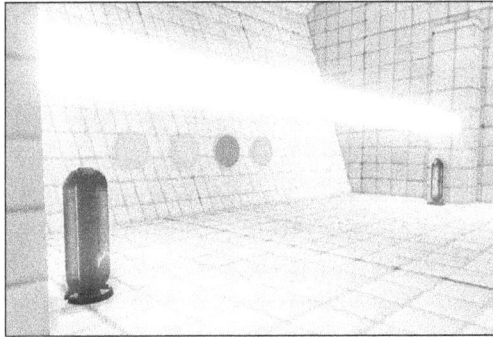

Toggling the state of a Trigger to disable or enable it based on another action is disarmingly simple. It can seem very difficult however without a push in the right direction. In Kismet, right-clicking on a node allows the user to expose a few properties to which one can give variables. For a Trigger event, one of these is called *bEnabled*. It is an easy mistake to think that this is a mechanism for changing the enabled state of the event, but it is more a way to get a result or report of the current state. You'd have to also supply a command to change the variable feeding the **bEnabled** nub.

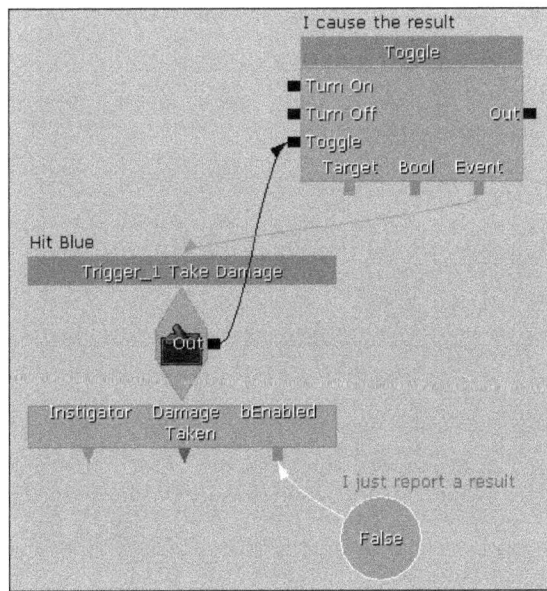

As shown here, it is a ***Toggle*** with a wire extending from its **Event** nub that does the trick. This leads into the top of the event one wants to either turn on, off, or toggle. This can be tracked in the log during PIE. We are going to examine a rather tangled up scene, with nodes and wire crossing all over the place. The goal is to shoot the two *PowerCores* in the level until the background blur clears and the generator sound turns completely off. What we want to avoid is any chance of canceling the process just by shooting the same Trigger over and over or winning if they get the order wrong.

Getting ready

Turn off UDK, then, in your UDK shortcut in the Windows **Start** menu, right-click and open the properties for the editor shortcut. In the path to the binary of the editor add *-log* at the end which will bring up a running log of everything UDK is doing while you run the editor, including PIE. This can help you trace the results of the kind of enabling and disabling that we'll do in this recipe. Restart UDK.

Load *Packt_05_DisableGenerator_Start.UDK* and set the **View | World Properties | GameType for PIE** to *UTGame*.

In the level we have a passage with angled sides. There is a beam in the center and two *PowerCore* meshes at either end. The events we are going to toggle on and off will draw on *Trigger_0*, by the purple *PowerCore*, and *Trigger_1*, by the blue *PowerCore*. Surrounding the scene are two **PostProcessVolumes**, one of which is on the purple side and tints the scene purple. The other is on the blue side and tints the scene blue. Toggling these clears the scene of the energy field (blur) and is our main goal. A color coding sequence shows the solution.

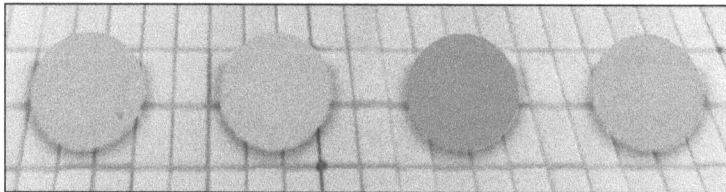

How to do it...

In the Kismet some parts already exist. These involve procedures that have already been covered.

For example, the Sub-sequence *Start* shown below consists of **Toggle Hidden** actions that expose color coded guide disks intended to reveal the order the player should shoot the *PowerCores*. There are four disks along one wall, and the PlayerStart faces these.

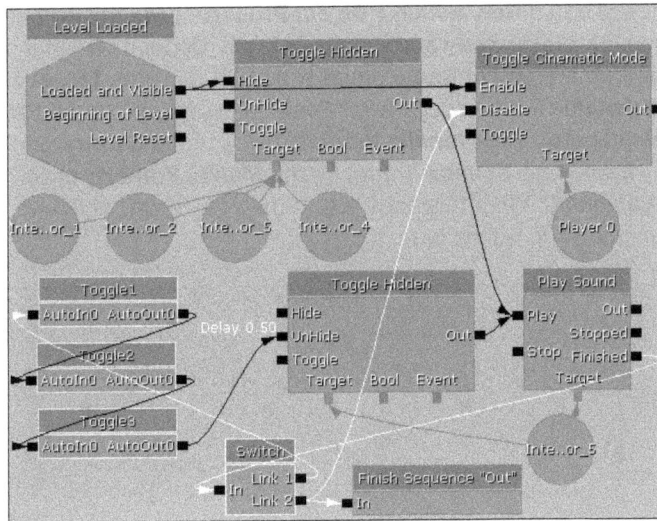

Doing the Damage

1. In Kismet, in the main sequence, add a **Player Spawned** event. Set its **Max Trigger Count** property to 0.

2. In the scene *Ctrl + Left-click* on *Trigger_0* and *Trigger_1* to select both.

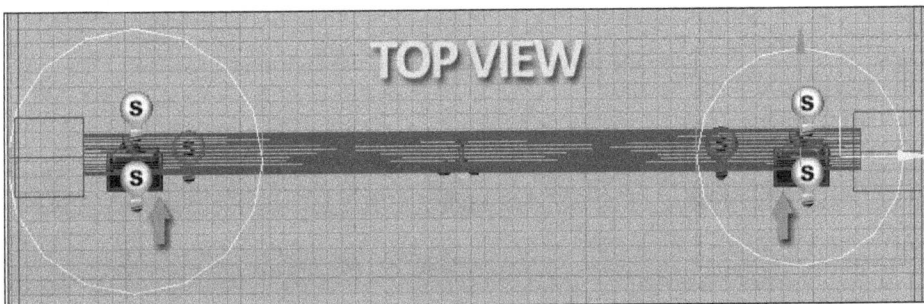

3. In Kismet, in the main sequence, right-click after the **Player Spawned** event and choose **New Events Using Trigger_0, ... | Take Damage**. For both expand their property **Damage Threshold** and set it from 100 down to 1. This is so it doesn't take much of a hit impact to trigger them. Also set their **Max Trigger Count** from 1 to 0, so that you can hit them as many times as you like.

4. *Trigger_0* is by a purple *PowerCore* so comment the **Trigger | Take Damage** event associated with it as *Hit Purple*. Comment the other **Trigger | Take Damage** event as *Hit Blue*. These comments will help later when connecting the toggles to them.

5. Hold *T* and click to add a **Toggle**. Comment this as *STARTSON*. Add another and comment it as *STARTSOFF*.

6. Right-click and add a **New Action | Object Property | Modify Property**. Connect its **In** nub to the **Player Spawned** event's **Out** nub. Under it assign a new **Named Variable** (with the **Find Var Name** property as *PPV_1*) to the **Target** of this. *PPV_1* is an **Object Variable** for the scene actor *PostProcessVolume_1*. Add an entry to the **Properties** property of the **Modify Property** using the **Add Entry** icon [⊙] and for **[0] | Property Name** type *bEnabled*. Turn on the **Modify Property** checkbox and set the **Property Value** to 0. What this does is turn the volume off, which we need because the first volume lit up will be blue.

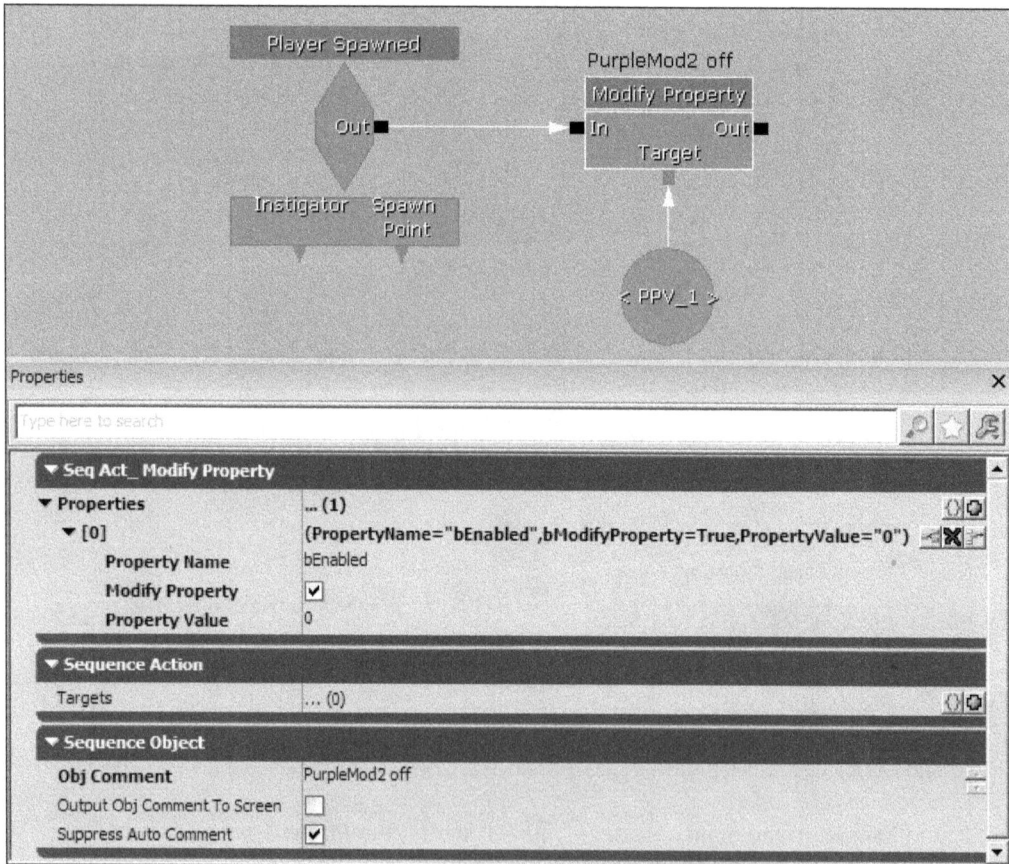

7. Now hook up the **Player Spawned** event to the **Toggle** *STARTSOFF* using the **Turn Off** nub. *Ctrl-drag* the **Event** nub of the **Toggle** and drag it to the left end of the node. Extend a wire from the **Event** nub to top of the event **Trigger_0 Take Damage**. Comment this event as *Hit Purple*. From the **Player Spawned** event to the **Toggle** *STARTSON* drag a wire to the **Turn On** nub.

8. *Ctrl-drag* the **Event** nub to the left of the node. Hook the **Event** nub to the top of the event **Trigger_1 Take Damage**. Comment this event as *Hit Blue*.

9. Hold S and click to add a ***Play Sound*** action and in its **Play Sound** property add
   A_Pickup_Ammo_Respawn_Cue from the Content Browser. Hook up the **Out** nubs of
   both ***Take Damage*** events into the **Play** nub of the ***Play Sound***. From the **Out** nub of
   the ***Play Sound*** extend a wire to the existing Sub-sequence *Beam*, as shown in the
   next screenshot.

10. In the **Play Sound** property, using the assign icon [◈], add the *PacktWavs.Cue.
    Energy_Cue* asset from the Content Browser . Right-click on the **Play** nub and
    choose **Set Activate Delay** and give that a duration value of 0.75. This is a good
    idea because otherwise the player's rather loud weapon shooting will cancel it out.
    You can also adjust pitch and volume in the properties to suit.

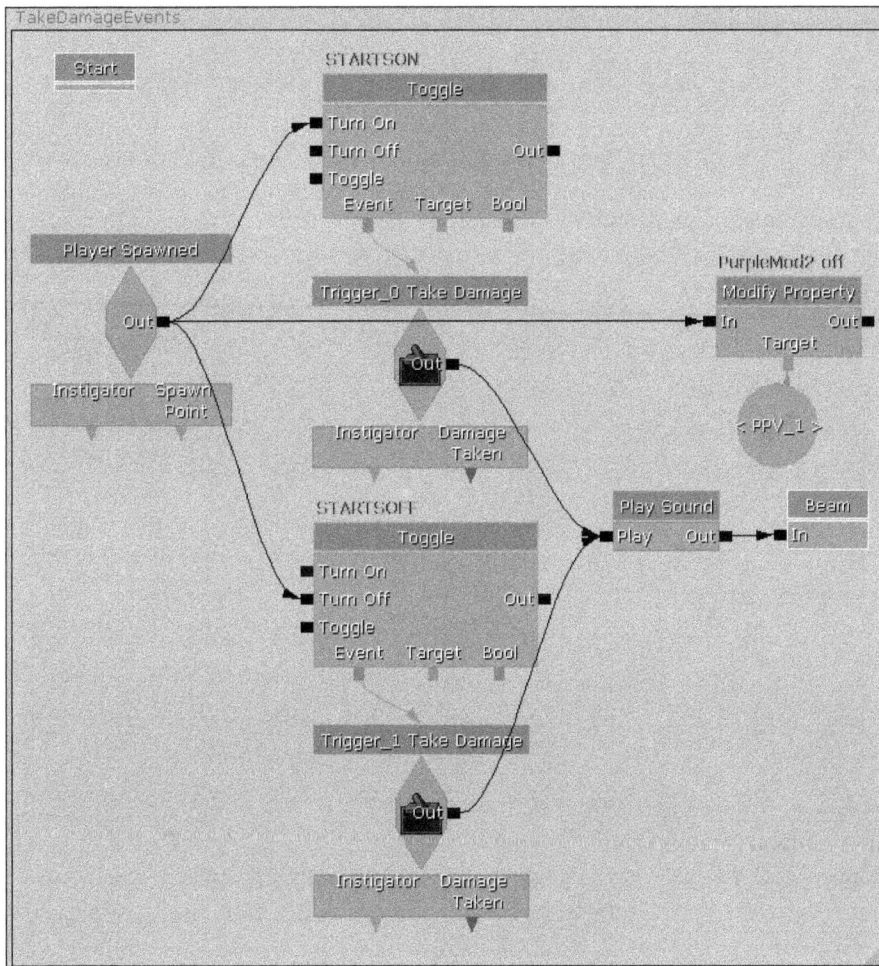

> When right-clicking on a nub that is a bit crowded by wires, you can highlight (but not apply) **Break Link To>** and you will see the names of the nodes involved. These take the **Obj Comment** labels applied to them, which makes tracking them easier. In addition it shows the nub type the wire joins to on the nodes. If you have a lot of **Named Variables** in the scene, you can right-click and expand **New Variable | Named Variables in Persistent Level** and a list of user defined **Named Variables** will show there. This gives you a quick way to assign variables if you use long or hard to recall **Var Names**.

Blue Blue Purple Blue

1. Create four **Toggle** actions (hold *T* and click) and comment them respectively *T1, T2, T3, T4*.

2. Right-click and choose **New Event | Remote Event**. Create five of these, and give them the **Event Names**: *OpenGate1, CloseGate1, OpenGate2, EnablePurple*, and *EnableBlue* respectively. Once named, these have **Activate Remote Event** analogs in the Sub-sequence *Settings*, which you can take a look at.

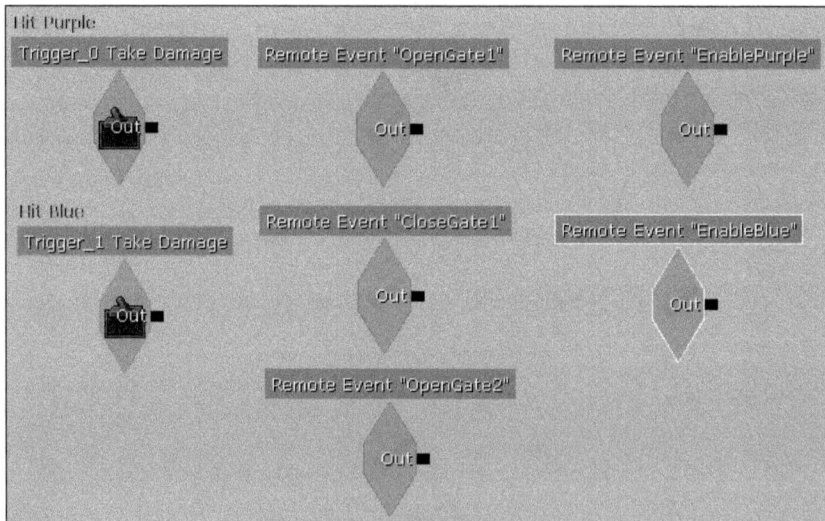

3. Add a new **Switch** action. In its properties set the **Link Count** to 2. Comment it as *S1*, then copy and paste another and comment that as *S2*. Then hold *G* and click to add a **Gate** action. Comment it as *Gate1*. Then create another and comment that as *Gate2*. This gives you all the nodes you'll need for this section. See the next screenshot to confirm that you have added these correctly:

4. The ***Toggle*** actions will affect the ***Trigger | Take Damage*** events. Connect the **Event** nubs of both *T1* and *T2* to the red title bar on the ***Trigger | Take Damage*** *Hit Purple*, which should already have a wire from the ***Toggle*** *STARTSOFF* created earlier. For the **Event** nubs of *T3* and *T4*, connect them to ***Trigger | Take Damage*** *Hit Blue*.

5. Add two more ***Toggle*** actions. Comment the first of these as *PurpleOn*, and the second as *BlueOn*. *PurpleOn*'s **Event** nub hooks up to *Hit Purple's* top bar. *BlueOn*'s **Event** nub hooks up to *Hit Blue's* top bar. The ***Remote Event*** *Enable Purple* feeds into the **Turn On** nub of the ***Toggle*** *Purple On*. The ***Remote Event*** *Enable Blue*, likewise feeds into the **Turn On** nub of the ***Toggle*** *BlueOn*.

6. Let's deal with the ***Gate*** *Gate1* action. Connect *Hit Purple* to *Gate1*'s **In** nub. Connect the ***Remote Event*** *OpenGate1* to *Gate1*'s **Open** nub. Connect the ***Remote Event*** *CloseGate1* to the *Gate1*'s **Close** nub. Connect the **Out** nub of *Gate1* to the **In** nub of the ***Switch*** *S1*.

7. **Link 1** of the ***Switch*** *S1* feeds back into the **Close** nub of *Gate1*. **Link 2** of the ***Switch*** *S1* feeds into the **Open** nub of *Gate2*.

8. For the ***Gate*** *Gate2*, connect the *Hit Blue* event to the **In** nub of *Gate2*. Connect the ***Remote Event*** *OpenGate2* to the **Open** nub of *Gate2*. Also connect the ***Remote Event*** *EnableBlue* to the **Open** nub. Feed the **Out** nub of *Gate2* into the **In** nub of the ***Switch*** *S2*. The **Link 2** nub of the same ***Switch*** should feed back into the **Close** nub of *Gate2*. Since we're developing a blue, blue, purple, blue firing pattern, these last steps help us control the ***Toggles*** which activate and deactivate the ***Take Damage*** events.

9. Earlier we set the **Toggles** to enable or disable the **Take Damage** events, but didn't specify what fires the inputs of the **Toggles** themselves. This comes from the **Switches** *S1* and *S2*. Here is the pattern:

   ❏ Hook up **Link 1** of the **Switch** *S1* to the **Turn Off** nub of **Toggle** *T1*

   ❏ Hook up **Link 2** of the **Switch** *S1* to the **Turn On** nub of **Toggle** *T2*

   ❏ Hook up **Link 1** of the **Switch** *S2* to the **Turn On** nub of **Toggle** *T3*

   ❏ Hook up **Link 2** of the **Switch** *S2* to the **Turn Off** nub of **Toggle** *T4*

   ❏ Hook up **Link 3** of the **Switch** *S2* to the **Turn On** nub of **Toggle** *T3*

   So *T3* has two inputs.

10. Next, string up the outputs, as shown in the following screenshot. The **Out** nubs of all those **Toggles** should feed into the respective inputs to the Sub-sequence *Settings*:

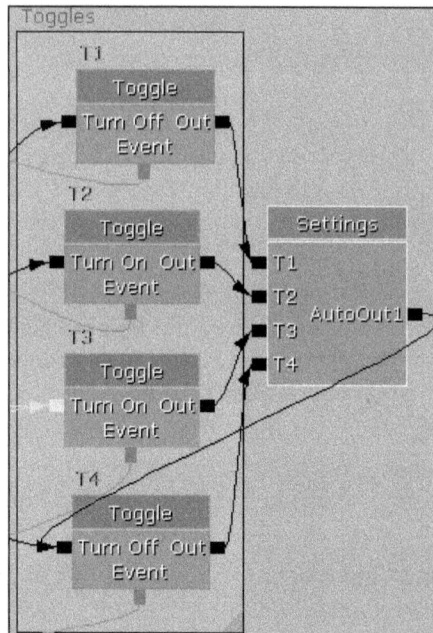

How it works...

Setting the nodes given above may take some time and consideration, but setting them up in a normal situation is much faster where you are coming up with the connection strategy yourself. What this example does is set up material swaps on the guide disks, changing them as they are successfully toggled, and it swaps the color of the blurry PostProcessVolumes accordingly. It disables the Triggers so that when you are firing at the wrong one nothing happens. It enables the Triggers in a pattern that allows us to shoot the right ones.

This particular example punishes us for choosing wrongly (or shooting haphazardly), simply by hurting the player if it takes them more than four shots to solve the problem. An **Integer Counter** or **Int Counter** has been used to calculate the actual incidents of hitting the **Trigger Take Damage** events, shown in the Sub-sequence *Ending*. The **Int Counter** takes an integer from **A**, increments it by 1 (or a value you set in the properties), and compares the result against a target integer **B**. Our targets are four shots, as there are four color coded disks giving us the shooting order.

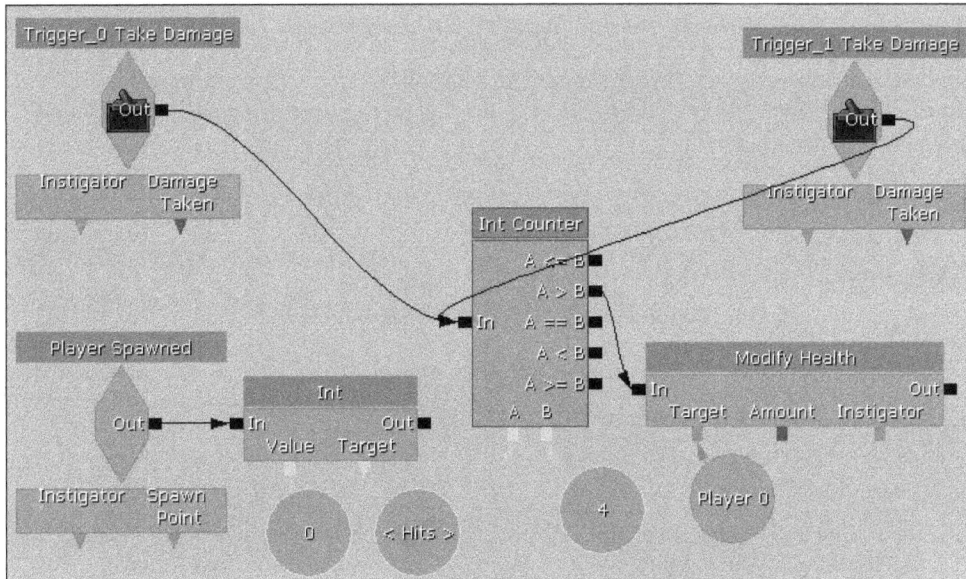

In the example, there are several Sub-sequences, which were given in order to isolate the **Trigger** toggling set up. There are two demonstrations for the scene. *Packt_05_DisableGenerator_DEMO.UDK* uses the Sub-sequence *Settings* and *Packt_05_DisableGeneratorLong.UDK* doesn't. Compare the difference in the connection patterns. Note that the maps are set to work with the **GameType** *UTGame*.

Allowing the player to pick up, carry, and place an object

UTGame comes with a PhysicsGun that lets you pick up RigidBody actors and hoist and throw them around. Sometimes however, you may want a controlled system to pick up objects and carry them around. The steps in this lesson provide a mechanic where you carry objects in front of you and uses shooting at the object to capture and release it. It uses an integer value comparison of the kind we've already covered, a switch for capture and release behavior, and offset triggers attached to the player to set a carrying location.

Getting ready

Load the scene *Packt_05_Carrying_Start.UDK*.

First examine the scene, noting the stair by the wall that has a missing step. Actually it is visible, but it will be hidden at level load. Select this and convert it to a Mover, so that it can be hidden. There is also another block like it lying on the ground nearby, shown in the next screenshot. Select this and convert it to a KActor. Our goal will be to place the KActor where the Mover is, with the Mover starting out hidden then being revealed by the KActor.

Press *K* so you can see actors in the screen get a green boundary to show they are being referenced in Kismet, as shown here. At first there will be none showing, since we have to add the objects one by one.

How to do it...

Setting up guides that follow the player:

1. The brief for this example is to have the carried object float in front of the player. To start out, we need to have a Trigger linked to the player. Select *Trigger_0*, *Trigger_1* and *Trigger_2* and open Kismet. Right-click and choose **New Object Vars using Triggers...** so we can refer to these in Kismet.

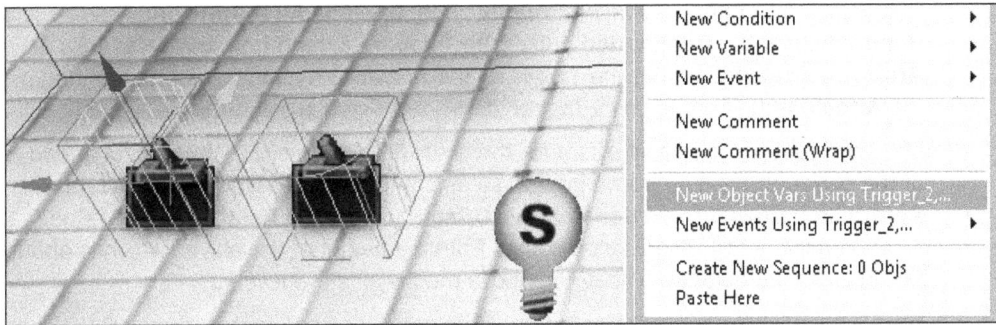

2. While we are setting up the scene elements, also select the block on the floor in the scene, the block that you converted to a KActor. In Kismet, right-click and choose **New Object Variable using KActor**. For this, set its **Var Name** property as *A*.

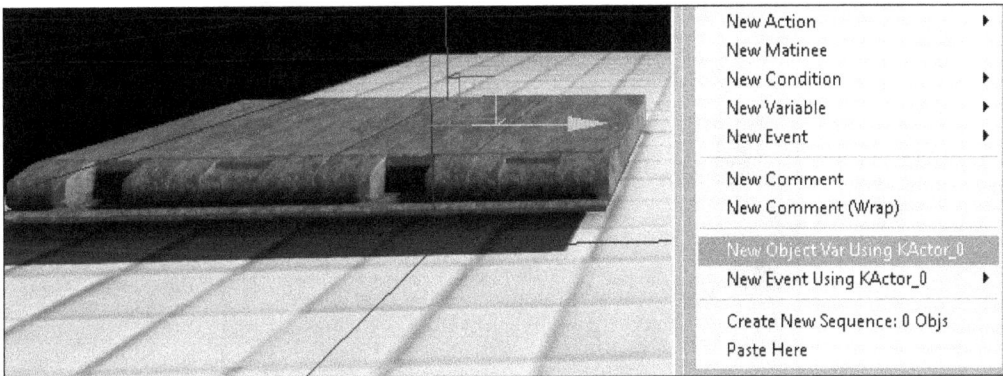

3. In the level, select the block against the wall that you converted to a Mover and in Kismet right-click and choose **New Object Variable using InterpActor**. For this, set its **Var Name** property as *B*.

4. Hold *Ctrl + L* and click to add a ***Level Loaded***, and hook up its **Level Loaded and Visible** to a new ***Teleport*** action. Set the **Target** for the ***Teleport*** to be the ***Object Variable*** *Trigger_2*.

5. Hold *P* and click to add a *Player Variable* and turn off its **All Players** property. Hook this up to the **Destination** nub of the *Teleport*. Extend from the *Teleport* a new *Attach to Actor* action. Set the **Target** as the *Player Variable* you just made, then set the **Attachment** variable using *Trigger_1*.

6. It is important to include an offset for the actor *Trigger_1* so the block floats ahead of the player and is a bit above ground so as not to block the view. In the **Attach to Actor**'s properties turn on **Use Relative Offset**, and set the **Relative offset** value to X = 400 and Z = 90. The Z value comes from the height of the player, which is about 96 units, so the object will float just above the player's eye level.

7. Hold *D* and click to add a *Delay* action. In its properties set its **Duration** to 0.001 and wire it so the **Out** nub of the *Teleport* action feeds its **Start** nub. Feed its **Finished** nub to the **In** nub of the *Teleport*. This creates a rapid loop back which will constantly situate the *Trigger_2* on the player.

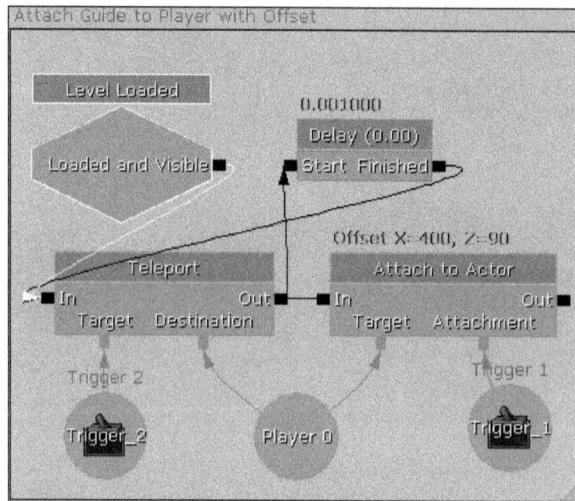

8. Comment the sequence starting from the *Level Loaded* event as *Attach Guides to Player with Offset*.

9. To see *Trigger_1* during play testing, right-click on the **Object Variable** *Trigger_1* in Kismet and choose **Select Trigger_1** in the level, then press *F4* in the scene to view the actor properties for *Trigger_1*. Go to **Display** and set **Hidden** off. When you confirm things are working, the Trigger may be hidden again. **Build All** [🔧] then press *F8* to PIE to check the result.

Handling Block A

1. In the scene, near the Mover you set earlier (the block against the wall), there is another Trigger actor. Select this Trigger and in Kismet right-click and choose **New Event Using Trigger_0 | Touched**. In the properties of this event set the **Class Proximity Types** as *KActor* instead of *Pawn*. Turn off **Player Only** and set the **Max Trigger Count** to 0. Turn on the checkbox for **Use Instigator** then set the *Object Variable Trigger_1* (which already exists in the Kismet) as the **Instigator** as in the following screenshot:

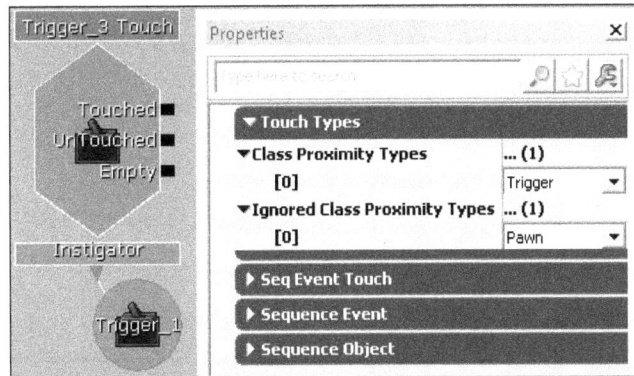

2. In Kismet, add a new **Teleport** action and set the **Target** for this to *Trigger_0* and the **Destination** as *Trigger_1*. Note where the actual Trigger actor *Trigger_1* is in the scene, by the steps.

3. Right-click on the **Object Variable** *KActor_2* under the **Trigger | Touched** event. **Choose Select KActor_2 in level**. Now right-click in Kismet and choose **New event using KActor_2 | Take Damage**. Set its **Max Trigger Count** property to 0. Hook its **Out** nub to the **In** nub of the **Teleport** action created in the previous step.

4. In the **KActor Take Damage** event's properties, set the **Min Damage Amount** to 0.0 and the **Damage Threshold** to 1. Also specify the **Damage Types** filter to be *UTDmgType_Rocket* using the add entry icon [⚙] and then choosing from the [0] list.

5. From the **Take Damage** event extend an additional wire from its **Out** nub to a new **Switch** action. Assign to the **Switch**, in its properties, a **Link Count** of 2. Also set it **Looping**.

6. In Kismet, right-click and choose **New Action | Set Variable | Int**. Comment this as *Hit*. Right-click on the **Value** nub and choose **Create New Int Variable**. In its properties set its **Seq Var_Int** value to 1. Next to it, hold *N* and click to add a **Named Variable** and set its **Find Var Name** property to *BlockAShot*. Hold *I* and click to create a new **Integer Variable**. Set its **Var Name** property to *BlockAShot*. The setting of this *BlockAShot* to 1 occurs when our **KActor** block takes damage, and *BlockAShot* will be subject to a comparison in the sequence later.

7. Connect the **Int** action *Hit* so its **In** nub goes to **Link 1** of the **Switch**. Copy the action *Hit* and its variable and paste them below. Change the action *Hit* so its **Obj Comment** field says *Released*. Also change the **Int Variable** connected to the **Value** nub so its value is 0 not 1 as shown here:

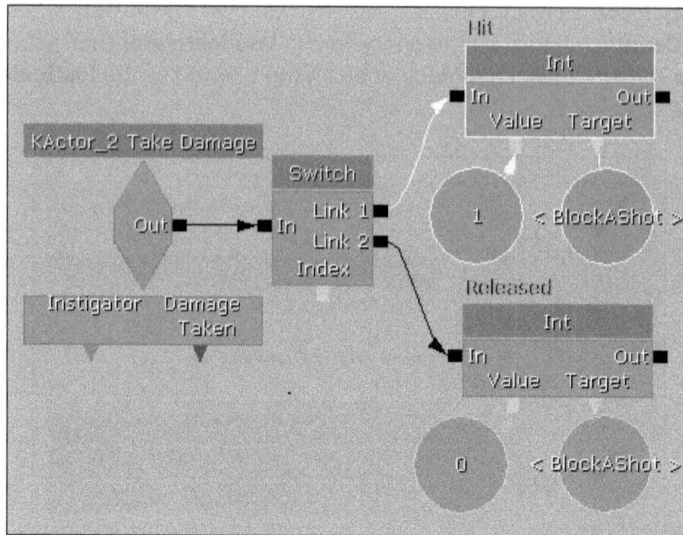

Creating Physics changes for the KActor

1. Add a **New Action | Physics | Set Physics** then press *Ctrl + C* and *Ctrl + V* so you have two of these. Comment the first as *Pick Up* and the second as *Release*.

2. For the **Set Physics** action *Pick Up*, set the **new Physics** property as *PHYS_Interpolating*. For the **Set Physics** action *Release*, set the **new Physics** property as *PHYS_RigidBody*. The **Target** for both actions will be an **Object Variable** using *KActor_2* (you can copy and paste it from the one already there in the sequence). What we now have is a way for the block to respond when picked up and released. Since it is a rigid body, when we release it we want to fall to the ground. While we are holding it, it should just follow the trigger, which is what we'll set up next.

3. Add a new **Teleport** action after the **Set Physics** action *Pick Up*. Make the **Teleport** action's **Target** the **Object Variable** *KActor_2*. Make its **Destination** the **Object Variable** *Trigger_1*. Both of these already exist in the sequence. Add a new **Attach to Actor** action extending from the **Teleport** action. Set the **Teleport** action's **Target** as the **Object Variable** *Trigger_1*, and its **Attachment** as the **Object Variable** *KActor_2*, which also exists in the scene and can be copied and pasted.

4. For the **Attach to Actor** action, edit its properties so **Use Relative Offset** is on, and there is a **Relative Offset** of X=100 and Y=100.

5. Copy and paste the **Attach to Actor** action and right-click on the pasted one and choose **Break All Connections**. Hook its **In** nub to the **Out** nub of the **Set Physics** action *Release*. For its **Target** set the **Object Variable** *Trigger_1* and the **Attachment** as the **Object Variable** *KActor_2*.

6. Hold *D* and click to add a **Delay** and hook the **Start** nub to the **Out** nub of the **Attach to Actor** action which extends from the **Teleport** action. Set the **Delay** action's **Finished** nub to the **In** nub of the **Teleport** action, creating a loopback. Set the **Delay** action's **Duration** to 0.000001 (the smallest possible number UDK will allow you to input). This means that when you pick up the block, it follows smoothly.

> UDK actually measures time in **Ticks**, which occur many times per second. The time a Tick takes depends on your CPU and scene complexity. The idea is that for every Tick the sequence at hand is evaluated. Frames, and seconds, by comparison are really massive giants in comparison to Ticks. But a 0.000001 delay is pretty fast. So the important thing is just to be sure that you don't need your sequence to have a Tick rate faster than the actual tick rate. In code, Tick is written as `event Tick (float DeltaTime)` where `DeltaTime` is the time since the last time Tick was actually called or given.
>
> Next time someone says they'll be back in a tick, you'd better not blink.

7. From the **Set Physics** action *Release*, drag a wire to the **Stop** nub of the **Delay**. This means that when the block is shot again, the following loop back will end. This is highlighted in the next illustration.

8. If you wish, comment the Kismet from the **KActor | Take Damage** event as *Fire to Attach Block A to Player – Fire Again to Release*.

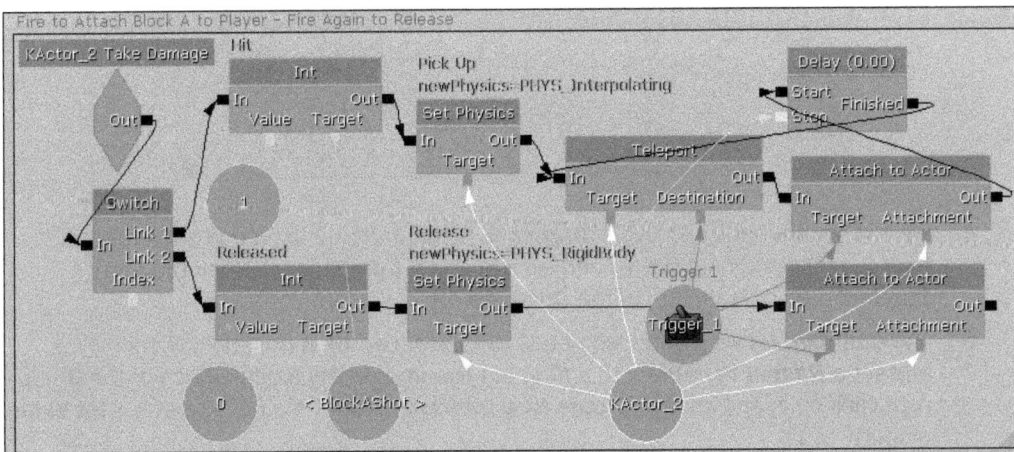

9. We've handled **Block A** but still need to handle **Block B**. Also we've set a *Hit* integer of 1 (True) for **Block A**, but we need to set a *Not Hit* integer of 0 (false) for **Block A** at the start of the level. Therefore, copy the **Int** action *Released*, and its two variables. Paste it nearby, then hook the pasted **Int** to a **Level Loaded** event.

Handling Block B and the Comparison Check

1. In Kismet, using the same **Level Loaded** you added before, add a new **Toggle Hidden**. Wire its **Hide** nub to the **Loaded and Visible** nub of the **Level Loaded** event. Its **UnHide** nub will be set later.

2. Set the **Target** of the **Toggle Hidden** as the **Named Variable** B.

3. Right-click and choose **New Action | Actor | Change Collision**. Highlight the action, press *Ctrl + C*, then *Ctrl + V* to paste a copy. Both need their **Target** set to the **Named Variable** B. For the first, comment it as *Collision OFF*. Hook the **In** nub of this up to the **Level Loaded** event. For the second, comment it as *Collision ON*. We will hook this up next. The property to set for *Collision OFF* is **Collision Type:** *COLLIDE_No Collision*. The property to set for *Collision ON* is **Collision Type***: COLLIDE_BlockAll*.

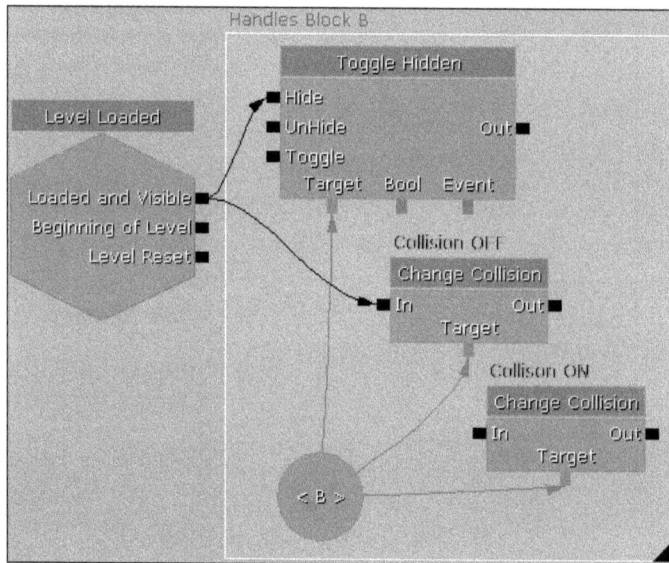

4. We already set earlier an event **Trigger_3 | Touch**. Now it is time to set it to work. Near it, press and hold *Ctrl + I* and click to add a **Compare Int**. Hook the event's **Touched** nub to the **In** nub of the **Compare Int**.

5. The **Compare Int** we just added needs variables. For the **A** nub, hold *N*, then click and set a **Named Variable** with a **Find Var Name** property *BlockAShot*. For the **B** nub, right-click on it, and choose **Create New Int Variable**. Set the new variable's **Int Value** property to 1.

6. From the **Compare Int**, extend a new wire to a new **Switch** action. Set its **Link Count** property to 2. Make sure that **Looping** is off. This is a one time only switch. For **Link 2** there will be no output. Near the **Switch** hold *T* and click to add a new **Toggle** and hold S and click to add a new **Play Sound**. The purpose of using a **Switch** here is so this part cannot recur after *Trigger_3* is touched. We are placing a block of concrete where it needs to go. Once it has happened, we're done.

7. Select in the scene *Emitter_0* which is a particle that gives a spark fizzle suitable to indicate that some kind of weld has occurred. You can press *Ctrl + B* to locate and check it in the Content Browser.

8. In Kismet, right-click the **Target** nub of the **Toggle** and choose **New Object Variable Using Emitter_0**. Ensure that the **Switch** action's **Link 1** wire goes to the **Turn On** of the **Toggle**.

9. Hold *D* and click to add a **Delay** after the **Toggle**. Set its **Duration** to 3.0 and wire the **Out** nub of the **Toggle** to the **Start** nub of the **Delay**. Then wire the **Finished** nub of the **Delay** to the **Turn Off** nub of the **Toggle**.

10. Press *Ctrl + Shift + F* to open the Content Browser. Here, search for *Armor_Chest_Cue* and highlight the resulting asset. Assign this in the **Play Sound** property of the **Play Sound** action in Kismet, using the assign icon [◈]. Set the **Volume Multiplier** property to 5.0 and make sure the **Play** nub of the **Play Sound** is hooked up to the **Link 1** nub of the **Switch**.

11. Hold *P* and click to add a **Player Variable**. Turn off its **All Players** property, and hook it up to the **Play Sound** action's **Target** nub.

12. From the **Compare Int** action's **A == B** nub, hook up a new **Destroy** action. Set the **Target** of this to use **Object Variables** based on *KActor_2* and *Trigger_1*. These variables already exist in the Kismet, so you can copy and paste them. The following screenshot shows the result so far:

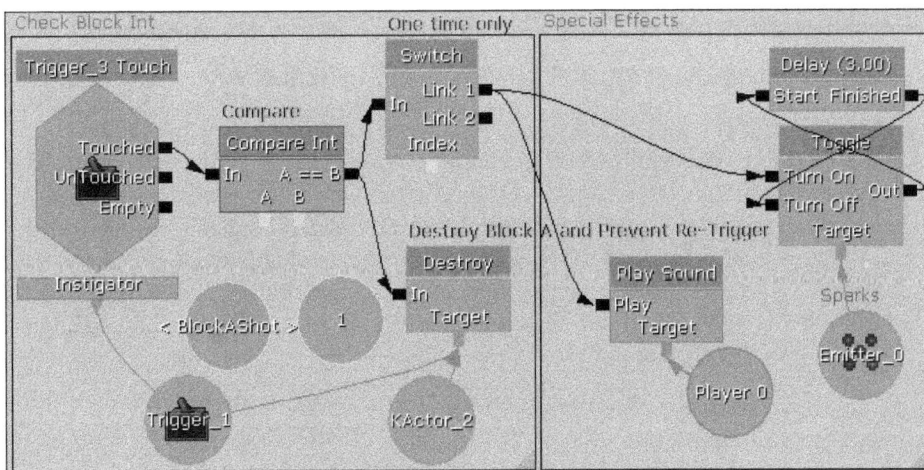

13. Now you need to connect the **Compare Int** up to other actions set earlier. Connect the **A == B** nub up to the **UnHide** nub of the **Toggle Hidden** action with its **Target** nub connected to the **Named Variable** B. Also connect **A == B** to the **In** of the **Change Collision** action Collision ON, which also has the **Named Variable** B connected to its **Target** nub.

How it works

The provided scene *Packt_05_Carrying_DEMO.UDK* shows the working scene. In essence, a trigger is attached to the player and enabled to make contact with only the block we want to carry and the destination where we want to place it. Since the block is a **KActor** (**kinematics actor**) it can work under physics, so if we shoot it it'll go pinging off into space. Changing its physics to *PHYS_Interpolating* and using a teleporting loop makes it follow the trigger, and changing its physics to *PHYS_RigidBody*, and breaking the teleport loop lets us drop it if desired. We use the Integer comparison at the end to verify if the block is currently being carried so that when the Trigger we use to carry the block around on (by an attachment and teleport loop) touches the destination, it will gives us the end results.

Exploring 'following' and 'attracting' behaviors

Suppose you have to guide an AI Bot from one location to another, but don't want to use a set path or ideal path based on PathNodes. The problems that can occur with having the Bot flexibly follow your position are as follows:

▸ The Bot can get stuck against geometry and lose its trace on you

▸ The Bot can block you as it encroaches on your position, in a corner especially

▸ The Bot may require respawning at its location and this can create a jitter

▸ The Bot can run out of the level trying to arrive at your location

If a level is flat, free of obstructions, and only needs a short time period, following behaviour will be easier to set up than if it involves climbing, moving obstacles and has interrupted or lengthy following times. Since there will never be a single way that will work in every case, we're going to focus on an example that provides an approach to each of the problems above. It not only requires the Bot to move to the player, but also has conditions to renew the Bot in the scene should it get stuck or be in a position we don't want, like encroaching too much on the player. The Bot is able to stop and resume walking, or, if we do manage to snag it, it can be unstuck just by walking up to it.

Getting ready

For this example, load the map *Packt_05_Kismet_Following_Start.UDK* and familiarize yourself with the scene by running around in it. The **GameType for PIE** is set to *MyGame*, so that will require you to set the config *DefaultEngine.ini* to point to `+ModEditPackage=MyGame` as in the previous recipe's *Getting ready* steps. There is a JumpPad, a ladder, and a swimming pool. The goal will be to lead the Bot from its spawn point up to a second room up the ladder without it getting stuck. All the actors and triggers that are in the scene have already been given their variables in Kismet.

How to do it...

Spawning the Bot and its guides

1. Open Kismet and double-click on the Sub-sequence *Spawns*. Right-click and choose **New Action | Misc | Finish Sequence**. This creates a route out of this Sub-sequence. When you select items in Kismet and choose **Create New Sequence** the *Finish Sequence* action and *Sequence Activated* Events are added automatically based on the content. Since this procedure is reverse engineered, here they'll need to be placed by hand.

2. Add a new *Player Spawned* event. Set its **Max Trigger Count** to 0. Also add a **New Event | Remote Event** and type *LoopBack* in its **Event Name** property. *LoopBack* won't go green just yet.

3. Hook up both of these events to a new *Actor Factory* action. For this, set the property **Factory** as *UTActorFactoryAI* and the **Controller Class** as *None*, and the **Pawn Class** as *MyPawnLookAtMorph*. This is a *MyPawn* variant that stares at the player. Turn off the property **Check Spawn Collision**.

> Don't set the *Actor Factory* type as *ActoryFactoryAI*. Without the *UTActorFactoryAI* variant, things won't work. If you want you can use the **View | World Properties | Gametype For PIE** as *UTGame* instead of *MyGame*, and instead of using *MyPawn* use **Controller Class** *UTBot* and **Pawn Class** *UTPawn*.

4. For the **Spawn Point** nub, add a *Named Variable BotLocator*. This should go green because the variables already exist in the main sequence. For the **Spawned** nub add a *Named Variable Bot*.

5. Following the *Actor Factory*, extend a new *Attach to Actor* action. Set its **Target** as the *Named Variable Bot* and the **Attachment** as the *Named Variable BotLocator*. Turn on the property **Use Relative Offset**.

6. From the **Out** nub of this, hook up one of the **Finish Sequence** actions we made then name its **Output Label** property: *BS_Out*.

7. Copy and paste the **Finish Sequence** action, and set the pasted one's **Output Label** to be *PS_Out*. Wire that up to the **Player Spawned** event, as shown in the next screenshot. Copy and paste the **Attach to Actor** action, and hook this up to the **Player Spawned** event. The **Target** should be the **Named Variable** *BotLocator* and the **Attachment** should be the **Named Variable** *BotOffset*. *BotLocator* and *BotOffset* both reference Triggers in the scene, but *BotOffset* is larger, so there's a certain distance between the two in terms of radius.

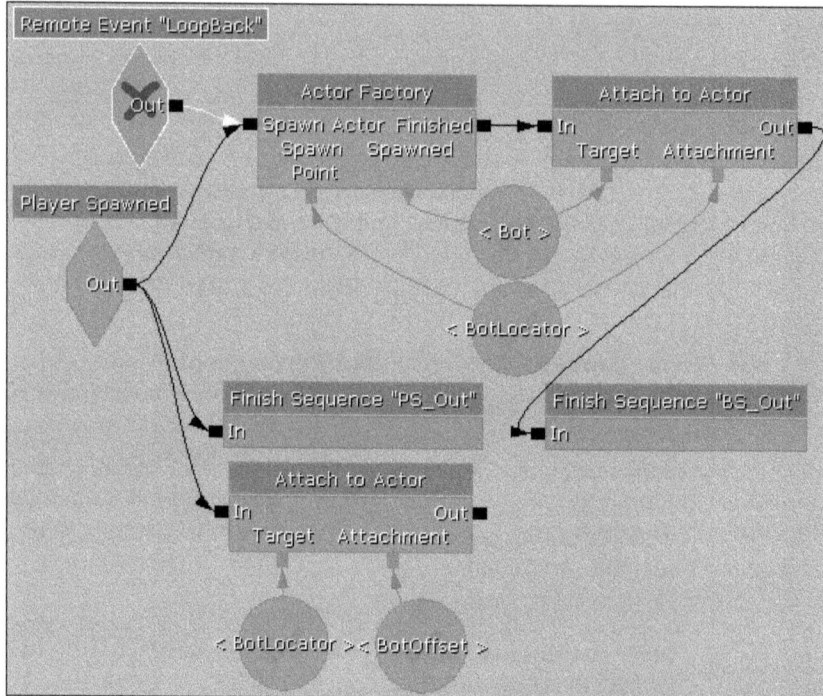

8. All we've done is spawn a Bot in the scene and attach Triggers to it. Now the Bot is followed around by the Triggers we have a reference for its position in case we need to respawn it or in case we want to fire off some Kismet from the attached Trigger.

The PlayerLocator

1. In the Sequences Window, ensure the Sub-sequences list is expanded, then click on *SetPlayerLocator*. Inside it add two **Sequence Activated** events. Give the first the **Input Label** property: *StopDelay* and the select the other and give that the **Input Label** property: *SetTeleport*.

2. From the event **SetTeleport** extend a new **Teleport** action. For the **Teleport** action's **Target** assign the **Named Variable** *PlayerLocator* and for the **Destination** hold *P* and click to add a **Player Variable**. Turn off the **All Players** property of that.

3. Hold *D* and click to add a **Delay** and hook up the **Out** nub of the **Teleport** action to the **Start** of the **Delay**. Hook up the **Finished** nub of the **Delay** to the **In** of the **Teleport** action. Set the **Duration** property of the **Delay** to 0.10. Finally, from the **Sequence Activated** event *PauseDelay* extend a wire to the **Stop** nub of the **Delay**. This gives us a rapid loop which will always put a Trigger on the player's position, unless the loop is deliberately interrupted by the *StopDelay*.

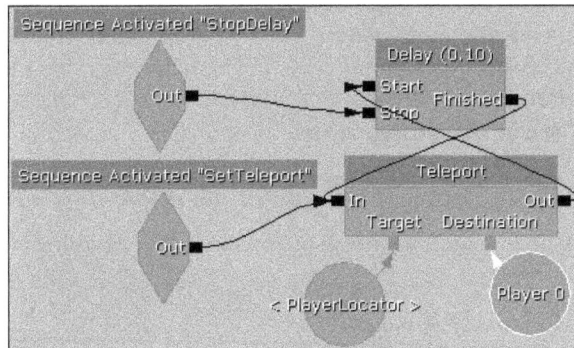

Handling the ladder

In our scene there's a ladder, and bots are not that great at handling instructions while climbing ladders, so we need to make a special case for it that, once it starts to climb it will finish doing so, then resume following. It is useful to know how to break off an action, do something else, then come back to it. One can imagine however, that if your level has dozens of ladders, then you'd have to elaborate things considerably. If you are working with a technical developer, it would be possible to create a custom condition *IsClimbing?* and use that instead. This method is quite fast with a single ladder though. It just forces the Bot to move on the ladder without interruption, then resume following once finished.

1. In the scene, at the base of the ladder volume, there is a Trigger actor (*Trigger_4*). Select *Trigger_4* then open Kismet and double-click on the Sub-sequence *Ladder*. In there right-click and choose **New Event Using Trigger_4 | Touch**.

2. In the **Trigger Touch** event's properties, add as an entry to **Touch Types | Class Proximity Types MyPawnLookAt** from the list of available types. To find this fast, you can press *M* to jump to items starting with *M*.

3. Add the **Named Variable** *Bot* to the **Instigator** nub of the **Trigger Touch** event, and make sure the property **Use Instigator** is on and **Player Only** is off. Set the **Max Trigger Count** to 0.

4. From the **Touched** nub of the *Trigger Touch* event, extend a **New Action | Event | Activate Remote Event**. Set its **Event Name** property to *ClimbingPausesDelays*. We'll add the event this should be associated with later, so don't worry that it is marked red.

5. Also from the **Touched** nub of the *Trigger Touch* event, extend a **New Action | AI | Move to Actor**. Set the *Named Variable* Bot as the **Target**, and assign the *Named Variable PathNode1* as the **Destination** and **Look At**. This references an existing *Object Variable* in the main sequence which is based on an actor in the scene. If you feel like looking for it in the scene, you'll find it at the top of the stairs.

6. In the properties of the *Move to Actor* action, ensure **Interruptable** is turned off (although it doesn't appear to matter, in theory it is just to let the Bot get from A to B without being told to do something else). Extending from the **Finished** nub of the action, add a *Delay* with a **Duration** of 0.10 and hook the **Finished** of the *Delay* to a **New Action | Misc | Finish Sequence**.

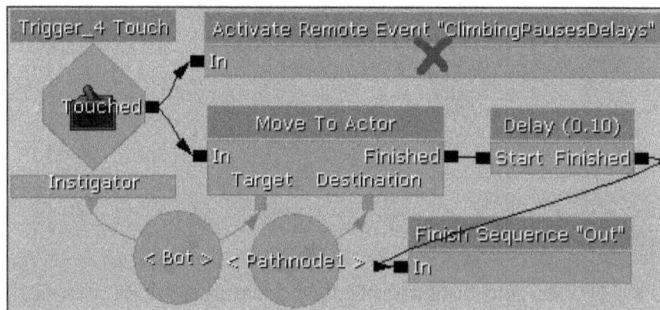

Teleporting locators

1. In the sequences list find *TeleportBottoPlayer* and open it. In here, add a **New Event | Sequence Activated**.

2. Extend from the event a new *Teleport* action, and extend from that an *Attach to Actor* action. Lastly, extend from that a **New Action | Event | Activate Remote Event**. Set the **Event Name** property for the last action to *LoopBack*. *LoopBack* should go green since we added the *Remote Event* it calls on earlier. Double-click *LoopBack* to step back and forth.

3. Assign the *Named Variable BotLocator* to the **Target** of the *Teleport* action and also to the **Attachment** of the *Attach to Actor*. Assign the *Named Variable PlayerLocator* to the **Destination** of the *Teleport* action and also to the **Target** of the *Attach to Actor*, as shown in the next screenshot. In the properties of the *Attach to Actor*, turn on **Use Relative Offset**.

4. Select the *Sequence Activated* Event and copy it by pressing *Ctrl + C*.

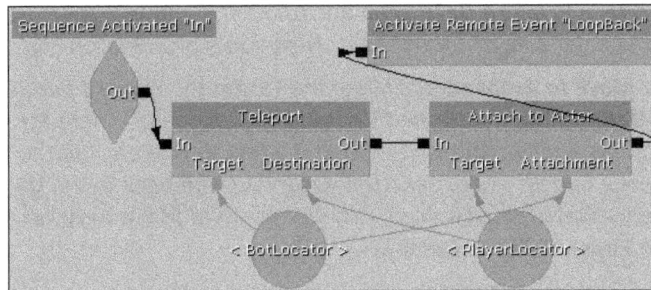

Bot stopping

1. Open the Sub-sequence *MoveSetVelocity* and press *Ctrl + V*. Set the event's **Input Label** property to *In*.

2. Extend from the event a **New Action | AI | Move to Actor**. Set the **Named Variable** *Bot* as the **Target** for this and set the **Named Variable** *PlayerLocator* as the **Destination**.

3. Extend from the **Move to Actor** action's **Finished** nub a **New Action | Actor | Set Velocity**. Right-click on the **Finished** nub of the **Move to Actor** and choose **Set Activate Delay**, then set the value as 0.10.

4. In the properties of the **Set Velocity** action, the defaults use zero for the **Velocity**, which is what we want. We just need to add the **Named Variable** *Bot* as the **Target** for the action.

5. Lastly, extend a **New Action | Misc | Finish Sequence**, and set its property **Output Label** to *Out*.

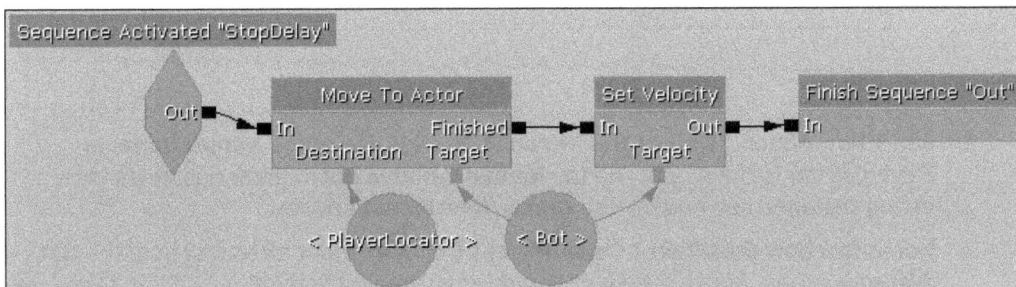

The fun part—putting it all together

1. We now have a range of Sub-sequences, but nothing connects. Go to the main sequence, and add seven **Delay** actions. Since there are so many, and we'll be wiring into them all over the place, comment them D1, D2, D3, D4, D5, D6, and D7 so they are easy to track through the steps that follow.

2. For D3, D4, and D7 set the property **Start Will Restart**.

3. Hold *G* and click to add a **Gate**, then add another. Comment them *Gate1* and *Gate2*. These will also get a lot of connections. Next add a new **Switch** action.

4. Add a new **Move to Actor** action. Make the **Target** the **Named Variable** *Bot*, and make the **Destination** the **Named Variable** *PlayerLocator*. There are going to be three **In** wires for this and two **Out** wires. Send the first **In** wire back to the **Out** nub of the Sub-sequence *Ladder* node. Send the second In wire back to the **BS_Out** nub of the Sub-sequence *Spawns* node. Also, connect the third **Move To Actor** action's **In** nub over to the **Finished** of the **Delay** *D3*.

5. The **Delay** *D3* needs a **Duration** of 0.20 and should have the property **Start Will Restart** turned on.

6. The **Finished** nub of the **Move To Actor** should extend to the **In** nub of *Gate1*. It should also extend to the **Start** nub of the **Delay** *D3* as shown here:

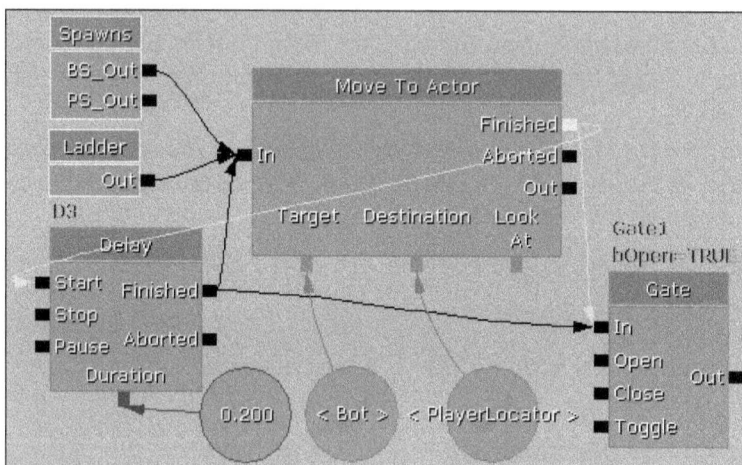

Distance Check

1. Add a **New Action | Actor | Get Distance**. For this assign the **Named Variable** *PlayerLocator* to the **A** nub, and the **Named Variable** *Bot* to the **B** nub. Right-click on the **Distance** nub and choose **Create New Float Variable**.

2. Now add a **New Condition | Comparison | Compare Float** extending from the **Get Distance** action. Assign the **Float Variable** just created to the **A** nub of this **Compare Float** as well. Right-click on the **Compare Float** action's **B** nub and choose **Create New Float Variable**. Set its **Float Value** as 175, which gives us a fair approximation of the distance we want the Bot to get to the player to look like it is encroaching but not getting too friendly.

3. The **Get Distance** needs a **Delay** loopback, so bring **Delay** *D6* over to it, and set the **Out** of the **Get Distance** to the **Start** of the **Delay** *D6*, and hook up the **Finished** of **Delay** *D6* to the **In** of the **Get Distance**. Set the **Duration** of the **Delay** *D6* to 0.20.

4. Wire back the **In** nub of **Get Distance** to the **BS_Out** nub of the *Spawns* Sub-sequence node.

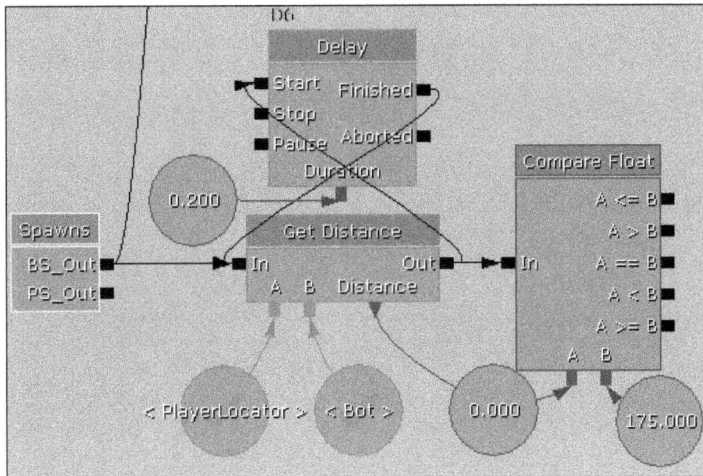

5. For the **Compare Float** action's **A <= B** output, follow the list given here (and notice they are mostly closing or stopping flow through the nodes they connect to):

   ❏ **A <= B** to *Gate1* **Close**

   ❏ **A <= B** to *Gate2* **Close**

   ❏ **A <= B** to **Delay** *D1* **Pause**

   ❏ **A <= B** to **Delay** *D2* **Pause**

   ❏ **A <= B** to **Delay** *D3* **Pause**

   ❏ **A <= B** to **Delay** *D4* **Pause**

   ❏ **A <= B** to **Delay** *D7* **Stop**

6. Also, for the **Compare Float** action's **A > B** output, complete the links given next. Essentially, if the Bot encroaches on the player within 175 units, everything stops. If the distance is greater than 175, everything flows again (so these wires open things up):

   ❏ **A > B** to the **Switch** action's **In**.

   ❏ **A > B** to *Gate1* **Open**

   ❏ **A > B** to *Gate2* **Open**

   ❏ **A > B** to the Sub-sequence *MoveSetVelocity* into the input *StopDelay*.

7. Those links above are shown in the following screenshot, though the layout is not necessarily that way, just the connections:

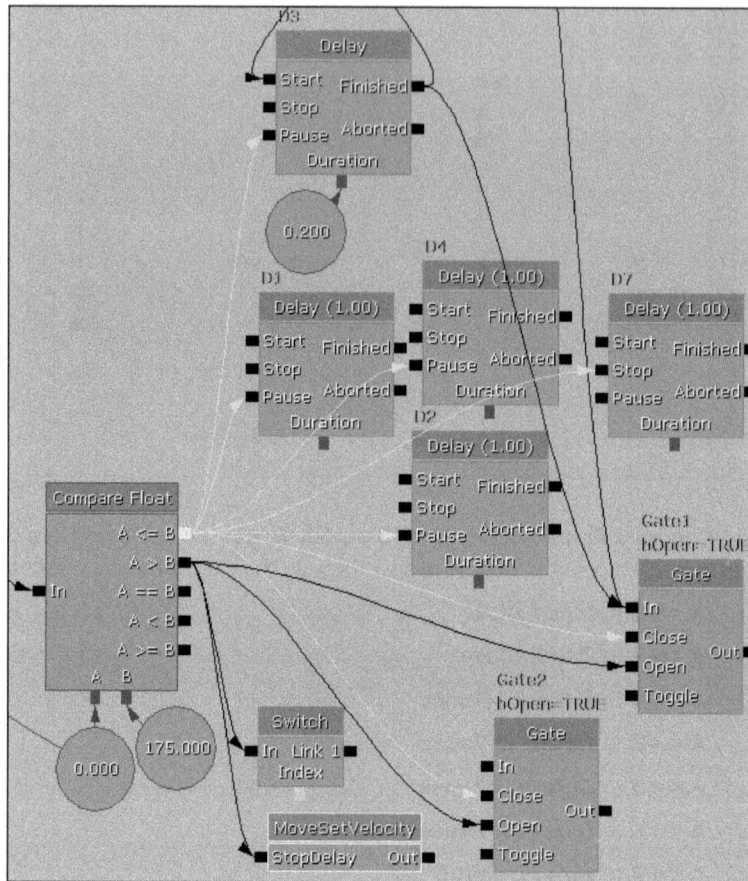

Velocity check

1. Move the *Delay D1* into some clear space. Extending from the *Delay D1* **Finished** nub add a **New Action | Actor | Get Velocity**. For this set the **Target** as the *Named Variable* Bot. Right-click on the **Velocity Vect** nub and choose **Create New Vector Variable**. This takes the velocity of *Bot* along the directions XYZ, so now we know how fast it is going. We're only interested in the Y component, so extend a **New Action | Math | Get Vector Components** from the *Get Velocity*. Then assign the *Vector Variable* from the last step to the **Input Vector** of the **Get Vector Components** action. Right-click on the action's Y nub and choose **Create New Float Variable**. This draws the Y value from the XYZ *Vector Variable*, and the specific value is what we'll be checking.

2. Extend the **Get Vector Components** action's **Out** nub to the **In** nub of a **New Condition | Comparison | Compare Float**. Assign the **Float Variable** from the last step that is capturing the Y value of the **Vector Variable** and hook it into the **A** nub of the **Compare Float**. Right-click on the **B** nub and choose **Create New Float Variable**, and adjust the resulting **Float Variable** so it has a **Float Value** property of 0.001.

3. From the **A < B** nub of the **Compare Float**, extend out a new **Attach to Actor** action. Although this is called **Attach to Actor** we are going to use it as a detach by turning on its **Detach** property. Also turn on **Use Relative Offset**. Comment the action as _Detach_ so you'll remember it has been set.

4. Assign the **Target** of the action as the **Named Variable** _Bot_ and the **Attachment** as the **Named Variable** _PlayerLocator_.

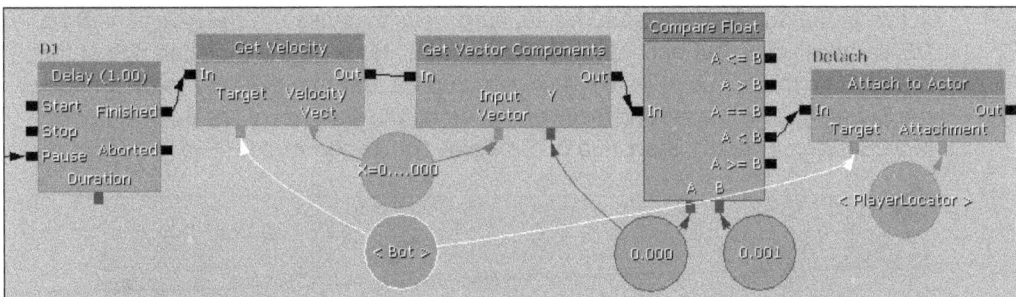

5. From the **A > B** node extend a wire to the **Start** nub of **Delay** _D4_. From the **Out** of the **Attach to Actor** action, extend wires to the **Pause** nub of the **Delay** _D3_ and to the **Start** nub of the **Delay** _D7_.

6. Select around the actions in the image above and create a Comment box called _VelocityCheck_. Now we have a method for telling the Bot to react if she's come to a stop which can help us avoid stalling issues. To solve the problem of stalling we're going to destroy and respawn our Bot. Since she'll be momentarily gone from the scene, enabling the **Detach** property of the **Attach to Actor** lets the guide that was following her stop doing so, and we use that subsequently as the re-spawn point for the Bot.

Putting it all together

1. In the _Global Variables_ section, find and select the **Object Variable** _Trigger_2_ which has the **Var Name** _PlayerLocator_. Right-click on this and choose **Select Trigger_2 in Level**. Then right-click on the canvas and choose **New Event Using Trigger_2: Touch**. This Trigger is joined to the player and it will be triggered by the Trigger joined to the Bot. So go into the event's properties and expand **Touch Types | Class Proximity Types**. Add an entry, and from the list choose _Trigger_. Make sure the **Use Instigator** property is on, and the **Player Only** property is off. Set the **Max Trigger Count** to 0. Set the **Re Trigger Delay** to 0. Set the **Named Variable** _BotLocator_ as the **Instigator** under the **Trigger_2 Touch** event.

2. The **Trigger_2 Touch** event connects to three nodes, the **Stop** nub of the **Delay** D3, the **In** nub of *Gate2*, and the **Pause** nub of the **Delay** D4.

3. While we are here, it is important to note for this scene the **Trigger** actors in the level have their properties adjusted so they differ from the defaults. They all have the property **Can Step Up On** turned off. *Trigger_3* (the Bot locator) has the **Collision Type** property set to *COLLIDE_NoCollision*. *Trigger_2* (the player locator) has its **Collision Type** property set to *COLLIDE_CustomDefault*. It also has **Block Rigid Body** and **No Encroach Check** ticked. The other Triggers don't. *Trigger_4*, at the base of the ladder volume, has its property **Trigger | AITrigger Delay** set to 0.1, which helps fire the command to send the Bot up the stairs.

4. Right-click and choose **New Event | Remote Event**, and give it the **Event Name** *ClimbingPausesDelays*. This is associated with an existing **Activate Remote Event** action in the Sub-sequence *Ladder*. Its purpose is to pause the **Delay** actions D4 and D5, so hook up its **Out** nub into their **Pause** nubs. Hook up the **Finished** nub of the **Delay** D5 to the **In** nub of *Gate2*. Also, hook up the **Out** nub of *Gate2* to the **In** nub of the Sub-sequence *MoveSetVelocity* and hook up the **Out** nub of the Sub-sequence *MoveSetVelocity* to the **Start** nub of the **Delay** D5, as shown:

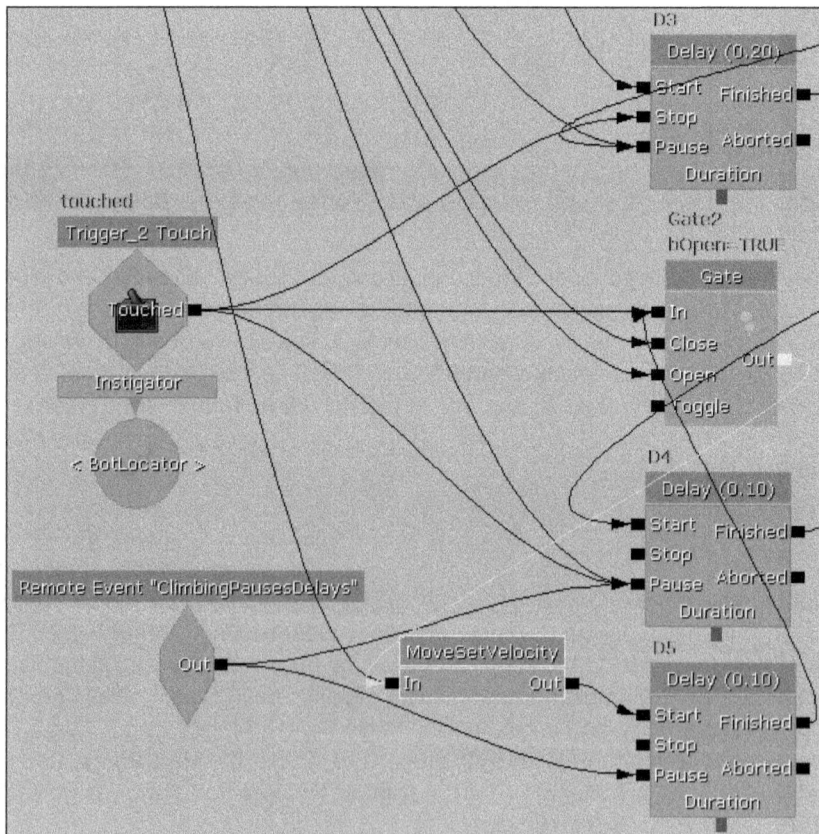

5. The Sub-sequence *Spawns* has a so far unused **PS_Out** nub. Hook this up to the **SetTeleport** nub of the Sub-sequence *SetPlayerLocator*. This situates a locator on the player once the player spawns.

6. After the ***Delay*** *D7* add a new ***Destroy*** action. Set as the **Target** the **Named Variable** *Bot*. From the **Out** nub of the ***Destroy***, extend to the **StopDelay** nub of the Sub-sequence *SetPlayerLocator* and also to the **In** nub of the Sub-sequence *TeleportBottoPlayer*, as shown:

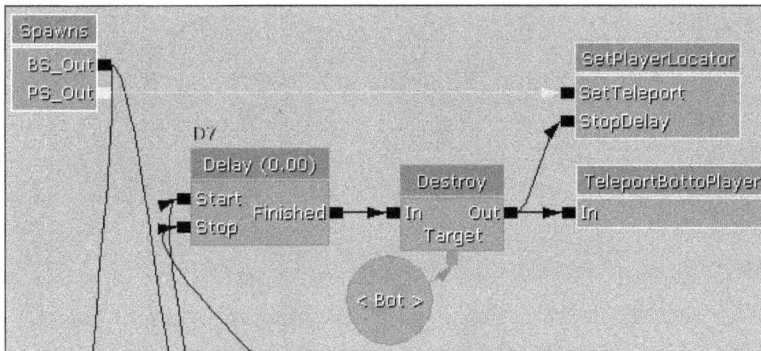

7. The ***Switch*** action we've already set so far has one input from the ***Compare Float*** action's **A > B**. Also add an input from the *Gate1* **Out** nub to the **In** nub of the ***Switch***. The ***Switch*** so far has one link output, which should hook up to the **Start** nub of the ***Delay*** *D1*. In the ***Switch*** properties set the **Link Count** to 2. From the new **Link 2** output, hook up a wire to the **Start** nub of the ***Delay*** *D2*. Hook the **Finished** nub of the ***Delay*** *D2* to the ***Get Velocity*** action's **In** nub, and also the **Finished** nub of the ***Delay*** *D4* goes there, so now it should have three inputs. This is shown in the highlighted links here:

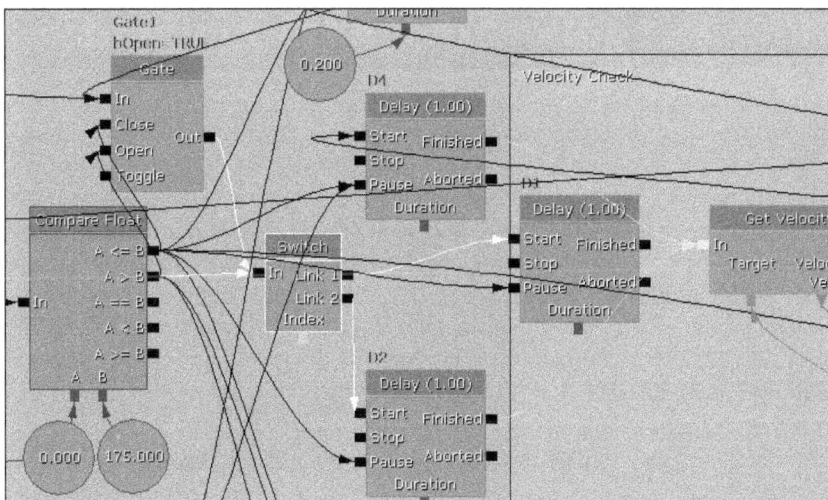

8. You should now be ready to PIE. You can also check out the working demonstrations: *Packt_05_FollowMyGame_DEMO.UDK* or *Packt_05_FollowUTGame_DEMO.UDK* in the provided content. Open up both and have a look at the differing organization of the Kismet network.

See also

▶ An interesting feature that can go along with the kind of attracting or following process discussed here is changing the speed at which the Bot or the player follows, particularly on ladders. Be sure to check out the recipe *Changing the speed of characters* in *Chapter 6, Under the Hood*.

Creating a regenerative health shield

There are many reasons why a designer may want to get the current value of the player's health. One reason might be to increment damage up to a certain point and no more, or to limit the aggression of opponents based on the health of the player. In this lesson we will log the player's health to an Integer and use that as a multiplier to create a regenerative, but temporary shield. There are many ways to build game mechanics around health, including damage to health based on distance, time, or number of hits. The method here is driven by Kismet. Often anything related to player properties is handled in code by a developer rather than in the level by a gamer, and not surprisingly this exception is fairly scene specific, not a generalized method to effect the player all the time. To provision permanent effects on player health, creating a class is better.

Getting ready

Load the scene from the provided content *Packt05_Health_Start.UDK* and familiarize yourself with its content. This scene is set in the **World Properties** to use *UTGame* as its **GameType** for PIE. The Kismet is functionally quite complete. There is already a Bot, and already a timer and all the multipliers we need are there to handle the damage. We are only going to look at a mechanism for capturing the value of the player's health.

This scene has the text 'OK' on one side. Once the player presses *E* to use a Trigger attached to them, the text 'OK' turns to a timer for 10 seconds. This timer marks a shield activation that protects the player from harm. The player is not armed, so to destroy the Bot they must fire off the Trigger opposite the OK once their shield has deactivated and they have visited that location. If they don't, the trigger is not ready and the Bot isn't destroyed, and the player takes damage normally. Open Kismet and note that all the Global Variables for objects in the level are placed already. Likewise, a lot of the basic Kismet we have handled in previous recipes is already set up. You may want to examine the Sub-sequence *SpawnBot* to see how once spawned it is given a weapon and then commences firing at you and chasing you.

How to do it...

1. In the scene, use the menu command **Edit | Find Actors** to search for and then select *Trigger_0*. In Kismet choose **New event using Trigger_0 | Touched**. The properties for this are default.

2. In the scene, select *Trigger_1* and in Kismet choose **New event using Trigger_1 | Used**. Turn off its **Aim to Interact** property.

3. Set the **Named Variable** *Player* as the Instigator for the **Trigger_1 Used** event. Extend from the **Trigger_1 Used** event's **Used** nub the Sub-sequence *CountDown*, the details of which are shown here:

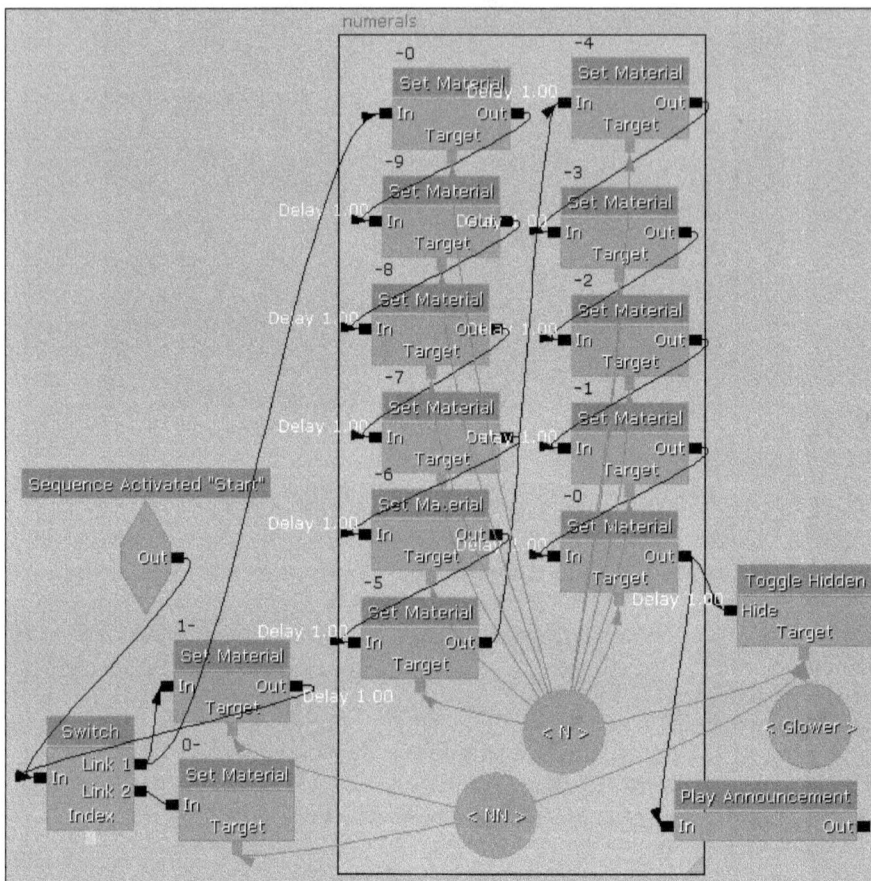

4. In the given screenshot, *NN* handles double digit numbers and *N* handles single digit numbers.

5. Also from the **Trigger_1 Used** extend a wire to the existing **Modify Property** *ON* action, which is set up to enable a PostProcess Volume in the scene. Notice that a wire from the **Player Spawned** event to the **Modify Property** *OFF* action already handles the off state of the same PostProcess Volume.

6. Hold *D* and click to add a **Delay** and hook up its **Start** nub to the **Used** nub of **Trigger_1 Used**. Set its **Duration** to 10.0. Extend its **Finished** nub to a new **Toggle** (hold *T* and click) to the right of it, into the **Turn On** nub. The **Turn Off** nub of this **Toggle** should wire up to the **Used** nub of the **Trigger_1 Used**. Its **Event** nub should extend to the top bar of the **Trigger_1 Used** event. For the **Toggle**, in its properties add the **Obj Comment** *Trigger Trip*. *Trigger Trip*'s **Out** nub should also hook up to the existing sound effect chain **Play Sound** *Shield Off* then **Play Sound** *Thunder*.

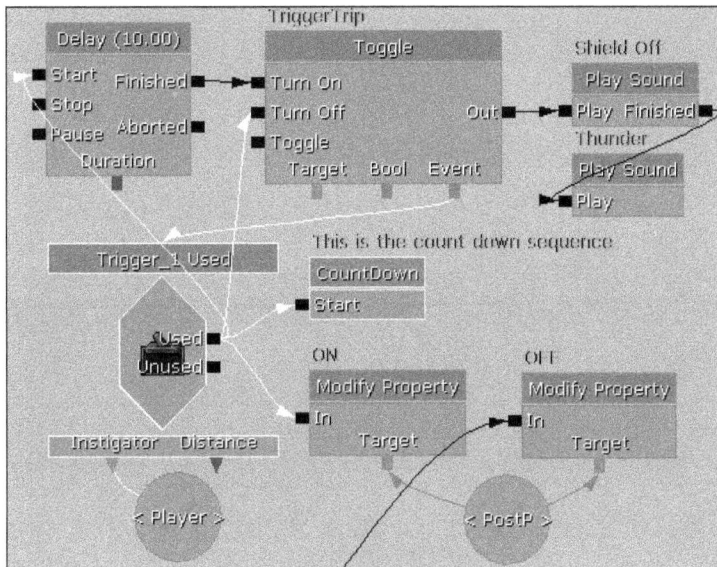

7. Hold *T* and click to add another **Toggle**. Comment this one as *Shields Depleted*. Extend a wire from the **Finished** nub of the 10 second **Delay** we made into the **Turn On** nub of the **Toggle** *Shield Depleted*.

8. Send a wire back from the **Turn Off** nub to the **Used** nub of *Trigger_1 Used*, and also to the **Out** nub of the existing *Player Spawned* event. The **Target** for this *Toggle* will be a *PointLightToggleable_0* in the center of the scene. This light creates a flash when the shields deplete. The **Turn Off** nub should also extend to a **New Event | Remote Event** with the **Event Name** *TurnOff*. This should go green as it is activated by the actions in the existing Sub-sequence *Ending*.

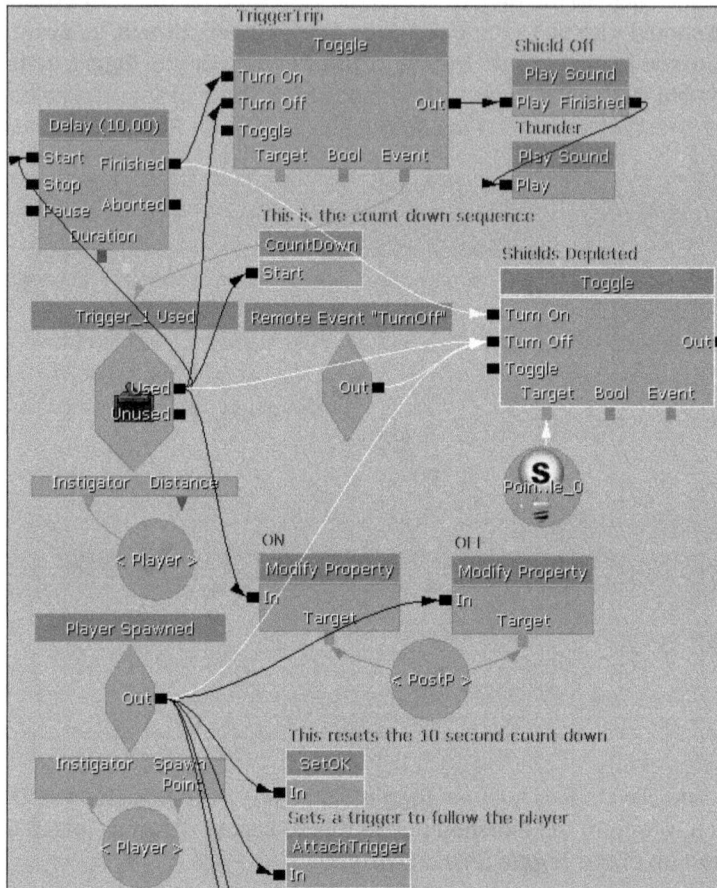

9. The *Player Spawned* event must also feed the Sub-sequences *SetOK*, *AttachTrigger*, and *SpawnBot*. This sets initial conditions for the Bot and triggers that follow the player, and the counter's start point.

10. Hold *G* and click to add a *Gate*. Comment it as *Gate1* and set its property **Seq Act | Gate | Open off**, so it starts with *bOpen=False*. Send a wire from the **In** nub of this to the *Trigger_1 Used* event's **Used** nub that we've been using a lot so far. Send a wire from the **Open** nub to the **Damaged** output nub of the Sub-sequence *DamageValue*. Extend the **Out** nub of *Gate1* to the **In** nub of the Sub-sequence *ModifyHealth*. Drag the Sub-Sequence *Modify Health* to the right of *Gate1*, so it sits nicely.

11. Copy and paste *Gate1* and name it *Gate2*. Add a new **Switch** action and give it two links. Ignore the **Link 1** nub, which should remain empty, and instead from the **Link 2** nub extend a wire to the **In** nub of *Gate2*. Extend the **Out** nub of *Gate2* into the **In** nub of the Sub-sequence *Ending*. Drag *Ending* over by *Gate2*. The **Switch** action's **In** nub should be fed by the **Trigger_1 | Used** event.

12. From the **Trigger_0 Touch** event we added earlier which so far has been left alone, extend the **Touched** nub to the **Close** nub of *Gate1*. Hold *Shift + G* and click to add a new **AND Gate**, then feed the **Touched** nub to the **AND Gate** action's **In** nub, and then from the **Out** nub to the **Open** nub of *Gate2*. The **AND Gate** is just an in-out conduit through which the flow will only pass if all the incoming nodes have already been fired. For this case, we also need the **Out** nub of the **Toggle** *Trigger Trip* to extend to the *In* nub of the **AND Gate**. Lastly, give the **Out** nub of the **AND Gate** another wire out, this time to the *DelayStopIn* nub of the Sub-sequence *ModifyHealth*.

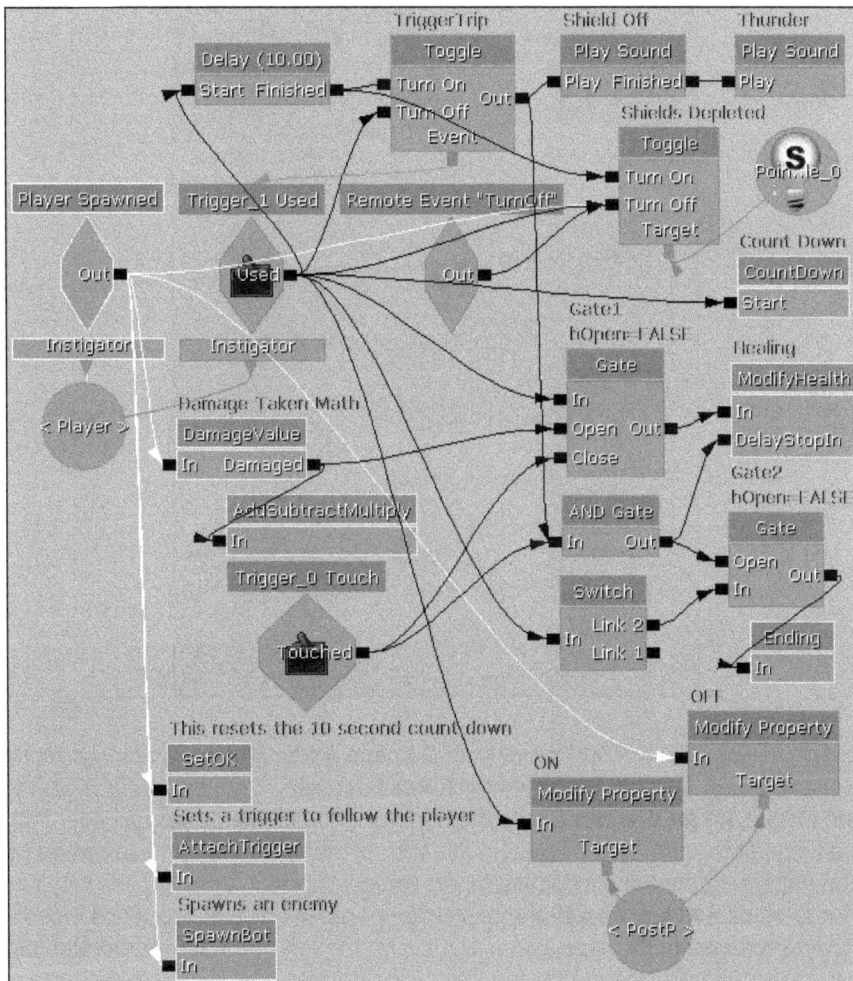

How it works

When the player is spawned an enemy Bot is also spawned. A trigger is attached to the player which is the activator for the shield when used. A timer counts down when the trigger is used, during which time the player is shielded. Be sure to check out the Sub-sequences in the demonstration, particularly the Sub-sequence *ModifyHealth*, which is a test for the amount of damage taken, and a healing result at a certain threshold, until the **Delay** stops this loop after 10 seconds in the main sequence. The **Modify Health** actions *Mod1*, *Mod2*, and *Mod3* do not have a **Damage Amount** property set, instead drawing on **Float Variables** assigned as **Named Variables** that call back and forth to keep the player's health balanced during the shielding period.

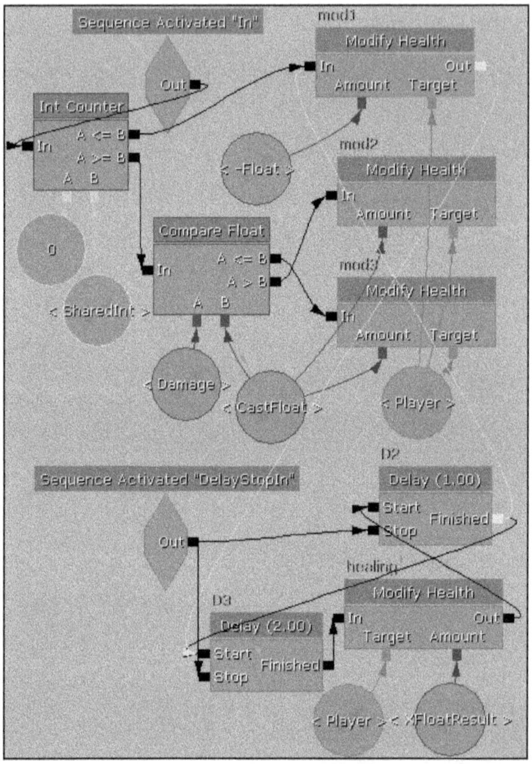

The actual math is done in the Sub-sequences *Damage Taken Math* and *AddSubtractMultiply*. When the player takes damage, the **Damage Taken** float value from the event is sent to an integer and logged. An **Int Counter** tracks the number of times the player has been hit, and logs it as an integer too. These two integers are then blended through an expression (where each action either subtracts the incoming target value, adds to it, or multiplies it by another value). That gives us a **XFloatResult** and this is compared in the Sub-sequence *Modify Health*. In the following screenshot *Damage Taken Math* is on the left and *AddSubtractMultiply* is on the right:

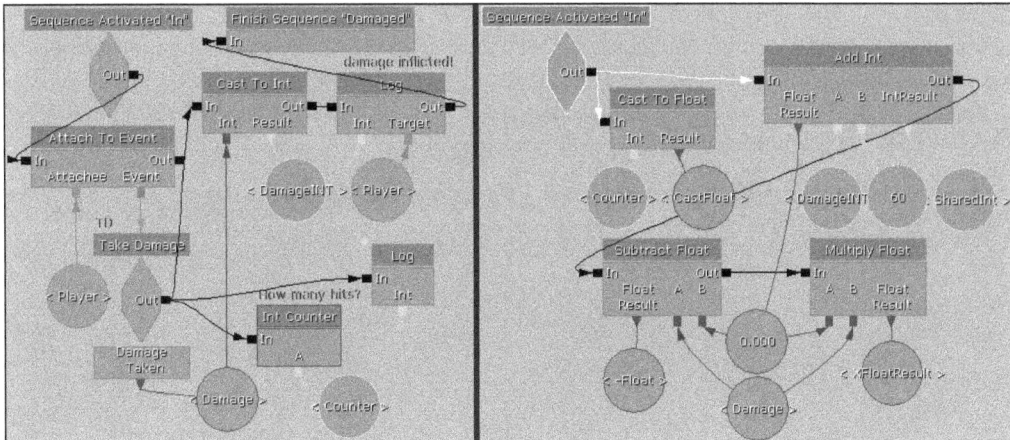

The shield is not completely impervious. If you stand in a rapid stream of bullets it will inevitably deplete, but if you get a moment to rest your health will bounce all the way back up.

You can review the entire sequence in the provided content *Packt_05_Health_DEMO.UDK*.

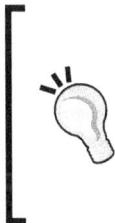

> You will notice in the illustration that all the nodes have had their unused nubs hidden, except for the **Switch**, because of its empty **Link 1**. To hide nubs, or expose hidden nubs, you can right-click on the node and access the item **Hide Unused Connectors** or **Show All Connectors**. If you want to expose a specific hidden nub, try **Expose Variable** and choose from the list which expands from it.

See also

The PostProcess effect and the light shafts that are toggled when we trigger the shield are discussed in detail in *Chapter 8, Then There Was Light!*

Creating a per-session checkpoint series

It's important to understand the difference between a "save game" and a "level checkpoint" right from the start. A save game writes information out to disk, external to UDK. This can be done with an understanding of DLLBind for example, or by using the SAPITU classes provided in UDK. For more information about this, take a look at the official documentation: http://udn.epicgames.com/Three/ConfigSavegameSystem.html.

In this case, the topic is on checkpoints, which enable a player to respawn on death in an updated location, according to navigation progress or other achievements. Our example is useful even though it doesn't save external data or permit closing the game and reloading its last status; it elaborates slightly on the toggling of Triggers by toggling PlayerStart actors, along with setting the appropriate properties so this will work.

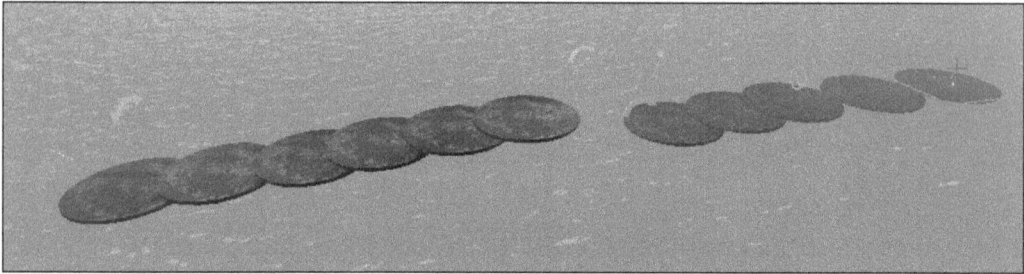

Getting ready

Load up *Pactk_05_CheckPoints_START.UDK*, a very simple scene with a string of platforms and some navigation guides. The platforms are colored. Run from green to red, then from blue to yellow. Even though it is not difficult to get to the end, an obstacle has been marked on the red platform that will kill us, since we want to test respawning. To test respawning it is also possible just to fall off the platforms into the water. The level has been set to the **GameType** *UTGame*.

How to do it...

The Kismet has some provided parts, to make things go a little faster. All the *Object Variables* are there for the Triggers and PlayerStarts in the scene. So we'll select them in the steps using the variables by right-clicking and choosing **Select in Level**.

Toggling the PlayerStarts

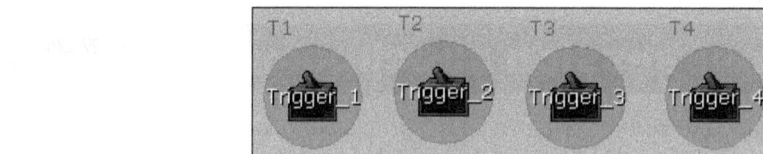

1. In Kismet find the row of *Object Variables* for the **Triggers** and highlight *T1*.

2. Right-click on it and choose **Select Trigger_1 in Level**. Then right-click and choose **New Event using Trigger_1 | Touch**. Repeat this with *T2*, *T3*, and *T4* so you have an event for each trigger.

3. Hold *T* and click to add a new **Toggle**, then copy it and paste till you have five of them. Comment them as *T0*, *T1*, *T2*, and *T3* respectively.

4. Extend a wire from the **Touched** nub of every **Trigger Touch** event to the **Turn Off** nub of the **Toggle** *T0*. Set the **Target** of the toggle as the **Named Variable** *Locations*. *Locations* references an **Object List Variable** we'll set to hold all our PlayerStarts. This means that whenever a trigger is touched all the PlayerStart actors are turned off.

5. Now we will turn on the PlayerStart actors one by one. Add a new **Switch** action. Set its **Link Count** property to 3. Hook up the **Out** nub of the **Toggle** *T0* to the **In** nub of the just added **Switch**.

6. Hook up each of the three links from the **Switch** to the **Turn On** nub of **Toggle** T1, T2, and T3:

   ▫ For the **Target** of the **Toggle** *T1* hooked to **Link 1**, assign the **Named Variable** *PS1*

   ▫ For the **Target** of the **Toggle** *T2* hooked to **Link 2**, assign the **Named Variable** *PS2*

   ▫ For the **Target** of the **Toggle** *T3* hooked to **Link 3**, assign the **Named Variable** *PS3*

   The variables represent PlayerStart actors in the scene.

7. Using a **Switch** in this case works because the order is linear and the Triggers are only fired once each. Alternatively, the toggling could be done instead with **Objectlists**, since integer math can be used to increment the Index it has.

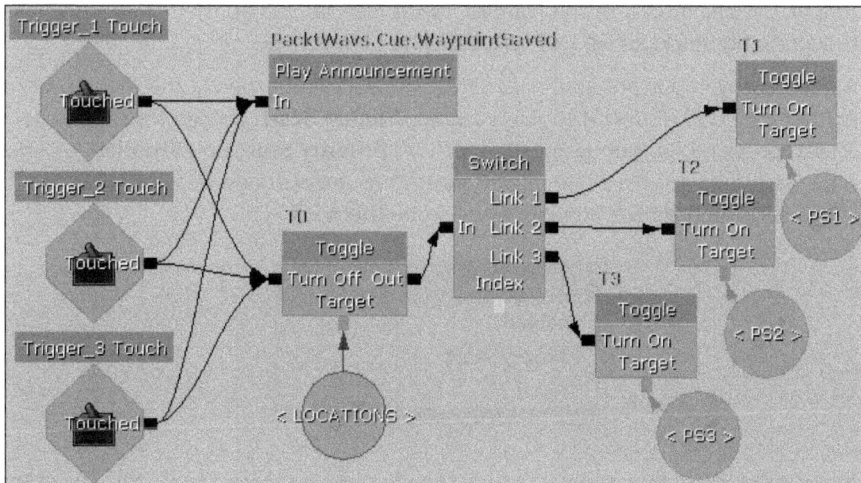

8. All these **Trigger Touch** events also feed into an action which gives us an audio cue: **New Action | Voice/Announcements | Play Announcement**. To fill the property **Announcement Sound**, open the Content Browser (*Ctrl + Shift +F*) and search for Waypoint. Highlight *PacktWavs.Cue.WaypointSaved* then assign it in Kismet using the assign icon [⧉].

9. Open the Sub-sequence *Ending*. The event **Trigger_4 Touch** needs to fire the *Ending* sequence. In the scene select the actor **Trigger_4 Touch** and in *Ending* right-click and choose **New Event Using Trigger_04 | Touch**. Hook this up as follows:

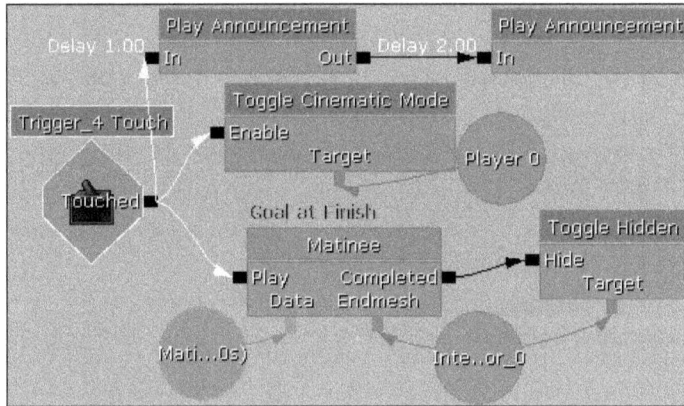

Provisioning the Object List

1. So far we have provisioned the **Toggle** actions, but the **Object List** *Locations* remains empty. Let's fill it up with the **Named Variables** that call on the PlayerStart actors. The reason to do this is so we can turn them all off at once.

2. A particularly important step is to set the default properties of the PlayerStart actors so that only *PS0* (PlayerStart_0) is set as **Primary Start**. Select PlayerStart 1, 2, and 3, and press *F4*. In their properties turn off **Primary Start** and **Enabled**, as shown here. They'll be enabled one by one when they are reached by the player and the triggered switch we set previously will wake them up.

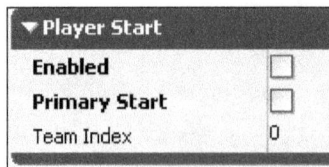

3. In the main Kismet sequence, where the **Object Variables** are for the PlayerStarts, hold *Ctrl + S* and click to add a **Level Loaded** event.

4. Hold *T* and click to add a **Toggle**, and hook its **Turn On** nub to the **Level Loaded** event's **Loaded and Visible** nubs. Set the **Named Variable** *PSO* as its **Target**.

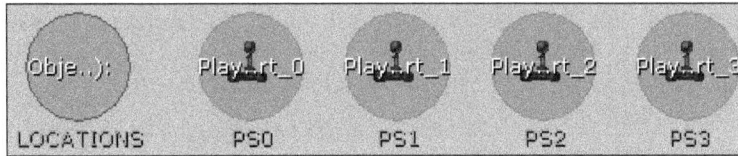

5. From the **Out** nub of the **Toggle** extend a chain of five **New Action | Object List | Modify ObjectList** actions. The **Out** nub of each hooks up to the next action's **Add to List** nub. They all share the same **Object ListVar**, which is the **Named Variable** *LOCATIONS*. In order, the **Object Ref** nubs to assign are the **Named Variables** *PSO*, then *PS1*, then *PS2*, then *PS3*, as shown here:

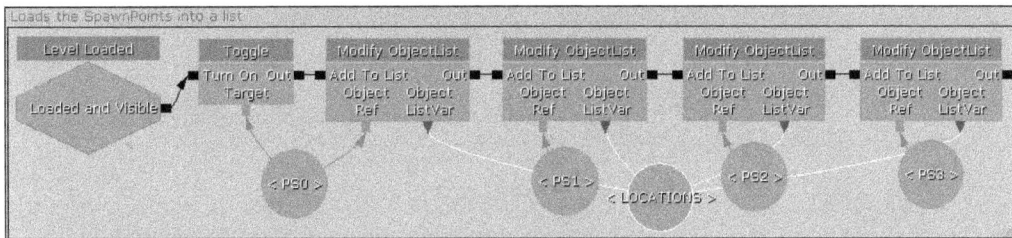

Setting the trap

1. Open the Sub-sequence *Start*. In the level there is a bouncy red trap for testing. The trap itself is a hovering warning object (*InterpActor_2*) which bounces up and down, and a **DynamicTriggerVolume** is attached to it that hurts the player if touched. This is marked with a single arrow in the next screenshot. The trap animation already exists in a **Matinee** called *Hovering Sign*, which is set to **Looping**. Also, the **Play Rate** is controlled by a **Random Float Variable** with a period of 0.66s to 2.33s for some variety, to prevent it being too predictable when dashing under it.

2. Extend out from the **Level Loaded** event in the Sub-sequence *Start* to a new **Attach to Actor** action. For this the **Target** will be the same as the **Object Variable** assigned to the **Hovering** track of the **Matinee**, which is *InterpActor_2*.

3. Right-click on the *Object Variable* Interpactor_2 assigned to *Hovering* and choose **Select in Level**. In the scene, click on the **Go To Actor** button in the tools panel or press *Home*. Select the InterpActor overlapping this, which is a copy of the already animated one. The copy faces backwards, because the source mesh is one sided. The *InterpActor_1* location is shown in the next screenshot using a double arrow, as there are two there:

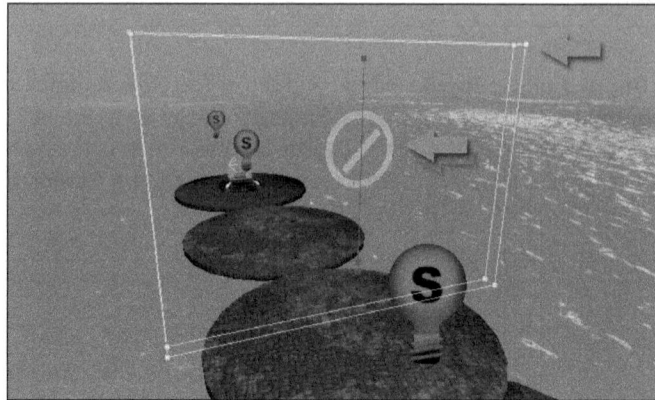

4. Back in Kismet, right-click on the **Attachment** nub of the *Attach to Actor* action and choose **Create New Object Variable using InterpActor_1**, then PIE to check that both objects are bouncing up and down.

> An alternative way to assign the variable is to copy the *Object Variable* InterpActor_2 then paste it, then in the pasted one, edit the **Obj Value** property to be *InterpActor_1*, right at the end of the string.

5. Presently you'd not be able to get underneath the bouncing object because it isn't the object that kills us, it is the **DynamicTriggerVolume** sitting there. We need this to follow the *Matinee* too. In the scene, select *DynamicTriggerVolume_0* which is indicated in the previous screenshot with a single arrow, and add it as the **Attachment** to a new *Attach to Actor* action. As before, connect the *Player Spawned* event's **Out** nub to the **In** nub of the *Attach to Actor*, and set the **Target** as the *Object Variable* InterpActor_2.

6. With the *DynamicTriggerVolume_0* still selected, right-click in Kismet and choose **New Event using DynamicTriggerVolume | Touch**. Set the **Max Trigger Count** for this to 0 and from its **Touched** nub extend a wire to a new *Modify Health* action.

7. In the **Modify Health** action's properties, set the **Damage Type** as *DmgType_Crushed* from the list. Set the **Amount** as 500, enough to kill anybody outright. Hold *P* and click and set the added **Player Variable** to *Player 0*, then hook it up to the **Target** of the **Modify Health** action.

8. Extending out of this action, add a **New Action | Voice/Announcements | Play Announcement**. From the Content Browser, set *PacktWavs.Cue.TryAgain* in the property **Announcement Sound** for this audio asset. Since the player dies while this sound plays it will be overlapping other sound effects, so right-click on the **Play Announcement** action's **In** nub, choose **Set Activate Delay**, and enter 1.

9. Hold *T* and click to add a new **Toggle**. Hook its **Turn Off** nub to the **Touched** nub of the **DynamicTriggerVolume_0 Touch** event. Add the **Named Variable** *Locations* as its **Target**. Finally, wire its **Out** nub to the **Turn On** nub of another **Toggle** action, and for this set the **Target** as the **Named Variable** *PS1*, as in the previous screenshot.

10. That should wrap up the required sequences to trigger checkpoints. Of course, you can just walk into the water each time you pass a checkpoint to see if the check point re-spawns you correctly. The provided scene *Packt_05_CheckPoints_DEMO.UDK* shows the final result.

See also

For further information about Kismet, bookmark and read closely the **UDN Kismet Reference**: http://udn.epicgames.com/Three/KismetReference.html.

6

Under The Hood
Configuration and Handy Tweaks for UDK

This chapter contains lessons in adjusting configuration, scripts, and even supplying additional actors and Kismet actions. Everything here is about altering the editor or gameplay settings to provision a customized playing experience:

- ▶ Groundwork for adjusting configuration defaults
- ▶ Enabling the remote control for game inspection
- ▶ Changing the Play in Editor view resolution
- ▶ Removing the loading hints and similar articles
- ▶ Editing DefaultEngineUDK to allow 4096x4096 texture compression
- ▶ Setting the preview player size reference object
- ▶ Binding a keyboard shortcut to a player action
- ▶ Adjusting player speed
- ▶ Creating your own Kismet node for Speed
- ▶ Changing the default player sounds
- ▶ Replacing the HUD
- ▶ DrawText and GameType concerns
- ▶ Handling level content streaming
- ▶ Spawning objects from a hit impact

Groundwork for adjusting configuration defaults

In this chapter we'll build up from simply changing some trivial configuration settings to orchestrating unique gaming experiences. To start out, we need to make clear how UDK configures content under the hood by introducing the layout and formatting for this kind of file. The experience in this recipe can be likened to savoring morsels of cake samples in a shop before committing to a purchase; while you're not actually changing major settings yet, the aim is to make some tasty observations so later the changes you make will come from informed decisions.

Getting ready

In your UDK installation, you have a folder called `C:\UDK\~\UDKGame\Config` and it is worthwhile to browse the files here and get to know them. Treat them like the faces of colleagues in a new company. It may take a while, but you'll eventually know all their names! You may want to make an alternative install of UDK before starting this chapter, to protect any content you've been working on. In these examples we're going to assume you are using ConTEXT, or a notepad alternative that highlights UnrealScript syntax, like those listed at `http://wiki.beyondunreal.com/Legacy:Text_Editor`. For more information about ConTEXT refer to *Chapter 3, It Lives!* We discussed its installation in the recipe *Configuring your character to use your AnimTree*. The advantage with ConTEXT is that you have a history of recently opened files, and several concurrently open files can be arranged in tabs; also, you can view specific lines in the file in response to line error warnings from the UDK log, should they arise.

> In ConTEXT, to display line numbers go to the **Options | Environment Options** menu then click on the **Editor** tab in the options dialog, tick on **Line Numbers** and press **Apply**.

How to do it...

1. Open the file `C:\UDK\~\UDKGame\Config\DefaultCharInfo.INI` using ConTEXT. Alongside it, open `C:\UDK\~\UDKGame\Config\UDKCharInfo.INI`, which is a rather similar file.

2. Values we set from an existing class are presented after a reference to the class in square brackets which surround the folder and class name, such as `[UTGame.UTCharInfo]`.

3. Commented out lines or notes are distinguished using ; and the entire line isn't parsed. This differs from the `//` used to comment out lines in UnrealScript.

4. In some configuration files you will see `BasedOn=...` followed by the path to another configuration file. This helps you track where the info is coming from.

5. Values for variables are set in the configuration file as in the example: `LOD1DisplayFactor=0.4`.

6. In ConTEXT, click on **File | Open...** and scroll down the list of files. Notice that it previews the contents of the highlighted .INI files before you open them.

7. Choose *DefaultWeapon.INI* and edit line 3 (strictly speaking line 1 is empty). Press *Ctrl + G* (or **View | Go to Line**) and enter the line number 3. This line specifies `CrosshairColor` for the weapon. If you change the value *A=255* to *A=0* you will effectively have hidden the weapon target.

8. Supposing you wanted to do so, you'd just have to save this file then reload UDK. No compiling is needed for adjusting configuration files, unlike classes, unless the configuration is defining custom scripts to be used in some way.

9. Let's assume for now that you don't want to hide the weapon cursor, so close the file without saving by pressing *Ctrl + W* and choose **No** for the file save option.

10. Open the file *UDKEditor.INI* and go to line 12: `Bindings=(Key="S",SeqObjC lassName="Engine.SeqAct_PlaySound")` then look at line 28: `Binding s=(Key="S",bControl=true,SeqObjClassName="Engine.SeqEvent_ LevelLoaded")`.

11. What's important here is the added `bControl=true` for the S key. S will create a **Play Sound** node in Kismet. *Ctrl + S* will create a **Level Loaded** event.

12. We really don't need to change anything but you can, for instance, change *Ctrl + S* to *Ctrl + L* in line 28, for adding a new **Level Loaded** event node in Kismet: `Bindi ngs=(Key="L",bControl=true,SeqObjClassName="Engine.SeqEvent_ LevelLoaded")`.

13. Make sure that UDK is closed before you save the change or the file will not be effected at all. Reloading UDK after saving the change will see it take effect. Unless you have very long hands you will probably want to test this using the right *Ctrl* button on the right-hand side of the keyboard so your fingers can hold *L* and *Ctrl* and *left mouse click* all at once. You should get the **Level Loaded** event in Kismet from this key combination now.

14. On that note, when you are specifying hotkeys for your game, bear in mind the idea of user friendly interface as you decide what keys to use. Often used keys should be easy to remember, fast to reach, and possibly semantically clustered together.

How it works...

What we looked at in this recipe were some formatting features that occur in every configuration file. In particular it is important to know that edits should be made while UDK is closed or they get scrubbed back out immediately. Also you will have noticed that the values we change reference UnrealScript classes from the `C:\UDK\~\Development\Src\` folder, and reading through their layout can help you learn how the default content in UDK is made to work during gameplay.

There's more...

Consider a version control software for editing UDK content

There is a free version control system called **Bazaar** (`http://bazaar.canonical.com`) that integrates with Windows folders. What version control software does is keep track of changes you have made to files, protecting them through a history based backup that lets you review and revert changes to a previous state if needed. You can **init** a folder, then browse it, add content and **commit** changes to changed files with comments that help you track what's going on. Where needed you can review the change history and **revert** files to any previously committed state. Alternatives to **Bazaar** are the commercial tool **Alienbrain Essentials for Artists**, or the free repository **TortoiseSVN**. The utility of version control in the case of UDK development is to prevent unrecoverable problems when doing a script compile when changes haven't been tracked and therefore can't be restored without re-installing from scratch, and to allow assets to be overwritten with a history.

Enabling the remote control for game inspection

This is a method for turning on an extra feature of UDK called the **Remote Control** that can be used to manipulate render nodes, inspect Actors, and evaluate performance.

How to do it...

1. In Windows, go to the **Start** menu or your desktop and find the shortcut for the UDK Editor and right-click on it to expose its properties.
2. In the **Target** field edit it to read: `C:\UDK\~\Binaries\UDKLift.exe editor -wxwindows -remotecontrol -log`.
3. The main point of this entry is so that we can launch a tool called **RemoteControl**. The usefulness of running the `-log` window increases over time. It is used for tracking what is happening while you run the editor and PIE. When trouble shooting problems in Kismet or with missing assets for example, it is a good first port of call for seeing where and when errors occur.

4. In the following screenshot, the log shows the creation of a **Trigger Touch** event in the main Kismet sequence based on the actor *Trigger_0* in the scene:

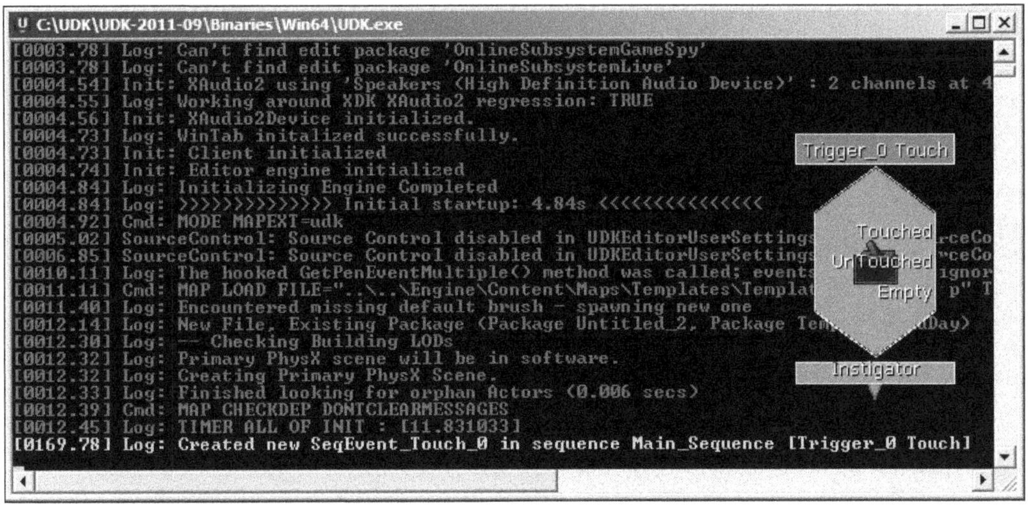

5. Having edited the UDK launch properties to allow **RemoteControl** to launch, now load the *Midday Lighting* map template and PIE (*F8*). If you press *Tab* and type *remotecontrol* you should get a pop-up window like this:

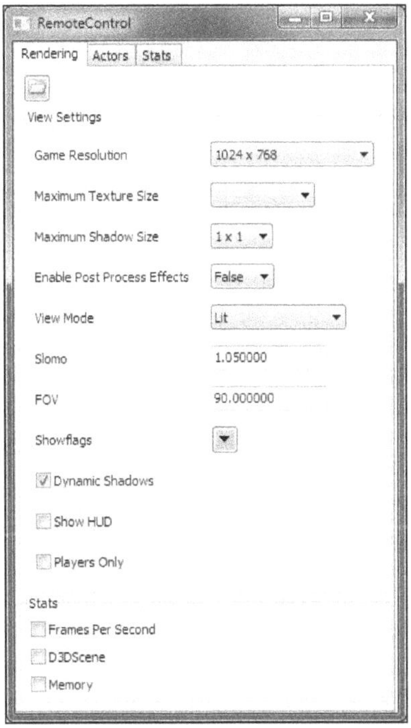

6. If you hit the **Actors** tab you get access to properties of certain actors, and you can change properties live while playing. For example, expand **Actors | DominantDirectionalLight** and double-click on *DominantDirectionalLight_0*. Then in the light's property **Movement | Rotation | Yaw** or **Pitch**, try out different angle values. However, the changed values will revert back to the editor state after PIE is closed.

7. See also: `http://udn.epicgames.com/Three/RemoteControl.html`.

8. An additional note: if you happen to minimize the **RemoteControl** window in some cases it may stay like that until you press *Alt + Space*. And to swap between the game and the **Remote Control** window press *Alt + Tab*.

9. Pressing **Show Flags** lets you display various elements of the scene such as Collision, Bones, and Bounds.

10. Go to the **Stats** tab and tick on **Memory** in the listing, then expand it and tick on the item within it called **Lightmap Memory**. This shows the cost of displaying lighting backed into lightmaps.

11. Further down in the **Stats** tab list, tick on the item **D3D9RHI** and look at the **DrawPrimitive** calls. In the game, look straight up at the empty sky and note the value. Now look at the box on the ground. Notice the value increases. This is because the view has to draw the added objects (ground and box). In a large scene, especially on iOS, there is a functional limit to the number of drawcalls.

How it works...

The **RemoteControl** tool is external to the game window and is created using **wxWindows**. It is meant for use during PIE, for evaluation of performance. The **Actors** tab shows us a tree list of what is in the level, along with filters. You can access **Actor Properties** for an actor under the crosshairs using the icon [▮] or access them from a list.

What you see in this screenshot is the result of turning the memory statistics on within a scene and the frame rate indicator (FPS = frames per second) through the **Rendering** tab in the **Stats** section, as well as the display of bones used in the scene. In **Remote Control**, you can set the **Game Resolution** (or game window size) under **Rendering | View Settings**. In the next recipe, we'll look at how to do this in UDK's configuration.

Changing the Play in Editor view resolution

This is a very short method for setting the view size for PIE sessions.

How to do it...

1. In `C:\UDK\~\UDKGame\Config\DefaultEngineUDK.INI` press *Ctrl + F* and search for `[SystemSettings]`. This should expose the lines:

   ```
   [SystemSettings]
   ; NOTE THAT ANY ITEMS IN THIS SECTION AFFECT ALL PLATFORMS!
   bEnableForegroundShadowsOnWorld=False
   bEnableForegroundSelfShadowing=False
   ResX=1024
   ResY=768
   ```

2. Change the `ResX` and `ResY` values to suit yourself, using screen resolutions that make sense, such as 1920x1080.

3. This will update *UDKEngine.INI* in the same folder so you will see the change reflected in these lines:

   ```
   PlayInEditorWidth=1920
   PlayInEditorHeight=1080
   ```

4. Load a level and PIE to see the difference. Note that if you update *UDKEngine.INI* directly it will just revert to whatever is set in *DefaultEngineUDK.INI*. There is a lot of redundancy built into UDK's configuration that takes some time and practice to get used to.

Removing the loading hints and similar articles

Quickly getting rid of all the peripheral text and imagery that wraps around a given level, especially in console mode, is not easy. A few options exist for removing the more distracting elements such as splash screens and menus. You may want to do this if you wish to show your work without any artwork made by someone else getting in the way of your own. One method is called **destructive editing**, where your delete or blank out assets at the source, and this isn't as safe as it is quick. Instead you can provide your own menus, splash, and UI by extending on the classes that call up the default ones.

How to do it...

Removing the console mode videos during map loading

1. Open `C:\UDK\~\UDKGame\Config\DefaultEngine.INI`.

2. Press *Ctrl + F* and search for *[FullScreenMovie]*, which should expose the startup and loadmap references.

3. Comment out the entries as follows:

   ```
   [FullScreenMovie]
   //+StartupMovies=UDKFrontEnd.UDK_loading
   //+LoadMapMovies=UDKFrontEnd.UDK_loading
   ```

4. Load a level and play in console mode [⬛]. You won't get the movies that precede gameplay. If you take out all the pre-loading content there may occur the problem of getting a look at the level too early and "pre-caching" showing up.

5. To learn how to instead swap out the .BIK files that constitute the loading movies between levels you can follow the video by **Michael J Collins**:
   `http://www.youtube.com/watch?v=SX1VQK1w4NU`.

Removing the level loading hints

1. To totally prevent .BIK movies during development, you can open `C:\UDK\~\Engine\Config\BaseEngine.INI` and search for *NoMovies*, then adjust the `FALSE` in the exposed lines:

   ```
   [FullScreenMovie]
   bForceNoMovies=FALSE to TRUE.
   ```

2. Open `C:\UDK~\Development\Src\UTGame\UTGameViewportClient.UC`.

3. Press *Ctrl + F* to search for *bAllowHints = true;*.

4. Change `true` to `false`.

Removing the map name

1. To remove the map name displayed during map loading, a sneaky method is to insert a transparent font into line 146 of: `C:\UDK~\Development\Src\UTGame\UTGameViewportClient.UC`.

   ```
   // Game Type name
   //class'Engine'.static.AddOverlay(
     LoadingScreenGameTypeNameFont, Desc,
       0.1822, 0.435, 1.0, 1.0, false);

   // becomes
   class'Engine'.static.AddOverlay(
     LoadingScreenGameTypeNameFont, Desc, 0.1822, 0.435, 1.0, 0,
   false);
   // and Map name
   // class'Engine'.static.AddOverlay(
   ```

```
LoadingScreenMapNameFont, MapName,
  0.1822, 0.46, 2.0, 2.0, false);
```

```
// becomes
class'Engine'.static.AddOverlay(
  LoadingScreenMapNameFont, MapName, 0.1822, 0.46, 2.0, 0, false);
```

What's happening here is that the last digit of four in an entry 1,1,1,1 is the Alpha value, controlling transparency, so 1,1,1,0 will be invisible. The first three numbers are RGB values, but they can be anything if the Alpha is 0.

Removing the default exit menu

1. Open `C:\UDK\~\UDKGame\Config\DefaultInput.INI` and press *Ctrl* + *F* to search for *Escape*. The first time will expose a removed key binding, so search from the cursor again to find in line 205: `.Bindings=(Name="Escape",Command="G BA_ShowMenu"` and comment it out with `;` then add this line underneath instead: `.Bindings=(Name="Escape",Command="quit"` if UDK should close directly.

2. If you want to provide a custom menu type: `.Bindings=(Name="Escape",Command="open Menu"`, where players pressing *Esc* will be sent to *Menu.UDK* (a scene of your own design) instead of the default menu. This won't do anything if you don't provision a *Menu.UDK* map first and cook it with your game levels. The map *Menu.UDK* would typically include some kind of clickable exit, resume, and reload buttons.

3. If you want *Esc* to automatically restart the level you're playing, put in `"open YOURMAPNAME"` but bear in mind the only way to exit then will be *Alt* + *F4*.

4. Possibly a strong way to approach the *Escape* option is to have a *Pause* command that permits a choice about leaving the game through a floating button: *Resume* or *Exit*. In addition you might have a similar floating button when the player dies: *Replay* or *Exit*, rather than the default **Fire to Respawn**.

See Also

For making inroads towards providing menus with clickable buttons, see *Chapter 10*, *The Way of The Flash UI*.

Editing DefaultEngineUDK to allow 4096x4096 texture compression

This is a method for enabling UDK to use textures larger than its default limit. Conventional wisdom says that game textures should be highly optimized, but large resolution artwork is always enticing for many designers, and computers are getting better all the time. Performance issues aside, it's a good goal to push the graphic envelope and larger textures allow detail to hold up better on close inspection.

Getting ready

We've provided one really large texture that is 4096x4096 that you may find convenient, intended for use as a Skydome. If you are going to use a large texture it would most likely be on a very important model like a key character always close to the camera or else of a very large model which is always visible, such as a Skydome, or Skybox. A simple tutorial for making a Skybox is at `http://www.worldofleveldesign.com/categories/UDK/UDK-how-add-skybox.php` but this recipe assumes the use of a provided one.

How to do it...

1. With UDK closed, open `C:\UDK\~\UDKGame\Config\DefaultEngineUDK.INI`.
2. Press *Ctrl + F* in ConTEXT and search for *Skybox*. You should be directed to line 127: `TEXTUREGROUP_Skybox=(MinLODSize=512,MaxLODSize=2048,LODBias=0,MinMagFilter=aniso,MipFilter=point)`.
3. Change the value for `MaxLODSize=2048` to `4096`. To really force it, you can also set the `MinLODSize=4096` too. Doing this for a Skybox is okay, since there's normally only one used in a map, but you'd risk slowing the game down to do this with regular textures. Note, the `TEXTUREGROUP_Skybox` will allow a texture for a Skybox to be large, but not other things like character textures. For that, you can edit the relevant values in the other `TEXTUREGROUP` lines. Further down, in the **SystemSettingsMobile** section, the texture sizes are much smaller, which is due to the relatively limited processing power of mobile devices.
4. Now save, and next we'll verify this in fact worked by adding a large sky to a scene in UDK.
5. Look in the Content Browser and search the *Packt* folder for *Packt_SkyDome*, which is a typical mesh for a sky. You can see there is a completed version, and a copy called *Packt_SkyDomeStart* which has no material.
6. Go to the *Packt* texture group. You will see there is already a provisioned 4096x4096 texture for *Packt_SkyDome*, but let's import a fresh one.

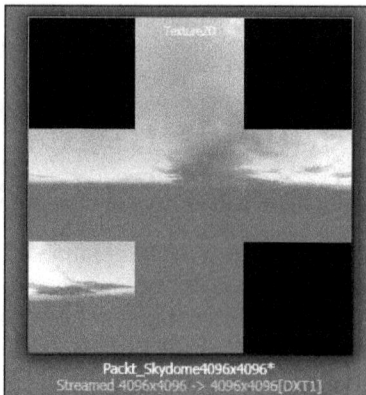

7. Right-click in the Content Browser panel and choose **Import**, and browse to find *Packt_SkydomeStart.PNG* which is just a copy of the already existing texture. The reason to import it, is to verify you understand the compression setting.

8. In the options you will see a panel that lets you specify the name info, which you should enter as *Packt.Texture.SkyDomeTest* or something unique. Further down you will see the compression settings. Choose **LODGroup** and from the expanding list choose *TEXTUREGROUP_Skybox*, as shown in the next screenshot, since this is what we have set to have 4096x4096 compression enabled in the configuration:

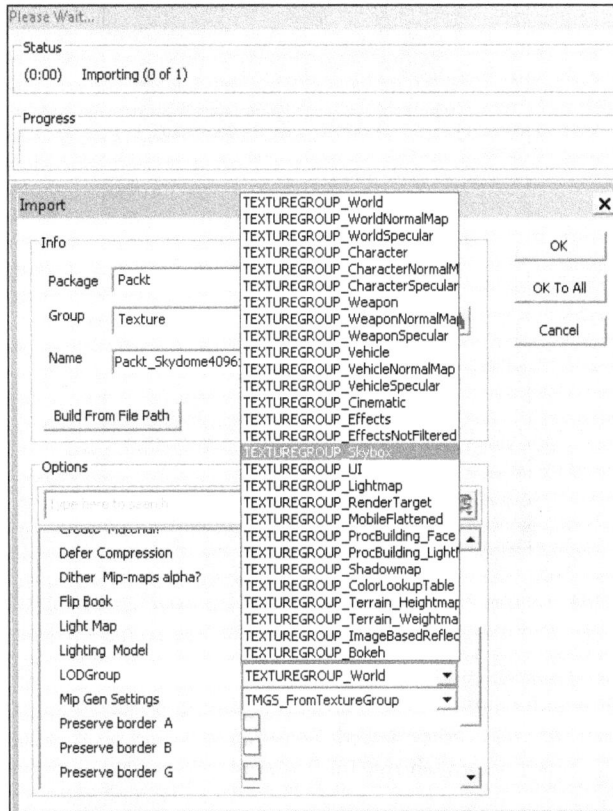

9. The file may take some time to process, given its size. Once it is complete you can create a new Material *Packt.Material.SkyDomeTest_mat*. Open it and in the Material Editor hold *T* and click to add the highlighted *SkyDomeTest* texture to the Emissive channel. Skies are self lighting, so in the **PreviewMaterial** node's properties, set the **Lighting Model** to *MLM_Unlit*.

10. The mesh *Packt_SkyDomeStart* is already UV mapped to match the texture, and if you double-click on it you can assign the new Material *Packt.Material.SkyDomeTest_mat* in the **LODGroupInfo** by expanding until you access the empty **Material** channel. Select the Material in the Content Browser then use the assign icon [🔄] to assign it.

11. Then you can save the package and place the mesh in the level. Be sure to access its properties (*F4*) and under the **Lighting** turn off **Cast Shadow** and set the **Lighting Channels** tick on **Skybox** and uncheck **Static**, as shown in the next screenshot:

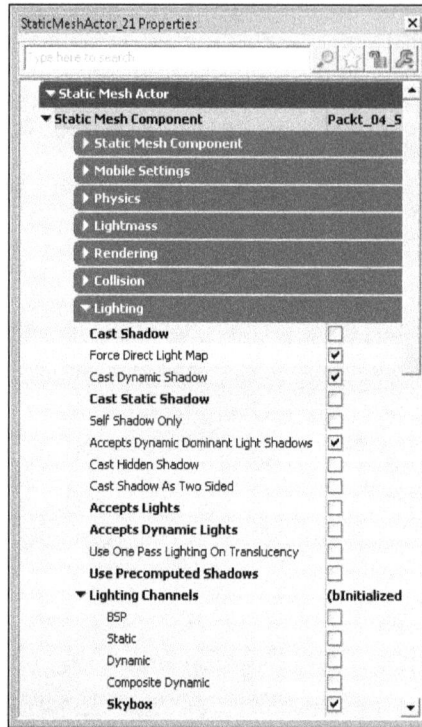

12. You could scale the mesh in the scene to suit, and perhaps drop it down below Z=0 a little. You could also use an **Exponential Height Fog** to hide the horizon.

13. Since there is a specific sun shown in the sky image, you will need to place a Dominant Directional light in the scene and rotate it so its arrow (representing its direction) approximates the direction the sunlight would be coming from. It would be appropriate to tint the light warmly for a sunset.

Setting the preview player size reference object

In UDK versions greater than April 2011, pressing the key \ in the editor Perspective view will show a mesh that represents the player height. By default this is just a cube. The mesh to display can be set in the configuration file *UDKEditorUserSettings.INI* and we'll look at how to adjust this. This is to help designers maintain proper level metrics. You'll be able to gauge how tall and wide to make doors so there's sufficient space for the player to move through without getting stuck.

Getting ready

Back up `C:\UDK\~\UDKGame\Config\UDKEditorUserSettings.INI` then open it in ConTEXT with UDK closed.

How to do it...

1. Press _Ctrl + F_ and search for _[EditorPreviewMesh]_. Under it, we will change the entry `PreviewMeshNames=" EditorMeshes.TexPropCube "`. Note the we need to replace this with a StaticMesh, and a good place to put it to ensure loading would be the _Engine\Content_ package _EditorMeshes_.

2. First, open UDK and in the Content Browser search using the type field for _TexPropCube_.

3. When this appears, right-click on the asset and choose **Find Package**. The packages list will show us _Engine\Content\EditorMeshes_ and in here right-click and choose **Import**.

4. You'll be prompted to browse in Windows, so from the provided content folder, find _SkinTail.ASE_ which is a character model and import this into EditorMeshes. There's no need to set a group name for this. Importing this file as a StaticMesh enables it to be used as a preview model. By contrast, the SkeletalMesh _Packt.Mesh.Packt_ SkinTail_ won't work for what we are trying to do. If you set up a SkeletalMesh for the preview model the log will return **cannot find staticmesh Yourmodelname** whenever you press \ in the editor.

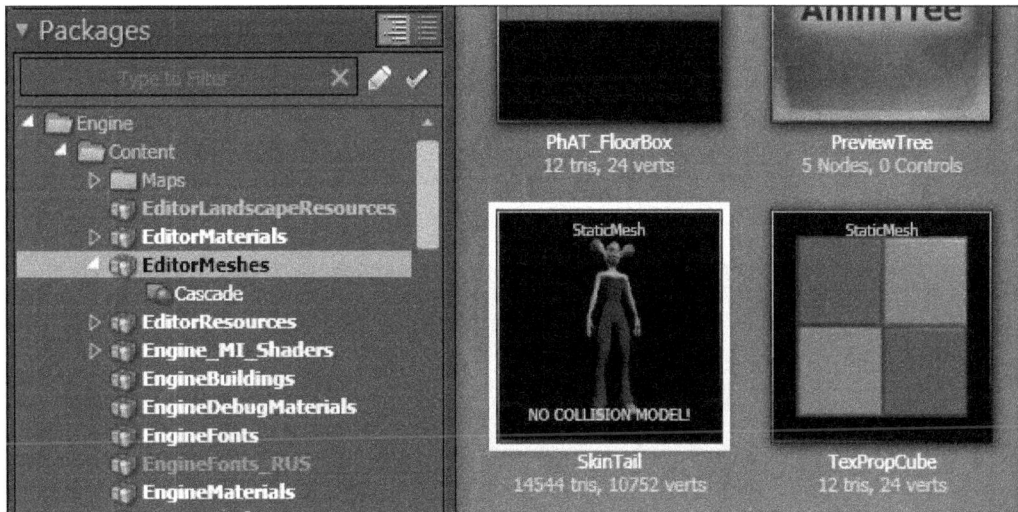

5. It is optional, but you can double click the imported StaticMesh and assign a Material to it after expanding the **LOD_Info** property to show the **Material** channel. For the *SkinTail* content, choose *Packt.Material.Packt_CharMat*.

6. Then save the *EditorMeshes* package including *SkinTail* and quit UDK.

7. Use ConTEXT to edit the file *UDKEditorUserSettings.INI* so that the line we were looking at in *Step 1* is changed to:

   ```
   PreviewMeshNames=" EditorMeshes.SkinTail "
   ```

   Eventually you'll opt to use your own StaticMesh.

8. Save, close, and restart UDK. Open a map, and press \ in the editor to see if *SkinTail* will display. If it doesn't, run UDK using the `-log` option and check for error warnings when \ is pressed.

9. Note that `PreviewMeshNames=" EditorMeshes.TexPropCube "` can also be adjusted in these configuration files: `C:\UDK\~\Engine\Config\BaseEditorUserSettings.INI` or `C:\UDK\~\UDKGame\Config\DefaultEditorUserSettings.INI`.

Binding a keyboard shortcut to a player action

It is relatively easy to reassign an existing action to a different keystroke in the files *UDKInput.INI* or *DefaultInput.INI*. It is somewhat harder to create a unique action. In this recipe we will be making the *O* key toggle a burst of light which lasts as long as you hold the key, then fades back out. I've chosen the letter O just because this key isn't defined by default in the **UDK** configuration. What this could be used for is triggering a flash light or lantern carried by the player, or illuminating the scene when casting spells.

Getting ready

The scene we'll use has a dark ambiance, *Packt_06_KeyChange_Start.UDK*.

The next screenshot is the result (when we've reached our goal) of flashing a bright light in the room:

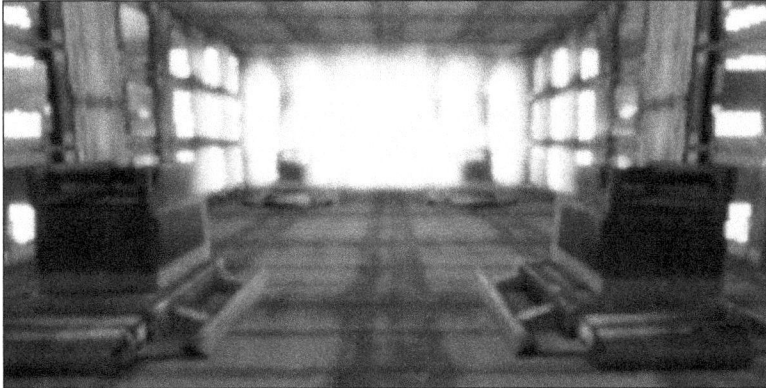

How to do it...

The configuration part

1. Open the scene if you like and look around, but eventually you should close it, and close UDK, as we need to set configuration with UDK closed.

2. Open ConTEXT and choose **File | Open** and browse for
   `C:\UDK\~\UDKGame\Config\DefaultInput.INI`.

3. Scroll down to the lines which start with:

   ```
   ;-----------------------------------------------------------------
   ; BINDINGS USED TO ORGANIZE ALL GAME BINDABLE ACTIONS IN ONE PLACE
   FOR SYSTEMS SUCH AS UI
   ; GBA - GAME BINDABLE ACTION
   ; "_Gamepad" - IS USED WHEN A CONTROLLER IS USING AN ALTERED
   MAPPING FOR AN ACTION
   ;-----------------------------------------------------------------
   ```

4. Enter the following line at the top of the list:

   ```
   .Bindings=(Name="O",Command=causeevent "Burst")
   ```

5. This will give us the ability to fire off a **_Console Event_** in Kismet with the **Event Name** _Burst_ and lets us add an extra layer of functionality. Extend the line:

   ```
   Bindings=(Name="O",Command=
       "causeevent Burst | OnRelease causeevent Belay")
   ```

6. Now we can use the release of the O key to fire off a secondary action from another **_Console Event_** in Kismet using the **Event Name** _Belay_.

7. We have to include the segment `causeevent` because otherwise *Burst* and *Belay* would need to be written up as functions in a class somewhere. Since we will only fire off a Kismet event, there's no need to go that far. The downside of using Kismet is that every scene where you want to press *O* to get *Burst* needs the console command and corresponding actions defined in Kismet, whereas a class would work in every scene. In a class, you would need to define a function "Burst" by declaring "exec function Burst()" and coding what you want to occur.

8. Just to show a little further refinement in this process, let's make *Shift + O* our desired key. Edit the line so the end has `Control=False,Shift=True,Alt=False`.

    ```
    Bindings=(Name="O",Command=
       "causeevent Burst | OnRelease causeevent Belay",
          Control=False,Shift=True,Alt=False)
    ```

9. Save the *UDKInput.INI* file that we've been editing. Now open up UDK and load *Packt_06_KeyChange_Start.UDK* and jump into Kismet [**K**]. You may notice that there is some functionality already there for a triggered door and lift. Those don't matter for what we're doing.

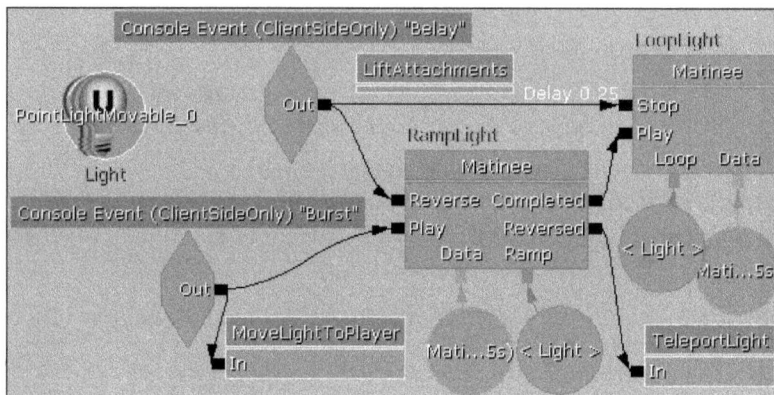

The Kismet part—making the light ramp

1. Look at the **Object Variable** *Light* for the scene's PointLightMovable actor in the middle of the main room. It is shown highlighted in the above screenshot, along with the network described below.

2. What we'll do is place this wherever the player is at the time of pressing a specific key and then turn it on. With the command `OnRelease` we'll turn it off again. It would be easy to just use the **Toggle** action but since a ramp is called for then a **Matinee** ought to be involved to control the light's brightness.

3. Select the provided **Object Variable** *Light* and choose **Select in Level** and then press *Home* to locate the actor. In the main sequence, right-click in Kismet and choose **New Matinee**.

4. Double-click on the *Matinee* action, then right-click in the dark gray tracks panel under **All** and choose **Add New Empty Group**. Name this group `Ramp`, right-click, and choose **Add New Float Property Track**.

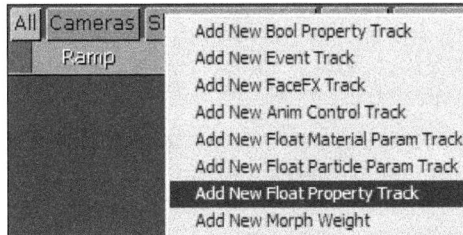

All	Cameras	S	Add New Bool Property Track
	Ramp		Add New Event Track
			Add New FaceFX Track
			Add New Anim Control Track
			Add New Float Material Param Track
			Add New Float Particle Param Track
			Add New Float Property Track
			Add New Morph Weight

5. From the list, choose *PointLightComponent0.Brightness*:

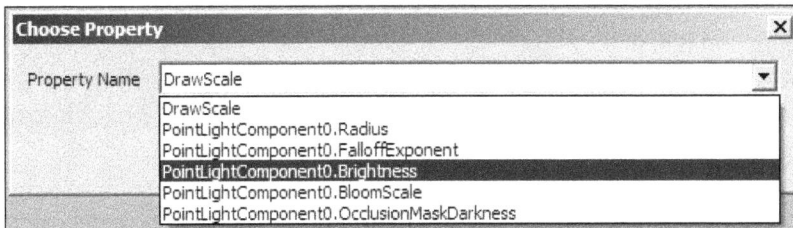

Choose Property ☒

Property Name | DrawScale ▼

DrawScale
PointLightComponent0.Radius
PointLightComponent0.FalloffExponent
PointLightComponent0.Brightness
PointLightComponent0.BloomScale
PointLightComponent0.OcclusionMaskDarkness

6. Key the **Brightness** track so the value ramps up from 0 to 4 over half a second. Zoom out in the Matinee Editor time line and find the red duration marker that is by default at 5.0s. Right-click on this and choose **Move to Longest Track Endpoint**, so now the time line will have 0.5s.

7. Hold *C* and click to comment the *Matinee* as *RampLight*, since we need another. Duplicate the *Matinee* action, and comment the pasted one as *LoopLight*.

8. For the *Matinee LoopLight* turn its **Looping** property on, then replace the value of its **Brightness** track 0.0s key so it has a steady curve of 4.0.

9. In Kismet, right-click and choose **New Event | Console Event.** Be sure to turn on its **Client Side Only** property. For the property **Console Event Name** type *Burst*. This is what our key binding in the configuration file calls up:

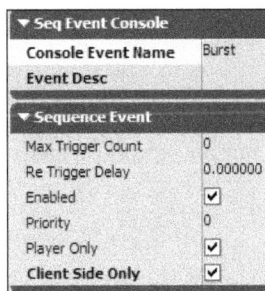

▼ Seq Event Console	
Console Event Name	Burst
Event Desc	
▼ **Sequence Event**	
Max Trigger Count	0
Re Trigger Delay	0.000000
Enabled	☑
Priority	0
Player Only	☑
Client Side Only	☑

10. Hook up the **Out** nub of the **Console Event** *Burst* to the **Play** nub of the **Matinee** *Ramp*. Also extend a wire from the same **Out** nub to the **In** nub of the existing Sub-sequence *MoveLightToPlayer*, which handles placing the light actor and its attachment so it follows the player.

11. In Kismet, right-click and choose **New Event | Misc | Console Event**. Be sure to turn on its **Client Side Only** property. For the property **Console Event Name** type *Belay*. This will drive our **OnRelease** action.

12. Hook up the **Out** nub of the **Console Event** *Belay* to the **Reverse** nub of the **Matinee** *Ramp*. From the **Reversed** output of the **Matinee** *Ramp* extend a wire to the **In** nub of the existing Sub-sequence *TeleportLight*, which handles placing the light actor out of the way when it is not in use. This is probably optional.

13. From the **Completed** output of the **Matinee** *Ramp* extend a wire to the **Play** nub of the **Matinee** *LoopLight*. Extend an additional wire from the **Out** nub of the **Console Event** *Belay* to the **Stop** nub of the **Matinee** *LoopLight*. Right-click on the **Stop** nub, choose **Set Activate Delay**, and enter 0.25 for this.

14. In the editor, press **Build All** [ ], then after it is ready, click on the **Play on PC** mode icon [ ] and run around a bit; then press *Shift + O* to check the light works. Hold it down then release to see if the **OnRelease** works.

15. You can load the provided map *Packt_06_KeyChange_DEMO.UDK* to check the completed result. Pressing *O* in this dark map will allow you to create a light which ramps up over 0.5s to be very bright. It will stay on as long as you hold the *O* key, as you move or look around. When you release, the same **Matinee** that ramps the light up will reverse again. Remember that what we've done here is set in Kismet a **Console Event** that fires actions specific to this map, so in another case the same *O* key that causes *Burst* could be used in a **Console Event** *Burst* that causes something else to occur, such as a burst mode for a weapon, or a burst of song, or a burst of speed. *Burst* itself is just a name allowing us to tie a keyboard key to an event.

Adjusting player speed

A good place to start getting to know the internal variables for the player is the web page `http://wiki.beyondunreal.com/UE3:Pawn_internal_variables_(UDK)`.

This page doesn't show you how to change values at our disposal but it can help elucidate ways a pawn can work.

One important variable to set for characters is how fast they move, particularly if their speed has to vary in different situations. This is what we'll deal with in this recipe, by creating a hotkey controlled sprint capacity for our player pawn class.

Getting ready

Open the file *Packt_06_Sprint_Start.UDK* and note the PlayerStart is within a long passage. We have to run really fast to clear a sinking door, and if we don't we're fried. One way to adjust player speed is through an edit to the *MyPawn.UC* class, so open this in ConTEXT: `C:\UDK\~\Development\Src\MyGame\Classes\MyPawn.UC`.

> You can also set a key for the player speed in Kismet using a **New Action | Misc | Console Command** action with a command entered such as: `setbind R setspeed 0.5` where *R* is the key and `0.5` is a multiplier on the default speed.
>
> The above **Console Command** will reduce walking speed by half when *R* is pressed. You can fire the action by hooking it up to a **Level Loaded** event or a **Trigger** event.

How to do it...

1. In order for any changes we make to our pawn class to work, if you haven't already done so, set in the `DefaultProperties` in the last few lines of this file: `C:\UDK\~\Development\Src\MyGame\Classes\MyGame.UC`.

    ```
    DefaultProperties
    {
    PlayerControllerClass=class'MyGame.MyPlayerController'
    DefaultPawnClass=class'MyGame.MyPawn'
    }
    ```

2. To be fair, there is more than one way to control player speed. To start with let's look at one way that can be achieved if you enable an existing chunk of code found in *Pawn.UC. MyPawn.UC*, which is provided in this book, extends from *UTPawn.UC* which itself extends from *Pawn.UC*, so there's a lineage at work here that is handed down even though *UTPawn.UC* doesn't itself declare `SetWalking` or a function using it. This is what we'll do now for *MyPawn.UC*:

    ```
    event SetWalking(bool bNewIsWalking)
    {
    super(Pawn).SetWalking(bNewIsWalking);
    }
    ```

3. The line `super(Pawn)` signifies that `SetWalking` comes from *Pawn.UC*. You then need only to specify in the `DefaultProperties` section of *MyPawn.UC* the following lines:

    ```
    Groundspeed=500 //this number defines the maximum run speed.
    WalkingPct=0.1 //between 0.0 and 1.0, since it is a percentage.
    ```

4. The left *Shift* key is already set by UDK for togging running and walking, based on this method.

5. Of course, just changing the speed doesn't automatically make the character's animation adapt to the change. This must be provisioned in the AnimTree used by the character, which can fire animation sequences using **BlendBySpeed** nodes. What you'll see if you PIE is just the same walk cycle but with less forward progress when you hold *Shift* to slow down.

6. Now, a more direct way to set the walk or run toggle works as follows. In *MyPawn.UC* add the following lines **above** the `DefaultProperties` section, where functions should go:

```
exec function Sprint()
{

GroundSpeed = speed+1000; // for 1000 set a value to suit
}


exec simulated function NoSprint()
{

GroundSpeed = speed-1000; // here the value is annulled
}
```

7. How this works is that when you press a *Sprint* hotkey an additional speed of 1000 (or whatever you set) is added to the default **Groundspeed** value, set in `DefaultProperties` of *MyPawn.UC* and what it is advised to do is set the hotkey's **OnRelease** part to be a *NoSprint* command, which takes off the added 1000 again, thereby resetting **GroundSpeed**. Make sure the values you set are the same for adding to `Sprint` and subtracting in the case of `NoSprint`.

8. Save *MyPawn.UC* and to complete this method, open the file `C:\UDK\~\UDKGame\Config\DefaultInput.INI` in ConTEXT. Scroll down to find the binding info below:

```
;----------------------------------------------------------------
; BINDINGS USED TO ORGANIZE ALL GAME BINDABLE ACTIONS IN ONE PLACE
FOR SYSTEMS SUCH AS UI
; GBA - GAME BINDABLE ACTION
; "_Gamepad" - IS USED WHEN A CONTROLLER IS USING AN ALTERED
MAPPING FOR AN ACTION
;----------------------------------------------------------------
```

9. Add the following lines directly after the previous lines (noting the . at the start):

```
.Bindings=(Name="F",
  Command="Sprint | OnRelease NoSprint")
```

10. Actually the *F* key is already assigned to *FeignDeath* (a play-dead action which is not really very useful), so scroll further down and use *;* to comment out the following line:

```
.Bindings=(Name="F",Command="GBA_FeignDeath")
```

11. Open the provided scene *Packt_06_Sprint_DEMO.UDK*, which is already complete. In the menu **View | World Properties**, make sure that the **Game Type for PIE** is set to *MyGame*. This will ensure our code from *MyPawn.UC* is used for this scene. We'll just test out the speed during PIE in order to see if holding the *Left-Shift* key will make us walk and holding the *F* key will make us sprint.

12. Don't forget to check the Kismet for the scene to see how the conditions and effects were set up for whether or not the player made it through the gateway. In the image below we see an **Integer Variable** named *Target* which is set after the player spawns. After a four second **Delay**, a **Matinee** locks a *Gatemesh* near the exit. The player has to rush there before they are trapped.

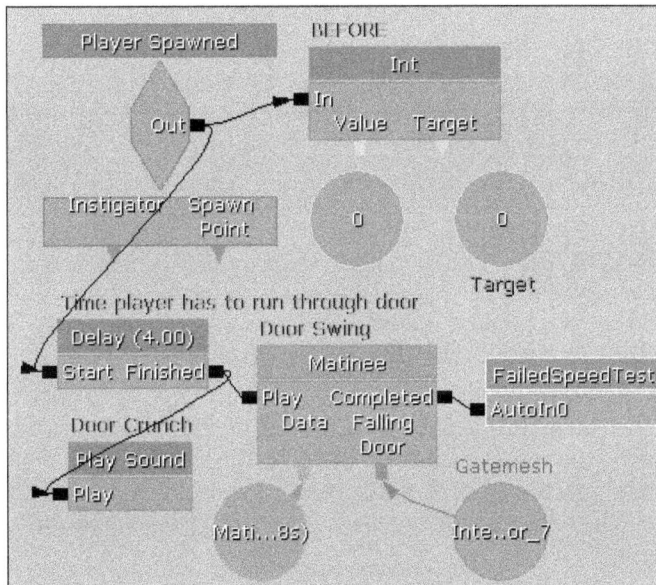

13. You may wonder why we don't just use a **New Event | Key/Mouse Input** to control speed. That would be fine for a change effected only in the current map, but one class setting can effect all the maps in the game.

14. The properties that drive the highlighted PostProcessVolume change are the same as in the *Chapter 4, Got Your Wires Crossed?* recipe on *Toggling the enabled or disabled state of triggers*. This is shown in the Sub-sequence *FailedSpeedTest* in the next screenshot, which compares *Target* using a **Compare Int** condition:

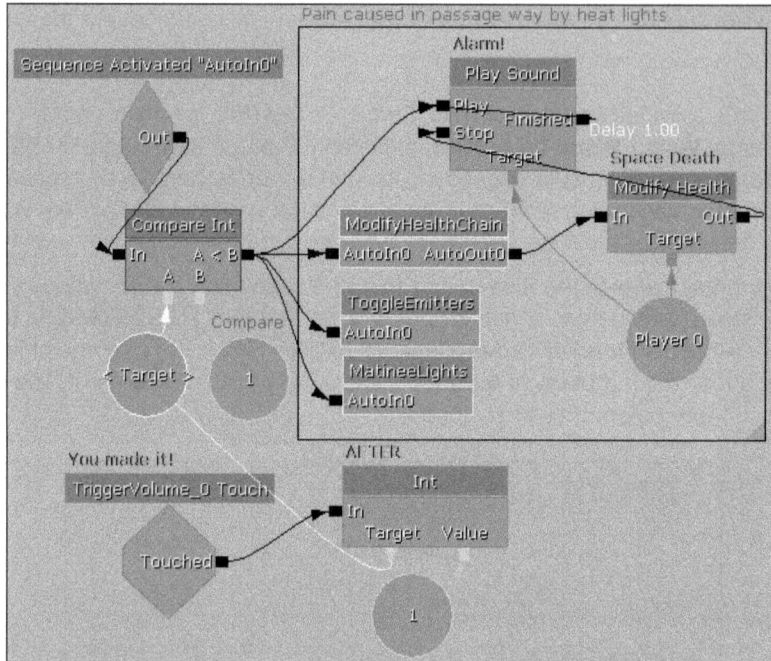

There's more...

Setting variable speed animations in the AnimTree

In *Chapter 3, It Lives!*, we set up an animation tree that includes instructions for our game's SkeletalMesh so it can animate. We should add a walk animation and run animation to reflect the change of speed in the actual translation of the model in the scene. Changing speed internally, within the character itself, is useful when creating combat dynamics or variability that might come from input other than the player like falling speed increases based on increases in distance.

1. Open the animation tree *Packt_CharTree_Aim*, a partially complete asset (for the completed version we're using *Packt.Mesh.Packt_SkinTailFBX* for the SkeletalMesh and *Packt.Anims.Packt_CharTree* for the AnimTree).

2. Add a **New Animation Node/BlendBy/AnimNodeBlendBySpeed** and in its properties expand the **Anim Node** part and type *Speed* in the **Node name** field. This name will appear on the header of the node. Also tick **On** the property **Anim Node Blend List | Play Active Child**.

3. Hook up the existing **AnimNodeBlendDirectional** which drives the directional animation sequences from the **AnimSet** into **Child 1** of the *Speed*, and hook up *Speed*'s **Out** into the next node in the chain, in this case the **Moving** output of the **UDKAnimBlendByIdle**.

4. Right-click on *Speed* and choose **Add Input**.

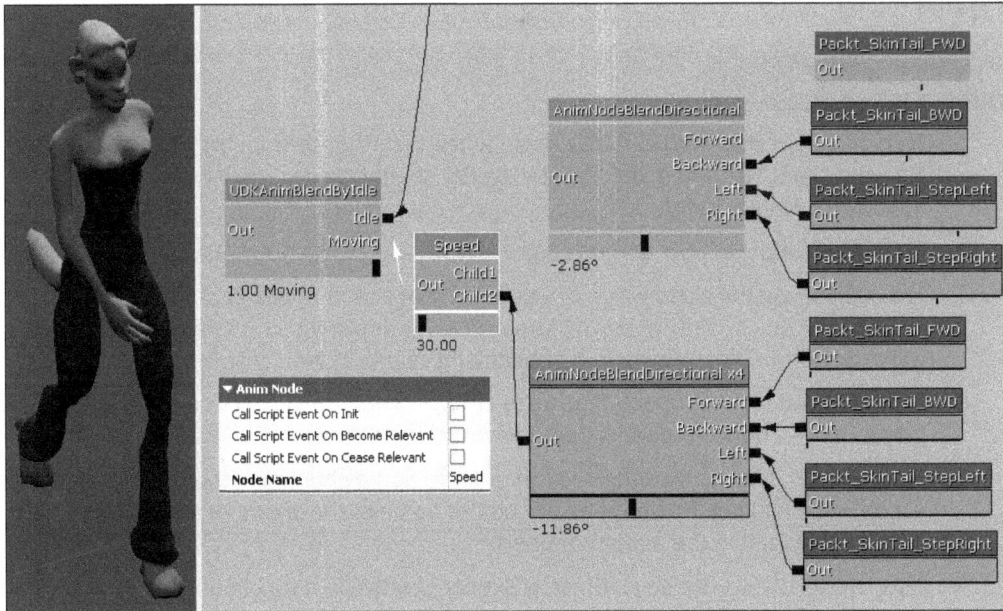

5. Select the **AnimNodeBlendDirectional** node and the four clips joined to it. Press *Ctrl + C* and *Ctrl + V* to reproduce them, and hook the copy into the newly added **Child 2** input of *Speed*.

6. For each clip joined to the pasted **AnimNodeBlendDirectional** set the speed to 4.0 (and make sure the first set of clips is set to 1.0) in their property **Rate**.

See also

There is a similar guide to setting up a player sprint control at 'UDK Central' and it includes functionality for a brief slowing down effect after sprinting, available at: `http://udkc.info/index.php?title=Tutorials:Sprint_button_(changing_speed_by_button)`.

Creating your own Kismet node for speed

In an earlier recipe in this chapter we discussed changing the player speed with a shortcut key. Being a designer, there will be times when you want the game to influence the player's speed. For this, the handiest way is probably by scripting a custom node we can hook up to events.

How to do it...

1. Turn off UDK, open ConTEXT, and begin a new file. Choose from the drop-down menu list which says **Text Files**, the item *UnrealEd*, so that the text we'll type is format friendly for UnrealScript.

2. The code starts: `class PawnGroundSpeed extends SequenceAction;`

3. This is because the class which drives all Kismet action nodes is `C:\UDK\~\ Development\Src\Engine\Classes\SequenceAction.UC`, and our changes will extend from that, adding to it or changing values it already sets up.

4. **Groundspeed** is the property that we're changing and it will only work on a pawn, be it player or NPC, hence the class name *PawnGroundSpeed*.

5. Type: `var() float PawnSpeed;` in order to add a channel in the properties of the action we're making. **PawnSpeed** will be the name of the channel, and users can set a float value for it in the action's property.

6. Type: `event Activated()` which is similar to starting a function.

7. Type in the following lines (for which credit goes to **PhoenixWing**):

```
{
   local SeqVar_Object ObjVar;
     local UTPawn P;
   foreach LinkedVariables(class'SeqVar_Object',
     ObjVar, "Target")
     {
     P = UTPawn( ObjVar.GetObjectValue();
     P.GroundSpeed = PawnSpeed;
     }
}
```

8. Above, we set `P` as a referent for `UTPawn`, tell `P` to be handled by an `ObjVar` called `"Target"`, and then we provide a means to change the **GroundSpeed** for `P`. What we have above is a way to make an **Object Variable** assigned to a **Target** nub for the action define `P` in the level, which means this will work on either the player or Bots spawned from an Actor Factory action using *UTActorFactoryAI*.

9. In Kismet, the custom ***PawnSpeed*** node will show us a property called **PawnSpeed** where we can enter a float value, and this will adjust the **GroundSpeed** value which is assigned in the `DefaultProperties` of *UTPawn.UC*.

10. For this script, we can add additionally some entries in the `DefaultProperties` that let us influence the **PawnSpeed** value through a ***float variable***. Add to the script:

```
DefaultProperties
{
ObjName="PawnSpeed"
ObjCategory="Pawn"

VariableLinks(1)=(ExpectedType=class'SeqVar_Float',
  LinkDesc="Speed",PropertyName=PawnSpeed) //This is all one line.
}
```

11. The `ObjName` and `ObjCategory` entries tell the action where to appear on Kismet's action list: **New Action | Pawn | PawnSpeed**.

12. The `VariableLinks(1)` part adds a **Speed** nub to the node which accepts ***Float Variables*** so the field for **PawnSpeed** can be influenced by other sequences in Kismet rather than just exist as a single value in the action's properties. You might use this to create a speed that randomly changes or matches some other dynamic value.

13. The following illustration shows the custom ***PawnSpeed*** action in use, along with the **PawnSpeed** property being taken over by a *Random **Float Variable*** through the **Speed** nub we added, shown here:

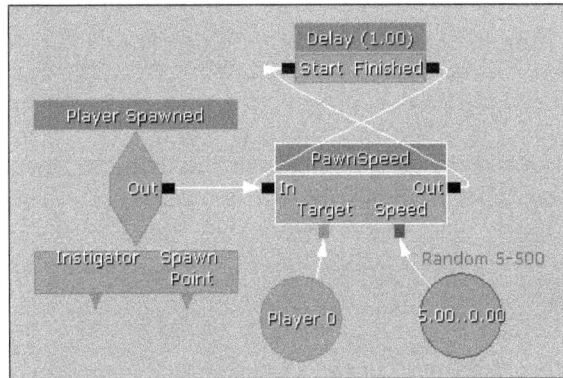

14. Save the file to
    `C:\UDK\~\Development\Src\Mygame\Classes\PawnGroundSpeed.UC`.

15. Start UDK to recompile your scripts. If you haven't done this in an earlier topic, don't forget to first direct UDK to your *MyGame* folder by editing `C:\UDK\~\UDKGame\Config\DefaultEngine.INI` to include after `[UnrealEd.EditorEngine]` an additional entry +`ModEditPackages=MyGame`, making sure it is the last entry after the default entries.

Changing the default player sounds

The default player sounds, such as grunts, footsteps and impacts, are set up in *UTPawnSoundGroup.UC* (and by extension *UTPawnSoundGroup_Liandri.UC* since the UDK generic Bot is from the Liandri family).

In *UTPawn.UC*, line 5497: `SoundGroupClass=class'UTGame.UTPawnSoundGroup'` we get the definition for the file that sounds will be established in. This is found in the file's `DefaultProperties`. Further down, we get additional **SoundCues** given for `ArmorHitSound=`, `SpawnSound=`, `TeleportSound=`, and `FallImpactSound=`, all of which can be overridden in your *MyPawn.UC* file's `DefaultProperties`. We also have some control over the audible distance with **MaxFootstepDistSq**, and **MaxJumpSoundDistSq**.

In this recipe we won't be considering changes to the weapon sounds for the default player, but these are, similarly, set in the `DefaultProperties` of the appropriate weapon class.

Getting ready

In **ConTEXT** you can open multiple files, so open up the `C:\UDK\~\Development\Src\UTGame\Classes\UTPawnSoundGroup.UC` first, then open up in another tab `C:\UDK\~\Development\Src\UTGame\Classes\UTPawn.UC` and look for line 5535, mentioned above using *Ctrl + G*. Since *MyPawn.UC* that we created in `C:\UDK\~\Development\Src\MyGame\Classes\` extends *UTPawn.UC*, if you have a line in the derived file which is the same as the base file, *MyPawn.UC* will act as an override. You can edit either *UTPawn.UC* or *MyPawn.UC* as you see fit, depending on what you have already provisioned in *MyGame*. Besides the two files from *\UTGame*, also open up `C:\UDK\~\Development\Src\MyGame\Classes\MyGame.UC`.

How to do it...

1. So that changes we make to our pawn class work, if you haven't already done so, in the last few lines of *MyGame.UC* set in the `DefaultProperties`:

```
DefaultProperties
{
PlayerControllerClass=class'MyGame.MyPlayerController'
DefaultPawnClass=class'MyGame.MyPawn'
}
```

2. In the `DefaultProperties`, also insert the following above the end curly brace }:

   `SoundGroupClass=class'MyGame.MyPawnSoundGroup'`

3. Make a copy of *UTPawnSoundGroup.UC*, renaming the copy to `C:\UDK\~\Development\Src\MyGame\Classes\MyPawnSoundGroup.UC` and also change the first line of your new *MyPawnSoundGroup.UC* to read `class MyPawnSoundGroup` extends **UTPawnSoundGroup**.

4. Delete everything between the class declaration and the `DefaultProperties` section. Leaving it there would just double up what's already in the class we're deriving from.

5. In the `DefaultProperties` for this class you will see there are a lot of SoundCue entries. Replace all the SoundCue paths as follows: *PacktWavs. Cue.Name*, where *Name* refers to the action you are setting the sound for:

   `DrownSound=SoundCue'PacktWavs.Cue.Drown_Cue'.`

> Any lines which you don't have a sound for you can be commented out with \\ and it will use the entry already established in *UTPawnSoundGroup.UC*. If you don't want to hear the **Epic Games** sounds, instead of a SoundCue name you could enter *none*, for instance: `DrownSound=none`.

6. There's a selection of SoundCues provided in the *PacktWavs* package and their names reflect the entries in the `DefaultProperties`. Later you can change these to whatever sounds you've sourced. After setting your SoundCue list, compile, then load a scene and set its **View | World Properties | GameType | Game Type** for PIE to *MyGame* and PIE to see what you get for your player sounds now.

7. The next screenshot is of the adjusted code for the *MyPawnSoundGroup.UC* file discussed here. There's a copy in the downloadable content provided for this book. Note that when you set it, you may be disconcerted by some of the regular UDK sounds like spawning and jumping sounding rather different. Notice that the footstep sounds listed here are all the same asset; but they are there to allow variety like walking in mud, walking in snow, walking in high heels ... if you have alternatives.

See Also

Chapter 3, It Lives! discussed footsteps assigned in the sequence properties of an AnimSet to create footstep sounds timed to the keyframed steps of the character. Check out the recipe *Sounds for non-Matinee controlled animation*.

```
defaultproperties
{
        DrownSound=SoundCue'PacktWavs.Cue.Drown_Cue'
        GaspSound=SoundCue'PacktWavs.Cue.Gasp_Cue'

        DefaultJumpingSound=SoundCue'PacktWavs.Cue.Shimmer_Cue'

        FootstepSounds[0]=(MaterialType=Stone,Sound=SoundCue'PacktWavs.Cue.FootSteps_Cue')
        FootstepSounds[1]=(MaterialType=Dirt,Sound=SoundCue'PacktWavs.Cue.FootSteps_Cue')
        FootstepSounds[2]=(MaterialType=Energy,Sound=SoundCue'PacktWavs.Cue.FootSteps_Cue')
        FootstepSounds[3]=(MaterialType=Flesh_Human,Sound=SoundCue'PacktWavs.Cue.FootSteps_Cue')
        FootstepSounds[4]=(MaterialType=Foliage,Sound=SoundCue'PacktWavs.Cue.FootSteps_Cue')
        FootstepSounds[5]=(MaterialType=Glass,Sound=SoundCue'PacktWavs.Cue.FootSteps_Cue')
        FootstepSounds[6]=(MaterialType=Water,Sound=SoundCue'PacktWavs.Cue.FootSteps_Cue')
        FootstepSounds[7]=(MaterialType=ShallowWater,Sound=SoundCue'PacktWavs.Cue.FootSteps_Cue')
        FootstepSounds[8]=(MaterialType=Metal,Sound=SoundCue'PacktWavs.Cue.FootSteps_Cue')
        FootstepSounds[9]=(MaterialType=Snow,Sound=SoundCue'PacktWavs.Cue.FootSteps_Cue')
        FootstepSounds[10]=(MaterialType=Wood,Sound=SoundCue'PacktWavs.Cue.FootSteps_Cue')


        JumpingSounds[0]=(MaterialType=Stone,Sound=SoundCue'PacktWavs.Cue.Stone_Cue')
        JumpingSounds[1]=(MaterialType=Dirt,Sound=SoundCue'PacktWavs.Cue.Dirt_Cue')
        JumpingSounds[2]=(MaterialType=Energy,Sound=SoundCue'PacktWavs.Cue.Energy_Cue')
        JumpingSounds[3]=(MaterialType=Flesh_Human,Sound=SoundCue'PacktWavs.Cue.Flesh_Cue')
        JumpingSounds[4]=(MaterialType=Foliage,Sound=SoundCue'PacktWavs.Cue.Foliage_Cue')
        JumpingSounds[5]=(MaterialType=Glass,Sound=SoundCue'PacktWavs.Cue.GlassPlate_Cue')
        JumpingSounds[6]=(MaterialType=GlassBroken,Sound=SoundCue'PacktWavs.Cue.GlassBroken_Cue')
        JumpingSounds[7]=(MaterialType=Grass,Sound=SoundCue'PacktWavs.Cue.Grass_Cue')
        JumpingSounds[8]=(MaterialType=Metal,Sound=SoundCue'PacktWavs.Cue.Metal_Cue')
        JumpingSounds[9]=(MaterialType=Mud,Sound=SoundCue'PacktWavs.Cue.Mud_Cue')
        JumpingSounds[10]=(MaterialType=Metal,Sound=SoundCue'PacktWavs.Cue.Metal_Cue')
        JumpingSounds[11]=(MaterialType=Snow,Sound=SoundCue'PacktWavs.Cue.Snow_Cue')
        JumpingSounds[12]=(MaterialType=Tile,Sound=SoundCue'PacktWavs.Cue.Tile_Cue')
        JumpingSounds[13]=(MaterialType=Water,Sound=SoundCue'PacktWavs.Cue.WaterDeep_Cue')
        JumpingSounds[14]=(MaterialType=ShallowWater,Sound=SoundCue'PacktWavs.Cue.WaterShallow_Cue')
        JumpingSounds[15]=(MaterialType=Wood,Sound=SoundCue'PacktWavs.Cue.Wood_Cue')


        DefaultLandingSound=SoundCue'PacktWavs.Cue.Extra_Cue'
        LandingSounds[0]=(MaterialType=Stone,Sound=SoundCue'PacktWavs.Cue.StoneLand_Cue')
        LandingSounds[1]=(MaterialType=Dirt,Sound=SoundCue'PacktWavs.Cue.DirtLand_Cue')
        LandingSounds[2]=(MaterialType=Energy,Sound=SoundCue'PacktWavs.Cue.EnergyLand_Cue')
        LandingSounds[3]=(MaterialType=Flesh_Human,Sound=SoundCue'PacktWavs.Cue.FleshLand_Cue')
        LandingSounds[4]=(MaterialType=Foliage,Sound=SoundCue'PacktWavs.Cue.FoliageLand_Cue')
        LandingSounds[5]=(MaterialType=Glass,Sound=SoundCue'PacktWavs.Cue.GlassPlateLand_Cue')
        LandingSounds[6]=(MaterialType=GlassBroken,Sound=SoundCue'PacktWavs.Cue.GlassBrokenLand_Cue')
        LandingSounds[7]=(MaterialType=Grass,Sound=SoundCue'PacktWavs.Cue.GrassLand_Cue')
        LandingSounds[8]=(MaterialType=Metal,Sound=SoundCue'PacktWavs.Cue.MetalLand_Cue')
        LandingSounds[9]=(MaterialType=Mud,Sound=SoundCue'PacktWavs.Cue.MudLand_Cue')
        LandingSounds[10]=(MaterialType=Metal,Sound=SoundCue'PacktWavs.Cue.MetalLand_Cue')
        LandingSounds[11]=(MaterialType=Snow,Sound=SoundCue'PacktWavs.Cue.SnowLand_Cue')
        LandingSounds[12]=(MaterialType=Tile,Sound=SoundCue'PacktWavs.Cue.TileLand_Cue')
        LandingSounds[13]=(MaterialType=Water,Sound=SoundCue'PacktWavs.Cue.WaterDeepLand_Cue')
        LandingSounds[14]=(MaterialType=ShallowWater,Sound=SoundCue'PacktWavs.Cue.WaterShallowLand_Cue')
        LandingSounds[15]=(MaterialType=Wood,Sound=SoundCue'PacktWavs.Cue.WoodLand_Cue')


        BulletImpactSound=SoundCue'PacktWavs.Cue.Impact_Cue'
}
```

Replacing the HUD

The HUD is provisioned in the file *MyGame.UC* and the example HUD **Epic Games** includes is 'UTGame.UTHUD', which has a dynamic compass, a health bar, and an ammo count, and a crosshair for aiming. These can be either modified or completely replaced, and there are various ways to make a working HUD, so what we will do here is just assume you want to remove the existing HUD and are comfortable adding your own content once you know what goes where. Most HUDs are now built upon Scaleform, and to get started with that, in respect of UI, it could be a good idea to look at `http://udn.epicgames.com/Three/ScaleformWorkflow.html`. An example of how the HUD and camera relate is at `http://forums.epicgames.com/showthread.php?t=721726`. *Chapter 10, The Way of the Flash UI* also discusses the basics of working with Scaleform.

In this section we are not going to cover comprehensive HUD provisioning, only some simple configuration tricks that are handy, that will expose users to the bare bones of this extensive body of content.

> The new default map types begin with no **GameType** and therefore no HUD. Others begin with *UTGame* (which was the default up till the July 2011 version and can still be set in **View | WorldProperties | Game Type**). In any scene it is worthwhile to know that to show no HUD at all we can use the ***Toggle HUD*** action or ***Toggle Cinematic Mode*** action in Kismet with **Hide HUD** ticked in its properties.
>
> Using UTGame, you may not only want to hide not just the HUD but the Unreal Tournament legacy weapon from the view too. After all, there's no point seeing a laser rifle bobbing in front of you when your game is a caveman simulator for instance. Neither of the HUD toggles will hide the *UTGame* weapon, but in this case you can also add a ***Player Spawned*** event in Kismet (not a ***Level Loaded*** since the player must spawn first) and connect to it a **New Action | Pawn | Give Inventory** action. Set the ***Give Inventory*** action so it has a new entry [🖳] with **None** set and tick on the property **Clear Existing**.

How to do it...

1. An original HUD design really sets the tone of any game. If you want to start your own *MyHUD* class, particularly now that Scaleform has been added to UDK, you can try:

```
class MyGame extends UDKGame
    config(MyGame);

DefaultProperties
{
```

```
    HUDType=class'MyGame.MyHUD'
//   bUseClassicHUD=true
// This code sample cannot use the line above as it does not
extend from UTGame but from UDKGame...


}
```

2. The highlighted line tells UDK to use the classic HUD type to avoid an error if your game extends *UTGame.UC*.

3. You can then continue to provision your *MyHUD.UC* with at least:

```
class MyHUD extends UDKHUD;
event PostRender()
{
DrawGameHud
}

//PostRender occurs after all the content of the game is sorted out.

function DrawGameHud()
{
  if ( !PlayerOwner.IsDead() && !PlayerOwner.
IsInState('Spectating'))

{

// Set the position on the screen...
Canvas.SetPos(Canvas.ClipX/2,Canvas.ClipY/2);

// Set the text colour to white...
Canvas.SetDrawColor( 255, 255, 255, 255 );

// Sets a medium font to use...
Canvas.Font = class 'Engine'.static.GetMediumFont();

///You can also use GetSmallFont or GetHugeFont

// Sets the text to display...
Canvas.DrawText( "This HUD is basic!" );
}
}

DefaultProperties
{
}
```

4. Comment out the `DrawText` instruction if you don't want it there. Instead, use **Draw Text** actions in Kismet. This example is just a starter. If you want to adjust text colour, remember that the 255,255,255,255 first three numbers are RGB values and the fourth is Alpha, for transparency.

5. Not everyone wants to write an entire HUD replacement, so if all you want to do is remove the rather large compass from the default HUD, you can go to line 481 of the file: `C:\UDK\~\Development\Src\UTGame\Classes\GFxMinimapHud.UC` and then comment out: `//Minimap.Update(CurZoomf);`

   By default the hotkeys *F2* (map) and *F3* (minimap) are for in game map toggling.

   If you like the minimap but want to make it smaller, leave the previous line as it was, and instead press *Ctrl + F* and search for *85*; which happens to be the scale value for the compass and should expose the lines:

   ```
   Minimap.SetFloat("_xscale", 85);
   Minimap.SetFloat("_yscale", 85);
   ```

6. Comment those out with `//`, so you don't have to remember the defaults, then add in this replacement underneath:

   ```
   Minimap.SetFloat("_xscale", 25);
   Minimap.SetFloat("_yscale", 25);
   ```

7. If all you want to do is remove the targeting crosshairs, open `C:\UDK\~\Development\Src\UTGame\Classes\GFxMinimapHud.UC` and in the `DefaultProperties` put in `false` instead of `true` in the line: `bDrawWeaponCrosshairs=true.`

8. Since there is a function `ToggleCrosshair(bool bToggle)` you can always add a hotkey to the *DefaultInput.INI* file, as we discussed in earlier recipes, such as: *Binding a keyboard shortcut to a player action*.

9. Another inroad into adjusting the HUD is to learn how the art assets are assigned for it, by looking in the editor in the Content Browser, under **UDKGame | GFx | UDKHUD** where you can access, change and replace the art or perhaps just find the name of the asset (right-click on it and choose **Copy Full Name to Clipboard**) so you can then locate it in the appropriate HUD class and swap it for the asset you want to use.

10. An example would be, again using the compass, to **Create a Copy** of *ut3_minimap_compass* which is in the package UDKHUD and place it into a *Backup._ut3_minimap_compass*. Here, *Backup* is a new package name and the prefixed underscore is to adjust the name, so we avoid a conflict while keeping it easy to remember in case this gets reversed later on.

11. Now search for the provided *Packt.Texture.AltCompass*, which is a 512x512 TGA with an embedded alpha channel, and looks square.

12. Right-click on this and choose **Create a Copy** and then set the info to *UDKHUD.ut3_minimap_compass* (the one we replaced out before).

13. If for some reason you have troubles juggling files, the original asset is found in: `C:\UDK\~\UDKGame\Flash\UDKHud\UDK_minimap\ut3_minimap_compass.PNG`.

14. Now PIE to see if a square compass shows instead of the round one, supposing you haven't already removed the compass as in step 2. Bear in mind that if you do an update to the UDK content this may be refreshed by the updater.

DrawText and GameType concerns

In this recipe we will look at how to get the ***Draw Text*** and ***Draw Image*** Kismet nodes working. These are actions and events that allow you to float a string of text or a texture on the screen during the game. In maps using the **GameType** *UTGame* these do not yield any results. So if you want a game with these you have to set up your own game type. They work with the **GameType** *SimpleGame*, so if you can't follow the class set up, you can still do the Kismet part of this recipe to see how **Draw Text** and **Draw Image** can be used. Using a font asset from the Content Browser, we will simply fire off some text: *"Walk to the Trigger please!"* and when the trigger event fires, fire another: *"You touched the Trigger!"* and have a texture based graphic display on the screen too.

Getting ready

Ensure that you have copied the provided classes for *MyGame* to `C:\UDK\~\Development\Src\MyGame\Classes\` and also allowed UDK to use *MyGame* by editing `C:\UDK\~\UDKGame\Config\DefaultEngine.INI` to include the line `+ModEditPackages=MyGame` as the last entry in the section `[UnrealEd.EditorEngine]`. We've covered this setup in detail in *Chapter 3, It Lives!* under the recipe *Configuring your character to use your AnimTree*.

How to do it...

1. Open the map template *Midday Lighting*. In the viewport, on the ground near the cube, right-click and choose **Add Actor | Trigger**. In the Trigger actor's properties turn off **Display | Hidden** so we'll see this Trigger in gameplay.

2. In Kismet [⎇], set up the following network. If you are new to Kismet, see *Chapter 4, Got Your Wires Crossed?*

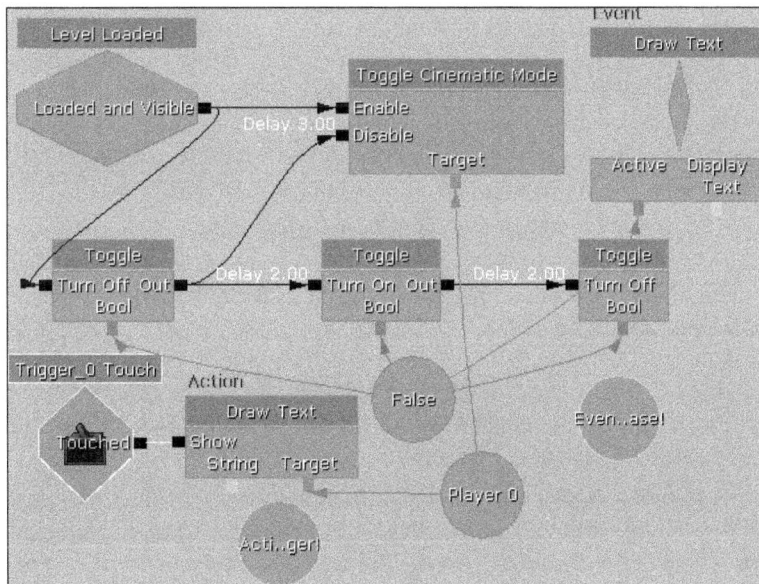

3. What may be new to you here is the ***Draw Text*** action hooked up to the ***Trigger Touch*** event, and the ***Draw Text*** event. These are closely related in terms of what they do, which is draw text on the screen (given the correct HUD settings). Let's go through their properties, starting with the ***Draw Text*** event.

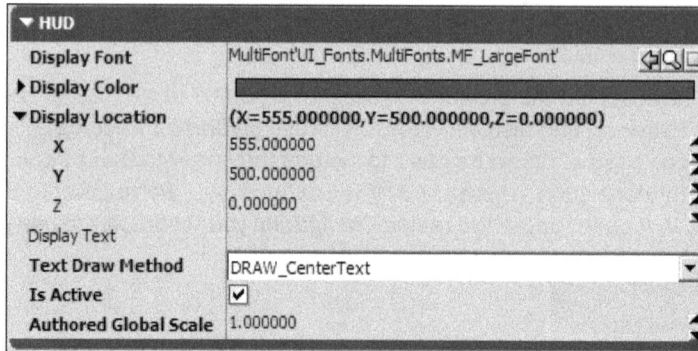

▼ HUD	
Display Font	MultiFont'UI_Fonts.MultiFonts.MF_LargeFont'
▶ **Display Color**	
▼ **Display Location**	(X=555.000000,Y=500.000000,Z=0.000000)
X	555.000000
Y	500.000000
Z	0.000000
Display Text	
Text Draw Method	DRAW_CenterText
Is Active	✔
Authored Global Scale	1.000000

4. The **Display Font** can be added using the assign icon [🖘] after searching for *font* in the Content Browser and choosing one of the available assets, in this case: *UI_Fonts. MultiFonts.MF_LargeFont*. **Display Color** is a color picker for the text that gets displayed. **Display Location** is where on the screen the text will be displayed, and it's closely related to **Authored Global Scale**. If you change that, then the relative screen position of the text will have to change. If you use a scale of 1 and your game screen resolution is 1024x768 then a centered text would be at **Display Location | X = 512**. You can also use the **Text Draw Method** *DRAW_CenterText* to align the text to the center of its location, instead of wrapping. This is a typical alignment setting for handling multiple lines of text. It doesn't put the text in the screen center. Lastly, tick on **Is Active**, which will ensure that the text displays on level load.

5. You can enter the actual text to display in the **Display Text** property's text field, by typing something there, or you can leave it empty, as shown above, and instead connect a ***String Variable*** (right-click and choose **New Variable | String**) to the **Display Text** nub of the event. In its **Str Value** property type *Touch the trigger please!* Using a variable lets you get more utility out of the event, by adding strings together or adjusting strings with a **Set Variable | String** action. For instance, the first time the event is fired the ***String*** could be set to *"Touch the trigger please!"* The second time it could be set to *"Find another Trigger!"*

6. Note the ***Toggle*** actions strung along in the Kismet screenshot a few steps back which turn on and off (with a brief delay) the ***Boolean Variable*** connected to the **Is Active** nub of the ***Draw Text*** event. The ***Boolean Variable*** has a b Value 0 = false / b Value 1 = true property that provides a control for making the text visible or not.

7. The network for the example also has a ***Toggle Cinematic Mode*** action which blocks player movement but still displays the character while waiting for the text to display. This is so players can't rush over and touch the Trigger before you've told them to go there. It would be bad if the text pops up too late.

8. For the ***Draw Text*** action, which is the friend of the event, these are the properties:

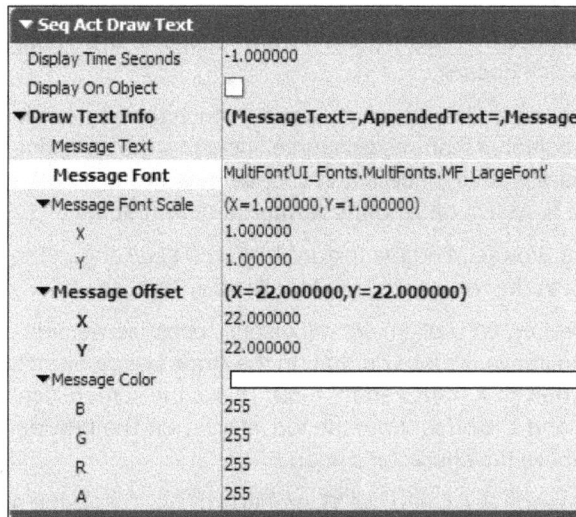

▼ Seq Act Draw Text	
Display Time Seconds	-1.000000
Display On Object	☐
▼ Draw Text Info	(MessageText=,AppendedText=,Message
Message Text	
Message Font	MultiFont'UI_Fonts.MultiFonts.MF_LargeFont'
▼Message Font Scale	(X=1.000000,Y=1.000000)
X	1.000000
Y	1.000000
▼**Message Offset**	**(X=22.000000,Y=22.000000)**
X	22.000000
Y	22.000000
▼Message Color	
B	255
G	255
R	255
A	255

9. Here, you can set a **Display Time Seconds** value if you want to control how long the text displays. A value of -1 means the text can display forever.

10. In this case, since the Player is the **Target** for the ***Draw Text*** action, we don't want to turn on **Show on Object**. Otherwise, we won't see the text as intended. However, if you set the Trigger actor in the scene as the **Target** for the action, then the text will lock to that and display over it, a bit like a tooltip.

11. Sticking with settings shown here, the **Message Text** can be left empty and instead, as before, we can use a ***String Variable*** to supply the displayed text. With the ***Draw Text*** event we had the **Display Text** nub that accepts a ***String Variable*** already showing there, but with the ***Draw Text*** action we have to right click on it and choose **Expose Variable | String—String**.

12. Add a ***String Variable*** and in its property **Str Value** type *You touched the Trigger*.

13. Going back to the properties of the ***Draw Text*** action, you can set the size and position of the message in the same way as with the ***Draw Text*** event. There's a **Message Font** channel where you can assign [⊕] from the Content Browser a font asset, such as *UI_Fonts.MultiFonts.MF_LargeFont*. There's a **Message Offset** which defaults to X=0, Y=0 which would give you a position at the top left corner of the screen, and needs to be about X=22, Y=22 to move to the center. The **Message Font Scale** gives you a sizing function for the text, but 1 will do fine. Also the **Message Color** picker set to white will do fine.

14. If you PIE now, you will probably not see any text at all. Whether or not the editor's HUD displays depends on the settings in the HUD class for the current **GameType**. If you set up *MyGame* using the provided classes then go to **View | World Properties | GameType** and set **Default Game Type** to *MyGame* and **Game Type for PIE** to *MyGame*, you should see the text display in game. If *MyGame* is not in the list for the **Game Type**, you haven't set that up. See the *Getting Started* section or choose *SimpleGame*. *MyGame.UC* sets properties for the HUD to use, which is *MyHUD.UC*. *MyHUD.UC* extends from *UDKHUD.UC* which supports **DrawText**, instead of extending *UTHUD.UC*, which doesn't.

15. Lastly, let's display an image, which is really much the same as displaying text but has a couple of additional features to handle, including the sampling size of the image and the use of alpha. Right click and choose **New Event | HUD | DrawImage** and for the event, set **Is Active** on, and the **Authored Global Scale** to 1.

16. In the Content Browser, find the texture *UDKHUD.skull* and in the **Draw Image** event properties press the assign icon [🔊] for **Display Texture**.

17. If you PIE currently, no skull image will display, because we didn't set the size or position of the image, so let's do that. In the **Draw Image** event's properties, set the **Display Location** so **X** = 485 and **Y** = 50. This is the screen location where the text will show up, and it is offset from the top left corner. The provided values will put the texture just above the character's head.

18. Set the **XL** property to 64 and the **YL** property to 64. This is the size the image will be on screen, which is twice the size of the source image. Now set the **UL** to 32 and the **VL** to 32. This value comes from the **UV** size of the source texture, and will show all the texture since the texture is 32x32 pixels. If you wanted to show just the top half of the skull, you'd enter **VL** as 16. Notice the source image for the skull already has an alpha channel built in.

19. An example that toggles the skull texture on and off is in the provided map *Packt_04_DrawText.UDK*. It also shows the **Draw Text** operations.

Handling level content streaming

In this recipe we are going to divide an existing scene into parts so that it can be streamed as required to unload parts that are no longer required, and ensure parts that are not yet required remain on standby. Streaming helps maximize performance by only loading areas the player can see. Moreover, streaming isn't only useful for performance optimization. In many storytelling scenarios, streaming can be used to selectively expose different features of a level based on player actions. This provides a nice way to generate a non-linear experience.

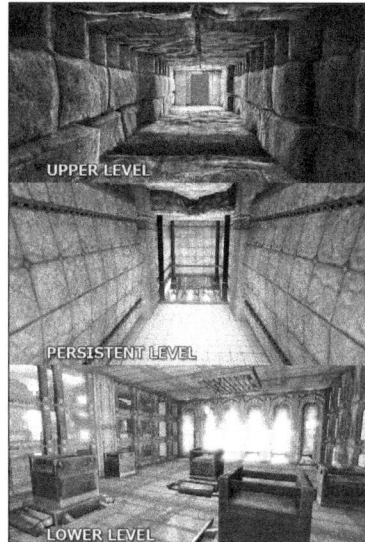

Getting ready

Open the file *Packt_06_Persistent_Start.UDK*, which represents the shared content persistent across the boundary between two streamed levels. The scenes we're going to stream have already been divided up from the scene we used in the previous recipe. In your own scene, you'd have to work out which elements would be saved to which scene. There is an upper level and a lower level, and the persistent level includes the elements which bridge those. Essentially this scene will be like an airlock between independent spaces.

How to do it...

1. For simplicity in this tutorial, the content is already divided up for you, since otherwise you would need to follow a long list of actor selection steps. As it is, this content is a mix of BSP and StaticMeshes.
2. Press *Ctrl + Shift + F* to browse and click on the **Levels** tab.
3. From the menu click **Level** to expand it, then choose **Add to Existing Level**.

4. Browse for and highlight both these scenes: *Packt_06_UpperLevel.UDK* and *Packt_06_LowerLevel.UDK*. When they are importing, from the drop-down list, choose **Kismet** as the streaming method. This means we must set up a Kismet sequence to tell the content to load and unload. It can also be done by **Distance**, or it can be **Always Loaded**.

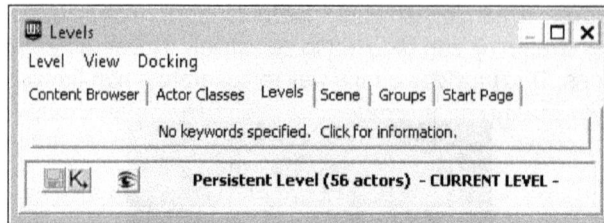

5. Right-click on the entry *LowerLevel* and choose **Make Current**. Any changes you make in UDK would then be saved out (like a Photoshop **Smart Object**) to the *Packt_06_LowerLevel.UDK* scene.

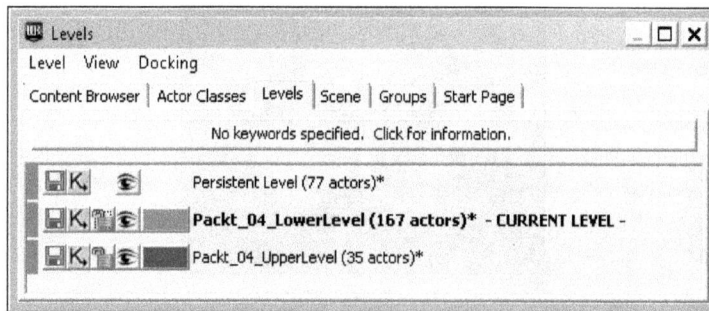

6. Build the scene [🔍] to look for duplicate items in the **Map Check** feedback that pops up after the build. There should be two copies of a type of StaticMesh beam in the floor and ceiling of the lower level.

7. Delete one of the floor beams and one of the ceiling beams, then select the two that remain. Right-click on them and choose **Level | Move to Selected Level**, or press *Ctrl +M*, which will place these into *Lower_Level*, since that's where they belong. A good way to check this is to use the **Eye** icons [👁] in the **Levels** dialog to toggle the visibility of level content.

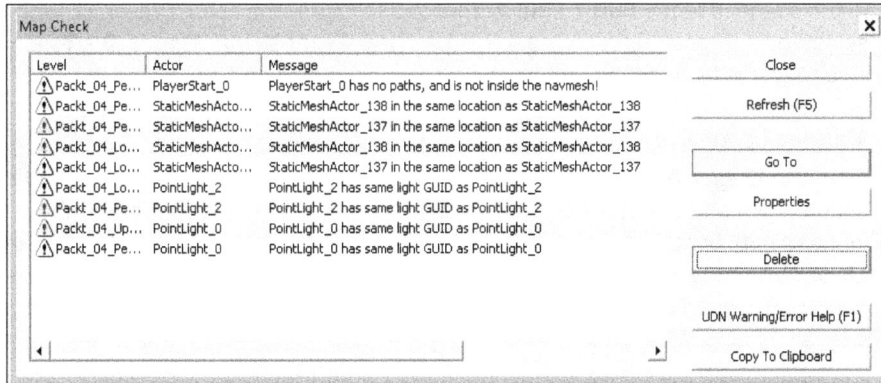

8. In the **Levels** list, right-click on the entry **Persistent Level** and choose **Make Current**.

9. You will also have two duplicate PointLights exposed during the **Build All** we did before. You can likewise deal with these in the **Map Check** feedback by selecting the extra ones and pressing **Delete**. Set the original two so they belong to the *Persistent level* by highlighting them, pressing **Go To**, then pressing *Ctrl + M*.

10. The erroneous duplicate objects and lights were included here to show how such problems may be solved easily. Save what you have, then PIE. You will notice that only the persistent level content is visible.

11. Press *Esc*, then go to Kismet [K]. Create a new **Level Loaded** event and hook this up to **Load** nub of a **New Action | Level | Stream Levels**.

12. In the **Stream Levels** action's property **Seq Act_Multi Level Streaming | Levels** add a new entry [ ] and in the **Level Name** channel type *Packt_06_LowerLevel*, and the node should get a green tick.

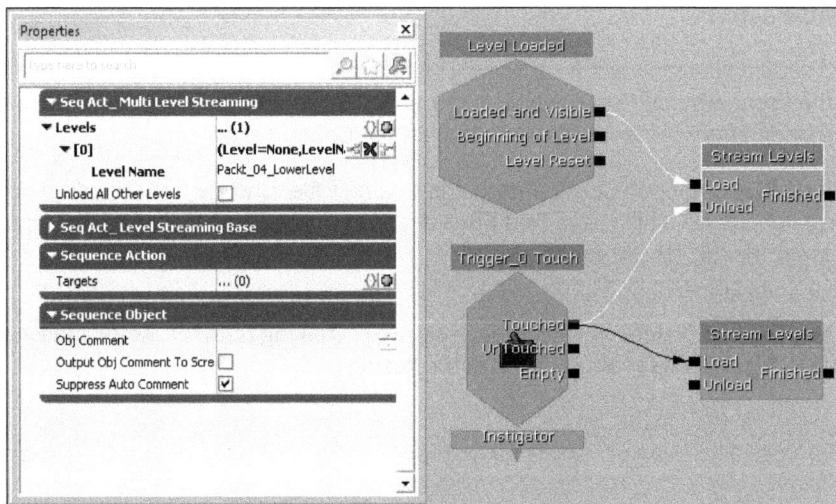

13. In the scene, use the **Edit | Find Actors** tool to locate the actor *Trigger_0*. With this selected, in Kismet, right-click and choose **New Event Using Trigger_0 | Touch**. This trigger is by a toppling metal door, so you can also find it by going into the Sub-sequence *Lift Attachments* and looking for the trigger event firing off the **Matinee** *UpperDoor*.

14. From the ***Trigger Touch*** event extend a wire to the **Unload** nub of the ***Stream Levels*** action. Then add another ***Stream Levels*** action, and hook the **Touched** nub up to its **Load** nub. For this second ***Stream Levels*** action, in its property **Seq Act_Multi Level Streaming | Levels** add a new entry and in the **Level Name** channel type *Packt_06_UpperLevel*, and the node should get a green tick.

15. You can do a lot of back and forth interchanges between streaming level content. If you want to see the level streaming before or after from what we've set up, PIE then after you trigger the metal door open, go back where you started from to see what has been unloaded. In normal gameplay, the elevator wouldn't let us go back down to the unloaded part unless it was reloaded again. An example is provided in the map *Packt_06_Persistent_DEMO.UDK*.

Spawning objects from a hit impact

This recipe is a guest tutorial. **Ryan Pelcz** gave me his kind permission to adapt his solution to spawning objects as a result of impacts upon another object. Imagine a vending machine that spits out plastic balls full of sweets each time it is hit. This is the kind of scenario we're going to create. The goal is to introduce the concept of **placeable actors**, **spawnable actors**, **actors taking damage**, and **applying impulses** to rigid bodies.

How to do it...

The placeable actor:

We have to code a placeable actor because it will have functionality a regular StaticMesh placed in the scene wouldn't have, which is the ability to produce other objects. Placeable objects are added from the **Actor Classes** tab not the Content Browser.

1. Close UDK and open ConTEXT and create a new file. Choose from the drop-down Highlighters list which says **Text Files** the item *UnrealEd* so that text we'll type is format friendly for UnrealScript.

2. The code starts: `class MyPowerCore extends Actor placeable;`

3. The `placeable` lets us select the asset we're making from the **Actor Classes** tab in the Content Browser and place it in the scene.

4. Adding the following lines gives us the mesh that will be placed using this class:

```
DefaultProperties
{
Begin Object class=StaticMeshComponent
  Name=PowerCoreMesh
//The line below sets the actual asset used, and can be replaced
to suit.
StaticMesh = Staticmesh'Packt.Mesh.PowerCore'
End Object
Components.Add(PowerCoreMesh)
}
```

5. So we have an object defined as a mesh from our Packt package, and now we can configure it. Add these lines also within the `DefaultProperties` brackets {}:

```
DrawScale=3 //may be adjusted to suit
bCollideActors=true
bBlockActors=true
```

6. `DrawScale` lets us declare how big or small we want the placed mesh to be, relative to the asset's built-in size. The next two lines ensure our mesh has collision when something touches it. The asset has already had a collision model defined in the Static Mesh Editor.

7. Save this code to `C:\UDK\~\Development\Src\MyGame\Classes\MyPowerCore.UC`.

The code above will work as it is, but it would give a warning about inefficient lighting following the game build. To avoid this, add below the first line's class declaration:

```
var() const editconst DynamicLightEnvironmentComponent
LightEnvironment;
```

Then, at the start of the `DefaultProperties` section, create a new object:

```
Begin Object Class=DynamicLightEnvironmentComponent
Name=MyLightEnvironment
bEnabled=TRUE
End Object
LightEnvironment=MyLightEnvironment
Components.Add(MyLightEnvironment)
```

Then you can add the lines:

```
LightEnvironment=MyLightEnvironment
bAcceptsLights=True
```

in the definition of the StaticMesh object you added already *PowerCoreMesh*.

8. Start UDK to compile the script changes, and re-run UDK, assuming the script compiles without a mistake. Once UDK loads, open any scene and press *Ctrl + Shift + F* and switch to the **Actor Classes** tab. Our placeable actor will show up in the **Uncategorized** category of actors as *MyPowerCore*. Highlight this and in the scene, right-click and choose **Add MyPowerCore Here**. Be sure it works before continuing.

The spawnable actor

1. Start a new class in ConTEXT to fulfill our *Ball* requirement:

```
class MyBall extends KActorSpawnable;

DefaultProperties
{
Begin Object Name=StaticMeshComponent0 //not Name = Static...
StaticMesh=StaticMesh'Packt.Mesh.BouncyBall'
bNotifyRigidBodyCollision=true
HiddenGame=false
ScriptRigidBodyCollisionThreshold=0.001
LightingChannels=(Dynamic=true)
End Object
Components.Add(StaticMeshComponent0)
CollisionComponent=StaticMeshComponent0
DrawScale=0.25
bCollideActors=true
bNoDelete=false
bStatic=false
}
```

2. As before the `DefaultProperties` define the mesh this class will use, and then describes the visibility, collision and lighting for it.

3. Save this code to `C:\UDK\~\Development\Src\MyGame\Classes\MyBall.UC`.

4. Right now if our object was spawned it wouldn't do much, so let's add some motion for it. Type the following in the *MyBall.UC* code under the first line:

```
simulated function PostBeginPlay()
{
local Vector SetDirection;
SetDirection.x = 15*FRand()-15*FRand();
SetDirection.y = 15*FRand()-15*FRand();
SetDirection.z = 150;
StaticMeshComponent.AddImpulse(SetDirection);
Super.Postbeginplay();
}
```

5. Save again. Here we are declaring a vector (direction from a position in space) randomly within the area the *Ball* spawns in X and Y and an upwards movement which is set to 150. Gravity will take over, given the object is a **KActor**.

Spawning upon Take Damage

1. Let's spawn the *Ball* up out of the top of the *PowerCore* when the *PowerCore* takes damage from being shot at by the player. Open up the *MyPowerCore* class and drop this rather long line in after the first line (it is an existing function in UnrealScript). All we need to know for now is that this will get called whenever the *Powercore* is shot:

```
var actor NewBall; //tells the function what it will create

simulated function TakeDamage(int DamageAmount, Controller
EventInstigator, vector HitLocation, vector Momentum,
class<DamageType> DamageType, optional TraceHitINfo HitInfo,
optional Actor DamageCauser)
```

2. Directly underneath, furnish the function with an instruction about what to do:

```
{
spawnNewBall();
}
```

3. This declaration of an actor variable to hold our soon to be spawned *Ball* now has a **TakeDamage** potential, but it doesn't have a spawn function yet. Enter the following code snippet next:

```
function spawnNewBall()
{
local Vector myLoc;
myLoc.x = Location.x;
myLoc.y = Location.y;
myLoc.z = Location.z+70;
newBall = spawn(class'MyBall',,,myLoc, Rotation);
'log("ShockRifle secondary fire (RMB) impacted on a PowerCore and
spawned:" @ NewBall);
}
```

4. Once again we are declaring a local vector variable and we're calling this one `myLoc`. We then set the 'x' and 'y' coordinates of `myLoc` to the 'x' and 'y' coordinates of the placed *MyPowerCore*. The 'z' coordinate will be placed 70 units above the box so that it is not spawned inside of the mesh (that would be bad). We spawn the *Ball* class at the location of `myLoc` using the line `newBall = spawn(class'Ball',,,myLoc, Rotation);` and we're done.

5. Having completed the two classes, all that needs to be done is load a level in UDK and press *Ctrl + Shift + F*, then look in the **Uncategorized** category of the **Actor Classes** tab, assuming you have the default **Show Categories** option ticked. Here you should see *MyPowerCore*. Highlight it, and in the scene, right-click and choose **Add MyPowerCore Here**. An example is provided in the map *Packt_06_Spawnable_DEMO.UDK* and you will notice a placed *ShockRifle* pickup. This is because the default *LinkGun* class doesn't include the ability to shoot up rigid bodies. You have to use the right-click fire method with the ShockRIfle.

6. An example scene is provided: *Packt_06_Spawnable_DEMO.UDK*. The example map uses the classes *PacktPowerCore* and *PacktBall* which are otherwise the same as *MyPowerCore* and *MyBall* you've just created.

> If you want to push the balls around using the character, open *MyPawn.UC* and add this line to the `DefaultProperties` section: `bPushesRigidBodies=true`.

How it works.

This was originally a tutorial by **Ryan Pelcz** (`http://pelcz.squarespace.com`). In essence all that's changed here are the actors used, and the formatting is arranged to match the book's recipe style. In short, this is what happens: The *Powercore* is declared as a placeable actor and that automatically means we'll find it in the **Actor Classes** tab, and then the *Ball* is declared as a spawnable and just needs something to spawn it. So we have a function which is a lot like the **Take Damage** event in Kismet but instead sits inside our *Powercore* class. Given there's some damage taken, it sets a location and impulse for a spawned *Ball*.

> Note, the DamageTaken depends on the secondary action of the ShockRifle in order to create a physics impulse on the placed Powercore. Other damage types won't work.

To have a bit of fun with this, and make the spawned balls bounce and float around, try changing gravity via Kismet using a *SetGravity -100* command inside a **Console Command** action (**New Action | Misc | Console Command**) hooked up to a **Level Loaded** event. For this to work, you'll have to **Play on PC** [🖥], so if you want to change it in config so that it works in PIE too, look to `C:\UDK\~\UDKGame\Config\DefaultGameUDK.INI` and scroll down to find the section `[Engine.WorldInfo]`. There you will see the next line is related to Gravity: `DefaultGravityZ=-520.0`. Changing that value will permanently affect gravity in game, so it would be best to comment out the line, then paste it in a copy of the line with the changed value. That way you won't have to remember the UDK's default value. You may also want to adjust RigidBody responsiveness by changing the next line: `RBPhysicsGravityScaling=2.0` to `0.02`, so there is a noticeable effect.

If you don't want the player to have control while they're off the ground, you can add: `AirControl=+0.005` and `DefaultAirControl=+0.0001` as an entry in your *MyPawn.UC* `DefaultProperties` section. Including the `+` here matters!

See also

The asset we're spawning in this recipe has a Physical Material Mask to set impact results. Hitting it in one spot may produce a different sound than in another spot.

See *Chapter 9, The Devil is in the Details!*

7
Hi, I'm Eye Candy!
Ways to Create and Use Particle Effects

In this chapter, we will cover the following topics:

- ▶ Editing the color graph of a particle over time
- ▶ Animating particles using SubUV charts
- ▶ Adding one particle's movement to another
- ▶ Making collision detection work for particles
- ▶ Controlling sort order for translucent Materials
- ▶ Making animated textures using particle systems
- ▶ Making trails with AnimTrail TypeData
- ▶ Assigning Level Of Detail (LOD) to a particle system
- ▶ Leaving a bloody trail

Introduction

UDK includes a bag of fireworks called **Cascade**. Cascade is not only a sprite particle generator but can also produce trailing ribbons, laser beams, and geometry arrays. Cascade has many features, and can be daunting to learn, but with patience proves to be a very complete and comfortable Particle Editor. Earlier in the book, in *Chapter 2, Notes From an Unreal World*, in the recipe *Creating a steamy plume in Cascade*, we covered the basics of a particle emitter's anatomy.

Now we'll look closer. One of the most important features of Cascade to learn early on is handling the **Distribution** values for the various modules, which provide a way to set values or value ranges to parameters of an emitter, such as direction, speed, age, color, and rotation. Unfortunately it is also a lot to cope with on your first try. Distributions are split up into **Constants** (static single values), **Vectors** (XYZ values), and **Particle Parameters** (named values something else can access and affect). The properties of each parameter can have **Min** and **Max** ranges to create variety and complexity. Particles move and they change color, so they also have **Point** entries [0], [1], [2], and so on, to add curves for animation through keys on a timeline. If there were a pipeline for creating particles that could be followed every time, it might begin with assigning a Material, deciding which modules will work to create the effect, then working out the distribution values to control how much, and how fast, and how big. Once you are comfortable with that you can look at making Emitters talk to each other through events and through Kismet and in code.

Editing the color graph of a particle over time

Changing colors in a particle using a curve is (for some reason) a little tricky to get used to in UDK. The UI design is probably to blame for this. Once you know how to enable curve display for a particular module, this topic can probably be considered rather easy. While we're going to focus on changing particle colors using RGB values, the same approach also works with changing alpha in order to fade visible particles and make them transparent.

How to do it...

1. Create a new particle system, *YourFolder.Cascade.ColorChanger*. In the **Required** module of this, set the **Material** to a white one, such as *Envy_Effects.flares. Materials.M_EFX_Flare_Burst_01* that comes with UDK.

2. We chose that Material because it has a **Particle | Vertex Color** node that the *TextureSample* is moderated by through a *Multiply* node, as shown in the next screenshot. Without it present, the color change we want to make won't work. You can read more information about this in the **Vertex Color** section of this page: `http://udn.epicgames.com/Three/ParticleExamples.html`.

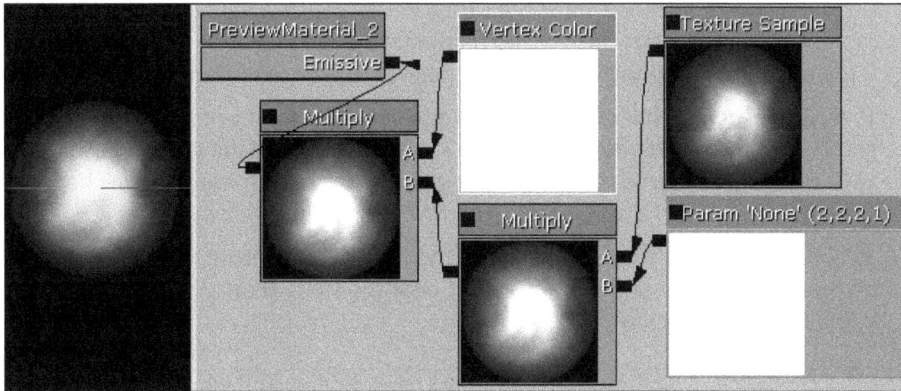

3. To change the color, in the default settings, we have a ***Color Over Life*** module with a **[0] Constant XYZ** for the emit time and **[1] Constant XYZ** for the end time. The constant XYZ gives us a Red-Green-Blue channel. 0 values are nothing, values which are 1 are 100%, and values above 1 will produce glows.

4. For this Material, set the **[0] Constant XYZ** to 5,0,0. This should make the particle stream a strong red. Now we want to animate this value.

5. Go to the ***Color Over Life*** module and click the green graph icon [🖼] on the right. You might expect this functionality to work through a right-click menu in the Curve Editor itself, but things get a lot easier once you know to click the green graph icon. Its location in the editor merits committing to memory, as there is no control in the Curve Editor to summon this toggle.

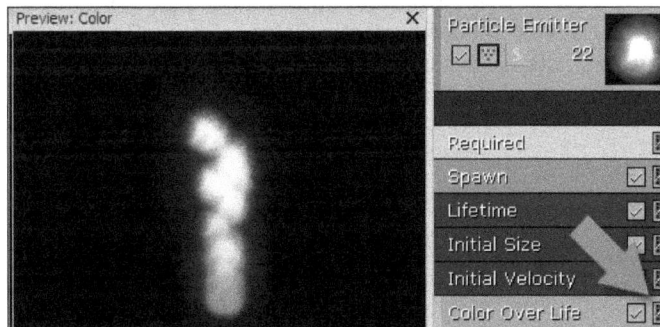

6. Once the curves are showing in the Curve Editor, you can right-click on them to remove them. It doesn't remove the animation, only the display of the graph. Right-click on the **AlphaOverLife** curve header, and choose **Remove Curve**.

7. To navigate the graph, there is a **Pan Mode** icon [✛] for moving the view of the graph, and a **Zoom Mode** icon [«] for scaling the view of the graph. A zoom with the *LMB* will vertically scale the view of the graph, a zoom with the *RMB* will horizontally scale the view of the graph, and *LMB + RMB* will uniformly scale.

8. To actually modify a curve, *Ctrl-drag* on the keys or handles on the curve. Drag down on the upper handle of the graph curve, near the value **5** (which we set for X = Red in the **Emitter**), as shown here:

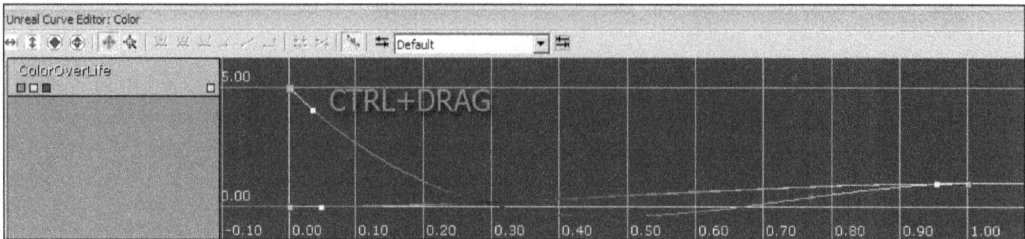

9. A nice feature of the **Color Over Life** curve is that the curve in the graph will show the color setting per frame. So the curve, as it starts to cross below zero, tints blue. Notice that we have thus produced three colors with only two keys.

10. Animating a change in this curve, to vary the emit or kill color over time, can be done by changing the **Distribution** type of the **Color | Color Over Life** property to a **DistributionVectorParticleParameter** and also adding a *Parameter Color* module under it. Enter *Colorful* in the **Parameter Color** module's **Color Param** field. The values aren't animated in the Cascade Curve Editor but instead through *Matinee*, using a **New Float Particle Parameter Track**, detailed next.

11. Now we know what's involved, first, change the particle. Set the particle values as shown below. These values can be altered to give different colors, so experiment with the **Min** and **Max** ranges. Make sure the **Min** values are always less than the **Max** values. Also, values between 0 and 1 are usually sufficient.

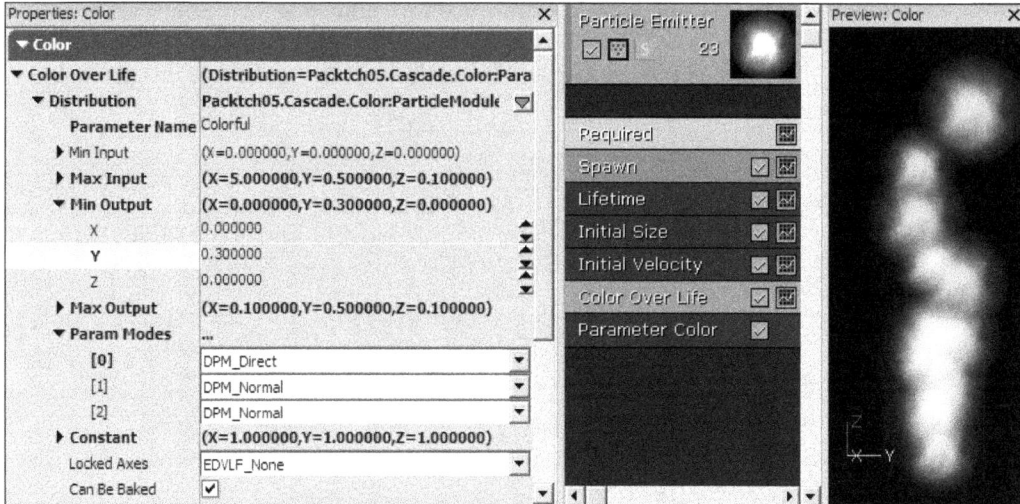

12. The downside of this change is that now we cannot set a different start and end color within the particle's life. Notice that there is a **Parameter Name** field. Type *Colorful* here. Also notice there are three **Param Modes**. Change the first to *DPM_Direct*. If this isn't changed, the colors will not be effected by Matinee.

13. Now save your particle system, and create a scene with a ground plane, a light, and a PlayerStart. Add your particle system as an **Emitter** actor in front of the player start, then open Kismet with the **Emitter** actor highlighted.

14. In Kismet, add a **New Event | Level Loaded** and a *Matinee* (M) hooked up to it. Double-click the *Matinee*. Right-click on the Matinee Editor in the dark gray space under **ALL** and choose **New Empty Group**. Name the track as you like, then right-click on that track and choose **New Float Particle Param Track**. For this new track, enter in the properties for **Param Name** that we typed in the Emitter modules just before, the **Color Param:** *Colorful*. With the track selected, add a key by pressing *Enter* or hitting the keyframe icon [⇥] in the top left corner under the **File** menu. Set keys that change the value of the parameter (which is limited to one value, not an RGB value) over about 12 seconds.

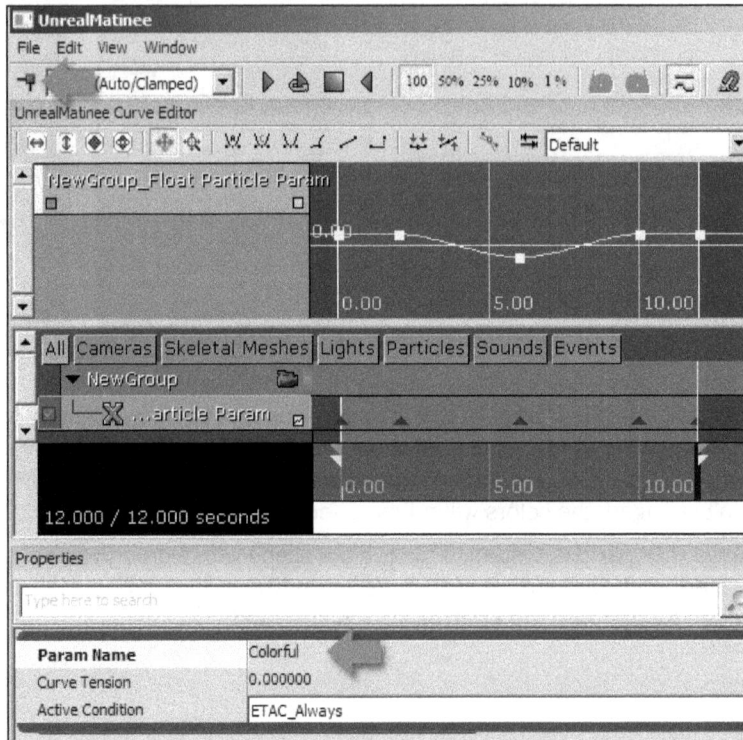

15. In Kismet, for the *Matinee* properties, set **Looping** on, supposing you have set the 0s and 12s frames for the color change to be the same, as above. Ensure the Emitter actor in the scene is assigned through an *Object Variable* to the *Matinee*. An example map is included: *Packt_07_ColorChange_DEMO.UDK*.

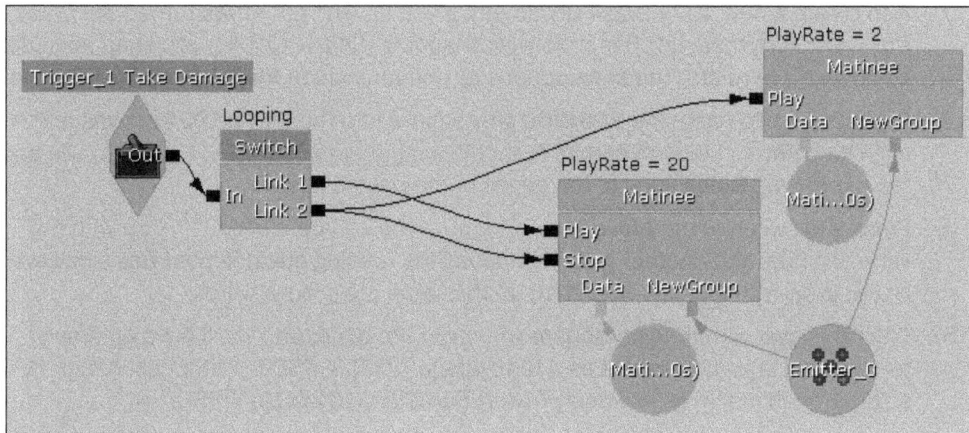

How it works...

This method exposes a named particle color track *Colorful* from the particle system to gradual change through keys in a Kismet **Matinee**. In some ways it seems a limitation that the Parameter method only allows animation of one track. It was pointed out that the **VertexColor** node in the Material Editor should be used to influence particle colors using the Material. You can additionally drive the **Opacity** or the **Emissive** channel of a Material using the **Alpha** of the **Texture Sample**, to create fading or dimming particles.

Animating particles using SubUV charts

Suppose you are creating an explosion effect for a film. You might go out and shoot video of flames against a black background so you can mix that footage into the effect. For a one second blast you'd wind up with 30 or so frames, which is no problem in a film, but in a game, you have to handle all those frames. One method is to spread the frames from the explosion onto a single grid and then read off each square in the grid in series. In Cascade, the term **SubUV** refers to rendering part of a texture onto a sprite. You can combine textures onto a grid, such as 4x4 or 8x8, and tell UDK to use SubUV for the texture and it will parse each of the grid squares for content to render. This can be done by stepping through the grid squares in order (linearly) or randomly.

Getting ready

Furnishing a 1024x1024 SUBUV texture card grid:

1. I'm going to assume the use of Photoshop for image processing in the book but you could use any equivalent image editor like GIMP from www.gimp.org. In Photoshop, create a 256x256 document. Fill the canvas with 50% gray. Press *Ctrl + A* to select all, then *Ctrl + C* to copy.

2. Also create a new 1024x1024 document. If you haven't got **rulers** turned on, press *Ctrl + R* to turn them on. This is so view snapping (*Shift + Ctrl + ;*) can snap to guides coming off the rulers. The snap options by default include **View | Snap To | Guides**.

3. Press *Ctrl + V* to paste the 256x256 gray square into the 1024x1024 canvas and align it up into the top left corner. It should snap there accurately. From the side and top rulers drag **Guide** lines to the edges of the pasted square.

4. Press *V* to switch to the **Move Tool**, and move the square along to line up with the vertical guide. Add another guide line along the leading edge. Repeat this sideways to fill the page with four squares, then do the same going downwards.

5. Clear the layer with the gray square when you are done, and you'll have an empty texture card layout. Save this as a template to *Grid4x4.PSD* for later use. A copy is also provided just in case: *Packt_TextureCardBlank1024x1024.PSD*.

If you use 3D software to create your textures, the rendered frames can be processed using contact sheet automation. For 32bit Photoshop, use Adobe Bridge. For 64bit Photoshop, you may want to check: http://sourceforge.net/projects/ps-scripts/files/ContactSheetX/ and get **ContactSheetX** which you can unpack then install by choosing **File | Scripts | Browse**. Choose the **CSX** install script, for instance *InstallCSX-1_5.jsx*. After installation, restart Photoshop; you'll then see the script available under **File | Automate | Contact Sheet X**; clicking this shows its dialog for processing a folder of rendered images into a grid directly.

In this recipe, we'll be putting this 4x4 texture card concept into practice, making a flock of dragons for the background of an environment. The source for the dragon is an animation in the included 3ds Max file *PACKT_Dragon_fly01.MAX*, which has a 16 frame loop, from the side view, of a dragon flapping its wings.

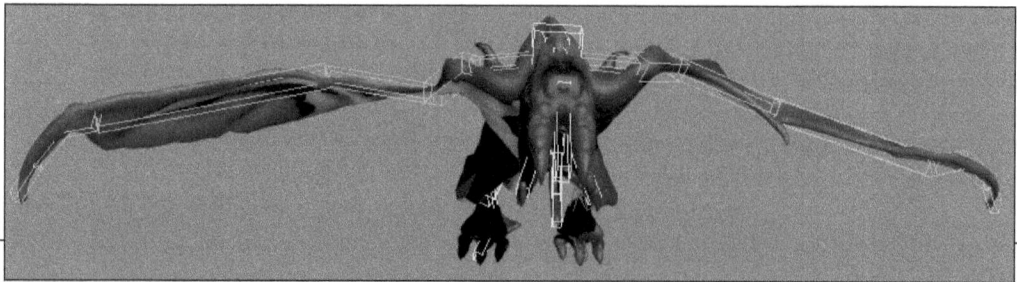

How to do it...

Making the SubUV texture:

1. The frames have been rendered to .TGA files which include an alpha in *MonsterFlySide####.TGA*. Open these in Photoshop, and your *Grid4x4.PSD* that you made previously, or if you didn't make the template, you can use: *Packt_TextureCardBlank1024x1024.psd*.

2. From each monster image, press *Ctrl + A*, then *Ctrl + C*, then switch to the grid and press *Ctrl + V*. Position the images sequentially going first along the top line 1,2,3,4, then the second line 5,6,7,8, then the third line 9,10,11,12, and the fourth line 13,14,15,16. There are 16 frames, so the layout fits neatly. Save this to your UDK content folder as: *Test_TextureMonster_Diff_1024x1024.PNG*. The result of this is shown in the next image, already imported into UDK.

3. We also need to generate a black and white cut out of the dragon frames. So go to the channels of the first .TGA monster image file and highlight the **Alpha** channel (so it appears selected) and press *Ctrl + A* then *Ctrl + C*. Now select the **RGB** channel and press *Ctrl + V*. The black and white content from the alpha channel will replace the colors.

4. Repeat that with every .TGA file for the monster flying, to provide you with just the alpha component, then select, copy, and paste the alpha content into the template, as in step 2. Save the result to your UDK content folder as: *Test_TextureMonster_Alpha_1024x1024.PNG*. Again, the result is shown below in the **Alpha** channel of the UDK *Texture Sample*, which we'll set up next.

5. In UDK, import *Test_TextureMonster_Diff_1024x1024.PNG* and *Test_TextureMonster_Alpha_1024x1024.PNG*, then create a new Material: *YOURFOLDER.Material.TestDragonFlock_Mat*.

6. For the *PreviewMaterial_0* node, set the property **Material | Blend Node** to *Blend_Translucent*. Set the **Lighting Mode** to *MLM_NonDirectional*, which will reduce the chance of the particle appearing unlit. And turn on **Two Sided** so we can see the dragon on the particle sprite no matter what angle it's viewed from (although it should be set to face the camera all the time anyway).

7. In the browser, highlight your imported alpha image *Test_TextureMonster_Alpha_1024x1024.PNG*, hold *T*, and then click in the Material Editor to bring it in. Hook the resulting texture sample to the **Opacity** channel of *PreviewMaterial_0*.

8. In the browser, highlight *Test_TextureMonster_Diff_1024x1024.PNG*, the diffuse texture image, and hook it up to the **Emissive** and **Diffuse** channels of **PreviewMaterial**, as in the next screenshot. Compile the Material, and save your package.

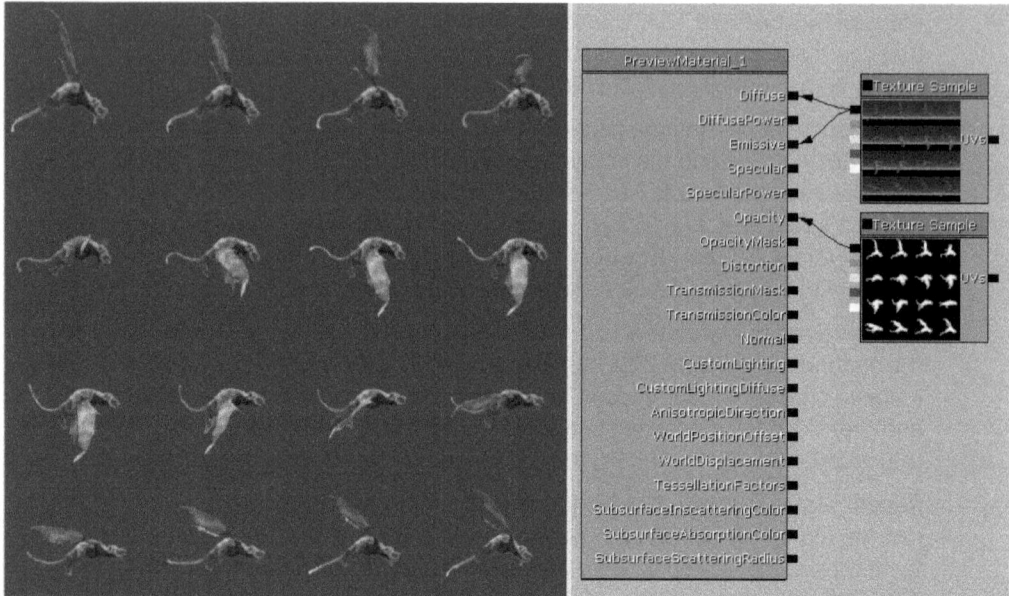

Setting up the particle asset to use the SubUV

1. The next step is to right-click in the content browser and choose **New Particle System**. At the prompt, set the asset to be *YOURFOLDER.Cascade.TestDragonFlock*.

2. The default particle system is not very inspiring, with a little upward jet of sprites with a *DefaultParticle* Material. Let's swap that texture for the *TestDragonFlock_Mat* you just made. Highlight that Material in the browser, then in the particle system, click on the **Required** module of the **Emitter** and in its properties expand **Emitter** to show the first channel **Material**. Here there is a green arrow [⬕] you can press to swap in your browser highlighted Material.

3. Set the property **Emitter | Sort Mode | PSORTMODE_ViewProjDepth**, which will mean dragons closer to the camera will render in front of dragons further away.

4. What you'll see is an upward plume of the texture sheet showing all the dragons in the grid, which may look kind of cool but isn't our goal. We need to tell the **Emitter** just to render part of the texture UV space. Scroll down in the properties to **Sub UV**. Set the **Interpolation Method** to *PSUVIM_Linear*, the **Sub Images Horizontal** to 4, and the **Sub Images Vertical** to 4. Now you will see lots of individual dragons shooting upwards.

5. At present the dragons aren't flapping their wings. To activate that, right-click in the space under the ***Color Over Life*** module of the **Emitter** and choose **SubUV | SubUV Movie**. In its properties turn on **Use Emitter Time**, and set the **Frame Rate | Distribution | Constant** to a value between 20 and 30. This sets the frame rate the animation will play, which was originally a snappy 30fps.

6. Move down from the ***Required*** module to the ***Spawn*** module. Set its **Spawn | Rate | Distribution | Constant** to 1 and **Rate Scale | Distribution | Constant** to 1.1. This changes the number of spawned dragons.

7. Move down from the ***Spawn*** module to the ***Lifetime*** module and set the property **Lifetime | Lifetime | Distribution | Min** 16 and **Max** 16. This means that all the dragons will live the same duration, which prevents dragons popping out of existence along their path. We won't be showing the moment of spawning and death of the dragons. It will be hidden from the player by scene rocks.

8. Move down from the ***Lifetime*** module to the ***Initial Size*** module and set the property **Size | Start Size | Max**: X=100, Y=100, Z=100 and **Min**: X=75, Y=75, and Z=75, which gives us a slight variety in the dragon sizes.

9. Move down from the ***Initial Size*** module to the ***Initial Velocity*** module, and change the property **Velocity | Start Velocity | Distribution | Max** to X=35, Y=0, Z=5 and the **Min** to X=30, Y=9, Z=5. This creates a sideways motion for the dragons so they fly along their facing axis. Then, the speed variation provides a touch of extra realism though you'll want values that aren't too extreme. You may need to swap the XY values to alter the direction the dragons travel.

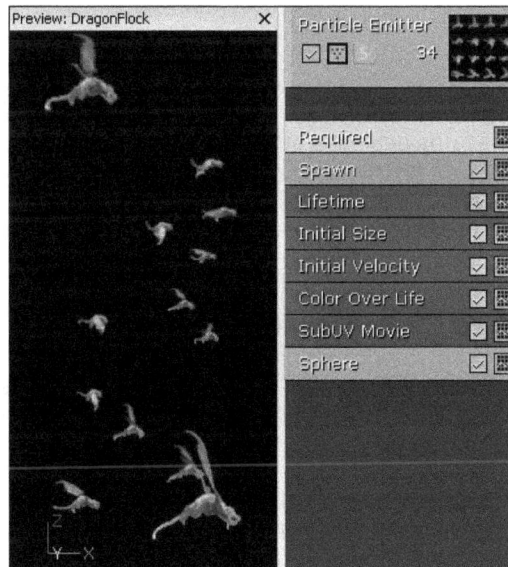

10. At the moment, the dragons disperse in a line, all from the same point. Let's spread them out. Under the **SubUV Movie** module you added, right-click and choose **Location | Sphere**. In the properties for the **Sphere** module, set **Surface Only** to be ticked on. Set the **Start Radius | Distribution | Constant** to be 200 or so. This sets the area for the flock, so really that is up to you. Too small a radius will make the dragons appear to overlap too closely.

How it works...

A demo scene is included in the provided content: *Packt_07_SubUV_DEMO.UDK* which includes the dragons flying against a sunset. They even react to the DominantDirectionalLight's light shafts, as shown in the previous screenshot.

SubUVs are generally used in situations where the particle content requires an animated source, such as flames, explosions, spinning objects, or flapping wings. In UDK the SubUV settings are a component of the **Required** module of an **Emitter**, but you also need to load an additional module of SubUV controls, called a **SubUV Movie**.

As we saw in Photoshop, the grid size must be a subdivision of the image resolution; for instance 64x64 goes into 1024x1024 16 times, which gives a 4x4 horizontal and vertical distribution.

You then set the type of interpolation for parsing the 4x4 grid. A sequential animation like wings flapping will be linear, while smoke might be random. Finally, we add a **Location** setting such as a *sphere* to situate the particle spawn points.

Adding one particle's movement to another

Event modules allow multiple particle systems within an **Emitter** to reference each other. For example, if you have a rocket particle dying, its location would be hard to predict, but it can send a notify about its pending death to another particle system, an explosion effect, which will then spawn at that point where the rocket particle died.

How to do it...

Setting up the base particle:

1. Open the particle system *PacktFX.Cascade.ParticleEventStart* from the *PacktFX* package.

2. Select the **Particle Emitter** label which includes the on/off checkbox and with this highlighted bright orange, look into the main properties, and change the **Emitter Name** there to *Circles*.

3. Under the label, in the *Required* module, the Material should be set to *Envy_Effects. Energy.Materials.M_EFX_Energy_Loop_Mesh*, which you can see in the next screenshot. Base parameters have already been set. Proceed on to the *Spawn* module.

4. Let's generate particles in discrete bursts rather than continually. For this example we will be using a **BurstList** to control particle spawning rather than a **Constant Rate**. Set the **Spawn | SpawnRate | Constant** to 0, to effectively cancel out the default stream. For the moment, you'll see no particles. Underneath, expand **BurstList** and press the add entry icon [🖳]. Set the **Burst List | [0] | Count** property to 2.

5. Ensure the *Lifetime* module's **Lifetime | Distribution | Min** and **Max** are both 5.0.

6. Set the Initial *Size* module's **Start Size | Distribution | Constant** to X=33.0, Y=33.0, Z=0.0, and set the *Initial Velocity* module's **Start Velocity | Distribution | Max | X = 222.0** and the **Min** to -222.0 so that you will get a generation of particles only sideways. This creates a result that might entertain fans of Mr. Feynman. We don't have any mechanism for knowing in advance whether the particle will break left, right, or both...

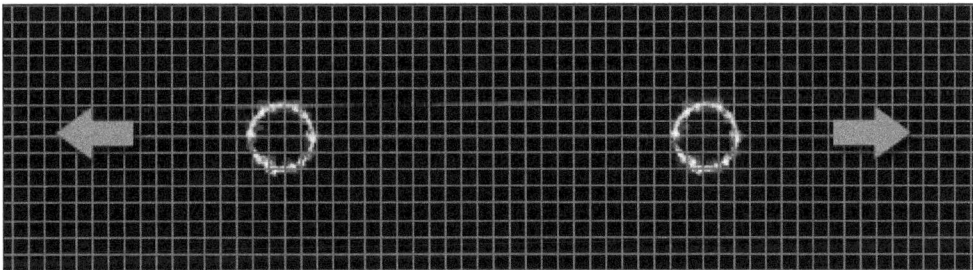

7. Digressions on the uncertainty principle aside, right-click underneath the **Color Over Life** module and choose new **Size | Size By Life** module. We'll make the particles grow as they age. In the properties of the **Size By Life** module, set the **Distribution** to **Constant Curve**. Add two **Points** entries and leave the [0] values alone, and for the [1] values, set the **In Val** to 2 and the **Out Val** to X=6, Y=6. This will cause the particles to appear to grow within that range from when they spawn to when they die.

8. To time the emission, in the **Required** module, set the **Duration | Emitter Duration** to 2.0, which will slow the rate of bursts slightly. Save for now.

Setting up the event for the secondary particles

1. Extend the particle system by right-clicking next to the existing one in the black space of the Cascade Editor. Choose **NewParticleSpriteEmitter**. Highlight its label and in the main properties change the **Emitter Name** to *Halos*.

2. Back in the new **Emitter** *Halos*, set the **Required** module so the property **Emitter | Material** is *JW_LightEffects.LensFlares.Material.M_LF_Ring02*.

3. In the same section, set the **Sort Mode** to *PSORTMODE_Age_OldestFirst*. Set the **Duration | Emitter Duration** to 5.0 and the **Delay | Emitter Delay** to 0.5. The sort order tells the oldest particles to be in front, and the **Duration** sets the length particles will emit for. The **Delay** will let us stagger the onset of this **Emitter** relative to the first **Emitter**.

4. In the **Spawn** module, set the **Spawn | Rate | Distribution | Constant** to 11, and the **Rate Scale** also. This means we'll get quite a lot of circular halos.

5. In the **Lifetime** module, set the **Min** and **Max Lifetime** property both to 1. This means the halos will all live the same time, but not overly long.

6. For the **Initial Size** module, set the property **Size | Start Size | Distribution | Max | XYZ** all to 12.0. Set the **Min XYZ** to 1.0. This means the halos will have a range of sizes they can have when spawned.

7. For the **Initial Velocity** module, set the property **Velocity | Start Velocity | Distribution | Max** to X=0.0, Y=0.0, Z=3.0. Set the property **Velocity | Start Velocity | Distribution | Min** to X=0.0, Y=0.0, Z=-3.0. The **Start Velocity Radial** property can remain at 0.0. Turn on the checkbox below: **In World Space**. This sets the speed and direction in Z, a bit up and a bit down.

8. So far the Halos will be emitted in the center of the view and more or less stay put. To get the particles in the **Emitter** *Halos* to follow those in the **Emitter** *Circles*, right-click below the **Color Over Life** module and add a **Location | Emitter InitLoc** module. In its properties, in the **Location | Emitter Name** field type *Circles*. Turn on **Inherit Source Velocity**, so the particles move with those from *Circles*, then adjust the **Inherit Source Velocity** scale to 0.1, so the new particles are slower.

9. Under this module, add a **Location | Sphere** module, which will make the new particles emit over a larger area. For the **Sphere** module, expand the **Location | Start Radius** and set the **Distribution | Constant** property to 2.0.

10. Lastly, add an *Orbit* module. Expand the **Chaining** property panel, and choose a **Chain Mode**. Note the differences. I chose *EOChainMode_Link*.

11. Add an **Offset Amount | Distribution | Max** X=0, Y=12, Z=0. This spreads the *Halo* particles over a wider area. Turn on the property below, **Offset Options | Process During Spawn**. This makes the particles attempt to circle around the Sphere their spawn location is based on. Just for fun, click on **Process During Update** to see what happens. It doesn't matter if you leave it on or off. We're just experimenting with different looks to get accidental effects.

Glowing beams

1. Now let's create a more orderly motion, a kind of flapping wings effects for two beams of glowing light. In the original **Emitter** *Circles*, right-click under the *Size By Life* module and choose **New Event | Event Generator**. This is empty until you press the add entry icon [⊚]. In its **Events | [0] | Type** properties, choose from the list *EPET_Spawn*.

2. The primary feature of the properties of the event is the **Custom Name** field. For this one, enter *EmitGlow*. This is just a memorable name we'll use for a third **Emitter**. It allows *Circles* to talk to other Emitter modules with that name.

3. Right-click to the right of the **Emitter** *Halos* and choose **New ParticleSpriteEmitter**. Call the new **Emitter** *Glows* (not *EmitGlow* ... that comes later) by clicking on the top panel where the image is, and going to the **Emitter Name** field in the properties.

4. Highlight the *Required* module, and set the **Emitter | Material** channel to be *VH_Raptor.Materials.M_Raptor_Soft_Lite_Flair* which is just a fuzzy white dot.

5. By now you'll realize every emitter needs a spawn count, a life time and a size and speed value of some kind. We are going to base the speed on another **Emitter**, so you can right-click on the *Initial Velocity* module and remove it.

6. Let's whip through the other common parameters. In the *Spawn* module, set the **Spawn | Rate | Distribution | Constant** to 0.01 and the **Rate Scale | Distribution | Constant** to 1.0. Turn on **Process Spawn Rate**. In the *Lifetime* module, set the **Lifetime | Distribution | Min** to be 1.0 and the **Max** to be 3.0. In the *Initial Size* module, set the **Size | Start Size | Distribution | Max XYZ** and **Min XYZ** all to 25.0.

7. Drag the *Size By Life* module from the **Emitter** *Circles* across to the **Emitter** *Glows*. They will be made instances of each other and get a **+** suffix to indicate they are linked.

8. Lastly, add an **Event | EventRcvr Spawn** module and set the **Source | Event Generator Type** to *EPET_Spawn*, and the **Emit Name** to *EmitGlow*. Above, in the **Spawn | Spawn Count | Distribution | Constant** field enter 200. This gives us quite a lot of particles. Probably at first they will all overlap in the same place. Turn on the **Velocity | Inherit Velocity** property. Ensure the **Inherit Velocity Scale | X** is 1.0. **Inherit Velocity** means the **Emitter** *Glows* particles will follow **Emitter** *Circles* particles.

9. Add an **Orbit** module, and set the **Chaining | Chain Mode** property to *EOChainMode_Link*. Set the **Offset | Offset Amount | Distribution | Max** to X=0, Y=0, Z=8 and turn on **Offset Options | Process During Spawn** and **Use Emitter Time** below. Rotation properties will have little effect on this particle since the Material is a small circular dot. If you do not turn on **Process During Spawn** you will not see the flapping effect, and instead see just a static glowing ball.

How it works...

This effect is built of three differently behaving particles. The first is a *Circle* that moves. The second is a scattering of *Halos* that follow it and have an orbit-like motion. The third is a dot that *Glows* and spins around the Circle with a period and spawn rate balanced to give an appearance of a kind of flapping motion. The ***Event Generator*** tells the ***EventRcvr Spawn*** what to do, using the **Event Name** *EmitGlow*. The shared ***Size By Life*** module means the circle and glows both grow as they age. You can get very interesting variations by changing just a few of the XYZ multipliers for **Size** and **Velocity**.

> Here's something of a hot tip, no pun intended. To create a *Heat Haze* effect, just create an almost totally translucent Material with a noisy panning or rotating texture feeding into the ***PreviewMaterial*** node's **Distortion** channel. What **Distortion** does is offset whatever is rendered behind the particle somewhat, and if the **Distortion** input is animated it creates a shimmer. An example is in the Material *PacktFX.Material.HeatHaze_mat*. Then set this as the **Material** in the **Required** module of a particle system. Attach it to whatever you want the *Heat Haze* to emit from in the scene. An example of this approach in action is the heat plumes from the *Cicada* vehicle that ships with UDK.

Making collision detection work for particles

Particle collision with the world is a common requirement for realistic effects. Imagine spent shells from a machine gun clattering onto the ground. This kind of interaction is built into Cascade through the **Collision** module, which can be added to each system from the right-click menu below **Color Over Life**.

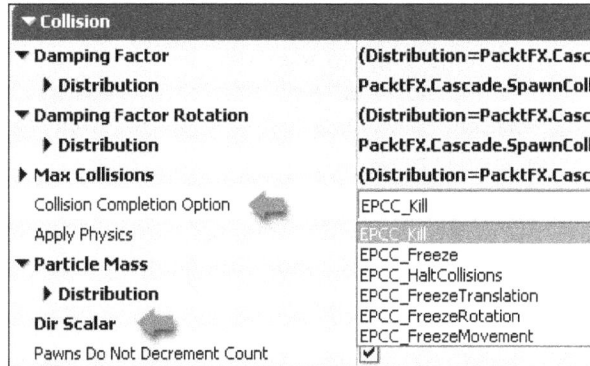

The main property for the **Collision** module is the **Collision Completion Option**, shown in the previous screenshot, which provides a roll-out list of possible results to occur upon a collision event. **Kill** will remove the collided particle. **Freeze** will stop it in its tracks. **HaltCollisions** will prevent further collisions. **FreezeTranslation**, **Rotation**, and **Movement** provide finer control over the stopping of the particle.

Another important property is **Dir Scalar**, further down, which is a value that can help close a gap or reduce overlap between killed particles and spawned particles in some situations. It will crop up in this example, which is going to not only show a particle collision but also spawn new particles at the hit location.

Getting ready

Open the map *Packt_07_CollisionSpawn_Start.UDK* from the provided content. This includes a ground plane, a tilted cube, lighting and a PlayerStart. Open the Content Browser and search for the particle system *PacktFX.Cascade.SpawnCollisionStart* which just includes two Emitters with Materials, the first being a red cross and the second a green tick. We won't be setting up the Lifetime, Size, Speed, or Spawn parameters. These have already been set, since otherwise we'd end up repeating the previous recipe all over again. Instead we'll focus on the Collision, Event, and Killing of the particles.

How to do it...

1. Double-click on the asset *PacktFX.Cascade.SpawnCollisionStart*.

2. In the **Emitter** *Cross*, click under the *Size by Life* module and choose
   Event | Event Generator. Right-click again and choose **Collision | Collision**.

3. Highlight the *Event Generator* module. In its properties, press the assign icon [✿]
   under **Events** to add an entry. Expand it to show **Events | [0] | Type** and from the list
   choose *EPET_Collision*. This means that when there is a collision it will fire the event.
   In the list, you will see other types to experiment with. If you were to choose *EPET_Any*
   for instance, the event would fire whenever there was a spawn, death, collision or call
   from Kismet. Further down the properties, enter *CollisionEvent* in the **Event Name**
   field. This sets what to listen for.

4. Highlight the *Collision* module you added to the **Emitter** *Cross*, and scroll down the
   properties to find **Collision Completion Option**. Choose *EPCC_Kill* from the list, but
   also note there are other options to try out. The particles will collide with actors in the
   scene and simply vanish. This may be okay in many situations, but let's add a result
   for the collision. We'll change the crosses to ticks.

5. In the **Emitter** *Tick*, right-click under the *Color Over Life* module and choose **Event
   | EventRcvr Spawn**. In this module's properties set the **Spawn | Spawn Count |
   Distribution | Constant** to 2.0 and in the **Velocity** property turn on **Inherit Velocity**.
   Under the **Source** property set **Event Generator Type** to *EPET_Collision*, so the
   Emitter knows what to listen for, and the **Event Name** will be *CollisionEvent*. Now the
   Emitter *Tick* can hear the event from the **Emitter** *Cross*.

6. At the moment, an Emitter actor in the scene based on the particle system asset
   would fire off *Cross* particles and when they hit an object they would turn into a
   stream of *Tick* particles. Let's add one last change to the system, which will be to
   adjust the direction of the spawn.

7. In the scene, there is already a cube. Drag the Particle System asset you've been
   making from the Content Browser into the scene, and place and rotate it so the
   stream of particles flows down from above towards the 45' upward facing side of
   the box. Check that the emitted *Cross* particles impact this and change to *Ticks*.

8. Double-click on the Particle System in the browser to re-open Cascade and in the
   Emitter *Tick*'s *EventRcvr Spawn* module, set the property **Velocity | Inherit Velocity
   Scale | Distribution | Constant** to X=0, Y=90, Z=1. This should force the stream of
   ticks to appear to deflect into the 45' angled surface.

9. A slight problem with the effect is that as the crosses turn to ticks there is a clear gap
   near the impact point. To adjust this, open the *Collision* module in the *Cross* system
   and for the property **Dir Scalar** change the default value to 20.0.

How it works...

This works because the **_Initial Velocity_** of the **Emitter** _Cross_ has a **Velocity | Start Velocity | Distribution | Max** and **Min** of X=1, Y=1, Z=90. The 1 is a very small increment for velocity. However, if it was set to 0.0 then we wouldn't be able to multiply it in the **Emitter** _Tick_'s inherit velocity scalar. The Z=90 provides the downwards speed. In the **Emitter** _Tick_'s **EventRcvr Spawn | Velocity | Inherit Velocity Scale** we multiply this Z value by 1.0 so it doesn't change. Then we take the Y value and multiple it by 90. So now we have two axes of speed ZY which gives us a 45' direction for the particles, which just appears to match the box. If, for instance, you rotate the Emitter actor 90' sideways and move it so the particles enter the box from a new angle, those values would not produce the same result. So some care has to be taken to get the conditions right. The screenshot below shows the intended result, and a completed Particle System asset _PacktFX.Cascade.SpawnCollisionDemo_ is used in _Packt_07_CollisionSpawn_DEMO.UDK_.

There's more...

Killing the particles

One reason to kill particles is to optimize performance. In our current example, the _Tick_ particles probably continue through the rainbow colored floor and continue downwards unseen and unneeded. To stop this, open the Particle System in Cascade and add to the **Emitter** _Tick_ a **Kill | Kill Height** module. Set it to so the **Absolute** property is turned on (so the height is measured in the world), have a **Height | Distribution | Constant** of 0.0 and the **Floor** property turned on (so particles will be killed below the height we set). The following screenshot shows the settings required to stop the particles. It works here because the floor geometry happens to be at the given world Z height of 0.0.

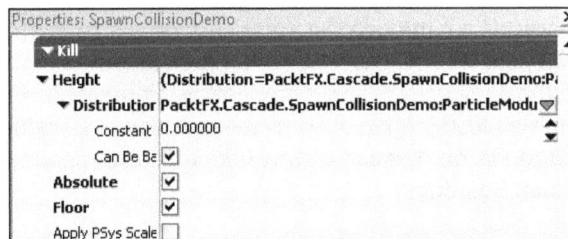

Controlling sort order for translucent Materials

Most particle emitters contain Materials with a translucent channel. If you have a few different particle Emitters overlapping, along with scene objects that also have translucent Materials, such as water or glass, you may see strange defects in the way the overlap occurs, as if objects behind are rendered in front. UDK requires us to set the priority of overlapping objects using, or the **sort order**, in the properties of each Emitter or object with a translucent Material. In the example, we're going to examine a simple waterfall scene with mist and swimmable water that has already been laid out, but needs the sort order fixed up.

Getting ready

Load and build the map *Packt_07_SortOrder_Start.UDK* and familiarize yourself with the layout. Notice that the waterfall is comprised of several Emitters stacked close to each other at the top and bottom of the waterfall.

How to do it...

1. Some of the particles cut through the water surface, which makes their effect look a little cramped. We'll fix this for each Emitter. Meanwhile, try selecting the water mesh in the perspective view. It probably won't respond. At the top of UDK's interface there is an icon [🔲] to allow direct selection of translucent surfaces in the viewport. Turn this on. You can do this from the **View** menu too, by clicking **Allow Translucent Selection**.

2. Select the water surface. This time it should be okay to do so, but there are a lot of transparent particle Emitters above the water mesh, so it is possibly best in this case to use the **Edit | Find Actors** tool [🔍] to grab it if clicking directly on it still doesn't work. The actor is called *StaticMeshActor_44.* You can also select the object in wireframe mode (*Alt + 2*) more readily.

3. Look at the misty cloud rising above the waterfall. It bisects the water surface, creating an edge. A way to handle the problem is with a **Depth Priority Group** change. This can be adjusted by setting their property **Static Mesh Component | Rendering | Depth Priority Group** from the default: **World** to: *SDPG_UnrealEdForeground*. In the waterfall scene, this is the solution for dealing with the misty cloud, which comes from *Emitter_14*. As seen in the following screenshots from another scene, the adjusted setting is shown on the right-hand side:

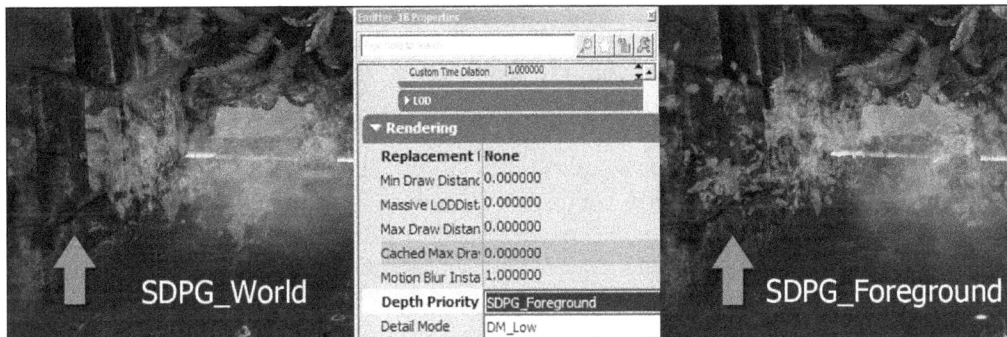

4. There is a limitation when using this solution. To illustrate it, select the yellow beam. Navigate the view so you are looking through it at the water and notice that where it crosses in front, the beam goes gray, as in the image below on the left. This could be fixed by setting it to have *SDPG_UnrealEdForeground* turned on, but then, if you view the beam from below the catwalk it is visible through the catwalk mesh, as shown in the next screenshot on the right. So what worked for the smoke doesn't work so well for the beam.

5. One related concern is that overlapping transparent content requires multiple draw calls to the same pixel on the screen, which demands more processing, and the larger the particle the more likely you'll have multiple screen draws. So it is good to keep the overall particle count under control. In the next screenshot, the left side shows the shader complexity (*Alt + 8*) of many overlapping particles, from an emitter with a high spawn count, and on the right there is a heavily reduced amount of particles. A darker value is better.

Making animated textures using particle systems

Particles generally render onto sprites, or cards, or little XY planes. This makes them great as sources for animated textures, which are usually square too. It's sometimes cheaper to render particles to a texture and place the texture in the scene instead of an expensive emitter. We've seen in the second recipe in this chapter that we can use the **SubUV** of a texture to have frame based animation within a particle system. This time we're going to capture a particle system playing to a video file, and process it back in as a texture card. In the texture import process we can set a special texture type called a **FlipBook** that will let us cycle the SubUV tiles of a texture just like we can in Cascade, but in the Material Editor. This will allow us to use the particles as a texture to moderate other texture components. Examples where this might be used in a real game are numerous. The effect created in this lesson looks like a turbulent foam. It could be projected as a LightFunction from a PointLight to create shifting shadows in a scene.

Getting ready

For this task we must do some work outside UDK, and you may need to grab a copy of CamStudio (free but feature light) or TechSmith's Camtasia (commercial but robust) screen recording tools. CamStudio can be obtained at www.camstudio.org.

How to do it...

1. In the Content Browser, open the particle system *PacktFX.Cascade.BlackWhite_01* and highlight the **Required** module. For the **Material**, press the find in Content Browser icon [🔍] and take a look at the asset *PacktFX.Material.DiamondGrid*, which is made from a somewhat random mash up of various black and white textures and operators. What we have at the end of this network, is a spinning, noisy, circle. Actually, any Material you like will do, since we're just provisioning the **Emitter** so we can generate particles from which to derive a new Material in later steps.

2. Back in the Particle System *PacktFX.Cascade.BlackWhite_01*, notice that the motion is mainly driven by an **Orbit** module and the Scale up/Scale down of the **Size Scale by Time** module and **Size By Velocity** module.

3. In the Cascade **Preview**, the background color has been changed to white to compare the particles on a different background. Change the background color to the default black by clicking on the three RGB circles icon [🔵] at the top toolbar of Cascade. Next to it, make sure, also, **Toggle Real Time** [⏱] is on and the particles are actually moving. Toggle off the grid too [▦].

4. There are probably many ways to capture a particle system as a texture, but a quick way is to use a screen capture tool. I'm going to assume you know how to use tools like CamStudio or Camtasia that let you record a section of the screen. Open up the tool of your choice and set a square frame size that captures the particles in the editor cleanly. Don't let the content overlap the edges. Enlarge the **Preview** window to get a good size, but a 512x512 area should be fine. Record about five seconds of 'footage'. To edit out the frames you will need to use an editing program such as Premiere or perhaps the **Videopost** tool in 3ds Max which can export frames to .PNG or .TGA that UDK can import.

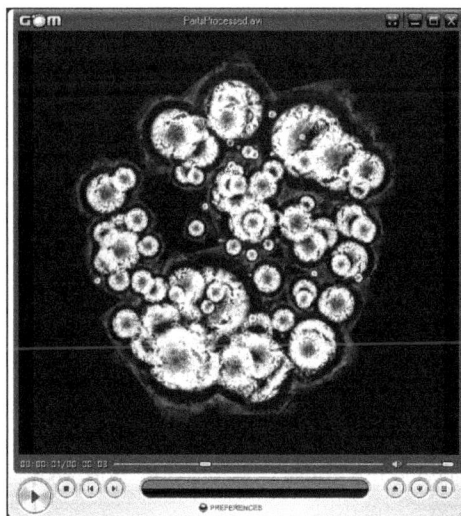

5. In your editor, isolate a 64 frame loop of frames. Don't take the first burst of particles as they spawn. A middle range of frames would be more likely to loop nicely. The screen capture utility will have captured a video format, so export the 64 frames to still frames. These will later be laid out into a single sheet as a grid. Make sure the output size doesn't have too much empty space and the frame size for the output is going to tile nicely into a 2048x2048 texture. 256X256 pixels will fit into that size at 8x8 tiles.

6. 64 frames are a lot of images to process by hand. Put your files into a folder and use the free Photoshop **ContactSheet X** script mentioned in the second recipe in this chapter to generate a combined grid of the source files. Note that amongst the settings in the next screenshot, there is an option to use a black **background** which should alleviate the need to remove white fringe edges from the image.

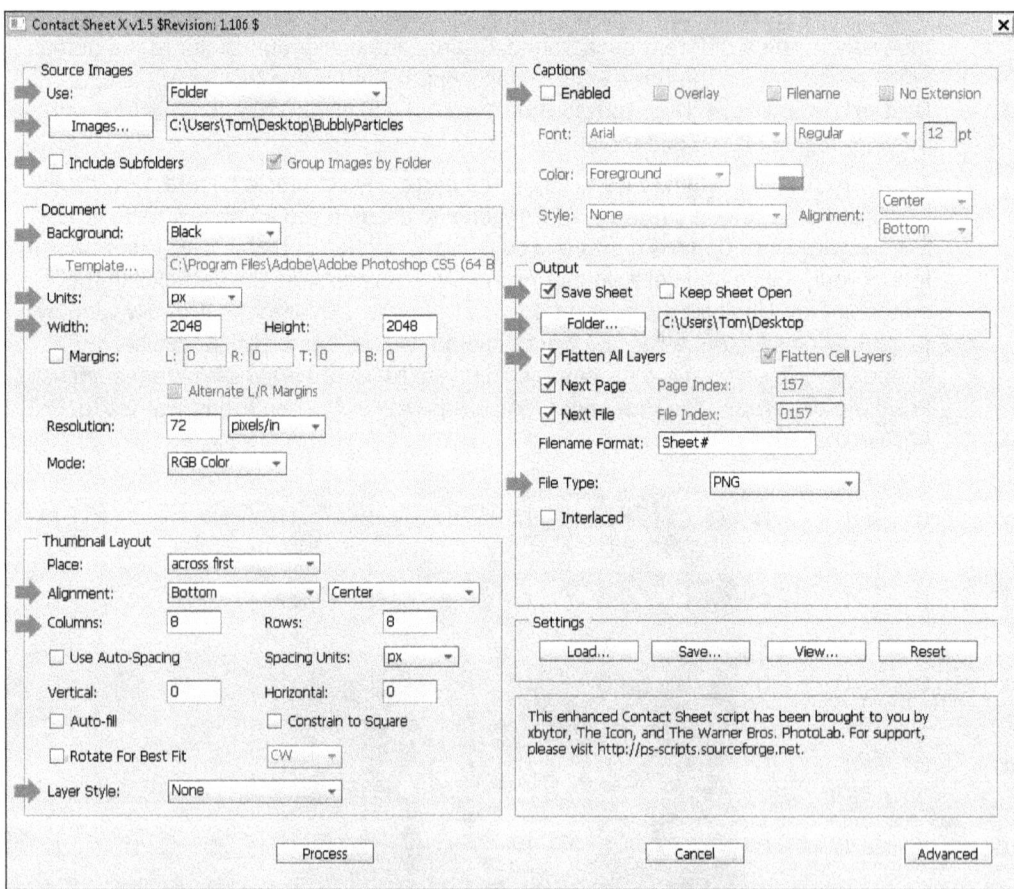

7. ContactSheet X will save the sheet to a .PNG. Be sure to check for any edge defects where the tiled images line up.

For designers who use GIMP rather than Photoshop, there are a number of plugins for GIMP that may do the same thing: http://www.sullockenzlin.demon.nl/Gimp.html or http://registry.gimp.org/node/120.

8. Transfer the final image to your package folder, or you can use the provided one, which has already been imported in two ways (one for particle system use and one as a flipbook for use in the Material Editor). The first is _PacktFX.texture. Packt_8x8_ParticleLoop_. This has default import settings. The second, _PacktFX. texture.Packt_8x8_ParticleFB_, needs to be told to be a **FlipBook** during import. In particular it needs its **horizontal** and **vertical** tile increment set, and its **Frame Rate** for playback. For this particle effect, we can choose to play the particles either in order or randomly, since they loop and just have a noisy distribution. Set the **FBMethod** to _TFBM_Random_.

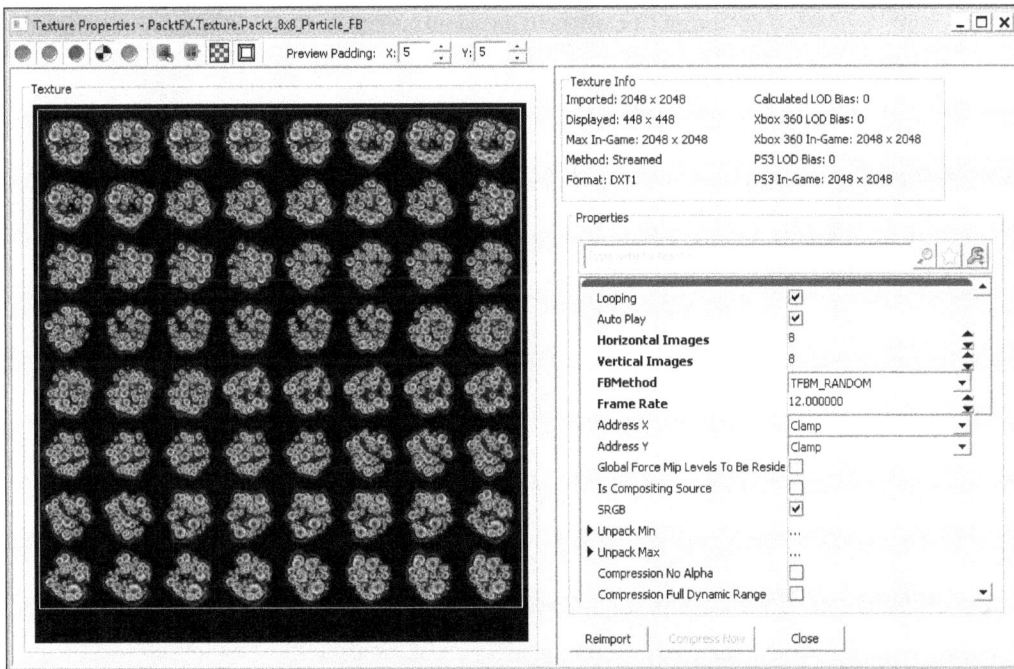

9. Once we have the **FlipBook texture** in UDK, we can create a Material which makes use of it. A Material transition could be modified by a FlipBook because of its animation. A **Decal** could be created using a particle rendering to save actual particle calculation in the scene.

10. To create a new Material network in this recipe would take up a lot of pages. Instead, let's examine the workings of an existing one already using our FlipBook texture, *PacktFX.Material.SubUVMat*, shown in the next screenshot, which you can open in the Content Browser in UDK to see in greater detail:

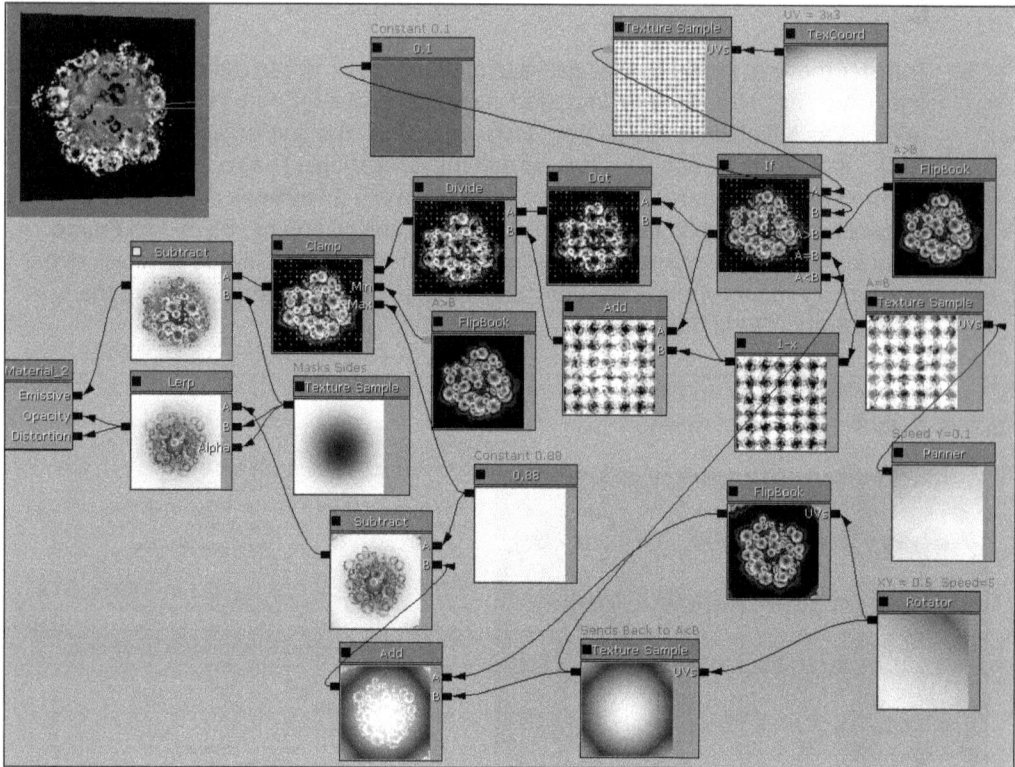

How it works...

Importing a FlipBook texture into the Material Editor is just a matter of right-clicking in the editor and choosing **Texture | New FlipBook Sample**, and assigning the texture highlighted in the content browser as usual.

This Material is set to **BLEND_Translucent**, as the use of the **Opacity** channel suggests.

If you vary the value of the two **Constant** nodes you will get considerably different looking patterns from the combination of the *Flipbook* with the diamond grid **Texture Sample**. The diamond grid texture is the same texture that was used to create the particle in the first place. The inclusion of the circular gradient texture (*PacktFX.Texture.BWdot* and *Packt.Texture.45degree_BWslope*) is to mask the effect as it rotates, and help influence the FlipBook's brightness.

It's anyone's guess what the resulting animated swirl might be used for in a game. Perhaps as a teleporter or wormhole effect, or possibly as an animated backdrop behind an object highlighted in the scene. Or maybe this might become the Material for another particle Emitter.

See also

For more information on the use of the *If* operator to help create Material transitions, check out *Chapter 9, The Devil is in the Details!*

Making trails with AnimTrail TypeData

Trails can be used for many purposes. They can be attached to machines to create exhaust. They can be attached as floating whiskers to Chinese dragons. How they are made is by drawing steps between particles. A stretchy sprite is interpolated in the space between particles rather than at each particle location. It is not very difficult to create a ribbon effect, but it can be tricky to get it to scale correctly into the scene and animate nicely over its lifetime.

How to do it...

1. Create a new particle system in your package called *MyTrailTest*.

2. In Cascade, set the *Required* module's settings to **Sort Mode:** *PSORTMODE_Age_NewestFirst* so new particles will be in front of older ones, and **Sub UV | Interpolation Method**: *PSUVIM_Linear*, with a **Sub Images Horizontal** and **Vertical** count of 4. This will mean the SubUV texture we'll use will render out in a linear order, as we discussed earlier in this chapter in the recipe: *Using SubUV charts to achieve particle diversity*.

3. Set the *Required* module's Material setting to *PacktFX.Material.SubUVMat*, the Material we made in the previous recipe.

4. As usual, we need to set the spawn, life, size, and speed parameters every particle requires. This time there is nothing remarkable about the ranges used. In the *Spawn* module, set the **Spawn | Rate | Distribution | Constant** to 12.0.

5. In the *Lifetime* module, set the **Lifetime | Distribution | Min** to 12 and **Max** to 24.

6. In the *Initial Size* module, set the **Start Size | Distribution | Max** X=2.0, Y=0.25, Z=0.01 and **Min** X=1.0, Y=0.1, Z=0.01. Later you can tweak these values, once the ribbon is applied.

7. In the *Initial Velocity* module, set the **Start Velocity | Distribution | Max** to X=1.0, Y=2.0, Z=55 and **Min** to X=-1.0, Y=-2.0, Z=55. This gives us a rapid upwards motion, and it is important that the Z values for **Min** and **Max** are the same or you may get a folding backwards effect in the ribbon, which looks weird here.

8. Add a *Size By Life* module, and set the **Size | Life Multiplier | Distribution | Constant Curve | Points | [0] | In Val** to 0.0, and **Out Val** XYZ to 2.0 for all three. Set the **Size | Life Multiplier | Distribution | Constant Curve | Points | [1] | In Val** to 1 and the **Out Val XYZ** to 0.0 for all three. What this does is make the particle grow a little during its life then shrink at the end.

9. That's it for the base particle. It probably looks like a lot of square cards going upwards, as in the following screenshot, on the left. The image has had its background color changed to better see the particles. Adding the ribbon trails to this should give us a result in Cascade similar to the image below, on the right:

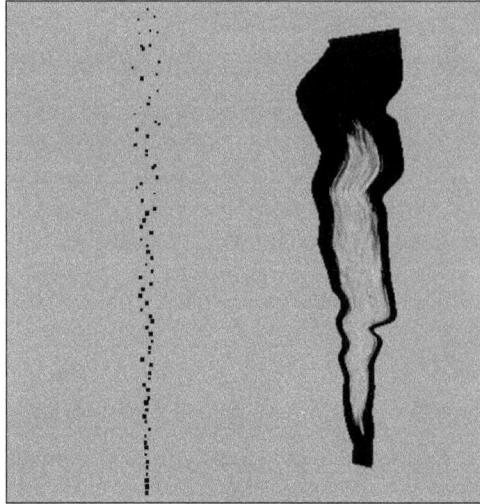

10. Right click under the *Size By Life* module and choose **TypeData | New Ribbon Data**. You could also experiment with **AnimTrail Data**. All that is needed to specify for the ribbon is its stepping values so it isn't too sparse, or chunky. The lifetime and velocity values heavily influence how the ribbon will look.

11. Set the properties for the *Ribbon Data* module so the **Sheets Per Trail** is 1, the **Max Trail Count** is 1, and the **Max Particle In Trail Count** is 22. Experiment with changing these values.

12. Set the properties **Enable Previous Tangent Recalculation** and **Tangent Recalculation Every Frame** both on. See what difference it makes to leave each one off.

13. Set the **Rendering | Tiling Distance** to 0.3, the **Distance Tessellation Step Size** to 0.3, and the **Tangent Tessellation Scalar** to 1.0. You should now have a ribbon that is trailing nicely upwards.

14. You may also want to experiment with changing the *Size By Life* module's **Size | Life Multiplier | Distribution | Constant Curve | Points | [1] | Out Val XYZ** so instead of being 0.0 it is 120, which really fans the ribbon out widely at its end.

15. Finally, if you can't see the particles start up in the Cascade Editor when you open the particle system, try turning it off and back on again. And now you are done, try changing the **Required | Material** to see how the effect changes. The provided Material: *Packt.Material.Digit0* looks interesting here, or the Material that ships in UDK: *UDK_ProceduralSky.Materials.M_Aurora_MASTER*.

16. The map *Packt_07_Ribbon_DEMO.UDK* shows the Emitter placed several times in a radial pattern to create streamers and these are all animated in Kismet through a *Matinee* using a **DrawScale3D** loop to make them shrink and grow. This scene uses ribbon data in the particle system *PacktFX.Cascade.RibbonDemo*.

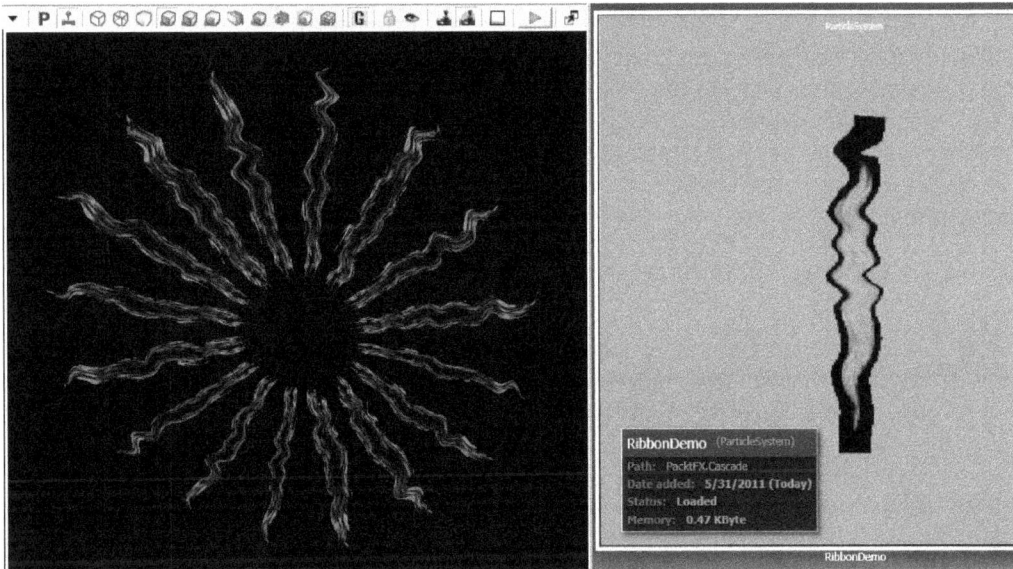

Assigning Level Of Detail (LOD) to a particle system

In Cascade, an LOD keeps the settings of level of detail for the particle system. LOD ranges define the point of change between set levels of detail, based on distance from the camera. Using LODs can reduce the processing load for the visual effect. The idea is to have optimal performance but maintain persuasive quality at close range, and smoothly ramp up the detail as the viewer gets closer to the Emitter actor. When passing the range, the transition between LOD settings should not be noticeable.

Getting ready

A little theory is probably a good thing to start with here. To take a particle system and create LOD variants, begin by selecting **Regenerate Lowest LOD**, to clear out any pre-existing levels. The lowest LOD is automatically generated from the highest LOD with a lower spawn rate. All the modules in the system will be grayed out, but can be edited per LOD by turning them back on to tweak their values to suit the current LOD. Before you start, it may help to read the UDN information about this topic, noting that it appears to be an incomplete system: `http://udn.epicgames.com/Three/CascadeUserGuide.html#Cascade LOD Controls`. In the documentation example each LOD is given a numbered sprite, so you can really see the difference in the levels to be sure they are working. It is important to understand that in your game, particles may behave a little differently than in the Cascade Editor. In terms of world space, the most likely choice when you are setting your LOD distances is to use **Automatic** mode, which is called *PARTICLESYSTEMLODMETHOD_Automatic*, as this will work out the Emitter distance from the camera at spawn time and as well as each time it loops, if looping. The distance is then compared to an **array** of distances to see which it should use. It also includes a time setting to control how often the array values will be re-checked.

Open the map *Packt_07_ColorChange_DEMO.UDK*.

How to do it...

1. In the scene an Emitter actor has already been placed. Select it and press *F4* to open its properties. Scroll down to the LOD section and expand it. You will notice the list there includes the choice we mentioned above *PARTICLESYSTEMLODMETHOD_ Automatic*. This is actually an **override**, taking over whatever method has already been set in the **Emitter** in the Cascade Editor. Recently a new method has been added, called **ActivateAutomatic mode**. This and **Direct mode**, are best set in code.

2. Click on the scene Emitter actor and press *Ctrl + B*. Right-click on the browser thumbnail and choose **Properties...** and expand the **LOD** section here. This shows the **Distances** array, which for now probably contains only one entry. Now right-click on the browser **Particle System** and choose **Create a Copy...** and call it *YOURFOLDER. Cascade.ChangeColorLOD_Test* or something similar.

3. Double-click the browser thumbnail to open the copied asset in Cascade. At the top of the Cascade Editor click the **Edit** menu and choose **Regenerate lowest LOD**. Since you only had one LOD to start with, this doesn't do a great deal.

4. The **LOD controls** that let us assign more levels are at the right of the icon row.

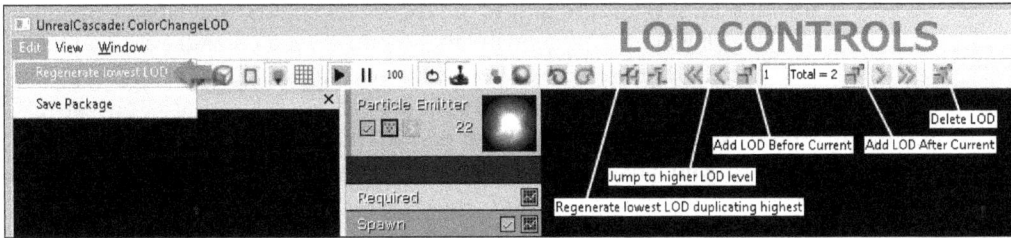

5. Click on the icon **Jump to Highest LOD Level** [«] and then press **Add LOD Before Current**, alongside [⚏]. Do so until the Total feedback says **Total=3**.

6. Next to **Total=3** is a number which shows the current level. Observe that 3 is the lowest, and 1 is the highest. You can tell from the watching the spawn rate change in the **Preview**: _ColorChange_ window.

7. Deselect any modules in the particle system and look at the properties panel. It should show an **LOD** section, and now you'll have more than one entry in the **LODDistances** array. Note that while your LODs number 1,2,3 your **LODDistances** entries number **[0],[1],[2]**. **[2]**=LOD 3 and gives the range for the furthest distance. It should be at 2500 currently. Set the distance for [1] to 888.0.

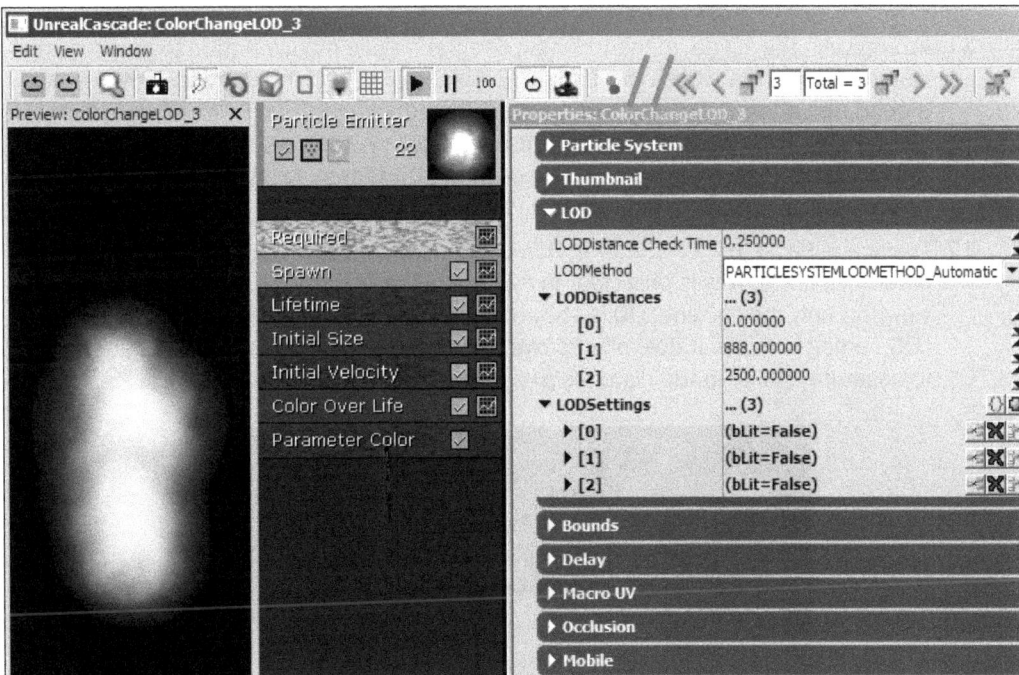

8. At level 3, the module settings are grayed out except for spawn, which has settings unique to this level. If you want to change other modules, you can right click on them and choose **Duplicate Highest LOD** or **Duplicate next higher LOD**. This will copy the value from that level and allow you to change it in here. For our example, on level 3, access the *Initial Size* module's properties, and set the **Start Size | Distribution | Max XYZ** to 75 and **Min XYZ** to 55 to make the somewhat sparser spawning particles larger.

9. For level 2, repeat this step but set the **Max XYZ** to 55 and the **Min XYZ** to 45, and for the highest level set the **Max XYZ** to 45 and the **Min XYZ** to 35. The idea here is that since now we are seeing more particles, they can be smaller and more detailed.

10. Go back to level 3, and set the **Spawn | Rate | Distribution | Constant** to 4.0 to better match the streamed look of the highest level, which has a rate of 20.

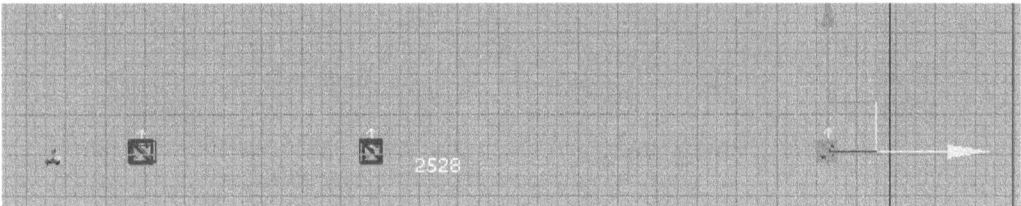

11. As shown in the scene, in the top view, use the middle mouse button to measure the distance 888 units across the ground and place a copy of the existing Emitter actor around about that distance from the first. Then measure 2500 units across from the first Emitter and place another copy at that distance. The idea here is to reproduce the Emitter at distances matching those in the **Distances Array** so the LODs will all be showing as specified. Rebuild and PIE to verify the effect.

12. The scene *Packt_07_LODSetting_DEMO.UDK* shows this using colors to highlight the difference LODs. This is only clear in PIE, not in the perspective viewport, as in the viewport only the current LOD is shown. Actually, color change is not that useful in an LOD setting because it doesn't improve performance, unless perhaps you are trying to desaturate color in the distance to enhance depth in the world space.

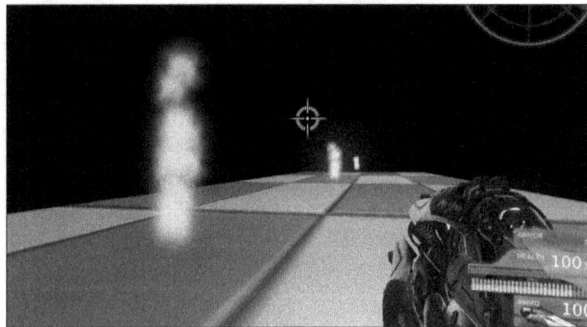

How it works...

An LOD, in Cascade, is just a copy of the main **Emitter** with changed values, usually reduced incrementally, so that particles further away have less computation without giving up the illusion of detail. In this example, for instance, we scaled up the distant particles size to compensate for their being fewer of them. Because the distance for the LODs proceeds in steps across a threshold, you may notice jumps in the graphics as you cross that threshold. That is where the true skill of LOD design comes in. In the provided map, if you walk forwards you will see an abrupt jump as the color changes, while the transition of the size and count for the LODs is fine.

Leaving a bloody trail

One way to improve the integration of a character into a game is through their footsteps left in snow, sand, or mud, or their wet footprints from stepping in water or, as in this case, a trail of their blood on the ground when they are injured. In this recipe we'll make a sprinkling of blood that spatters on the ground when an injured character is moving. Then when the character dies we'll pool the blood around them. It is customary in games to fade this kind of effect over time to avoid rendering too many particles.

Getting Ready

Open the map *Packt_07_BloodTrails_Start.UDK* and note that there is already a Kismet sequence set up. If you want an explanation of the functionality here, look to *Chapter 4, Got Your Wires Crossed?* Everything here is also covered there. We will be adding variables after we make the particle system.

How to do it...

1. In the content browser, right-click and choose **New Particle System**, and call it *Yourfolder.Cascade.BloodSplatter*. In its **Required** module add the Material *PacktFX.Material.BloodSplatter*. Below, set the property **Sort Mode** to *PSORTMODE_Age_NewestFirst*.

2. Below is the Material for the particle *PacktFX.Material.BloodSplatter*, which you can inspect in UDK too. The texture is *PacktFX.Texture.Droplet*. The shader simply has color, an opacity mask, and luminance so it doesn't appear black. Adding reflections and highlights in the Material might be a nice touch.

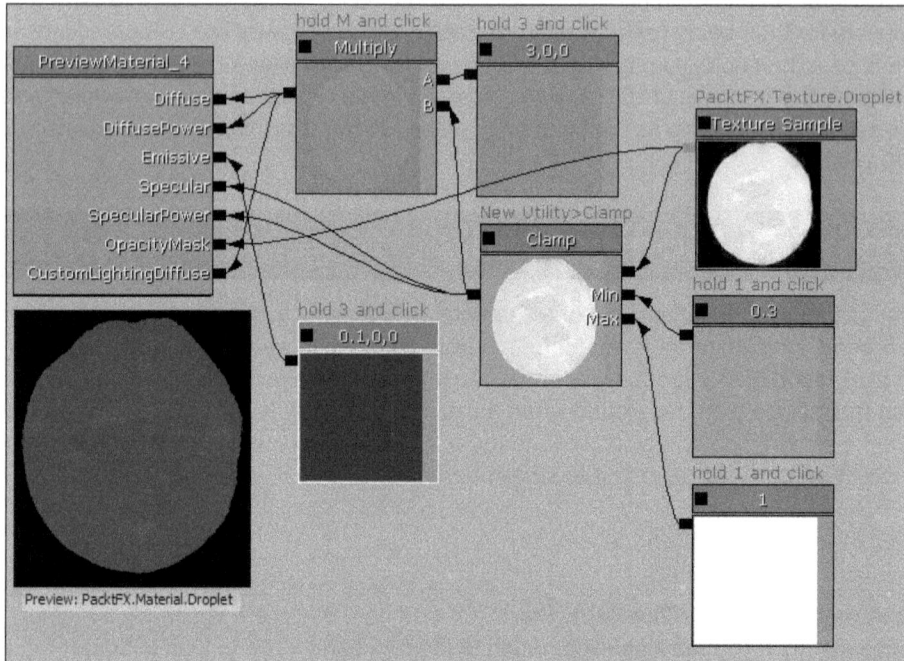

Preview: PacktFX.Material.Droplet

3. Save the particle system. Place it in the scene where the **Note** actor is below the Bot's spawn point. The spawn point is set at the floor height. We'll spawn a blood pool from Kismet to handle when the Bot dies and is no longer moving. We could spawn the particles straight off the Bot location via Kismet, but for this example it suffices to just place the Emitter in the level. That way, you can see what is happening as we edit its base values.

4. The first feature to set for the particles is their life time, which should be very long. When blood splatters appear on the ground they don't really fade out. Over a long time they might dry up to a black color, but by then you'd probably have moved on to another level in the game. Anyway, plausibility concerns out of the way, set the **Lifetime** module's **Lifetime | Distribution | Min** and **Max** properties to 55555 or some really high number.

5. The second feature to set up for the particles is their movement and facing direction. How we'll get around the problem of the particles moving (blood droplets spatter and stick), is by adding an **Orientation | Lock Axis** module and deleting the default *Initial Velocity* module. Set the **Lock Axis** property, of which there is only one, to *EPAL_Z*.

6. The *Initial Size* module sets the particle size, and really depends on how big your character and scene are. For the scene we're using, set the **Size | Start Size | Distribution | Max XYZ** to 6.0 and the **Min XYZ** to 3.0.

7. Delete the *Color By Life* module. Add a **Location | Cylinder(Seed)** module, and turn off the check boxes for its **Start Height | Positive Z** axis and **Negative Z** axis. This will turn the cylinder we'll spawn the particles on to a disk.

8. Down at the bottom of the **Cylinder(Seed)** module turn on the **3DDraw Mode** so you can see the cylinder in the **Preview** window. Make sure the **Start Radius | Distribution** type is a **Constant Curve**. Expose the curves for this module in the Curve Editor and press **Fit to View [⊙]**. Right-click and remove all the curves except **StartRadius**. We don't need to change those. Now press *Ctrl + LMB* click on the **StartRadius** curve a few times at even spacing and set the resulting keys so they range between 0 and 1 (which represents a percentage), so the radius of the cylinder changes, something like the following:

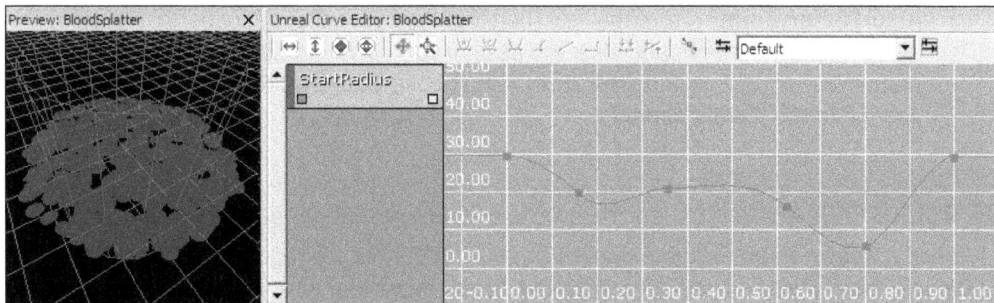

9. Last, set the *Spawn* module so it uses a **Burst List** rather than a **Constant**. The **Spawn | Rate | Distribution |Constant** should be 0.0 and the **Rate Scale** too. Set the **Burst | Particle Burst Method** to *EPBM_Interpolated*. Add two entries to the **Burst List** array by pressing the add entry icon [⊕]. For **Burst List | [0]** set the **Count** to 5.0 and for **Burst List | [1]** set the **Count** to 1.0 (these are values that varying will produce interesting varieties in the amount of blood, effectively with a high and low amount). Expand **[1]** and set its **Time** value to 1.0 so the spawn amount changes over time. Make sure **Process Burst List** is checked.

10. Now save your particle system. Check you have placed an Emitter actor for the particle system on the *Note* mentioned earlier, and select this. Open Kismet [K], and right-click on the *Object Variable* commented as *EmitterScene* in Kismet, which has the **Var Name** *Blood*. Choose **Assign Emitter_# to Object Variable(s)**.

11. In the Content Browser, highlight the particle system that you've been making, then right-click and choose **Create a copy...** to duplicate it and name it *Yourfolder. Cascade.BloodPool*. Next we'll make it emit only one particle that grows over time. The system already has a long *lifetime*, so we don't need to change that. Its *Initial Size* is fine too. The *Lock Axis* module takes care of orienting the particle to the floor. So we only need to alter the *Spawn* module settings. Change **Burst List[0]** to have a **Count** value of 1.0 and delete the entry **[2]** since it's not needed here, by pressing the **X** icon [✖].

12. Right-click under the *Lock Axis* module and choose **Size | Size Scale By Time** and highlight it. In its properties, make sure the **Distribution** type is a **DistributionVectorConstantCurve** and add two entries to it. **For Points | [0] | In Val** enter 0.0, for the **Out Val** set **XYZ** to 1.0. For **Points | [1]** set the **In Val** and **Out Val XYZ** all to 12. A bit further down, turn off the check box for **Enable Z**.

13. In Kismet, highlight the *Actor Factory* at the end of the sequence called *Spawn Emitter: BloodPool*. In its properties, hit the **Factory Selector** icon [▼] and choose **ActorFactoryEmitter** from the list. Then highlight your *BloodPool* particle system in the content browser, and click the assign icon [◉] in the channel in the Kismet properties (or right-click on the asset and choose **Copy Full Name to Clipboard** and paste it in the Kismet channel).

How it works...

In Kismet, a **Spawn Point** for the *BloodPool* spawned Emitter is already set to the location of the *BloodSplatter* particles when the **Trigger | Touch** event that kills the Bot is fired. In a real game, this would have to be set so the particle appears when the Bot takes damage enough to kill them from any source not just a Trigger in the scene. This recipe is intended to reduce the complexity of the concept enough to illustrate the effect, but you'd probably want to build on it a lot more layers of integration such as disposing of particles after a while, or aligning the blood pool better, or adding footprints in the blood, and making the event that causes the blood based on player action. For now, when you build and PIE, you should see blood trailing the Bot which then pools around his body when he falls down. This effect is not highly polished but should get you going in terms of handling the particle modules.

An example is provided: *Packt_07_BloodTrails_DEMO.UDK*. This uses *MyPawn* rather than *UTPawn*, and when the injured pawn dies the spawned AI actor is destroyed and substituted for an unhidden SkeletalMesh actor driven by *Matinee* so it can fall to the ground as the blood spreads around it.

8
Then There Was Light!
Manipulating Level Light and Shadows

After a level is created, its look can be moderated by an art director to have a certain color tint, blur, bloom, or intensity. This is conducted through simple post-process filtration. We will be discussing the features of PostProcess and we'll also discuss lighting approaches and their features, including custom lens flares, types of shadows, ambient occlusion, God Rays and light types, and their settings for achieving nice illumination under different conditions.

In this chapter, we'll cover the following topics:

- Emissive lighting
- Comparison of static and dynamic lighting
- Light exclusivity using channels and levels
- Adjusting shadows through light environments
- Distance field shadows
- Penumbras and hotspots
- Accessing the main PostProcessChain
- Ambient occlusion
- Depth of field
- Ensuring shadows work with translucent or alpha based materials
- Enabling and controlling light shafts
- Enhancing sunrays using lens flares
- Creating caustics using projected imagery
- Translucent colored glass

Introduction

Lighting in UDK is built around real-time requirements. **Epic Games** provides the neatest explanation of the features that UDK includes in terms of Rendering, Shaders, and "Eye-Popping Lighting and Shadows" on their front page at `http://www.UDK.com/features`.

> ▶ **Illuminate**
>
> UDK gives you all the options to perfectly light any scene. Ambient occlusion, per-pixel lighting, fill lighting, and fully dynamic specular lighting and reflections are all possible.

> ▶ **Unreal Lightmass**
>
> Unreal Lightmass is an advanced global illumination solver, custom built to fully take advantage of all that Unreal Engine 3 has to offer. Light your world with a single sun, give off soft shadows, and let the diffuse inter-reflection (color bleeding) do the work.

> ▶ **Detailed Shadows**
>
> Advanced shadowing with support for three techniques:
>
> ❑ Dynamic characters casting dynamic soft shadows.
>
> ❑ Ultra high-quality and high-performance pre-computed shadow masks.
>
> ❑ Directional light mapping with static shadowing and diffuse normal-mapped lighting. An unlimited number of lights can be pre-computed and stored in a single set of texture maps.

Scene lighting that you can put to work immediately is one of UDK's biggest perks. This area does however require some familiarity with the parlance of CG lighting and rendering. A good place to start would be the UDN documentation on lighting in UDK at `http://udn.epicgames.com/Three/UDKLevelCreationHome.html`.

Here are some of the terms that you would want to explore immediately:

▶ **Lightmass**—*The Global Illumination system for UDK.*

▶ **DominantLight**—*Helps you set up a direct sunlight. Normally just one is used.*

▶ **PointLight**—*Omni-directional light for artificial lighting, fills, and local lighting.*

▶ **LightEnvironments**—*Used to optimize dynamic object lighting.*

▶ **Modulated Shadows**—*The default shadow type.*

▶ **Distance Field Shadows**—*A newer type of shadow.*

Emissive lighting

This scene reproduces the **Cornell box** commonly used for CG rendered lighting tests and exploration. In this case, rather than use light actors in the scene, we'll see how far we can get by just using the Emissive property of a Material assigned to a BSP in the scene. There are numerous cases where this would be a good way to go; it all boils down to being able to get realistic dispersion of light around the form of the light source. If your light is a cable or tube, or is enclosed (as shown next) then it is inefficient, and sometimes difficult, to manage several PointLights spread around the area.

Getting ready

Load the provided map *Packt_08_CornellEmissive_Start.UDK*. There are two BSP boxes in the scene and a **PlayerStart** actor.

How to do it...

1. Select the BSP floor surface, right-click, and choose **Select Surfaces | All Matching Brush** (*Shift + B*).

2. In the Material Editor, highlight the Material *Packt.Material.Packt_CornellBase* and then right-click in the editor and choose **Apply Material**: *Packt_CornellBase*.

3. Now select the side wall and from the Content Browser apply the Material *Packt. Material.RedWall*, which just has a Diffuse input from a **Constant 3** set to R=0.5, G=0, B=0, and a slight Emissive to brighten it up. For the other side wall, apply the Material *Packt.Material.GreenWall*, similarly.

4. Select the surface of the box in the ceiling, then press *Shift + B* to select all the surfaces of the brush. In the Content Browser, highlight *Packt.Material.HotLight* and in the scene, right-click and choose **Apply Material**: *HotLight*.

5. With this still selected, press *F5* to open the **Surface Properties** dialog. In the **Lightmass Settings** section turn on **Use Emissive For Static Lighting**. Set the **Emissive Light Falloff Exponent** to 0.33 and, above, turn on **LightingChannels | Static** and **Dynamic** as well as the default **BSP**.

6   Build and PIE. At the moment you will notice some red and green color spill, or radiosity, across the ceiling, but it looks quite blotchy. Back in the **Surface Properties** dialog, set the **Lighting | Lightmap Resolution** to 2 for all the scene surfaces and build again. It will take longer, because tightening up this value generates a larger Lightmap. A value of 2 means there is one Lightmap every 2 units. Here a small value will give more precise results. Mainly, shadows will be better. PIE again, and this time you should notice the ceiling has much smoother gradients. You may also want to switch from the quick and average looking **Preview** quality build to the slower but better looking **Production** quality setting for **Build Lighting**.

7. Experiment with scaling and moving the ceiling lamp BSP, adjust the **Emissive Light Falloff Exponent**, and change the base gray wall Material (try out the *Packt_Glossy* and *Packt_Matte* Materials).

8. In the Content Browser search for a **Prefab** called *Packt.Prefab.PrefabBuckyBalls*. Place this in the scene on the floor, directly under the light. The meshes will help to show the color spill more clearly, since the empty room doesn't really reveal that much. Light has to hit various objects and cast shadows to look interesting.

9. An experiment at this point, in sampling for UDK, could be to subdivide the BSP walls by pressing *Shift + F2* and select and wall edges then use the **Split** option. If you need to alter the Material or surface properties for the subdivided BSP walls, in this case, you can select all the parts of one wall surface by choosing one square then right-clicking and going **Select Surfaces | All Coplanar**. To make sure the red spill and green spill work correctly, you may need to set for the walls the property **EmissiveLightExplicitInfluenceRadius** to 500 or so.

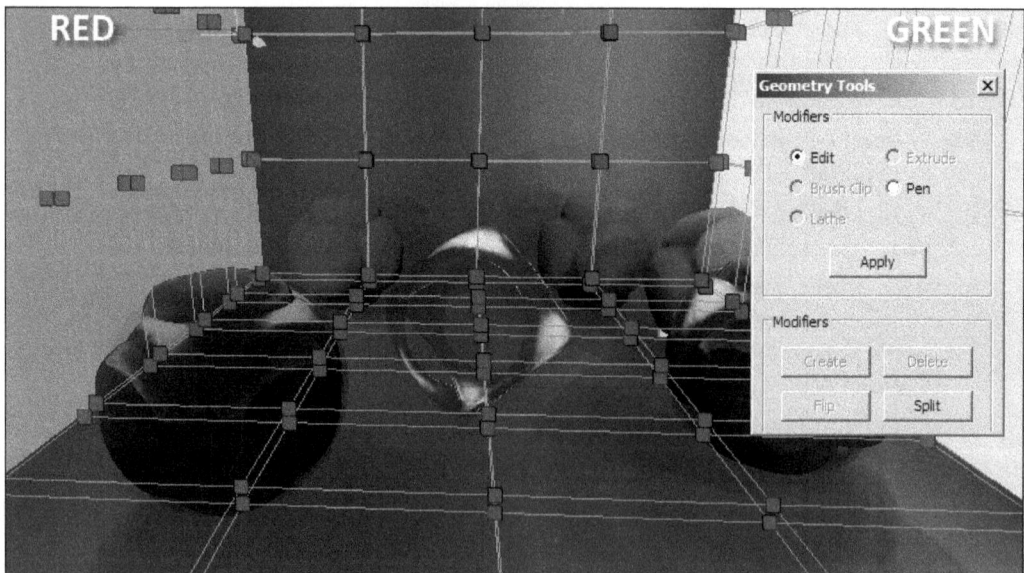

10. To improve the look of the lighting there are some world Lightmass settings we can bump a little, in particular the **Ambient Occlusion**, which is globally set. Go to the **View** menu and choose **World Properties**. Expand the **Lightmass** section, and locate the option to **Use Ambient Occlusion** and tick that. What we've done here is allowed shadows to be calculated for areas around objects that occlude, or block, the ambient light. This topic is discussed in more detail later in this chapter.

11. If you have the time, do a rebuild each time you change a major setting to compare the change. Turn on **Enable Image Reflection Shadowing** just to see the difference; in the real world, reflective surfaces don't receive shadows as obviously as non-reflective surfaces, but having it turned off, UDK can make a surface look like it is receiving no shadows. Set the **Num Indirect Lighting Bounces** to 5. As the rollover tip for this property explains, values above 3 or 4 come virtually free but it can be hard to see the difference. This is really worth doing as a *comparison*. To do so, screen grab (*Prt Scr*) your builds to Photoshop (*Ctrl + N* then *Ctrl + V*) and overlay them and step through the layer visibility to compare the images).

12. Set the **Static Level Lighting Scale** a little lower, around 0.9. This value approximates world scale relative to level lighting, and will affect scene dependent values in the lighting. If you raise it very high your scene will brighten. If you reduce it quite low the scene will take much longer to build.

13. Another factor to consider is that the soft shadows from a surface emitting light will not show up well on other surfaces that are also emitting light.

14. We used a BSP surface for Emissive lighting. Now try a StaticMesh. Delete the BSP ceiling lamp, rebuild, then place a scaled down sphere in the scene, such as *Packt. Mesh.BouncyBall* and assign it the Material *Packt.Material.HotLight.* With that selected, press *F4* to go set its **Lightmass | Use For Emissive Lighting** property to be on. Under the **Lighting | Lighting Channels** section, turn on the checkbox to use with **BSP** and **Static**. With no other lights in the scene, you will be able to see how a small light surface can transmit a lot of energy.

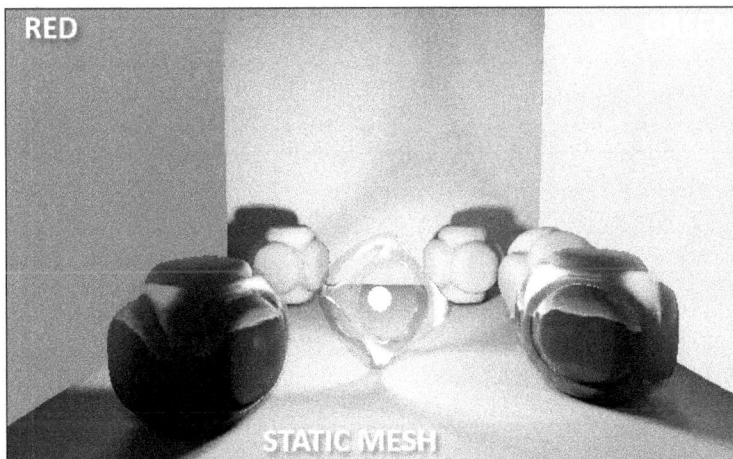

How it works...

There are three main contributing factors to basic lighting quality in UDK: **Emissive lighting** (as an area light effectively) from a Material onto an object is just one, light from **PointLights** and **DominantDirectionalLights** and their shadows, and finally, **Ambient Occlusion**, where indirect lighting is blocked by objects encroaching on each other. We explore this in a later recipe in this chapter. Besides **Lightmass** settings, there is a **World Info** setting that could make a difference, as well as the maximum **Packed Light and Shadow Map Texture Size**.

Comparison of static and dynamic lighting

Static lighting is best for objects that never move, especially with respect to their shadows.

Dynamic lights allow a shadow which is very crisp to update with changes in the model animation (both changes in deformation and changes in world position).

Static shadows are baked in place, and are only built once. Dynamic shadows are rendered on the fly, constantly updating as scene elements change.

In the real world, of course, all shadows would therefore come under the dynamic category, but that is quite expensive in a computed world, so static lighting's mission is to give us a fast render which, while looking nice comes with the limitation that it will only hold up if nothing is moving. The problem is that, in a game, lots of things move.

If you have ever placed a **UTTeleporter** in your level and wondered why it renders black, or not at all, you will have confronted the need for dynamic lighting. Some objects require a dynamic light to perform properly. One way to fix this is to use **DominantDirectionalLights**, which are dynamic by default. The other way is to **convert** a PointLight to a dynamic light by setting it to be **Dynamic** in its **Lighting Channels** property.

You will likely receive this warning when placing a teleporter and building lighting:

```
Performance Warning - UTTeleporter_0 - Static Mesh Component
[Pickups.Base_Powerup.Mesh.S_Pickups_Base_Powerup01] not
Lightmapped and not using a light environment, will be inefficient
and have incorrect lighting! Set bUsePrecomputedShadows=True to
use Lightmaps or enable the light environment.
```

In this recipe we'll be dealing with the problems involved in this kind of performance warning by taking an asset which requires dynamic lighting and showing how it looks with normal lighting and with dynamic lighting, and how to enable dynamic lights.

Getting ready

Load the provided map *Packt_08_CornellTeleporter_Start.UDK*.

How to do it...

1. Setting up the teleporter is also a handy lesson, to get us going. Open the Content Browser and switch tabs to **Actor Classes**. Expand the **Navigation** category to show **Teleporter | UTTeleporter**. With that highlighted, right-click in the scene and choose **Add UTTeleporter here**.

2. *Alt +LMB-drag* the teleporter actor so there are two. Here it might be good to place one on the floor and one up on the block by the PlayerStart.

3. For the teleporter up on the block, open its properties (*F4*) and expand the **Object** section (at the bottom), and in the **Tag** field type *Destination*. Select the other teleporter actor, and in its properties expand the **Teleporter** section. In the **URL** field type *Destination*. So, we've set up a one way teleport from the ground level up onto the block.

4. As is, if you build now, you will get the performance warning mentioned earlier. Select both teleporters and press *F4* to edit their properties together.

5. Expand the **Lighting** section and turn on **Use Precomputed Shadows**. Rebuild, PIE, and see the difference. The teleporter on the ground looks fine, but the one on the block by the PlayerStart (*Destination*) isn't right. The shadow is there, but the mesh isn't. This is because that teleporter also needs a URL.

6. Give the teleporter on the ground level the **Object | Tag** *Origin*. But if the URL for the upper teleporter is to *Origin*, given the location of the PlayerStart, we'd get a nasty transferal. So, a way round this is to have *Destination* disabled. There is a check box for **Enable** in its **Teleport** properties. It will still act as a destination from origin, and still be visible, but you won't be able to teleport to its URL, *Origin*.

About now it would help to inspect examples. The next screenshot marked **A** shows the destination teleporter using pre-computed shadows and it is enabled but, without a **URL** to send out to, it is void. The image marked **B**, captured from a reverse angle, shows the destination teleporter disabled and with a **URL** Origin. It does not use pre-computed shadows and is not lit by any light. The image marked **C**, by comparison, has a specific PointLight assigned to it using the dynamic channel and using the **Gameplay1** channel (for both light and teleporter), to make it only affect the teleporter, not the surroundings too. It hasn't got use pre-computed shadows turned on, so renders gray, unaffected by the bright surrounding coloration. The image marked **D** shows the teleporters both with pre-computed shadows on, with the correct **URL** for each, with a dynamic light effecting them through the **Gameplay1** channel, and consequently lit and tinted by the scene coloration.

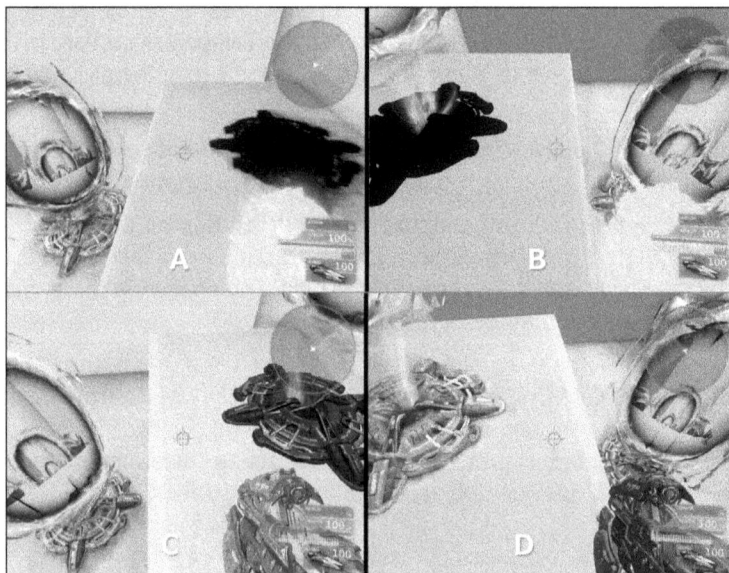

7. The teleporter can render if you turn on **Use Precomputed Shadows** or give it a dynamic light. There is a way to improve the calculations of pre-computed shadows, which is to create a **BSP cube** fitted to and enclosing the room and generate from it a **Precomputed Visibility Volume** from the **Volumes** list while the BSP is selected. Add, similarly, a **Lightmass Importance Volume**.

Light exclusivity using channels and levels

The previous recipe touched on the use of **lighting channels** to specify that lights will exclusively affect objects given the same lighting channels. In this recipe the intention is to learn how levels and channels can be employed to make sure lights influence only what you want them to. Levels are actual division of content into distinct maps, loading as required. Channels relate content according to which channel an object is assigned to, something like layers. Either way, lights will effect objects in the same level or channel that they are assigned to.

How to do it...

1. Grab any PointLight and press *F4* to expose its properties and look in the **Lighting | Lighting Channels** section, which is a long list of channels such as **Unnamed1**, **Cinematic1**, and **Gameplay1**.

2. Add a PointLight to the scene we've been using, or you can otherwise open: *Packt_08_CornellChannels_Start.UDK* and set its **Lighting | Lighting Channels | Unnamed1** checkbox to be ticked on. By default the light will have the **BSP**, **Static**, and **Composite Dynamic** channels already ticked. Turn those off, or the light won't be exclusive at all.

3. Select the prefab meshes (you may have to right-click on the prefab and choose **Convert PrefabInstance to Normal Actors**) and set the gray ones at the back through their properties to also use the lighting channel **Unnamed1**, as with the light, as shown in the following screenshot:

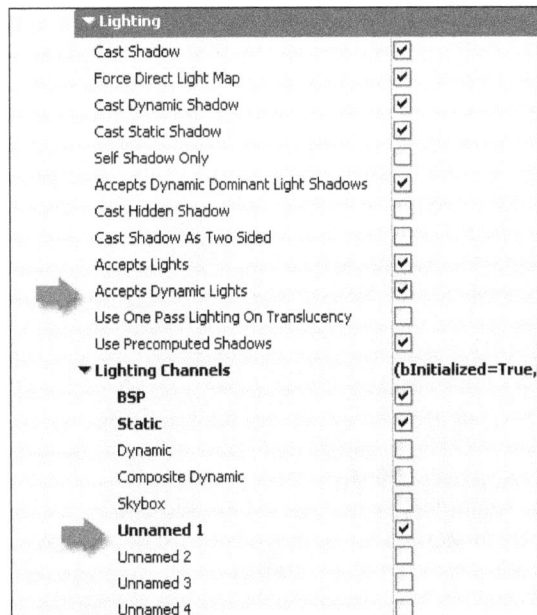

4. Set the light's **Light | Light Component | Light Component | Brightness** to 3.0 and, just underneath, the **Light Color** to a chromatic blue R=0, G=0, B=1, as this is a color not used elsewhere in the scene.

5. Repeat this using a new light that has the **Lighting Channel | Unnamed2** ticked and also set some other scene objects to use their **Lighting Channel | Unnamed2**, and set the new light's color to a strong yellow.

6. It should be apparent in the editor that only the **Unnamed1** objects are affected by the **Unnamed1** light, and only **Unnamed2** objects are effects by the **Unnamed2** light, but when you rebuild and PIE there will be a lot of spill and fill.

7. So how to solve that? In the light properties, for both lights, turn off the property **Use Direct Light Map**. If this is set to true, the light will be baked into a Lightmap for all static primitives it affects. Since we are concerned with a live, dynamic light we don't need that here. Tick on **Force Dynamic Light**. Setting this option will preclude any pre-computation for that light (no Lightmaps or ShadowMaps), forcing it to be a dynamic light casting stencil shadows. So we're doubly covered.

8. For the objects that were assigned a unique lighting channel, turn on the property **Lighting | Accepts Dynamic Lights**. This makes sure they won't be discarded from the dynamic light calculated during game play. Add a small fill light (with an intensity of 0.1) to light the BSP and to cast shadows. Or you could use an Emissive BSP, as in the previous recipe.

9. You should end up with a result similar to the next screenshot, which comes from *Packt_08_CornellChannels_DEMO.UDK*. It is worth noting that experimenting with changes to the values and settings will help you figure out what to expect as you go. Try not to change too many properties all at once or you can lose track of what is contributing to the result.

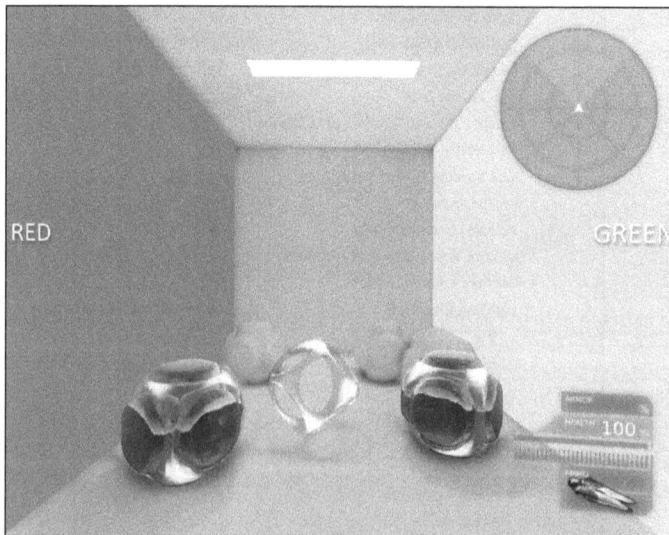

There's more...

Light exclusivity using levels

UDK's editing environment is in a way layered, in the sense that content can be assigned to individual, mutually exclusive levels. This feature allows us to leverage lighting effects only for objects in the same level that the light occupies. We discussed the use of levels for streaming in *Chapter 6, Under the Hood*. It works much the same way for lighting control. Here's a quick example:

1. Create a hollow BSP box with a blue PointLight placed at one end and an orange PointLight placed at the other. Add some Static Meshes inside the room.

2. Open the Content Browser and switch across to the **Levels** tab, shown below. Select the PointLight, and all the objects you want to be lit by it and choose **New Level from Selected**. In this example, set the option **Always Loaded** on when creating levels. The other PointLight and objects will remain in the default layer. Select those and make a new level for them, the same way.

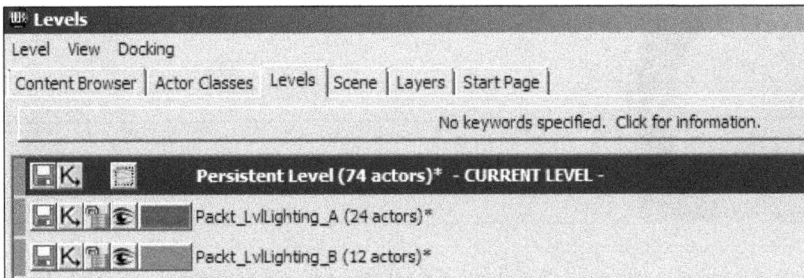

3. To move objects back and forth between levels you can use copy objects, switch active levels, then paste. To switch active levels, right-click on the level you're aiming for and choose **Make Current**.

4. You can actually navigate the level content easily by switching over to the **Scene** tab next to it, which lists the actors according to their level. If you tick the **AutoFocus?** checkbox, when you highlight an actor the view will jump to it. In the next screenshot, the **Scene** tab is shown, with a highlighted actor selecting and framing in the viewport, as well as displaying its properties. To gain familiarity with this tool, try selecting, copying, and pasting content from one level to another to re-arrange the lit meshes into a new lighting pattern.

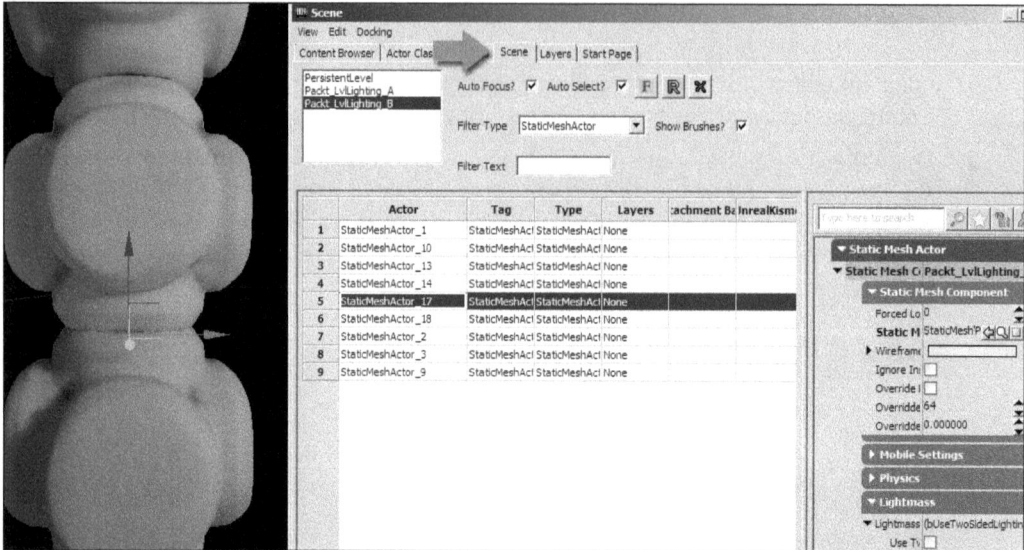

5. Right-click on each level and choose **Self Contained Lighting**. You should notice the lighting distribution for the objects is now exclusive. In the next illustration, only the foremost StaticMesh and the BSP room are in the persistent level.

6. The next screenshot shows the result of containing the lights to light their current level only. This is a powerful feature, because of the unique map files it generates that can be independently updated, allocated, and managed.

Adjusting shadows through light environments

We mentioned that there are three main light types in UDK: an **Emissive component**, **static** and **dynamic light actors**, and a **Light Environment**. Light Environments apply to InterpActors, RigidBody actors, and SkeletalMeshes. Every InterpActor (aka Mover) and KActor (aka RigidBody) has a dynamic light environment by default. Light environments provide level designers with an automated way of controlling dynamic lighting by approximating the effect of relevant static lights. With that in mind, this recipe gives a guided tour of light environment staging in a scene so a SkeletalMesh can be lit dynamically in a way that reduces harsh shadows.

Getting ready

Load the provided map *Packt_08_LightEnvironment_Start.UDK*. This scene shows a small enclosure with a **DominantDirectionalLight** (Sun), a Skydome, and some weak fill lights. The next screenshot shows the scene, and the XYZ axis is the location of the **DominantDirectionalLight** as it shines along its X axis, tilted down over the walls. In the light properties, **Light Shafts** are enabled. This scene is fairly empty, and we're just going to add some SkeletalMeshes to examine the **Light Environment** settings.

How to do it...

1. From the Content Browser drag an instance of *Packt.Mesh.Packt_SkinTailFBX*. Place copies in each of the four wall spaces like the one shown below. Keep them all selected at once and press *F4*.

2. In the SkeletalMesh properties assign the appropriate **Physics Asset** from the Content Browser. The *Packt_SkinTailFBX* asset uses *Packt.Mesh.Packt_Character_Physics*. Look in the properties for the **Physics Asset** channel. There, press the assign icon [◄] with *Packt_SkinTailFBX* highlighted in the Content Browser. In theory, this improves the shadow casting calculation and at least it removes a build performance warning.

3. In the next screenshot you can see the expanded properties of the *Packt_SkinTailFBX* **SkeletalMesh** actor.

4. With all the SkeletalMeshes selected choose **Lock Selected Actors** [🔒] from the **Properties** window icons.

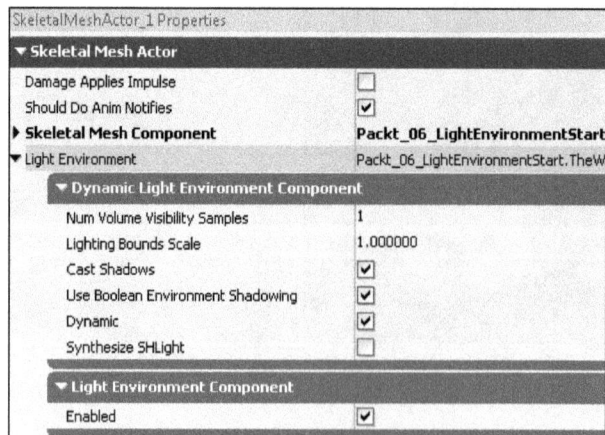

5. Once the mesh properties are locked, or pinned, select the **DominantDirectionalLight** in the scene (it is probably easiest to search for it using **Edit | Find Actors**) and expose its properties too. Under **Light Component** make sure **Cast Composite Shadow** is ticked on. Under **Light Component | Lighting Channels** make sure **Dynamic** and **Composite Dynamic** are turned on.

6. Under the **SkeletalMesh** properties turn off **Use Boolean Environment Shadowing**. Turn on **Synthesize SHLight**.

> The next screenshot shows comparisons in the editor of these properties in different combinations. The first uses the defaults **Use Boolean Environment Shadowing** on, and **Synthesize SHLight** off. The second uses **Boolean Environment Shadowing** off, and **Synthesize SHLight** off. This causes a shadow to fall across the body from the scene that isn't shown in the quick computation of the Boolean setting. Notice the darkness of the dynamic shadow. The third: **Use Boolean Environment Shadowing** off, and **Synthesize SHLight** on. Notice the fill light that now appears, and the internal shadow on the character is lighter. The cast shadow is still very dark.

7. Now that the meshes have their settings in place, go to the main editor's **View** menu and choose **World Properties**. Scroll down to the **Light Environment** section, and examine the globals there that allow you to adjust the brightness, contrast, and indirect brightness and contrast. For the most part these values range between 0.5 and 5.0. I chose 1.

8. The shadows cast from the character are very black. To fix this, select the **DominantDirectionalLight** and expand its **Light Component | Light Component | Mod Shadow Color** properties, which are below the **Lighting Channels** section.

9. Set the **Light Shadow Mode** to *LightShadow_Normal*. This is important because otherwise the modulated shadows multiply against the background and go black when rebuilding lighting.

10. Set the **Mod Shadow Color** so the **Alpha A** is about 0.75 (or close to the static shadow darkness) and set the **Shadow Filter Quality** to *High*. Depending on your scene, and here it is unlikely to matter, you can set the **Min** and **Max Shadow Resolution** to force a certain level of quality, for instance making both to be 1024 will force a set shadow resolution. If you set a **Max** of 1024 and a **Min** of 2.0 and in game walk backwards away from the cast shadow you can watch it changing resolution based on the distance.

11. A limitation of the shadows cast this way is that you will get a drop-out of the shadow if the camera goes far enough away from the actor. This is obviously an optimization step. A way to fix it is to set the property **Shadow Fade Resolution** in the **Dominant Directional Light** to 2.0; this is very small, and therefore the dropping out will be less likely to occur.

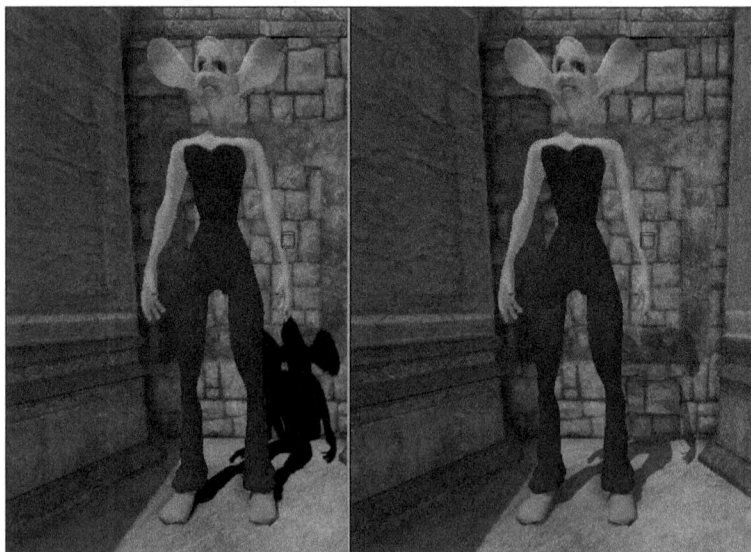

How it works...

The previous screenshot shows a dark, unpleasantly heavy shadow on the left. That is the default for a dynamic object. On the right, the effect of adding a light environment for the actor is clearly more subtle. A **Light Environment** pertains to a specific actor. From the static and dynamic lights that affect it, the lighting is reproduced for the object with a fixed rendering cost. This approximation is done using a **spherical harmonic** light and a **directional light**. A quick explanation is that spherical harmonics are part of a solution to Laplace's equation. Spherical harmonics help game developers code lighting complexity. For those with a coding bent, it may open your eyes to some CG math. An explanation of this can be found at http://www.research.scea.com/gdc2003/spherical-harmonic-lighting. pdf. **Epic Games** provides documentation about **Light Environments** and some common troubleshooting: http://udn.epicgames.com/Three/LightEnvironments.html.

An important thing to consider is that this method discards lights from the scene that don't affect the model, does a kind of fuzzing of light from those that do, to simulate light bounces, and then creates a direct light in favor of the strongest incident light affecting the model to produce a key light effect.

Light Environments can be told to cast a shadow (from the direct light only) which is based on the scene lights the spherical harmonics are derived from, if they happen to be casting a shadow already. A limitation of this is that if you enable shadows for it, and there are no shadows in the derivation source lights, then the resulting shadow will go straight down.

Distance field shadows

This recipe is quite short, but too sweet to be just a quick tip. Besides what was discussed in the previous recipe, there is a further pre-computed shadow type that is off by default. The full name for it is a **signed distance field baked shadow**. But what does that mean? UDK has this method built into its dominant lights, and once enabled it replaces the native shadows. Besides being distance based, a key difference is in the compactness of the information stored. The technology is derived from Valve's **Alpha Tested Magnification** and effectively stores the lighting information in the separate RGB channels of a texture. For more information, explore Valve's paper, which discusses limited texture artifacts: http://www.valvesoftware.com/publications/2007/SIGGRAPH2007_ AlphaTestedMagnification.pdf.

Getting ready

Open the provided scene *Packt_08_LightEnvironment_DEMO.UDK*. This is the same scene as was used previously. Roll the camera over some area of the ground where the trees are casting shadows.

How to do it...

1. There is really only one thing to worry about, the **Whole Scene Dynamic Shadow Radius**. Remembering this only works with **DominantDirectionalLights**, go to the **Edit | Find Actors** then search for *Dominant* and you should get the actor which is performing as the scene's sun. This also works in the default map templates (post-June 2011), which all have a DominantDirectionalLights already provisioned.

2. Open the selected light's properties and under **Lights | Light Component** expand the **Cascaded Shadow Maps** section, and in the property **Whole Scene Dynamic Shadow Radius** enter a value of 1024. Build and PIE to try and see any difference in the shadow detail.

3. In the left-hand side screenshot, we have **Whole Scene Dynamic Radius** set to 1024. For that image, in the DominantDirectionalLight properties, the value for **CascadedShadowMaps | NumWholeSceneDynamicShadowCascades** was 10. A value of 1 would be less detailed, but its softness would be equal all around. In the right-hand side screenshot, it is set to 0, which disables the dynamic shadow.

How it works

The distance field method gives us a cheap shadow type that is good for sharp, detailed shadow situations. The downside is that we don't have a penumbra or Falloff we can access, and the calculation is from the camera, not distance from the base of the object. If you must have shadow penumbras, try using a DirectionalLightToggleable, which can do those, but is more expensive over a whole scene. Penumbras are covered in depth in the next topic.

Overall, we have a few ways to generate shadows in UDK (static shadows, dynamic shadows, composite shadows, and cascaded shadows). Until there's an uber lighting solution, it is enough for most cases.

Penumbras and hotspots

The goal in this recipe will be to achieve a nice resolution shadow with a convincing shadow Falloff. As we've seen, not all of the available lighting solutions support penumbras. If you are not sure what a penumbra is, place the tip of your finger on the table and look at the shadow your hand casts. Around the tip of the finger the shadow will look darker and sharper than it looks as the distance between the table and your hand increases. Hotspots, the bright part of a spotlight, also have a penumbra caused by distance from the light to the surface. What causes the penumbra? Since the source of light is not an absolute point but in fact a surface, the angle of light isn't really coming from one place. Not all of the light is blocked equally around an object's edges, which leads to soft gradients in the shadow.

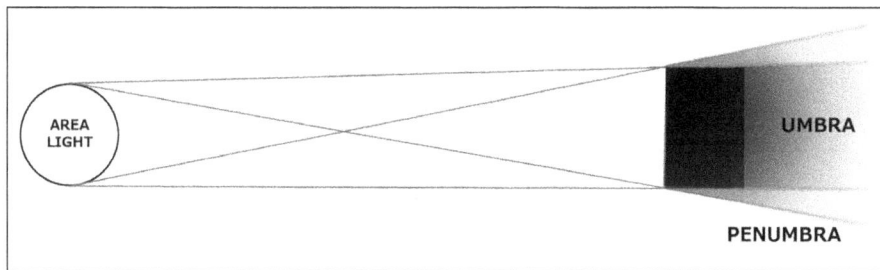

Before we begin, it is strongly suggested that the initial step when delving into shadow casting in UDK would be to look over the documentation provided by **Epic Games** at `http://udn.epicgames.com/Three/ShadowingReference.html`.

There are three main ways by which shadows can be resolved, and the key thing to remember is that lights can move or be static. On top of that, objects can also move or be static, and shadows have to be calculated in the most efficient way possible. It is helpful to keep the following in mind:

- The base class of each light type is a static version. It uses **per-object dynamic shadows** combined with **pre-computed lighting**. For instance, a PointLight.
- The movable subclass of that light may be moved at runtime. It uses **whole-scene dynamic shadows**. For instance, a PointLightMoveable.
- The toggleable subclass of that light may not be moved, but it can change color and brightness at runtime. It uses **per-object dynamic shadows** combined with shadow maps. For instance, a PointLightToggleable.
- The dominant subclass of that light is similar to Toggleable lights, but **distance field shadow maps** are available for it. For instance, a DominantPointLight.

Getting ready

Open up the map *Packt_08_Penumbra_Start.UDK*. You should have views which show two groups of figures at different scales, including BSP boxes the figures are seated on. The left-hand side screenshot given next shows the unlit scene, and the second shows lighting only that comes from a single spotlight (*Alt+ —*). For the ground, the density increases on the front side of the characters. At the back of the scene the lighting is sparse, so shadows at the back area will receive less indirect fill.

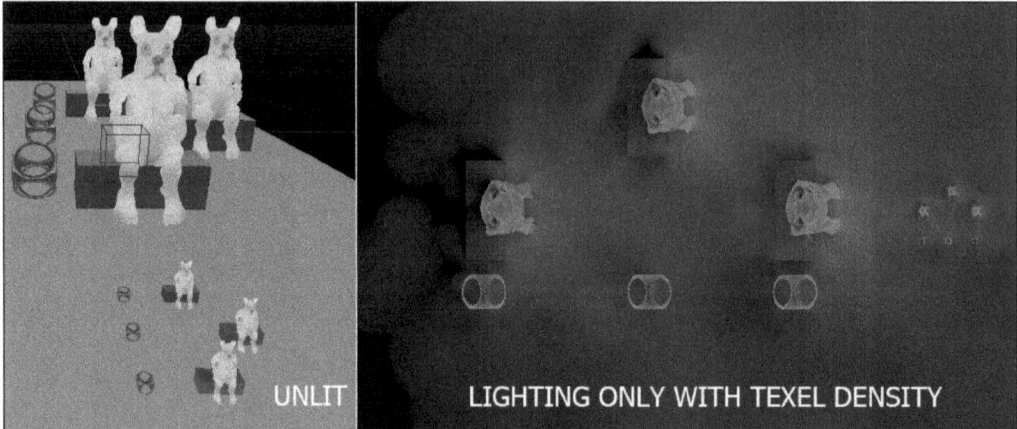

UNLIT LIGHTING ONLY WITH TEXEL DENSITY

How to do it...

1. Place a regular PointLight on the floor and scale it so its range fits the scene, which is about 5000 units in length. Open its **Movement** properties and set the light's XYZ location in the world to (X=400.0, Y=3300.0, Z=2000.0).

2. In its **LightComponent** properties set the property: **LightComponent | ModShadow | Color | A** to 0.7 to make the shadows a little less solid. Set the **Light Source Radius** to 128, which sets the area light size. Build with the current settings to get a result similar to the following screenshot:

3. Set your perspective view to **Lit Mode** (_Alt + 4_). The PointLight shadows are reasonable but not spectacular. Note that **ambient occlusion** has been enabled in the **World Properties** for this scene. Notice the shadows have fuzzy edges, but uniformly, and also seem uniformly dark, which is not what we're after. We need the base of the shadow to be sharp and dark, then fade and blur as it stretches far away from the object.

4. Click on the BSP floor and press _F5_. In its **Surface Properties**, the **Lightmap Resolution** is set to 36. Drop this right down to 2 so shadows falling on it are calculated at a higher resolution. In the next image the BSP floor has been split down the middle; the left half is set to the default 32, and the right half is set to 2 and the shadow there looks a lot more defined. Interestingly, when dealing with StaticMesh actors shadowing rather than BSP, their **Lightmap Resolution** property requires increased values.

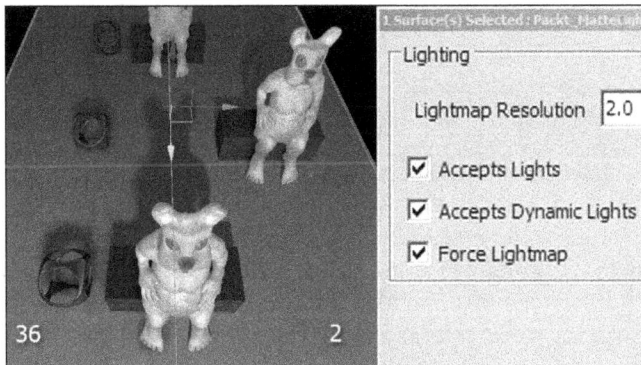

5. If you compare the end and the base of the shadow on the more defined side, the top is fuzzy and light as compared to the base. So there's our penumbra.

There's more...

Dominant light shadow penumbra

Convert the spotlight we've been adjusting by right-clicking on it in the view and choosing **Convert Light | PointLights | Dominant PointLight**. If you rebuild lighting the penumbra effect will be gone, replaced by a somewhat weird but much stronger shadow. The scene build time by now may well have doubled.

Make sure both surfaces for the floor have a **Lightmap Resolution** of 2. Further down, notice the default **Shadow Filter Quality** is *SFQ_Low*. It is usual for 3D applications to have low default settings, to allow good scene performance.

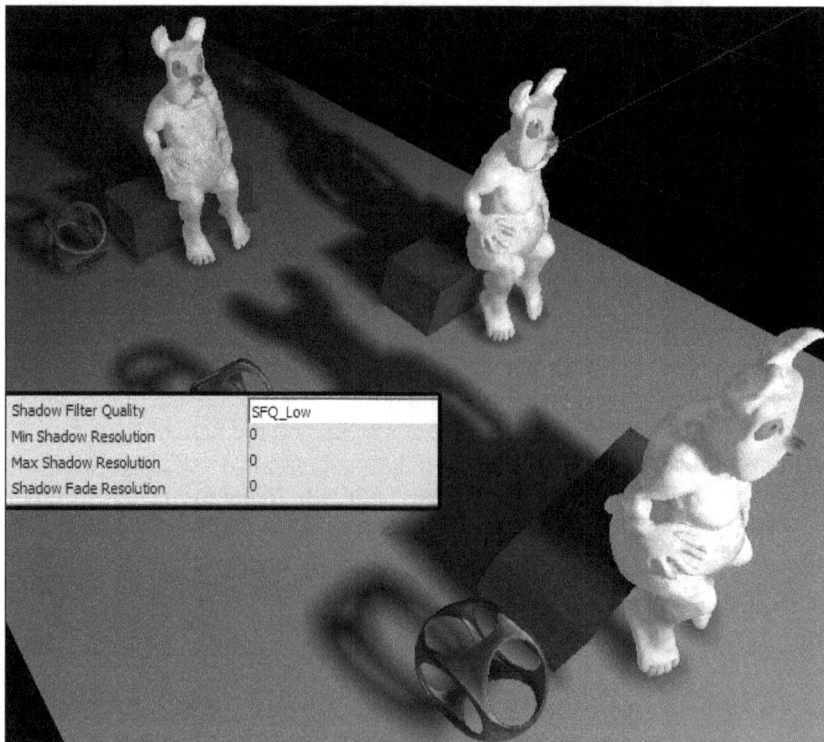

1. In the light's properties, confirm that its **Light Source Radius** is 128. Increase its **Brightness** to 2.0, and further down set the **Shadow Filter Quality** from *SFQ_Low* to *SFQ_High*. Change the **Min** and **Max Shadow Resolution** from 0 to 2048. The result is a bit cleaner, but the penumbra is not convincing, as the base of the object is pretty fuzzy.

2. Convert the light again by right-clicking on it and choosing **Convert Light | Directional Lights | DirectionalLightToggleable**. Rebuilding lighting now will flip all the previously set values for the light properties to defaults, hence the abruptly different shadow, shown here on the left-hand side:

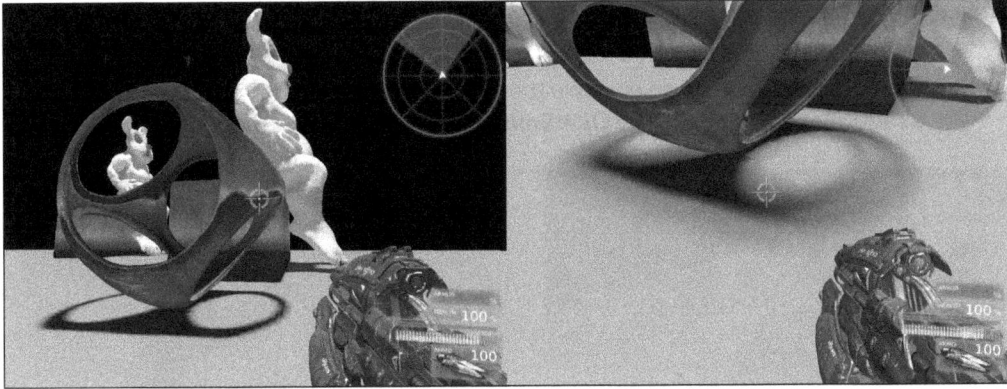

3. The new shadows are very solid. This is controlled through the property **Light | LightComponent | Lightmass | LightmassSettings | LightSourceAngle**, and its default is 1.0 (shown on the left-hand side in the previous screenshot).

4. Increase it to 10.0 to force up the angle at which the directional light's Emissive surface extends relative to an object receiving light. That influences penumbra sizes for its cast shadow (shown on the right-hand side in the previous screenshot). The **Shadow Exponent** property will also contribute to the Falloff of the penumbra.

5. The light is still not quite right in terms of its direction. Notice that the shadow comes directly from overhead, even though the light we created was placed well in front of the characters. What's happened is that we've switched from a PointLight to a directional light, so you need to rotate the light to face in a certain direction which by default is downwards. Instead, rotate the light so its small blue direction arrow points towards the figures, at around 33 degrees.

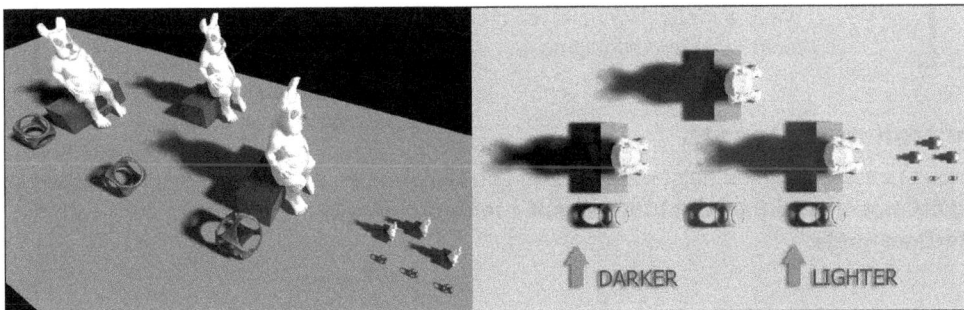

6. To finish up, while enduring much slower lighting builds, try changing up some of the values for the **Light Source Angle**, **Shadow Exponent**, and **Min** and **Max Shadow Resolution**. In the previous screenshot the penumbra is really forced, and the samples are quite clear. The great thing about this penumbra compared to the one from the default PointLight is that it works well even for the small scale models in the foreground. The values were: **ShadowExponent** = 4.444 and **LightSourceAngle** 3.333.

7. The next screenshot is an example that uses even broader settings: **ShadowExponent** = 2.0 and **LightSourceAngle** 10.0.

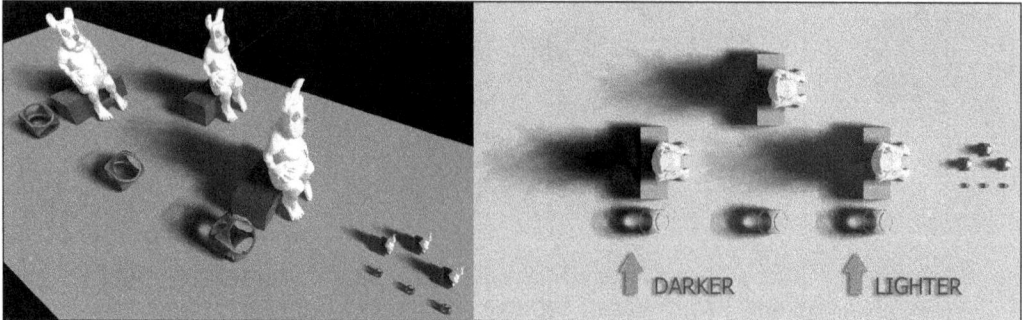

8. A peculiarity of this scene is that the rearmost shadow is noticeably darker than the foremost shadow. This is because the last one isn't receiving any bounce lighting. The light bounces from the last big statue back into the shadow of the first one, making it look less dark. Distance from the light source is irrelevant with directional lights—only direction matters. So, adding a wall at the rear of the scene would help deflect light back to fill the shadow.

> It can be costly in terms of production time to continually test out lighting, because of the build, so use a simple scene to test, and then you can save this scene as a template for high level scenes using copy and paste. Do model layout and play testing in a fast building preview mode. Normally you'd expect to add globals first and then local lights and spotlights.

Controlling hotspots

It is quite easy to adjust a hotspot for a spotlight. Simply open its properties and find the **Light | LightComponent | SpotLightComponent | InnerConeAngle** and adjust it, along with the **OuterConeAngle**.

In the next screenshot, there are two spotlights. The background one has an **InnerConeAngle** of 20 and **OuterConeAngle** of 30. Its **Brightness** is ramped up to 4.0.

The foreground spotlight is set to a lower intensity and much wider **OuterConeAngle** to create a very broad, weak hotspot in order to subtly lighten the tail end of the character's cast shadow. Its hotspot is barely noticeable, but the fill it produces in the shadow is, which assists the penumbra effect. In this recipe, the shadow penumbras were from strong directional lights, and the space was wide open. In most lighting situations shadows are filled from many different angles by multiple direct lights or filled by bounced, indirect light dissipating throughout the surroundings or by ambient sky light.

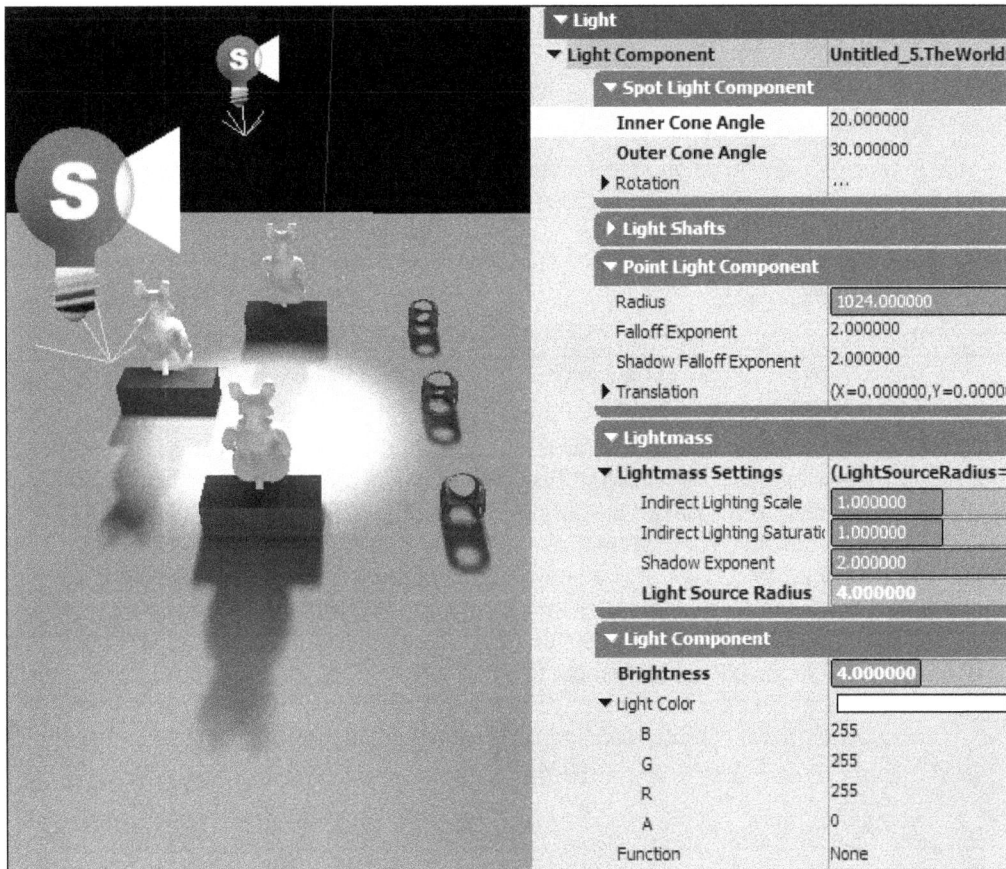

Accessing the main PostProcessChain

PostProcess is an area where UDK shines. It offers three ways to grade the look of the game render in real-time. One way affects all the maps in your game, called the **PostProcessChain**, which is an asset set in the *DefaultEngine.INI* configuration. Another deals with the current map, called the **World Info**. Another deals with parts of the current map, through a BSP volume, called a **PostProcessVolume**. Besides changing the coloration of the level, the PostProcess grading can be used to add DOF (Depth of Field is the measure of focus), blur, motion blur, bloom, and shadow fidelity control, which was discussed briefly in the first recipe of this chapter. Right now, we're going to step through the handling of the primary PostProcess in your game.

How to do it...

1. In ConTEXT, or your chosen text editor, open `C:\UDK\~\UDKGame\Config\DefaultEngine.INI` and search for the line `DefaultPostProcessName=FX_HitEffects.UTPostProcess_Console`. Change this to *Packt.PostProcessChain* or *Yourfolder.PostProcessChain*. Later, you'll create your own asset using the name that you give here.

2. Open UDK, and in the Content Browser, look for the asset *FX_HitEffects. UTPostProcess_Console*; right-click on it and choose **Create A Copy...**, then when prompted give it the same name that you set in the previous step.

3. Double-click the copy to open this in its editor. In the next screenshot it is important to understand that the **MaterialEffect** nodes are all turned off, but certain functions in code might turn them on in some situations. The next screenshot shows that the **UberPostProcessEffect** node is the one doing most of the work. Your network may be strung out in a line, a little differently. The nodes chain together in order of their calculation after the scene renders. The use of the word *Uber* in **UberPostProcessEffect** suggests an effect on the scale of Superman. Actually, it just supersedes previous attempts to create an all-in-one method of controlling the rendered image after its raw calculation by the engine. For the most part, what is already there works pretty well and not much needs to be changed.

4. Notice there's a **Scene | ImageGrain** setting in the *UberPostProcessEffect* properties which takes over the work of the disabled **MaterialEffect** *Film Grain*.

5. **Film Grain** is seen in old photos, ones that used the coarse medium of silver halide suspended in photographic gelatin—or film. The material adds fine noise, which reduces the smoothness of the image overall but also softens edges and can create a unifying effect. Essentially this effect is cosmetic.

6. The **Hit Impact** effect is where the whole screen may go red when the player is heavily wounded.

7. The **AmbientOcclusionEffect**, we'll discuss in the next recipe on **Ambient Occlusion**.

8. A **Vignette** is a dimming of the screen borders to help focus the central part of the image. It is often used in games where the art director wants to leverage its psychological effects. To turn any **MaterialEffect** nodes on, just tick on the check boxes for **Show in Editor** and **Show in Game** in the node's properties.

9. The next screenshot shows that the asset used to generate the vignette is actually quite complex, and the key node in the Material network is the **Scene Texture Sample** based on *SceneTex_Lighting*, which the rest of the nodes modulate.

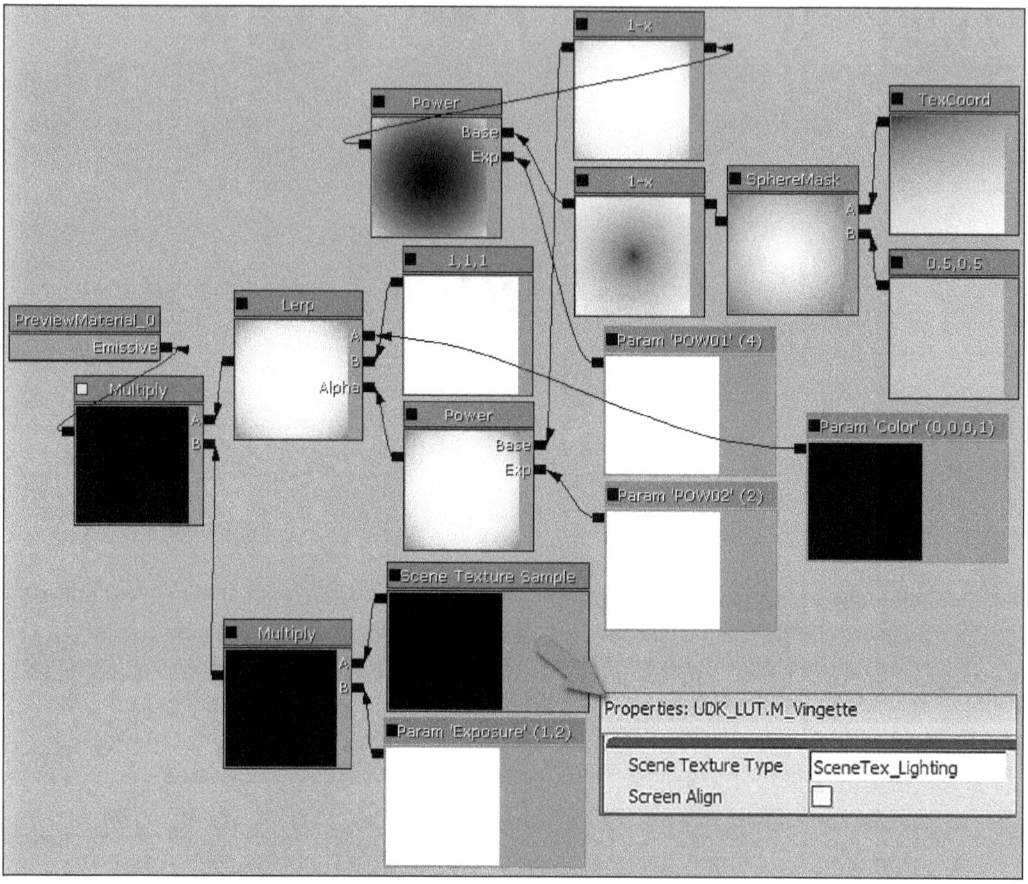

10. Given here is the **Parent Material** of the **Material Instance Constant** (**MIC**) assigned to the *Vignette* **MaterialEffect** node. The **Parameter** nodes *Exposure* and *Color* influence the vignette's appearance, and can be accessed through a **Material Instance Actor** placed in the scene from the **Actor Classes** list.

11. After the **MIC** is assigned to the **MIA** actor, it can be controlled by a *Matinee* in Kismet using a **New Float Material Param** track which has the same **Param Name** in its properties as is used by the node in the initial material network. In the next screenshot the **Param 'Exposure'** is keyed in *Matinee* through the **MIA** actor in the scene it refers to (with the **MIC** set in its **Mat Inst** property). We can now adjust the PostProcess settings parametrically. All of this is discussed step by step in a bonus downloadable PDF recipe: *Creating an animated day to night transition* (available at `http://www.packtpub.com/sites/default/files/downloads/1802EXP Unreal Development Kit Game Design Cookbook_Bonus Recipes.PDF`).

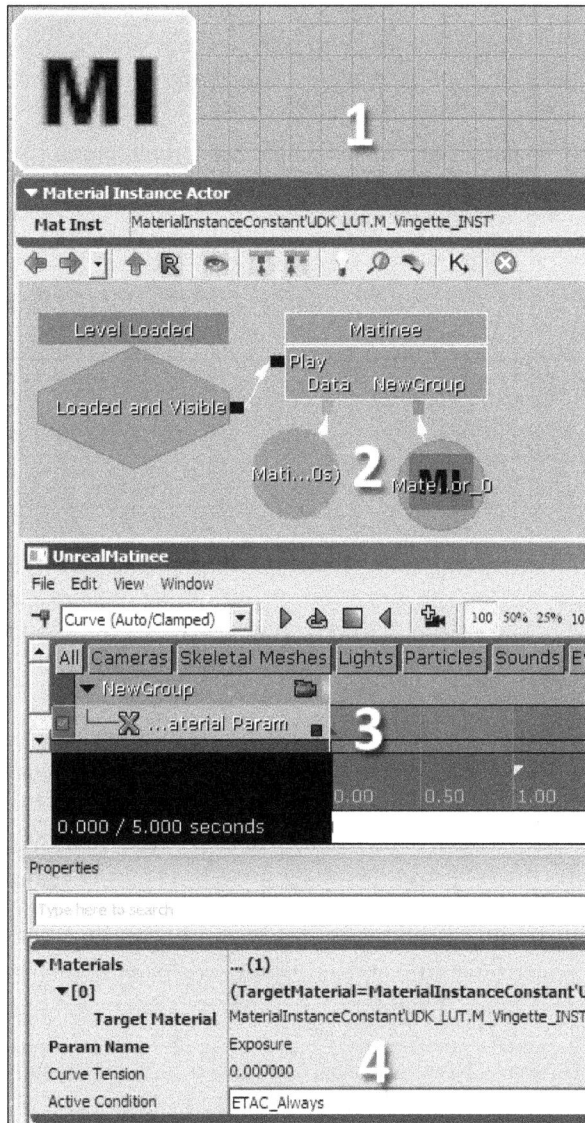

12. What's important to know here is that we've set the configuration of UDK to use the PostProcessChain we've just been examining as the main one. All levels will use its settings. If you want a unified look across your game, no matter what level is loaded, you'd change things such as **DOF** and **Bloom** here.

13. In the **UberPostProcessEffect** node, expand the **Depth of Field** property section and set the **Depth of Field Type** to *BokehDOF*. Bokeh reproduces the effects of a camera aperture's shutter blades. This will create hexagon like patterns if your DOF rendering includes particles producing raindrops or other small highlights. You will need to include a texture for the blades. A good source is the UDK forums: `http://forums.epicgames.com/threads/769625-Free-Bokeh-textures!`

    Here users occasionally post sets and guides, but any black and white hexagon, pentagon, octagon, or even star or cross like shape will do fine, saved as a small, square texture and imported into your package.

14. You can quickly generate one in Photoshop using the **Shapes | Polygon** tool [🖌], setting the number of sides low enough the edges don't blend to a circle. For a finishing touch, add a dim radial gradient over the top. One is provided: *PacktFX.Texture.Bokeh_9*.

15. Add it, or one of your own, to the **UberPostProcessEffect** node's **Depth of Field | Bokeh Texture** channel.

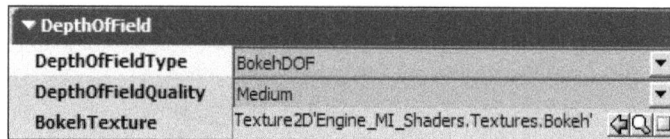

▼ DepthOfField		
DepthOfFieldType	BokehDOF	▼
DepthOfFieldQuality	Medium	▼
BokehTexture	Texture2D'Engine_MI_Shaders.Textures.Bokeh'	◁🔍☐

16. DOF can be set here either using a distance from the camera or the radial distance from a set position in the scene (which is an unusual method best used in a cinematic or loading menu background where you don't have player movement and want to limit the focus around a target object). If your camera to player distance in a top-down game or side-scroller is always locked to a relative offset, then the **FOCUS_position** method might prove useful.

17. The remaining values specify blur amount and distance thresholds for the focus. For now, leave them on their defaults, or game levels you make in future may turn out fuzzy. We will be adjusting DOF in a controlled way in an upcoming recipe.

18. At this time, the PostProcessChain you want to have in your scene is up to you; it just depends whether you are satisfied with the base UDK settings. It's useful to know that UDK's default settings are derived here and there from **Gears of War** by **Epic Games**, which uses strongly colored textures that are then slightly desaturated and tinted to help make things look a bit worn out. You may also notice that the overall values for shadows, mid-tones, and highlights haven been shifted a little in the **UberPostProcess | Scene** properties. This is probably to clamp them to prevent bright spots and overly black darks.

There's more...

MaterialEffects in the PostProcessChain

Let's extend what we've just been through in a somewhat lecture-like way as a practical example by using the PostProcessChain to create a unique depth fog.

On 'UDK Central' there is a great video from the adroit designer **Micahpharoh**: `http://udkc.info/index.php?title=Tutorials:Post_Process_Chain_Material_Example`. It explains how a Material can be set up, using **Math** nodes mainly, to drive the scene coloration to create desaturated toning, edge detection effects, and even distance based distortion. A Material can be built around the **Utility | New Desaturate** operator. To make this kind of effect you can either build a simple operation using a few nodes or a carefully crafted network that drives for a highly art directed look.

To reproduce the desaturated look, the Material that you make should be set to have a **Blend Mode** that is *BLEND_Translucent* and a **Lighting Model** that is *Unlit*. You can use other types, but the default **Opaque** blending won't work. This is because the key operator, a **Scene Texture Sample**, needs transparency. In the next example, we will create a fog effect in a similar way:

1. Start a new Material called *Yourname.Material.PPChainFog*.

2. In the **PreviewMaterial** node's properties, set **Material | Blend** mode to *Blend_Translucent* and the **Material | Lighting Model** to *Unlit*. The operators for the Emissive channel in the Material are shown next. The Emissive channel will be derived from the **Scene Depth** and the scene **DepthofFieldFunction**. The result we're after is a foggy z-depth style Material with a soft circular influence.

3. Hold *1* and click to add a **Constant** and set its **R** value between 0.1 to 0.8 then hook the node up to the Opacity channel of the **PreviewMaterial** node. Later you'll have to tweak the **R** value to taste.

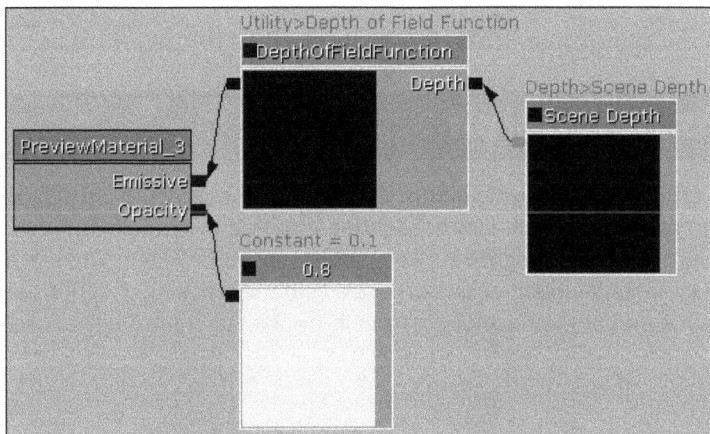

4. The **Scene Depth** node takes the distance from camera pixels to the objects the camera sees. It feeds a **DepthofFieldFunction** node from the **Utility** category, which is the major player here, and we're effectively rendering the scene depth in increasing brightness. Compile the Material but don't close it.

5. In the Content Browser search for *UTPostProcess_Console* or whatever PostProcessChain you have assigned. Highlight it, then go to the **View | World Properties | Rendering** menu and in the **World Post Process Chain** click the assign icon [🔄] to assign it.

6. Open the PostProcessChain in its editor, and click on the **MaterialEffect** node that is reserved for the **Vignette** effect, which is currently not used. The default Material for this is *UDK_LUT.M_Vingette* (sic). Replace this with the Material we just created and compiled: *Yourname.Material.PPChainFog*. You can also use *PacktExtra.Material. PPChainLow* if you prefer.

7. In the **MaterialEffect** properties, also turn on **Show in Editor** and **Show in Game**. You should see the effect of a depth fog occur in the viewport. Try changing the values for the **Constant** node feeding the Opacity channel section in the Material you kept open.

8. In the following screenshot on the left-hand side, the enabled **Vignette** effect darkens the frame edges. On the right, the 'pseudo fog' effect clouds the background.

Ambient occlusion

Scene ambient occlusion is off by default in UDK, and generally speaking just turning it on will be enough to get a nice result. Indirect lighting is not off by default. The main distinction is that indirect light is a fill from light bounces, adding secondary light onto surfaces not lit by direct lights or key lights. Ambient occlusion deals with the blocking of light from the sky (the indirect light source and any bounced light from it) by objects in proximity to each other.

Think about it like this. If you hold up one hand, with your knuckles facing a lamp, you'll still see some light on your palm (unless the lamp is weak and you are in a huge empty room). The light on your palm is bounced light, or indirect lighting. Now, if you lift your other hand too, so your palms are facing, you will notice the palm surfaces get darker and darker the closer your hands get. The indirect light is occluded. So ambient occlusion is the occlusion of the sky light (usually thought of as a soft, diffuse, evenly spread light from all directions), not the bounced direct light, although that is occluded too.

Having said that, it really only makes sense to calculate ambient occlusion in an outdoors setting. The main reason to trouble with Ambient Occlusion settings in UDK is to choose between **real time calculated ambient occlusion** and **baked ambient occlusion** (which can take a while to pre-calculate but tends to look better since it is stable). That's what we'll cover in this example.

Getting ready

From the provided content, open the file _Packt_08_AmbientOcclusion_Start.UDK_, and note that in the Kismet there is a locked off **_Matinee_** set camera for PIE so we can be sure to capture the same view each time we rebuilt lighting.

How to do it...

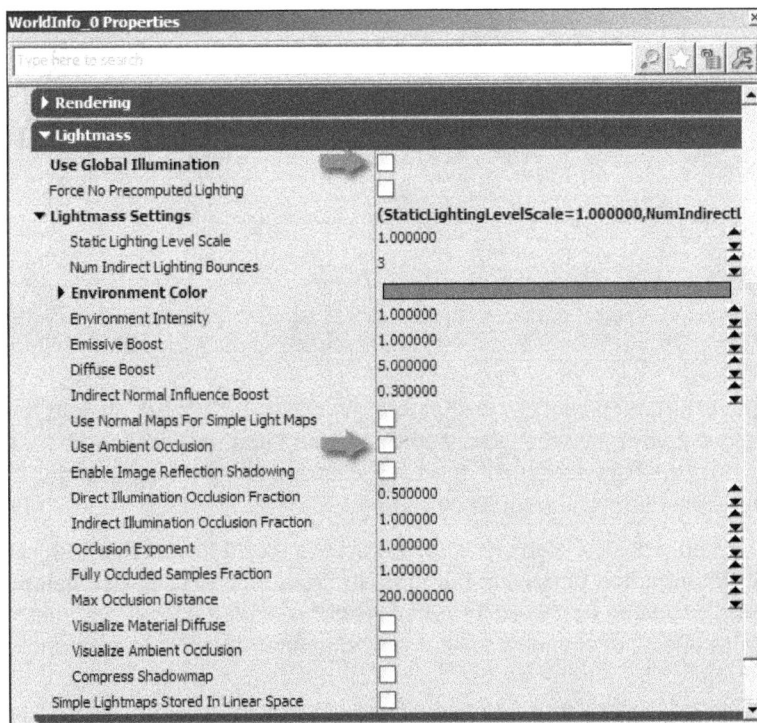

1. You can see the **World Info | Lightmass** settings in this screenshot. Both **Use Global Illumination** (indirect lighting) and **Use Ambient Occlusion** are off. The result of building light gives us very black shadows. This is shown in the next image, marked **NO GI**.

2. Turn on **Use Global Illumination** and rebuild the lighting, and compare the results. A nice way to do this is to screen grab (*Prt Scr*) and paste into Photoshop layers and then hide/unhide the layers to make comparisons easier. In the next image, marked **GI**, you can see the indirect lighting fills the shadows.

3. Turn on **Use Ambient Occlusion**, rebuild the lighting, and compare the results. The next image, marked **AO+GI**, shows that surfaces encroaching on each other, such as around corners, cavities, and beneath objects get darker.

4. Increase the **Occlusion Exponent** to 3.0 and rebuild the lighting. You can see that the occluded surfaces are given a stronger contrast.

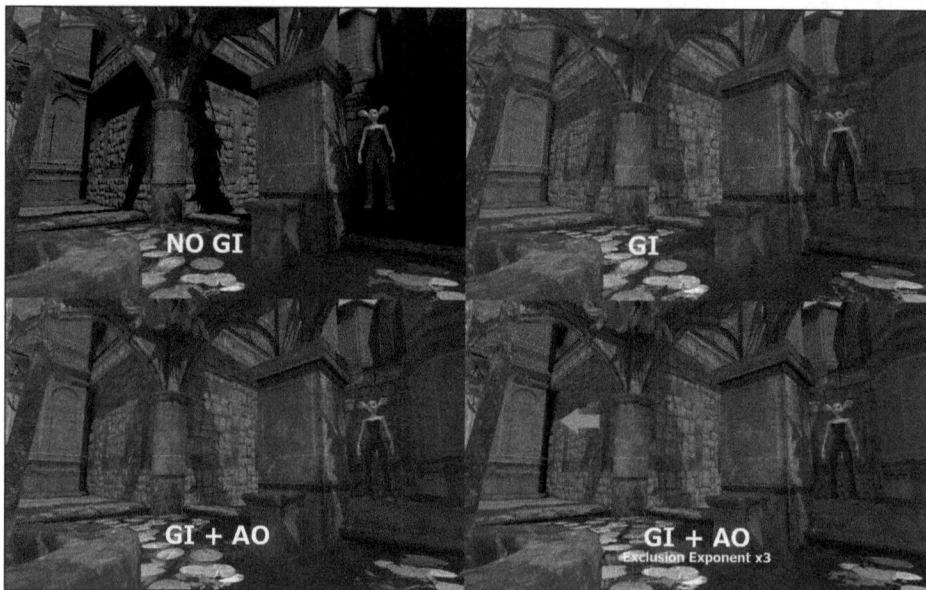

5. The initial difference is easy to spot, but the occlusion is more obvious if we push it. In the previous image, the increased **Occlusion Exponent** is seen where the arrow points into the tight wall crack. It is also apparent along the pond water line. This is because the surfaces are quite close to each other.

6. To spread out the occlusion, you can adjust the **World Properties | Lightmass | Direct Illumination Occlusion Fraction**, **Indirect Illumination Occlusion Fraction** settings, and **Fully Occluded Samples Fraction**. Here it is probably best to trial and error the effects of changing the values. Some changes will be dramatic and others subtle. Note that sometimes you won't notice a change through a static camera that you may notice when moving around the level.

7. Besides the **Occlusion Exponent**, which adjusts the power of the AO, an important value to keep tabs on is the **Max Occlusion Distance**. If you have two blocks facing each other (and their shadows don't fall across each other due to their angle to the main light) then you can measure the **Max Occlusion Distance** by increasing it in steps. In the next screenshot, the blocks are 70 units apart, a distance obtained in the top view using the *MMB* tape measure.

> A tip related to this kind of comparison: use **Detail Lighting** (*Alt* + 5) and the **Lighting Only** (*Alt* + 6) to see how your scene shadows look without the interference of textures. It is harder to evaluate shadows in dark scenes with a lot of contrast than it is to evaluate shadows in mid contrast scenes.

Depth of field

There are three depth of field looks you'll want to learn to achieve. The *first* is when the background is out of focus and the foreground is sharp, which is fairly easy, and the *second*, which is somewhat more difficult, is the opposite, where the background is sharp while the foreground is blurred. The *third* case is where both foreground and background are blurry but a telephoto style patch of the middle distance is sharp.

UDK gives us two ways to create Depth of Field, and these handle two of the above goals well. A **Position** based blur, being locked to a world location, is good for the third case, middle ground focus, but isn't dynamic. A **Distance** based blur method defocuses the background far better than it handles the foreground.

DOF can be applied in the scene based on a BSP volume created by the designer. If you use these, only the volume you are in yields a result to the screen draw, and if you are outside a volume you won't see its effects. On top of that, post-processing volumes compete with each other if they overlap, and only one DOF setting will win out, so having multiple DOF volumes layered on each to get near and far focus will not work. It is possible to successively expose volumes with different settings through Kismet, which is demonstrated at the end of the recipe. In the meanwhile, we'll go through the three basic settings needed to make **Depth of Field** work within a volume.

Getting ready

Open the scene *Packt_08_DOF_START.UDK*. The view is set to a locked **Matinee** camera and player movement is constrained. This is so we can compare DOF values from an exact position. When we're done, the *Matinee* and *Cinematic Mode* can be released.

How to do it...

1. Let's start with the easiest method, where the background is blurred out. You should check that your **UberPostProcessEffect** in the assigned PostProcessChain asset has **Use World Properties** ticked on.

    > If you aren't sure which PostProcessChain is set for UDK, this is defined in `C:\UDK\~\UDKGame\Config\DefaultEngine.INI`, in the `[Engine.Engine]` section. An example would be: `DefaultPostProcessName=Packt.PostProcessChain`. This way you can set DOF in the PostProcessChain for all your maps. We covered this earlier in the recipe on *Accessing the main PostProcessChain*.

2. We're just going to effect the current level. Open the **View | World Properties** menu and expand **World Info**. **DOF** settings are under the **Default Post Process Settings** category.

3. Turn on the unchecked tick box in the channel for **Enable DOF** (the one to the right-hand side, not the one on the left that is ticked by default). For now make sure the **DOF Focus Type** is set to *FOCUS_Distance*.

4. Set all the values for DOF to 0.0, from **DOF Blur Bloom Kernel Size** down to **DOF Interpolation Duration**. This removes all chance of seeing DOF from the world settings. The first value to ramp up is the **DOF Blur Kernel Size** (which affects the radius of the DOF/Bokeh effect, and how blurry the scene gets). Set a value of 10.0.

5. If you want to blur the entire image (which is useful if your scene is just the backdrop for some kind of game menu overlay) set the **Min** value to 1.0.

6. Having done so, put it back to 0.0 as apart from total blurry vision, there's not much use in raising it. Instead, set the **MaxFar** value to 1.0. You will see that, again, the entire image is blurred. This is because the start distance for the blur is 0.0 units from the camera, and everything past that distance gets blurred. So, we also need to set a distance for the focal point (or a target distance), and a radius of effect, or a focal range.

7. Set the **DOF Focus Distance** to 512, and the **DOF Focus Inner Radius** to 256. The camera will focus 512 units ahead of itself, and all around it for 256 units outwards will be in focus, with a Falloff set by the **DOF Falloff Exponent**, which you can set from 0.5 to 1.0.

8. In the previous screenshot we see a background blur and foreground focus. In the examples coming up next, we can add middle distance blur just by shifting the settings, as in **A**, and reverse the focus, as in **B**, and also have a focus only in the middle distance, as in **C**. Example **D** shows that foreground blur, when it is ramped up high, cause an edge detection artifact where the surface is blurred but the edge is not.

The next image shows the DOF properties for A, B, C, D:

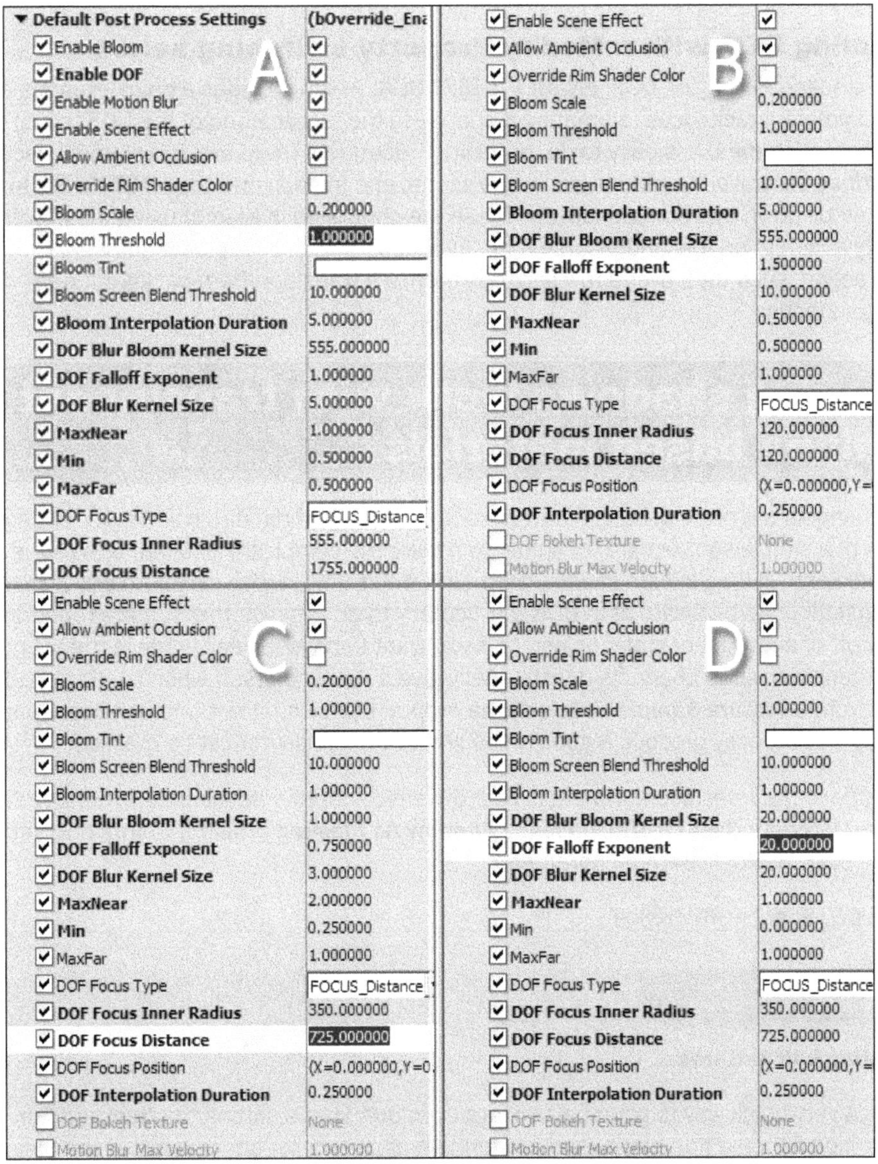

Default Post Process Settings	(bOverride_Ena
Enable Bloom	✔
Enable DOF	✔
Enable Motion Blur	✔
Enable Scene Effect	✔
Allow Ambient Occlusion	✔
Override Rim Shader Color	☐
Bloom Scale	0.200000
Bloom Threshold	1.000000
Bloom Tint	
Bloom Screen Blend Threshold	10.000000
Bloom Interpolation Duration	5.000000
DOF Blur Bloom Kernel Size	555.000000
DOF Falloff Exponent	1.000000
DOF Blur Kernel Size	5.000000
MaxNear	1.000000
Min	0.500000
MaxFar	0.500000
DOF Focus Type	FOCUS_Distance
DOF Focus Inner Radius	555.000000
DOF Focus Distance	1755.000000

A

Enable Scene Effect	✔
Allow Ambient Occlusion	✔
Override Rim Shader Color	☐
Bloom Scale	0.200000
Bloom Threshold	1.000000
Bloom Tint	
Bloom Screen Blend Threshold	10.000000
Bloom Interpolation Duration	5.000000
DOF Blur Bloom Kernel Size	555.000000
DOF Falloff Exponent	1.500000
DOF Blur Kernel Size	10.000000
MaxNear	0.500000
Min	0.500000
MaxFar	1.000000
DOF Focus Type	FOCUS_Distance
DOF Focus Inner Radius	120.000000
DOF Focus Distance	120.000000
DOF Focus Position	(X=0.000000,Y=
DOF Interpolation Duration	0.250000
DOF Bokeh Texture	None
Motion Blur Max Velocity	1.000000

B

Enable Scene Effect	✔
Allow Ambient Occlusion	✔
Override Rim Shader Color	☐
Bloom Scale	0.200000
Bloom Threshold	1.000000
Bloom Tint	
Bloom Screen Blend Threshold	10.000000
Bloom Interpolation Duration	1.000000
DOF Blur Bloom Kernel Size	1.000000
DOF Falloff Exponent	0.750000
DOF Blur Kernel Size	3.000000
MaxNear	2.000000
Min	0.250000
MaxFar	1.000000
DOF Focus Type	FOCUS_Distance
DOF Focus Inner Radius	350.000000
DOF Focus Distance	725.000000
DOF Focus Position	(X=0.000000,Y=0
DOF Interpolation Duration	0.250000
DOF Bokeh Texture	None
Motion Blur Max Velocity	1.000000

C

Enable Scene Effect	✔
Allow Ambient Occlusion	✔
Override Rim Shader Color	☐
Bloom Scale	0.200000
Bloom Threshold	1.000000
Bloom Tint	
Bloom Screen Blend Threshold	10.000000
Bloom Interpolation Duration	1.000000
DOF Blur Bloom Kernel Size	20.000000
DOF Falloff Exponent	20.000000
DOF Blur Kernel Size	20.000000
MaxNear	1.000000
Min	0.000000
MaxFar	1.000000
DOF Focus Type	FOCUS_Distance
DOF Focus Inner Radius	350.000000
DOF Focus Distance	725.000000
DOF Focus Position	(X=0.000000,Y=
DOF Interpolation Duration	0.250000
DOF Bokeh Texture	None
Motion Blur Max Velocity	1.000000

D

Animating DOF with a Modify Property switching series

Open the scene *Packt_08_DOF_ENABLINGTEST.UDK*, which provides a quick example of how to animate a rack focus (animating a change in the target plane of the DOF focus) using **PostProcessVolumes**. It is easy to do, but a little repetitive. There are 10 volumes placed over the *Matinee* controlled Camera Actor in the scene, and in each one their **DOF Focus Inner Radius** steps down by 100 respectively. These are controlled in Kismet using the *Modify Property* action to enable and disable them in series through a loop back through a *Switch* action, such that, over a few seconds there's a transition from background to foreground focus.

Ensuring shadows work with translucent or alpha based materials

Alpha channels are often used to control opacity (of leaves, hair, dirt in windows, or decals). The use of a simple square card, or sprite, to render the complexity of a leaf or a tuft of fur is highly efficient. Getting a 'hair' shadow off a card with translucency isn't hard but there are some limitations to be aware of in UDK, particularly to do with whether you are rendering a shadow off of a moving or static object, or if you want to have moving lights in the scene. Light from Material Emissive channels doesn't really give a detailed result when casting shadows derived from a *Texture Sample* node's **Alpha** output. Light from the DominantDirectionalLight type also won't readily produce a good alpha shadow because it must be masked.

> To make the translucent Materials cast dynamic shadows as masked Materials, set the Material's **Cast Lit Translucency Shadow As Masked** property to true and set the Opacity Mask Material parameter
>
> —UDN: Shadow Reference

Generating hair textures

1. A very quick way to get a hair texture from 3ds Max is setting the **Hair and Fur** modifier on a thin plane, and rendering it against a flat background (if the hair is to be dark, render on white). You can set the background color by pressing 8 and adjusting the **Color** sampler. The background color will be ignored in the Alpha calculation when saving the image to a 32bit .TGA.

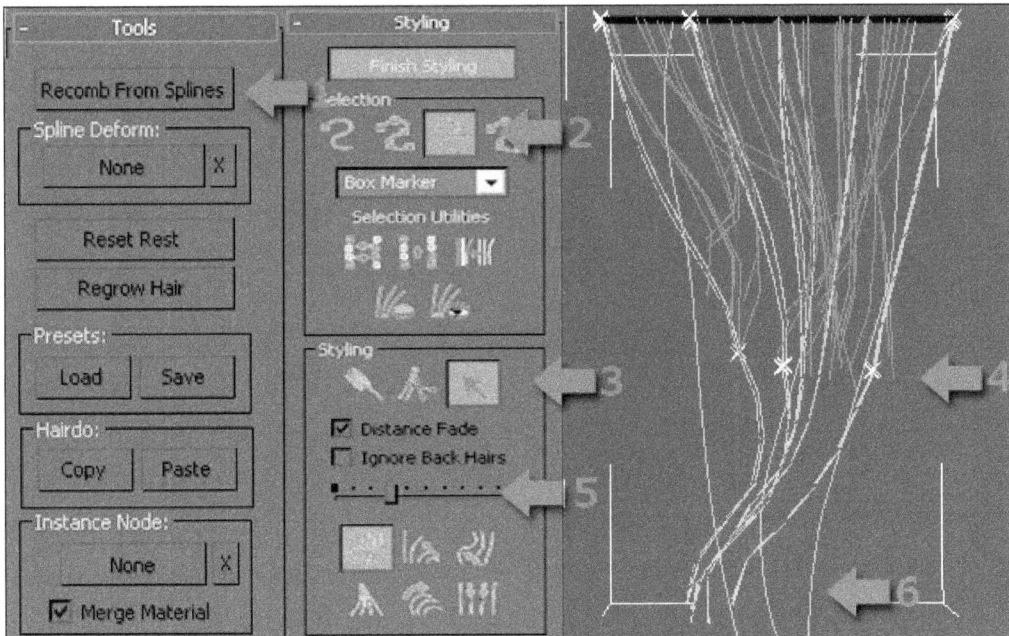

Above, the properties of the **Hair and Fur** modifier are highlighted in so far as they help give a quick result. For **1, Recomb from Splines** lets you choose a **Spline Shape, 6**, that you've made in the viewport from which to drive the look of the hairs. **Styling, 2**, using points gives you most control of custom styling. Drag on just the hair ends. To adjust the hair in points mode you have to use the **Select** tool, **3**. The points in the viewport highlight with an X, **4**, and brushing them directly will allow you to shape the hair using the transform tool, for which there is a **brush size** slider, **5**. In the previous screenshot the actual hairs (red) are shorter than the guides (orange). Further down in the modifier there are numerical values for **root and tip width**, **scale of the hair**, **cut length**, and so on. In the end, ensure that you render a square (512x512) image of the hair.

2. In UDK, import the .TGA to your package, setting in the import options the *BLEND_Translucent* setting instead of *BLEND_Opaque*. You can tell the importer to automatically create a Material for you using the **RGB** channel for Diffuse and the **Alpha** for Opacity. Set the Material type to *Anisotropic* so it handles shine in a hair-like way, and to be *Two Sided* since we'll be using the Material on a plane. This can also be done after importing the texture, within the Material Editor.

3. Open the Material, and set up its ***MaterialPreview*** properties as shown next, noting the additional **Translucency** properties that target how hair will respond to lighting and shadowing:

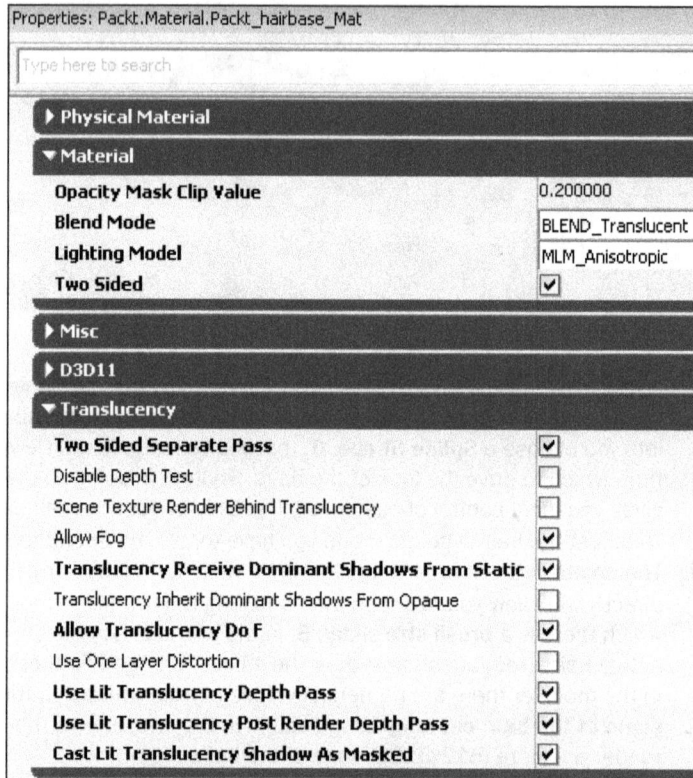

Properties: Packt.Material.Packt_hairbase_Mat

Type here to search

▶ Physical Material

▼ Material

Opacity Mask Clip Value	0.200000
Blend Mode	BLEND_Translucent
Lighting Model	MLM_Anisotropic
Two Sided	☑

▶ Misc

▶ D3D11

▼ Translucency

Two Sided Separate Pass	☑
Disable Depth Test	☐
Scene Texture Render Behind Translucency	☐
Allow Fog	☑
Translucency Receive Dominant Shadows From Static	☑
Translucency Inherit Dominant Shadows From Opaque	☐
Allow Translucency Do F	☑
Use One Layer Distortion	☐
Use Lit Translucency Depth Pass	☑
Use Lit Translucency Post Render Depth Pass	☑
Cast Lit Translucency Shadow As Masked	☑

4. For the network, set it up something similar to what's given next so that you have a color influence and a specular influence. **Multiply** the **Texture Sample** content using a **Constant** so you can raise and lower the result as required.

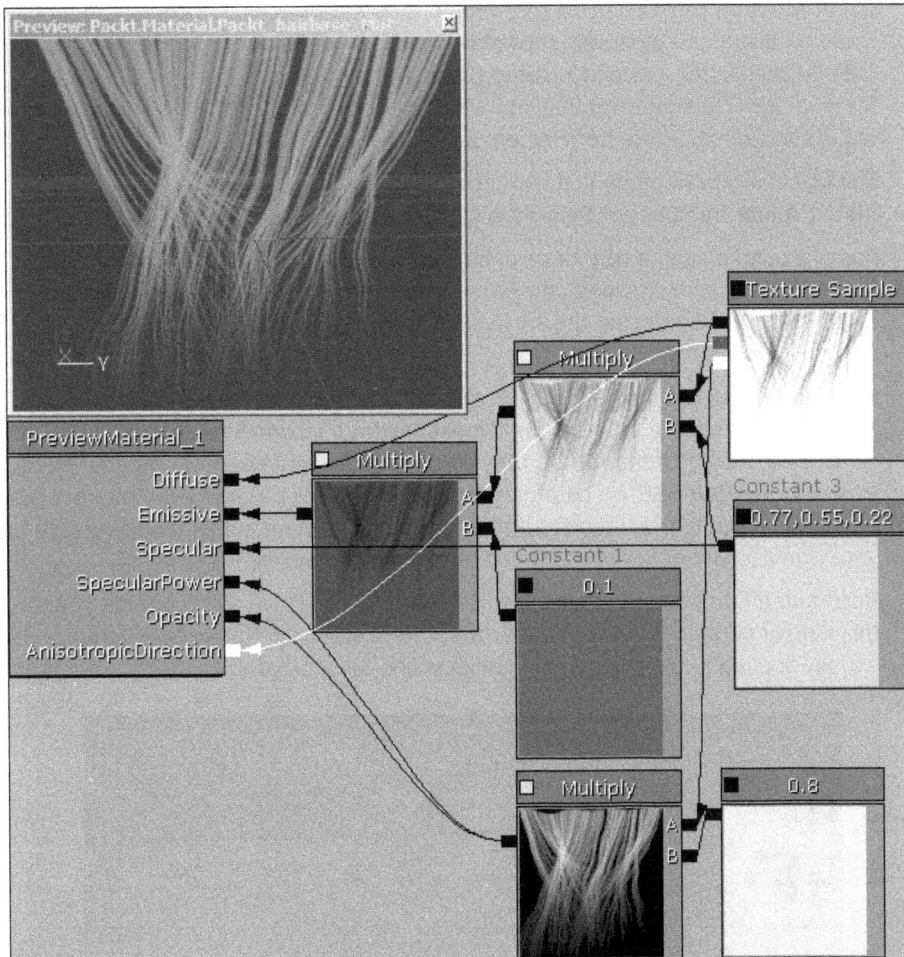

5. Compile and save the Material. Temporarily unhook the **Anisotropic Direction** channel from the **Texture Sample** and set the **Blend Mode** to *MLM_Unlit* to show only the Emissive contribution. The hair will darken dramatically, so it's clear the gleam of the hair needs the Anisotropic setting. An **Anisoptropic Direction** should ideally be biased to R, G, or B, given they represent an X, Y, or Z direction. Close the Material Editor without saving this change.

Shadows for transparent surfaces

1. Keep the Material asset highlighted in the Content Browser. In the main editor, place the provided StaticMesh *Packt.Mesh.HairMesh* and apply your Material to that. In a real situation you'd be using many small sets of hair meshes. The same process could be used for long grass, cobwebs, or branches, but it is good to test this out for the first time using just one isolated piece. Remember that the situation works for any Material with transparency that you want shadows from, and the point is to learn how static shadowing differs from dynamic shadowing.

2. The Material you've made is translucent so it can only be selected directly when **View | Allow Translucent Selection** [🖼] is active.

3. Add a ground object, a BSP box will be fine, with the 'hair' placed above it. Select all the BSP surfaces by clicking one BSP surface in the perspective view and pressing *Shift + S*, then *F5*, and set the surfaces' **Lightmap Resolution** to 1 or 2, for the best shadowing possible.

4. Hold *L* and click to add a PointLight, and build to see how the defaults turn out. Press *F4* and edit the property **LightmassSettings | LightSourceRadius** to a small value, because the default 32.0 may cause a significant shadow spread if placed closed to the *Hair* BSP. Be careful what angle you view the hair BSP from because its anisotropic highlight will tend to only show from a certain angle. Realizing this may save time, so just orbit around the object to check this.

5. Build and PIE to see the results. A base PointLight will give a reasonable shadow for this kind of situation, but remember that this is static lighting or BSP lighting. Hair is usually applied to moving dynamic objects like SkeletalMeshes.

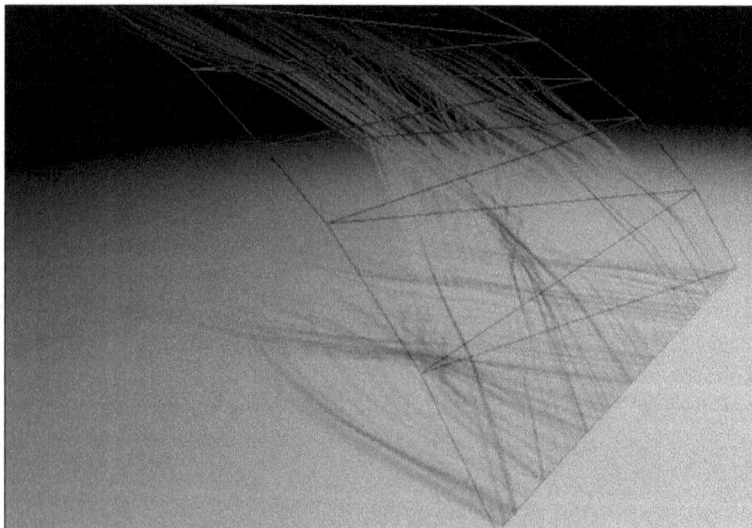

6. Certain lights are designed for dynamic objects, and the shadow we have built is not really going to work. Select the Hair BSP and right click and choose **Convert | Convert to Static Mesh**. Name it *YOURFOLDER.Mesh.HairTest*. Place this in the scene beside the BSP using the right-click method (choose **Add RigidBody**: *YOURFOLDER.Mesh.HairTest*). This is important as we want a RigidBody not a StaticMesh in the scene.

7. For the light, enable its **Dynamic** properties in the lighting channel and shadow casting sections. No matter what you change and how much you fight with the light and object settings, you won't get a dynamic shadow for the hair. The reason lies in the Material, which is set as translucent. Switching to dynamic lighting means we need to switch to a masked opacity.

8. Right-click on the *HairTest* RigidBody and choose **Material | Find in Content Browser**. Right-click on it and choose **Create a copy**. Name the copy *YourFolder. Material.HairMasked_Mat* and open it up.

9. Unhook the feed into the Opacity channel and hook it up instead to the Opacity Mask channel directly below. In the ***PreviewMaterial*** properties, set the **Blend Mode** as *BLEND_SoftMasked*, and ramp the **Opacity Clip Mask Value** to 0.2 or so. Notice how the alpha gets chewed away the higher this value is. Find a nice balance for the mask, around 0.12, then save the Material and make sure it remains highlighted.

10. Right-click on the RigidBody actor in the scene and choose **Material | Assign from Content Browser**. Immediately you should see solid, dynamic shadows appear. You can adjust these as in the previous recipe to soften the shadow or generate a penumbra for it. Reduce the darkness of the cast shadow using the color picker in the property **Mod Shadow Color**, below **Lighting Channels**.

11. In this example, notice the dynamic shadow even affects the SkeletalMesh actors added to the scene. The hair is now a RigidBody, and the D/S is using a **Whole Scene Dynamic Shadow Radius** of 1024 in its properties.

12. The next example shows a similar result using only the light calculation from a StaticMesh whose Material includes an Emissive channel. *Emissive lighting* was the topic of the first recipe in this chapter. The distance Falloff for the shadow on the hair (a RigidBody) and the SkeletalMesh is set up through the property for each object: **Light Environment | Dynamic Light Environment Component | Lighting Bounds Scale**, which has been set from 1 to 4. Notice the shadow from the StaticMesh is lighter than the hair's solid dynamic shadow.

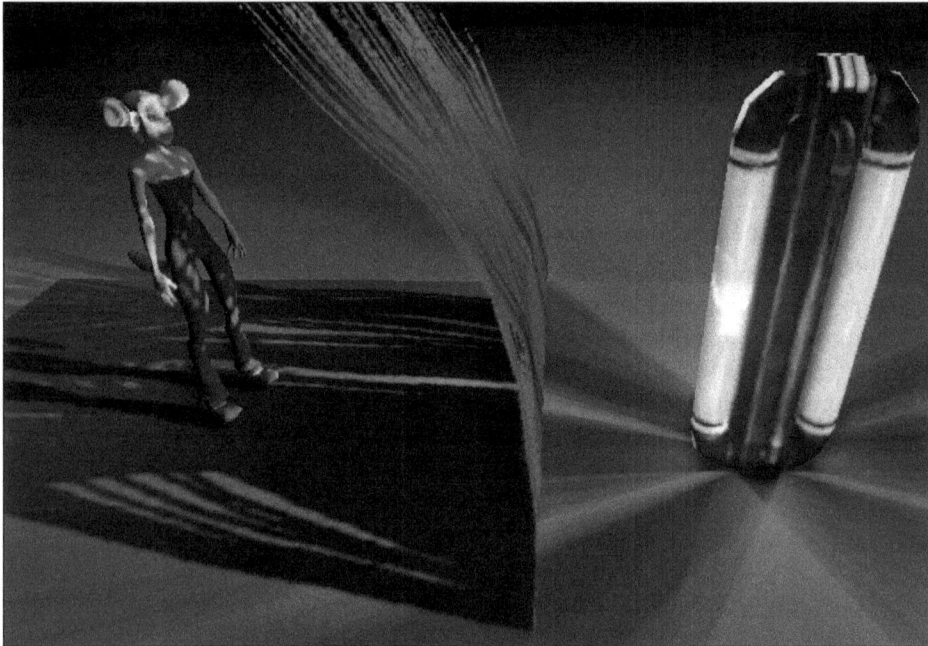

How it works...

As we've discussed, moving objects require their dynamic shadows to use Opacity Mask settings for clip masks, while StaticMesh actors can use the higher quality **Translucent** settings. Some light types (base PointLights for instance) favor static objects and others (DominantDirectionalLight) favor dynamic objects. For clipping masks, to get the best result, it is useful to consider the resolution of the surface you're casting the shadow against, and also the resolution of the Material itself. Notice how the final images show a few floating or stray endings, because clipping masks use a clipping value to chew into the texture.

Enabling and controlling light shafts

In previous scenes we have already seen the use of **Light Shafts** (or God Rays) which disperse around objects occluding any light on which rays are enabled. The classic use for light shafts is as a feature of sunlight, but any light can have Light Shafts enabled in its properties, and this can be used to create a 'beams through fog' effect without really doing anything more than turn them on for a given light. There are a few properties worth exploring, to tune the look of light shafts when they're used.

1. The given screenshot shows a sequence from an animated light casting light shafts around a 'sun' mesh, which is just an Emissive sphere. The example comes from our online bonus recipe (PDF), that supplements the book *Creating an animated day to night transition* and can be found at `http://www.packtpub.com/sites/default/files/downloads/1802EXP Unreal Development Kit Game Design Cookbook_Bonus Recipes.PDF`.

2. For the current scene, which you may wish to do first, we're just dealing with the basics. Open the scene *Packt_08_LightShafts_Start.UDK*. It includes a DominantDirectionalLight and a Skydome, which are necessary for the effect.

3. In the center of the map's compound there is a D/S light giving us a sunlight. It has light shafts turned on, but the contribution is subtle. Add some trees or any tall mesh you can look up past towards the sun. We've used the *Banana Plant* asset for this book.

4. From the Content Browser, add the same Emissive sun sphere that we used in the previous scene, *Packt.Mesh.SampleSphere*. Look at the Skydome and see where the brightest spot is, and place the sun in line with it. It should be moved high above the scene, as the Skydome is really big. A parallax effect is needed where the sun doesn't appear to move against the sky while the foreground elements should.

5. Add an **Exponential Height Fog** actor to the scene with a **Fog Density** of 0.1 as this will increase the effectiveness or interest of the light shafts.

6. Frame the *Banana Plants* against the sun, open the D/S light's properties and set the **Light Shaft | Occlusion Depth Range** to 88, then 888, then 8888, then 300000 to see the effect of this change. Above that, it won't change much. You should notice the sun glow and its light wrapping effect reduce as you step up. Go with 8888 to have significant bloom, and move on to the next step.

7. Adjust the **Radial Blur Percent** in steps. 15 is the lowest value, and 100 is a fairly hefty spread. Choose 88.

8. The value **OcclusionMaskDarkness** sets the darkness of where the rays are blocked. 1 is a minimal darkness, and 0.1 is quite dark. Choose 0.88.

9. Set the **BloomScreenBlendThreshold** to 8. This value is a bloom control based on whether the scene object is brighter than this value. Higher values bloom more.

> The settings that we just went through are shown in the upper part of the next screenshot, and reduced values are shown underneath. Neither set of values is wrong. The point is to show that a variety of looks can be achieved with the light shafts beyond simply enabling the feature.

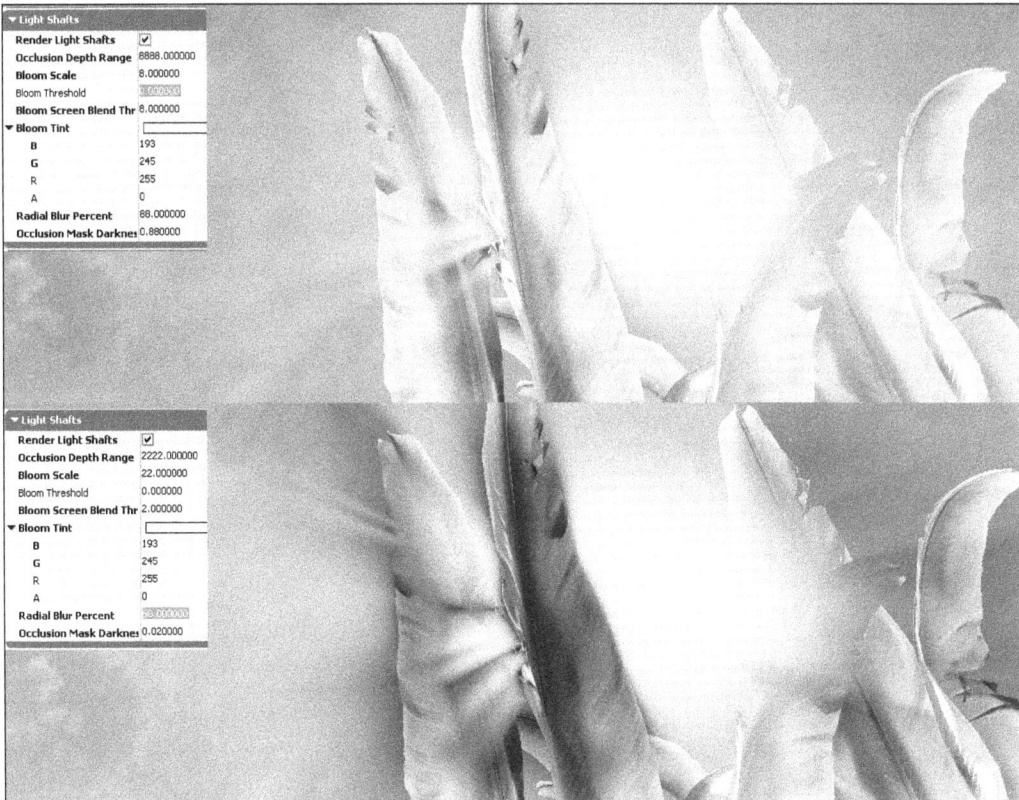

See also

The next recipe tunes the compound scene that we just worked with, adding lens flares.

Enhancing sunrays using lens flares

A lens flare is a *distraction* in an image caused by stray light in the camera lens. There are two kinds of lens flares. One is directional, based on a cone (much the same as is used by a spotlight) and the other is radial (standard). Flares are a modified version of a particle, and have an editor much like Cascade, and their elements are made through the Material Editor. If you have been thorough with the chapters so far, you'll be kind of familiar with a lot of the steps required. The order of ceremonies is outlined in the UDN page: http://udn.epicgames.com/Three/LensFlareEditorUserGuide.html. In this recipe we are going to construct a lens flare from scratch to place in an existing lit scene.

Getting ready

From the provided content, open *Packt_08_LensFlare_Start.UDK* and note the big sun sphere hanging under the Skydome. Our lens flare effect will serve to complement it.

How to do it...

1. In the Content Browser, in your folder, right-click and choose **New LensFlare**. Name the asset `Yourfolder.LensFlare.Test_LensFlare`. The **Unreal LensFlare** Editor will open. The key idea to grasp is that each element the user adds to the lens flare has a distance value based on an offset from a **Source element**. A lens flare can include different 'shapes' spread at varying apparent distances.

2. Search in the Content Browser for *PacktFX.Texture.Packt_FlareShape_A*. Highlight it, right-click, and choose **Find Package**. You'll find five flare shape textures (plus a few others used for DOF that would also work fine). They have a black backdrop and a radial pattern. These were generated quickly in Photoshop using Gradients and the Shape tool and some blurring filters.

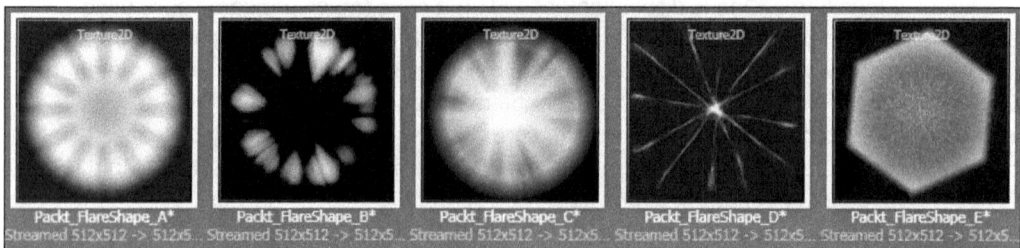

3. Highlight these, right-click and choose **Properties**. In the properties dialog, expand **Texture2D** and choose **Clamp** instead of the default **Wrap**. This will allow us to rotate the texture without the corners suffering any overlap problems.

4. Create Materials for the textures. You can select them all, then right-click and choose **Create New Material** and UDK will generate the **Texture Samples** for you. Hook the **Texture Sample** to the Emissive and Opacity channels. Then set the Material **Blend Type** to _BLEND_Translucent_, set it to be **Two sided** and use the **Lighting Model | MLM_Unlit**.

5. If you want to, add a **Coordinate | Rotator** node to the UV inputs for each Material's **Texture Sample**. Set a rotation speed to 0.05. This gives the lens flares a spin. This is not a realistic feature of a lens flare, but does look interesting.

6. For the Materials that will be used with a lens flare, in the **_PreviewMaterial_** properties the **Usage | Used With Lens Flare** property should be ticked on.

7. Double-click your **LensFlare** asset, and in the **Source** element set the **LFMaterials** entry to _PacktFX.Material.Demo_FlareShape_F_mat_. Right-click on the element and choose **Add Element After**. Here, set the **Element Name** to _A_, and set the **LFMaterials** entry to use the Material you made driven by the texture _Packt_FlareShape_A_, and continue to repeat the pattern to add more elements, as shown next. The order is unimportant in this example.

8. The distance given to each element determines the spreading out of the shapes. It should increment automatically if you use the **Normalize Radial Distance** in each element's properties.

9. Excluding the **Source Element**, newly added elements are all created with a **Size | XYZ** of 0.2 by 0.2. Change this so no two elements are the same, within a range of 0.1 to 1. The **Source Element** default size is 75x75x75. It can be used as a sun. You can also effect the size using a **Scaling | Distribution | Constant**, and, if you want the LensFlare to be, for instance, a stretched oval rather than round, you can use the **Axis Scale** parameter. A very important thing to note is that if _bNormalizeRadialDistance_ is enabled, 1.0 will represent the camera distance from the source to the edge of the screen. Using this, you want to use small numbers indeed, such as: A= 0.01, D=0.1, C=0.2, F=0.66, E=0.75, B=0.95.

10. Further down, you'll see an **Alpha | Distribution | Constant** that will allow you to fade the Material for each element. The **Color | Distribution | Constant | XYZ** lets you tint each shape in the regular XYZ = RGB style.

11. For now, let's go with the way things are, having set the distances and some size variation. We need to set the LensFlare asset in the scene to further tweak it. Press the **Save Thumbnail Image** icon [🖻], close the **LensFlare** Editor, and save your package, or use the prepared asset *PacktFX.LensFlare.Sun_LF* instead.

12. With the asset highlighted in the Content Browser, right-click in the scene and choose **Add LensFlare**: *Sun_LF* (or use yours).

13. You may notice that light shafts affect the lens flare actor, but this is only the icon being affected. If you observe this, press G to toggle game mode and check out the difference. The **LensFlare** actor displays as a particle Emitter.

14. Place the **LensFlare** actor right up by the sun sphere that we added earlier, just beneath it. You can see the lens flare affect the editor by pressing the toggle for **Real Time** playback [🔊] *Ctrl + R*. Now you will be able to adjust the relative distances, sizes, and opacity of the lens flare elements back in the **LensFlare** editor.

15. The values of the Emissive component in the flare Materials can also be altered to taste.

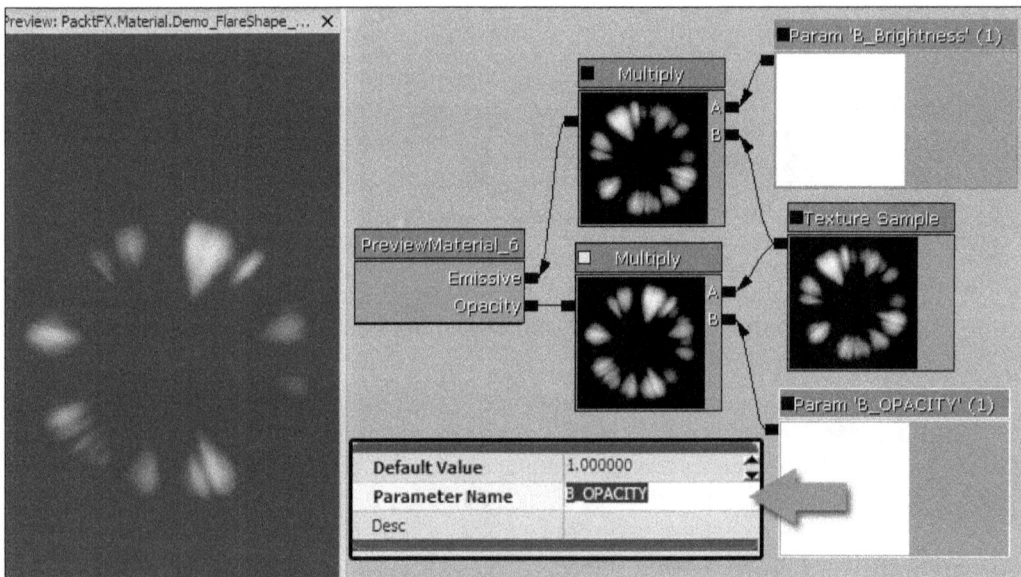

Here we set *B_OPACITY* as a parameter. Next, we drive *B_OPACITY* in the lens flare.

▼ Lens Flare Editor Property Wrapper	
▼ Element	(ElementName="B",RayDistance=0.950
Element Name	B
Ray Distance	0.950000
Is Enabled	☑
Use Source Distance	☐
Normalize Radial Distance	☑
Modulate Color By Source	☑
▶ **Size**	(X=0.660000,Y=0.660000,Z=0.660000)
▶ **LFMaterials**	... (1)
▶ **LFMaterial Index**	(Distribution=Transient.LensFlareEditor
▶ **Scaling**	(Distribution=Transient.LensFlareEditor
▶ **Axis Scaling**	(Distribution=Transient.LensFlareEditor
▶ **Rotation**	(Distribution=Transient.LensFlareEditor
Orient Towards Source	☐
▶ **Color**	(Distribution=Transient.LensFlareEditor
▶ **Alpha**	(Distribution=Transient.LensFlareEditor
▶ **Offset**	(Distribution=Transient.LensFlareEditor
▶ **Dist Map Scale**	(Distribution=Transient.LensFlareEditor
▶ **Dist Map Color**	(Distribution=Transient.LensFlareEditor
▼ **Dist Map Alpha**	(Distribution=Transient.LensFlareEditor
▼ Distribution	Transient.LensFlareEditorPropertyWrap
Parameter Name	B_OPACITY
Min Input	0.000000
Max Input	0.250000
Min Output	0.250000
Max Output	1.000000
Param Mode	DPM_Normal
Constant	0.000000

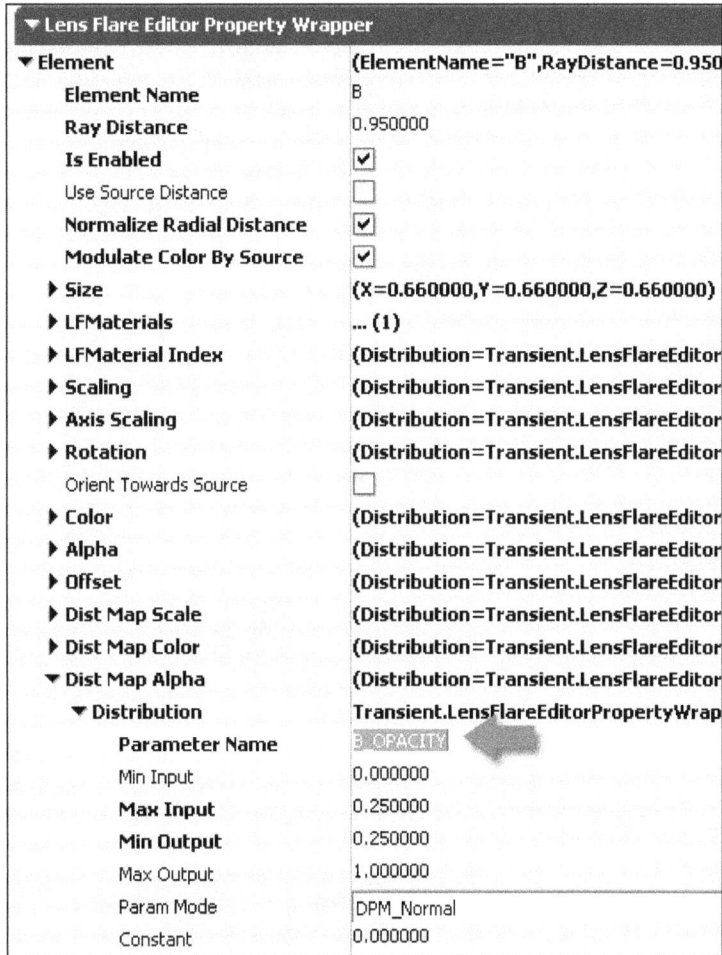

16. As shown here, some features of the element can be driven by animatable vector parameters. Supposing you add vectors to the flare Materials, within the bottom properties of each **LF Element** you can see parameters that are prefixed "Dist Map". These are **Dist Map Scale**, **DistMap Color**, and **Dist Map Alpha**. These can map to values in the Material depending on their distance and the camera distance from the **LF Source**.

17. As a demonstration, open the **Lens Flare Editor Property Wrapper** for **LF Element** *B*, expand the **Dist Map Alpha** property, and right-click on the **Distribution** channel's blue triangle [▽] which sets the type of distribution it will use. Choose from the list, **DistributionFloatParticleParameter**. This has a parameter name field where you can type *B_Opacity*, which is also assigned in the parent Material of the **Material Instance Constant**: *PacktFX.Material.Demo_FlareShape_B_Mat_INST*, which you can assign to this element (under **Element | LFMaterials | [0]**). Open the Parent Material and inspect the Opacity channel, which is set to **Multiply** the **Texture Sample** with a **Constant** converted to a **Parameter**.

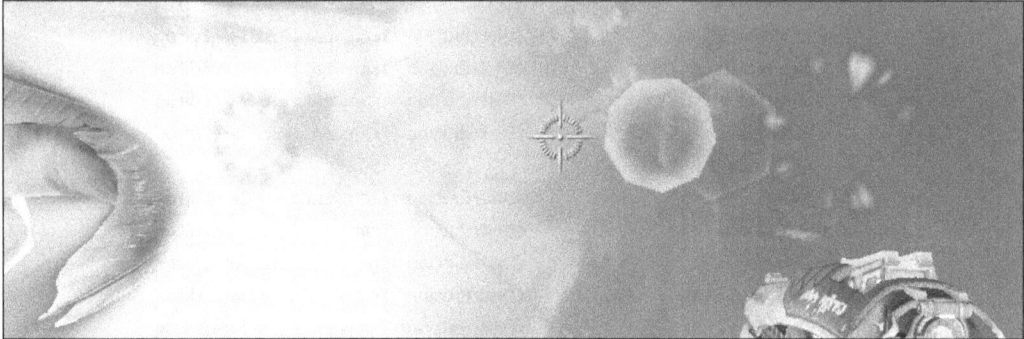

See also

If you are not sure how **Named Parameters** work in UDK, look up the **Material Instance Constants** recipe in *Chapter 9, The Devil Is In the Details!*

Creating caustics using projected imagery

The property of a light that allows imagery to be projected from it is called the **LightFunction** in UDK. In this recipe we'll briefly cover the process to assign it, using an animated example: pool caustics through a FlipBook. Caustics is an effect called by refraction of light through surfaces such as glass and water. Pool caustics is a well known example. Reflective objects can also cast caustics, such as a gold ring's reflection onto a table. In a game you can use a LightFunction to recreate those effects, but you can also use it for any projected imagery, such as the aberration in a torch hotspot, or to fake the effects of stained glass window light splashes (though a way to create stained glass lighting is covered in the chapter following this one). A quick note—pool caustics show on the bottom of the pool (refraction) but they also reflect up onto walls surrounding the pool.

Getting ready

For this example the caustics content is processed through Photoshop after being generated in a free tool, **Caustics Generator**, from `www.dualheights.se/caustics/`. This is distributed under a GNU license, though the Pro version is better, and cheap.

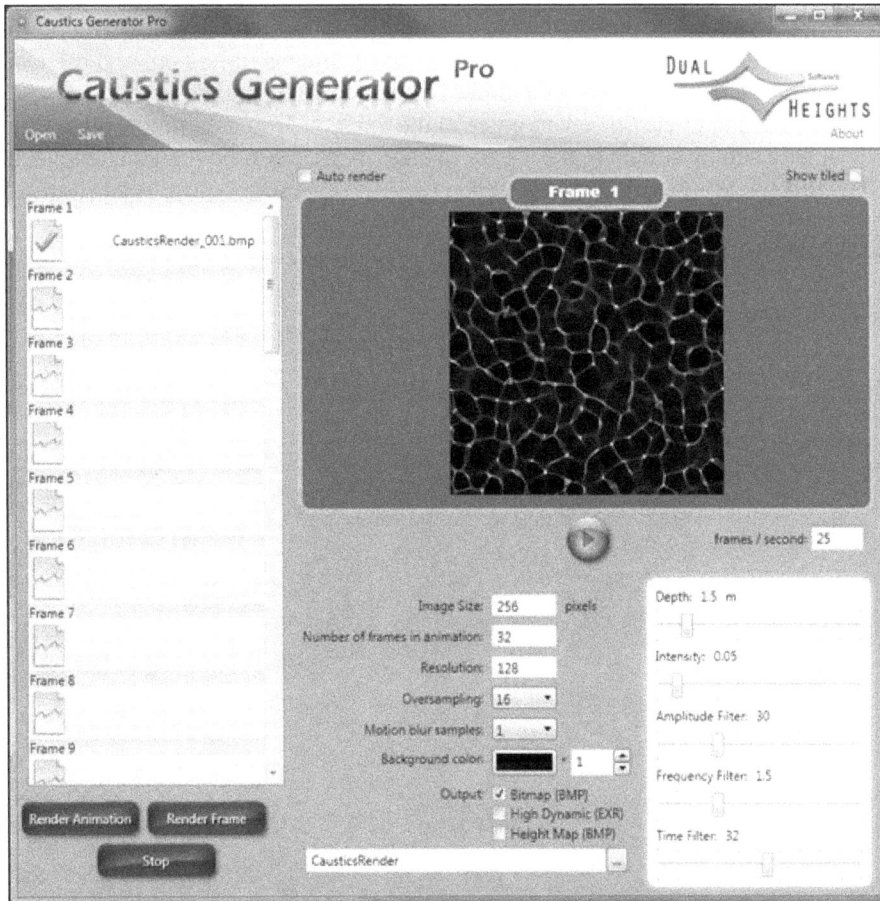

How to do it...

1. First let's create the caustic texture, which will be a 2048x2048 FlipBook based on tiled frames. Run _Caustics Generator.EXE_, which has just one dialog, and experiment with the **Depth**, **Intensity**, **Amplitude**, **Frequency**, and **Time** filters. You can use the **Render Frame** button to get a sense of the caustic generation.

2. Set the **Number of Animation Frames** value to 16 (to fill a 4x4 grid) and ensure the **Time filter** is also set to 16 to ensure content that can be looped.

3. Set the **Width** and **Height** to 512x512. Change the **Background Color (RGB)** to 0,0,0 since we will be using an opacity translucency with the texture. Set an **Output Filename** into a subfolder somewhere, and tick the **Save output** checkbox. **Press Render Animation**.

4. In Photoshop, create a new 2048x2048 document, and then open all the frames from the rendered sequence. Make sure **View | Snap** is turned on, and then, in order, highlight each image then press *Ctrl + A*, *Ctrl + C*, and go to the 2048x2048 document and press *Ctrl + V* to paste in the images. Arrange them as tiles. The snapping setting should make it easy to align them. Save the resulting image as: `C:\UDK\~\UDKGame\Content\Yourfolder\CausticTest2048x2048.TGA`.

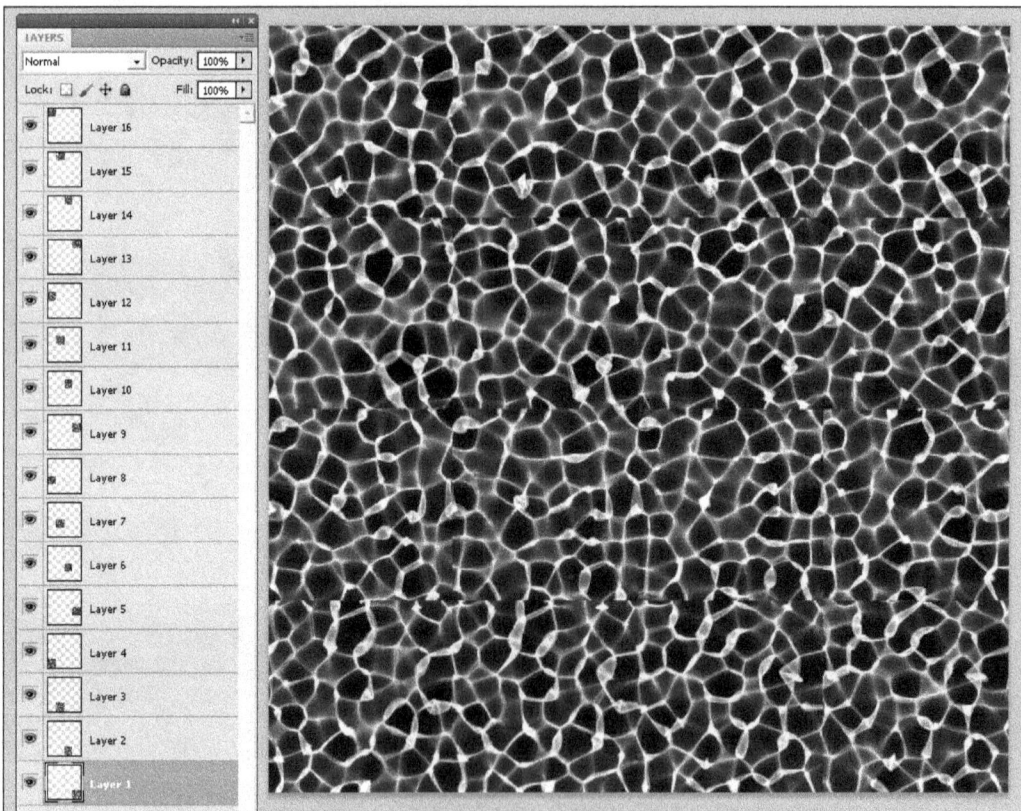

5. In UDK, highlight your package in the Content Browser, and choose **Import**. Select the image you just saved, and in its properties be sure to tick on **FlipBook**. Create a new Material, *Yourfolder.Material.CausticFlipbook*, which uses the imported texture as in the next screenshot. In the Material, rather than use a *Texture Sample* as usual, right-click and choose **Texture | New FlipBookSample**.

6. In the Content Browser, highlight the imported FlipBook texture, right-click, and choose **Properties**. Here, expand the category **Flip Book**.

7. Make sure **Looping** and **Autoplay** are ticked on, and the number of **Horizontal** and **Vertical** images are both set to 4. The frame rate should be 16, though you can experiment with it.

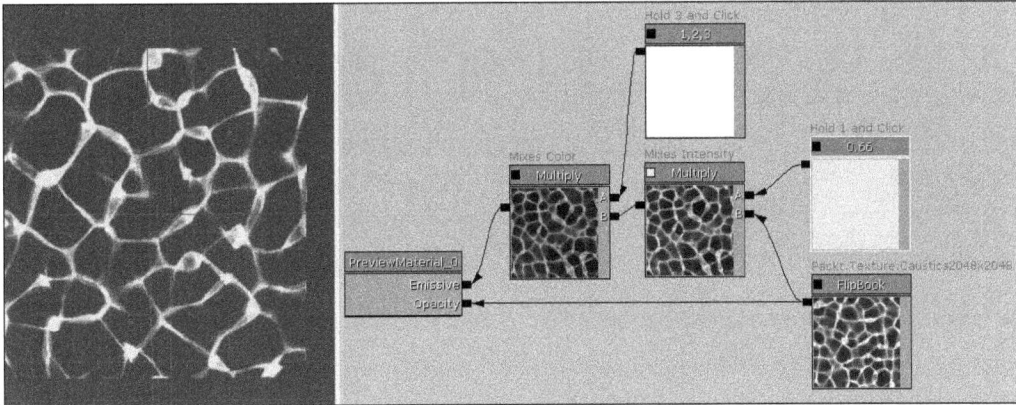

8. In the *PreviewMaterial* settings, set the **Material** to have a **Blend Type** that is *BLEND_Translucent*, to be **Two Sided**, and to have the **Lighting Model** as *MLM_Unlit*. Further down, expand the **Mutually Exclusive Usage** section, and tick on **Use as Light Function**. Remember, for a Material to work as a light function it must have this property set true in order to work as intended.

9. Now we can tie this Material into a spotlight's **LightFunction**. Save your package, then open the scene *Packt_08_Caustics_Start.UDK*, a courtyard with a central pond. Sunlight interacting with water causes caustics where light hits a surface, both above and below the water table.

10. Hold *L* and click in the scene on a surface such as a wall to place a light there. Every light has a property **Light | LightComponent | Function** to which you can add the Material by enabling it with the blue triangle icon [▽] and effectively adding a **LightFunction** entry. This will have a **Source Material** field into which you can paste the name of the caustic Material you've made (or you can use the provided *Packt. Material.CausticsFlipBook_mat* instead). Set its **Scale XYZ** property to 512x512x512, which reflects the generated caustic size.

11. Although the caustic will work either with an omni-directional PointLight (you can experiment with the standard versus dominant light effect of this), a PointLight may create weird distortions because it tries to project in all directions. It would therefore be best in this case to **convert** your default PointLight to a **Spotlight**, and this will allow you to face the caustic in a single direction. You may need to add a few around the walls by the pond to get an even spread. It would probably help to disable shadows for the light also.

12. The following screenshots show the result in the provided map *Packt_08_Caustics_DEMO.UDK*; on the left-hand side is the **Lighting Only** (*Alt* + *6*) and on the right is the final lit scene, though the caustic animation doesn't show up so well in a still image:

How it works...

The **LightFunction** is independent of any object which may be causing the projected light. It can be used for *gobos* (occluded light patterns), projection of screen images, light caustic through colored glass, and water caustics. All that is required is to make an **Emissive Material** with the **Mutually Exclusive Usage | Use For LightFunction** enabled, and add this as the **Source Material** to a light with its **LightFunction** property enabled in the scene. Directional lights work best.

There's more...

A forum example

A great UDK tutorial from **Sjoerd De Jong** (`http://www.hourences.com/tutorials-ue3-light-function/`) shows how to get some extra functionality out of a LightFunction, including the splash of a searchlight, flashing, and pulsing lights, and in particular how to make a texture non-tiling when used as a LightFunction.

An extension on this tutorial is the feedback from the user **Flava-Fly** at `http://www.game-artist.net/forums/support-tech-discussion/13315-udk-light-function-bleed-stretch.html`, in which some problems that were encountered in the process are detailed, and fixed up. These include not clamping the U and V components of the texture in its properties, which is easy to forget. The use of **Preserve Border A** (also a texture property) is explained. Where the color of a texture spills beyond the desired clamp, you can build a black border into the texture (which shows up as invisible in opacity) and the border is what spills, and the opacity negates it.

A further example of using LightFunctions that is worth checking out is about creating the effect of cloud shadows: `http://udn.epicgames.com/Three/DevelopmentKitGemsUsingLightFunctions.html#Cloud%20light`.

Translucent colored glass

UDK lighting can pick up the color from a Material used by a translucent, shadow casting object, and cast it as a kind of caustic onto another surface. This **Transmission** is calculated automatically. For **Lit** Materials it uses the Material's Diffuse channel, plus white, linearly interpolated (**Lerp**) by the Opacity channel to work out the **Transmission**. For **Unlit** Materials it uses the Emissive channel, plus white, linearly interpolated (**Lerp**) by the Opacity channel to work out the **Transmission**. **Modulated** Materials are calculated slightly differently, using just the Diffuse or Emissive channel depending on whether they use the **Lit** or **Unlit** lighting model. That's a mouthful to digest, certainly, so we are going to do an example which shows on one hand a **Lit** Material using **Translucency**, and alongside it, an **Unlit** Material using **Additive** mode.

In this recipe we'll be creating a stained glass window effect, based on the concept of **Transmission** outlined above. First we'll generate a texture, then we'll set up the scene.

Getting ready

Open the scene *Packt_08_GlassShadowsStart.UDK*. This scene is just a BSP shell of a room in which we'll place windows and lights then compare some interaction of light. Note first that all the surfaces, in the **Surface Properties** dialog (*F5*), have their **Lightmap Resolution** changed from the default 32 to 1, which means we'll get a better shadow detail on these surfaces. This was covered in our earlier recipe on shadows.

How to do it...

1. Open the Content Browser and search for the StaticMesh asset *Packt.Mesh. ThinWindow*. This is just a simple plane. Quite deliberately it has the Material *Packt. Material.Hotlight* applied to it, which we won't be using for the window. Place an instance in each of the BSP subtracted windows.

2. Instead of keeping the *Hotlight* texture, we'll make a quick stained glass. This can be done on a new layer over white using **Paths** in Photoshop. **Stroke** the path shapes black with a thickish brush. The intermediate space can be given faux-shadows using soft gradients.

3. Color can be laid into the pattern in a layer above using a **Paint Bucket** with the **All Layers** turned on in its options. Admittedly, the following example is simple:

4. The image should be saved as a .TGA with 32bit alpha at 512x512 and imported to UDK as *Yourfolder.Texture.StainedGlass*.

5. Create a new Material *Yourfolder.Material.StainedGlass_Lit* with the texture added in a **Texture Sample**. Save it and create a copy called *Yourfolder.Material.StainedGlass_Unlit*, since we'll be comparing the two types.

6. For *Yourfolder.Material.StainedGlass_Lit*, set its **PreviewMaterial** properties as **Light Model | MLM__Phong**, and the **Blend Mode | BLEND_Translucent**. Turn on **Two Sided**. Under the **Translucency** settings tick on **Cast Lit Translucency Shadow As Masked**.

If you just want the shadow of the translucent Material (the frame) you can turn this on in the **Lightmass | Lightmass Settings | Cast Shadow As Masked**. This will show only the shadow, not the transmission color.

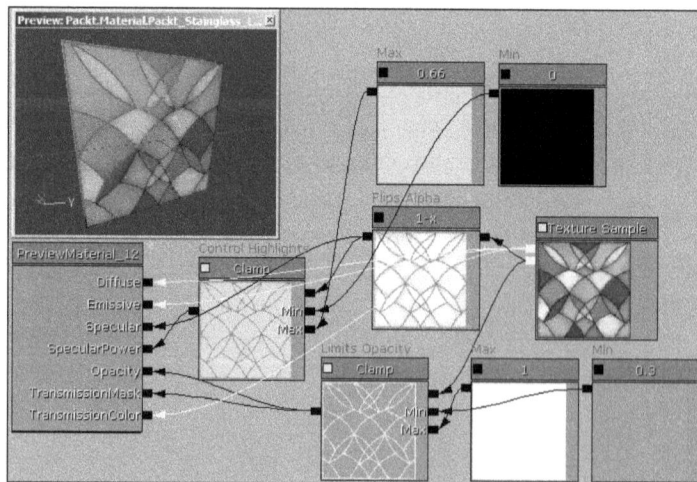

7. Above, the network of nodes feeding from the ***Texture Sample*** includes the **RGB** output of the texture linking to the Diffuse and Emissive channels. The **Alpha** output hooks up to a **Math | New OneMinus** (1-x) and this in turns hooks to the input of a **Utility | New Clamp**. This controls highlights, and is moderated by two ***Constant*** nodes (hold *1* and click) with a **Min** value of 0.0 and a **Max** value of 0.66. The ***Clamp*** feeds the Specular Power channel. The Specular channel is fed by the inverted alpha. The **Alpha** from the texture also feeds a second ***Clamp***, and this limits the Opacity channel using two ***Constant*** nodes. The **Min** value is 0.3 and the **Max** value is 1.0. This is more important than the specular component. If the opacity is not altered, in the **Lit** Material the black parts of the alpha will be totally transparent.

8. Select all the nodes and press *Ctrl + C*. Compile and save the Material.

9. That deals with the **Lit** Material, so now open up the **Unlit** one: *Yourfolder.Material. StainedGlass_Unlit*. This time set the ***PreviewMaterial*** properties so the **Lighting Model** is *MLM_Unlit*. Set the **Blend Mode** to be *BLEND_Additive*. Turn on **Two Sided**. Further down, under **Translucency**, turn on *CastLitTranslucencyShadowAsMasked*.

10. The network itself will be no different from the previous one except that the Diffuse channel is not needed. You can press *Ctrl + V* to paste the copied nodes (from step 9), and hook up the Emissive, Opacity, Specular, and Specular Power as before. Don't connect the Diffuse channel. Compile and save.

11. Select one of the *ThinWindow* actors and with the **Lit** Material highlighted in the Content Browser, right-click over the actor and choose **Materials | Assign From Content Browser**. For the other *ThinWindow* actor, assign the Unlit Material.

12. Hold *L* and click on the window to create a PointLight. Right-click over the light and choose **Convert Light | Spotlights | Spotlight**. Position and orient the light so it is about 200 units outside the room, directly facing the window, then raise it a little and orient it to slope downwards.

13. In the light's properties, set the **Light | Light Component | Spot Light Component | Inner Cone Angle** to 22.0 and set the property **Light | LightComponent | Lightmass | LightmassSettings | LightSourceRadius** to 0.1. This small value tightens up the light to give a better transmission result.

14. Add a StaticMesh (such as *Packt.Mesh.FlatCyl_COL*) into the room on the floor to interrupt the cast light through the windows. Find the Material: *Packt.Material.Packt_Matte* and assign it to the StaticMesh.

15. In the next screenshot there is also a StaticMesh with the Material *Packt.Material. Hotlight* providing a weak fill light so the dark corners of the room get extra lighting. The **Emissive Boost** is set to very low 0.1 in the mesh's **Lightmass** properties. Also in the screenshot, on the left, is the top view in Brush Wireframe display, to show the relative position of the two lights and windows.

16. In the demonstration map which is provided: *Packt_08_GlassShadow_DEMO.UDK*, one spotlight has a **Light Resolution** of 5.0 and the other has a **Light Resolution** of 0.1, and this yields a sharper result.

> Try adjusting the **Emissive** intensity to get a brighter, pure color in the Transmission for the **Unlit** Material. This can be done by adding a *Multiplier* (and a *Constant*) in the Material, or in the StaticMesh **Lightmass** properties or even as a global multiplier in the **View | World Properties | Emissive Boost** menu.

How it works...

It is important to realize that this effect is not projected imagery as in the previous recipe, but a transmission by a light through a mesh surface into the mesh's cast shadow. The transmission is handled by a _Lerp_ using the Material's **Alpha** and either the Emissive or Diffuse channel depending on whether the Material is **Unlit** or **Lit**. The light resolution of the light actor and the surface resolution of the BSP that the light shines on influence the look of the transmitted color. In this additional comparison render, the Emissive fill light on the thin mesh in the center of the room has been removed so the room is darker. The windows have been duplicated and the global **Emissive Boost** has been increased.

9
The Devil Is In The Details!
Making the Most of Materials

This chapter's recipes cover some of the Material Editor's deepest, darkest secrets. Most of the solutions pave the way for further exploration; exposure to a new tool often means that other functionality is also exposed. The recipes presented here are not tailored exclusively for a game level (for simplicity's sake), but their use in game construction is explained too.

In this chapter, we'll discuss activities such as:

- Animating a Material Instance Constant in Kismet
- Forcing a mesh to always face the camera
- A cloth-like effect using WorldPositionOffset
- Creating murky liquid
- Creating a scanning effect
- Quick glass
- Creating transitions between materials
- Static Cubemap creation and real-time reflection
- Wet surface reflections with dynamic actors
- Making a holographic effect using Bump Offset
- InteractiveFoliageActors
- Getting varied hit impacts off models using a PhysicalMaterial

Introduction

The Material Editor is easy to get a hang of in terms of provisioning the **Diffuse**, **Normal**, **Specular**, **Opacity**, and **Emissive** features of a model asset, but UDK's editor offers far more functionality than just loading up and controlling imported textures. In particular, a range of nodes access the scene itself. You can call on the scene lighting, distance of pixels from the camera, the reflection for a given surface normal, and you can even drive Materials in the scene through Scalar parameters in your code. In many of the recipes so far we have already discussed the everyday operators that you can use in the Material Editor, from **Fresnel** Falloff to **FlipBooks**. Here, we're going to focus mainly on the more difficult, but equally useful scene driven operators (and a few others that we haven't touched on so far).

From UDK versions after September 2011, a new ease of use feature has been added to the Material Editor. Material Functions are encapsulated fragments of commonly used operations (like the **HeightLerp** function which mixes two textures based on a heightmap and would be really helpful when texturing landscapes) or custom operations created by users. To get started using this new feature, in any Material, look to the right-hand side panel where the **Material Function Library** now sits below the **Material Expressions** list. You can also right-click and browse the **Functions** and **FunctionUtility** categories of nodes in the Material Editor. A description of their usage is available at `http://udn.epicgames.com/Three/MaterialFunctions.html`.

Animating a Material Instance Constant in Kismet

In this recipe we'll go through the steps to create a **MaterialInstanceConstant** (**MIC**), and show how a MIC can be used to set up player influence over the qualities within a Material. This was already set up and used in the final recipes from *Chapter 4, Got Your Wires Crossed?* They were active in the night-to-day transition in the scenes. A MaterialInstanceConstant exposes a parameter to animation such as an RGB color channel, a brightness channel or the strength of an Alpha channel. In practical applications, you could use this as a way to alter Materials on assets; making the tattoos on a magic creature glow for instance, as its powers charge up.

Getting ready

From the provided content, load the scene *Packt_09_MIC_Start.UDK*.

The scene shows a quite abstract special effect. If you don't want to see this looping in the perspective viewport, press the **Real time** toggle (*Ctrl + R*), which is the joystick icon [🕹].

How to do it...

1. In the Content Browser, search the provided content for *Packt.Material.GridPanner*, right-click on it and choose **Create a Copy**.

2. Name the copy *Yourfolder.Material.GridPanner_Params*.

3. Double-click on the result. The Material Editor will open, and you can see the nodes for the Material are fairly diverse. While this Material setup possibly merits some explanation, we'll just focus on the nodes that allow us to expose values to Kismet. See the upcoming *How it works* section for more information.

4. Along the top are **Constant** nodes marked *A*, *B*, and *C*. These have values that will be interesting to change.

5. Select *A* = **Constant 1** and right-click on it. Choose **Convert to Parameter**. Notice that there is now an entry in the properties of the new ***Parameter*** node called **Parameter Name**. Here, type in *Saturation*.

6. Select *B* = **Constant 3** (RGB) and right-click on it. Choose **Convert to Parameter**. As before, we need to add a **Parameter Name** in its properties. This time, type in *Color Shift*.

7. Select *C* = **Constant 1** and right-click on it. Choose **Convert to Parameter**. Again, we need to add a **Parameter Name** in its properties. This time, type in *Brightness*.

8. What you see in this screenshot is our goal, a radiant digital furnace. When we shoot the four globular floating balls, each produces a change in the furnace Material. Now that each **Parameter Name** has been set up, right-click on the Material *GridPanner_Param* in the Content Browser and choose **Create New Material Instance Constant**. Call it *GridPanner_MIC1*.

9. Double-click on *GridPanner_MIC1* and in the window that pops up, turn on the params. Adjust the **color, brightness,** and **saturation** params to suit our needs.

10. Make three more copies: *GridPanner_MIC2, GridPanner_MIC3,* and *GridPanner_MIC4*. Change each one's params to a somewhat different color, brightness, and saturation than the rest.

11. In Kismet, examine the current set of events and actions. These are explained in the *How it works* section after this recipe.

12. Hook up to each **Trigger | Take Damage** event's output a **New Action | Actor | Set Material** action. In the properties of each event, assign a different colored *GridPanner_MIC* until all four triggers have a unique one. Also, create a **Delay** and one more **Set Material** action in some clear space. Set the **Delay** to 5.00 and the Material assigned to the extra **Set Material** action to be the main *GridPanner*. In the scene, select the two big meshes *InterpActor_0* and *InterpActor_1* and then assign them to the **Target** of the **Set Material** action.

13. Right-click in Kismet and choose **New Event | Remote Event**. In the properties of this, assign the **Event Name** to *DelayStart*. With the **Remote Event** selected, press *Ctrl + C* then *Ctrl + V* to spin off a copy. In the properties of the copy, assign the **Event Name** to *DelayStop*.

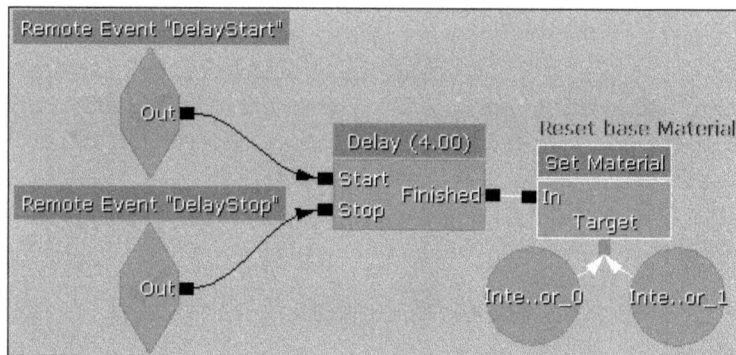

14. As shown here, hook up the *DelayStart* output into the **Delay** (*4.00*)'s **Start** nub. Hook up the *DelayStop* output into the **Delay** (*4.00*)'s **Stop** nub.

15. Right-click in Kismet and choose **New Action | Event | Activate Remote Event**. In the properties of this action set the **Event Name** to *DelayStart*. For both the **Remote Event** *DelayStart* and the **Activate Remote Event** *DelayStart* its tick should go green. You can click on each to jump from one to the other.

16. Create three more copies of this node and distribute them near each **Play Sound** action. To each event's **Out**, hook up the **Finished** nub of a **Play Sound**.

17. Paste one more **Activate Remote Event**, and set the **Event Name** in its properties to *DelayStop*. Make sure that it's highlighted, then copy it, and paste three more.

18. Hook up each of these to a **Take Damage** event. They perform the task of stopping any current delay that may be ticking over when an actor takes damage. You could just hook up all the events to one **Activate Remote Event**: *DelayStop* but then inevitably wires would start crossing all over the place and possibly be hard to read. Each of the four **Take Damage** events will have a similar network, as shown here, with different MIC assets applied to the **Set Material** action, *MIC1*, *MIC2*, *MIC3*, and *MIC4*.

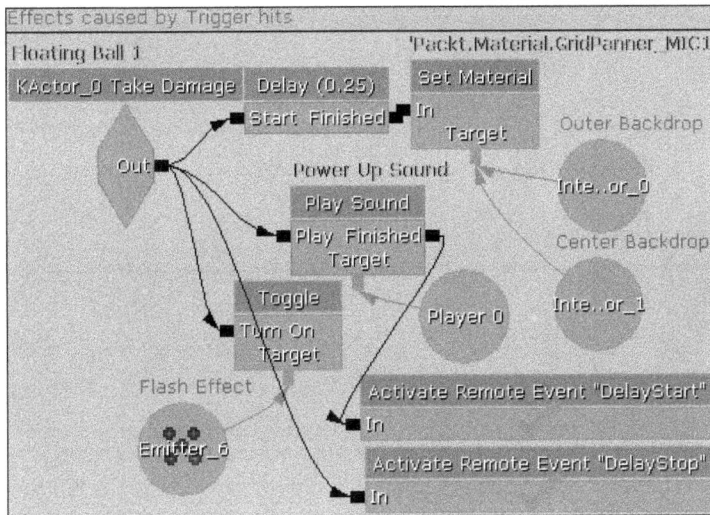

To get the most out of this image, open up the Kismet in the demo map *Packt_09_MIC_DEMO.UDK*. The toolbar toggle **Hide Unused Connectors** [ ] has been turned on to save some room. You will notice that there are four copied sets of nodes that work on the four particle emitters, and the four globular meshes.

How it works...

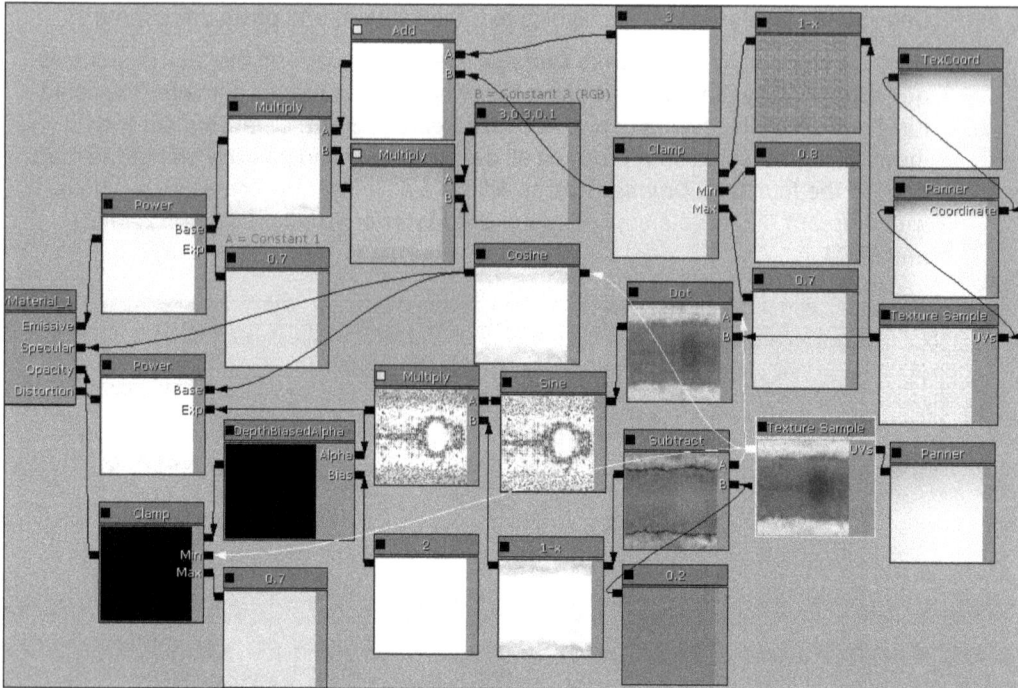

The parent Material *Packt.Material.GridPanner* is not as complicated as the clustered nodes in the image might look. All the nodes can be added in the Material Editor by typing in the search field on the right-hand side panel of the editor, which is called the **Material Expressions list**. The read order to follow the description of the nodes is from right-to-left. Each node adds a slight change to the two loaded textures. The first node is a ***TexCoord*** tiling node, which tells a texture to repeat or tile across whatever object it winds up on. The second two nodes are **Panners**. These control the vertical movement of the two textures on a surface at different speeds. The texture coordinates feed into ***2D Texture Samples***. This example uses a grid-like texture and a gradient-like photo of surf. The next group of nodes are mostly **Constants**. These include fixed values that modify the textures in terms of the amount of brightness or saturation taken from them. There is also a ***One Minus*** or (***1-x***) node which inverts the grid texture. These are like filters in Photoshop essentially; they adjust the incoming content by a fixed rule. The ***fourth vertical*** line of nodes from the right includes a **Sine** (which creates a noisy wave-like perturbation) in the incoming data and another ***One Minus***. The fifth vertical line of nodes from the right includes **Multiply** nodes which mix together two inputs, a **Dot Product** and a **Subtract** operation feeding into them. The thumbnails show the effect of these nodes. The ***fourth*** line of nodes includes the ***Constant 3*** we made into our **color parameter vector** (RGB values we can access externally). The final group of nodes going into the Material's Diffuse and Emissive channels just pull together the elements on the left, with value adjustments to tweak their intensity. ***The bottom group of nodes control*** the Material Opacity channel, and the operators include a ***DepthBiasedAlpha*** so edges close to the camera fade, and a ***Clamp*** to limit the extend of the inputs from the animating texture. The ***PreviewMaterial*** node's properties are set to **Blend Type** = *Translucent*, and **Lighting Mode** = *MLM_Unlit*, since the Emissive channel generates the brightness of the Material in the scene.

There's more...

Animating a value in a Material Instance Constant in Matinee

In this example we changed the Material parameters using a ***Set Material*** action in Kismet. We can also animate values exposed by the ***Parameter*** node.

1. In the Content Browser, right-click and choose **Create New Material**. Keep the Material Editor open, then, back in the Content Browser, search for and highlight *Texture2DPackt.Texture.FrazettaMask*.

2. In the Material you just created, add a ***Texture Sample*** (hold *T* and click), using the texture asset *Packt.Texture.FrazettaMask*, a white circle.

3. Add a ***Multiply*** (hold *M* and click) node and a ***Constant*** (hold *1* and click) node. Hook the ***Texture Sample*** node's **RGB** nub and the ***Constant*** into the ***Multiply*** **A** and **B** nodes, then hook the ***Multiply*** into the Material's Emissive channel.

4. Right-click on the ***Constant*** and choose **Convert to Parameter**. In its properties, set the **Parameter Name** as *Varying*. Save the Material as *TEST_MAT*.

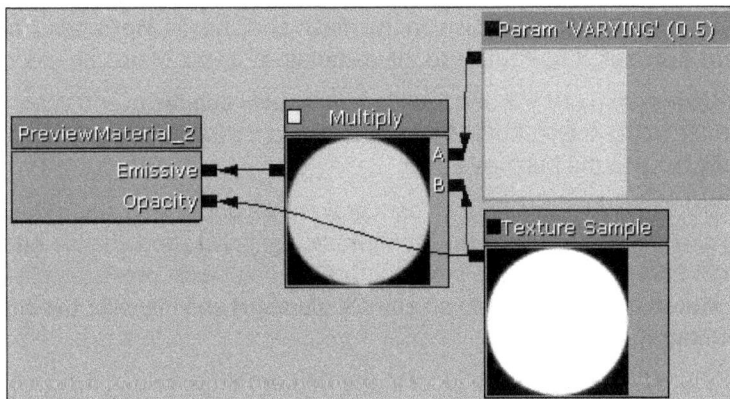

5. Right-click on the Material you created in the Content Browser and choose **Create new MaterialInstanceConstant**.

6. Open the new MIC asset and tick the scalar value *VARYING*. If you don't, it won't be found by a ***Matinee***. Save the asset as *TESTVarying_MIC*.

7. In the scene, press *Ctrl + Shift + F*, then switch to the Content Browser's **Actor Classes** tab. Uncheck the filter **Show Categories** and highlight in the list **MaterialInstanceActor**. This actor acts a sole conduit through the MIC to a single *Object Variable* in Kismet, given that many actors might possibly use the MIC in the scene. Any animation effecting the MIA affects all the actors using its assigned MIC.

8. Right-click in the scene and choose **Add MaterialInstanceActor Here**. This will create an MIA in the scene [**MI**]. It can sit anywhere as it is just a placeholder actor. In its properties assign *TESTVarying_MIC* in the **Mat Inst** channel.

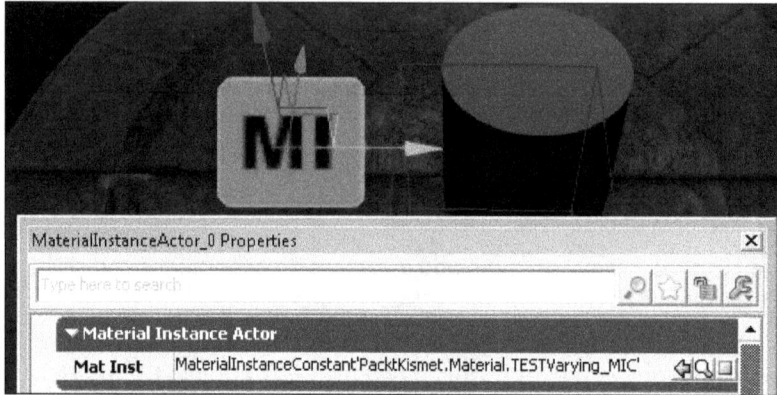

9. Also add a PlayerStart actor, a PointLight, and a floor to stand on. Drag any StaticMesh into the scene. Right-click on it and choose **Convert | Convert StaticMesh to Mover**. With the Mover selected, highlight *TESTVarying_MIC* in the Content Browser, then right-click on the mesh and choose **Materials | Apply from Content Browser**. It now refers to the same asset as the MaterialInstanceActor.

10. Open Kismet, hold *Ctrl + S* and click to add a **Level Loaded** event. While the MIA actor is selected in the scene, hold *M* and click to add a new **Matinee**. Double-click the **Matinee** to open the Matinee Editor.

11. Right-click in the Matinee Editor's dark gray tracks panel, and add a **New Empty Group** and call it *MyTrack*. Highlight *MyTrack*, right-click, and choose **Add New Float Material Param Track**. In the properties of the new track, press the assign icon [🎛] in the **Material** channel to add an entry. Expand **[0]** and highlight the channel **Target Material**.

12. Select your *TESTVarying_MIC* asset in the Content Browser and assign it here using the green arrow [⬅]. Under this entry, change **Param Name** to *VARYING* (the parameter name we set earlier in *Test_Mat* that *TestVarying_MIC* can access).

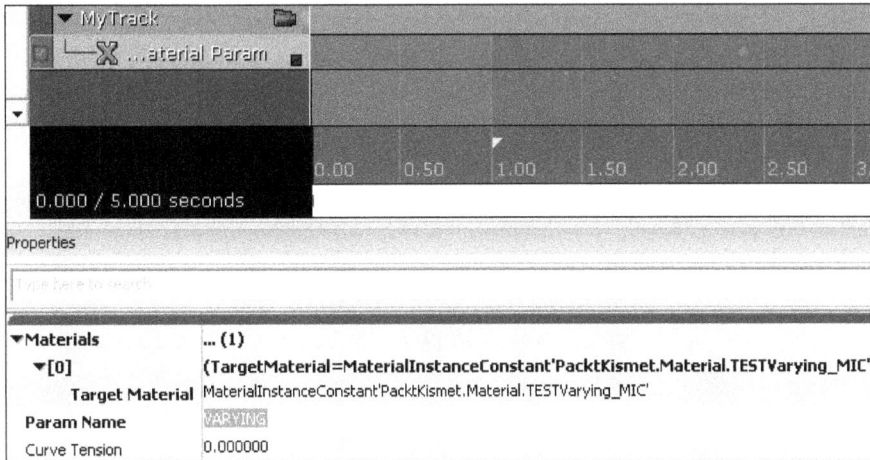

13. Highlight the **Float Material Param Track** in the Matinee Editor timeline, and key it (using *Enter* to add keys). This track takes the **Float** value (0.5) in the original Material's *Parameter* node and lets us control it. Right-click on each key and choose **Set Value** to adjust them as desired to create varying values for the Parameter *VARYING*. The default value for the key is 0. The Material's 100% amount is a value of 1.

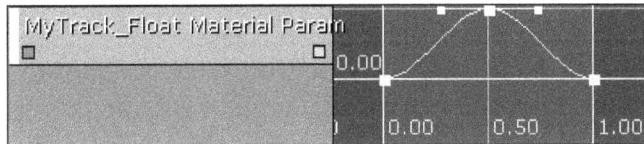

14. If you used 0 and 1 for the curve, as shown here, the Material should fade in and out. Don't forget to set the time-line range to the longest key time.

15. To make this loop, in Kismet, select the **Matinee** action and in its properties turn on **Looping**. Build the scene and PIE to verify whether the *VARYING* amount that we set appears to be pulsing. An example is the disc floating by the PlayerStart in the provided scene *Packt_09_MIC_DEMO.UDK*.

Creating an animated RGB color shift

1. In the original *Material TEST_MAT*, right-click and choose **Parameters | New Vector Parameter**. Call the parameter name *COLOR* in its properties.

2. As before add a **Multiply** node, then hook the **Vector** and **Multiply** up so the parameter *COLOR* can affect the Emissive channel. Compile and save.

3. Open the *TESTVarying_MIC* asset and turn on auto-activate for the *Color* parameter.

4. Double-click the **Matinee** in Kismet, highlight *MyTrack*, and add a new **Vector Material Parameter Track** under the existing parameter track. Highlight the new track to expose its properties.

5. In the properties, under **Material**, hit the add entry icon [🔘] and expanding **[0]** to show **Target Material**. Make sure *TestVarying_MIC* is highlighted in the Browser and press the assign icon [🔄]. Underneath, enter *COLOR* as the **Param Name**.

6. Key-frame the RGB components of the **Vector Material Parameter** track. To do so, tick on the small square on the end of the vector track in the Matinee Editor so it goes yellow. You should see a Graph Editor above with **TimeVarying_Vector Material...** displayed, and RGB squares below it.

7. Ticking the RGB squares on and off will expose individual RGB tracks to key frame. For example, leave only the Red square on, key frame it from 0 to 1 over 2 seconds. Then leave only the Blue square on, and key frame it from 1 to 0 over 2 seconds. You will get a blend from one hue to another.

Forcing a mesh to always face the camera

This example uses the **RotateAboutAxis** node and a **Custom** node in the Material Editor, so we'll be covering how to enter a custom expression into the node too. An example that's practical for the use of a mesh constrained to the camera could be distant trees, or any large billboard style geometry standing in for a more detailed asset to save memory: airships circling in the sky, fish schooling in the sea. As we'll see, it's best used where the player can't get up close to the sprites however.

Getting ready

Open the scene *Packt_09_FacingPlanes_Start.UDK* and note that there are three BSP cards which we can use for testing. PIE and note that the cards don't orient towards the camera as you run around them. For this method of rotating the objects, StaticMesh planes won't work. You can try applying the Material created in this recipe to the StaticMesh objects in the scene (the small planes) and you'll see they shrink to thin lines. BSP will work better.

How to do it...

1. In the Content Browser, create a new Material: *Yourfolder.Material. CameraFacing_mat*.

2. Near the bottom of the **PreviewMaterial** there is a channel called WorldPositionOffset. We also look at WorldPositionOffset later in the chapter.

3. Set the Material to have a **Blend Mode** which is *BLEND_Translucent*. Since we have a Translucent Material, turn on **View | Allow Translucent Selection**.

4. Right-click next to this and choose **Utility | New RotateAboutAxis**. Hook its output into the WorldPositionOffset channel. To start with there'll be a red warning, but this will resolve out as we proceed further.

5. Right-click next to this and choose **Coordinates | New WorldPosition**. Hook this into the **Position** nub of the **RotateAboutAxis**.

6. Also right-click and choose **Coordinates | New ObjectWorldPosition**. Hook this into the **PositionOnAxis** nub of the **RotateAboutAxis**.

7. Now we enter our **Custom** node, which we'll call *HywelThomas BillBoardRotation* since that's who the expression comes from. Right-click and choose **Custom | New Custom**. Open ConTEXT and in there the file from the *Packt**Files**Provided Content* called *HywelThomas BillBoardRotation.TXT* and copy it. Back in UDK, in the **Custom** node properties, press the **Code | Click to Show Editing Box** bar. Paste the following code into the floating box and press **OK**:

```
float4 output;
float3 CameraToObjVector;

//Get Camera to Object Vector
CameraToObjVector = normalize(CameraWorldPos -
  ObjectWorldPositionAndRadius);

//Set RGB of output to the object's Z-Axis.
output.r = ObjectOrientation.r;
output.g = ObjectOrientation.g;
output.b = ObjectOrientation.b;

//Transform Vector into Radians.
output.a = atan2(CameraToObjVector.y,CameraToObjVector.x);

return (output);
```

8. In the properties of the custom node, set the **Description** to *HywelThomas BillBoardRotation*. Set the **Output Type** to *CMOT_Float4* (or you will see an error warning). Hook up the ***Custom*** node to the **NormalizedRotationAxisAndAngle** nub of the ***RotateAboutAxis*** node.

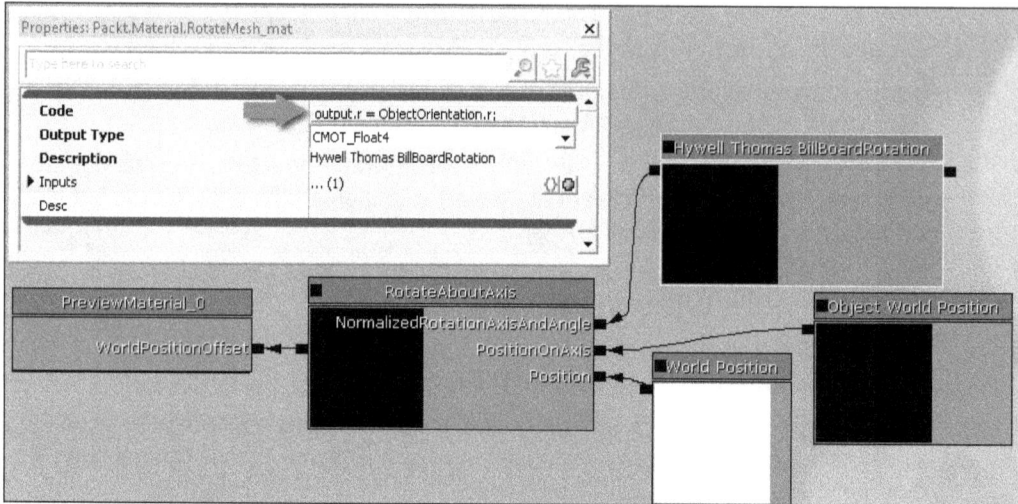

9. In the Material's Emissive channel, add the **RGB** of a ***Texture Sample*** using *Packt. Texture.FrazzettaMoon* (which is just a circle) or something similar, and also hook its **Alpha** into the Opacity channel. Then you can check the result of the rotation expression by compiling the Material then placing it on the cards. Select the surface of one card (they are BSP), right-click, and press *Shift + T* or choose **Select Surfaces | Matching Texture**. With the Material that we've made highlighted in the Content Browser, right-click and choose **Apply Material: ...**

10. You can see the effect in the editor, and the cards will turn as you navigate through them. Since the cards have a wide base and their pivot is central, the edges will appear to move, so for facing behavior you'd be limited to objects with floating forms, like clouds, or skinny forms, such as trees or individual blades of grass (rather than large sheets of grass or hedge rows). The expression doesn't take into account any rotation already applied to the object.

11. Now that you know how the WorldPositionOffset channel works and how to enter expressions into a Custom node, it should open up some ground for experimentation in this area. UDN provides an example at http://udn.epicgames.com/Three/ MaterialsCompendium.html#Custom. An example scene using the Material *Packt.Material.RotateMesh_mat* comes with the provided content: *Packt_09_ FacingPlanes_DEMO.UDK*.

How it works

The Material's ability to turn the mesh is derived from the fact that UVW coordinates and RGB colors are similar mathematically to world coordinates. All can be represented as vectors, which are a way to express directions in space as XYZ values. For each vertex of the model in the scene, or for its pivot, the WorldPositionOffset channel in the Material really only applies a shunt to the value the vertex or pivot already has. The coordinates that draw on object or world parameters can be used to create conditional shaders, for instance on wet Materials where water runs down an object's surface only if the surface is perpendicular to the world Z direction. An example is at `http://udn.epicgames.com/Three/MaterialExamples.html#Wet`.

A cloth-like effect using WorldPositionOffset

In this recipe we'll go through the steps to generate a wavy surface in the mesh, which could be used for a variety of effects, including swaying objects such as hanging plants, cloth, or magical effects.

How to do it...

1. Start a new scene, and in the Content Browser, search the provided content for *PacktKismet.Mesh.MyWavyMesh* and right-click on it; choose **Create a Copy...** and place this to *Yourfolder.Mesh.WaveTest*. Right-click this and choose **Copy Full Name to Clipboard**. It is just a thin BSP box that has had its edges split a few times before being converted to a StaticMesh. A BSP itself wouldn't work because it doesn't respond to the vertex offsets we'll be doing to the converted geometry. Place the asset in the scene, above the ground. Right-click on it and choose **Convert | StaticMeshActor to Mover**.

2. In the Content Browser, right-click and choose **New Material**; name it *Yourfolder. Material.Wave_mat* and open it up.

3. In the Material's **PreviewMaterial | Material Interface | Preview Mesh** paste the copied mesh name.

4. Right-click and choose **Coordinates | New World Position**. Next to it, hold *C* and click (to create a **Component Mask**). In the mask properties, set it so only **R** is ticked. Hold *1* and click to add a **Constant** and name it *Range*. Enter an **R** value of 0.2. Hold *M* and click to add a **Multiply**.

5. Connect the **Constant** *Range* to the **B** nub of the **Multiply**. Connect the **R** output of the **Mask** to the **A** nub.

6. Right-click and choose **Utility | New Time**. Tick on the *Time* node's **Ignore Pause** property if you want the effect to continue playing at all times. Hold *A* and click to insert an **Add**, then hook the **Time** into the **A** nub of the **Add** node, and the **Multiply** node's output into the **B** nub.

7. Right-click and choose **Math | New Sine**, and set its **Period** property to 6.0 and hook up the **Add** output into the **Sine**. The **Sine**, and the **Constant** *Range* together make the frequency of the wave. Next we'll add the amplitude, or height. Hold *3* and click to add a **Constant 3 Vector**, and set it to **R = 0, G = 0, B = 100**.

8. Name the **Constant 3 Vector** Height. Hold *M* and click to add a **Multiply** and call it Wave. Connect the **Sine** into *Wave*'s **A** nub and the **Constant** *Height* into the *Wave*'s **B** nub. Connect *Wave* to the Material's WorldPositionOffset channel. Compile and assign the Material to the actor that you placed at the start. It should begin to wave like a cloth in a steady wind, or seaweed in a current.

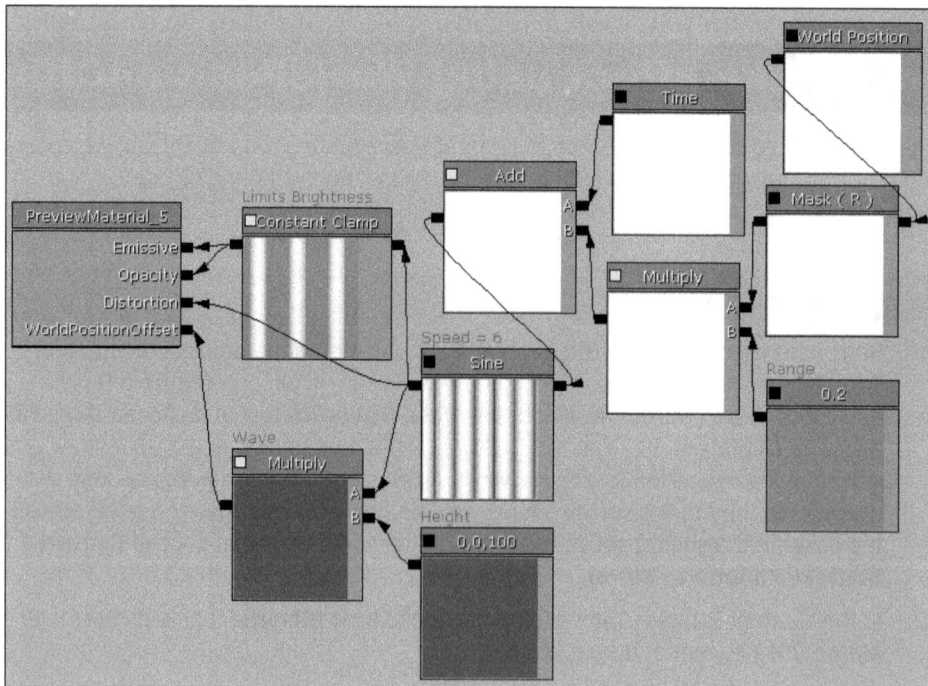

9. This is all that's needed. The rest of the process would be adding Opacity and Emissive parameters and such. To give variable speed to the wave, the constant values in the Material could be converted to **Parameters** and animated in a **Matinee**.

10. A final touch could be to make a Mexican wave effect, where the 'cloth' resembles the flat, rolling wave shown next. Drive a **Constant Clamp** in between the **Sine** and the **Multiply** Wave. You can then change the **Min** and **Max** properties in the **Constant Clamp** to generate flat or stepped waves. Try 0.4 and 0.8.

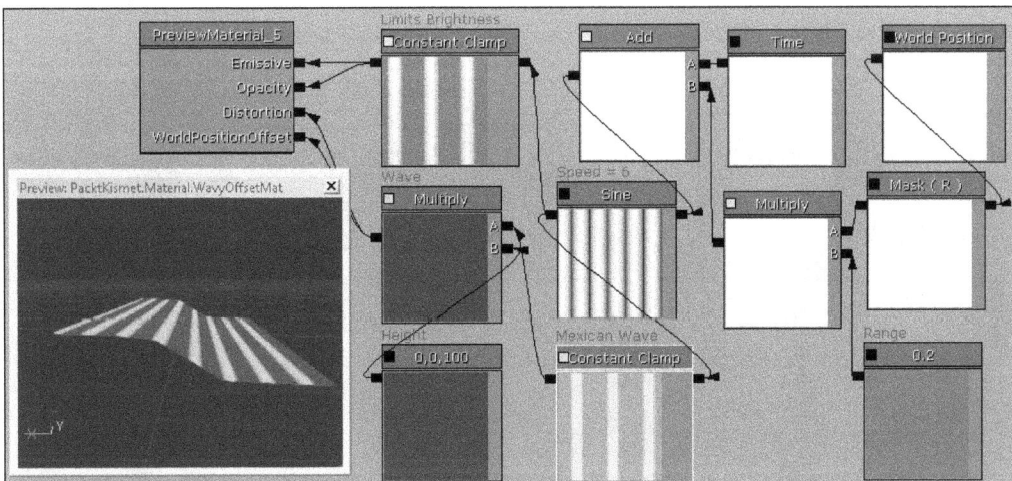

11. Note that when you PIE the mesh will have no collision, and collisions assigned in the StaticMesh asset won't animate with the animated Material. So you'd have to reserve use of the effect to geometry that's visible but not reachable or to objects that are not touchable, like energy fields. An example is in the provided content: *Packt_09_WavyCloth_DEMO.UDK*.

Creating murky liquid

It is possible to change an object's surface visibility based on its distance from the camera. You can also get the distance to the next surface underneath it or behind it, even where it varies pixel for pixel. Some kinds of netted curtain fabric exhibit this effect; where the fabric is close to the window it is see through, and where it's further off the surface, it isn't. In a game environment, a fringe of transparency created by a **DepthBiasedAlpha** node is often used at the converging edge of water and land so that some of the shore is visible under shallow water, while the water opacity increases further out. It is also possible to create holographic or scanning effects using this node. In this recipe and the next we'll do both, creating a murky pool and a passageway scanner.

Coverage of **DepthBiasedAlpha** and other depth based Material nodes can be found at http://udn.epicgames.com/Three/MaterialsCompendium.html. Look up **SceneDepth** and **PixelDepth** too.

Getting ready

Open the scene *Packt_09_DepthBiased_Start.UDK*. You will see a large pool and an enclosed passageway, both filled with objects. The objects are there to help us get a sense of the changes in depth or distance in the scene. In this recipe, what we're interested is the Material on the surface of the pool.

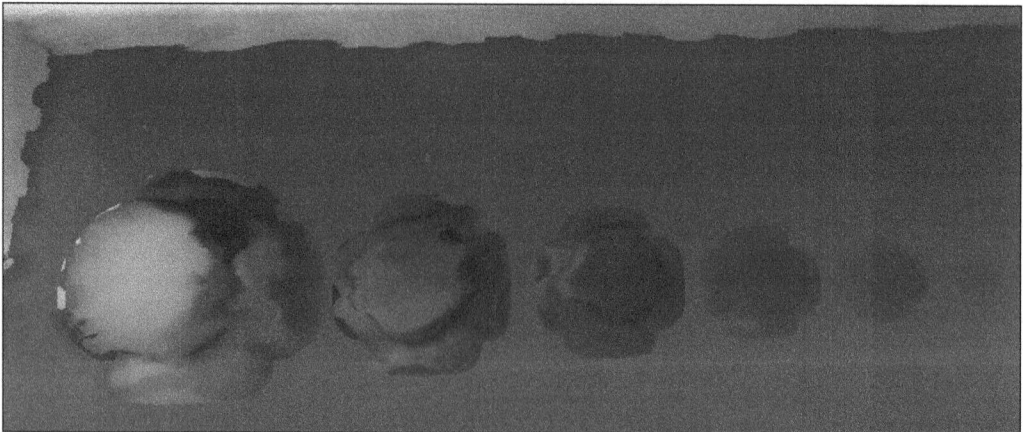

How to do it...

1. In the Content Browser, create a new Material: *Yourfolder.Material.PoolDepth_mat*. Apply it to the surface of the pool, which is a Mover animated to go up and down by a Kismet **Matinee**.

2. Open your new Material in the Material Editor. Set its **PreviewMaterial** properties so **Lighting Model** is *MLM_Unlit* since it won't require scene lighting, and set the **Blend Mode** to *BLEND_Translucent*. That means it can handle variable transparency. Turn on **Two Sided** also, which means if you have the Material on a plane it will show on both sides.

3. Right-click and choose **Depth | New DepthBiasedAlpha** and in its properties set the **Bias Scale** to 100. The **Bias Scale** value determines the extent of the alpha based on the distance between two surfaces. Hook up the **DepthBiasedAlpha** into the Opacity channel of the Material.

4. Right-click and choose **Utility | New ConstantClamp** and hook this up into the **DepthBiasedAlpha** input. Set the **Min** value to 0.2 and the **Max** value to 0.95. Again, these values are fairly touchy, and it would be good at the end of the procedure to experiment with the effect of changing them.

5. Hold *L* and click to add a **Lerp**. Hook this up to the **ConstantClamp** input. Hold *1* and click to add a **Constant** and then add another. Set the first to **R = 0.5**, name it MIN and then hook it up to the **A** nub of the **Lerp**. Set the second to **R = 1.5**, name it MAX and then hook it up to the **B** nub of the **Lerp**. Once again, the values entered here make a big difference to the final result. What these will finally control is the wideness of the blending at the surface. Hold *D* and click to add a **Math | New Divide**, and hook it into the **Alpha** input of the **Lerp**.

6. Hold *1* and click to add a **Constant**, name it *Depth*, and set **R** to 1024. This value determines the overall depth of the water, as a scalar value. Varying this, the *Min* and *Max*, as well as the **Bias Scale** affects the look of the transparency. Hook the **Constant** *Depth* to the **B** nub of the **Divide**.

7. Right-click and choose **Math | New Subtract**, then hook it to the **A** nub of the **Divide**. Right-click and choose **Depth | New DestDepth**, then choose **Depth | New PixelDepth**. The **DestDepth** hooks into the **A** nub of the **Subtract**, and the **PixelDepth** hooks into the **B** nub of the **Subtract**.

8. Essentially that deals with the Opacity for the Material. The **DestDepth** node handles the depth from the camera to the nearest surface behind this Material (think of water and the bottom of the pool). The **PixelDepth** handles the depth from the camera to the surface. Subtracting **PixelDepth** from **DestDepth** gives us the depth of the water at every point.

9. If you compile the Material, then build and PIE you should notice the water is a foggy black and static. Since the `Lighting Model` is set to *MLM_Unlit*, it needs color, reflectivity, movement, and highlights to be driven through the other Material channels, such as a Distortion animation, and an Emissive tint.

10. There are many ways to proceed from here, so take this solution with a pinch of salt. Right-click in the Material Editor and choose **Vector | New ReflectionVector**. Right-click again and choose **Math | New SquareRoot (Sqrt)**. Add a *Constant*, name it *Density*, and set its **R** value to 0.2. Right-click and add a **Math | New CrossProduct (Cross)** and hook up the *Constant Density* to its **A** nub and the *ReflectionVector* to its **B** nub.

11. Right-click, choose **Coordinates | New ObjectOrientation**, then hold *M* and click to add a *Multiply*. Connect the *ObjectOrientation* to nub **A** of the *Multiply*, and connect the *Cross* to nub **B**. Hook up the *Multiply* to the Material's Emissive channel. This will allow you to produce a color tint for the water.

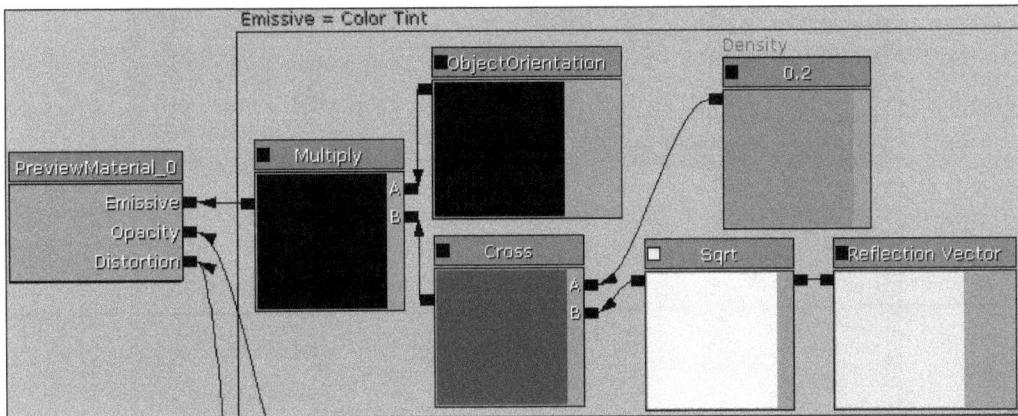

12. Now for the Distortion of the surface, so we can ripple the water. There is a great deal of room to alter the values provided here. Right-click and add a **Coordinates | New Rotator**. Set its **Center X** property to 1.0, its **Center Y** property to 0.0, and its **Speed** property to 0.03 or thereabouts.

13. Hook this up to a **Math | New Cosine**, and set the **Period** property of the *Cosine* to 0.66. Hook up the *Cosine* to a **Math | New Frac**.

14. Hold *P* and click to add a *Panner*, and then set its **Speed X** property to 0.03 and its **Speed Y** property to 0.05. These values determine the speed of the texture across the water. It produces a sliding effect rather than a rippling effect.

15. Right-click and choose **Math | New Sine**. A Sine is what adds a wave-like property to the pattern. Add another, and hook up the output of the *Panner* to it. For the second hook up the output of the *Frac* to it. Also hook up the *Frac* to the *Panner* node's input. The first *Sine* should have a **Period** of 0.33 and the other one a **Period** of 3.33 (or thereabouts). For each *Sine*, hook its output to a separate *Normalize* node (hold *N* and click). The period of the *Sine* creates an amplitude like effect in the wave.

16. Right-click and add a **Math | New DotProduct**. A *DotProduct* creates a Falloff effect. Check out the example at http://udn.epicgames.com/Three/ MaterialsCompendium.html#DotProduct.

17. Feed one **Normalized Sine** into the **A** nub of the **DotProduct** and the other into the **B** nub. Connect the **DotProduct** output into the Distortion channel of the Material. These changes break up the ripple so it doesn't appear too uniform. Compile and check that the surface of the water is now rippling.

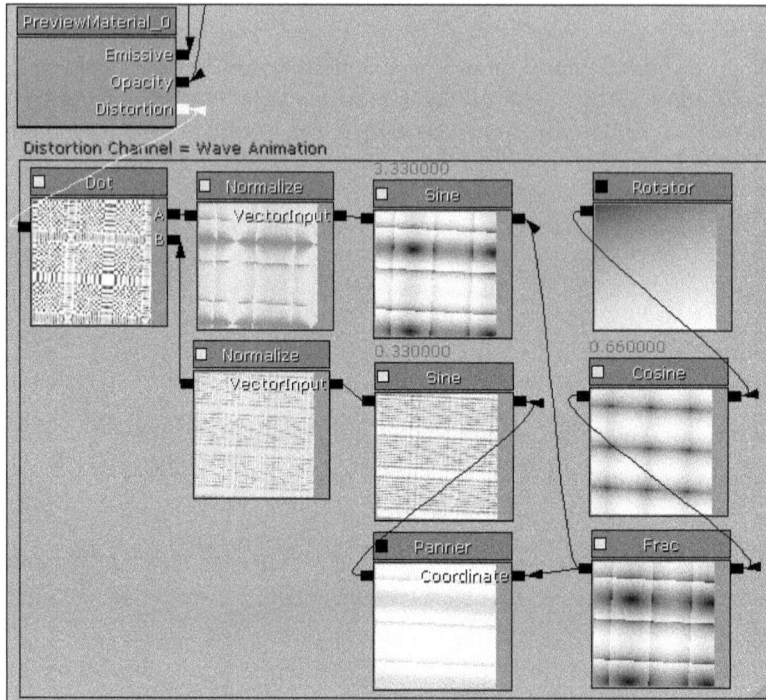

18. If you start to vary the *MIN* and *MAX* **Constant** nodes you will notice that as you range up the values the apparent thickness of the water will change, and the apparent depth, and the apparent tilt of the water fog near the camera (since it's driven by **PixelDepth**), as in the next screenshot. The effect is actually best used from directly above the water so you'd expect to see it in a top down strategy game rather than a first person shooter.

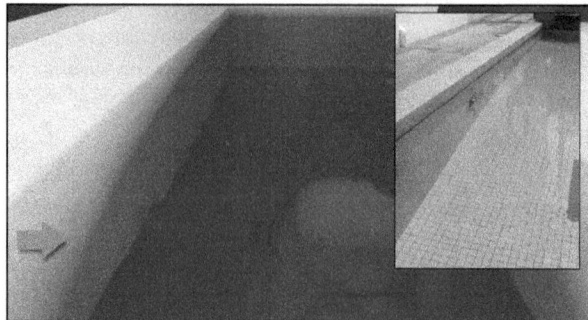

19. At first I considered the curving tilt to be visually unpleasant and tried to fix it. Then I noticed a similar real-world effect, shown here, which is caused by refraction of the water. UDK doesn't even attempt to calculate refraction for transparent surfaces based on their Material, so maybe there's something here to chew on for those who ponder such problems.

20. Compile and experiment with the value changes to see the range of looks the **DepthBiasedAlpha** network can produce. An example is provided: *Packt_09_DepthBiased_DEMO.UDK*.

Creating a scanning effect

This recipe continues on from the previous one. Open the scene *Packt_09_DepthBiased_ Start.UDK*. You will see a large pool and an enclosed passageway, both filled with objects. What we're interested in is the Material for the energy field in the passageway. It should sweep over the objects (as it's already animated in a **Matinee**). When the surface touches an object, we're going to make the surface of the energy field glow where contact occurs.

How to do it...

1.   In the Content Browser, right-click and choose **New Material**. Call it *Yourfolder. Material.DepthScanner*. In the passageway in the scene, select the Mover that goes back and forth (*InterpActor_0*). Apply your new Material to it.

2.   Open the Material. Set its **Lighting Model** to *MLM_Unlit* and its **Blend Mode** to *BLEND_Translucent*.

3.   Hold *L* and click to add a **Lerp**; name it *Emissive*. Hook this **Lerp** up to the Material's Emissive channel.

4.   Hold *3*, click to add a **Constant 3 Vector**, and set it to **R = 20, G = 1, B = 1**. This serves as the brightness boost for the *Rim* of the Material. Add another **Constant 3 Vector** and set it to **R = 0.66, G = 0.12, B = 0.1**. This serves as the basic *Color* of the Material.

5.   Right-click and choose **Depth | New DepthBiasedAlpha** and hook it up to the **Alpha** input of the **Lerp** *Emissive*. Set the **Bias Scale** value to 100. This determines the spread of the energy field's rim. Hold *1* and click to add a **Constant** and set its **R** value to 1.0. Feed the **Constant** into the **Alpha** input of the **DepthBiasedAlpha**.

6.   Hold *L* and click to add another **Lerp**, and name it *Opacity*. Hook it up to the Material's Opacity channel. Feed the **Constant** with a value of 1.0 into the **A** nub of the **Lerp**.

7. Right-click and choose **Depth | New DepthBiasedAlpha** again, and set its **Bias Scale** value to 5.0. Hook up the **Constant** with a value of 1.0 also into this **DepthBiasedAlpha**, into its **Alpha** nub. The **Constant** feeds three nodes. Feed the **DepthBiasedAlpha**'s output into the **Alpha** nub of the **Lerp** *Opacity*. Finally, hold *1* and click to another **Constant** and set its **R** value to 0.25, and hook it up to the **B** nub of the **Lerp** *Opacity*. This value drives the overall transparency of the Material, besides the *Rim*.

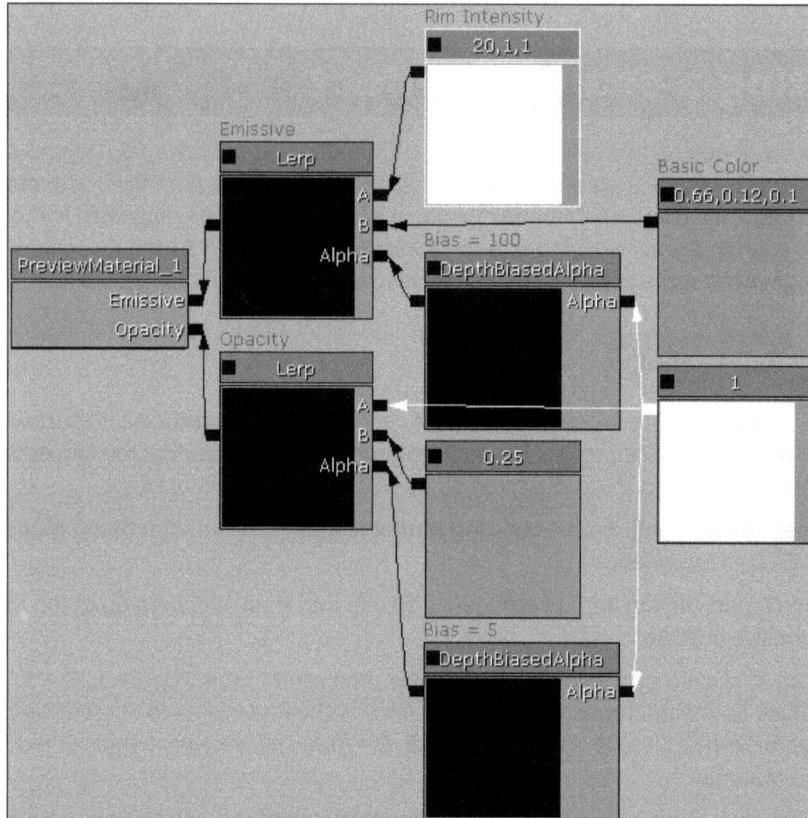

8. Open the **View | World Properties** menu and set the **Game Type for PIE** to *UTGame*. Compile, and PIE to see if the scanner, as it passes along the passageway, brightly outlines the surface of objects it passes over. Press *Tab* and type in *behindview* to see it effect the player bot too (although you may have to be running at the time because the player is pretty small and the scanner moves fairly quickly).

Quick glass

In this recipe we'll go over a way to generate a reasonable glass material. In reality, glass reflects the local environment, which is a tough call in a game environment. In this example we'll fake reflections, while in a later recipe we'll look at recording reflection maps from the actual scene too.

How to do it...

1. In the Content Browser, right-click and choose **New Material**. Name it *Yourfolder. Material.Quickglass_mat*.

2. In the Material *PreviewMaterial* properties, set the **Blend Mode** to *BLEND_Translucent* and also turn on **Two Sided**.

3. It's good to preview this kind of Material on a complex model, so highlight *Packt. Mesh.Statue* in the Content Browser. Right-click and choose **Copy Full Name to Clipboard**. In the *PreviewMaterial* properties, expand **Material Interface** and paste into the field the mesh name. Note that the eyes, which have their own Material, won't be affected, just the statue body.

4. In the Material Editor, hold *1* and click to add a *Constant* and set its **R** value to 0.5. Press *Ctrl + C* with the node highlighted, then *Ctrl + V* till you have four.

5. Right-click and choose **VectorOps | New Fresnel**, then hold *M* and click to add a *Multiply*. Hook one of the *Constants* to the **A** nub of the *Multiply*, and the *Fresnel* to the **B** nub of the *Multiply*. Hook the *Multiply* to the Opacity channel.

6. Hook one *Constant* to the Diffuse channel. If you want, *Multiply* this by a *Constant 3 Vector* so you can tint the glass.

7. Hook one **Constant** to the Specular Power channel. The higher its value is, the glossier it will look. Test out values such as 1, 11, 111, 1111.

8. Try a **Depth | PixelDepth** for the Specular channel.

9. Hook the **Pixel Depth** and the **Fresnel** that we already have to a **VectorOps | New DotProduct**, then hook that up to the Distortion channel to produce an illusion of refraction. Compare the result of changing the **A** and **B** order of the incoming nodes.

10. Right-click and choose **Vector | New ReflectionVector** and hook this up to the DiffusePower channel. You may want to unhook and hook it up a couple of times to see the difference that it makes. Compile the Material and save your package. Note that in the Content Browser this Material will just look gray.

11. Also test the Material on a StaticMesh in any scene with surroundings. In the Material Editor there is only a black background, which influences the appearance of the object. Sometimes a transparent object in the preview looks okay but in a scene looks too transparent.

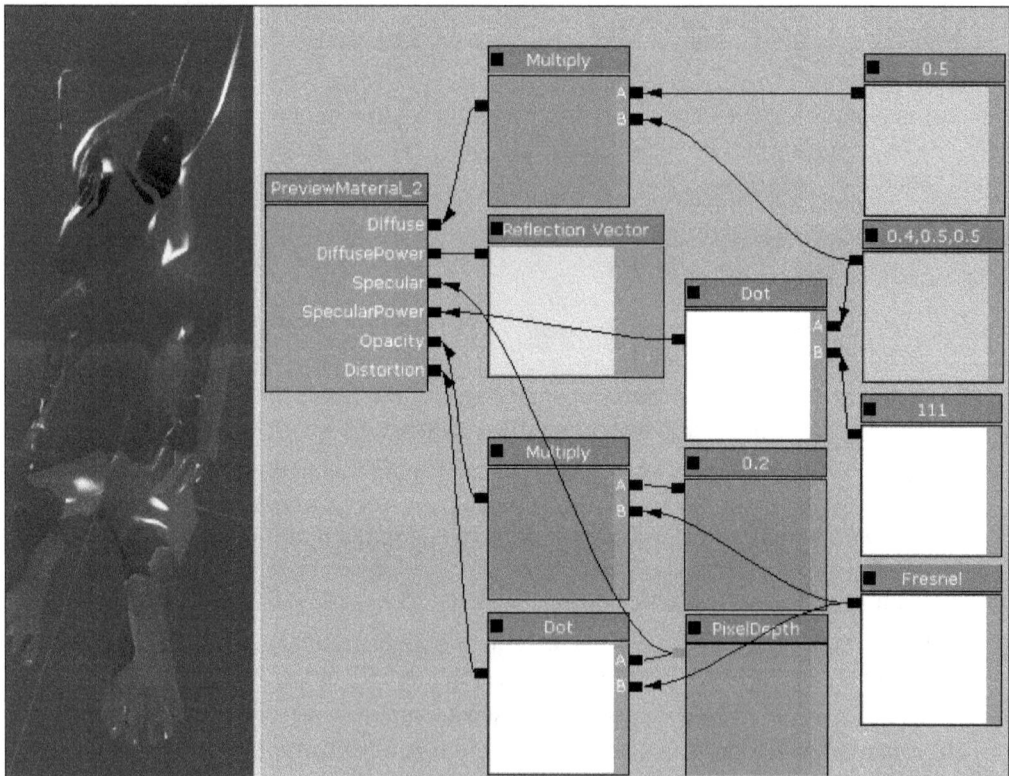

Creating transitions between Materials

There are a number of ways to transition between two Materials, where a mesh changes from having one to having another. Some Material changes can be sudden, simply using the *Set Material* action in Kismet. Some transitions can be done using a linear opacity dissolve, where a parameter is animated to adjust a *Lerp* node's **Alpha** to weight from **A** towards **B** for instance. Others require a more organic blend though, such as a dry to wet transition through spattering rain drops, or a burning transition that crawls over a surface. The method explained here assumes that three Materials will be used: a Material set before the transition, another set during the transition, and another set afterward. The design of the blending is where the creative problem-solving lies, and there are numerous ways to come up with an interesting mask. Masking can reveal an underlying texture, or simple fade out to nothing. A lot of artists blend to transparent using noise textures to hide destroyed items or dead characters. It can also be used for wet, dry, burning, or burnt effects.

How to do it...

1. Let's start with a kind of burning transition, which is simplified so that the *Before* surface is red, rather than wood or skin for instance. The *After* surface is blue, rather than burned wood. You could put any texture you want into the *Before* or *After* states. We'll also have a *During* texture represented as yellow.

2. So, to get started, in the Content Browser right-click and choose **New Material**. Call it *Yourfolder.Material.TransitionBurn*.

3. Open it in the Material Editor and add a **Constant 3 Vector**, name it *Before*, and set it to 1,0,0 and then add another, name it *After*, and set it to 0,0,1. Add one more, name it *During*, and set it to 1,1,0 (which is yellow).

4. Right-click and choose **Texture | New FlipBookSample**. In the Content Browser search for *Packt.Texture.Packt_Burning*. Highlight it and then assign it to the **FlipBookSample** in the Material Editor.

5. You may cry unfair, since we're using an existing texture. So let's look over how this was generated. In 3ds Max there is a map type called a **Gradient Ramp**, which is really convenient for making a wiping effect between two colors with noise added. There are quite a lot of steps, but fairly easy ones. Open the Material Editor (*M*) and right-click in **Slate** and choose **Maps | Standard**. Looking in the **Gradient Ramp Parameters** dialog, you will see a black to white ramp with three flags. At one end click to add flags so that you get a sharp white to black change, with a thin band of gray. Edit the gradient properties to assign a higher **Noise Amount** and **Noise Size** value, similar to the example shown in the next screenshot. You may want to squeeze them closer together.

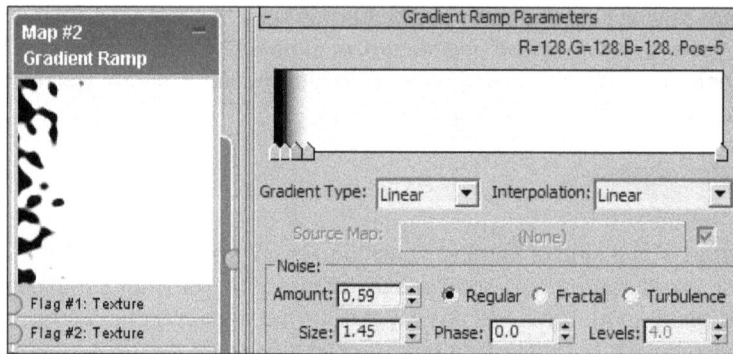

6. In the 3ds Max main workspace, press *N* to turn on **Autokey** mode and go to frame 15 on the time line (since we're going to render only 16 frames and it counts frame 0). Slide the flags for the gradient ramp along to the white end, keeping their order the same. If you wish, animate the noise values too.

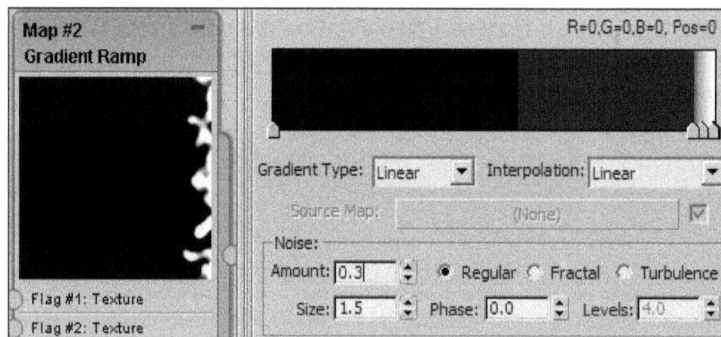

7. In the **Slate** Material Editor, right-click on the map and choose **Render map**. A dialog will appear in which you can set the **output size** (256x256) and the file name and path. Render out to *Gramp.PNG* and set the **frame range** to 0-15.

8. In Photoshop, combine the resulting *Gramp* frames into a tiled FlipBook image. This procedure was detailed in *Chapter 7, Hi, I'm Eye Candy!* When you import the image into UDK, make sure that you set the **FlipBook** checkbox on and name it *Yourfolder. Texture.Burning* (or you can use the provided *Packt.Texture.Packt_Burning*).

9. Also in Photoshop, use a white brush and rub out the empty black parts on the left-hand side of the image behind the advancing gradient ramp's noisy edge. This generates a mask for the currently burning part, distinct from the unburned and burned parts, as in the following image:

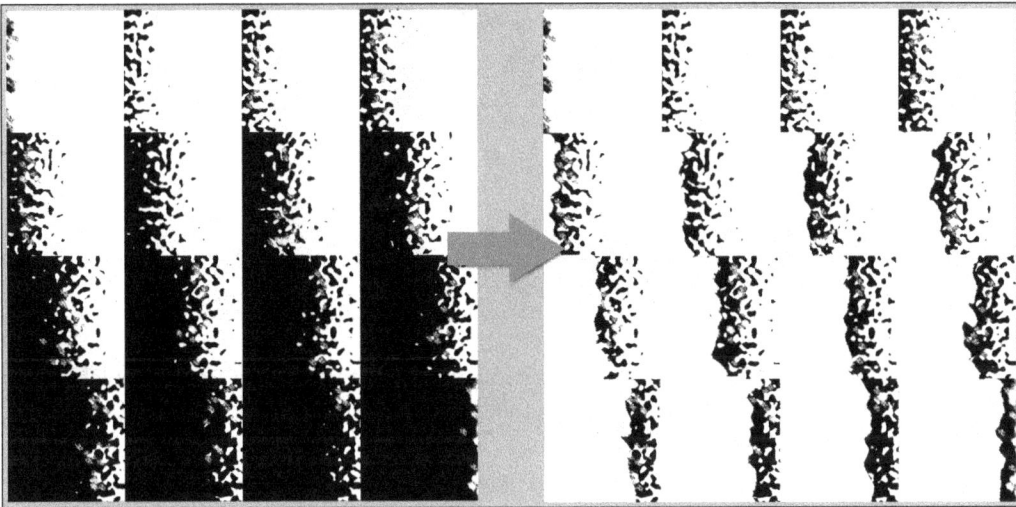

10. Save the result and import it as *Yourfolder.Texture.BurningMask*. Remember to set the imported texture so the **FlipBook** checkbox is ticked.

11. Back in the Material that we've been working on, highlight the **FlipBook Sample** and press *Ctrl + C* then *Ctrl + V* to make a copy of it. In this one, place your imported *BurningMask* asset (or you can use *Packt.Texture.Packt_BurningEdge*). Hook up these as seen in the following network screenshot:

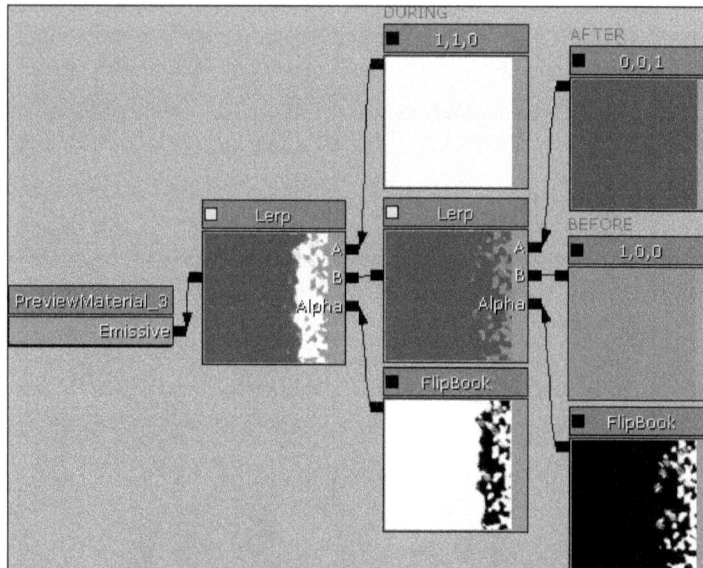

12. To realize the effect, you will need to make a new Material called *Before* (which will be red, used for the first surface type in the transition), and another Material called *After* along the same lines.

13. Open any map, and apply *Before* to a new KActor placed in the scene (it must be a dynamic actor or the process won't work), and also place a Trigger. Create a Kismet sequence where a **Trigger Touch** event fires a **Set Material** action to swap in the transition Material we've been making on the InterpActor, and then, after a 1 second delay (since the FlipBook frame rate is 16 frames per second) link to another **Set Material** node which will fire the *After* Material.

14. A final note in case your **Set Material** just doesn't want to work. The KActor is derived from a StaticMesh, and if you see (when you double-click on the StaticMesh in the browser) that its tick box for **Can Become Dynamic** is off, then you won't be able to get the effect. In the provided example the mesh *Packt.Mesh.Card* is used. Find this in the Content Browser, note that this setting is on and the effect is working. Turn it off, and the **Set Material** action reverts the Material to the **LOD Material** *Packt.Material.RotateMesh_mat*. The example is found in the map *Packt_09_Transition_DEMO.UDK*.

15. In the next screenshot, the Kismet is shown on the left-hand side and the final result is shown on the right-hand side. There is a limitation to the example: its one second duration can only be slowed down by adjusting the **FlipBook frame rate**, and that introduces jerky motion (more frames would be needed). Also, using *Texture Samples* as masks means the transition can only do what the source texture does. In the Content Browser, in the *Packt* content, you will also notice a similar transition mask *Packt.Texture.BuildUp*.

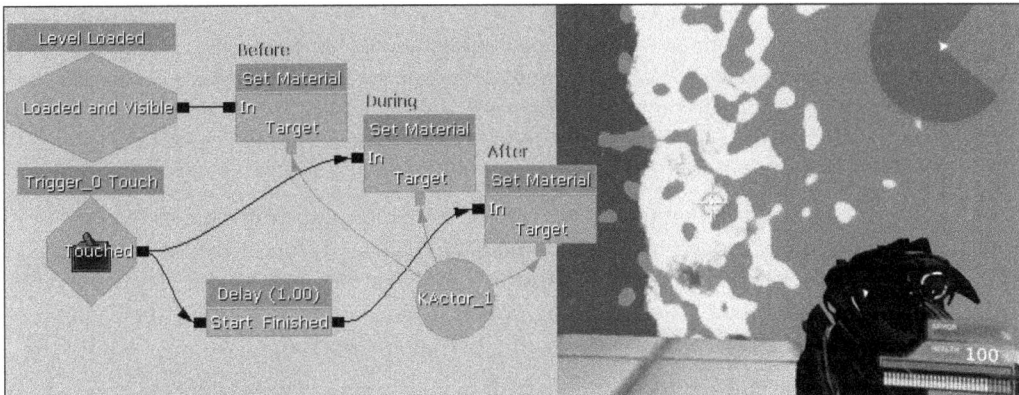

See also

For an alternative method to doing transitions, which uses *Matinee* animation of **MIC Parameter** nodes, consult the excellent demonstration by Eat3D in their DVD specifically on this topic, **Unreal VFX—Material Transitions**, from `http://eat3d.com/vfx`.

Static Cubemap creation and real-time reflection

To create a reflection of the live scene requires feeding a camera view from six different angles to a Material on an object, such as a screen or water surface. The first way to do this is by creating a Cubemap (which is static) and the other is by creating a RenderToTextureCube (which works in real time). A **RenderToTextureCube** is an extension from the single surface **2D RenderToTexture** asset, which is good for security camera footage and portals.

Getting ready

Open the scene *Packt_09_ReflectProces_Start.UDK*, which shows an energy chamber.

How to do it...

1. Open the Content Browser and switch to the **Actor Classes** tab. Look in the list for **Uncategorized | SceneCaptureCubeMapActor** (or else uncheck the Show Categories checkbox and look in the list under **SceneCaptureActor | SceneCaptureCubeMapActor**).

2. Highlight this and right-click in the middle of the scene and choose **Add SceneCaptureCubeMapActor Here**. A big black ball will appear and you'll need to place it in the room so it doesn't overlap the floor, ceiling or walls. Expand the properties of this actor to show: **SceneCaptureActor | SceneCapture | Capture | TextureTarget** which requires a **Texture** entry. Lock [🖼] the properties, then in the Content Browser right-click and choose **NewTextureRenderTargetCube**. Call it *Yourfolder.Texture.RoomCube*.

3. Set 512 as the **Size X** amount. Turn off **Needs Two Copies** (which saves memory, as in this case you don't need two). **ForcePVRTC4** can be left unchecked for this example (it doubles the size of the texture). Highlight this new asset in the browser, then back in the properties of the scene actor that was pinned, assign the highlighted asset to the **Texture Target** channel. The ball should update.

4. You don't really have to adjust the default properties to get a result, but you may want to mouse-over each to get a description of its purpose and experiment with changing them, in particular the **Max View Distance Override**, which sets how far from the actor the reflections will be shown. If you change the **View Mode** to *SceneCapView_Lit* then it will get more of a contribution from scene lighting. Similarly, if you tick **Enable Post Process** and then tick **Use Main Scene Post Process Settings**, the reflections will take into account bloom and focal blur if there's any in the environment.

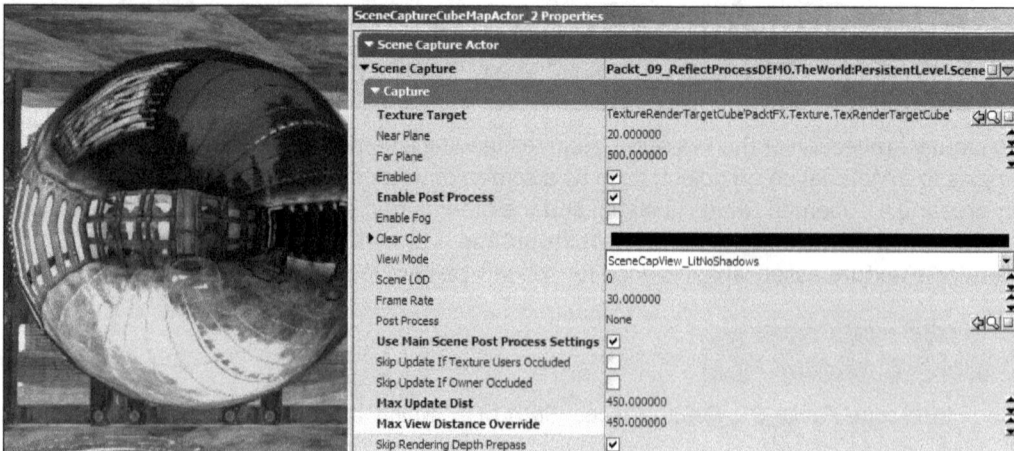

5. Right-click on the generated asset in the Content Browser and choose **Create New Static Texture**. This will render out six views based on the scene actor position and compile them into a static **TextureCube** (it won't update). Name it *Yourfolder.Texture. RoomCube_Result*.

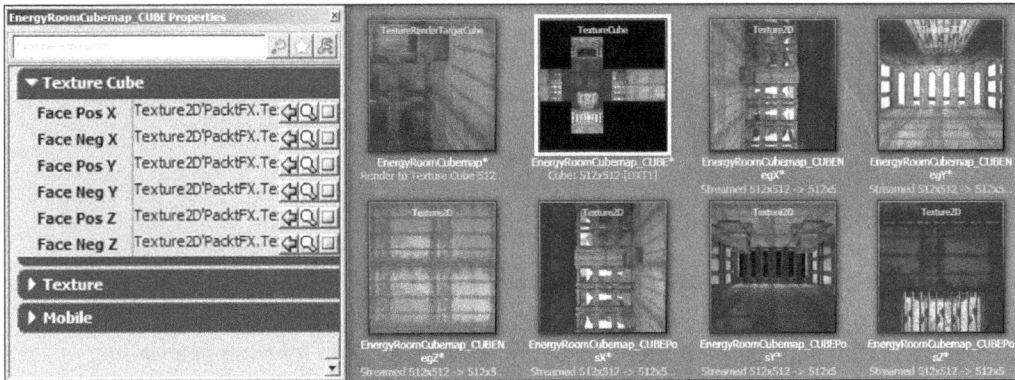

6. Besides generating the Cubemap, you can use real-time capture in a Material too. Create a new Material, *Yourfolder.Material.ReflectCubeTest* and within it, right click and choose **Texture | New TextureSampleParameterCube**. Set its **Parameter Name** property to *Cube*, just to shorten it. In the **Texture** channel, assign the **TextureRenderTargetCube** asset you created. Be sure not to confuse this with the static **TextureCube**.

7. Right-click and choose **Vector | New ReflectionVector** and hook this into *Cube*'s UVs input.

8. Right-click and choose **Utility | New LightmassReplace**, then hook Cube to it. This can connect to the Diffuse and/or Emissive channels.

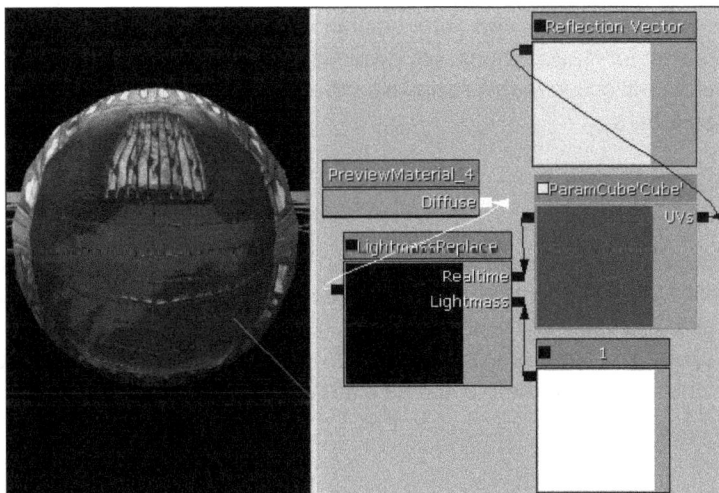

9. Compile the Material, save your package, and assign the Material to a new StaticMesh placed in the scene in the middle of the floor.

10. In the scene there is a ***Matinee*** driving a platform which drops down. You should see the reflection of this movement in the StaticMess actors Material when you PIE. An example is provided: *Packt_09_ReflectProcess_DEMO.UDK*. This uses a slightly more complex iteration of the Material, which blends in a base texture and creates more of a glossy coating effect: *Packt.Material.ReflectProcessSpecular*. It is a little bit like the pumping up of specular suggested in the documentation for simulated HDR: `http://udn.epicgames.com/Three/MaterialExamples.html`.

There's more...

Image based reflections and Material usage

The Cubemap that we generated can be used in many ways. It is also possible to directly use real-time capture from a 2D scene actor (for creating a mirror for example) where the reflection must be updated live. The Material Editor sequence for this using a 2D capture is provided by **Epic Games** (in their **Gems**): `http://udn.epicgames.com/Three/rsrc/Three/DevelopmentKitGemsCreatingDistortedReflection/07_MirrorMaterialLayout.jpg`.

As it happens, there is now a new process for this sort of situation, called an **Image Based Reflection**, which uses its own actor type, an **ImageReflectionActor**, described at `http://udn.epicgames.com/Three/ImageBasedReflections.html`. Our next recipe discusses this process.

Wet surface reflections with dynamic actors

It is possible to generate efficient planar reflections on planar surfaces using Image Based Reflections, and these have their own actor type and process. This can include variable reflectivity, but is best for static lighting. For dynamic actors, a shadow plane must be included where the reflection will occur. In this recipe we will make a wet floor which reflects in some places more than others.

Getting ready

Enabling **DirectX11** will be necessary for some users (depending on future updates to UDK). To do this, open in ConTEXT `C:\UDK\~\Engine\Config\BaseEngine.INI`, search for *AllowD3D11*, and if you find that it's set to `False`, change it to `True`. A couple of lines below that you'll also see `AllowImageReflections=True`, hopefully. If it isn't set to true, try setting it, but actually if it's not there could be a larger issue to solve.

In the properties for the icon which starts your UDK, for instance, in the Windows Start menu, in the Unreal Development Kit category, where it says **UDK Editor**, edit the **Target** command line so that `-D3D11` is appended to the line `C:\UDK\~\Binaries\UDKLift.EXE editor -D3D11`. It is helpful to append `-log` after it also.

When you re-launch UDK you will know what version of DirectX UDK is using by looking at the top of the editor where it says **Unreal Development Kit (64 bit, DX11)** ... or **DX9**. If it says DX9 perhaps you should look closely at your hardware and system.

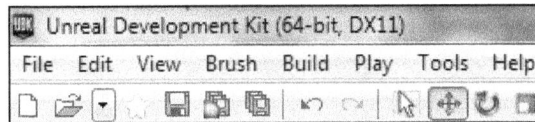

Assuming that everything is okay on this score, open *Packt_09_IBReflect_Start.UDK*.

How to do it...

1. Ensure that **View | Enable Translucent Selection** [🔲] is toggled on in the editor, and that you're in **Lit mode** (*Alt + 4*).

2. Add a **LightmassImportanceVolume** around the room, by creating a BSP cube, scaling it to fit, and choosing [🟢] **Volumes | LightmassImportanceVolume**. This volume speeds up lighting calculation and is useful generally to bound any scene, but in this case it is required if you tick **Enable Image Reflection Shadowing** in the **View | Lightmass | Lightmass Settings | World Info** menu, which you should do to get a good shadow result from any SkeletalMesh that interacts with an image-based reflection.

3. Select one of the lights in the scene, right-click on it, and choose **Select | Select All PointLight Actors**. Press *F4* then scroll down the properties to turn on **Light | LightComponent | Image Reflection | Use Image Reflection Specular**.

4. Create a Material called *Yourfolder.Material.IBRTest_mat*. For its Specular channel, hook up a Constant (hold 1 and click) and set the Constant's **R** property to 1.0. In the *PreviewMaterial* properties, expand the **D3D11** section and turn on the property **Use Image Based Reflections**. Compile the Material. This is just a quick Material to cover the whole scene. In a game level you would have to include the above steps for every texture involved along with the rest of their settings.

5. In the scene, select one of the StaticMesh actors, right-click, and choose **Select | Matching Material**. All the StaticMesh actors should select. Now drag the *IBRTest_mat* Material onto the objects to assign it to all of them at once.

6. Press *Ctrl + Shift + F* and switch to the **Actor Classes** tab. From the list, add an **ImageReflection** actor. Don't confuse it with an **ImageReflectionSceneCapture** actor, which is something else altogether. The first requires you to set a texture to base the reflection on, which is great for things such as capturing neon signs, while the second captures the scene itself, within a bounding box that sets its range, and is heavier to compute.

7. Also add an **ImageReflectionShadowPlane**. The shadow plane is needed so dynamic objects can cast shadows on the ground. It displays with the same icon as a **Fog** in the scene.

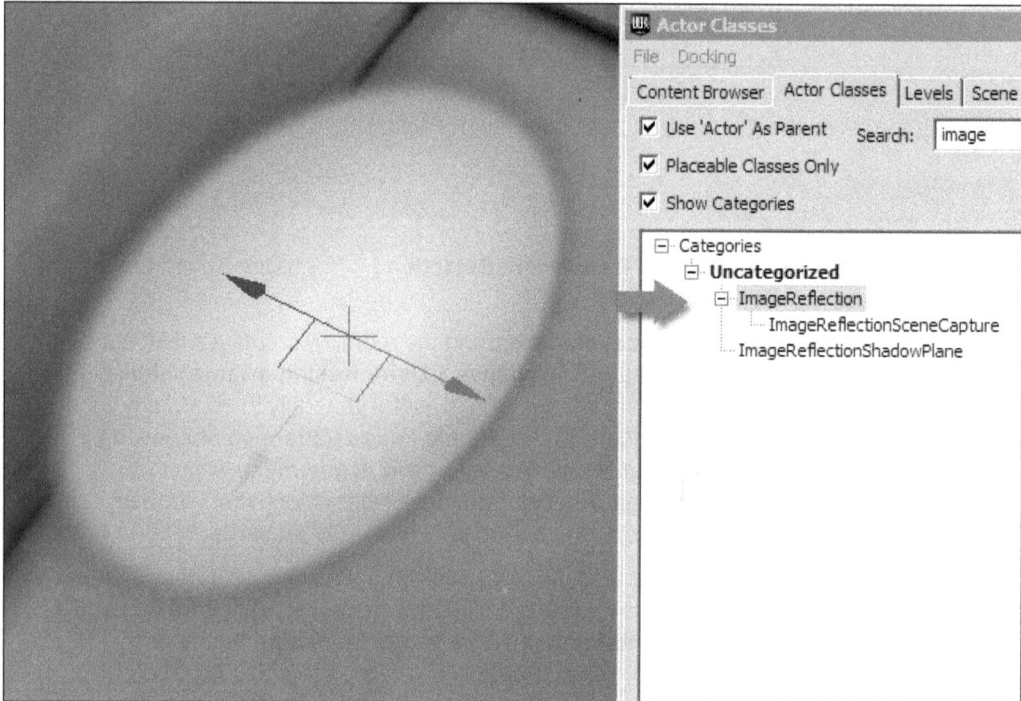

8. The **ImageReflection** actor probably has a glowing circle icon, as shown in the previous screenshot. This will change once you apply your own texture to it. Note that the actor is one sided by default.

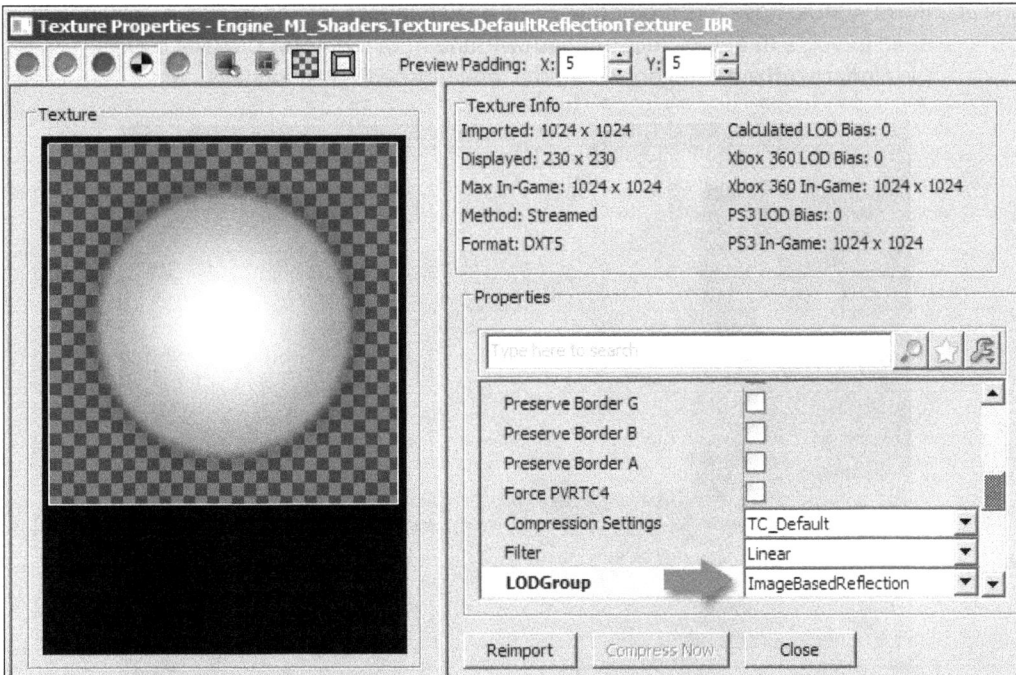

9. The texture assigned to it has the **LODGroup ImageBasedReflection** in its properties. Any texture that you use with this actor should also have the same. You can set this by right-clicking on the texture in question within the Content Browser and choosing **Properties** and assigning this from the drop-down list, as shown on the right-hand side in the previous screenshot. The texture used must be 1024x1024.

10. To make the surface that you're trying to get the reflection to show on look wet, the specular channel in the Material (for the floor or wall not the ImageReflection actor) should have a variable degree of Specular Power, so that some parts are glossy and some are not. You can even animate the specular power with a **FlipBook** or **Panner**. A bit of roughness from a normal map will contribute a lot too. For any grayscale texture you add to create varying glossiness, it is a good idea to also **Multiply** the input with a **Constant** (perhaps even a **Parameter**) so that you can moderate the intensity of the effect.

11. The ImageReflection actor itself does not render in-game, it just displays in the editor. You will have to add a plane with the relevant Material on it to also render a source for the reflection, as shown in the next screenshot. A demo scene is provided: *Packt_09_IBReflect_DEMO.UDK*.

12. If you want to have this method work with SkeletalMeshes in the scene, you'll need to add a **ImageReflectionShadowPlane** from the **Actor Classes** list in the **Uncategorized** category where the image-based reflection falls.

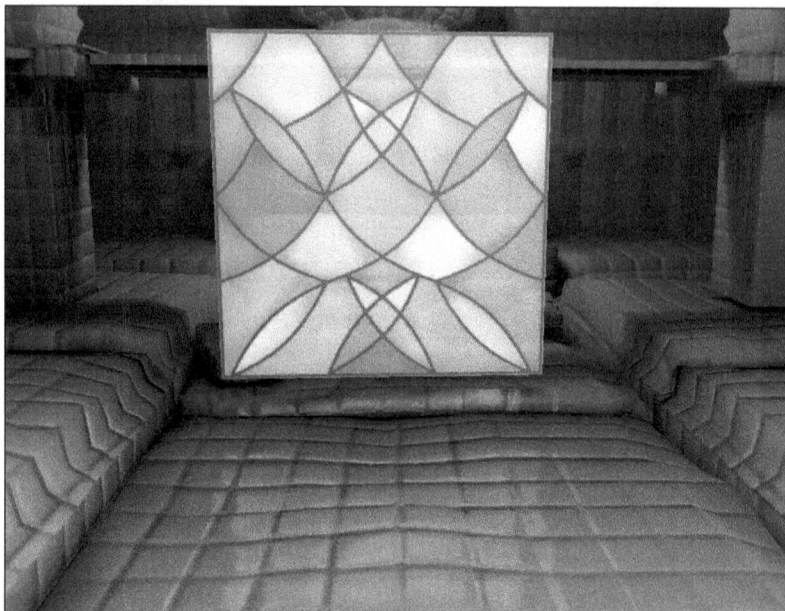

There's more...

Panoramic reflected environment textures

World Info has some properties that allow specifying reflections coming from an infinitely distant hemisphere over the level. This lets us add ambient reflections that appear like they are coming from the distance, and to bring out the detail that the shadowing methods provide. You have to set an **ImageReflectionEnvironmentTexture**, which is a panoramic environment texture for image reflections. It looks like a regular spherical environment map but the ground portion is cut off so that the image content's 'horizon' is along the bottom of the image (V = 0) and straight up in world space is along the top (V = 1). The U direction of the texture then corresponds to rotation around the Z world axis.

The look of this kind of panoramic projection (which is a dome really) is something similar to the next screenshot. We've made a rough outline over the example that UDK provides in order to indicate the typical pattern that you'd see in this kind of projection.

Making a holographic effect using Bump Offset

Bump Offset provides us with a way of doing a stacked effect within a Material so that the Material doesn't appear completely flat. It projects content based on a height value to simulate displacement. It is really good for enhancing bumpy surfaces like courtyard cobble stones. Still, on top of this, we can offset different elements in a Material so they float, or appear to, which can form the basis for a convincing holographic image.

Getting ready

The artwork for the texture is already provided. It is worth looking at the construction of it in Photoshop first. Open up *MaskRGBA_DEMO.PSD* and got to the menu **Window | Channels**.

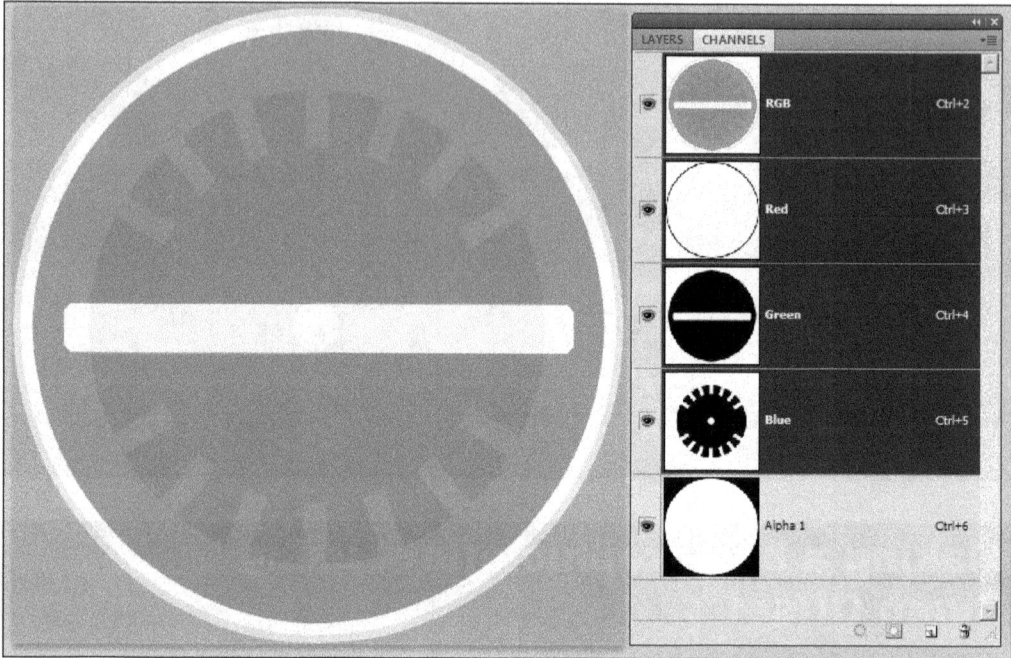

Each channel includes a distinct image in black and white. UDK can access the channels of a texture individually, and this is really handy for mask usage, since masks are usually a single channel. The image also includes an Alpha, which is really just an additional channel. The 512x512 image has to be saved as a .TGA in 32bit format. Once imported, this texture will provide multiple elements to generate the holographic asset from.

How to do it...

1. In the Content Browser, right-click and choose **New Material**. Call it *Yourfolder. Material.Hologram_mat*.

2. Apply the Content Browser filter **Texture**, and search for *Mask* in the *Packt* content, and notice the textures available include *Packt.Texture.MaskRGBA*. Highlight this and in the Material you just made add it to a ***Texture Sample*** (hold *T* and click). Right-click on *MaskRGBA* in the Content Browser, choose **Properties**, and set the **Texture2D | Address X** and **Address Y** set to **Clamp** for both (which will ensure any later **Rotator** coordinate used with the texture will treat the corners correctly).

3. Set the ***PreviewMaterial*** so its **Blend Mode** is *BLEND_Additive* and its **Lighting Model** is *MLM_Unlit*. Switch the Material preview to display a plane using the icon [🔲] at the top of the Material Editor.

4. Hook up the **Alpha** output of the ***Texture Sample*** into the Opacity channel.

5. One by one, hook up the **R** then the **G** then the **B** output's of the ***Texture Sample*** to the Material's Emissive channel in order to verify how each looks. They show in black and white. To tint them we'll need to **Multiply** them by a **Constant 3 Vector**.

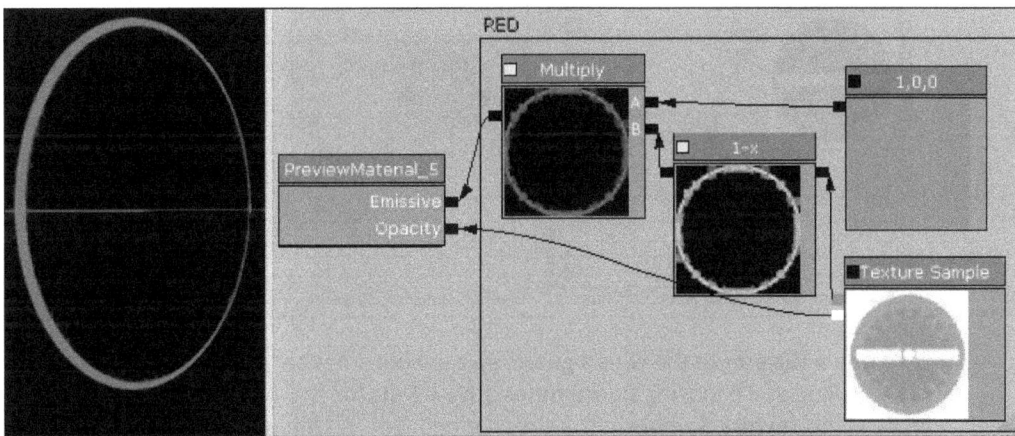

6. Notice the ***1-x*** (**Math | New One Minus**) used to invert the ***Texture Sample*** node's **Red** channel's black and white pixels.

7. Select, copy, and then paste this group, then change the **Texture Sample** output for the pasted group so that the **Green** channel feeds the value inverting *1-x*. Repeat this once more to make a group using the **Blue** channel. In the next screenshot, the *1-x* has been deleted from the **Green** channel's contribution:

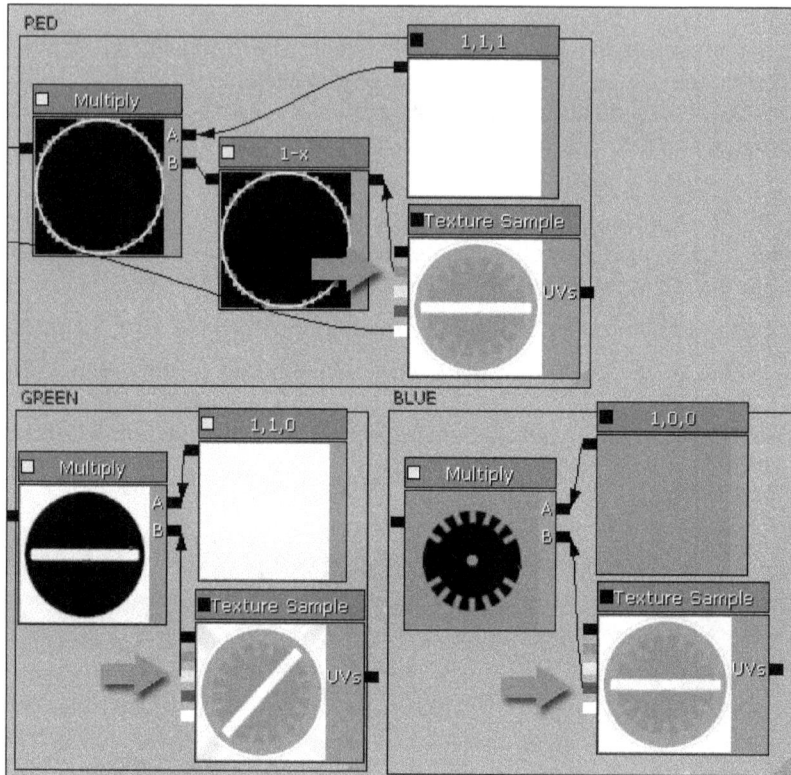

8. Let's add a **Rotator** to the *Green* group, so the horizontal bar spins. Do this by right-clicking and choosing **Coordinates | New Rotator** and hooking it into the **UVs** input of the **Texture Sample** in the *Green* group. Set the **Speed** property as you like.

9. The next process is to add the nodes together. Hold *A* and click and feed the *Red* group's **Multiply** output into the **A** nub of the **Add**, and the *Blue* group's **Multiply** output into the **B** nub of the **Add**. Create another **Add** and feed the first **Add**'s output into the new **Add**'s **A** nub and feed the *Green* group's **Multiply** output into the **B** nub of the second **Add**. Send the combined **Add** into the Emissive channel of the Material.

10. For the **Bump Offset**, right-click and choose **Utility | New BumpOffset** and hook its output to the **Rotator** in the *Green* group. Also, hold *1* and click to provide a **Constant** and name it *Height*, as it will give us a height value. Set the **Constant** to 0.66 and in the **Bump Offset** node's properties, set **Height Ratio** to 0.66 and **Reference Plane** to 0.5.

11. Set another *BumpOffset* feeding the **UVs** of the Blue group's *Texture Sample* and give it a **Height Ratio** and **Reference plane** value of 0.33. Make sure to feed its **Height** input the *Constant* Height also, though you could also create a new *Constant* if you prefer a different value here.

12. For the colors used by the *Red*, *Green*, and *Blue* groups (which are called this because of the channel usage) you can set the **Constant 3 Vector** RGB values to whatever you like, but notice how they add together, since the *PreviewMaterial* has its **Lighting Model** as *Additive*. The next screenshot shows the result of setting up the network, then playing with color combinations so that each channel yields a distinct color. The impact of the *Bump Offset* can be seen by rotating the preview to the side, then to the front, where it appears to have a certain depth or floating quality.

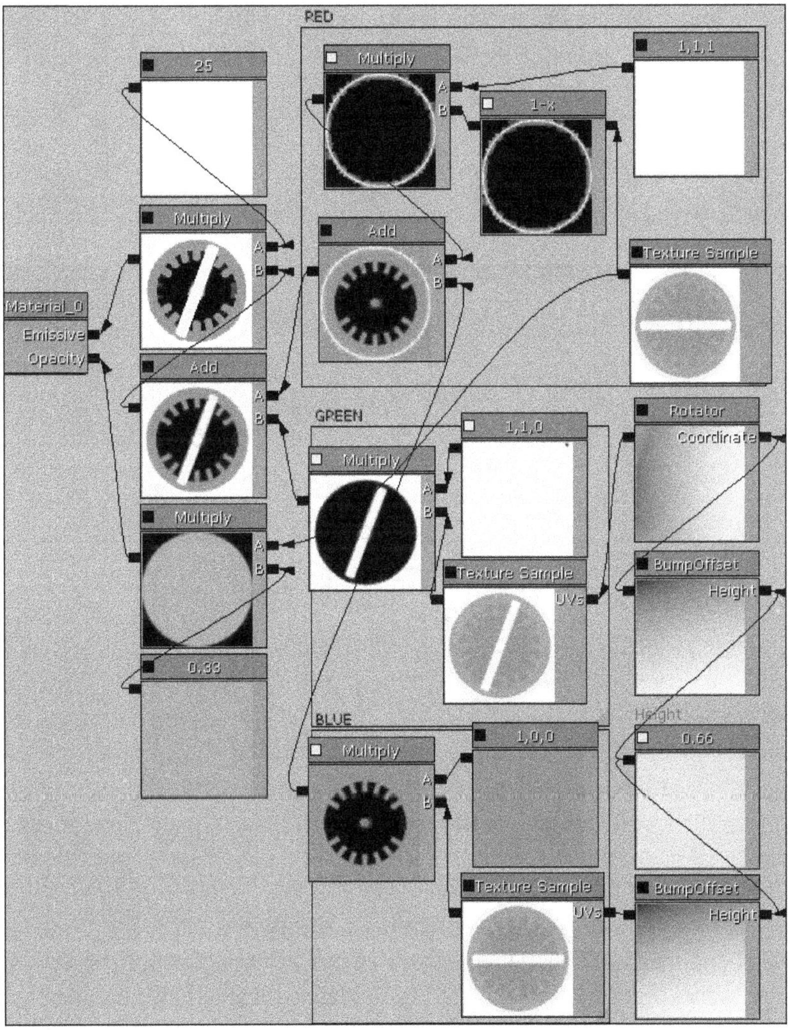

13. To complete the Material you may want to **Multiply** the feed from the **Texture Sample** in the *Red* group by a **Constant** with a value of 0.66 or so. Then **Multiply** the Emissive feed by a **Constant** of about 25 to boost it up so it glows. An example is included in the Material *Packt.Material.HologramBumpOffset*.

Interactive Foliage Actors

WorldPositionOffset was discussed in a couple of cases earlier in this chapter, and there's one more interesting case: how **Interactive Foliage Actors** use this feature. An Interactive Foliage Actor needn't have anything to do with foliage, but that is what it is often used for. **Epic Games** provides a video of the actor being used to create a field of undergrowth which reacts to the bounds of a Bot as it runs around amongst it: `http://udn.epicgames.com/Three/rsrc/Three/InteractiveFoliageActor/WalkingThroughFields.mp4`. A spring system automatically applied to the actor (it can be any StaticMesh) drives the interaction.

In this recipe we'll look at what we can do with the Material nodes that are involved, using the node which possibly has the longest name of all: **FoliageNormalizedRotationAxisAndAngle**.

How to do it...

1. In the Content Browser, find *Packt.Mesh.PowerCore* and highlight it. Right-click in the scene and choose **Add InteractiveFoliageActor: Packt.Mesh.PowerCore**. Don't be surprised if it appears quite high off the ground. Lower it using the **Translation Mode** widget. The *End* hotkey won't work here.

2. Press *Alt + C* to show object collision in the viewport. You will notice that the *PowerCore* actor has a huge bounding cylinder. With the *PowerCore* actor selected in the scene, press *F4* and look for the **Collision | CollisionComponent | CollisionHeight** property and set it to 60. Set the **CollisionRadius** to 10.

3. Set the **DrawScale** of the *PowerCore* actor to 3 (down in the entry field at the bottom of the editor) or in the property **StaticMeshActor | StaticMeshComponent | PrimitiveComponent | Scale3D** and set X=3, Y=3, Z=3.

4. In the Content Browser, search for *Packt.Material.PowerCore_IFA*. Right-click on it and choose **Create a copy...** then name the copy *Yourfolder.Material.PowerCoreIFATest*. Drag this onto the power core, then hold *Alt* and drag out a few copies of the actor. Open the Material in the Material Editor.

5. Right-click in the Material Editor and choose **Math | New RotateAboutAxis**. Hook this up to the World Position Offset channel of the Material (it will return an error warning but that's because we didn't load anything into this node yet). So, right-click and add a **Coordinate | New WorldPosition** and then a **Coordinate | New ObjectWorldPosition**. The *WorldPosition* hooks into the **Position** nub of the *RotateAboutAxis*. The *ObjectWorldPosition* hooks into the **PositionOnAxis** nub.

6. Right-click and add a **Coordinates | FoliageNormalizedRotationAxisAndAngle** node. Right-click and choose **Custom | New Custom**.

7. Hook its input to the output of the *FoliageNormalizedRotationAxisAndAngle*. In the properties of the **Custom** set the name to *Custom: FloatAngle*. Press **Click to Show Editing Box** and enter the following code snippet:

```
float angle = b;
float cosAngle = cos(angle);
float sinAngle = sin(angle);
float3 A = float3((a.x*cosAngle - a.y*sinAngle),
   (a.y*cosAngle + a.x*sinAngle),a.z-20);

return A;
```

8. Press **Apply** and close the window. In the properties of the custom node, there needs to be two inputs, one called **a** and one called **b** (these are what the code refers to). Add the inputs by clicking the **add entry** icon [🔧] and ensure the node's **Output Type** property is set to *CMOT_Float 3*. Make sure there are no typos. If there are you'll see a red error warning in the Material statistics.

9. If you don't put the -20 after the z in the expression, you will get rotation around a different axis. As it is, the impulse applied to the *PowerCore* actor will turn it to spin around its vertical axis, a bit like a Tibetan prayer wheel.

10. Hold *N* and click to add a *Normalize*, and hook the **Custom** node to its **VectorInput** nub. Right-click and choose **VectorOps | New AppendVector**. Hook up the *Normalize* output to the **A** nub of this *Append* node. Hook the *Append* output to the *NormalizedRotationAxisandAngle* nub of the *RotateAboutAxis*.

11. Hold *M* and click to add a *Multiply* and name its **Desc** property as 1. Add another, and name it 2.

12. Right-click and choose **Constants | New VertexColor**. Hook it to *Multiply 1* in the **A** nub.

13. Hold *1* and click to add a **Constant**, set its **R** value to 1.5 and hook it up to the **Multiply** *1* in the **B** nub.

14. Hook the output of **Multiply** *1* to the **A** nub of **Multiply** *2*.

15. Hold *C* and click to add a **Component Mask**, and in its properties uncheck all but the **A** checkbox. Hook the **Mask**'s output to **Multiply** *2* in the **B** nub. Hook up **Multiply** *2* to the **B** nub of the **Append** node.

16. Compile, save, and build. To check things are working, you have to PIE. First, open the menu **View | World Properties**, and scroll down to **Game Type** and set the **Game Type for PIE** to *UTGame*. When you PIE, press *Tab* and type *behindview* in the text field. Run up to the *PowerCore* meshes and check they spin as you bump them.

How it works...

This example's functionality comes from the mathematics that output a float angle depending on the direction from which the player hits the actor in the scene. This is fed in to the **RotationAboutAxis** node, and the **Constant** in the expression defines the intensity of the spring. You could also effect the spring setting by opening the **InteractiveFoliageActor** properties and expanding the **Foliage Physics** section to expose the values for its Impulse Scaling, Stiffness, and Dampening.

There's more...

Bobbing from the base

In the previous example, we set the code segment in the custom node *FloatAngle*:

```
...
float3 A = float3((a.x*cosAngle - a.y*sinAngle),
  (a.y*cosAngle + a.x*sinAngle),a.z-20);

return A;
```

If you set it as follows, which is only a small change, you can change the nature of the bobbing of the object:

```
...
float3 A = float3((a.x*cosAngle - a.y*sinAngle),
  (a.y*cosAngle + a.x*sinAngle),a.z);
return A;
```

You then will probably want to adjust the nodes as seen in the next screenshot (in particular by **Subtracting** 25 from the *ObjectWorldPosition* so as to lower the **PositionOnAxis**):

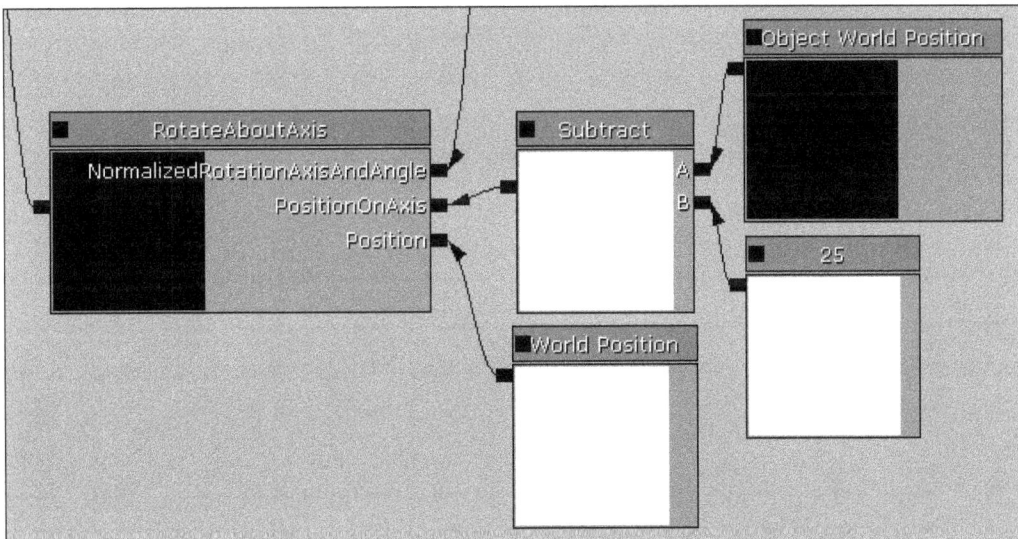

By default, it bobs around its center, which only looks okay when it is spinning around its up axis. If you want a sideways rocking motion, dropping the **PositionOnAxis** works because we set the **Collision Height** for the *PowerCore* to be 60, so the subtraction of 25 puts it at the base (or just above). The **Constant** driving the spring intensity should be reduced as the rocking motion looks more extreme than the spinning motion. A demo is provided: *Packt_09_IFA_DEMO.UDK*. Two of the *PowerCore* actors are set to rock and another two are set to spin.

Getting varied hit impacts off models using a PhysicalMaterial

Our model can have different reactions to hit impacts based on a mask component in its Material which defines areas with different surface properties, such as metal or skin. Most often, Physical Materials are used to control what sound effect will play following a hit impact on a given part of the body.

How to do it...

1. Right-click in the Content Browser and choose **Create New PhysicalMaterial**. Name it *MyCharPhysBlack*. Create another called *MyCharPhysWhite*.

2. A Physical Material is assigned to an object inside the properties of the **PreviewMaterial_0**, the main node everything flows into in the Material Editor. Therefore, in the Content Browser, right-click and **Create a Copy** of the Material for *Packt_Character*, which is *Packt_CharMat*. Name the copy *MyCharMat_Phys*.

3. Open *MyCharMat_Phys* and click on the *Material_0* node, look to its properties, and expand **PhysicalMaterial**.

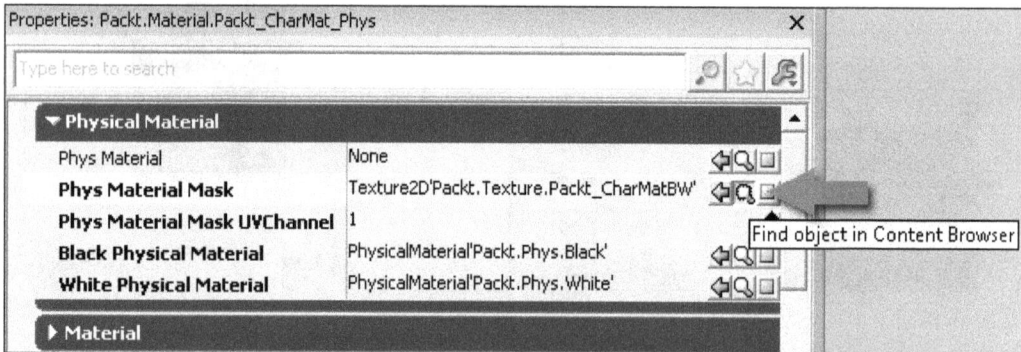

The **Phys Material Mask** in this case is the image file: *Packt_CharMatBW1.BMP*. This black and white image was derived from *Packt_Female_Diffuse.TGA* and it defines the clothes as black and the skin as white. It was painted directly on the model using the 3ds Max 2011 **Viewport Canvas** tool. The pure black and white tone range was obtained using the **Legacy Brightness and Contrast** in Photoshop. Then the **Image | Mode** was changed first from **RGB** to **Greyscale** and then to **Bitmap**. Saving the result as .BMP allows 1bit compression.

According to the UDN documentation on 1bit masks, their compression can handle information in images with more than straight black and white values, it will just squeeze the values higher than half of 255 as white and those lower than half of 255 as black. However, it may help to ensure that this procedure is done according to your own image processing, rather than computed, unless you really trust your computer.

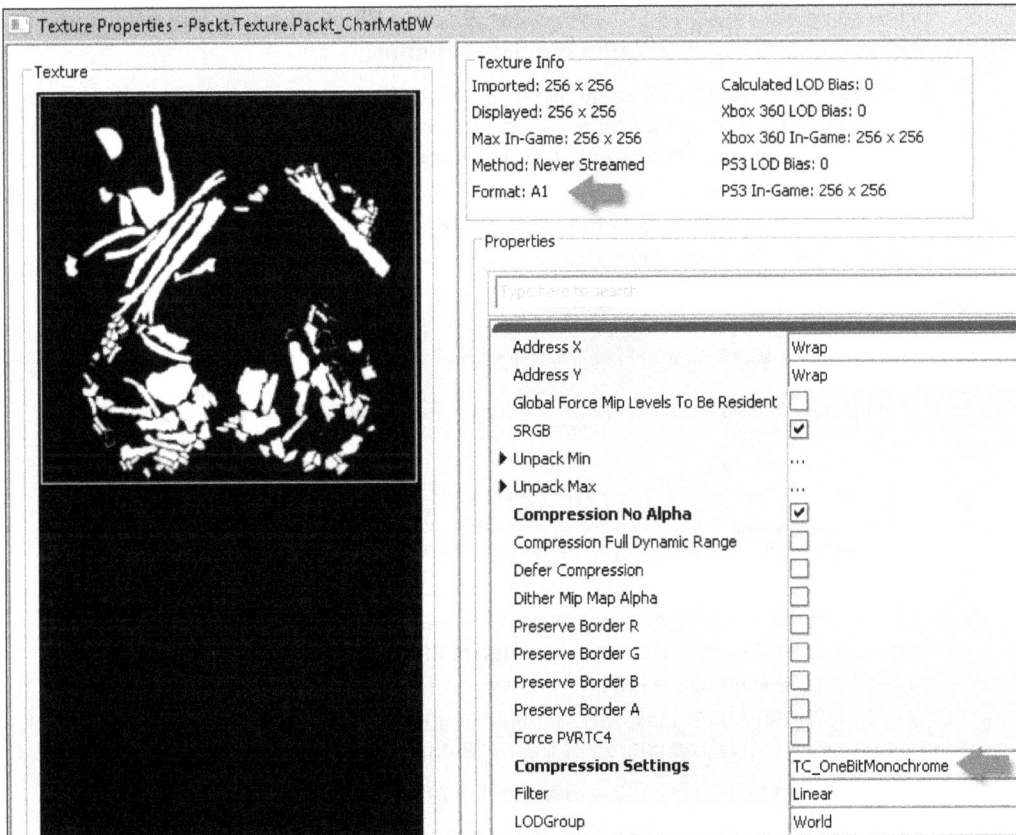

4. Right-click in the *Packt* folder of the Content Browser and choose **Import** then select *Packt_CharMatBW.BMP*. Set the texture name as *Yourfolder.Texture.CharMask*. Unlike the usual import of a texture, here we need to set the texture compression option upon import to *TC_1bitMonochrome*.

5. On import, or by double-clicking the imported .BMP texture, you can access texture properties and set this, and it is very important to check that the **Format** result of the compression says **A1**, rather than, for instance, DXT1. Anything other than **A1** will not produce a result for the Physical Material Mask. The Format: **A1** feedback has been marked in the previous screenshot.

6. Highlight the imported texture then assign [⟲] this to the *Phys Material Mask* channel in the properties of *MyCharMat_Phys*'s **PreviewMaterial_0** node. You should end up with a result similar to what you see in the screenshot after step 3, using your imported texture.

7. In the same way, assign *MyCharPhysMat_Black* to **Black Physical Material**, and *MyCharPhysMat_White* to **White Physical Material**.

8. In the browser, double-click on *MyCharPhysMat_White* and type *impact* in the search field to isolate the relevant properties, as shown in the next screenshot. Assign the particle system *SmokePlume* in the channel **Impact Effect** (this is just a random particle system so we can see the effect). In the **Impact Sound** channel assign *PacktWavs.Cue.one_Cue*, so we have a distinct audio to check whether the **Physical Material** mask will work.

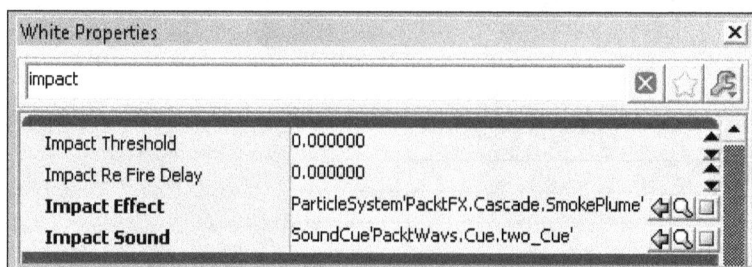

9. Likewise, in the browser, double-click on *MyCharPhysMat_Black* and assign the particle system *Beam* in the channel **Impact Effect** (another random particle system). In the **Impact Sound** channel assign *PacktWavs.Cue.two_Cue*. So now we have two different hit impact effects that the **Physical Material** mask will expose depending on where the character takes damage, on their skin or on their clothes.

10. Click the green tick [▨] in the Material Editor to compile the changes.

11. Drag *Packt_Character* as a SkeletalMesh into a scene. Make sure that, in her properties (*F4*) that **Skeletal Mesh Actor | Damage Applies Impulse** is turned on. This will ensure that she'll react to physics collisions and the **Physical Material** will activate.

12. Likewise, for any character to which a **Physical Material** is assigned, in its properties (*F4*) the setting **Skeletal Mesh Actor | Skeletal Mesh Component | Skeletal Mesh Component | Physics | Notify Rigid Body Collision** must be turned on. A SkeletalMesh dragged into the scene will also need **Collide**: *Block All* set as well.

13. PIE and scroll the mouse to cycle to the PhysicsGun (since we need a physics impulse). Hit her to see whether or not the Physical Material Mask gives us a different style hit off the Black and White components.

The **Physical Material Mask** won't work by default with the LinkGun as a weapon, since that doesn't apply a physics impulse, so scroll the mouse wheel to set the physics gun active then left-click to poke the model in the scene.

> The example we've made is based on a Physical Material setting for the *Packt_CharMat* Material. An example map showing a rigid body ball with a masked Physical Material is included in the provided content: *Packt_09_PhysMatMask_DEMO.UDK*. It shows a bare scene with rigid bodies that one can hit with the physics gun, which should help clarify the intended result. You should be able to drag any SkeletalMesh using *Packt_CharMat* or the example that you've set up into the scene and test the Physical Material in the same way.

See also

Given that a Material appears on just about every geometric asset in a level, there are many examples of Materials which you can look at in the UDK content. For more discussions of Materials for special effects see: *Chapter 7, Hi, I'm Eye Candy!* look at the recipe *Making animated textures using particle systems.*

10
The Way Of
The Flash UI

Scaleform, CLIK, and Flash Interfaces

Scaleform is now considered the premiere tool for generating **user interface (UI)** components for many games. Its use requires in-depth knowledge of Flash and ActionScript and the **GFx nodes** in Kismet. Awareness of the UnrealScript classes that govern **HUD** behavior is also needed.

In this chapter, we will cover topics such as:

- ▶ Setting yourself up to work with Scaleform
- ▶ Working with images to skin a button
- ▶ Cursor design and script for cursors
- ▶ Importing SWF content to UDK
- ▶ Placing an SWF on a BSP surface using Render to Texture

Introduction

Formerly, UI implementation was done in UDK using **UIScenes**, a part of the Canvas tool. These were internally integrated in the editor but in some ways limited (although it is possibly a shame UIScenes were deprecated completely). Scaleform Corporation, just before it was acquired by Autodesk, paired up with **Epic Games** to allow Flash based .SWF content to be imported into UDK. This allows designers access to the timeline-based, vector-based graphic animation Flash permits, and also access to ActionScript commands that drive cursors, button rollovers, clicking actions, and user input. Additionally, adding the Scaleform GFx Media Player extension within Flash provides a way for designers to preview how the UI content will look in game directly as they work, since they don't have to export, compile and build their game, and so forth.

The overall design process incorporating Scaleform for UI is to come up with a plan for the UI features, then do the art (or at least placeholder art) and animation, then set the properties of the art, then write the script that controls the asset's usage in Flash, and then export the content, import it to UDK, and then refer to the imported assets in Kismet to determine the situations and order in which they will be called on. The same references can be added in custom UnrealScript classes, where the designer may be going for a unified HUD system so the Scaleform script linkage can be edited easily and with more complexity. In this chapter, we will be discussing common ways that users can create and handle UI elements in UDK, and then provide an example to shine some light on the challenge of making a core element in a game UI, the inventory system.

Setting yourself up to work with Scaleform

Scaleform does not require Adobe Flash, but that is the working environment for building UI content that is generally accepted and that Epic endorses through their documentation (`http://udn.epicgames.com/Three/Scaleform.html#Setting up Adobe Flash Environment`). It is best to work with a later version such as CS5, but CS4 also works. ActionScript 2 is easier to use, but ActionScript 3 is also supported, with increasing documentation (although none of the examples in this book depend on it). Autodesk provides lessons on using Scaleform within UDK: `http://gameware.autodesk.com/scaleform/support/documentation`.

Getting ready

This recipe assumes you already have Adobe Flash CS5 working. If you don't have it, and don't want to own it, you could try one of several free routes (such as using Vectorian Giotto and FlashDevelop).

How to do it...

Setting up Scaleform in Flash

1. In Flash, open a new .FLA, set to ActionScript2. In the menu **Help | Manage Extensions** click **Adobe Extension Manager**. Click **Install** located at the top of the Launcher application's interface. Navigate to your `C:\UDK\~\Binaries\GFx\ CLIK Tools\` folder and choose *Scaleform CLIK.mxp*. This sets up the **Scaleform Workflow Enhancement**.

2. Restart Flash, and then go to the menu **Window | Other Panels**, and choose **Scaleform Launcher**.

3. The **Launcher** needs some paths assigned so **CLIK widgets** will work. Click the **+** icon to add a new **Profile**. Type the profile name: FXMediaPlayer. The profile needs a **Player**. Click on the **+** icon next to the **player EXE** channel. You'll need to then navigate to and choose `C:\UDK\~\Binaries\GFx\FxMediaPlayer.exe`.

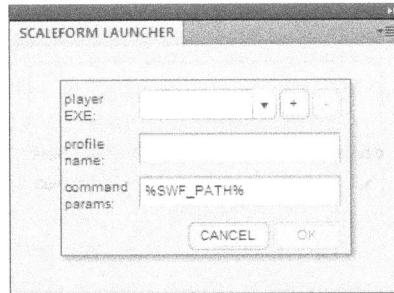

4. The usage for the **Launcher** is to have your **Profile** active when you hit the button labeled **Test with FXMediaPlayer**. Refer to the UDN documentation for information on multiple resolution previewing and different debugging modes. It isn't required just now to set those up. Of course, we need some content in our .FLA for the **FXMediaPlayer** to actually show anything in its preview mode, but first we have to continue setting things up.

5. While still in Flash, so that CLIK components will actually work, set up the **Scaleform CLIK Class Paths**. Choose the menu **Edit | Preferences**. Choose **ActionScript**, then click **ActionScript 2.0 Settings**. Add a new entry with the **+** button there. Set the path `C:\UDK\~\Development\Flash\CLIK` and make sure (by using the up and down arrow icons) that the newly added path is second from the top.

6. Open the menu **File | Publish Settings**, and in the **Formats** tab, turn off the **HTML** checkbox (or **HTML Wrapper** checkbox in CS 5.5). Switch to the **Flash** tab. Set the **Player** entry to **Flash Player 8**. In CS 5.5 this is in the same tab. Also make sure the **Script** method is set to **ActionScript 2.0**.

7. For every .FLA you make, set the **File | Publish Settings** path for the **Flash (.swf)** output so that it goes to `C:\UDK\~\UDKGame\Flash\YourfolderUI\` with the name of your file added.

There's more...

Adding new CLIK Objects to your library

In Flash you have two ways to proceed. You can add objects from the provided UDK components, or you can assign a CLIK class to a selected movie clip in its properties.

1. For the first method, in Flash open: `C:\UDK\~\Development\Flash\CLIK\ components\CLIK_Components.FLA`.

2. If you do not have the **Mobile Slate** font type that is embedded in the components you'll get a font swap dialog where you are prompted to chose a replacement font. There are various workarounds to this, which you can explore at `http://forums. epicgames.com/threads/805632-Slate-Mobile-font-Missing` but if you don't know what you are doing with fonts, just choose a new one when prompted and go with that, as there's a good chance you or the designer you work with will want a different font anyway.

3. The following is already set up, but is worth taking a look at. Copy the button symbol from the *Clik_Components.FLA* to the library of a new .FLA file. Then right-click on it and choose **Duplicate**. Right-click on the object and choose open **Component Definition...** and then in the **class** field, select and copy the class assigned in the **Properties**: *gfx.controls.Button*. Right-click on the movie clip that you want to deal with in the **Library** and choose **Properties**. Expand the **Advanced** section. There, tick on **Export for ActionScript**. In the class field, enter which class you want to use, for example: `gfx.controls.Button`, then click **OK**. Click **OK**.

4. The above steps matter because CLIK components that you duplicate within your **Library** will not retain their class in the advanced properties. They will also have some auto-naming issues with the **linkage Identifier** as well, being called 'Button Copy' and the like. For every CLIK component, set its **Identifier** to the name of the symbol by going to the **Window | Properties** panel (*Ctrl + F3*) and setting the **<Instance Name>** to match the symbol's **Name** (given when you right-clicked on it and set in its **Properties**).

See also

In the recipe *Building CLIK functionality within UDK*, the function of CLIK components and set up concerns are covered in depth.

Working with images to skin a button

Since the UI components that come with Flash are not optimized to run in GFX, UDK users should not use those, and instead base their UI on the Scaleform **Common Lightweight Interface Kit** (**CLIK**) components. This kit ships with UDK, and can be found in the folder `C:\UDK\~\Development\Flash\CLIK\components`. The end of the previous recipe details setting that up. However, those components are merely functional, and in most cases designers will want to adapt them, or 'skin' them, to their own taste. In this recipe this is what we'll do, using the standard **Button** component as an example because almost every game requires one at some point or another, and because its user interaction is amongst the first steps one usually takes when learning Flash too. A key point to note is that the 2D components in a CLIK object are converted by UDK at render time into 3D **Draw Primitives**, so in the artwork, there are several issues of control of these. For instance, drawing text on the screen requires a **Draw Primitive** (**DP**) and if you add a background behind the text that requires another. Autodesk provides a **Best Practices** PDF guide which addresses such concerns at: `http://www.scaleform.com/udkusers`, along with video guides and CLIK documentation, which is undoubtedly the logical place to go when getting started.

Getting ready

Assuming you have finished the previous recipe, but are otherwise starting from scratch, in Flash open: `C:\UDK\~\Development\Flash\CLIK\components\CLIK_Components.FLA`.

How to do it...

Creating simple button art

1. In the Library, highlight the *Button* type and right-click on it. Choose **Copy**.
2. Press *Ctrl + N* to open a new Flash file, and in this one's **Library** right-click and choose **Paste**. Select the **Button**, and drag it to the middle of the stage.

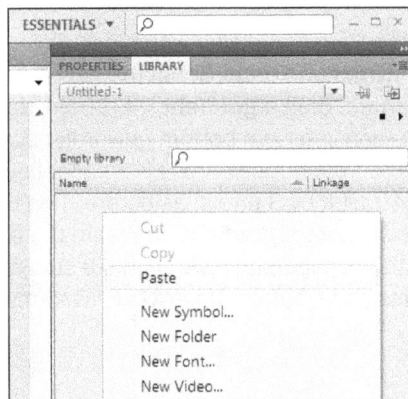

3. The button looks pretty uninspiring, and we're going to dress it up, but let's first consider its layer structure. On the stage, right-click on the button instance and choose **Edit**. Above the stage, on the left-hand side of the timeline you should see the layers *actions*, *labels*, *textField*, and *button*. These can be renamed or rearranged; however, note that the button will not work as intended if the ActionScript in the *actions* layer and labeled keyframes of the *labels* layer are not present in their proper positions. Also, each state of the button must be included at the proper positions relative to the *labels* keyframes on the timeline.

4. So, what is a state? The button we're using only has four, which are **up**, **over**, **down**, and **disabled**. More advanced buttons, such as **Toggles**, include **selected_up**, **selected_over**, **selected_down**, and **selected_disabled**. An **Animated Button** adds four more states: **release**, **out**, **kb_down**, and **kb_release**. These have to do with user cursor and mouse action, and in the case of animations, when the end of the animation occurs. Script can be driven by the state changes just as triggers are used in Kismet in UDK.

5. For each state, a different graphic is interposed for the button's look. Often it is just a change of tint or brightness, or size, but sometimes entirely different artwork is called for, particularly in the case of games. In the example given next, the artwork remains largely the same (at a pixel level) and the borders are what are altered for each state: *inactive*, *over*, *down*, and *active*. There is a different look for the button when the game mode it represents is available or not.

6. With that in mind, a UI artist has to know how the content will be deployed. Generally differences are systematic and restrained. Ours will have a different image per state. We'll make it in Photoshop then import it to the Library.

7. In Photoshop, create a document which is 128x128. Press *Ctrl + Shift + N* to create a **New Layer**. Set the **Marquee** selection tool to **Ellipse** [○] and make sure it has **Fixed Ratio** set in its control bar at the top of the screen.

8. Make a circle within the frame, and fill it with black. Select the filled area and choose **Select | Modify | Contract** and enter 3. **Fill** the next area with medium gray, then, with the area still selected, drag a **gradient** [■] from black to transparent upwards. Drag the gradient creation line from bottom upwards because that will make the ring appear shadowed on the bottom. Make a smaller circular selection and **fill** it with a bright gray. Contract it by 3 pixels, as before. This time, **fill** the selection with a downwards black to transparent **gradient**, to create the appearance of a shadowed recess. Finally, clear the background layer to make sure our layer is showing against transparency. Save this as *Mybutton_up.PNG*. .PNG format must be used.

9. Now simply effect the button in four different ways to give you four different states. Save each variant respectively as *Mybutton_over.PNG*, *Mybutton_down.PNG*, and *Mybutton_disabled.PNG*. If you prefer, you can use the ones from the provided content. They were made by using gradients and the **Stroke** selection command (right-click on a selection after defining the brush setting and color of your choice).

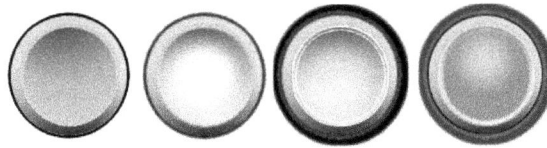

Importing the artwork to Flash and setting the art in place:

1. Your PNG files should be placed in a structure like: `C:\UDK\~\UDKGame\Flash\YourfolderUI\MyButton` after you've completed them. *YourfolderUI* is a subfolder you create for all your Flash, possibly named for your project or game. The folder *MyButton* refers to the name of the particular .FLA scene you are making, or going to make, where its content will be stored. Each scene would need a different name. In this case, I called mine `C:\UDK\~\UDKGame\Flash\PacktUI\MyButton\`.

2. In Flash, choose the menu item **File | Import | Import to Library**, and choose your artworks. Symbols for the images are also automatically generated, named Symbol #. If you like, rename the symbols by right-clicking on them and choosing **Rename**.

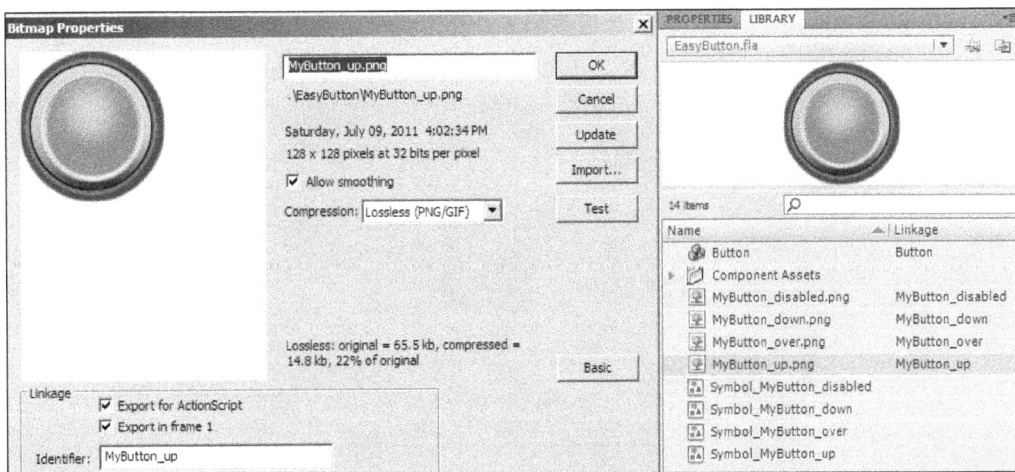

3. You next need to set a **Linkage ID** for each imported asset, which serves the purpose of letting UDK know where to find the original artwork. To do so, right-click the button images you've added to the Library (one at a time) and choose **Properties**. For each one, set the **identifier** which is just the name of the file, excluding the suffix. It is advised to also turn on **Allow Smoothing** in the same dialog and set the compression as **Lossless** (**PNG/GIF**). It is also possible to turn on **Export for runtime sharing** if you want the images contained in the SWF (that will result from the whole process) as a resource to be called on by other SWFMovies as well as by UDK packages. If you want to try it, see udn.epicgames.com/ScaleformImport.html#Resource sharing for more information on that, but in this case it isn't required.

4. The whole point of this is that the button provided in the CLIK resources from UDK is already scripted for us, and we are now just going to replace its art with ours. On the Timeline, in the button layer, highlight the first keyframe, which should highlight the button content on the stage. Delete that, then pull in your imported artwork. The first keyframe is the **Up** state, so bring in *MyButton_up*'s symbol and place it more or less where the old button image was. If you want to line things up nicely, adjust the rulers so they line up with the edge of your imagery. Then shift to the next keyframe, clear the CLIK button image for the over state, and drag in your *MyButton_over* symbol. Repeat this for down and disabled, using the respective imagery. Check the content is nicely aligned.

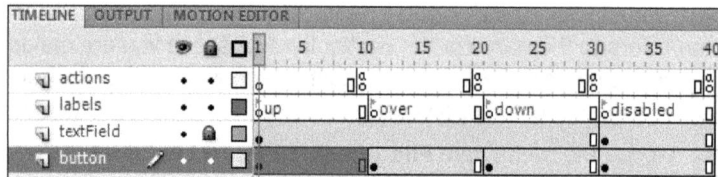

5. Save your .FLA at C:\UDK\~\UDKGame\Flash\YourfolderUI\ and call it *MyButton.FLA*. Your PNG folder would be C:\UDK\~\UDKGame\Flash\ YourfolderUI\MyButton\.

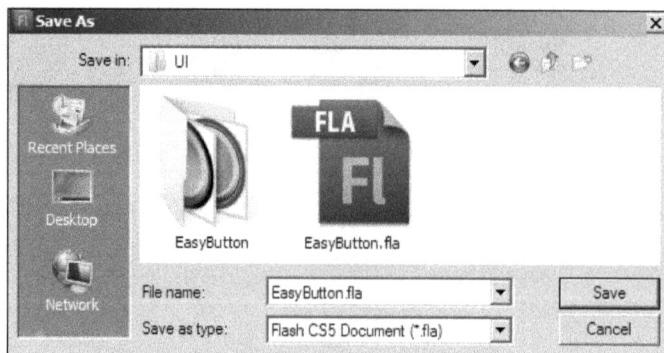

Cursor design and script for cursors

To interact with UI assets in UDK, the player needs to jump from targeting using the camera to clicking on menu items. This is done by gaining control of the XY screen space using a cursor. In this recipe, we'll provide a bare bones procedure for getting a simple cursor working while also giving an overview of how ActionScript and Kismet communicate. Note that at the time of writing UDK has only just implemented ActionScript 3 support for Scaleform. Also, now Scaleform 4 is out with more bells and whistles. Because this is only a recent development, all the lessons from here on in are written in ActionScript 2, which is still fully supported and an excellent starting point.

How to do it...

First, decide for yourself. Do you want a cursor that has a lot of thematic character or a cursor that is simple and clear? Usually, a simple cursor is less obtrusive than a highly decorative one.

Creating simple cursor art

1. In Photoshop, create a 256x256 document. Click on the **Path** tool (*P*), and put down a few points to generate a closed triangle. The shape outline must be closed. Hold the **Path** tool icon [✎], to access its variants. Choose the **Add Anchor Points** tool [✎] and use it to refine the triangle so it has additional points. Then position them till you start to get a pointer or arrow shape that you like.

2. If you lose focus on the line, *Ctrl* click it to select it, since just clicking on it may add a point where you don't want it. Try to use as few points as possible and use the **Handles** to drive the shape curves. If you add too many, use *ALT* and click on the unwanted points. You can use the **Convert Point** tool [◢] to change a corner to a bezier curve, and vice versa. Use as much of the canvas space as you can. The next image shows a clean shape made of just a few points.

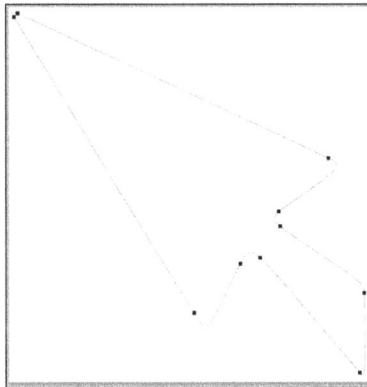

3. Right-click on the shape and choose **Stroke Path** using a black, small size brush.

4. Create a new layer then right-click on the path again (still with the **Path** tool (*P*) or **Direct Selection** tool (*A*) active) and choose **Make Selection**. If it happens to select the inverse, just press *Ctrl + Shift + I* to flip this. You want the arrow interior only selected. Save the selection as *Arrow* in the **Select | Save Selection** menu.

5. Pass a black to transparent gradient up the screen. With the *Arrow* selection showing, choose **Select | Modify | Contract** by about 6 pixels, and fill the smaller selection with white. Then stroke it with black to outline the white.

6. Make sure your content is not on the background layer, and then delete the surrounding white from the image using the magic wand to select it. The arrow should now sit on a transparent layer. Zoom out to 12.5% to see how the result will likely appear when the cursor is set up in Flash. It's better to make large scale art and shrink it down in Flash. Depending on your game, you may want to make different cursor art for things such as 'CPU thinking' and 'dragging' states.

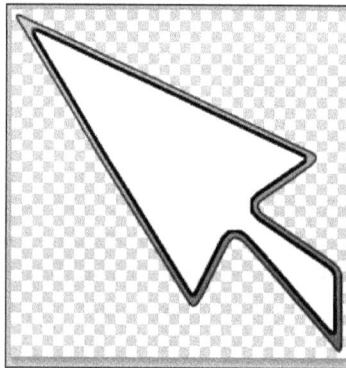

7. Save the mouse as `C:\UDK\~\UDKGame\Flash\YourfolderUI\Mouse\Mouse.PNG`. In Flash, import this .PNG into your library. You can either use the imported .PNG as the mouse, or create a shape using the vector art tools in Flash, as detailed next.

8. Create a new **Movieclip** symbol in your library and name it *MouseCursor*. Double-click on it to open it up, and you will see a large, blank canvas. If you want to create a vector cursor, you can use the **Brush** tool (*B*) or the **Rectangle** tool (*R*) with a little adjustment of the corners. Right-click on the vector and choose **Distort or Free Transform** to alter it so it looks like a pointer. If you want to use the imported *Mouse.PNG*, drag it from the library onto the stage and place it so that its tip is in the center of the stage, where the "+" shaped marker is.

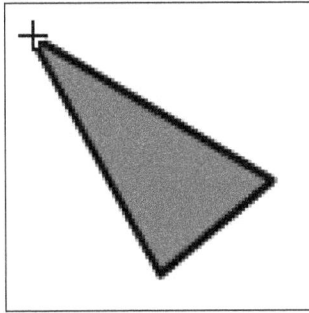

You can think of this marker as being much like the pivot point of a model; essentially it determines where the "center" of an object is. In this case, though, we want it to be at the end of the mouse cursor so that we can use it to detect where the user is trying to click.

9. We're using ActionScript 2, which means that we want to attach our code for making the cursor move directly to the mouse cursor symbol itself. With the *MouseCursor* symbol still open, look down at the timeline; this timeline is unique to this symbol, separate from everything we do on the main stage. Name the first layer *Cursor*.

10. Right-click on the first frame of the *Cursor* layer, then click on **Actions** in the pop-up menu to open up the ActionScript Editor.

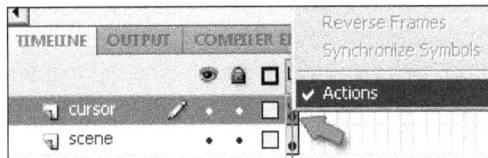

11. The following cursor script is standard across many of the UI elements you'll build using CLIK components in Flash for Scaleform translation to UDK. In the ActionScript Editor, enter the following , without the // comments:

```
// this hides the Windows mouse
import flash.external.ExternalInterface;
Mouse.hide();
//the next line fires up CursorInst when you drag the mouse
startDrag("CursorInst", true);
//the next line tells us we're going to listen for the mouse
var mouseListener:Object = new Object();
//the next function starts to listen and gives the mouse XY values
to CursorInst
mouseListener.onMouseMove = function()
{
   CursorInst._x = _root._xmouse;
   CursorInst._y = _root._ymouse;
```

```
// The next line is a command UDK can understand to hear what we
listened for,
// which is the mouse XY. It is similar to an FSCommand ... but more
official.
   ExternalInterface.call( "ReceiveMouseCoords", _root._xmouse, _
root._ymouse );
// and the last lines keeps updating all this
   updateAfterEvent();
}
Mouse.addListener(mouseListener);
```

12. As we said, that goes on frame0 of the *Cursor* layer. Now select the *MouseCursor* symbol and press *F9* to open its script and enter:

```
onClipEvent(enterFrame)
{
    _X = _root._xmouse;
    _y = _root._ymouse;
}
```

13. Go back to the stage. Click-and-drag a copy of the *MouseCursor* symbol from the library onto the stage, and name its layer *Mouse Cursor*.

14. Save your Flash scene (*Mouse.FLA*) and export your (*Mouse.SWF*) both to `C:\UDK\~\UDKGame\Flash\UI\Mouse`.

15. This mouse cursor would not do anything in the game except move around on the screen, if invoked. Instead, it's handy as a template. Copy the *Cursor* layer (to do so right-click frame0 and choose **Copy Frames**), and paste it into other Flash scenes which contain your menu or whatever UI you want to have in your game. You can use it over and over again. Indeed, we use it again, next. In fact, if you have some troubles getting a cursor working, open *PacktSlider.FLA* and copy out the cursor layer at keyframe 0 to your own document.

Importing SWF content to UDK

Once you have made some SWF cursors, buttons, menu content and so on, you'll want to try it out in UDK. UDK allows users to run a commandlet (**gfximport**) external to the editor. This process assumes your content is in the correct relative file structure, as it should be, which has been discussed in previous recipes. So if you wanted to bring in your *Mouse.SWF* and your *EasyButton.SWF* you'd type in the windows **Run** command line `C:\UDK\~\UDKGame\Binaries\Win64>UDKGame.exe gfximport UI\Mouse.SWF\EasyButton.SWF` and all the subfolders involved would be parsed into UDK, to a package saved as `C:\UDK\~\UDKGame\Content\Gfx\UI`. Naturally this is like an express service.

Let's assume that you want to take a more hands-on role in handling your belongings, and will import content yourself.

How to do it...

1. If you didn't already, in Windows, make a folder in the `UDKGame\Flash\` path of your UDK installation called *YourfolderUI*. That's where your Mouse.SWF and MyButton. SWF need to be, along with the related subfolder \MyButton. Restart UDK, and in the content browser, highlight this *YoufolderUI* folder. Right-click and choose **Import**.

2. Choose the *MyButton.SWF* you'll be dealing with. During the import, all images used by the SWF will be imported as Texture Objects into the package you specified.

3. You can also flag, in the import options, to use a **Texture Atlas**, which combines into one large texture all the texture content the SWF references. To do so enable the **Pack Textures** option. **Pack Texture Size** sets the maximum size of the atlas. You can also set rescaling settings here. This is for when your SWF uses lots of little graphics, and they can be fitted to one large texture. In our example, it's not needed.

4. The **sRGB** checkbox is there so you can switch textures from Flash's Adobe RGB to sRGB, although to many this will be a subtle distinction. You can read more about the terms at: `http://www.cambridgeincolour.com/tutorials/sRGB-AdobeRGB1998.html`.

5. Save your package. In Kismet, you can add an SWF into an ***GfxMovie*** action's **Movie** property, fired from a ***Level Loaded*** event to check that it works as intended.

Placing an SWF on a BSP using Render to Texture

Once an SWF is imported, it usually displays full screen. This can be changed so the SWF is drawn on a BSP surface (or CSG Additive surface really) anywhere in the level you like. In this recipe we will use a simply skinned **Slider** built upon a CLIK component, set it on a BSP surface, and ensure it still operates when triggered. The biggest problems for SWF displayed on a BSP surface are to do with the cursor having to track just the surface of the BSP, not the whole screen (so you may face registration problems), and getting the SWF to take focus. There are simple solutions to both of these issues.

How to do it...

1. Import to a new package the provided file *BSPSlider.SWF*, and save its new package as *BSPSlider.UPK*. In the same package in the Content Browser, right-click and choose **New TextureRenderTarget2D**. Call this *BSPSlider.Texture.SWFtoBSP* (or anything you want). All this does is serve as a placement proxy for the SWF. Right-click on it and choose **Edit Using Texture Viewer**. There, set the size to 256 x 256 if it isn't already. This matches the Flash document that *BSPSlider.SWF* came from.

2. Right-click in the content browser and choose **New Material**. Name it *BSPSlider. Material.SWFtoBSP_mat*.

3. Highlight the **TextureRenderTarget2D** asset *SWFtoBSP* in the Content Browser, then hold *T* and click on the Material Editor. This adds it to a **Texture Sample** node. Set the **PreviewMaterial** properties so the **Render Texture Mode** is *RTM_Alpha Composite*. Hook up the **Texture Sample** to both the **Diffuse** and **Emissive** channels, and the **Alpha** channel to the **Opacity Mask** channel of the **PreviewMaterial** node. Compile the material [   ] and save the package.

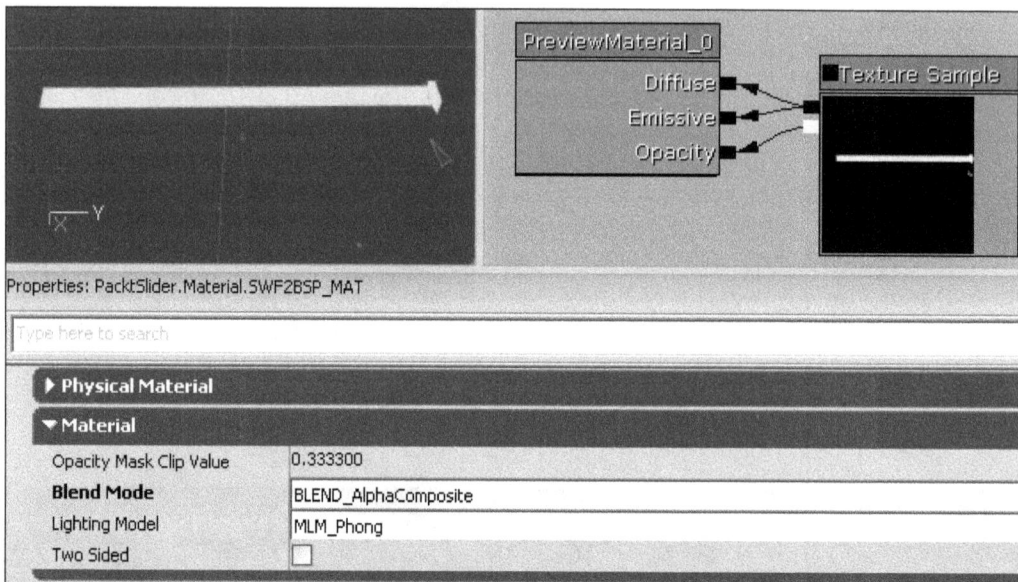

4. Open a map, for instance the template *Midday Lighting*. Press **Go to Builder Brush** [   ], then press *Ctrl + A* to add a CSG box. Delete or move the StaticMesh box that overlaps the Builder Brush in the template.

5. In the Content Browser, find the Material *BSPSlider.Material.SWFtoBSP_mat* and drag it onto the front face of the CSG additive cube that you built. In certain cases you may need to press *F5* to access the **Surface Properties** of the BSP and adjust its UV scale or orientation. Try a value of 0.5 x 0.5 UV then click **on Apply**.

6. On the ground, near the BSP brush, right-click and choose **Add Actor | Trigger**. With the Trigger selected, open Kismet [**K**], then right-click and choose **New Event using Trigger_0 | Touch**. Extend from this a **New Action | GFx UI | Open Gfx Movie** as shown in the next screenshot.

7. In the **Movie** property of the **Open GFx Movie**, add the SWF asset *BSPSlider.SWF*. Tick **Take Focus** and **Capture Input**, though this depends on what SWF you're using. Ticking these enables the mouse to take over from directing the player camera when the **Open GFx Movie** action is fired by the *Trigger_0 | Touch* event. Clicking is an input, but you could also set up hotkeys to work with the SWF, which is discussed in a later recipe.

8. Go to the properties of the **Open GFx Movie**, and in the property **Render Texture** add the asset _BSPSlider.Texture.SWFtoBSP_ from the Content Browser using the assign icon [⊕]. After that, highlight _BSPSlider.SWF_ and assign it to the **Movie** channel using the assign icon [⊕].

9. Currently, the SWF will render opaque. Since we already enabled transparency in the Material we're using, set the property **Render Texture Mode** to _RTM_Alpha Composite_.

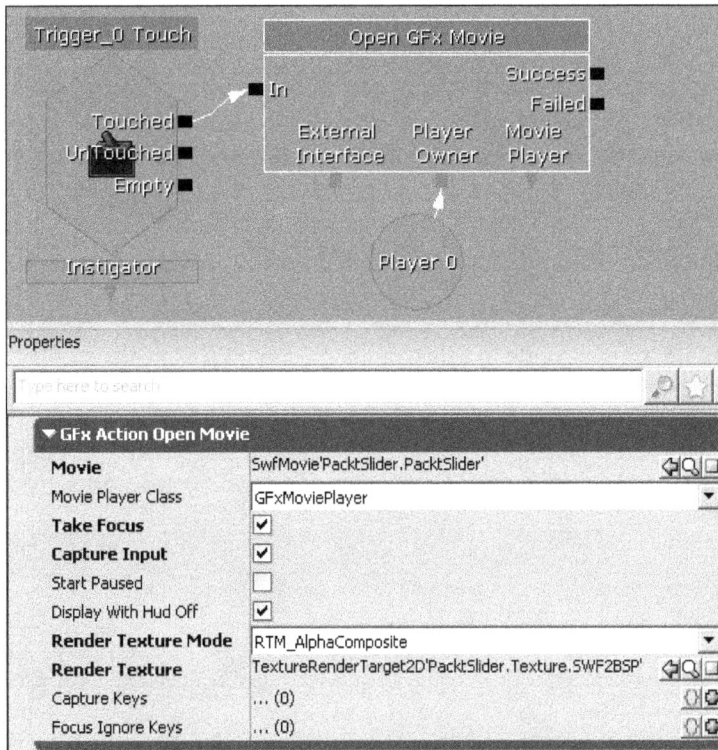

10. The default **View | World Properties | Game Type | Game Type for PIE**: _None_ has no HUD, so if you are using that, tick on the **Open Gfx Movie** action's **Display With HUD Off** property or you won't see the SWF displayed. Anyway, if you aren't using a special HUD type, use _SimpleGame_. This lets us pop up some text later to inform the player what to do with the slider.

11. Right-click in Kismet and choose **New Action | Misc | DrawText**. Connect the **Touched** nub of the **Trigger_0 | Touch** event to its **Show** nub.

12. In the Content Browser search for _UI_Fonts.MultiFonts.MF_HudSmall_. This is a font that we can use to display text in the **Draw Text** action. Highlight this asset, and in the **Text Info | Message Font** property of the **Draw Text** action, click on the assign icon [⊕]. In the **Message Text** property type: _Drag the slider to quit!_

13. In order that the text aligns nicely on the screen, set the **Message Font Scale** so its X and Y values are both 0.25. For its screen location, set the **Message Offset** values so X = 1000 and Y = 20. This assumes you have a 1920x1080 resolution.

14. Last in this setup stage is to fire a ***Toggle Cinemetic Mode*** action so the player can't move after the touching the Trigger. Right-click and choose **New Action | Toggle | Toggle Cinematic Mode**. In its properties, uncheck **Disable Input** and **Hide HUD**. We want to see the HUD, and we want the player to be able to input something even though we don't want them to run around. Connect the **Touched** nub of the ***Trigger_0 | Touch*** event to its **Enable** nub.

15. If you PIE and run up to the asset you should see the instruction text pop up above the cube, so you know that the Trigger is working. The SWF will display, but you won't be able to drag the slider, even though we enabled **Take Focus** in the ***Open GFx Movie*** action. Functionality for the slider dragging is provided in the CLIK Slider component that comes with UDK. This can be tested in Flash using the Scaleform **Gfx Media Player** launcher. So why does nothing happen?

16. The cursor isn't happy about launching in the BSP surface in the scene. It wants to work in full-screen mode. We can make it happy again by adding another ***Open Gfx Movie*** node playing an empty SWF between the **Trigger_0 | Touch** event and the **Open Gfx Movie** node to which our *BSPSlider.SWF* is assigned. To do so, in the Content Browser import a new SWF called *Dummy.SWF* into the same package as the *BSPSlider.SWF*. In Kismet, copy-and-paste the **Open Gfx Movie** node and in its **Movie** property assign *Dummy.SWF* instead. Also turn off **Take Focus** and **Capture Input** for this pasted node. Connect it up in between, as shown in the next screenshot:

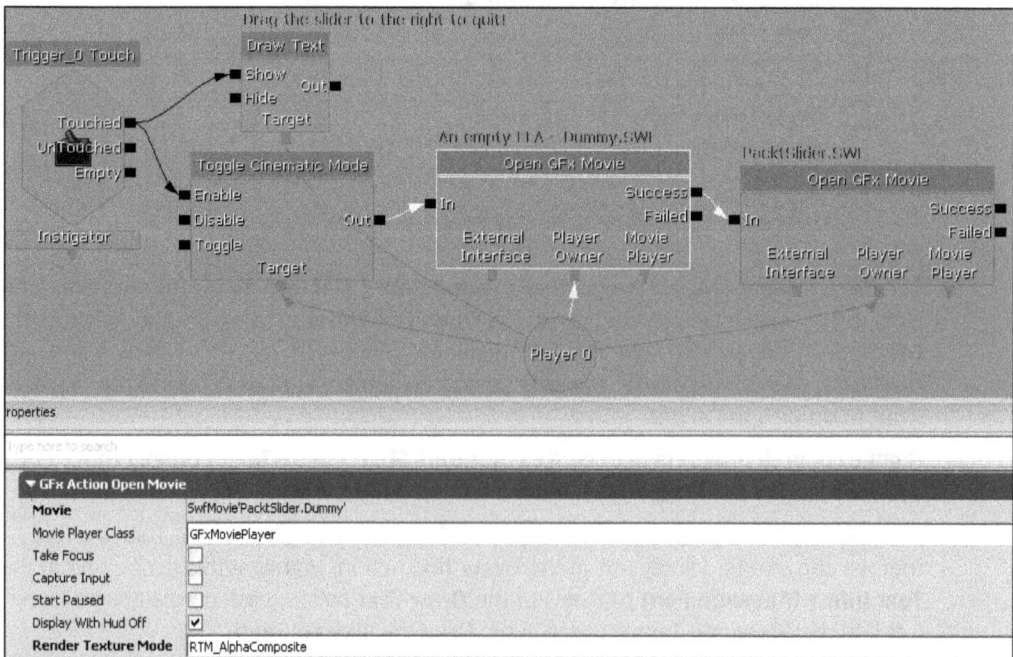

17. PIE to test this out, to see if the mouse now appears and lets you move the slider about. Cool; but we're not quite done. Even though the slider now moves, nothing is scripted to happen. Let's make the slider quit the game when the player moves it all the way to the right. Slide to close … like an iPad.

18. In the slider component of the SWF you will need to add some more code. So save what you have and open up Flash CS5 and load the provided `\Packt\UDKGame\Flash\PacktSlider\BSPSlider.FLA`. All you need to do is highlight the *Slider* layer in the Timeline, noting the other layer is the *Cursor* layer pasted directly in from our previous recipe, then right click on the first frame of the *Slider* layer and choose **Actions**. In the ActionScript Editor, enter the following script:

```
BSPSlider.addEventListener("change", this, "onValueChange");
function onValueChange(event:Object)
{ if (BSPSlider.value) == BSPSlider.maximum)
 { fscommand("SliderMax"); }
}
```

19. What this does is fairly simple. It makes the symbol in the scene called *BSPSlider* listen for a value change in the slider. In particular, if the slider value is the maximum value it can be, then it will fire a **FSCommand** *MaxSlider*.

20. Click on the *BSPSlider* symbol, either on the stage or in the library. You should see its **Properties** panel showing on the right-hand side of the screen. Here you can see the `Maximum` value for the slider defaults to 10. In this case it doesn't matter what the value is. When the slider reaches the right-hand side, its at maximum. Make sure that the **liveDragging** checkbox is on and also the **snapping** checkbox, as shown in the next screenshot. The value **snapInterval**, set to **1**, ensures that the slider uses Integer values.

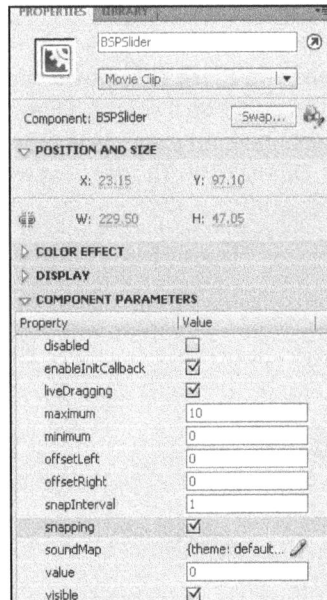

21. Publish the adjusted *BSPSlider.FLA* file to update your current *BSPSlider.SWF* and in the UDK Content Browser, highlight *BSPSlider.SWF* and choose **Reimport**.

22. In Kismet, right-click and choose **New Event | GFx UI | FSCommand**. In its properties, assign the SWF asset *BSPSlider* to the **Movie** channel. Under that, in the **FSCommand** channel, type: *SliderMax*. This matches what we entered into the ActionScript previously. Next, extend from the event a **New Action | Misc | Console Command** and in its **Commands | [0]** field type *quit*. This will close the map, but you could swap in any action or command you prefer.

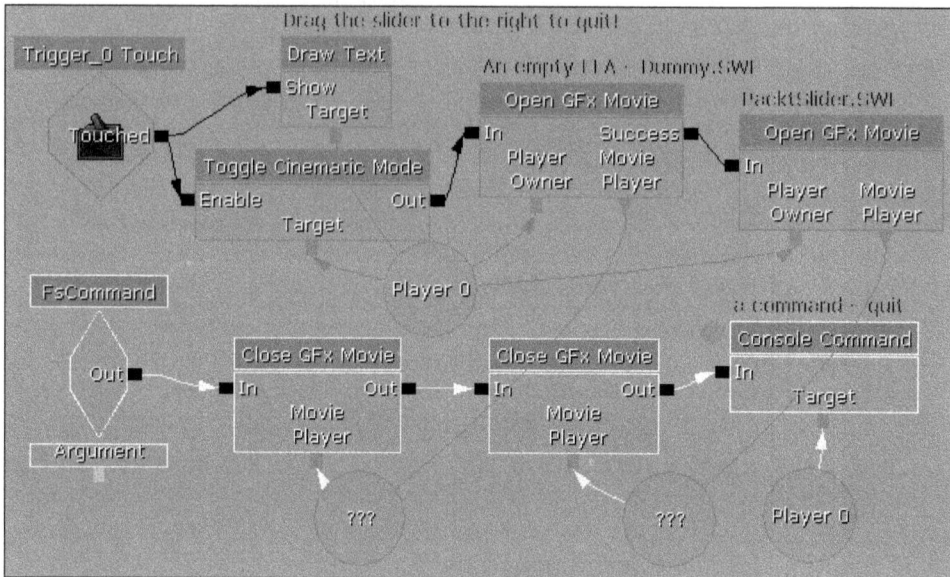

23. In the example shown here, two **Close GFx Movie** nodes have been added to the sequence to show what you might do if your quit event was replaced with something where gameplay should continue. An example is provided using *PacktSlider.SWF* in *Packt_10_PacktSlider_DEMO.UDK*. The map file was made in the January 2012 version of UDK.

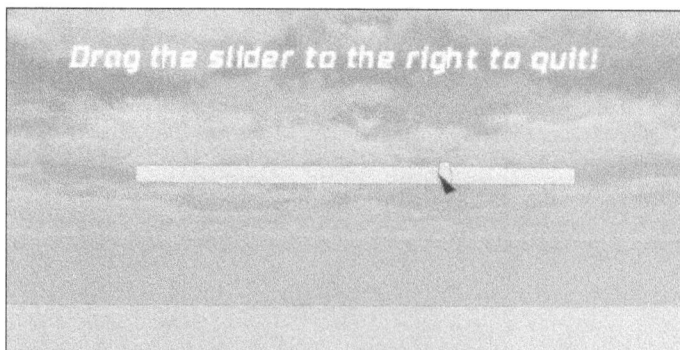

This recipe involved getting a slider to close the level. You can script a slider to do many things. It is particularly suited to adjusting the volume of music that's playing. My thread on this is posted on the UDK forums. It details where I got stuck, which seems to be a common stumbling point for others too, and how I found the solution (after trial and error) and there's a clean, working example provided: `http://forums.epicgames.com/threads/885824-Live-slider-music-volume-change-from-actionscript`.

Additional content

Some more content available at `http://www.packtpub.com/sites/default/files/downloads/1802EXP_Unreal_Development_Kit_Game_Design_Cookbook_Bonus_Recipes.pdf` contains more recipes based on the following topics:

- Building a Dialog Box using CLIK for use in UDK
- Setting up Dialog Box functionality in Kismet
- Adding ActionScript for keyboard control to a Dialog Box
- Triggering unique dialog by toggling FsCommands
- Adding menu functionality to the Dialog Box in Flash
- Setting up the menu in Kismet with Invoke ActionScript
- Scripting for CLIK components and the importance of Focus
- Creating an animated day-to-night transition

Index

[PACKT]
PUBLISHING

Thank you for buying
Unreal Development Kit
Game Design Cookbook

About Packt Publishing

Packt, pronounced 'packed', published its first book "*Mastering phpMyAdmin for Effective MySQL Management*" in April 2004 and subsequently continued to specialize in publishing highly focused books on specific technologies and solutions.

Our books and publications share the experiences of your fellow IT professionals in adapting and customizing today's systems, applications, and frameworks. Our solution based books give you the knowledge and power to customize the software and technologies you're using to get the job done. Packt books are more specific and less general than the IT books you have seen in the past. Our unique business model allows us to bring you more focused information, giving you more of what you need to know, and less of what you don't.

Packt is a modern, yet unique publishing company, which focuses on producing quality, cutting-edge books for communities of developers, administrators, and newbies alike. For more information, please visit our website: www.packtpub.com.

Writing for Packt

We welcome all inquiries from people who are interested in authoring. Book proposals should be sent to author@packtpub.com. If your book idea is still at an early stage and you would like to discuss it first before writing a formal book proposal, contact us; one of our commissioning editors will get in touch with you.

We're not just looking for published authors; if you have strong technical skills but no writing experience, our experienced editors can help you develop a writing career, or simply get some additional reward for your expertise.

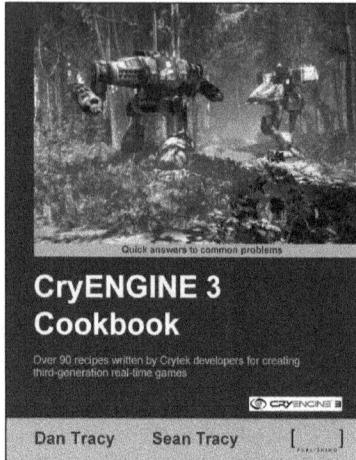

[PACKT]
PUBLISHING

CryENGINE 3 Cookbook

ISBN: 978-1-84969-106-2   Paperback: 324 pages

Over 90 recipes written by Crytek developers for creating third-generation real-time games

1. Begin developing your AAA game or simulation by harnessing the power of the award winning CryENGINE3

2. Create entire game worlds using the powerful CryENGINE 3 Sandbox

3. Create your very own customized content for use within the CryENGINE3 with the multiple creation recipes in this book

4. Translate your design into CryENGINE by following the easy step by step recipes exploring flow graph, track view, and many of the other tools within CryENGINE

Unity 3.x Game Development Essentials

ISBN: 978-1-84969-144-4   Paperback: 488 pages

Build fully functional, professional 3D games with realistic environments, sound, dynamic effects, and more!

1. Kick start your game development, and build ready-to-play 3D games with ease.

2. Understand key concepts in game design including scripting, physics, instantiation, particle effects, and more.

3. Test & optimize your game to perfection with essential tips-and-tricks.

Please check **www.PacktPub.com** for information on our titles

[PACKT]
PUBLISHING

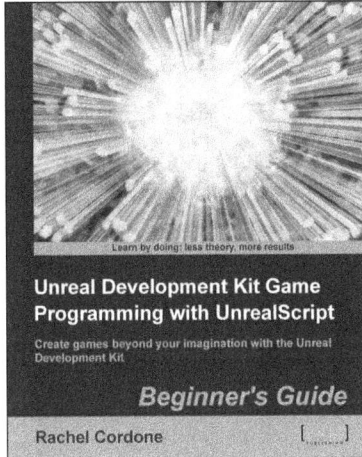

Unreal Development Kit Game Programming with UnrealScript: Beginner's Guide

ISBN: 978-1-84969-192-5   Paperback: 466 pages

Create games beyond your imagination with the Unreal Development Kit

1. Use features of the popular NetBeans IDE to improve Java EE development

2. Careful instructions and screenshots lead you through the options available

3. Covers the major Java EE APIs such as JSF, EJB 3 and JPA, and how to work with them in NetBeans

4. Covers the NetBeans Visual Web designer in detail

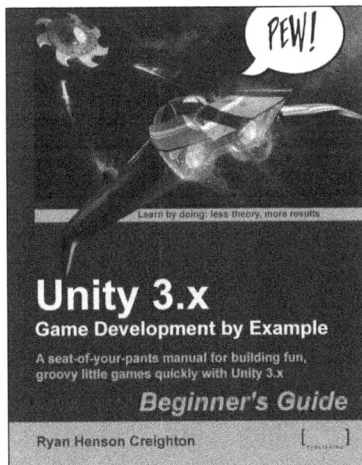

Unity 3.x Game Development by Example Beginner's Guide

ISBN: 978-1-84969-184-0   Paperback: 408 pages

A seat-of-your-pants manual for building fun, groovy little games quickly with Unity 3.x

1. Build fun games using the free Unity game engine even if you've never coded before

2. Learn how to "skin" projects to make totally different games from the same file – more games, less effort!

3. Deploy your games to the Internet so that your friends and family can play them

4. Packed with ideas, inspiration, and advice for your own game design and development

Please check **www.PacktPub.com** for information on our titles

www.ingramcontent.com/pod-product-compliance
Lightning Source LLC
Chambersburg PA
CBHW060952210326
41598CB00031B/4804